22.99

The Essential Guide

Excel
5.0 for Windows

About the author

Anne Prince is the author of VS COBOL II and co-author of our assembler books. Over the years she also used her skills as a programmer and her technical knowledge of mainframe computers to edit other books on mainframe subjects such as CICS, TSO, and DB2. Many readers who are familiar with Murach books are familiar with her work.

Anne also worked as the editor on the revision of one of our best-selling PC books, *The Only DOS Book You'll Ever Need*. Most recently, she authored *The Essential Guide: 1-2-3 for Windows Release 4*. These experiences combined with her educational background (a B.A. in Mathematics from CSU Fresno) made her the perfect choice to write this book.

About the cover

Steve Huschle is the artist whose photography you see on the cover of this book. A native of Minnesota, Steve says about his work, "I attempt to exploit the camera's innate ability to transform the mundane into the marvelous."

The Essential Guide

Excel 5.0 for Windows

Anne Prince

Mike Murach & Associates
4697 West Jacquelyn Avenue, Fresno, California 93722-6427
(209) 275-3335

Graphics designer: Steve Ehlers

Project coordinator: Steve Eckols

Development Team: Lee Chae
Michael Farino

Other books for *Windows* users

The Least You Need to Know about Windows 3.1
The Essential Guide: Word 6.0 for Windows
The Essential Guide: 1-2-3 for Windows Release 4
The Essential Guide: WordPerfect 6.0 for Windows

Books for DOS users

The Least You Need to Know about DOS, Second Edition
The Only DOS Book You'll Ever Need, Second Edition
The Least You Need to Know about Lotus 1-2-3
The Practical Guide to Lotus 1-2-3
The Least You Need to Know about WordPerfect 5.0 and 5.1
The Essential Guide: WordPerfect 6.0 for DOS

10 9 8 7 6 5 4 3 2 1

ISBN: 0-911625-78-9

Library of Congress Cataloging-in-Publication Data

Prince, Anne.
The essential guide. Excel 5.0 for Windows / Anne Prince.
p. cm.
Includes index.
ISBN 0-911625-79-8 (alk. paper) :
1. Microsoft Excel for Windows. 2. Business--Computer programs.
3. Electronic spreadsheets. I. Title.
HF5548.4.M523P75 1994
650'.0285'5369--dc20 94-4932
CIP

Contents

What this book will do for you

This book will help you upgrade or convert to *Excel 5.0 for Windows* as quickly, as easily, and as thoroughly as possible. To make this possible, this book has features that you won't find in any competing book. Here, then, are four ways that this book will help you get the most from *Excel 5.0 for Windows*.

Upgrade or convert to *Excel 5.0 for Windows* in just a few hours

Excel 5.0 for Windows is easier to use than any of the previous versions of *Excel*. And it's as easy to use as any other spreadsheet program on the market today. Still, it has so many new features and functions that learning to use it can take many hours. And if you haven't used *Windows* before, the problem is compounded.

That's why the goal of section 1 in this book is to help you upgrade or convert to *Excel 5.0 for Windows* in just a few hours. To accomplish that, this section is divided into three chapters.

Chapter 1 is for PC users who have never used *Windows* before. It presents the essential *Windows* skills that you need for working with *Excel 5.0 for Windows*. Of course, if you already know how to use *Windows*, you can skip this chapter.

Chapter 2 gets you started with *Excel* as quickly as possible. It does this by assuming you already have some experience with an earlier version of *Excel* or another spreadsheet program like *Lotus 1-2-3* or *Quattro Pro*. So it doesn't waste your time reviewing fundamentals (but don't worry, it doesn't assume that you're an expert spreadsheet user, either). When you complete this chapter, you'll be able to use *Excel 5.0 for Windows* about as well as you use the spreadsheet program that you're upgrading or converting from...maybe better!

Chapter 3 takes you beyond the point where you were with your previous spreadsheet program. It does this by presenting 10 features that are new or improved in *Excel 5.0 for Windows*, so you can start using them right away. Then, it introduces you to all the other new or improved features of Version 5, so you'll have some idea what you want to learn next.

Learn new skills
whenever you need them, in just 10 or 15 minutes each

As you've worked on your own spreadsheets, you've probably realized that there must be better, quicker ways to do certain functions. But it would take so long to figure out the new ways, that you stick to what you know. You don't have time to waste spinning your wheels.

That's why the goal of the last four sections in this book is to help you learn new skills in just 10 or 15 minutes each. To accomplish that, most of the chapters in these sections are independent of each other, so you can read them in whatever sequence you prefer. The exceptions are that you should read chapter 11, which presents the basic skills for creating and modifying a chart, before you read chapter 12, which presents advanced charting skills. And you should read chapter 14, which shows you how to set up a list, before you read the other chapters in section 4, which present other features for working with lists and databases. The features in all of these chapters are arranged by function, not by menu choices, so you can learn a new function in a single chapter...you don't have to skip from one chapter to another, flipping back and forth to the index in between.

In addition, these chapters are chock-full of practical examples that show what *Excel* can do, procedures that show how to do it, and summaries that present the information that you need in condensed form. As a result, you can learn how to use a function or a feature just by reviewing the related figures...you don't even have to read the text. The text is there to give you additional perspective on when and how to use a feature.

Although the chapters in sections 2 through 5 will help even competent spreadsheet users improve their work, these chapters are even more valuable if you've never had the time to master your previous spreadsheet program. By learning new skills whenever you have a few minutes to spare, you'll soon be working better and faster than you ever have before.

If you're wondering whether a book this thin presents all of the functions and features of *Excel 5.0 for Windows*, it does. The only features that it presents lightly are (1) writing macros using Visual Basic, (2) the use of some of the commands and @functions for scientific and mathematical analysis, and (3) the use of some of the add-in programs that come with *Excel*, such as *Microsoft Query*. If you have experience with those features, though, the treatment in this book should be adequate for your purposes. And if you don't, you probably won't ever need them. For the typical business user of *Excel 5.0 for Windows*, this book presents everything you need to know...and a lot more.

Refresh your memory about how to use any function in just a few minutes

Most modern programs provide so many functions that no one can remember how to use all of them. And *Excel 5.0 for Windows* is no exception. What's the technique for revealing column A or row 1 after you've hidden it? How do you enter, edit, and format the data in all the worksheets in a file at the same time? What do you have to do to create a mixed chart? These are the kinds of details that you forget when you don't use a feature often.

That's why the third goal of this book is to provide a reference that lets you brush up on any function or feature in just a few minutes. Because the book consists of independent chapters, you can find what you need to know in a single chapter...you don't have to waste time skipping from one chapter to another. And because the figures present all the information that you need, you can refresh your memory just by reviewing them...you rarely have to read the text.

Increase your productivity as well as the quality of your work

Because each new version of a program provides more features than the previous versions, you ought to be able to improve the quality of your work whenever you upgrade or convert to a new program. When you use *Excel 5.0 for Windows*, for example, you should be able to improve the appearance of your worksheets, the clarity of your charts, and the sophistication of your analysis. Often, though, improvements in work quality are accompanied by a decrease in productivity as you spend time fiddling with new options, trying to figure out if they'll give you the results you want.

That's why the fourth goal of this book is to help you increase your productivity as well as the quality of your work. To get you started in that direction, section 2 presents the essential skills that will help any *Excel* user work more productively. So these are the skills you'll want to learn right away. In contrast, sections 3, 4, and 5 cover skills that are useful, but not essential to every *Excel* user. So you can read the chapters in these sections when (and if) you need the skills they present. In short, you won't waste any time on functions you don't really need.

This book also helps you work more productively by presenting the functions in most chapters in a top-down sequence, starting with the functions that are most useful and moving on down to those that are least useful. This gives you some perspective for deciding which functions to use. Beyond that, the text in each chapter continually provides the perspective you need to use a feature productively. Sometimes, this means that you're advised to use the basic functions of a feature, but to avoid the advanced functions because they're counterproductive.

Please let us know what you think of this book

With so many new PC books published each year, we didn't want to publish "just another" *Excel* book. There are too many on the market already. And yet, none them even tries to provide the four benefits that I've just described: getting you going right away, teaching you new skills when *you* decide you need them, serving you as a quick reference, and giving you the perspective you need to work more effectively each day. To us, that means the other books haven't yet focused on what people need to know to get the most out their software. With this book, we've tried to remedy that.

If you have any comments or criticisms, we would appreciate hearing from you. That's why there's a postage-paid comment form at the back of this book. With your help, we can continue to create books that let you get the most out of your software, as quickly as possible.

Mike Murach, Publisher
Fresno, California
March 1994

Anne Prince, Author

Section 1

Get started right with *Excel* 5.0 *for Windows*

This section contains three chapters that are designed to get you going quickly and productively with *Excel*. The first chapter is for PC users who have never used *Windows* before. It presents the essential *Windows* skills that you need for working with *Excel*. If you already know how to use *Windows*, you can skip this chapter.

The second chapter in this section is designed to get you started with *Excel* as quickly as possible. It assumes that you already have some experience with a previous version of *Excel* or with another spreadsheet program like *Quattro Pro* or *Lotus 1-2-3*. As a result, this chapter takes advantage of what you already know to get you started more quickly. Although it doesn't presume that you're an expert spreadsheet user, it doesn't waste your time reviewing fundamental concepts either. When you complete this chapter, you should be able to use *Excel* about as well as you use the spreadsheet program that you're upgrading or converting from.

The third chapter in this section is designed to take you beyond the point you were at with your previous spreadsheet program. It does this by introducing you to features of *Excel* 5.0 that can make a big difference in your productivity. By taking advantage of these features, you should be able to get more from *Excel* than you got from your previous program.

When you complete the three chapters in this section, you should be a competent *Excel* user. Then, you can use the remaining chapters in this book to learn new skills whenever you have the need for them. If you want to learn how to use pivot tables, for example, you can read chapter 16. If you want to learn more about charting the data in a worksheet, you can read chapters 11 and 12. And if you want to learn more about working with two or more worksheets in a single file, you can read chapter 9. Because the chapters in sections 2, 3, 4, and 5 are written as independent modules, you can read them in whatever sequence you prefer. And that means you can learn new skills whenever you have 10 or 15 minutes to spare.

Chapter 1

Learn the essential *Windows* skills

This chapter presents a quick introduction to *Microsoft Windows*. Although you won't learn everything there is to know about *Windows* here, you will learn the essentials that you need for using *Excel*. If you already have some experience using *Windows*, you can probably skip this chapter.

In this chapter, I assume you're using *Windows* version 3.1. If you're using *Windows* 3.0, the skills you'll learn here still apply, but the screens will look somewhat different on your monitor than they do in the illustrations in this chapter. If you're using *Windows* 3.0, though, I recommend that you upgrade to version 3.1 right away. It's an improved product that's faster and more reliable, and it also offers more features.

An introduction to *Windows*

Simply put, Microsoft *Windows* is an operating system that improves upon DOS by providing features such as multitasking, a standard graphical user interface, an improved facility for managing files and directories, and improved memory management. From a purely technical standpoint, though, *Windows* isn't a complete operating system because it still requires that DOS be installed on your PC. Once you start *Windows*, however, it replaces DOS as your PC's operating system. As a result, you can use *Windows* to start your application programs, to manage directories and files, and so on.

How to start *Windows* On many PCs, the command that starts *Windows* is already in the AUTOEXEC.BAT file so *Windows* starts automatically when you turn your PC on. If *Windows* doesn't start when you turn your PC on, you can start it from the command prompt by entering this command: *win*. Although you can specify some options when you use the *win* command, it's unlikely that you'll need to. That's because *Windows* inspects the configuration of your PC and sets the appropriate defaults as it starts up.

As *Windows* starts, it displays a logo screen. After a moment, the logo disappears and a blank screen appears with an hourglass on it. The hourglass means that you should wait for the start-up process to finish before you try to do anything.

During start-up, *Windows* always starts at least one program called the *shell program*. On almost all *Windows* systems, this shell program is the Program Manager. Its opening screen is shown in figure 1-1. You can use this program to start application programs like *Excel* or *Word*.

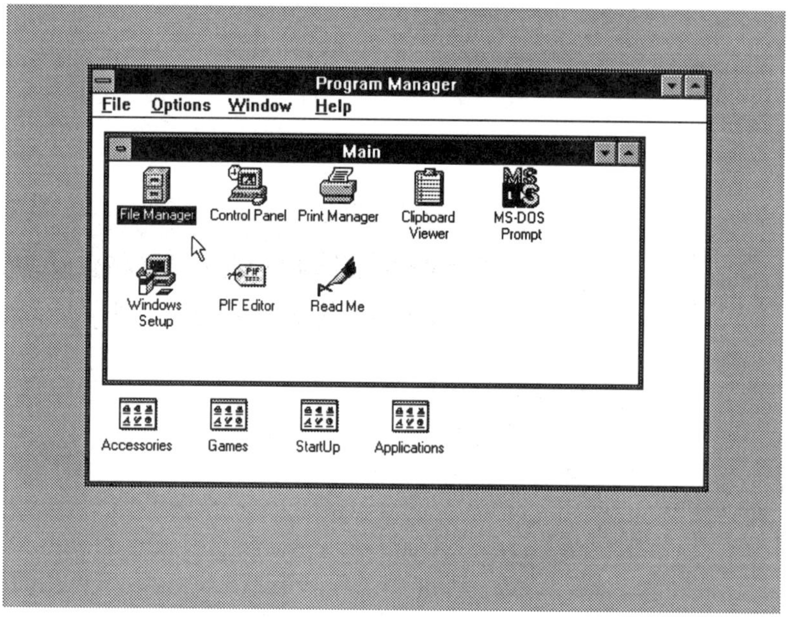

Figure 1-1 The starting display of a new *Windows* system with the Program Manager as the shell program

When you start *Windows* for the first time after it has been installed, the starting display looks like the one in figure 1-1. After that, though, the starting display will vary because the *Windows* display changes as you work with it. On some systems, for example, the starting *Windows* screen looks the way you left it at the end of your last work session. In addition, you can customize *Windows* so the starting display looks the way you want it to.

The parts of the *Windows* display Figure 1-2 identifies the most important parts of the *Windows* display. As you can see, the background portion of the screen is called the *desktop*. Upon this desktop, *Windows* creates a workspace for each program that is running called an *application window*. In figure 1-2, only the Program Manager is running so there's only one application window on the desktop.

Within an application window, most programs create their own windows called *document windows*. These windows always belong to the program that creates them, and they are always displayed inside their program's application window. Although the name "document window"

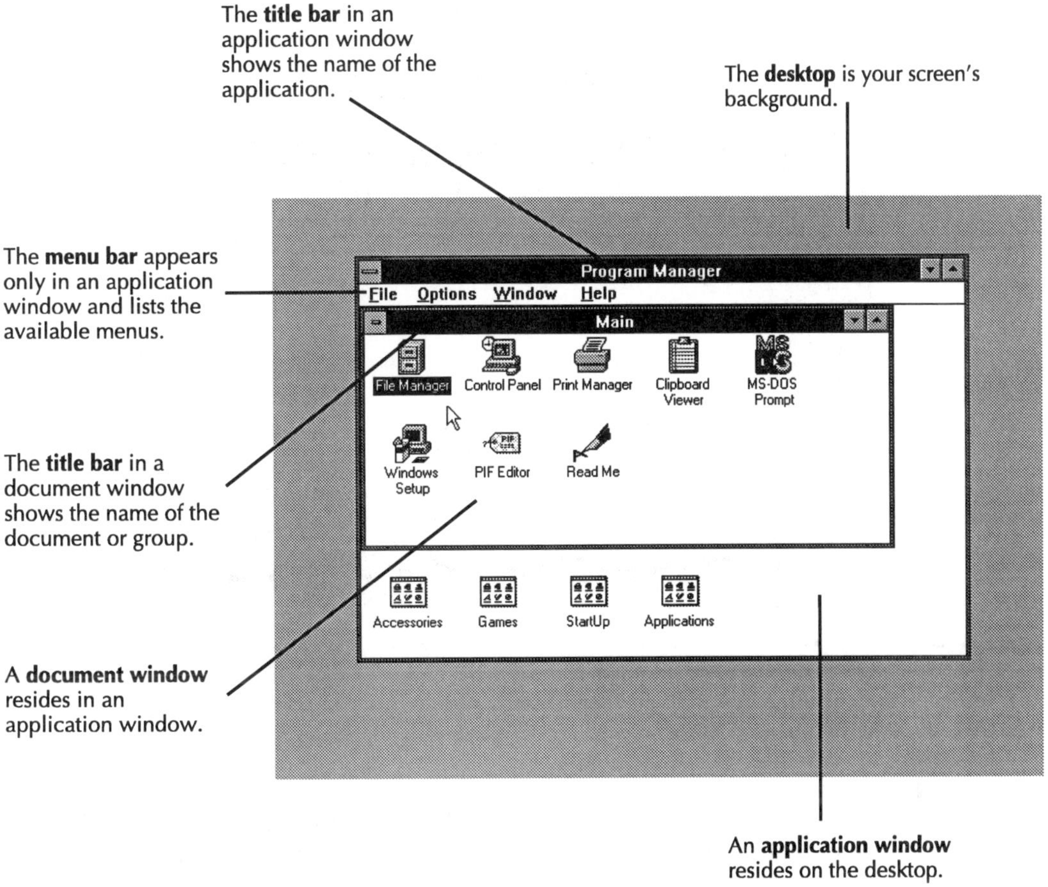

Figure 1-2 The parts of a *Windows* display

makes sense for a program like a word processor that actually creates documents, all windows that are used by application programs are called document windows. In figure 1-2, for example, the application window for the Program Manager contains a document window labeled "Main."

Nearly all windows have *title bars* across the top. The title bar of an application window shows the name of the program that owns the window. The title bar of a document window depends on what the window contains. If a document window contains a document like a word processing file or a spreadsheet, the title bar shows the name of the document. When you work with more than one window at a time, you'll come to depend on title bars because they identify the various windows on your screen.

Beneath the title bar of an application window, you'll always find a *menu bar*. You can see the menu bar for the Program Manager in figure 1-2. The menu bar lets you access *program menus* so you can issue commands to the program. Usually, you can use the menu bar to help identify an application window because document windows don't have menu bars.

How to end *Windows* Before I show you how to end *Windows*, you should know that most *Windows* users never need to leave the *Windows* environment. Once you end the application programs you're using and return to the Program Manager, it's safe to turn your computer off with *Windows* still running. Since you can run most DOS programs from within *Windows*, you usually don't have to leave *Windows* for that purpose either. But in the unlikely event that you need to run a DOS program without *Windows* running, you need to know how to end *Windows*.

To end *Windows*, you just close the Program Manager's application window. To do that, you can use several different methods. One of them is pressing the F4 key while you hold down the Alt key (Alt+F4). Later in this chapter, you'll learn how to end a *Windows* program by using the mouse.

When you end the Program Manager, *Windows* warns you that it's about to end and gives you a chance to change your mind. If any application programs are currently active, *Windows* also warns you if you've made changes that haven't been saved. Then, you can return to the application program and save your work, or you can choose to abandon the work you were doing and end *Windows*.

Basic mouse skills for working with *Windows*

Windows was designed to be used with a mouse. That's why you can perform many of the *Windows* functions more easily with a mouse than you can with a keyboard. Once you learn the basic mouse actions, you can use the actions to minimize, maximize, and restore windows; to move a window; to change the size of a window; and to scroll through the contents of a window.

The four basic mouse actions To use a mouse with *Windows* or any *Windows* application program, you need to know how to use four mouse actions. These are summarized in figure 1-3. Although these actions may

Action	How to do it
Point	Move the mouse so the mouse pointer is positioned on the object or control that you're interested in.
Click	Without moving the mouse pointer off the object you're pointing to, press the left mouse button down, then release it.
Double-click	Without moving the mouse pointer off the object you're pointing to, press the left mouse button down, then release it, then press it down again, then release it again. Do this quickly, in less than a second.
Drag	After you point to an object, press and hold down the left mouse button, move the mouse pointer to a new location, then release the left mouse button.

Figure 1-3 The four basic mouse actions

seem a little difficult if you haven't used a mouse before, you'll quickly become adept at using the mouse. All it takes is the practice that you'll get as you use the skills presented in the first section of this book.

The first mouse action is to *point*. This means to move the mouse so the *mouse pointer* is on an object. You use pointing in combination with the other three actions.

After you point to an object, you *click* the mouse to tell *Windows*: "That's the one I want," or "I want to do that." To click, you press the left mouse button down and release it. A click isn't completed, though, if you move the mouse pointer off the object you were pointing to before you release the button. This is an intentional part of the *Windows* design. If you have second thoughts about an operation, you can often cancel it by not completing a click while the pointer is on an object.

Some *Windows* operations require that you *double-click* on an object. To do that, you point at the object and quickly click the left mouse button twice. You may have to practice a bit before you're able to click twice quickly enough, but it's easy once you get the hang of it. To start an application program from the Program Manager, you just double-click on the symbol for the program.

If you need to move an object from one place to another, you can use the mouse to *drag* it. To do that, you point to an object, press and hold down the left mouse button, move the mouse pointer to the new location while the object is dragged along with it, and release the mouse button so the object is dropped at the new location. When you use *Excel*, you can use the drag action to highlight a range of cells. You can also use it to select commands from menus.

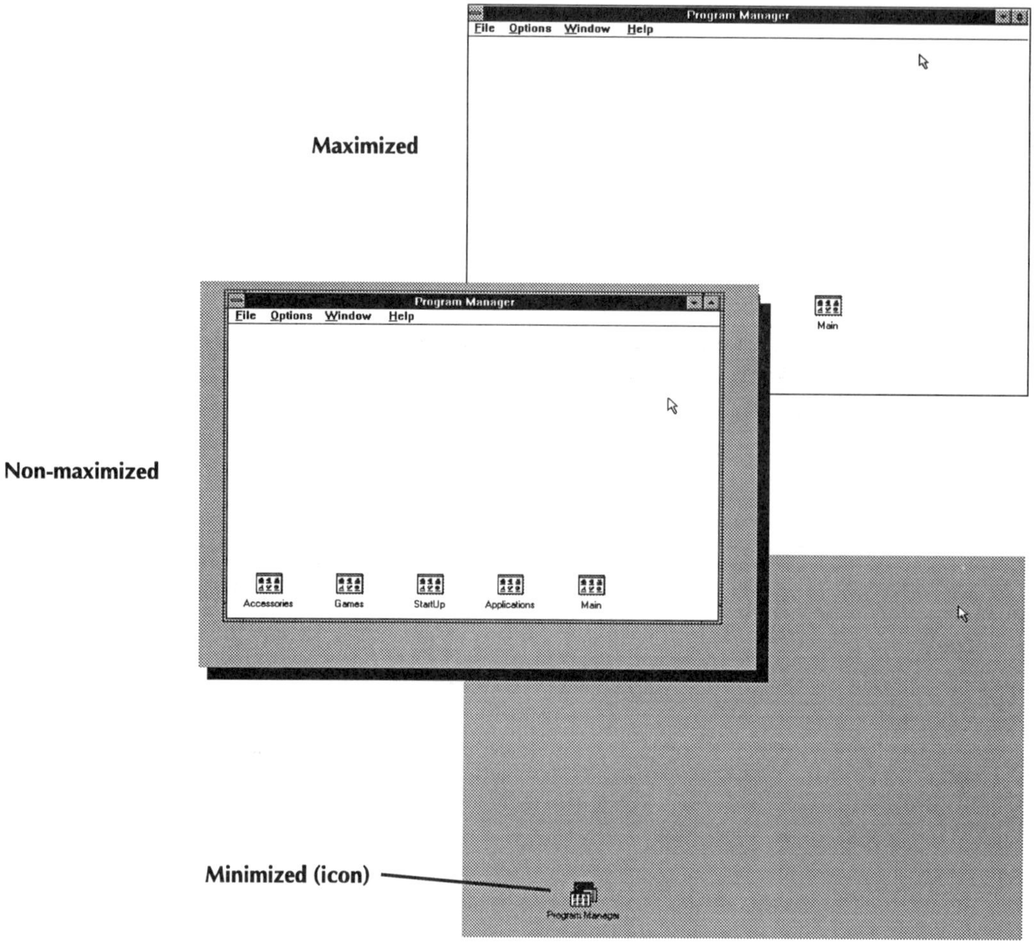

Figure 1-4 The three states of an application window

How to minimize, maximize, or restore a window A window can exist in any of the three states shown in figure 1-4: maximized, non-maximized, and minimized. As you can see, a *maximized* application window fills the entire screen, so the desktop background isn't visible at all. A *non-maximized* application window does not fill the entire screen, so the desktop background (or perhaps another window) is visible behind it. And a *minimized* application window is reduced to a symbol called an *icon* that represents the window. When you minimize an application window, its icon is always displayed on the desktop.

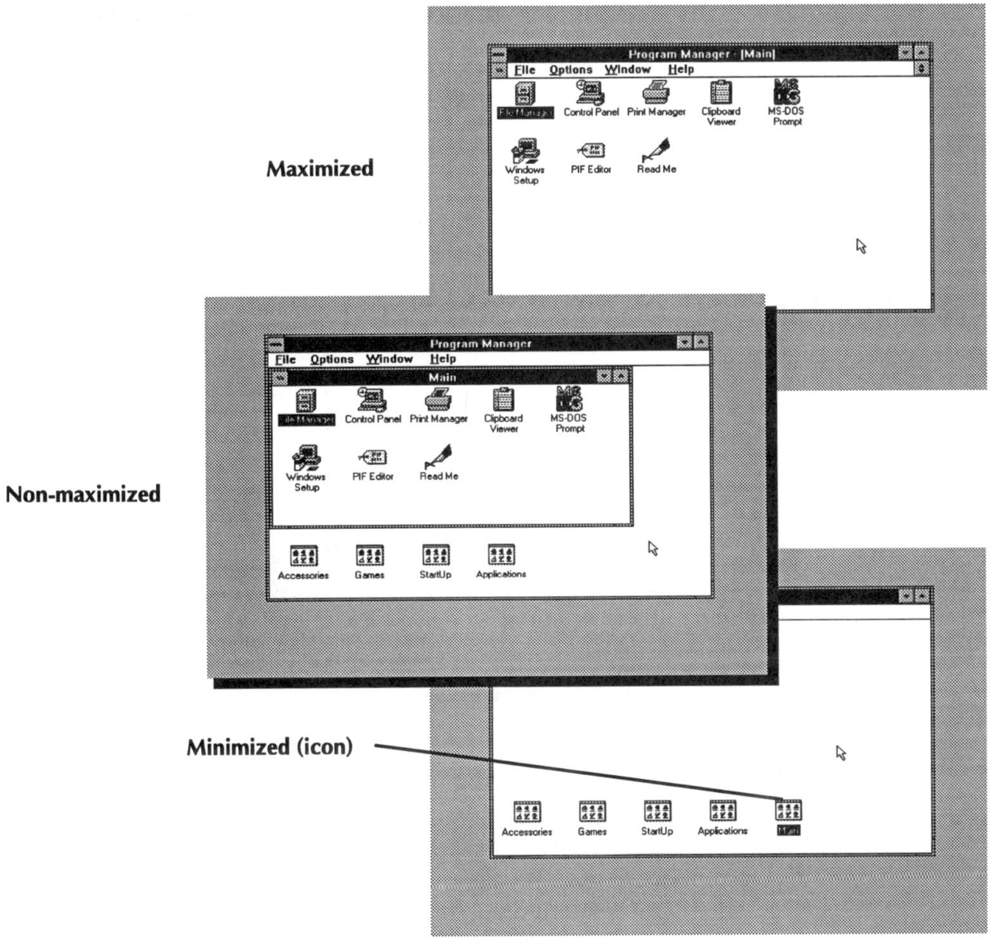

Figure 1-5 The three states of a document window

In contrast, figure 1-5 shows how document windows appear in these three states. As you can see, a maximized document window fills its entire application window, so no other document windows are visible. A non-maximized document window partially fills the application window, so other document windows in the application window may be visible. And a minimized document window is displayed as an icon in the application window.

To change the state of an application or document window, you use the control boxes in the top right corner of a window as shown in figure 1-6. To

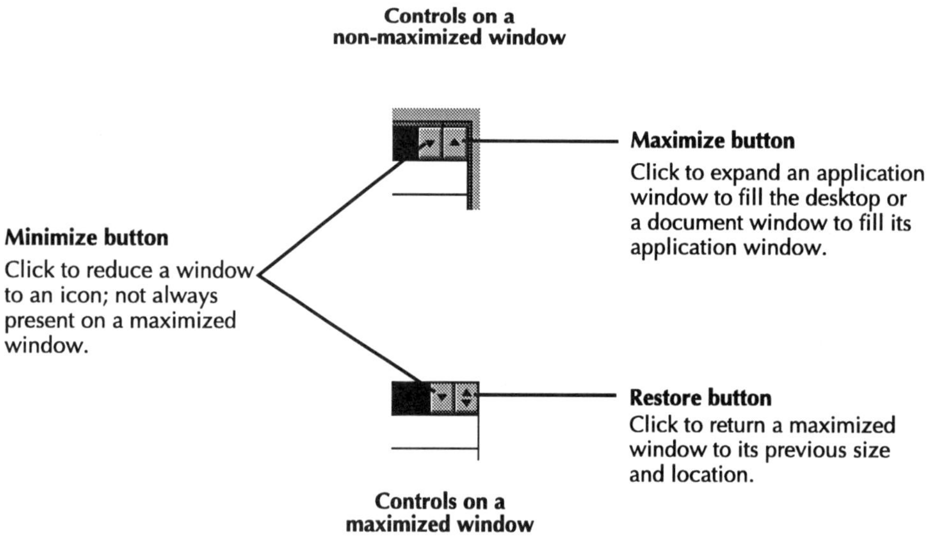

Figure 1-6 The controls for minimizing, maximizing, and restoring windows

minimize a window, you click on its *minimize button.* To maximize a window, you click on its *maximize button.* To restore a maximized window, you click on its *restore button.* And to restore a minimized window from its icon, you double-click on the icon. Because *Windows* remembers the previous size and position of the window when you minimize or maximize it, it's returned to its previous size and position when you restore it. Note in figure 1-6 that a maximized window doesn't have a maximize button, and a non-maximized window doesn't have a restore button.

How to move or size a window One of the benefits of *Windows* is that it lets you decide where your windows are placed on the screen and how large they are. To move a window from one position on the screen to another, you drag the window by its title bar as illustrated in figure 1-7. Then, when you release the mouse button, the window is moved to the new location.

To control the size of a window, you drag different portions of the window's border as summarized in figure 1-7. As you can see, you can change a window's width by dragging its left or right border, and you can change a window's height by dragging its top or bottom border. If you drag

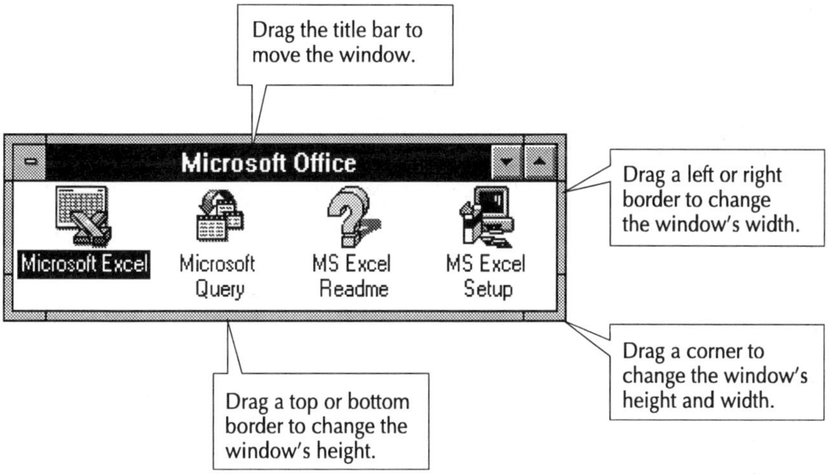

Pointer shape	Function
	Normal
	Resize window width
	Resize window height
	Resize window height and width

Figure 1-7 How to move and resize a window

one of the four corners of a window, you can adjust both its height and width at the same time. To perform any of these sizing operations, you carefully move the mouse pointer over a border or corner until its normal arrow shape changes to a double-headed arrow. Then, you drag the border or corner until the window is the size you want. When you release the mouse button, the size of the window is changed.

How to scroll through the contents of a window If a window is too small to show all of its contents, the application program automatically adds *scroll bars* to it. Then, you can use the controls on the scroll bars to move the contents of the window as summarized in figure 1-8. As you can see,

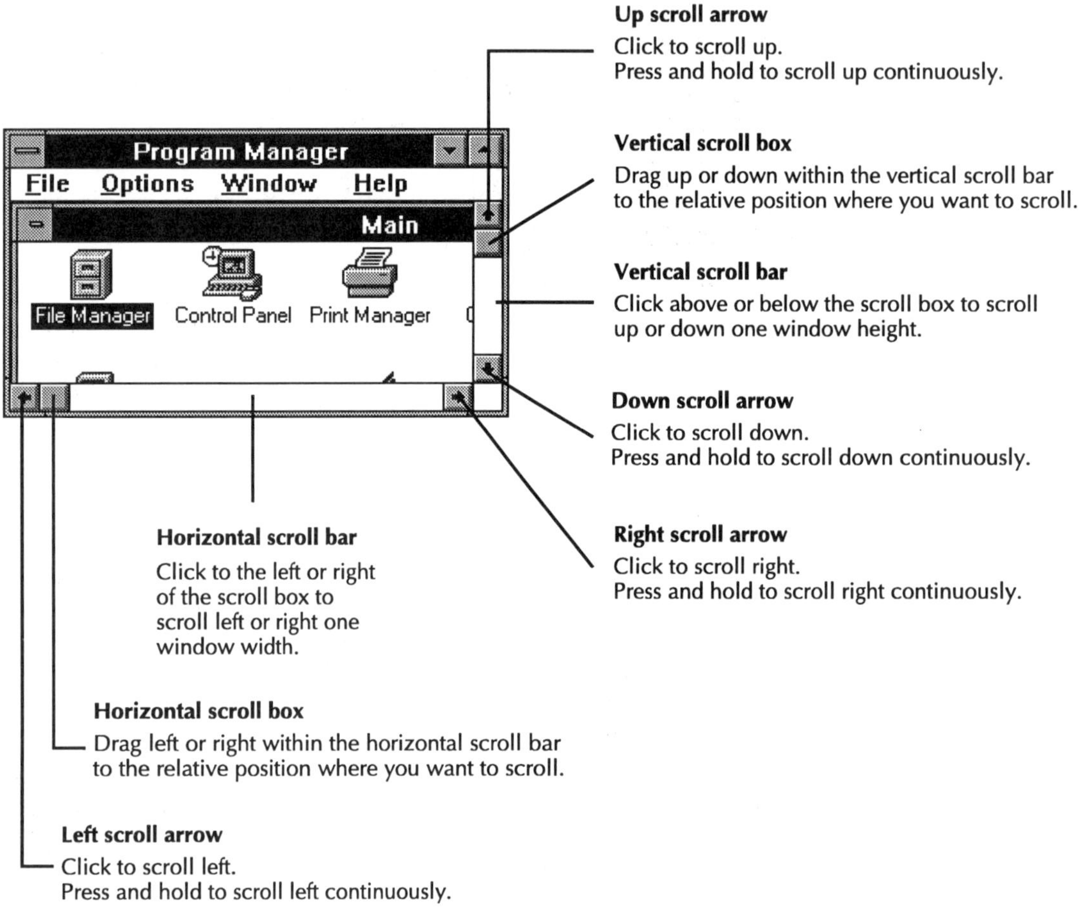

Figure 1-8 How to scroll the contents of a window

you can click on a *scroll arrow* to scroll one unit at a time. You can click on the scroll bar to scroll one window height or width at a time. And you can drag a *scroll box* to scroll a varying number of units based on the distance that you move the scroll box.

If you experiment with these controls for a few minutes, you shouldn't have any trouble using them so I won't describe scrolling in more detail. You should realize, though, that the location of a scroll box on a scroll bar indicates the position of the current contents of the window relative to the total contents for the window. If the scroll box is at the bottom of a vertical scroll bar, for example, the window displays the last portion of the total contents for the window. If the scroll box is halfway down a vertical scroll bar, the window displays the middle portion of the total contents for the window.

How to start your application programs, switch between them, and end them

Before you can use an application program under *Windows*, you need to know how to start it from the Program Manager. Then, to take full advantage of the multitasking feature of *Windows*, you need to know how to switch from one application program to another. Last, you need to know how to end an application program.

If a program is designed for use with *Windows*, it can be referred to as a *Windows application program*, or just as a *Windows application*. You should realize, though, that you can also run DOS application programs under *Windows*. In fact, most of the skills that follow work for both *Windows* applications and DOS application programs. Because *Excel* is a *Windows* application, though, the emphasis in this chapter is on *Windows* applications.

How to start a *Windows* application In all, *Windows* provides seven different ways to start an application program. In practice, though, you can use one simple mouse technique for starting any *Windows* application from the Program Manager. You just double-click on the icon for the program.

When *Windows* first starts, however, the icon for the program you want to start may not be visible in the application window for the Program Manager. That's because the Program Manager organizes its icons into collections called *program groups*. Each of these groups is represented by an icon that can be called a *program group icon*, or just a *group icon*. Then, when you double-click on a group icon, a group window is *opened*. This window contains the icons for the programs that are in the group, and these icons are called *program item icons*, or just *program icons*. To start one of the programs in the group, you double-click on its icon.

In figure 1-9, you can see how you can use these techniques for starting *Excel*. In part 1, you locate the group icon that contains the program. In this example, the group icon is named "Microsoft Office" and it is clearly visible. Sometimes, though, you have to close the windows that are on top of the group icon before you are able to see it. Once you locate it, you double-click on the icon to open its window.

As you can see in part 2 of figure 1-9, the Microsoft Office group contains four program icons, including the one for *Excel*. Then, when you double-click on the *Excel* icon, *Windows* starts (*launches*) the program as shown in part 3. Here, the application window for *Excel* is maximized so you can no longer see the Program Manager.

How to switch from one *Windows* application to another Because *Windows* provides a feature called *multitasking*, you can start two or more programs at the same time. However, you can work on only one program at a time. That program is the *active program*, and it runs in the *active application window*. If several application windows are displayed on the desktop, the active window is always the one on top, and the title bar of the active program is always highlighted. In part 3 of figure 1-9, for example, *Excel* is the active program, and its application window is on top of the Program Manager's.

Windows provides several methods for switching from one program to another, and four of them are summarized in figure 1-10. The first method is the most direct way to switch to another program because all you do is click on any part of an inactive application window. When you do, *Windows* brings that application window to the top of the stack and makes it the active window. Of course, some part of the application window has to be visible for you to click on it.

The second way to switch from one application to another is to use a *Windows* option called *Fast Alt+Tab Switching*. This feature lets you scan through the names of the programs that are running and switch to the one you want. To use this feature, you hold down the Alt key and press the Tab key repeatedly. Each time you press Tab, a panel appears with the name of a program in it. When the name of the program you want appears, you release the Alt key and that program becomes the active application. You should realize, though, that this feature can be deactivated by using one of the setup options. So if this switching method doesn't work on your PC, you should find out how to reactivate it.

The third way to switch from one program to another is to use the Alt+Esc keystroke combination. Each time you press this combination, the next program in sequence becomes the active program. If just two programs are running, that's what you want. But if several programs are running, this can be inefficient. Unlike Fast Alt+Tab Switching, Alt+Esc Switching can't be turned off, so it's always available.

Part 1: To start *Excel*, find the group icon named "Microsoft Office" and double-click on it.

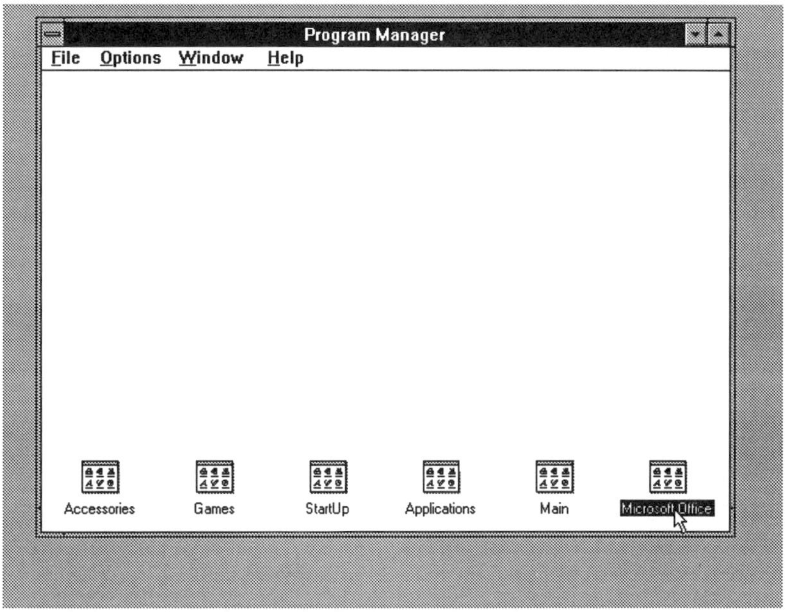

Part 2: *Windows* opens a document window that contains the icons for the programs that come with *Excel*. To start *Excel*, double-click on the "Microsoft Excel" icon.

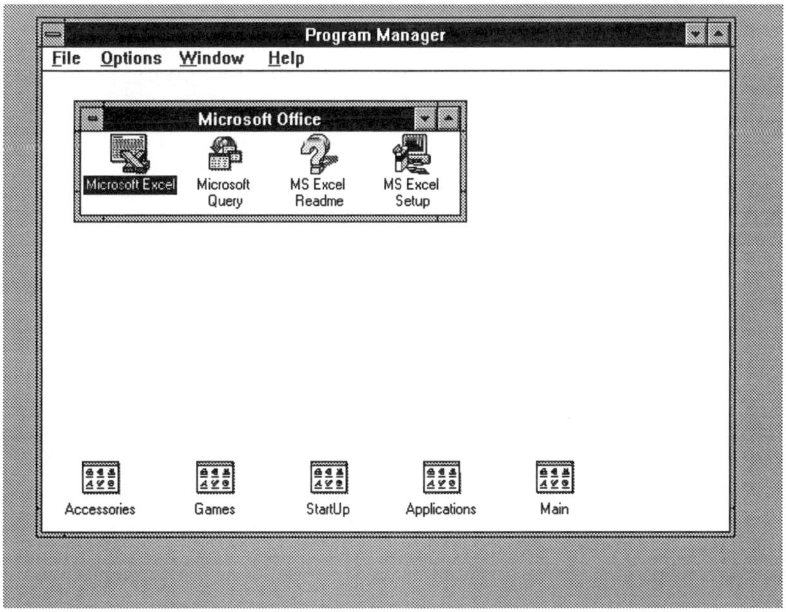

Figure 1-9 How to start a *Windows* application like *Excel* (parts 1 and 2 of 3)

Part 3: *Windows* starts the *Excel* program.

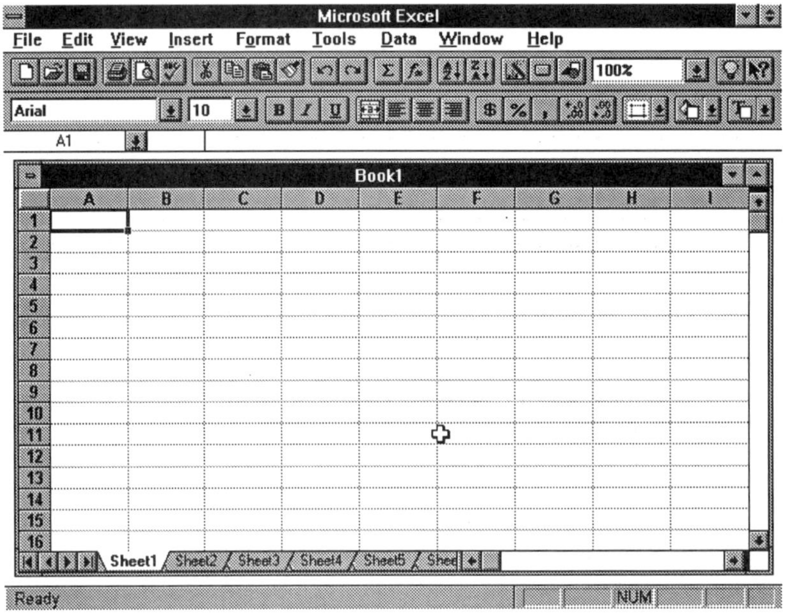

Figure 1-9 How to start a *Windows* application like *Excel* (part 3 of 3)

The first three ways to switch from one program to another leave the application windows unchanged. In contrast, the fourth way uses the minimize and restore functions, which change the state of a window. When you want to switch to another program, you click on the minimize button for the current program. This reduces the active window to an icon that appears at the bottom of the desktop, but the program is still running. Then, to switch to another program, you double-click on its icon. When you use this method for switching between programs, you usually start by minimizing all of the program windows. Then, when you activate a window, you maximize it so you can use the full screen while you work with it.

How to end a *Windows* application The easiest way to end any *Windows* program is to double-click on the *control-menu box* in the upper left corner of the application window for the program as shown in figure 1-11. If you've haven't saved your work, the application program will warn you before it ends. Then, you can return to the program to save your work. Or, you can abandon your work and end the program.

1. Click on an inactive application window.
2. Use Fast Alt+Tab switching.
3. Use Alt+Esc switching.
4. Minimize and restore application windows.

Figure 1-10 Four ways to switch between programs

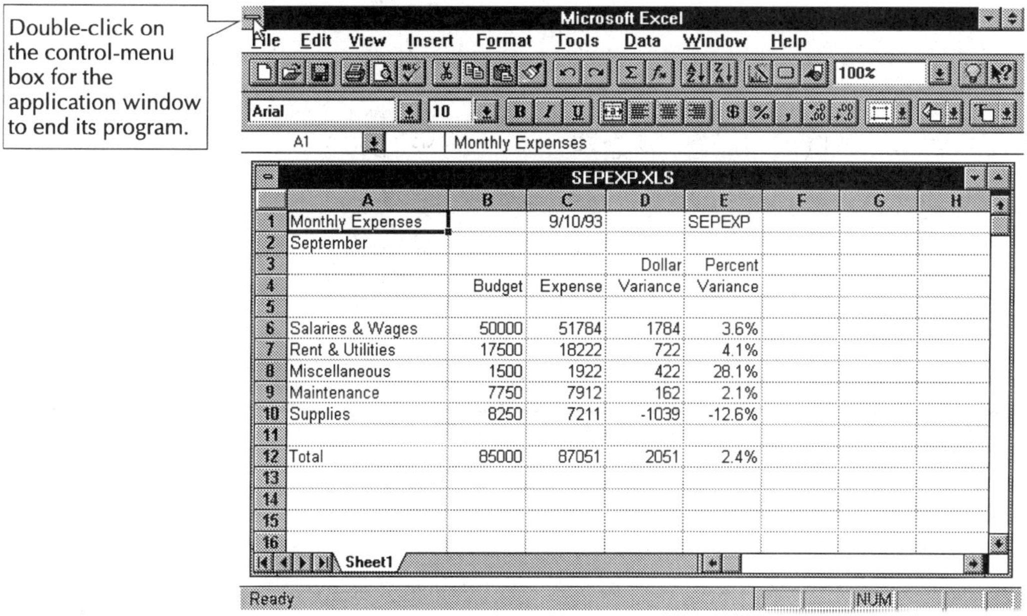

Figure 1-11 How to end a *Windows* application like *Excel*

Since the Program Manager is a *Windows* program, double-clicking on the control-menu box for its application window will end the program. Then, if the Program Manager is the shell program, *Windows* also ends. However, if other programs are still running, *Windows* will give you a chance to save any work before it ends all the programs.

Incidentally, if you accidentally click on a control-menu box instead of double-clicking on it, a *control menu* will drop down from the box. Don't let this menu bother you, though. To end the program, you can just double-click on the control-menu box as if the menu weren't there. Or, to remove the menu, you can click anywhere on the desktop outside of the control menu.

Figure 1-12 The programs in the Main and Accessories groups of the Program Manager

Other *Windows* programs for *Excel* users

Thus far, you've been introduced to just one of the programs that comes with *Windows*, the Program Manager. But if you look at figure 1-12, you can see that the Main program group contains program item icons that start eight other programs that come with *Windows*, and the Accessories group contains 13 other programs that come with *Windows*. In addition, the Games group contains a couple of games that come with *Windows*.

For *Excel* users, the *File Manager* in the Main group is the most important of these *Windows* programs because you use it for managing the files and directories that are on your hard disk. In general, the File Manager provides all of the functions that are available through DOS, but it does so with a graphic interface that lets you work without remembering so many

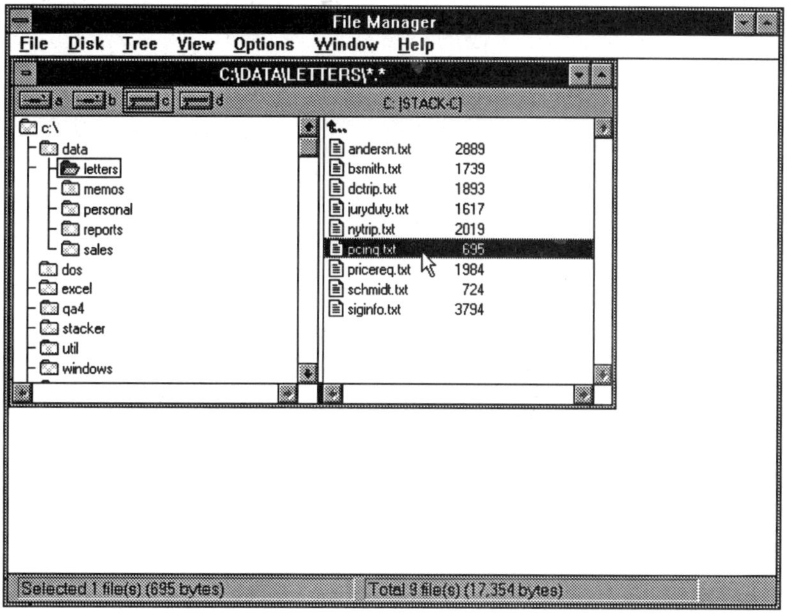

Figure 1-13 A typical application window for the File Manager

details. In addition, the File Manager lets you perform most functions more efficiently than you can with DOS.

To use the File Manager, you can switch from *Excel* to the Program Manager, then start the File Manager. Its opening screen will look something like the one in figure 1-13. Then, you can use the File Manager to perform functions like creating directories, copying and moving files from one directory to another, renaming files, and deleting files. When you're through, you can switch back to *Excel* from the Program Manager and continue your spreadsheet work. Or, you can end the File Manager by double-clicking on its control-menu box before returning to *Excel*.

Some of the other programs that come with *Windows* may also be of interest to *Excel* users, even though they aren't essential. In the Main program group, for example, you can use the Control Panel to set some of the options for your *Windows* system, and you can use the Print Manager to install a new printer on your system. In the Accessories group, you can use the Write program for word processing and the Calendar program for keeping track of your appointments.

The benefits that you get from using *Windows*

Now that you've finished this chapter, you can start to see why *Windows* is so popular. First, the multitasking feature lets you run two or more application programs at the same time so you can switch from one program to another in just a few seconds. This feature also makes it easy for you to transfer data from one program to another. If, for example, you normally use a spreadsheet program and a word processing program, you can start both at the start of a work session and switch from one to another as needed. Then, if you want to transfer data from the spreadsheet program into the word processing program, or vice versa, you can do so with just a few keystroke combinations or mouse actions.

Second, the File Manager makes it easier for you to manage your files because you don't have to use the DOS shell or the even more cumbersome DOS commands. Once you learn how to use this feature, you can use the File Manager for managing all your files and the Program Manager for starting all your programs. From that point on, you probably won't ever want to use DOS again.

Third, *Windows* provides a *graphical user interface*, or *GUI* (pronounced gooey), so all *Windows* programs look similar and operate in consistent ways. This makes it easier for you to learn how to use new *Windows* applications. In this chapter, you've learned the standard techniques for working with *Windows*, and you'll learn the standard techniques for entering data and using commands in the next chapter. Once you learn those techniques, you'll be able to apply them to almost every other *Windows* program that you use.

Fourth, as part of the graphical user interface, *Windows* provides for WYSIWYG (What You See Is What You Get). That means that what you see on the screen is going to closely resemble what you get when you print what you're working on. That's true whether you're using a word processing or a spreadsheet program.

Last, if you've ever received an "out of memory" message from a DOS spreadsheet program, you'll appreciate *Windows*' improved memory management. In particular, because *Windows* eliminates the 640KB memory limit that's inherent to DOS, you don't have to fuss with expanded or extended memory configurations. On most *Windows* systems, that means you can work on large spreadsheets without worrying about memory limitations.

Perspective

This chapter presents the minimum set of *Windows* skills that you need for getting started with *Excel*. However, there's a lot more that you need to know if you want to get the most from *Windows*. For instance, you need to know how to use the File Manager if you want to manage your files and directories from *Windows*. You need to know how to use the Control Panel or Print Manager if you want to change some of the *Windows* options or install a new printer on your PC. And you may need to know how to use the PIF Editor if you want to run some of your DOS programs from *Windows*.

To help you learn these other *Windows* skills as quickly and easily as possible, we've created a book called *The Least You Need to Know About Windows 3.1*. The tutorial section of this book will help you become a competent *Windows* user in six hours or less. When you complete that section, you'll know how to use the Program Manager, the File Manager, and the standard features of all *Windows* programs. After that, you can use the reference sections to learn other *Windows* skills whenever you have 10 or 15 minutes to spare. For ordering information, please refer to the back of this book.

Summary

- You can start *Windows* from the DOS command prompt by entering *win*. On many PCs, this command is in the AUTOEXEC.BAT file, so *Windows* starts automatically when the system starts.
- When it starts, *Windows* can load more than one application program, but one of them will always be the *shell program*. The default shell program is the Program Manager, and it lets you start application programs.
- When you start an application program, *Windows* creates a workspace on the *desktop* for it called an *application window*. Inside its application window, a typical program can create its own workspaces called *document windows*.
- You can use the mouse to perform any *Windows* function. To use the mouse, you need to know only four basic mouse actions: *point*, *click*, *double-click*, and *drag*.

- Nearly every application and document window has a *title bar* across the top that identifies its contents, *borders* and *corners* that let you resize the window, and some combination of *minimize*, *maximize*, and *restore buttons*. You can use the mouse to minimize, maximize, restore, move, and size a window by working with the buttons, title bar, borders, and corners of a window.
- When a window is too small to show all of its contents at the same time, *scroll bars* are added to it. Then, you can use the mouse to scroll through the window by working with the scroll bars, scroll arrows, and scroll boxes.
- The Program Manager organizes your programs into *program groups* that are displayed in document windows called *group windows*. When a group window isn't open, it appears as a *group icon*. When a group window is open, the programs within in it are displayed as *program icons*.
- To *open* a group window, you double-click on a group icon. To start a program, you double-click on its program icon.
- *Windows* provides several methods for switching from one application window (or program) to another. One of the easiest is to click on any part of an inactive window. Another is to use *Fast Alt+Tab Switching*.
- To end a *Windows* application, you double-click on the *control-menu box* for the program's application window. You can also end the Program Manager in this way.
- When you use *Excel*, you can use the *File Manager* for managing files.
- Some of the benefits that you get from using *Windows* are *multitasking*, improved file management through the File Manager, a standard *graphical user interface* for all *Windows* programs, built-in WYSIWYG, and improved memory management.

Chapter 2

Get up to speed with *Excel 5.0 for Windows*

An introduction to *Excel*

The program items for *Excel* in the Microsoft Office group window
The parts of the *Excel* window

Basic spreadsheet skills that still work with *Excel*

The keystroke combinations for working with *Excel*
How to enter labels into a worksheet
How to enter values into a worksheet
How to enter formulas into a worksheet
How to enter functions into a worksheet

How to use a mouse with *Excel*

To scroll through a worksheet
To select a cell, row, column, range, or the entire worksheet
To enter or edit the contents of a cell
To start a function, adjust column width, or adjust row height

How to issue *Excel* commands

How to use the mouse or the keyboard to issue a command
How to use shortcut keys to issue a command
How to work with a dialog box

This book assumes that you already have some experience with another spreadsheet program. If you do, it shouldn't take you long to learn how to use Version 5.0 of *Microsoft Excel*. That's true whether you've been using a DOS spreadsheet program or a *Windows* spreadsheet program. And that's true whether you've been using an earlier version of *Excel* or a completely different program like *Lotus 1-2-3* or *Quattro Pro*.

The purpose of this chapter is to get you up to speed with *Excel* 5.0 as quickly as possible. To do that, you'll start by learning how to use the spreadsheet skills you already have with *Excel*. Next, you'll learn how to use *Excel*'s graphical user interface. Then, you'll learn how to use the *Excel* commands that correspond to the types of commands you used with your old spreadsheet program. Last, this chapter introduces you to all of the commands offered by *Excel*. When you complete this chapter, you should be able to work at least as efficiently with *Excel* 5.0 as you worked with your old spreadsheet program.

An introduction to *Excel*

In chapter 1, you learned how to start a *Windows* program from the Program Manager. To start *Excel*, you double-click on the icon for the Microsoft Office group. Then, you double-click on the *Microsoft Excel* icon.

The program items for *Excel* in the Microsoft Office group window Figure 2-1 shows the Microsoft Office *group window*. As you can see, this window contains four program item icons. The first icon is the one that you use for starting *Excel*.

The other three icons are for programs that most *Excel* users aren't likely to need. For instance, the *Microsoft Excel Setup* program lets you install parts of *Excel* that you didn't install initially. And the *Microsoft Query* program lets you do complex database operations.

The parts of the *Excel* window When you start *Excel*, an *application window* like the one in figure 2-2 opens. To a large extent, this window looks like the display for any other spreadsheet program. In addition, most of the terms that are used for the components of the window are like those used for any other spreadsheet program. Nevertheless, it's worth taking a couple of minutes to review the components of the window and the terms that are used to describe them.

Icon	What it does
Microsoft Excel	Starts the *Excel* program.
Microsoft Query	Starts the MSQUERY program so you can retrieve information from external data bases.
MS Excel Read Me	Starts the *Windows* Notepad program and retrieves the file named README.TXT so you can read last-minute product updates for *Excel.*
MS Excel Setup	Lets you install or remove components of *Excel.*

Figure 2-1 The Microsoft Office program group with the program item icons for *Excel* 5.0

In this example, the *document window* contains an *Excel workbook*. As a result, you can also call the document window a *workbook window*. The workbook in this example contains one *worksheet* that summarizes monthly expenses. In the next chapter, you'll see an example of a workbook that contains multiple worksheets.

Within the workbook window are the *columns* and *rows* you'd expect in any spreadsheet. The *current cell,* also called the *active cell,* is identified by the *cell pointer*, which is indicated by a dark outline around the cell. You identify a cell with a *cell reference*, called a *cell address* in some spreadsheet programs. A cell reference consists of the letter of the column and the number of the row found in the *worksheet frame* (not identified in figure 2-2). So the cell reference of the current cell in figure 2-2 is C12.

Above the workbook window are five bars that contain different controls: the *title bar*, *menu bar*, *Standard toolbar, Formatting toolbar,* and *formula bar*. In the *name box* of the formula bar, you can see the address of the current cell. In the *entry area* of the formula, you can see the contents of the current cell. In this case, cell C12 contains a function that gets the total of cells C6 through C11.

The two toolbars contain rows of buttons. Each button gives you easy access to a frequently used command just by clicking on it. If you haven't used toolbar buttons like these before, you'll see how they can quickly improve your productivity in the next chapter.

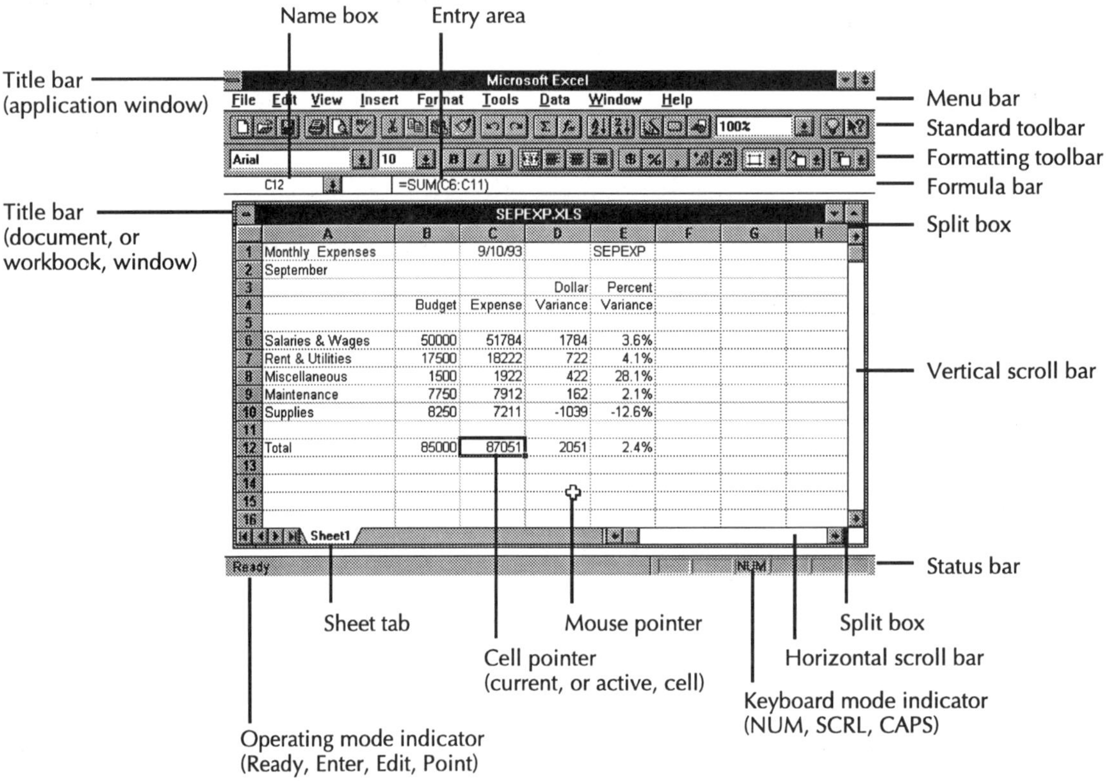

Figure 2-2 The *Excel* screen

At the bottom and on the right of the workbook window are *scroll bars*. In chapter 1, you learned how to scroll through a window by clicking on these bars. When you use *Excel*, you can use the same techniques for scrolling through a worksheet. Above the vertical scroll bar and to the right of the horizontal scroll bar are *split boxes* you can drag to split the window into *panes*. Panes lets you look at different parts of a worksheet at the same time.

At the bottom of the document window is the *status bar*. On its left side, it shows what operating mode *Excel* is in at any given moment. In the example in figure 2-2, *Excel* is in Ready mode. On the right side of the status bar, indicators show current keyboard modes. In this example, the NUM indicator is on, which means that the keyboard is in Num-lock mode.

Keys that change keyboard modes	
Caps-lock	Turns Caps-lock on or off.
Scroll-lock	Turns Scroll-lock on or off. This changes the way the screen scrolls when you use keys that move the cell pointer. Usually, you want this off.
Num-lock	Turns Num-lock on or off. When Num-lock is on, you can use the numeric keypad to enter numbers. When Num-lock is off, you can use the numeric keypad to move the cell pointer.
Keys that move the cell pointer	
Right-arrow or Tab	Moves the cell pointer right one cell.
Left-arrow or Shift+Tab	Moves the cell pointer left one cell.
Down-arrow or Enter	Moves the cell pointer down one cell.
Up-arrow or Shift+Enter	Moves the cell pointer up one cell.
Page-up	Moves the cell pointer up one screen.
Page-down	Moves the cell pointer down one screen.
Alt+Page-up	Moves the cell pointer left one screen.
Alt+Page-down	Moves the cell pointer right one screen.
Home	Moves the cell pointer to the first column in the current row.
Ctrl+Home	Moves the cell pointer to cell A1.

Figure 2-3 Some of the keystroke combinations that you can use with *Excel* (part 1 of 2)

Near the lower left corner of the workbook window is a *sheet tab* with the name Sheet1. Because *Excel 5.0* lets you store more than one worksheet in a single workbook file, a sheet tab identifies each worksheet. In the next chapter, you'll learn more about this feature.

Basic spreadsheet skills that still work with *Excel*

Many of the spreadsheet skills that you already have will still work with *Excel*. In particular, you can enter and edit labels, values, formulas, and functions in much the same way that you did with your old program.

The keystroke combinations for working with *Excel* Figure 2-3 presents the keystroke combinations for working with *Excel*. You can use these keystrokes for moving the cell pointer, for editing an entry in a cell, and so on.

Keys for editing the contents of a cell	
F2	Enters Edit mode.
Left-arrow	Moves the cursor left one character.
Right-arrow	Moves the cursor right one character.
Down-arrow or End	Moves the cursor to the end of the entry.
Home	Moves the cursor to the start of the entry.
Backspace	Erases the character to the left of the cursor.
Delete	Erases the character to the right of the cursor.
Keys for completing entries	
Enter	Completes the entry and moves the cell pointer down one cell.
Shift+Enter	Completes the entry and moves the cell pointer up one cell.
Tab	Completes the entry and moves the cell pointer right one cell.
Shift+Tab	Completes the entry and moves the cell pointer left one cell.
Esc	Cancels the changes in the current cell, leaves the cell pointer in the current cell, and returns to Ready mode.
Arrow	Completes the entry and moves the cell pointer in the direction of the arrow. Can't be used when editing an entry.
Keys for highlighting a range of cells	
Shift+*pointer-movement*	Hold down the Shift key while you use the keys that move the cell pointer to highlight the range. Release the Shift key to complete the selection.
. (period) or : (colon)	Lets you extend a range selection.
Ctrl+Spacebar	Selects the entire column where the cell pointer is located.
Shift+Spacebar	Selects the entire row where the cell pointer is located.

Figure 2-3 Some of the keystroke combinations that you can use with *Excel* (part 2 of 2)

The keystroke combinations in the last group in this figure are for highlighting a range. A *range* consists of a rectangular group of cells. Although some spreadsheet programs refer to a range of cells as a *block*, *range* is the term that has always been used with *Excel.*

The first way to highlight a range from the keyboard is to move the cell pointer to the first cell in the range, then hold down the Shift key as you move the cell pointer to the far corner of the range. If you're entering a range in a formula, you can also use a period or a colon to anchor the first cell in the range. Then, you can use the pointer-movement keys to highlight the range. *Excel* also provides shortcuts you can use to select an entire column or row.

How to enter labels into a worksheet Figure 2-4 summarizes what you need to know for entering *labels* into a worksheet. Simply move the cell pointer to the cell where you want to enter the label, type it, then press Enter. As you type, the entry appears in the cell as well as in the entry area of the formula bar.

Excel does a better job than other spreadsheet programs of identifying labels by the characters they contain. It does this by using a default cell format called *General format*. In particular, *Excel* assumes that an entry is a label if it contains a letter or any other non-numeric character, as long as the entry doesn't match a pattern for a number, a formula, a date, or a time. For example, if you enter 12-31, *Excel* interprets the entry as a date and displays 31-Dec in the cell. If you enter 13-31, however, *Excel* interprets the entry as a label because it doesn't match the pattern for a date or a formula.

If you want *Excel* to interpret an entry as a label even though it matches a number, formula, date, or time pattern, you have to enter an apostrophe prefix. For example, if you want *Excel* to interpret 12-31 as a label rather than as a date, you type '12-31. Then, *Excel* displays 12-31 in the cell.

If you're a *1-2-3* user, you may also expect to use prefixes to specify how a cell entry should be aligned. In *Excel*, however, you don't use prefixes for this purpose. Instead, you can use the alignment buttons in the Formatting toolbar. You'll learn how to use *Excel's* toolbar buttons in the next chapter.

How to enter values into a worksheet Figure 2-5 summarizes what you need to know for entering *values* into a worksheet. If you've been using an earlier version of *Excel*, you can enter values as you always have. Each value can consist of one or more digits, a decimal point, and a leading plus or minus sign.

A value entry can also include a leading dollar sign, commas, and a percent sign in any cell with General format. If you use any of these characters in a cell with a numeric format, they're ignored if they're not appropriate to the format. If you enter any of these characters in a cell with General format, however, *Excel* changes the format of the cell to the format indicated by the characters you entered. If you enter a value with a leading dollar sign, for example, the format of the cell is changed to Currency. Similarly, if you enter a value with a comma and no dollar sign, the format

The labels of a worksheet

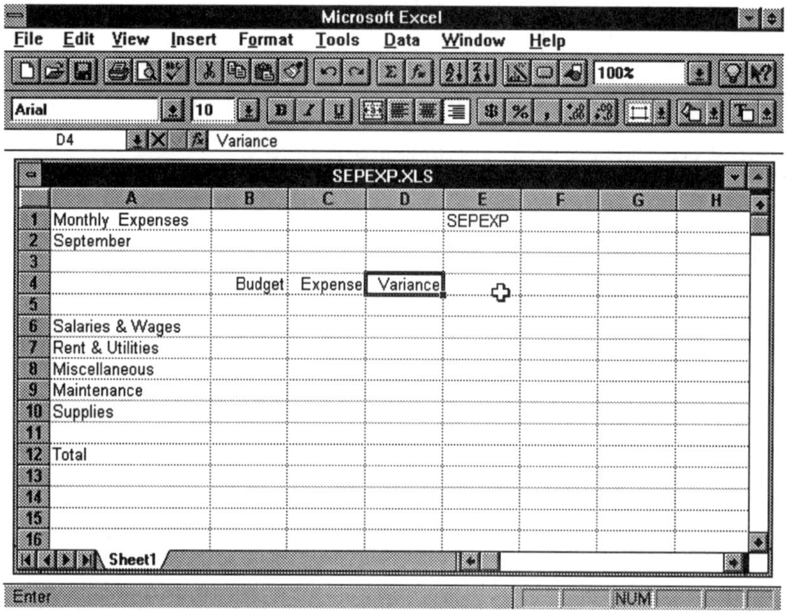

General procedure

1. Use the keyboard or the mouse to move the cell pointer to the cell where you want to enter the label.
2. Type the text for the label.
3. Press the Enter key.

Notes

- *Excel* assumes an entry is a label if it contains a letter (it doesn't have to start with a letter) and doesn't match a standard pattern for a number, formula, date, or time.
- If you want *Excel* to treat a number, formula, date, or time as a label, type an apostrophe as its first character. If, for example, you want to enter 1-2 as a label, you must type an apostrophe before it. Otherwise, *Excel* will interpret the entry as a date and display 2-Jan.
- If a label is too long for the current cell, the extra characters are displayed in the empty cells to the right. If the cells to the right aren't empty, the extra characters aren't displayed, although they are still stored in the current cell.

Figure 2-4 How to enter a label into a worksheet

The values of a worksheet (shaded)

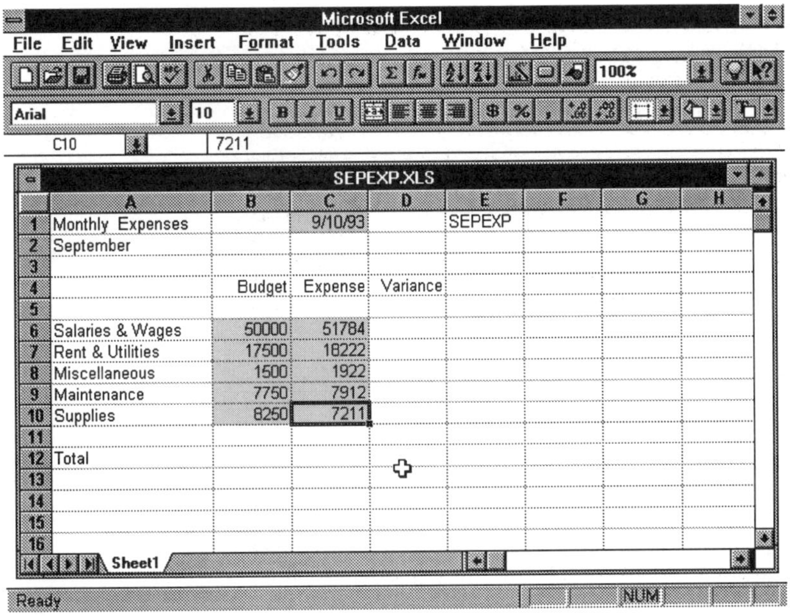

General procedure

1. Use the keyboard or the mouse to move the cell pointer to the cell where you want to enter the value.
2. Type the number, date, or time.
3. Press the Enter key.

Valid characters	**Example**
The digits zero through nine	189
Leading plus or minus sign	-97.5
One decimal point (period)	123.45
Leading dollar sign	$123.45
Comma	1,234.56
Trailing percent sign	45%
Hyphen (in a date)	1-1-95
Slash (in a date)	1/1/95
Colon (in a time)	7:30
Text as part of a date or time	August 15

Figure 2-5 How to enter a value into a worksheet (part 1 of 2)

Entries in cells with General format

Entry	Value displayed	Value stored	New format category
12345	12345	12345	General (no change)
12,345	12,345	12345	Number
12,345.67	12,345.67	12345.67	Number (with 2 decimal places)
$12,345	$12,345	12345	Currency
$12,345.67	$12,345.67	12345.67	Currency (with 2 decimal places)
12%	12%	.12	Percentage (with 0 decimal places)
12.345%	12.35%	.12345	Percentage (with 2 decimal places)
12-3-45	12/3/45	16774	Date
12:34	12:34	0.523611	Time

Notes

- General is the default format. When you enter a value in a cell that has General format, the format of the cell is changed as in the examples in the preceding table. The format affects only how the value is displayed, not the actual value that is stored in the cell.
- When you enter a value with a dollar sign, comma, or percent sign in a cell that doesn't have General format, the symbols are ignored if they're not appropriate to the numeric format of the cell.
- If a value is too wide to be displayed in its column, the cell is either filled with pound signs (########) or the value is displayed in exponential notation (like 1.2E+08). Figure 2-12 shows how to change the width of a column.

Figure 2-5 How to enter a value into a worksheet (part 2 of 2)

of the cell is changed to Number. And if you enter a value with a trailing percent sign, the format of the cell is changed to Percentage.

You can also include other characters in date and time entries. For example, 1-2-94, 1/2/94, 2-Jan-94, Jan 2, and January 2 are all valid date entries. In each case, the format of the cell is changed to Date, and the data is displayed in an appropriate format.

How to enter formulas into a worksheet Figure 2-6 summarizes what you need to know for entering *formulas* into a worksheet. These are the entries that perform arithmetic operations. If you've been using an earlier version of *Excel*, you can enter formulas just as you always have. Start the formula with an equal sign, identify the cells in the formula by moving the cell pointer to them or by typing their actual cell references, and type arithmetic operators as necessary to construct the formula.

Figure 2-7 illustrates a typical procedure for entering a formula that subtracts the contents of cell B6 from the contents of cell C6. To start, type

General procedure

1. Type an equal sign (=). Then, type the first value or identify the first cell that's required in the formula.
2. Type the first operator that's required. Then, type the next value or identify the next cell that's required.
3. Continue in this way until the formula is complete.
4. Press the Enter key.

Three ways to identify the next cell that's used in a formula

1. Use the mouse to select the cell.
2. Use the pointer-movement keys to move the cell pointer to the cell.
3. Type the cell reference into the formula.

Valid operators

Operator	Meaning
^	Exponentiation (raising to the power of)
*	Multiplication
/	Division
+	Addition
-	Subtraction

Parentheses ( )

You can use parentheses whenever you want to clarify the sequence in which operations will be performed. The operations in the innermost sets of parentheses are performed first.

Typical formulas	Description
=C5-B5	Subtract the contents of cell B5 from the contents of cell C5.
=C3+C4+C5	Add the contents of cells C3, C4, and C5.
=C3*D3	Multiply the contents of cell C3 by the contents of cell D3.
=(C5-B5)/B5	First, subtract the contents of cell B5 from the contents of cell C5; then, divide the result by the contents of cell B5.
=D10*.065	Multiply the contents of cell D10 by .065.

Figure 2-6 How to enter a formula into a worksheet

an equal sign and move the cell pointer to the first cell in the formula. Then, type an operator (in this case, the minus sign), and move the cell pointer to the next cell in the formula. To complete the formula, press the Enter key.

1. Type the equal sign, then move the cell pointer to the first cell used in the formula. Here, the formula is going to be placed in cell D6 and the first value to be used is in cell C6.

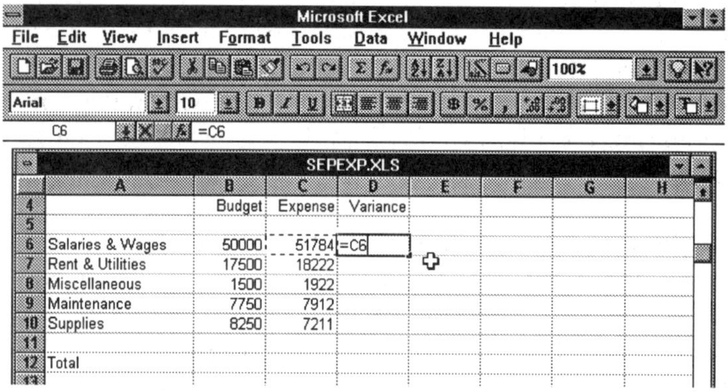

2. Type the first operator that's required. Then, move the cell pointer to the next cell that's required. Here, the operator is the minus sign and the next cell is cell B6.

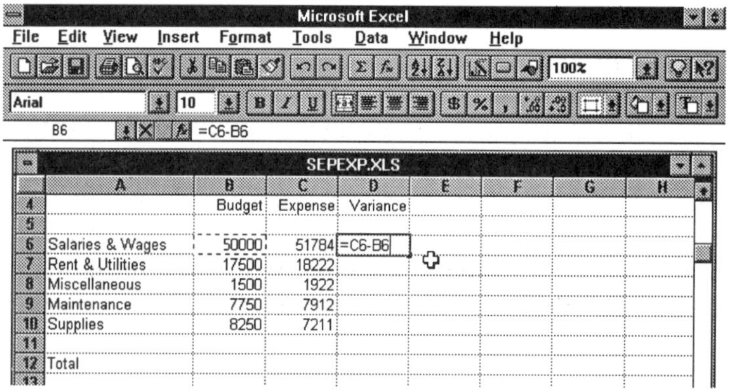

3. Press the Enter key, and *Excel* calculates the result of the formula and moves the cell pointer down one cell.

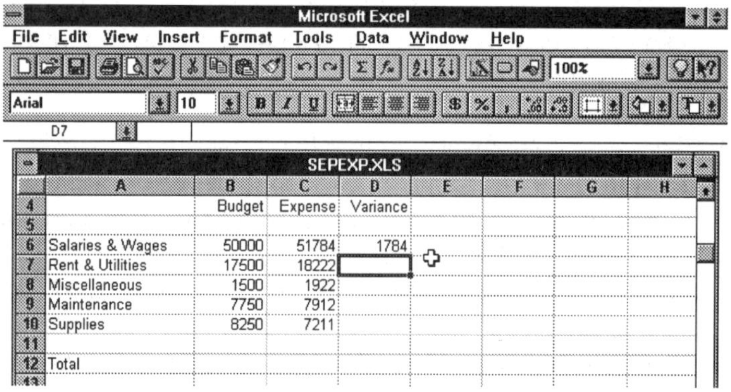

Figure 2-7 A typical procedure for entering a formula

If you've been using some other spreadsheet program, you shouldn't have any trouble adapting to the form required by *Excel.* The only thing that's likely to be different is that you start a formula with an equal sign instead of a plus or minus sign. And if you prefer to enter formulas as you do in *Lotus 1-2-3*, you can set an *Excel* option that will let you continue to enter formulas in *1-2-3* format. You'll see how to set that option at the end of this chapter.

How to enter functions into a worksheet Figure 2-8 summarizes what you need to know for entering *functions* into the formulas of a worksheet. These are the entries that perform specific functions like adding the values in a range or getting the average of the values in a range.

Figure 2-9 illustrates a typical procedure for entering a function that operates upon the values in a range. To start, type the equal sign and the name of the function (in this case, SUM) followed by a left parenthesis. Next, identify the range and complete the entry using one of the methods presented in figure 2-8.

If you've been using some other spreadsheet program, you shouldn't have any trouble adapting to the form required by *Excel.* You just have to get used to the new function names, which unlike *Lotus 1-2-3* functions, don't start with the at sign (@). *Excel*'s notation for identifying ranges (B5:B9) may also be different from what you're used to. If you've been using *Lotus 1-2-3*, though, you can continue to identify ranges in the form you're used to (B5..B9). When *Excel* sees this form, it automatically converts it to its own format.

How to use a mouse with *Excel*

All *Windows* programs provide a *graphical user interface*, or *GUI* (pronounced gooey), that is designed for use with a mouse. In fact, many of the features offered by *Excel* depend on the use of the mouse.

To scroll through a worksheet Scroll bars appear on a window whenever all of the contents of that window can't be seen at one time. If you refer back to figure 2-2, you can see the scroll bars on the workbook window. To scroll the worksheet one row or column at a time, you click on the scroll arrows at the ends of the scroll bars. To scroll the worksheet one window height or width at a time, you click on the scroll bars themselves. And to scroll to a relative position in the worksheet, you drag the scroll boxes.

The procedure for entering a function into a formula

1. Type the equal sign to start the formula.
2. Type the name of the function and a left parenthesis.
3. If no arguments are required, skip to step 6.
4. Supply the first argument. If the argument is a range, identify the range using one of the methods below. In the function that's displayed, the corners of the range will be separated by a colon (:).
5. If necessary, supply additional arguments. For each, type a separator (a comma), then the argument itself.
6. If the function is the last item in the formula, press the Enter key. Otherwise, type a right parenthesis to complete the function, then continue entering the formula.

Four ways to identify a range

1. Move the cell pointer to one corner of the range; type a colon (:) or one period (dot); and move the pointer to the other corner of the range.
2. Move the cell pointer to one corner of the range. Then, hold down the Shift key while you move the pointer to the other corner of the range. When you release the Shift key, the range is added to the function.
3. Use the mouse to highlight the range.
4. Type the cell reference for one corner of the range; type a colon (:) or one period (dot); and type the cell reference for the other corner of the range.

Four of the most useful functions

Syntax	Entry example	Function
TODAY()	=today()	Gets the current date.
SUM(range)	=sum(b5:b10)	Adds the values in the range.
COUNT(range)	=count(b5:d10)	Counts the cells in the range that aren't empty.
AVERAGE(range)	=average(b10:f10)	Derives the average of the values of the cells in the range that aren't empty.

Figure 2-8 How to enter a simple function into a worksheet

To select a cell, row, column, range, or the entire worksheet Figure 2-10 shows you how to use the mouse to select various parts of a worksheet. To select a cell, you just click on it. To select a row or column, you click on the column letter or row number in the worksheet frame. To select two or more rows or columns, you drag the pointer through those row numbers or columns letters in the worksheet frame. To select all the cells in a worksheet, you click on the Select All button, the rectangle in the upper left corner of the frame.

1. Type = (the equal sign) and the name of the function (SUM). Then, type a left parenthesis and identify the range. In the display of the function, the corners of the range will be separated by a colon. Here, the function is in cell B12 and the range is B6:B10.

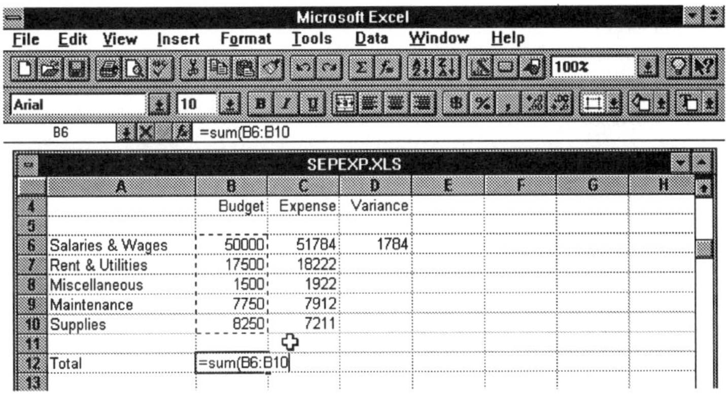

2. Press the Enter key to complete the function. Then, *Excel* calculates the result of the function and moves the cell pointer down one cell.

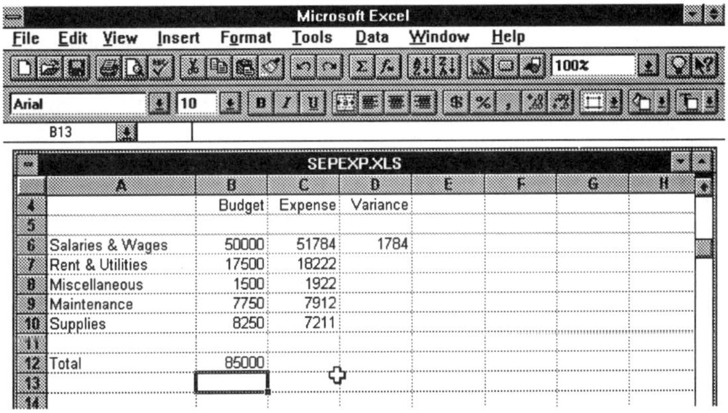

Figure 2-9 A typical procedure for entering a simple function

With *Excel*, you often highlight a range before you start a command, and using the mouse is the most efficient way to highlight the range. To do this, point to the first cell in the range, hold down the left mouse button, and drag the pointer to the last cell in the range. Then, when you release the mouse button, the range remains highlighted.

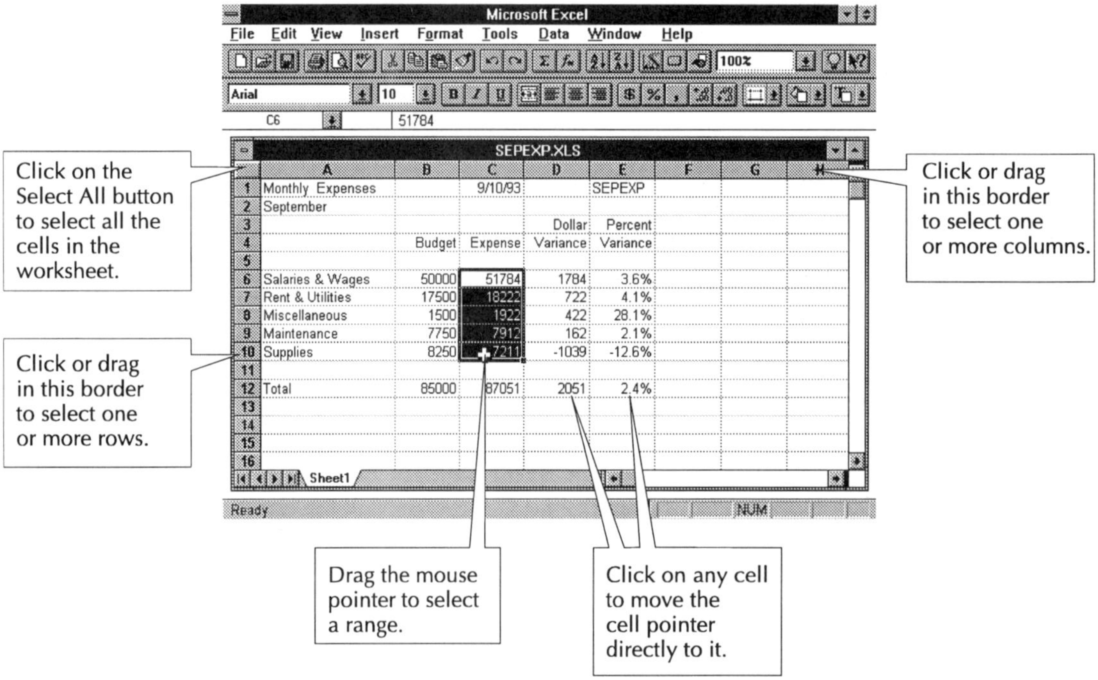

Figure 2-10 How to use the mouse to select a cell, row, column, range, or worksheet

To enter or edit the contents of a cell Figure 2-11 shows you how to use the mouse as you enter and edit labels, values, or formulas. In contrast to DOS spreadsheet programs and earlier versions of *Excel*, *Excel* 5.0 lets you enter and edit data directly in a cell. To enter data, click on the cell to select it and start typing. To edit an entry, double-click on the cell.

If you want to enter or edit a value in the entry area of the formula bar, you first move the cell pointer to the appropriate cell. Then, you click on the formula bar to enter or edit the data there. If you want to use the mouse to cancel or complete an entry, you click on the Cancel or Enter boxes that are displayed in the formula bar. In most cases, though, it's easier to enter and edit data in the cells, not in the formula bar. It's also easier to use the Enter key to complete an operation and to use the Esc key to cancel an operation.

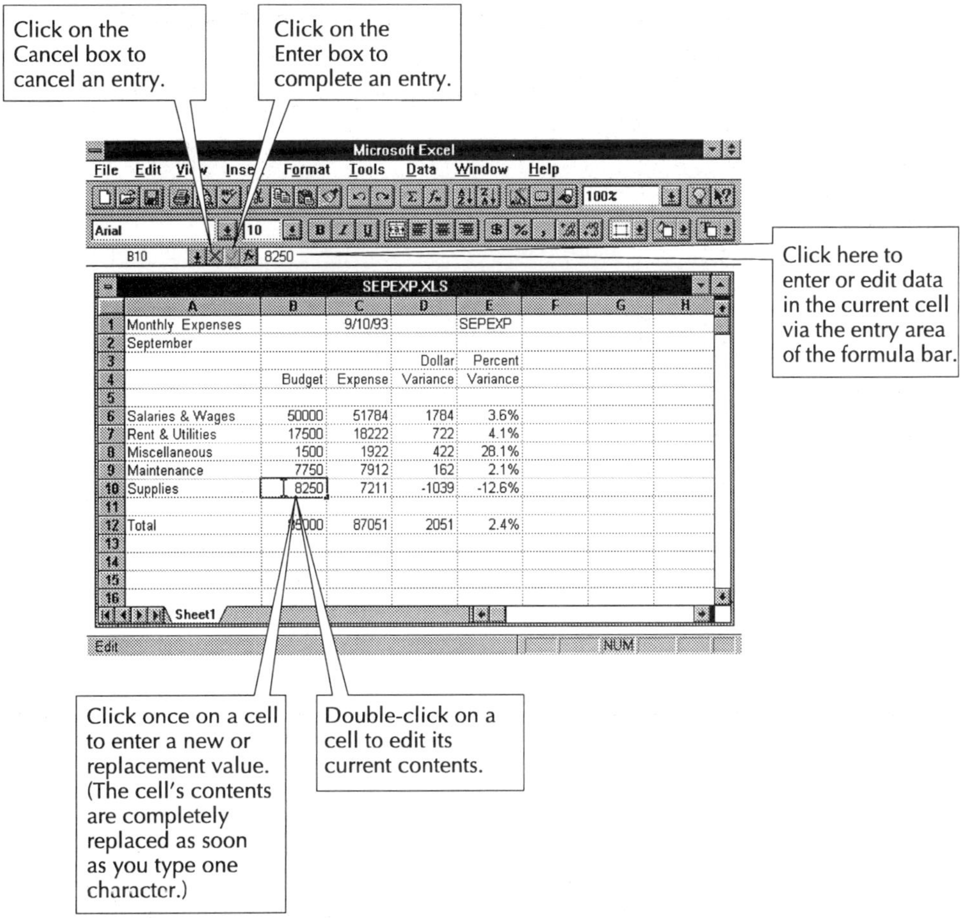

Figure 2-11 How to use the mouse as you enter or edit data

To start a function, adjust column width, or adjust row height
Figure 2-12 shows you how to use the mouse for some other purposes. First, you can click on the Function Wizard button in the Standard toolbar to start a function. When you click on this button, *Excel* displays a dialog box that contains a list of the available functions. When you select one of these functions, it's entered into the current cell complete with parentheses and placeholders for the arguments the function requires. Then, all you have to do is supply the arguments. If you experiment with this, you'll

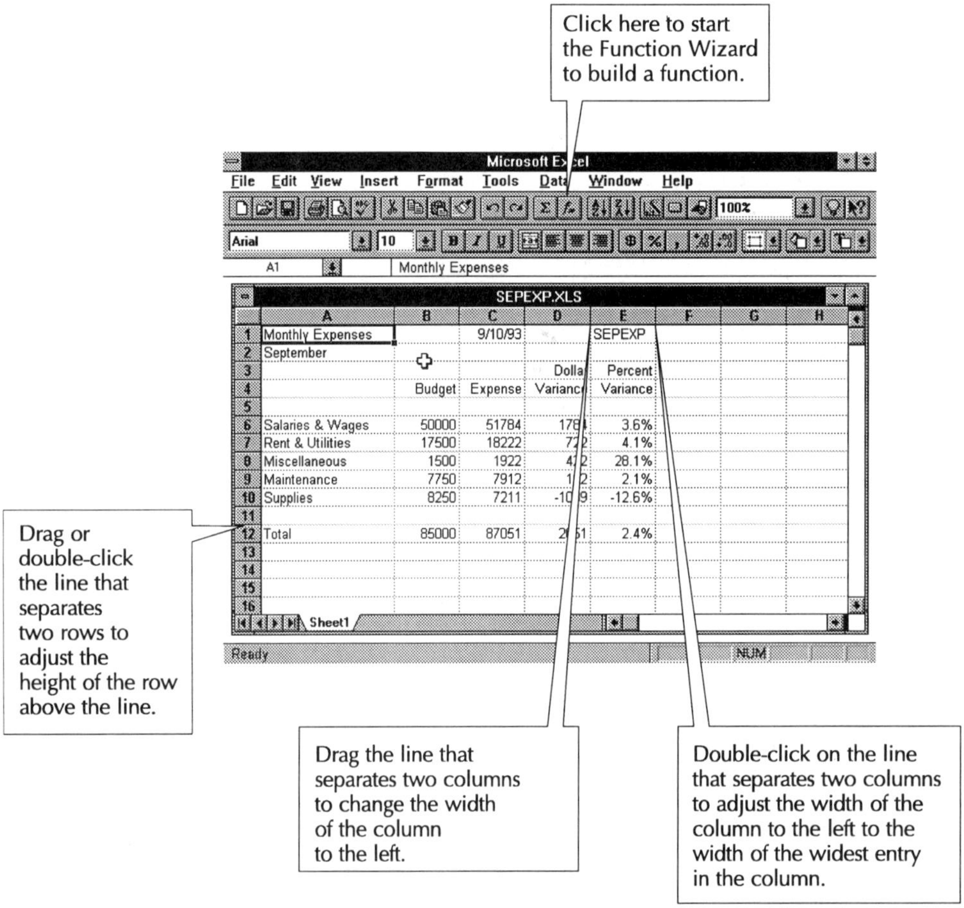

Figure 2-12 How to use the mouse to start a function, adjust column width, or adjust row height

quickly see how easy the Function Wizard makes it to enter functions. You can also use the Function Wizard to help you construct arguments for the function you chose. But this is usually more trouble to use than it's worth.

You can also use the mouse to adjust column widths and row heights. All you do is drag the line in the frame that separates two columns or rows. This changes the width of the column to the left or the height of the row above. If you double-click on the separating line, the width or height is automatically adjusted to provide for the largest entry in the column or row.

If you select a range of columns or rows by dragging through them in the worksheet frame before you start one of these mouse operations, the operation applies to all of the columns or rows in the range.

How to issue *Excel* commands

All of the *Excel* commands are available through menus that you can access from the menu bar. Because these menus appear to be pulled down from the menu bar, they are often referred to as *pull-down* menus. To use *Excel* effectively, you need to know how to issue commands from these menus and how to work with the dialog boxes for the commands.

If you're experienced with another *Windows* program, you probably know how to use the menus and dialog boxes for *Excel.* That's because the menus and dialog boxes for all *Windows* programs generally work the same way. In that case, you can skim through the topics that follow until you get to information that's specific to *Excel.*

How to use the mouse or the keyboard to issue a command Figure 2-13 summarizes the procedures you can use to issue commands from the pull-down menus. Because the procedures are simple, you won't have any trouble using them. Mostly, it's a matter of using the one that fits your working style.

How to use shortcut keys to issue a command Figure 2-14 presents *keyboard shortcuts* for issuing some of the most frequently used commands and formats. If you experiment with shortcut keys, you'll find that using them is often faster than accessing the same function through a menu. If you want to boldface the labels in a range, for example, you can select the range, then type the letter *b* while you hold down the Ctrl key.

How to work with a dialog box When *Excel* requires additional information before it can complete a command, it displays a *dialog box* like the one in figure 2-15. This is the dialog box for the Options command in the Tools menu. This dialog box contains several types of controls: *drop-down list boxes*, *text boxes*, *check boxes*, *command buttons*, and so on. To complete the command, you set the options in the boxes the way you want them and click on the OK command button. If you want to change the user name, for example, you type a replacement value in the User Name text box, then click on the OK command button.

The Tools menu after it has been pulled down from the menu bar

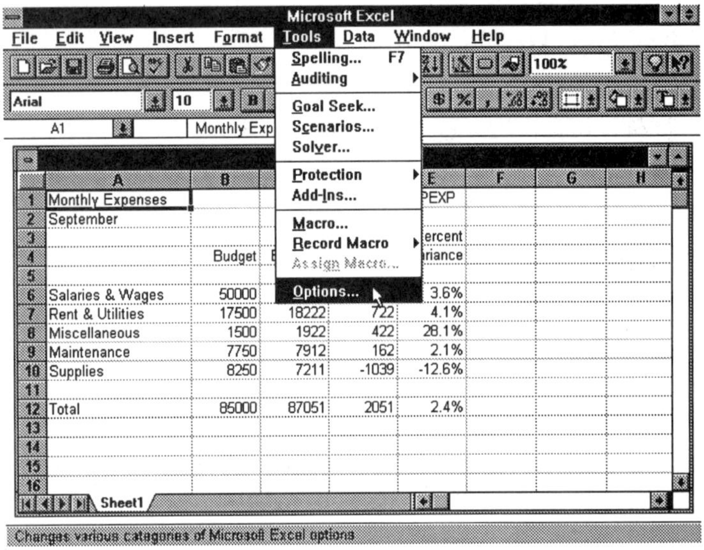

How to use the mouse to issue a command

Method 1:

1. Click on the name of the menu that contains the command you want to issue.
2. Click on the name of the command you want to issue.
3. If a submenu appears, click on the name of the subcommand you want to issue.

Method 2: Drag the highlight from the menu name to the command and, if a submenu appears, to the subcommand you want to issue. Then, release the mouse button.

How to use the keyboard to issue a command

1. Press the Alt key to activate the menu bar.
2. Press the underlined letter of the menu you want to pull down. Or, use an arrow key to move the highlight to the menu and press the Enter key.
3. Press the underlined letter of the command you want to issue. Or, use an arrow key to move the highlight to the command you want and press the Enter key.
4. If a submenu appears, press the underlined letter of the subcommand you want to issue. Or, use an arrow key to move the highlight to the subcommand you want to issue and press the Enter key.

Note

You can also use *shortcut menus* to issue many commands. A shortcut menu pops up from the mouse pointer when you press the right mouse button. The commands on a shortcut menu are context-sensitive. In other words, the specific commands that appear depend on the operation you're performing or on what you're pointing to when you access the menu. The next chapter shows you how to use shortcut menus.

Figure 2-13 How to issue a menu command

For File menu commands

Open	Ctrl+O
Save	Ctrl+S
Print	Ctrl+P

For Edit menu commands

Undo	Ctrl+Z
Repeat	F4
Cut	Ctrl+X
Copy	Ctrl+C
Paste	Crtl+V

For applying formats

Bold	Ctrl+B
Italic	Ctrl+I
Underline	Ctrl+U

Figure 2-14 The keyboard shortcuts for some common *Excel* operations

Access

Select the Options command from the Tools menu, then click on the General tab.

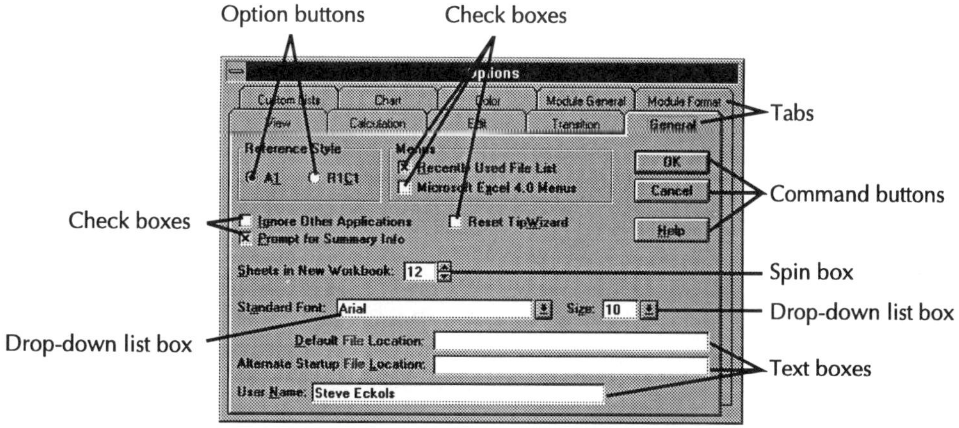

Figure 2-15 A typical dialog box

Figure 2-16 shows the different kinds controls that you're likely to find in a dialog box for *Excel* and how to use them. If you've used other *Windows* programs, you're already familiar with most of the controls for *Excel.*

The easiest way to work with the controls in a dialog box is to use the mouse. However, you can also use your keyboard. To move the *focus* forward from one control to another, you press the Tab key. To move the focus backward, you press Shift+Tab. If you press the Tab key when the focus is on the last control in a dialog box, the focus wraps around to the first control. If the name of the control has an underlined letter in it, you can also move the focus to that control by holding down the Alt key and pressing that letter. If the control is a command button, this technique also activates the button. Sometimes, it's hard to tell which control has the focus on it, but *Excel* often marks the control that has the focus with a light dotted line.

The keyboard technique that you use to change the setting of a control depends on the type of control. When the focus is on a text box, you type a new value through the keyboard. When the focus is on an option button, you use the arrow keys to change the setting. When the focus is on a check box, you turn the option on or off by pressing the Spacebar. And when the focus is on a command button, you activate it by pressing the Enter key.

In most dialog boxes, one command button responds to the Enter key whether or not the focus is on it as long as the focus isn't on another command button. This means that you don't have to move the focus to it before you press the Enter key. This button is indicated by a dark outline around it as illustrated by the OK button in figure 2-15. The default command button is usually the one that will have the least serious consequence if you choose it accidentally.

Some dialog boxes have many controls. *Excel* uses *tabs* to group and organize controls on a complex dialog box. For example, the Options dialog box in figure 2-15 has 10 tabs, each with a different set of controls. The controls you can see are for the active tab, in this case, the General tab. If you want to see and set options in another category, click on the appropriate tab or press Ctrl+Tab to display the next tab.

How to use the primary commands of the File menu

Figure 2-17 shows the File menu and summarizes its commands. Most of these commands correspond to commands that are offered by all spreadsheet programs. For instance, the Open command is like the /File Retrieve command of *Lotus 1-2-3* for DOS; the Save command is like the /File Save command; and the Print command is like the /Print Printer command.

How to use dialog box controls	Before	After
Command button Click on the button to issue the command.		
Text box Click in the box to activate it for entry.	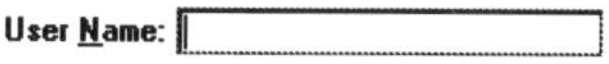	
Check box Click on the box to turn an option on or off.	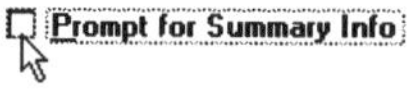	
Option button Click on a button to select an option and cancel the other ones in the array.		
Spin box Click on the arrows to change the value in the text box. Or, type a new value in the text box.	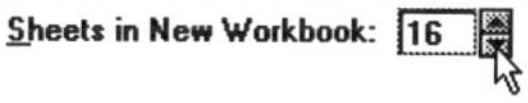	
List box Click on an item in the list to select it.	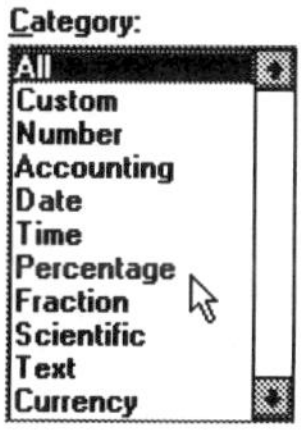	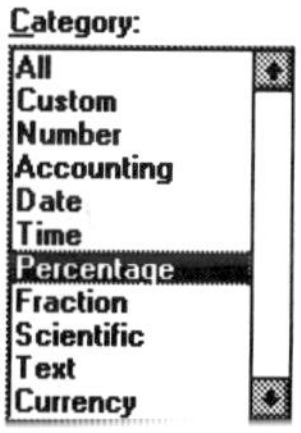
Drop-down list box Click on the down arrow to display the list. Click on an item to select it.		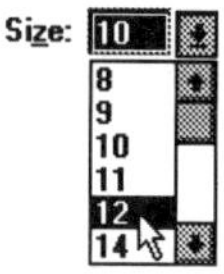

Figure 2-16 How to use the common controls in a dialog box

The File menu

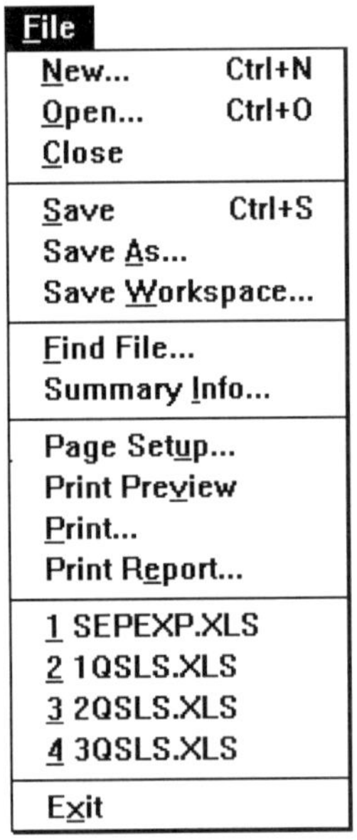

Command	Function	Presented in
New	Creates a new workbook file.	Chapter 2
Open	Retrieves a file from disk.	Chapters 2 and 17
Close	Closes the current workbook file.	Chapter 2
Save	Saves the current workbook file to disk.	Chapter 2
Save As	Saves the current workbook to disk using a new file name.	Chapter 2
Save Workspace	Saves open workbook files to disk and preserves their arrangement on the screen.	Chapter 24
Find File	Searches specified disks for files that meet criteria you specify.	Chapter 24
Summary Info	Sets identifying information for the current workbook such as title, subject, author, and comments.	Chapter 24
Page Setup	Sets options that affect the layout of the printed page.	Chapter 10
Print Preview	Displays an image of the current worksheet as it will appear when printed, including headers, footers, etc.	Chapter 10
Print	Prints the current worksheet.	Chapters 2 and 10
Print Report	Prints views or scenarios.	Chapter 24
file name	Opens the file that's named. The files that are listed are the last four files you worked on.	Chapter 2
Exit	Quits *Excel*.	Chapter 2

Figure 2-17 The commands of the File menu

In this chapter, you'll learn how to use the New, Open, Close, Save, Save As, Print, and Exit commands. You'll also learn how to use the numbered file names at the bottom of the menu. Then, if you need help with the other commands of the File menu, you can read the chapters referred to in figure 2-17.

The Open command You use the Open command to retrieve an existing file from a hard disk or diskette. When you retrieve a file, it's loaded into a workbook window. With *Excel*, you can work on more than

Access

Select the Open command from the File menu.

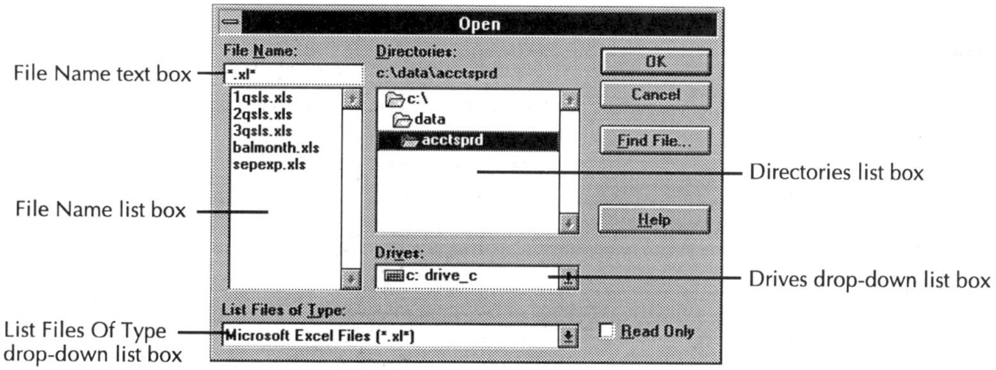

Procedure

1. Use the Drives drop-down list box to select the drive that your file is on.
2. Use the Directories list box to select the directory that your file is in. To select a directory, click on it. To start a new path, double-click on the root directory (the one at the top of this box). Then, double-click on the icons for the lower-level directories that you want to see. When you select a directory, its files are displayed in the File Name list box.
3. Use the List Files Of Type drop-down list box to select the type of file you want to retrieve. For example, if you want to retrieve a *1-2-3* file for use by *Excel*, you can access the box and make that selection.
4. To select the file that you want to retrieve, you can type the file name in the File Name text box or select the file name from the File Name list box. To select the file and complete the command, double-click on the file name in the list box.
5. If you don't double-click on the file name in step 4, click on the OK button to complete the command.

Figure 2-18 How to retrieve (open) a file

one file at a time, and each file has its own window. Then, you can switch from one window to another using the *Windows* techniques that are presented in chapter 1.

Figure 2-18 shows the dialog box for the Open command and how you use its controls to identify the file you want to retrieve. For a complete file specification, you need to use the controls to supply the drive, path, and file name. However, you don't have to go through this tedious process every time you want to retrieve a file if you work in one directory most of the time. Instead, you can set the default directory *Excel* uses to your work directory. To do this, access the General tab of the Options dialog box as described in figure 2-15. Then, type the path of the directory you use most often in the Default File Location text box.

If you're converting to *Excel* 5.0 from an earlier version of *Excel*, you'll be happy to learn that the Open command retrieves the files created by earlier versions with no problems. Similarly, if you're converting from *Lotus 1-2-3*, you can use the List Files Of Type drop-down list box to specify that the files you want to retrieve are in *1-2-3* format. In either case, *Excel* 5.0 converts the file to its format and loads the file.

The file name commands If you look at the four items in the File menu just above the Exit command in figure 2-17, you'll see four file names. These are the last four files that you worked on. To open any one of them, you just select the file name as if it were a command.

The New command When you start *Excel*, it displays an empty window where you can start a new workbook. Later, if you want to start another new workbook file, you use the New command. When you select this command, *Excel* displays a dialog box that asks you if you want to create a workbook or slides. If you select the Workbook option, a workbook window is opened for the new file. To create slides, the Slide Show *add-in program* must be installed. You'll learn more about add-in programs in chapter 24.

The Save and Save As commands *Excel* has two commands for saving a workbook file. You use the Save command to save changes to an existing file. When you issue this command, the file is saved immediately with no intervening dialog box, thus replacing the earlier version of the file. In contrast, you use the Save As command to save a new file for the first time or to save an existing file with a new name. In this case, a dialog box is displayed so you can give a proper file specification for the file.

Figure 2-19 shows the dialog box for the Save As command. As you can see, it is much like the dialog box for the Open command. If you don't want to save the file in the default directory that's shown, you can use the controls to specify the new path. If you don't type a new name, *Excel* creates a generic one for you like book1.xls, but you usually don't want that.

If you opened a file that was created by an earlier version of *Excel* or another spreadsheet program, you have to use the Save As command to save the file in the Version 5.0 format. To indicate that the file is now in Version 5.0 format, you should change the Save File As Type setting to

Access

Select the Save or Save As command from the File menu.

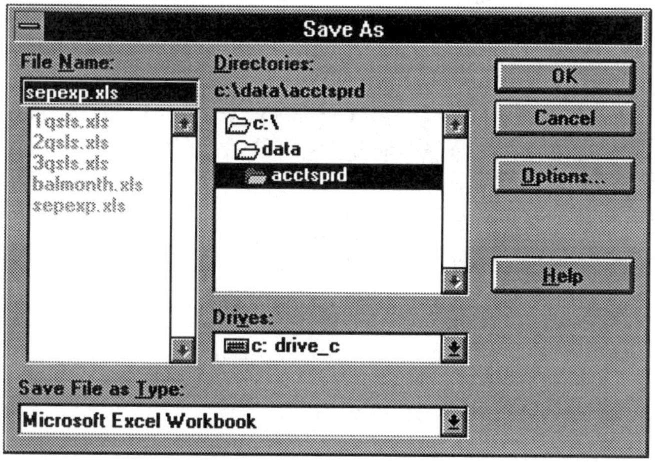

Procedure

1. Use the Drives drop-down list box and the Directories list box to select the drive and directory where you want to save the file.
2. Use the Save File As Type drop-down list box to select the type of file you want to save. For example, if you choose Microsoft Excel Workbook, the file is saved in *Excel* 5.0 format. You can choose other options, including several *Lotus 1-2-3* formats.
3. Type a file name in the File Name text box.
4. Click on the OK button to complete the command.

Notes

- The Save As dialog box is displayed the first time you save a new file with the Save command. After that, the Save command saves the file without displaying a dialog box.
- The Save As dialog box is displayed each time you use the Save As command. This lets you save the current file with a new name.

Figure 2-19 How to save a file

"Microsoft Excel Workbook." If you want the file to keep its original format, use the Save command instead.

The Close command When you issue the Close command, it closes the active workbook window. If you haven't saved your most recent changes to the workbook, a dialog box is displayed that lets you save or ignore the changes. Otherwise, the workbook window disappears. If the window that you're closing is the only one that's open, the workbook is cleared, but the application window remains open so you can retrieve another workbook file. When this is the case, the only menus that are available are File and Help.

The Print command *Excel* has four commands for printing: Print Report, Page Setup, Print Preview, and Print. If you experiment with the four printing commands, you shouldn't have much trouble using them. But if you need help, you can refer to chapter 10 for more information.

Figure 2-20 shows the dialog boxes for the Print command. The first one appears when you issue the Print command. It lets you specify the pages that you want to print and the number of copies that you want. You can use the Print command to print the current worksheet, a selected range within the current worksheet, or all of the worksheets in the current workbook file.

The Print dialog box also provides command buttons that let you access the Page Setup and Print Preview commands. The Print Preview command is useful because it lets you see how a worksheet is going to look before you print it. Then, if something isn't right, you can return to the worksheet and correct it before printing. You can use one of the other command buttons, Printer Setup, to change the default printer. When you click on it, the second dialog box in figure 2-20 appears.

The Exit command When you issue the Exit command, the program ends. This is the same as double-clicking on the control-menu box in the upper left corner of the application window. If you haven't saved the last changes you made, a dialog box appears that gives you a chance to save the changes. Otherwise, you are returned to the program that you started *Excel* from (usually, the Program Manager).

How to use the primary commands of the Edit menu

Figure 2-21 shows the Edit menu and summarizes its commands. These commands let you perform many of the functions that you need when you modify a worksheet. For instance, the Fill command lets you duplicate the contents of a cell through a range; the Delete command lets you delete cells, rows, or columns; and the Cut, Copy, and Paste commands let you move or copy a range of cells.

Access

Select the Print command from the File menu.

Operation

- To print the current worksheet on the default printer, click on the OK button. The default settings are to print one copy of all pages of the current worksheet.
- If you want to print a selected range in the current worksheet, you can select the range before you start the Print command. Otherwise, you can specify starting and ending pages in the From and To spin boxes.

Notes

- The Page Setup and Print Preview buttons start the commands with the same names.
- To change the default printer, click on the Printer Setup button. When you do, this dialog box appears:

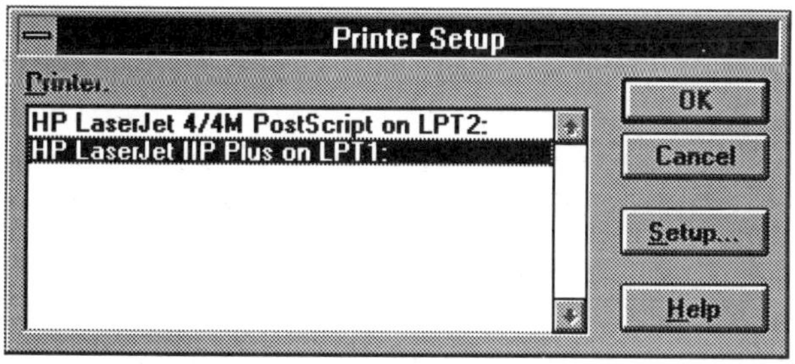

Select the printer you want to use, then click on the OK button.

Figure 2-20 How to print a file

The Edit menu

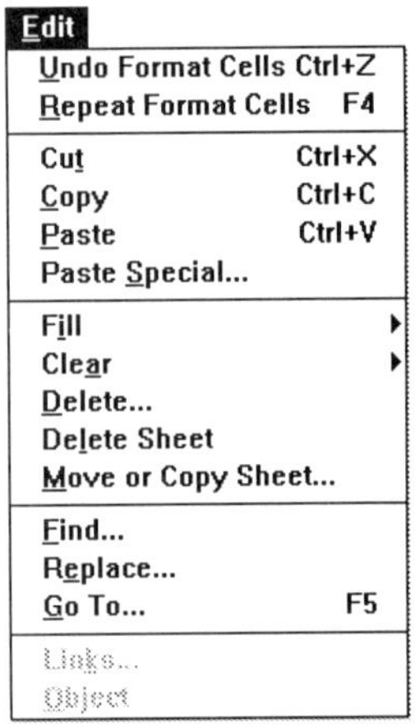

Command	Function	Presented in
Undo *function*	Reverses the effect of the most recent command or operation. (Available after most commands and operations, but not all; if not, Can't Undo appears on the menu.)	Chapters 2 and 7
Repeat *function*	Repeats the most recent command or operation. (Available after most commands and operations, but not all; if not, Can't Repeat appears on the menu.)	Chapters 2 and 7
Cut	Removes the selection from the worksheet and places it on the clipboard.	Chapters 2 and 7
Copy	Places the selection on the clipboard without removing it from the worksheet.	Chapters 2 and 7
Paste	Inserts the contents of the clipboard at the current location in the worksheet.	Chapters 2 and 7
Paste Special	When a selection from a worksheet has been placed on the clipboard, this command lets you paste the contents, format, or calculated values at the current location. Also supports pasting objects with Object Linking and Embedding.	Chapters 7, 8, and 23
Fill	Opens a submenu with commands that duplicate the contents of the first cell or cells in a range in the other cells of the range; generate a series; or justify text into even lines.	Chapters 2, 5, and 7
Clear	Opens a submenu with commands that delete the contents, formatting, or notes from the selected range, but leave the cells in place.	Chapters 2 and 7

Figure 2-21 The commands of the Edit menu (part 1 of 2)

The Edit menu (continued)

Command	Function	Presented in
Delete	Deletes the selected cells, rows, or columns.	Chapters 2 and 7
Delete Sheet	Deletes the selected worksheet(s) from the current workbook.	Chapter 9
Move or Copy Sheet	Moves or copies the selected worksheets to another location in the current workbook or to another workbook.	Chapter 9
Find	Searches for specific characters.	Chapter 7
Replace	Replaces specific characters with other characters.	Chapter 7
Go To	Selects the cell or range you specify.	Chapter 7
Links	Lists external documents that are linked to the current worksheet and lets you modify the links.	Chapter 23
Object	Opens a submenu with commands for working with linked and embedded objects.	Chapter 23

Figure 2-21 The commands of the Edit menu (part 2 of 2)

The Cut, Copy, and Paste commands When you move or copy data from one range to another, you use a *Windows* feature called the *clipboard.* This is a temporary storage area that you use to transfer data from one range to another in a single worksheet or from one worksheet to another. To put data on the clipboard, you use the Cut or Copy command. To insert it into a worksheet, you use the Paste command.

Figure 2-22 summarizes the procedure for copying or moving a range of cells using the clipboard. To copy a range, you select the range of cells and issue the Copy command. The range that you selected is then copied to the clipboard, thus replacing whatever was on the clipboard before. To complete the copy operation, you move the cell pointer to the cell where you want to insert the contents of the clipboard and issue the Paste command. This pastes the range into the worksheet, but the range also remains on the clipboard. As a result, you can use the Paste command again to paste the range in another location.

Procedure

1. Select the range of cells that contains the data you want to move or copy.
2. Issue the Copy command to copy the range to the clipboard.
   Issue the Cut command to move the range to the clipboard.
3. Move the cell pointer where you want to copy or move the range.
4. Issue the Paste command to insert the contents of the clipboard.

Notes

- You can use these procedures to copy or move data within one worksheet or from one worksheet to another, whether they're in the same workbook or not. You can even use them to copy or move data from one *Windows* program to another.
- The data on the clipboard remains there after a Paste operation so you can paste the data into more than one location. However, the data remains there only as long as the source range is marked with a moving border.

Figure 2-22 How to move and copy data using the Cut, Copy, and Paste commands

To move a range of cells, you use the Cut command instead of the Copy command. This puts the selected range on the clipboard and removes it from the worksheet. To complete the move function, you use the Paste command. Here again, the contents of the clipboard remain in it after you issue the Paste command.

The contents of the clipboard change each time you issue a Cut or Copy command. If you've used other *Windows* programs, you know that the Cut, Copy, and Paste commands are a standard part of *Windows*. But if you haven't used these commands before, it may take you a while to get used to them. Once you do, you'll realize that they're every bit as efficient as the Move and Copy commands that you may have used with your old spreadsheet program. Besides that, you can use the clipboard when you want to transfer data from any other *Windows* program to *Excel*, and vice versa.

To speed up your copy and move operations when you use these commands, you can use the keyboard shortcuts that are shown on the Edit menu: Ctrl+X for the Cut command, Ctrl+C for the Copy command, and Ctrl+V for the Paste command. To help you remember these shortcuts, you can think of the letter X as a scissors, which represents cutting; the letter C as the first letter in Copy; and the letter V as the editor's caret mark for inserting text.

If you're an experienced *Windows* user, you know that in most cases, whatever you cut or copy to the clipboard remains there and is available to be pasted until you cut or copy something else. In a program like a word processor, you can leave a selection on the clipboard while you work, and it will still be there when you want to Paste it. In *Excel*, when you copy or cut a range to the clipboard, it remains there only while the source range is marked with a moving border. If you proceed with other editing, you may be surprised to find that the contents of the clipboard have disappeared.

The Fill command The Fill command lets you perform some copy operations more efficiently than you can with the Cut, Copy, or Paste commands or with the Copy command that you used with your old spreadsheet program. When you select the Fill command, a submenu is displayed with several Fill options. Figure 2-23 shows how you can use the Down subcommand of the Fill command to copy a formula to the four cells below it. After you select the cell that contains the formula and the rows below it in a single range, you just issue the Fill Down command to complete the operation.

It's an *Excel* convention to combine the names of the commands on a main menu and a submenu. So Fill Down really is an abbreviation for "the Down command on the Fill command's submenu. As a result, you'll see command names like Fill Down, Fill Right, Fill Series, and Fill Justify throughout this book.

The Clear command The Clear command lets you delete the data in a range of cells. As you can tell from the arrowhead next to the Clear command in the Edit menu, it has a submenu. Its commands are Clear All, Clear Formats, Clear Contents, and Clear Notes.

The Delete and Delete Sheet commands To delete cells, columns, or rows, you use the Delete command. Just select the range you want to delete before you issue the command. To delete an entire worksheet, you use the Delete Sheet command. Before you issue this command, make sure that the worksheet you want to delete is current.

If you want to delete one or more columns or rows, the easiest way is to select them by dragging the mouse pointer over the column letters or row numbers. Then, the columns or rows are deleted immediately when you select the Delete command. You can also delete columns or rows by selecting a range that contains at least one cell in each column or row you want to delete. If you use this method, however, *Excel* displays a dialog box that asks you if you want to delete the selected range or the rows or columns the range occupies. If you want to delete the range, you then have to specify

1. Select the cell or cells that contain the data you want to copy along with the cells below them where you want to copy the data:

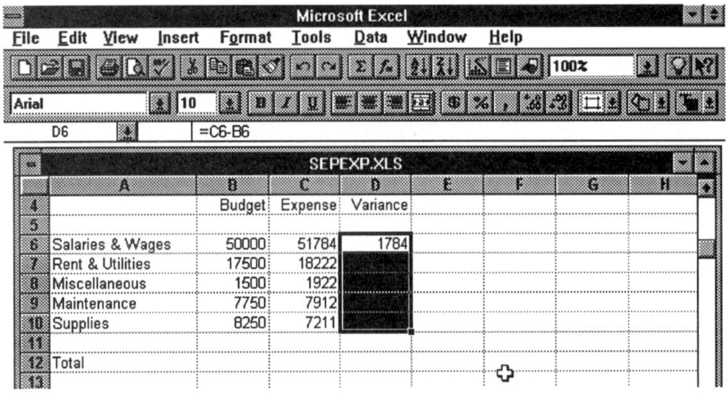

2. Select the Fill command from the Edit menu and this submenu appears:

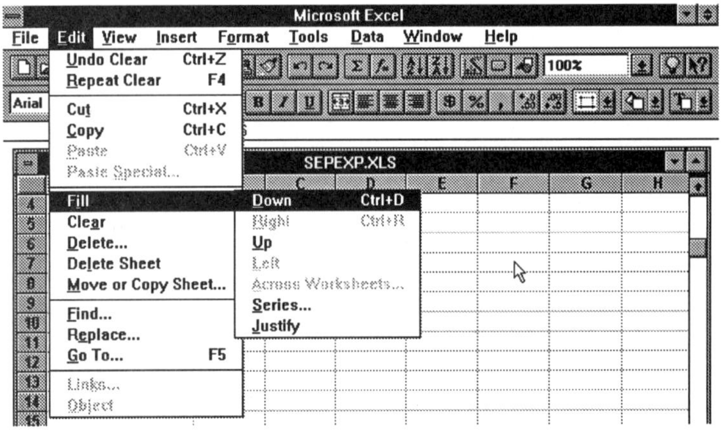

3. Select the Down command and *Excel* copies the contents down into the selected range:

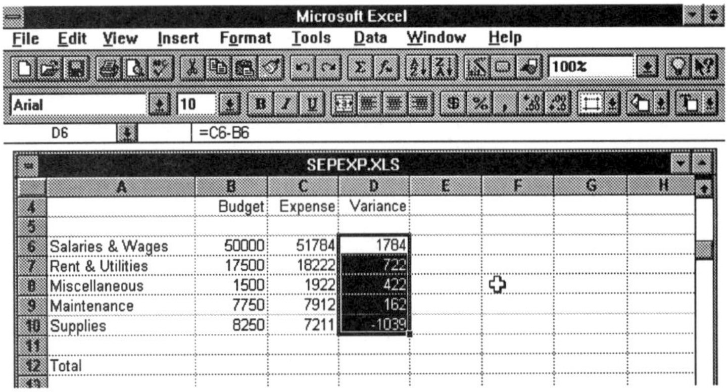

Figure 2-23 How to use the Fill Down command

whether the data beneath the range should be moved up or the data to the right of the range should be moved left.

The Undo and Repeat commands The Undo command lets you cancel the last change you made to a worksheet, and the Repeat command repeats the last command or action. The shortcut keys for these commands are Ctrl+Z and F4. Because the Undo command applies only to your most recent change, you must issue the command immediately after you make the change that you want to undo. You can undo and repeat most, but not all commands. For example, you can't undo some clipboard operations.

How to use the Help feature of *Excel*

Figure 2-24 shows the Help menu and summarizes its commands. When you issue any of these commands, a window opens for the Help information. This window is actually an application window for a separate program that provides the Help information. As a result, you can often minimize, maximize, restore, move, and size the window using the techniques presented in chapter 1. When you end *Excel*, its Help program also ends.

If you experiment with the commands of the Help menu, you'll see that the *Excel* Help feature provides a wide variety of information. In general, this information is most useful when you already know how to use a function or feature, but you just can't remember some detail. If you need to look up the syntax for the ROUND function, for example, using the Help feature is probably more efficient than using any other reference.

In contrast, the Help information is least useful when you're trying to learn how to use a new feature or function or you can't remember how a feature or function works. If you're trying to chart the data in a worksheet or you're trying to figure out how to use the Scenario Manager, for example, the Help information is likely to frustrate you. For those purposes, a book like this one is easier to use than the Help information. Similarly, if you need to learn the basics of using *Excel*, you're usually better off with a printed tutorial than you are with the examples and demos that are available through the Help menu. When you use printed materials, you can read about a feature or function and experiment with it on your PC at the same time.

How to get context-sensitive Help information Figure 2-25 shows you how to get *context-sensitive* Help information. To do that, you press the F1 key or click on the Help button in a dialog box. Then, *Excel* opens a

The Help menu

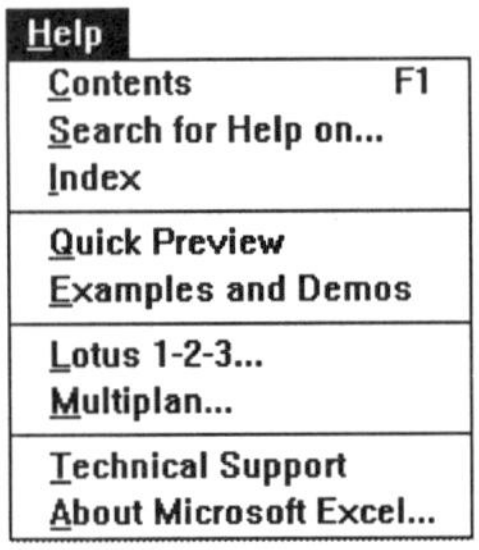

Command	Function
Contents	Displays the table of contents for the Help information.
Search for Help on	Searches for help on a particular topic.
Index	Displays an alphabetical list of topics.
Quick Preview	Presents four tutorials on how to work with *Excel* 5.0.
Examples and Demos	Presents examples of and practice activities for common *Excel* features.
Lotus 1-2-3	Displays reference and tutorial information on *Excel* equivalents of *Lotus 1-2-3* features.
Multiplan	Displays reference information on *Excel* equivalents of *Multiplan* commands.
Technical Support	Lists answers to common technical questions and describes how to get technical support from Microsoft.
About Microsoft Excel	Displays copyright and other information about *Excel*.

Figure 2-24 The commands of the Help menu

Help window that displays information about the function you're trying to perform. In many cases, this type of context-sensitive information is more useful than the information you get through the Help menu.

In figure 2-25, you can see the context-sensitive Help information for the Print command. This illustrates both the strength and weakness of the Help information that you get with *Excel*. The strength is that the Help window offers a large amount of information. The weakness is that the information introduces complexities (like embedded charts) that are likely to confuse and distract you rather than help you.

How to navigate through the Help information Figure 2-26 shows the opening window for the Contents command of the Help menu. Here, you can see the table of contents. To pick a topic, you just click on it. These options lead to lists of subtopics that you can choose from.

If you don't find the information you want, you can click on the Search button that's in the Help window. This leads to a Search window like the one in the bottom of figure 2-26. In the text box at the top of the Search

Two ways to access context-sensitive Help information

- Press the F1 key after you've started an operation.
- Click on the Help button in a dialog box.

The Help information that you get when you press F1 when the Print dialog box is displayed

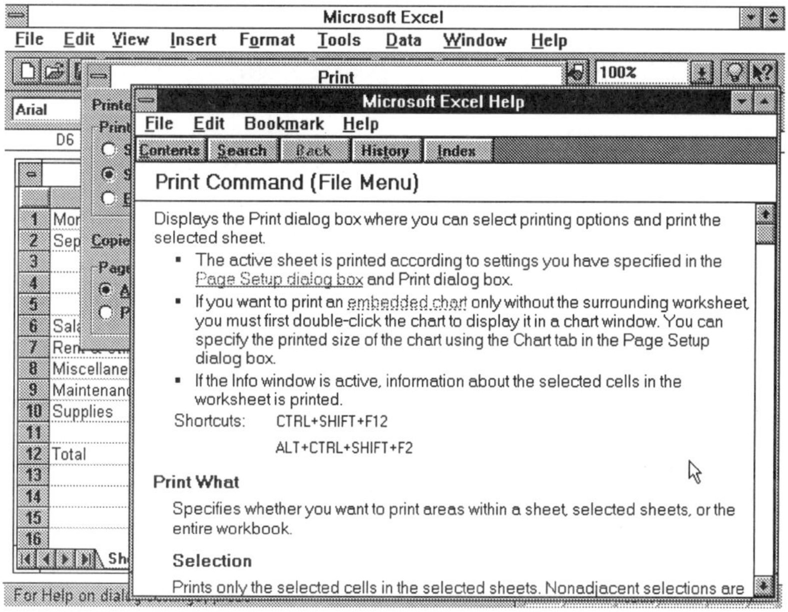

Figure 2-25 How to get context-sensitive Help information

window, you can type the name of the topic that you want information about. As you type, the list of topics in the first list box changes to reflect what you've typed. When you see the topic that you want, you can select it and click on the Show Topics button to display a list of the related topics in the second list box in the Search window. Then, you can select the topic you want and click on the Go To button to display the Help information for that topic.

The Back and History buttons provide two more ways to navigate through the Help information. When you click on the Back button, it takes you back one screen or topic. When you click on the History button, it presents you with a list of the topics that you've used in the current Help session. Then, you can return to any one of these topics by double-clicking on the topic in the list.

The Help window for the Contents command

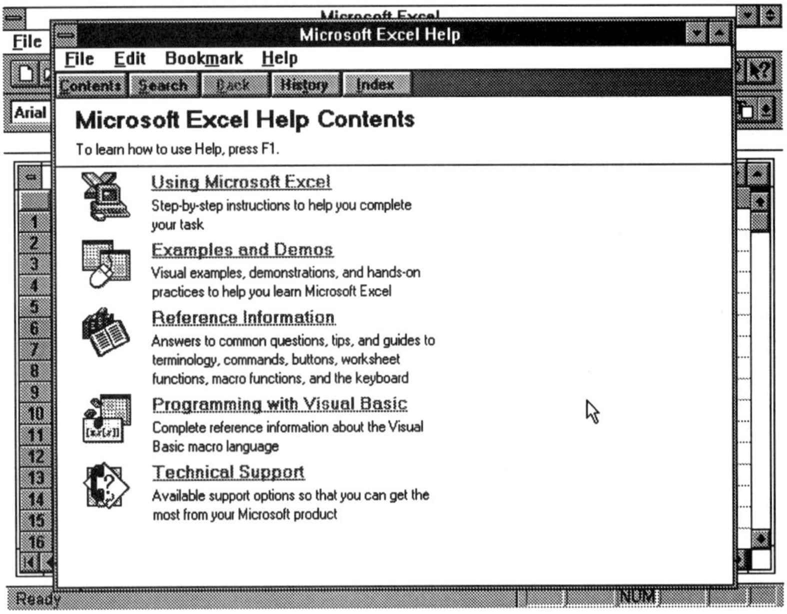

The Help window for the Search for Help on command

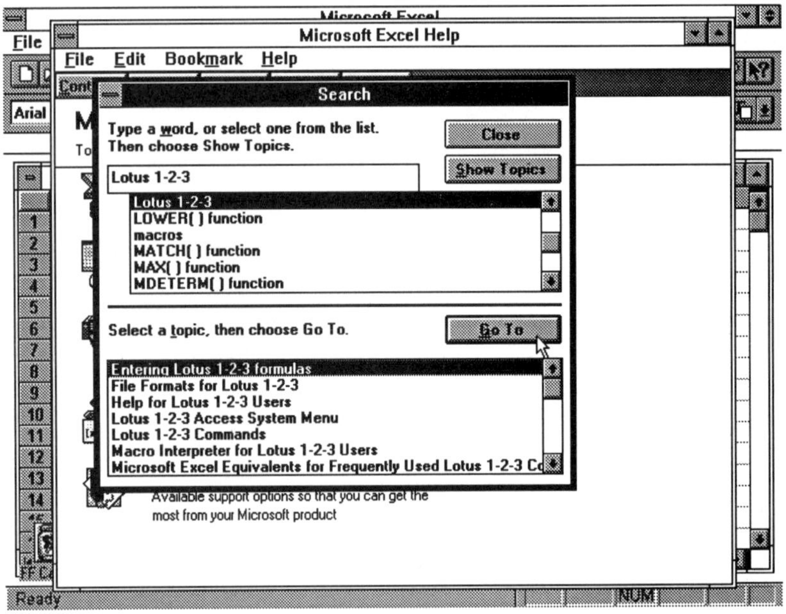

Figure 2-26 Typical Help windows

How to print Help information If you want to keep a permanent copy of the information that you find through the Help feature, you have a couple of options. First, you can print a copy of the current topic by issuing the Print Topic command from the File menu of the Help application window. Second, you can copy a topic or a portion of a topic to the clipboard by issuing the Copy command from the Edit menu of the Help application window. Then, you can paste the information into a word processing program before printing it from that program.

An introduction to the commands in the other menus

Now that you know how to use the commands of the File, Edit, and Help menus, you should have no trouble using many of the commands in the other menus. That's particularly true if you know what functions they perform. In the rest of this chapter, then, I'll introduce you to the commands in the other menus.

The View menu Figure 2-27 shows the View menu and summarizes its commands. You can use these commands to change the display of the application window and the workbook windows it contains. For instance, the Zoom command increases or decreases the size of the display. The Formula Bar, Status Bar, and Toolbars commands let you specify what elements appear in *Excel*'s application window. These commands are easy to use so it's worth taking the time to experiment with them. You'll learn more about these commands in chapter 7.

The Insert menu Figure 2-28 shows the Insert menu and summarizes its commands. If you know how to add cells, rows, and columns to a spreadsheet using an earlier version of *Excel* or some other spreadsheet program, you should be able to use the Cells, Rows, and Columns commands right away. Similarly, if you know how to use range names, you should be able to use the Name command too. Otherwise, you can refer to the chapters listed for more information about the commands.

The View menu

Command	Function	Presented in
Formula Bar	Displays or hides the formula bar.	Chapter 7
Status Bar	Displays or hides the status bar.	Chapter 7
Toolbars	Displays or hides any or all of the toolbars that are available with *Excel*; customizes toolbars.	Chapters 7 and 20
Full Screen	Toggles between the default display and full screen display where *Excel*'s application window is maximized and the title bar, the Standard and Formatting toolbars, and the status bar are hidden.	Chapter 7
Zoom	Changes the magnification of the current window.	Chapter 7
View Manager	Creates, applies, and deletes views (sets of display options) for the current worksheet.	Chapter 7

Figure 2-27 The commands of the View menu

The Format menu Figure 2-29 shows the Format menu and summarizes its commands. Of all of the Format menu's commands, you'll probably use Cells more than any of the others. However, most of these commands are easy to use, and most of them are closely related to commands that are provided by other spreadsheet programs. For more information, though, you can refer to the chapters that are listed for the commands.

Because you can perform the functions available with some of the commands of the Format menu in different ways, you may not need to use some of the commands. In the next chapter, for example, you'll learn how to perform some of the functions of the Cells command more easily by using buttons in the Formatting toolbar. Similarly, you can apply character formatting to cells by using the shortcut keys in figure 2-14. And you can adjust column widths and row heights by using the mouse techniques in figure 2-12.

The Tools menu Figure 2-30 shows the Tools menu and summarizes its commands. Two commands that you should be able to use right away are the Spelling and Options commands. All of the commands are covered in detail in the chapters that are listed.

The Insert menu

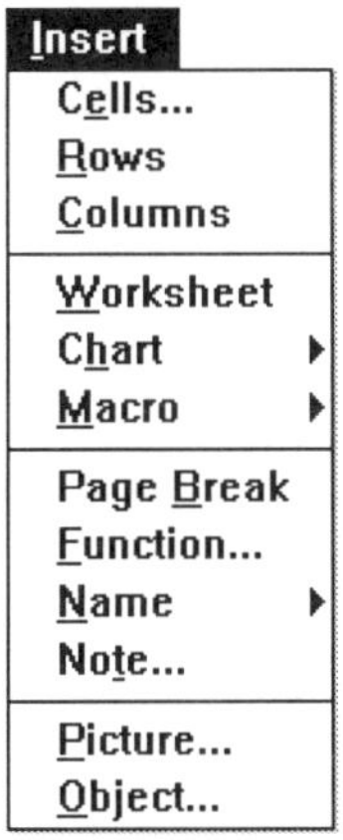

Command	Function	Presented in
Cells	Inserts cells in the selected range.	Chapter 7
Rows	Inserts one or more rows above the selection. This command inserts the same number of rows as the selection spans.	Chapter 7
Columns	Inserts one or more columns to the left of the selection. This command inserts the same number of columns as the selection spans.	Chapter 7
Worksheet	Inserts a new worksheet to the left of the selected sheet tab. This command inserts as many worksheets as the selection spans.	Chapter 9
Chart	Opens a submenu with commands that access the ChartWizard to help you create either an embedded chart in the current worksheet or a new chart sheet in the current workbook.	Chapter 11
Macro	Opens a submenu with commands that insert a Visual Basic module, a dialog sheet, or an *Excel* 4.0 macro sheet in the current workbook.	Not presented
Page Break	Inserts a page break. (If the cell pointer is next to an existing page break, Remove Page Break appears in the menu instead of Page Break.)	Chapter 10
Function	Starts the Function Wizard to add a function to the formula in the current cell.	Chapters 2 and 6
Name	Opens a submenu with commands that create, delete, and insert named ranges.	Chapter 7
Note	Attaches a comment to the current cell.	Chapter 18
Picture	Inserts a graphic object from an external file into the current worksheet.	Chapter 13
Object	Uses Object Linking and Embedding to insert an external object into the current worksheet.	Chapter 23

Figure 2-28 The commands of the Insert menu

The Format menu

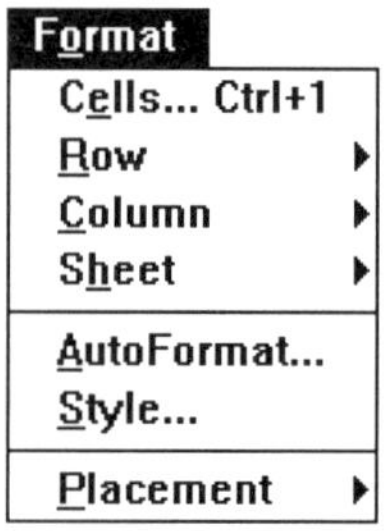

Command	Function	Presented in
Cells	Applies format, alignment, font, border, pattern, and protection options to the selected cells.	Chapters 8 and 24
Row	Opens a submenu with commands that change the height of selected rows, hide rows, and unhide rows.	Chapters 7 and 8
Column	Opens a submenu with commands that change the width of selected columns, hide columns, and unhide columns.	Chapter 7
Sheet	Opens a submenu with commands that rename, hide, and unhide worksheets in the current workbook.	Chapter 9
AutoFormat	Applies a set of formatting options called an *autoformat* to the selection. Autoformats are built into *Excel*.	Chapters 3 and 8
Style	Applies predefined sets of formatting options called *styles* to the selection; creates, modifies, and deletes styles.	Chapters 3 and 8
Placement	Opens a submenu with commands that change the layering and grouping of graphic elements.	Chapter 13

Figure 2-29 The commands of the Format menu

The Data menu Figure 2-31 shows the Data menu and summarizes its commands. Although *Excel* is primarily a spreadsheet program, you can use it for many tasks you might otherwise do with a database management program. *Excel*'s list management features make it easy to keep track of information that lends itself to tabular organization. Plus, you can retrieve information from a dedicated database program into an *Excel* spreadsheet. The commands related to list and database processing are covered in detail in the chapters that are listed.

The Window menu Figure 2-32 shows the Window menu and summarizes its commands. This menu is a standard feature of *Windows* programs that lets you work with the windows for two or more open files at the same

The Tools menu

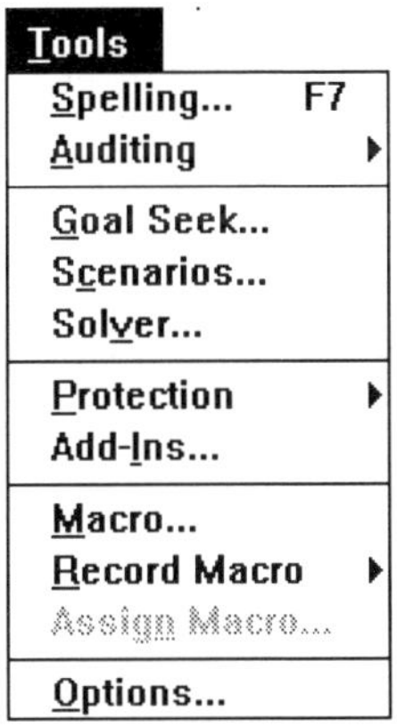

Command	Function	Presented in
Spelling	Checks for and corrects spelling errors.	Chapters 3 and 7
Auditing	Opens a submenu with commands that detect and diagnose worksheet problems.	Chapter 18
Goal Seek	Changes the value in the selected cell until a formula in another cell that depends on it reaches a specified result.	Chapter 22
Scenarios	Manages different sets of data (scenarios) that you can use for what-if analysis.	Chapter 21
Solver	Starts *Excel*'s Solver feature.	Chapter 22
Protection	Opens a submenu with commands that prevent changes from being made to worksheets and workbooks.	Chapter 24
Add-Ins	Loads or removes add-in components.	Chapter 24
Macro	Executes, changes, or deletes macros.	Chapter 19
Record Macro	Opens a submenu with commands that record mouse and keyboard actions as macros.	Chapter 19
Assign Macro	Assigns a macro to a toolbar button or a graphic object.	Chapters 19 and 20
Options	Displays a dialog box with 10 tabs you can use to set a variety of *Excel* options.	Chapter 4

Figure 2-30 The commands of the Tools menu

time. For example, the Arrange command lets you organize the windows for the open files by *tiling* or *cascading* them. And you can switch to any one of the open files that are listed at the bottom of this menu by selecting the file name. If you open two workbook windows and experiment with these commands, you'll see how easy they are to use.

The Data menu

Command	Function	Presented in
Sort	Arranges selected rows in a specified sequence.	Chapters 7 and 15
Filter	Opens a submenu with commands that display only those rows in a list that meet specific criteria.	Chapter 14
Form	Displays a dialog box called a *data form* that you can use to view, enter, change, and delete data from a list or database.	Chapter 14
Subtotals	Inserts rows in a sorted list with subtotals for selected columns.	Chapter 15
Table	Creates a data table based on different values in one or more formulas.	Chapter 24
Text to Columns	Starts the TextWizard to help you split text in one column into multiple columns.	Chapter 24
Consolidate	Collects data from multiple locations in a table.	Chapter 24
Group and Outline	Organizes rows with matching values in specified columns in outline form to create summary reports.	Chapter 7
PivotTable	Starts the PivotTable Wizard to help you create or change a pivot table.	Chapter 16
PivotTable Field	Defines a calculated field in a pivot table.	Chapter 16
Refresh Data	Updates a pivot table or a query.	Chapter 16
Get External Data	Retrieves data from another source (like a database file) using *Microsoft Query.*	Chapter 17

Figure 2-31 The commands of the Data menu

The Window menu

Command	Function	Presented in
New Window	Creates a new workbook window for the current workbook.	Chapter 9
Arrange	Changes the layout of open workbook windows.	Chapter 9
Hide	Hides a workbook window.	Chapter 9
Unhide	Reveals a hidden workbook window.	Chapter 9
Split	Divides the current workbook window into two or four panes. (If the window is already divided into panes, Remove Split appears in the menu instead of Split.)	Chapter 7
Freeze Panes	Locks the top pane, the left pane, or both to keep titles on the screen while you scroll. (If panes are already frozen, Unfreeze Panes appears in the menu instead of Freeze Panes.)	Chapter 7
file name	Makes the workbook window for the selected file active.	Chapter 9

Figure 2-32 The commands of the Window menu

How to make the transition to *Excel* from *Lotus 1-2-3*

As you've seen throughout this chapter, the experience you have with any other spreadsheet programs will help you learn *Excel*. However, if you're a *Lotus 1-2-3* user, you can benefit from several features of *Excel* that were designed to make the transition even easier. To use these features, you activate the appropriate options in the Transition tab of the Options dialog box shown in figure 2-33.

One of the most useful options is Transition Navigation Keys. After you activate this option, you can use the *1-2-3* keystrokes to move the cell pointer from place to place in a worksheet.

If you want to be coached as you learn *Excel*, you can activate the Lotus 1-2-3 Help option. When it's active, you can type in a *1-2-3* command (like /fr), and *Excel* displays a dialog box that describes how to accomplish the same operation in *Excel*. If you like, you can watch an

Access

Select the Options command from the Tools menu, then click on the Transition tab.

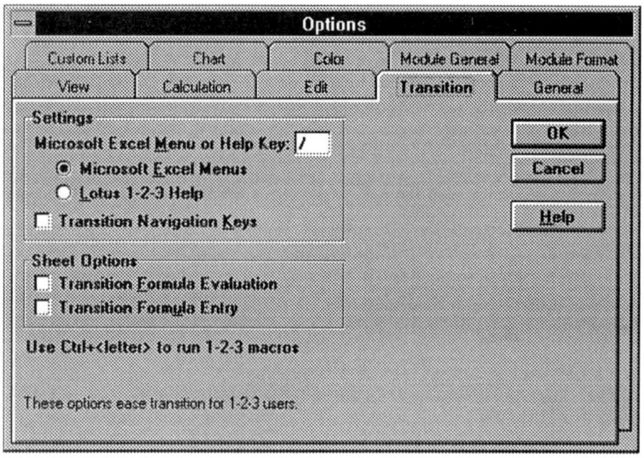

Option	Description
Microsoft Excel Menu or Help Key	Lets you specify a key that accesses either *Microsoft Excel* Menus or *Lotus 1-2-3* Help. The default is the standard *Lotus 1-2-3* command key, the slash (/).
Microsoft Excel Menus	Specifies that the key above will access *Excel*'s menu bar.
Lotus 1-2-3 Help	Specifies that the key above will invoke a coaching system that recognizes *1-2-3* operations, then describes and demonstrates the *Excel* equivalent.
Transition Navigation Keys	Uses *1-2-3* navigation key conventions instead of *Excel* conventions.
Transition Formula Evaluation	Lets you open complex *Lotus 1-2-3* files without losing or changing information. Needed only if a *1-2-3* file uses advanced features like numeric evaluation of text strings, Boolean expressions, and database criteria.
Transition Formula Entry	Converts formulas with *Lotus 1-2-3* release 2.2 syntax to *Excel* syntax. Makes names defined in *Excel* behave like names defined in *1-2-3*.

Figure 2-33 The Transition tab of the Options dialog box

animated demonstration of how to do it. Although you won't want to use this feature all the time, it's an efficient way to learn new skills as you move from *1-2-3* to *Excel.*

Perspective

As you work with *Excel,* I think you'll find that this program is easier to use than your old spreadsheet program. In fact, with just a few hours practice, you should be able to work more efficiently with *Excel* than you did with your old spreadsheet program.

On the other hand, there's a lot more to *Excel* than this chapter has shown. That's why chapter 3 introduces you to the new or improved features of *Excel.* In particular, it presents ten features that you should start using right away.

Summary

- To start *Excel,* you double-click on the icon that opens its *group window* (usually Microsoft Office). Then, you click on the icon for *Microsoft Excel.* This opens the *application window* for *Excel,* which contains one *document,* or *workbook, window.*
- You can still use the basic keyboard skills and techniques that you used with your old spreadsheet program for entering labels, values, formulas, and functions into a *worksheet.* However, the General format makes it easier for you to enter labels and values.
- Like all *Windows* programs, *Excel* has a *graphical user interface* that's designed for use with a mouse. In many cases, the mouse technique for performing a function like selecting a range is more efficient than the comparable keyboard technique.
- *Excel's* menu interface is a standard feature of all *Windows* programs. You can use either the mouse or the keyboard to pull down menus from the *menu bar* and issue commands from the menus.
- *Shortcut keys* make it easy for you to issue some of the more common *Excel* commands.

- When a command needs more information, a *dialog box* is displayed. Then, you set the options in the dialog box the way you want them.
- You use the commands of the File menu to open files and their windows, to save files, and to close files and their windows. You use other commands in this menu to print worksheets.
- You use the commands of the Edit menu to copy and move ranges of cells and to delete the contents of cells. The Undo command in this menu lets you undo the last operation.
- The Cut, Copy, and Paste commands are standard *Windows* commands that work through a *clipboard*. You can use these commands to copy or move data from one range of a worksheet to another or from one *Excel* workbook to another. In addition, you can use them to move data from one *Windows* program to another.
- You can access the Help feature through the Help menu, by pressing the F1 key, or by clicking on the Help button in a dialog box. When you use the F1 key or the Help button, the information that you get is *context-sensitive*.
- Many of the commands in the View, Insert, Format, Tools, Data, and Window menus are easy to use because they correspond closely to the commands in other spreadsheet programs or in other *Windows* programs.

Chapter 3

Start taking advantage of the new and improved features

Ten new or improved features that you can start using right away
- Expanded toolbars
- Shortcut menus
- Drag-and-drop editing
- AutoFill data entry
- Spell checking
- Nonadjacent selections
- TipWizard
- Customized view options
- Multiple worksheets in a single workbook file
- Multiple Document Interface

Nine other new or improved features of *Excel* 5.0
- Styles and autoformats
- Charting
- Drawing
- Lists and filters
- Pivot tables
- External databases
- Macros
- Analytical tools
- Object Linking and Embedding

Perspective
Summary

Version 5.0 of *Microsoft Excel for Windows* provides many new or improved features. Ten of them are so easy to use that you can start using them right away to improve your performance. In this chapter, you'll learn about these ten features. Then, you'll be introduced to nine more extensive features that are presented in other chapters in this book.

Ten new or improved features that you can start using right away

Excel 5.0 provides ten new or improved features that you need to know to use it effectively. Because these features are easy to use, you'll want to start using them right away. Although some of these features are presented in more detail later in this book, the material in this chapter should be enough to get you started with them.

Expanded toolbars As you can see in figure 3-1, the default *Excel* screen has two *toolbars* that are displayed between the menu bar and the formula bar: the *Standard toolbar* and the *Formatting toolbar*. Each has a row of *toolbar buttons*. When you click on one of these buttons, it starts a command just as though you accessed the command through the menus or through shortcut keys. So if a command operates upon a range, you should select the range before you click on the toolbar button for the command.

Figure 3-2 summarizes the buttons in the Standard and Formatting toolbars. Although most of these buttons just start commands, some of them seem to have "intelligence." If, for example, you click on the AutoSum button when the current cell is immediately below a column of numbers, a SUM function is created that sums the numbers above the current cell. If you click on this icon when the current cell is immediately to the right of a column of numbers, a SUM function is created that sums the numbers to the left. Now isn't this an improvement over entering the SUM function from scratch?

The buttons on the Standard and Formatting toolbars let you access the functions that you're most likely to need. However, *Excel* has 11 other toolbars with buttons for special functions, such as working with charts, drawings, and tables. *Excel* automatically displays some of these toolbars when you issue an appropriate command. You'll see these toolbars in later chapters in this book.

The Standard and Formatting toolbars are called *docked toolbars* because they're in fixed positions in *Excel*'s application window. In

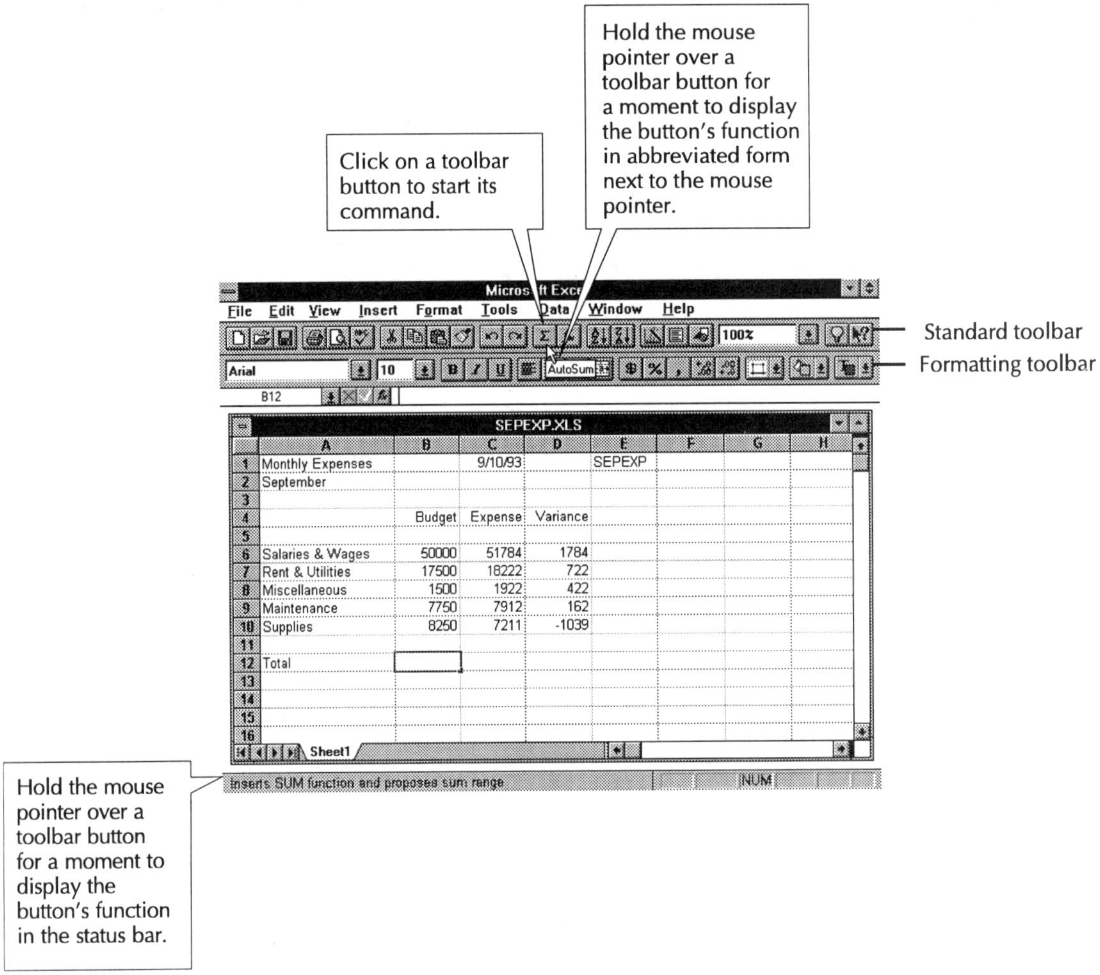

Figure 3-1 How to use toolbar buttons

contrast, most of the other toolbars are *floating toolbars* that appear as palettes of tools that you can move, resize, and close. However, you can easily change a docked toolbar to a floating toolbar by pointing to its background and dragging it down into *Excel*'s workspace. To change a floating toolbar to a docked toolbar, do the opposite.

If you like the idea of using toolbar buttons, *Excel* lets you customize them in several ways. For instance, you can rearrange the buttons on a toolbar, delete buttons, and add new buttons for functions you use often but

Standard toolbar buttons and drop-down list box

Control	Function
	Creates a new workbook file.
	Opens a workbook file.
	Saves a workbook file.
	Prints a worksheet.
	Previews the printed output.
	Checks spelling.
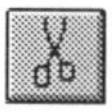	Cuts the selection to the clipboard.
	Copies the selection to the clipboard.
	Pastes the contents of the clipboard to the current cell location.
	Copies cell formats (Format Painter).
	Reverses the effect of the most recent command or operation.
	Repeats the most recent command or operation.
	Inserts the SUM function and proposes a range.
	Starts the Function Wizard to help you build a function.
	Sorts the selection in ascending sequence.
	Sorts the selection in descending sequence.
	Starts the ChartWizard to help you create or modify a chart.
	Creates a box for text not associated with a cell.
	Shows or hides the Drawing toolbar.
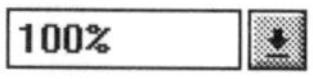	Changes the magnification in the current window.
	Opens the TipWizard to help you with the actions you perform.
	Displays help on a part of the screen or a selection.

Figure 3-2 The toolbar buttons and drop-down list boxes in the Standard and Formatting toolbars (part 1 of 2)

Formatting toolbar buttons and drop-down list boxes

Control	Function
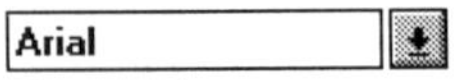	Changes the font for the selection.
	Changes the font size for the selection.
	Makes the selected cells bold.
	Makes the selected cells italic.
	Makes the selected cells underlined.
	Left-aligns the selected cells.
	Centers the selected cells.
	Right aligns the selected cells.
	Centers text across multiple cells.
	Applies Currency format to the selected cells.
	Applies Percentage format to the selected cells.
	Adds commas to the number format of the selected cells.
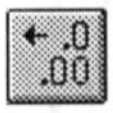	Adds one decimal place to the number format of the selected cells.
	Removes one decimal place from the number format of the selected cells.
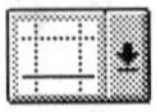	Adds border lines to the selected cells.
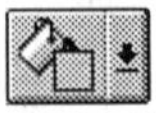	Changes the background color of the selected cells.
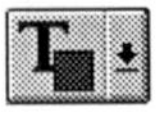	Changes the color of the text in the selected cells.

Figure 3-2 The toolbar buttons and drop-down list boxes in the Standard and Formatting toolbars (part 2 of 2)

that don't have buttons in the toolbars that come with *Excel*. In chapter 20, you can learn these skills and others that will help you get the most from using toolbar buttons.

The shortcut menu when a range is highlighted

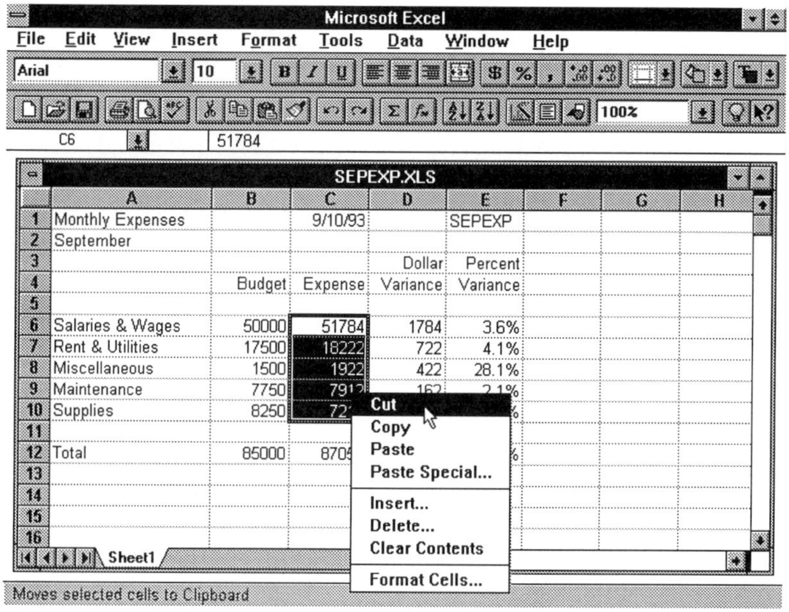

Procedure

1. Point to the area of the screen related to a command you want to issue (like the title bar, a sheet tab, or a window border) or select the cell, range, or object you want a command to affect.
2. Press the right mouse button to display the shortcut menu.
3. To issue a command, continue to hold the right mouse button down and drag the highlight to the command, then release the right mouse button. Or, click the left mouse button on the command after you pop up the menu.

Figure 3-3 How to use a shortcut menu

Shortcut menus In figure 3-3, you can see a *shortcut menu.* To pop up this type of menu, you point to an *object* such as a cell, a range, a chart, or a graphic and hold down the right mouse button. Then, you select the command you want to issue.

Shortcut menus can help you work more efficiently because they're easy to access and because they display the most commonly used commands for the object that you've pointed at. In figure 3-3, for example, you can see that the shortcut menu for a range contains appropriate commands from the Edit, Insert, and Format menus. In other words, the shortcut menus are *context sensitive.* If you pop up a shortcut menu for another object like a chart, the commands in the menu change to the most commonly used ones for that type of object. If you experiment with shortcut menus, you'll soon realize how efficient they are to use.

Drag-and-drop editing In *Windows* terminology, *drag-and-drop* refers to the ability to move or copy an object from one screen location to another by dragging it with the mouse. In figure 3-4, you can see how this technique is used to move a cell or a range of cells in *Excel*. First, you select the range of cells that you want to move. Next, you move the mouse pointer just over the border of the range so it changes to an arrow. Then, you hold down the left mouse button and drag the object to another location in the worksheet. When you release the mouse button, the range is "dropped" into the new location.

You can also use this technique to move a chart or graphic object. In addition, you can use a similar technique to copy any object. To do that, select the object, then hold down the Ctrl key as you grab it and move it to another location. You'll know that you're copying the object instead of moving it because a small plus sign appears just above the arrow. When you release the mouse button, the object is copied to the new location.

AutoFill data entry When you need to copy the data in a cell to a range of adjacent cells, you can use the *AutoFill feature* as illustrated in figure 3-5. In this example, a formula in one cell is copied to the two cells to its right. To use this feature, you begin by selecting the range that contains the data you want to copy. Then, you point to the *fill handle* in the lower right corner of the selection and drag it through the cells where you want to copy the data. Although you can also copy data to adjacent cells using the Fill Down, Fill Right, Fill Up, and Fill Left commands in the Edit menu, it's easier to use the AutoFill feature.

You can also use the AutoFill feature to enter a series of labels or values like those shown in figure 3-6. First, you enter the first one or two labels or values in the range. By default, the only series *Excel* recognizes from a single entry are the months of the year and the days of the weeks, but you can create your own custom series. You'll learn how to create a custom series in chapter 5.

After you enter the starting entries, you select them and drag the fill handle through the cells you want to fill. If *Excel* recognizes the starting entries as a series, it continues the series through the range. Otherwise, *Excel* copies the starting values into the range. You can also create series using the Fill Series command in the Edit menu, but it's usually easier to use the AutoFill feature.

How to move a range of cells

1. Select the range that you want to move:

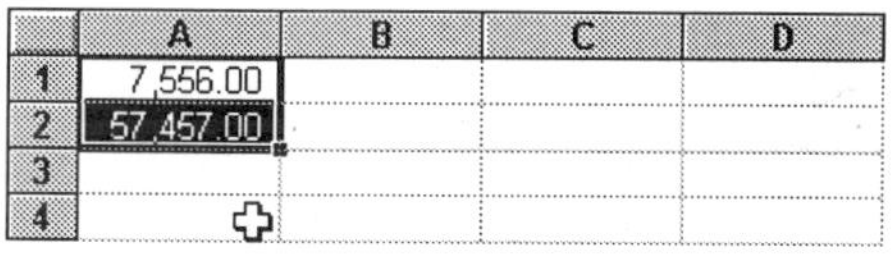

2. Position the pointer over the border of the range so it changes to an arrow:

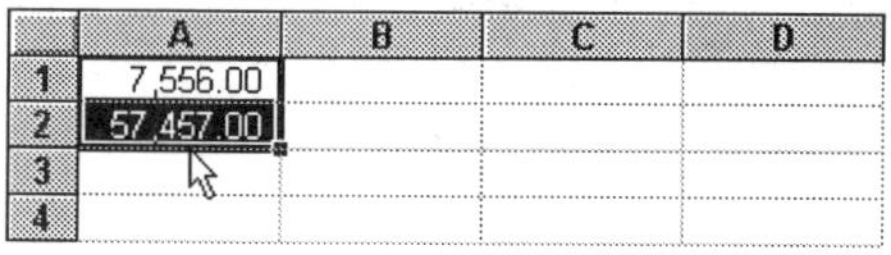

3. Drag the range to its new location:

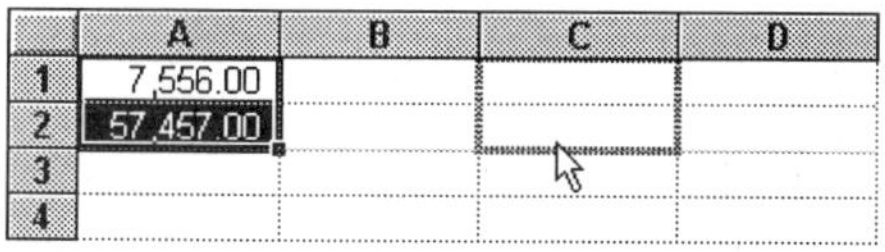

4. Release the mouse button to "drop" the selection into position:

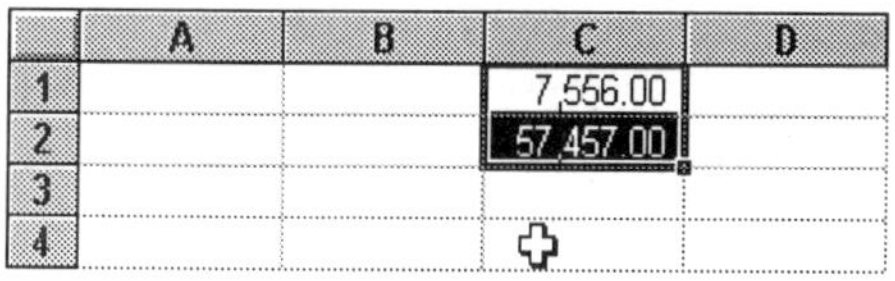

How to copy a range of cells

Use the same procedure that you use for moving a range of cells, but hold down the Ctrl key while you perform the drag operation.

How to move or copy another type of object

The procedures above work for moving or copying any object that can be selected. For instance, you can use the same procedures to move or copy a cell, a chart, or a graphic object.

Figure 3-4 How to use drag-and-drop editing to move or copy an object

Spell checking If you've been using a spreadsheet program that didn't have a spelling checker, you'll welcome the addition of this feature. To check the spelling in a worksheet, you issue the Spelling command from the Tools menu. When the command finds an error, it displays a dialog box like the one in figure 3-6. Often, the command recommends the correct spelling for the word as shown here. Then, you just click on the Change button to correct the word.

Procedure

1. Select the cell or range of cells that contains the data you want to copy, and place the mouse pointer over the fill handle so the pointer turns into a cross:

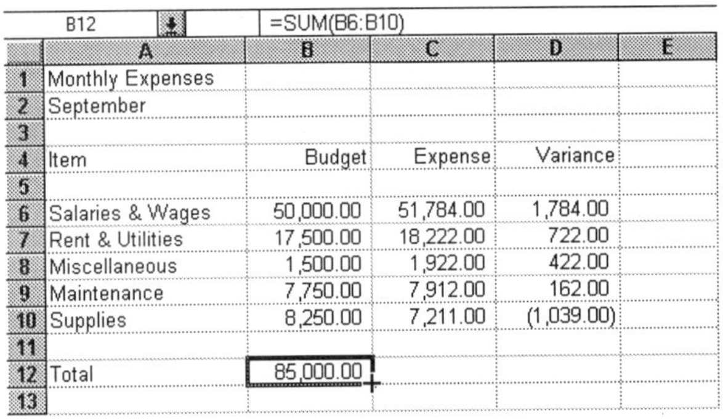

B12 =SUM(B6:B10)

	A	B	C	D	E
1	Monthly Expenses				
2	September				
3					
4	Item	Budget	Expense	Variance	
5					
6	Salaries & Wages	50,000.00	51,784.00	1,784.00	
7	Rent & Utilities	17,500.00	18,222.00	722.00	
8	Miscellaneous	1,500.00	1,922.00	422.00	
9	Maintenance	7,750.00	7,912.00	162.00	
10	Supplies	8,250.00	7,211.00	(1,039.00)	
11					
12	Total	85,000.00			
13					

2. Drag the fill handle across the range you want to copy the data to:

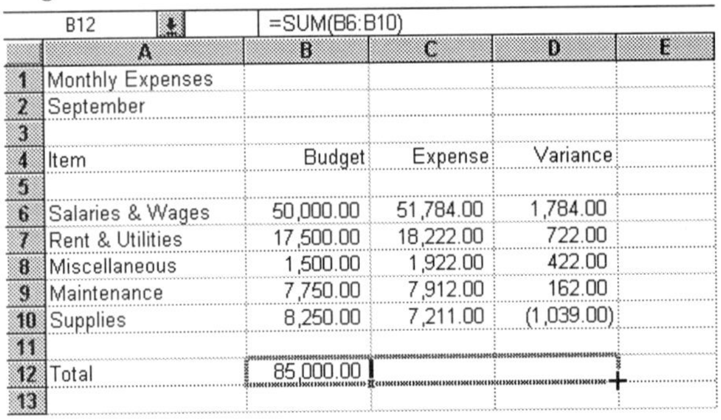

B12 =SUM(B6:B10)

	A	B	C	D	E
1	Monthly Expenses				
2	September				
3					
4	Item	Budget	Expense	Variance	
5					
6	Salaries & Wages	50,000.00	51,784.00	1,784.00	
7	Rent & Utilities	17,500.00	18,222.00	722.00	
8	Miscellaneous	1,500.00	1,922.00	422.00	
9	Maintenance	7,750.00	7,912.00	162.00	
10	Supplies	8,250.00	7,211.00	(1,039.00)	
11					
12	Total	85,000.00			
13					

3. Release the mouse button and the data is copied into the range:

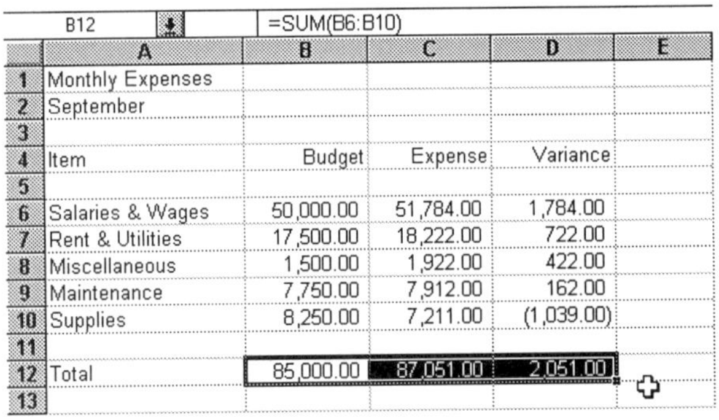

B12 =SUM(B6:B10)

	A	B	C	D	E
1	Monthly Expenses				
2	September				
3					
4	Item	Budget	Expense	Variance	
5					
6	Salaries & Wages	50,000.00	51,784.00	1,784.00	
7	Rent & Utilities	17,500.00	18,222.00	722.00	
8	Miscellaneous	1,500.00	1,922.00	422.00	
9	Maintenance	7,750.00	7,912.00	162.00	
10	Supplies	8,250.00	7,211.00	(1,039.00)	
11					
12	Total	85,000.00	87,051.00	2,051.00	
13					

Note

If *Excel* recognizes the initial entry as part of a series, it continues the series into the extended range instead of copying the data. By default, the only series *Excel* recognizes from a single entry are the months of the year and the days of the week.

Figure 3-5 How to use the AutoFill feature to copy data

Procedure

1. Enter the first one or two labels or values in a series.
2. Select the labels or values that you've entered, then drag the fill handle in the lower right corner of the selection down through the cells you want to fill:

	A	B	C	D	E	F	G	H	I
1	Numbers	Numbers	Days	Days	Months	Months	Quarters	Dates	Dates
2									
3	1	2	Monday	Mon	January	Jan	Q1	11/1/93	11/1/93
4	2	4	Tuesday	Tue	February	Feb	Q2	11/2/93	11/8/93
5									
6									
7									
8									
9									
10									
11									
12									
13									
14									
15									
16									
17									
18									

3. Release the left mouse button and the series are entered into the range:

	A	B	C	D	E	F	G	H	I
1	Numbers	Numbers	Days	Days	Months	Months	Quarters	Dates	Dates
2									
3	1	2	Monday	Mon	January	Jan	Q1	11/1/93	11/1/93
4	2	4	Tuesday	Tue	February	Feb	Q2	11/2/93	11/8/93
5	3	6	Wednesday	Wed	March	Mar	Q3	11/3/93	11/15/93
6	4	8	Thursday	Thu	April	Apr	Q4	11/4/93	11/22/93
7	5	10	Friday	Fri	May	May	Q1	11/5/93	11/29/93
8	6	12	Saturday	Sat	June	Jun	Q2	11/6/93	12/6/93
9	7	14	Sunday	Sun	July	Jul	Q3	11/7/93	12/13/93
10	8	16	Monday	Mon	August	Aug	Q4	11/8/93	12/20/93
11	9	18	Tuesday	Tue	September	Sep	Q1	11/9/93	12/27/93
12	10	20	Wednesday	Wed	October	Oct	Q2	11/10/93	1/3/94
13	11	22	Thursday	Thu	November	Nov	Q3	11/11/93	1/10/94
14	12	24	Friday	Fri	December	Dec	Q4	11/12/93	1/17/94
15	13	26	Saturday	Sat	January	Jan	Q1	11/13/93	1/24/94
16	14	28	Sunday	Sun	February	Feb	Q2	11/14/93	1/31/94
17	15	30	Monday	Mon	March	Mar	Q3	11/15/93	2/7/94
18	16	32	Tuesday	Tue	April	Apr	Q4	11/16/93	2/14/94

Note

If *Excel* is able to interpret the starting entries as a series, it continues the series into the extended range. Otherwise, *Excel* copies the data into the range.

Figure 3-6 How to use the AutoFill feature to enter a series of values into a range

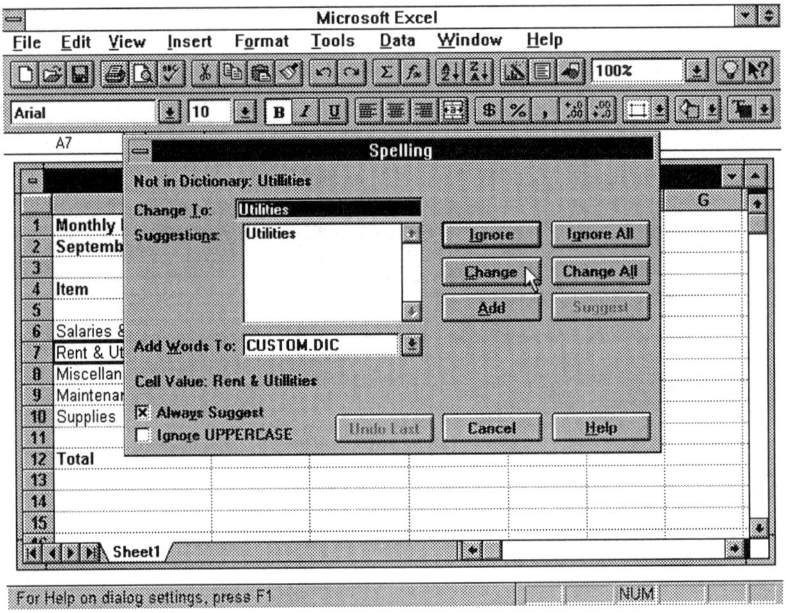

Figure 3-7 The dialog box for the Spelling command in the Tools menu

Nonadjacent selections A *nonadjacent selection* consists of one or more ranges as shown in figure 3-8. Here, two ranges are highlighted. To make a nonadjacent selection, highlight the first range. Then, hold down the Ctrl key as you highlight each additional range. When you issue a command, it operates upon all of the ranges in the selection.

To make a nonadjacent selection, you have to use the mouse in combination with the Ctrl key; there are no keystroke equivalents. However, you can type a reference for nonadjacent ranges directly into a text box. To do that, just separate the ranges in the selection by commas as in this example:

A1:E4,A6:A12

Usually, though, it's easier to use the mouse when you want to make a nonadjacent selection.

TipWizard Figure 3-9 shows one of the best ways to learn how to work efficiently with *Excel*: using the TipWizard. To turn on the TipWizard, you click on the TipWizard button and the TipWizard toolbar appears. Then, the TipWizard monitors your work and suggests easier and more

A nonadjacent selection that contains two ranges

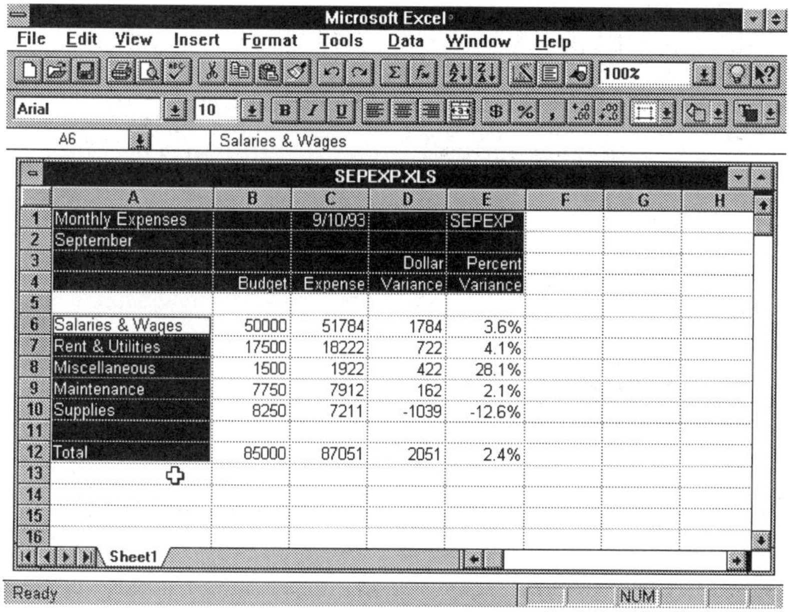

Procedure

1. Use a standard technique to highlight the first range.
2. Hold down the Ctrl key while you highlight each subsequent range in the nonadjacent selection.

Figure 3-8 How to make a nonadjacent selection

efficient ways to do the same operations. These suggestions remain available during your work session, and you can scroll back to review them. Because the TipWizard's suggestions are based on your actions, they're likely to be quite useful, especially if you're just starting to work with *Excel.*

Customized view options If you want to adjust the view in the application or workbook window as you work, you can use the commands in the View menu as summarized in figure 3-10. If you want to make the data easier to read, for example, you can use the Zoom command to enlarge or reduce the displayed data. The Zoom command lets you choose the magnification level you want to use. You can also select several standard zoom percentages from the drop-down list box in the Standard toolbar.

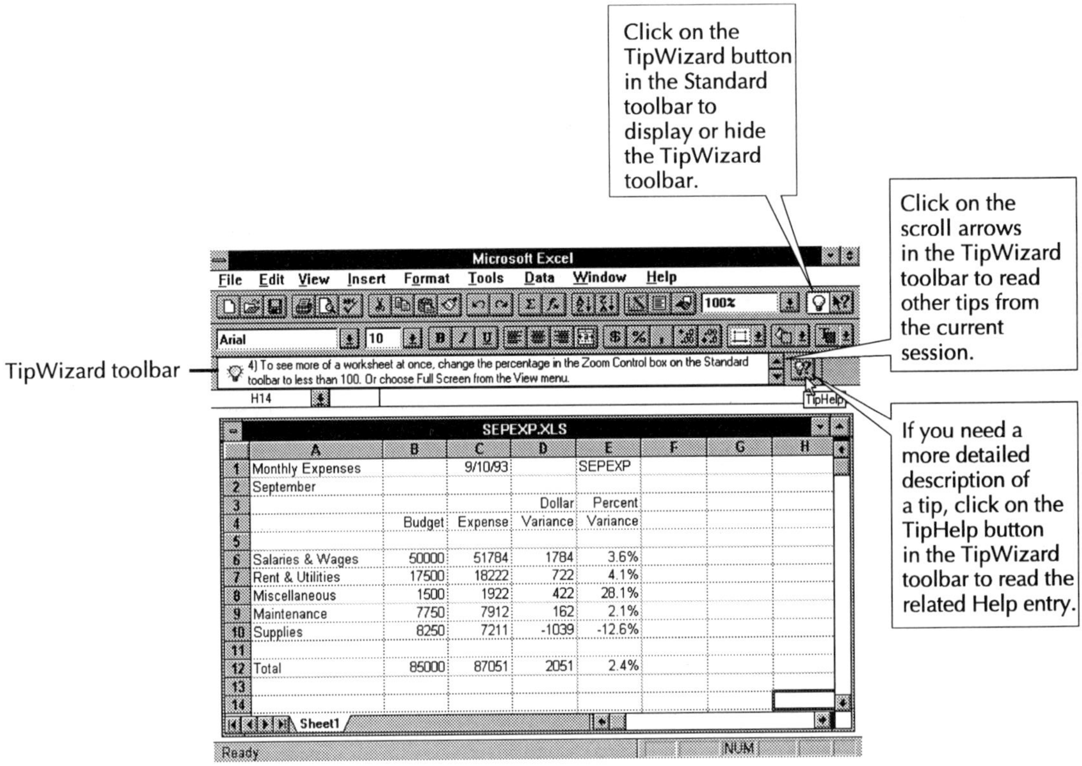

Notes

- The TipWizard monitors your work and offers suggestions for how to accomplish tasks more easily or efficiently. For example, the TipWizard made the suggestion in this example because the cell pointer was moved just outside the block of cells displayed on the screen (to cell I15), then back.
- All of the suggestions the TipWizard makes in a session remain available in a scrolling list in the TipWizard toolbar. You can review them at any time.

Figure 3-9 How to use the TipWizard

To make more lasting view changes, you can use the View tab of the Options dialog box. The options in the Show group affect *Excel*'s application window and are in affect from one session to the next. In contrast, the options in the Objects and Windows Options groups affect only the current file. These options are saved with the file so they're used the next time you open it. In figure 3-10, you can see that I used the View tab to remove the status bar, scroll bars, and sheet tabs from the display. I also used the Zoom command in the View menu to reduce the screen to 75%, and I used the Toolbars command to remove the Formatting toolbar.

Access

Select the Options command from the Tools menu, then click on the View tab.

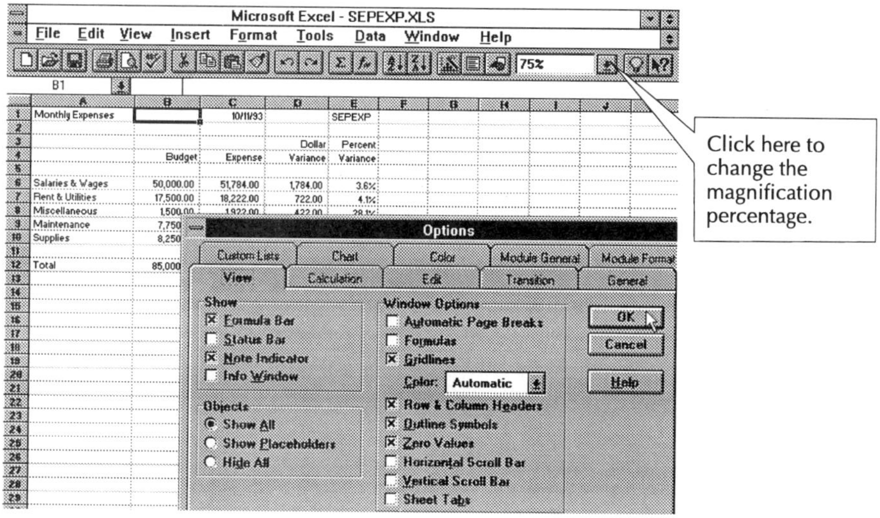

View menu command	Function
Formula Bar	Displays or hides the formula bar.
Status Bar	Displays or hides the status bar.
Toolbars	Displays or hides any or all of the toolbars that are available with *Excel*, and lets you customize the toolbars.
Full Screen	Toggles between the default view and full-screen view where *Excel's* application window is maximized, and the title bar, the formula bar, the Standard and Formatting toolbars, and the status bar are hidden.
Zoom	Changes the magnification percentage for the workbook window. You can also change the magnification by selecting a percentage from the drop-down list box in the Standard toolbar.

Figure 3-10 How to use the commands of the View menu and the options of the View tab to adjust the appearance of the worksheet screen

If you have a long or wide spreadsheet and you want to view two portions of it at the same time, you can split the worksheet view vertically or horizontally. To do this, you use the split boxes, the small black boxes located above the vertical scroll bar and to the right of the horizontal scroll bar. When you move the mouse pointer to a split box, the pointer changes to the splitter symbol. Then, to split the view, you drag the split box to where you want it and release the mouse button. If you want, you can save your file with a split view so it's displayed that way the next time you open it.

Or, you can return the file to normal view by dragging the split box back to its original location.

Multiple worksheets in a single workbook file When you use version 5.0 of *Excel*, each workbook file can consist of one or more worksheets as summarized in figure 3-11. When you create a new file, it starts off with 16 worksheets. You can delete and add worksheets at any time. In figure 3-11, for example, the workbook contains 12 worksheets; the other 4 that were available when this file was created have been deleted.

To help you identify a worksheet, each one is assigned a name: Sheet1, Sheet2, and so on. These names are on the *sheet tabs* along the bottom edge of the workbook window. You can rename a worksheet at any time by double-clicking on its sheet tab and typing in a new name. In figure 3-11, for example, the tabs are named with the months of the year.

To switch from one worksheet to another, you click on a sheet tab. To copy or move data from one worksheet to another, you can use the Cut, Copy, and Paste commands of the Edit menu. And if you want to display more than one worksheet on the screen at the same time, you can use the New Window command in the Window menu to open another workbook window for the file.

If you want to create a formula that operates upon the data in more than one worksheet, you can switch from one worksheet to another as you identify the cells that are used in the formula. For instance, the formulas in a Total row of one of the worksheets can summarize data from the other worksheets in the workbook. When a formula in one worksheet refers to a cell in another worksheet, its cell reference is preceded by the name of the worksheet. In the formula

=Jan!B10+Feb!B10+Mar!B10

for example, the values in cell B10 in worksheets Jan, Feb, and Mar are added together.

If you aren't used to working with more than one worksheet in a single file, you should start experimenting with this feature right away. Often, if you treat a job as several small worksheets rather than one large worksheet, your work is simplified so you can work more accurately and efficiently. For more information about this feature, please read chapter 9.

Multiple Document Interface When you use *Excel*, you can open more than one workbook file. *Excel* provides for this by following a standard *Windows* convention known as the *Multiple Document Interface,* or

A single workbook file that contains 12 worksheets

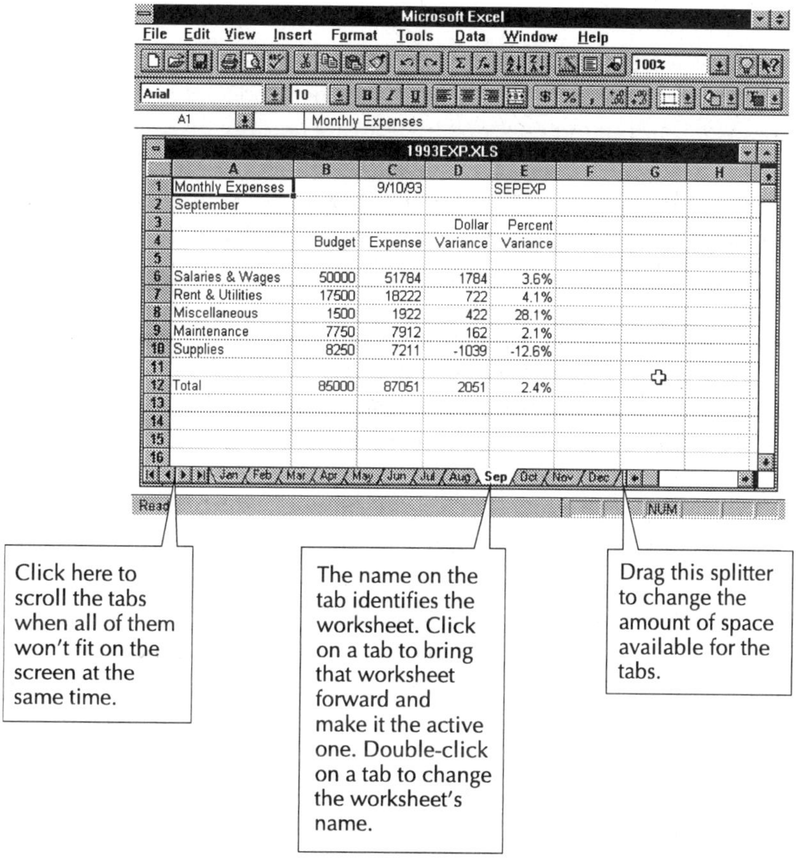

Operation

- To delete a worksheet, select its tab. Then, issue either the Delete Sheet command from the Edit menu or the Delete command from the shortcut menu.
- To insert a new worksheet, first select the tab to the right of the position where you want to add the new worksheet. Then, issue either the Insert Worksheet command from the Insert menu or the Insert command from the shortcut menu.
- You can use the New Window command in the Window menu to open additional windows for the workbook file. Then, you can view a different worksheet in each window.

Figure 3-11 How to work with two or more worksheets in a single workbook file

MDI. If you've used another MDI application like Microsoft's *Word for Windows*, you won't have any trouble using more than one workbook file with *Excel*.

When you work with *Excel*, each workbook file is displayed in its own workbook window. To illustrate, figure 3-12 shows the *Excel* display after two workbook files (windows) have been opened. To arrange the workbook windows as shown, the Cascade option of the Arrange command in the Window menu was chosen. Often, though, the workbook windows are maximized so you see only one window at a time.

To switch from one window to another, you use the standard *Windows* techniques. If you click on an inactive window, for example, it comes to the top and becomes the active window. Or, you can use the Window menu to switch between files. Similarly, you can use standard *Windows* techniques to move, size, maximize, minimize, or restore a window.

Because the *Excel* 5.0 facility for using multiple worksheets in a single workbook file is so efficient, you may have little need for working with two or more separate workbook files at the same time. So when you start using *Excel* 5.0, you may want to combine some of your old worksheet files into one workbook file that contains two or more worksheets. To do that, you can open the old files along with the new file. Then, you can copy data from the old files into the worksheets of the new workbook using the clipboard. For more information about working with more than one file at a time, please read chapter 9.

Nine other new or improved features of *Excel* 5.0

Figure 3-13 lists nine of the more extensive new or improved features of *Excel*. Each of them offers benefits that can make your work easier and more productive. In the remainder of this chapter, I'll introduce you to them quickly. Then, you can refer to the chapters listed for more information on them.

Styles and autoformats If you've used *styles* with your old spreadsheet program, you know that a style can consist of a font, a size, and attributes like boldface or italics. In *Excel*, styles can also include borders, alignment, and fill colors and patterns. Once you create styles, you can apply them to ranges of cells. For instance, you can apply a style to the cells that are used for column headings so they are printed in boldface type, in a larger size than the data in the rest of the worksheet, and with a dark underline as a border. Because *Excel* has built-in WYSIWYG, what you see on the screen is what you're going to get on the printer.

Another *Excel* 5.0 improvement that can make it easier for you to prepare polished worksheets is *automatic formatting*. When you select the AutoFormat command from the Format menu, *Excel* lets you apply a set of

Excel **after two workbook files have been opened and displayed in cascaded arrangement**

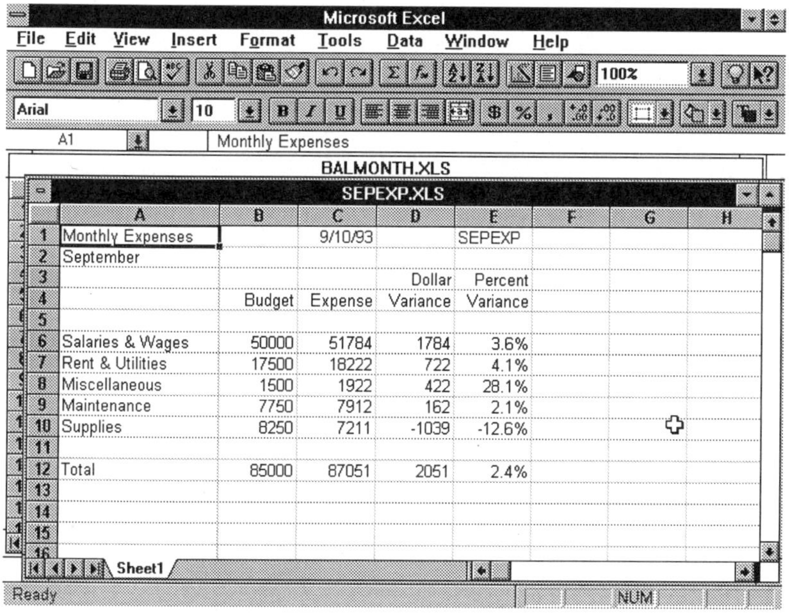

Operation

- Use the Open command in the File menu to open another file and its workbook window.
- Use the Close command in the File menu to close the active file and its workbook window.
- To arrange the workbook windows, select the Arrange command from the Window menu, then select an option from the Arrange Windows dialog box:

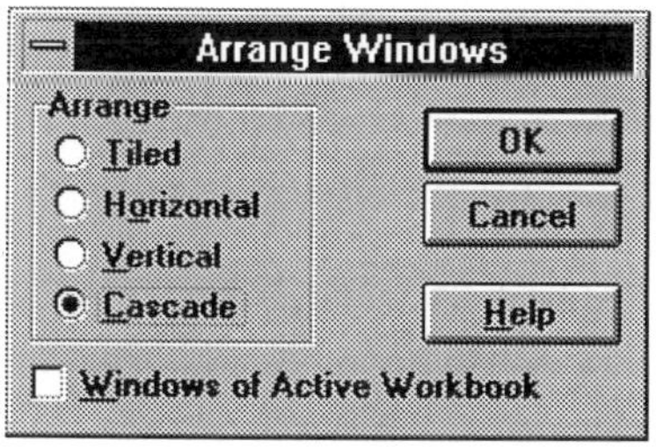

- Use the file names in the Window menu to switch from one workbook window to another.
- Use the Cut, Copy, and Paste commands in the Edit menu to transfer data from one file to another through the clipboard.
- Click on any part of an inactive window to make it the active window.
- Use *Windows* techniques to move, size, minimize, maximize, or restore a workbook window.

Figure 3-12 How to work with two or more open workbook files

Feature	Presented in
Styles and autoformats	Chapter 8
Charting	Chapters 11 and 12
Drawing	Chapter 13
Lists and filters	Chapter 14
Pivot tables	Chapter 16
External databases and *Microsoft Query*	Chapter 17
Macros	Chapter 19
Analytical Tools	Chapters 21 and 22
Object Linking and Embedding	Chapter 23

Figure 3-13 Nine other new or improved features of *Excel* 5.0

pre-defined formatting options, called an *autoformat*, to a range. *Excel* recognizes the differences between headings, totals, and data ranges in the selection and formats them differently. You can choose from 16 different autoformats.

Charting The *charting* feature of *Excel* 5.0 is an incremental improvement over the already excellent charting capabilities of *Excel* 4.0. You can create a chart by highlighting the range of data and labels for the chart and selecting the Chart command from the Insert menu or clicking on the button for charting in the Standard toolbar. Then, *Excel*'s *ChartWizard* walks you through a series of dialog boxes to help you construct a chart just the way you want it. Usually, *Excel* makes the right assumptions about what to chart and what labels to use. As a result, you can create a useful chart with just a few mouse actions and keystrokes. Then, after you create a chart, you can get the chart the way you want it using some improved editing features.

Drawing The *drawing* feature of *Excel* lets you enhance a worksheet or a chart with lines, text boxes, and other graphic devices. This feature is easy to use, and it's an improvement over the drawing feature that was available with earlier releases of *Excel*. Although this feature isn't for everybody, it can be useful when you need to make a graphic presentation.

Lists and filters Many people use their spreadsheet programs to store, manage, analyze, and print data organized in lists. In effect, a list is a simple database. *Excel*'s AutoFilter feature lets you hide and show rows that meet selection criteria you specify. And the Form command creates a dialog box you can use to enter new "records" into a list and do queries. With these features alone, *Excel* is able to meet the data management needs of many users.

Pivot tables Pivot tables are a new feature of *Excel* 5.0. With this feature, you can select an existing tabular range and have *Excel* automatically generate cross-tabulations and summary values from it. Then, you can "pivot" the table to change its arrangement and recompute its summary values.

External databases *Excel* 5.0 can work with data from several external database management programs, including *dBase III* and *dBase IV*, *Paradox* 3.0 and 3.5, *Microsoft Access*, *SQL Server*, and *Oracle Server*. To retrieve information from a database managed by one of these programs, you use the *Microsoft Query* program that comes with *Excel* 5.0. *Microsoft Query* retrieves the data to satisfy a query request, then passes it to *Excel* as a results table. However, this is a one-way communication; you don't update the source data from either *Excel* or *Query*,

Macros *Excel* 5.0 replaces the macro features that were available in earlier releases with a powerful programming language called *Visual Basic Programming System: Applications Edition*. Frankly, most *Excel* users won't need to worry about writing macros in Visual Basic. That's because *Excel* has a "watch and learn" macro recorder that lets you perform an action, then converts your actions into the code required for Visual Basic. *Excel* 5.0 can also convert macros from previous versions of *Excel* and from DOS versions of *Lotus 1-2-3*.

Analytical tools If you pull down the Tools menu, you'll see three commands that provide analytical tools: Goal Seek, Solver, and Scenarios. Goal Seek provides a relatively simple function that is occasionally useful in business worksheets. In contrast, Solver provides a powerful analytical capability that can be overwhelming to the average *Excel* user. The

Scenarios command lets you access the *Scenario Manager*, a new feature of version 5.0 of *Excel.* It lets you create more than one "what if" version of the same worksheet by changing the variables from one worksheet to the next. However, a new worksheet isn't actually created for each version. Instead, the Scenario Manager keeps track of all the versions in a single worksheet and lets you display or print each version as needed.

Object Linking and Embedding *Object Linking and Embedding* (or *OLE*) is actually a *Windows* feature that is supported by *Excel.* This feature makes it easy for you to link an *Excel* worksheet to a word processing document for a program like *Word* or *Ami Pro*. Then, when you change the data in the worksheet, the data is automatically changed in the word processing document. Similarly, you can embed an object from other applications into your workbook file. Then, the object becomes a part of the workbook file, and it's no longer linked to the program that created it.

Perspective

Once you master the ten new or improved features that are presented in this chapter, you should be a competent user of *Excel* 5.0. Then, you can use the remaining chapters in this book to learn how to use other functions and features. Because the remaining chapters are written as independent modules, you can read them most of them in whatever sequence you prefer. Because they're heavily illustrated, you can often learn from the figures without even reading the text. That means you can learn new skills whenever you have 10 or 15 minutes to spare.

Summary

- *Toolbar buttons* invoke many common *Excel* functions such as opening and closing a file and printing a worksheet. In some cases, the buttons are intelligent so they do more than just start a command.
- If you click the right mouse button while pointing at a worksheet object, *Excel* displays a *shortcut menu* that lists the commands you're most likely to use for that object.
- You can move or copy a cell, a range of cells, or another object with the mouse by using the *drag-and-drop* feature.

- You can fill a range of cells by entering just one or two labels or values in the range and using the *AutoFill* feature.
- You can check the spelling of the labels in your worksheets using the Spelling command in the Tools menu.
- You can select *nonadjacent ranges* by holding down the Ctrl key while you highlight two or more ranges with the mouse.
- You can use the *TipWizard* to monitor your work and suggest better ways to perform the same operations.
- To make a worksheet easier to work with, you can adjust the view by using the commands in the View menu, the options in the View tab of the Options dialog box, or the split boxes.
- You can create more than one worksheet in a single workbook file. Then, the workbook file can consist of several simple worksheets rather than one large worksheet. To switch from one worksheet to another, you can click on the *sheet tab* for a worksheet.
- You can open more than one workbook file at a time. Then, you can use standard *Windows* techniques to manipulate the windows and switch from one window to another.
- *Excel* provides many other new or improved features including enhanced styles, charting, list management, and database features; a new macro language in Visual Basic; powerful analytical tools in the Scenario Manager, Goal Seek, and Solver; and tighter integration with other *Windows* programs through Object Linking and Embedding.

Section 2

The Essential *Excel 5.0 for Windows* skills

This section presents the essential skills that all *Excel* users should have. For ease of use, each chapter in this section is treated as an independent module so you don't have to read the chapters in sequence. However, you should take the time to read all of the chapters in this section because the skills they present can help you work more productively.

The chapters in this section and the three sections that follow are designed for both training and reference. To help you learn as quickly as possible, the figures for each function and feature include just about everything you need to know to use it. As a result, you can often learn how to use a function or feature just be reviewing the related figures...you don't even have to read the text. This helps you learn more quickly, and it makes this the ideal reference book.

When you use the chapters in these sections for training, though, we recommend that you read both the text and the figures. Since the text provides additional perspective on when and how to use a function or feature, it will help you get the most from *Excel*. But later on, when you use the chapters for reference, you shouldn't need the text at all. Instead, you should be able to refresh your memory about how to use a function or feature just by reviewing the figures.

Chapter 4

How to set *Excel* options

An introduction to the *Excel* options

How to set the View options

How to set the Calculation options

How to set the Edit options

How to set the General options

Perspective

Summary

When you install *Excel 5.0 for Windows*, the installation program sets up several values and codes that affect the way *Excel* works. These are called *default options*, *default settings*, or just *defaults*. For instance, one default determines whether you can use the drag-and-drop feature to move and copy cells, another determines whether the formula bar is displayed, and a third determines the size of the data that's displayed in the workbook window. Although you can use *Excel* without ever changing the starting defaults, you'll probably want to change some of them so *Excel* will work the way you want it to.

This chapter begins by introducing you to the Options command of the Tools menu. This command displays a dialog box with 10 tabs that you can use to change the *Excel* defaults. Then, this chapter shows you how to use four of these tabs. First, you'll learn how to use the View tab to change the defaults that affect *Excel*'s display. Next, you'll learn how to use the Calculation and Edit tabs to specify the way *Excel* operates. Last, you'll learn how to use the General tab to change the defaults that apply to workbooks.

An introduction to the *Excel* options

When you select the Options command from the Tools menu, *Excel* displays the dialog box shown in figure 4-1. From this dialog box, you can select one of ten tabs that contain controls for different sets of defaults. To switch between tabs, you click on the name of the tab you want to access.

Figure 4-1 summarizes the options provided by each tab in the Options dialog box. Six of the tabs contain specialized options. Unless you're working with an advanced feature, you probably won't need to adjust the defaults for these options.

How to set the View options

Figure 4-2 shows the View tab of the Options dialog box and summarizes its options. As you can see, the options in this tab are divided into three groups. The options in the Show group apply to *Excel* and stay in effect from one work session to the next. In contrast, the options in the Objects and Window Options groups apply to the current file, and they are saved with the file. If you experiment with these options, you can quickly see how they change the view of either the workbook window or the *Excel* window.

Most of the controls in the View tab are check boxes. If an option is selected, an X appears to its left, and that feature is included in the display.

Access

Select the Options command from the Tools menu.

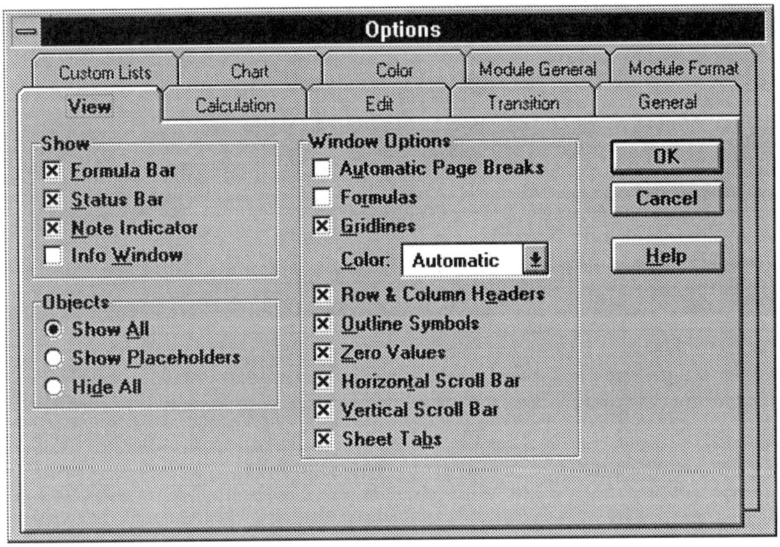

Operation

To switch between tabs, click on the name of the tab you want to access or press Ctrl+Tab.

Figure 4-1 How to use the Options command (part 1 of 2)

If an option isn't selected, that feature is omitted from the display. In figure 4-2, most of the options are selected, which is the *Excel* default. These defaults are okay for most jobs, but you may want to change a few of them to suit your work habits. For instance, you can remove the Formula bar and the Status bar from the screen if you don't like using them. Notice that you can't remove the default toolbars using the View tab. Instead, you use the Toolbars command in the View menu as you'll learn in chapter 20.

Some of the View options do more than display or hide the standard features of the *Excel* screen. The Note Indicator option in the Show group displays a small dot in the upper right corner of cells that contain notes. And the Info Window option opens a separate window that contains information on the contents and formats of selected cells. The Show Placeholders option in the Objects group displays placeholders in place of graphic objects. The Formulas option in the Window Options group displays formulas in cells that contain them instead of the values they produce.

Tab	Description	Presented in chapter(s):
View	Changes the way workbooks, objects, and windows are displayed.	4
Calculation	Changes the way cells in a workbook are calculated.	4
Edit	Controls how you can enter, edit, copy, move, and update data and objects.	4
Transition	Contains options that help you switch to *Excel* from another spreadsheet program, especially *Lotus 1-2-3*.	2
General	Controls basic defaults for all new files. These defaults include the number of sheets, the standard font and font size, the default file location, and the user name to attach to each file.	4
Custom Lists	Creates custom lists that you can use with the AutoFill feature or to custom sort a list or pivot table.	5
Chart	Specifies a default chart format and controls how empty and hidden cells are plotted in line charts; also controls how chart sheets are sized within a window.	Not presented
Color	Creates custom colors and adds them to the default color palette; also lets you copy color palettes from other workbooks.	8
Module General	Contains options for running and displaying Visual Basic procedures; also controls the language and country settings for procedures.	Not presented
Module Format	Customizes the format of various types of code you write and record in Visual Basic.	Not presented

Figure 4-1 How to use the Options command (part 2 of 2)

And the Zero Values option determines whether a cell that contains a zero value displays a zero or a blank.

How to set the Calculation options

Figure 4-3 shows the Calculation tab of the Options dialog box and summarizes its options. As you can see, most of the options in the Calculation tab let you change the way cells in a workbook are recalculated. The Automatic option is selected by default, which means that cells are recalculated each time you change the data in a cell. Because this recalculation goes on in the background, though, you can continue working. As a result, the Automatic default setting is usually the one you want for all of your work. The only

The View tab

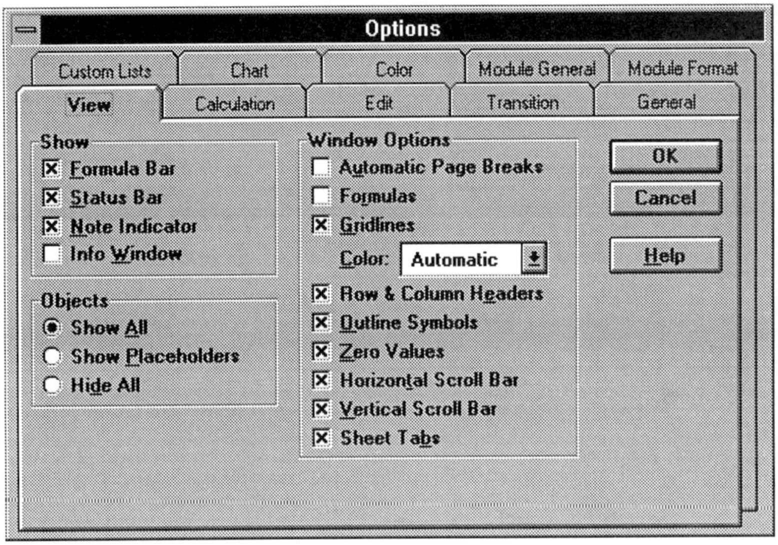

Show group

The options in this group apply to the application window for *Excel*. They are saved by *Excel* so they're used each time you run the program. They stay in effect until you change them again.

Objects and Windows Options group

The options in these two groups apply only to the current file. They are saved with the file so they're used the next time you open it.

Figure 4-2 How to set the View options

time you might want to change this is when you're working with a worksheet so large that automatic recalculation is slowing down the operation of *Excel*. Then, if you change the default to Manual, you can tell *Excel* when you want recalculation to take place either by pressing the F9 key to recalculate cells in all open workbooks or by pressing Shift+F9 to recalculate only the cells in the current worksheet. Whether you select Automatic or Manual, though, the defaults in the Iterations and Workbook Options groups should work okay the way they are.

The Calculation tab

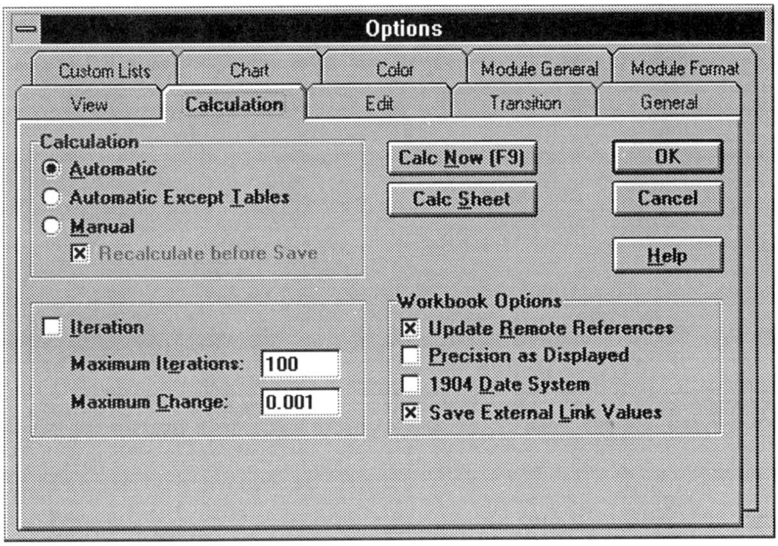

Option	Description
Automatic	Calculates all dependent formulas whenever a value or formula is changed.
Automatic Except Tables	Calculates all dependent formulas except data tables.
Manual	Calculates open workbook files when you press either the Calc Now button or the F9 key.
Recalculate before Save	Calculates all formulas whenever you save changes to a workbook. This is available only for those workbooks that are in the Manual calculation mode.
Iteration	Limits the iterations used in a goal seeking operation or to solve formulas that contain circular references. Operates according to the Maximum Iterations and Maximum Change settings.
Update Remote References	Calculates formulas that contain references to other applications. If this option isn't selected, formulas are calculated using the last value received from the other application.
Precision as Displayed	Changes the values stored in cells from full precision (15 digits) to the displayed format.
1904 Date System	Calculates dates from the starting date of January 2, 1904 instead of the default date of January 1, 1900.
Save External Link Values	Saves a copy of linked values in the worksheet that contains the links. If this option isn't selected, linked values are recalled from the external document as needed.
Calc Now (F9) button	Calculates all open workbooks, including data tables, and updates all charts. You can also perform this operation by pressing the F9 key.
Calc Sheet button	Calculates the active worksheet, including its data tables, and updates all charts associated with it. You can also perform this operation by pressing Shift+F9.

Figure 4-3 How to set the Calculation options

How to set the Edit options

Figure 4-4 shows the Edit tab of the Options dialog box and summarizes its options. As you can see, most of the controls are check boxes that let you turn an option on or off. When you install *Excel*, all of the options except Fixed Decimal are on. Normally, that's what you want, but you may need to change some of these options under special circumstances.

How to set the General options

Figure 4-5 shows the General tab of the Options dialog box and summarizes its options. The options on this tab apply to all new workbooks. One option you'll definitely want to change is Default File Location. This option identifies the default *working directory Excel* uses when you open or save a workbook file. When you install *Excel*, this default directory is C:\EXCEL, but that's not where you should save your files. Instead, you should change this directory to the one that you are currently using for most or all of your workbook files. If, for example, you're saving your files in C:\DATA\DEPTXL, that should be the setting for the Default File Location option.

You may also want to change the Standard Font and Size defaults to the font and size you use most often. Then, you won't have to change them for each new workbook or worksheet. And you may want to change the Sheets In New Workbook option to the number of worksheets you typically store in each workbook. Note that these defaults don't go into affect until the next time you start *Excel*, so they don't affect the new workbooks or worksheets you create during the current session.

Perspective

Since most of the starting *Excel* defaults work the way you want them to, you should need to change only a few of them to suit your working habits. To start, you should use the General tab to change the working directory for your workbooks. You may also want to use the General tab to specify a different default font and font size. Since these defaults apply to *Excel*, they stay in effect from one work session to another. Then, whenever you start a new workbook, you can use the View tab to change the view of that workbook. Often, if you take the time to set the right defaults for a workbook, you can improve your overall efficiency.

The Edit tab

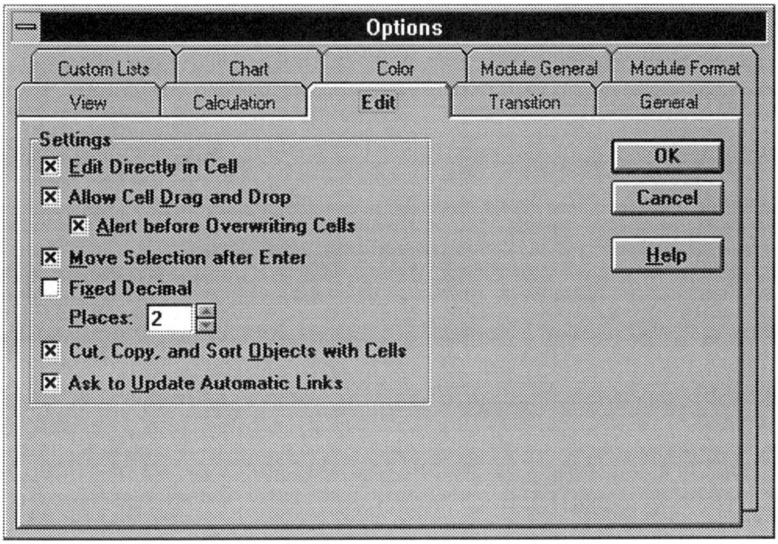

Option	Description
Edit Directly in Cell	Determines whether you can use the in-cell editing feature to edit the contents of a cell.
Allow Cell Drag and Drop	Determines whether you can use the drag-and-drop feature to move and copy data.
Alert before Overwriting Cells	Displays a warning message when you drag-and-drop data into a cell that already contains data.
Move Selection after Enter	Shifts the cell pointer down one row after you press the Enter key to enter data into a cell.
Fixed Decimal	Adds a decimal point to all numbers you enter as values in a worksheet. The position of the decimal place depends on the number you specify in the Places spin box.
Cut, Copy, and Sort Objects with Cells	Determines whether objects stay attached to the cells where you've placed them when you cut, copy, filter, or sort the cells.
Ask to Update Automatic Links	Displays a message box asking if you want to update links when you open a file that contains OLE links.

Figure 4-4 How to set Edit the options

The General tab

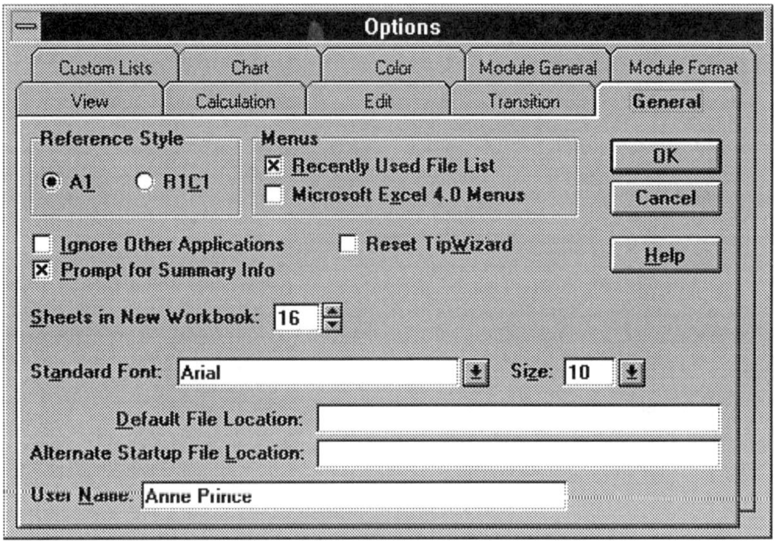

Option	Description
A1	Labels column headings alphabetically and row headings numerically.
R1C1	Labels both column and row headings numerically.
Recently Used File List	Displays a list of the last four files used in the File menu.
Microsoft Excel 4.0 Menus	Displays the menus used in *Excel* 4.0 in place of the 5.0 menus.
Ignore Other Applications	Ignores requests made from other applications using Dynamic Data Exchange.
Prompt for Summary Info	Displays the Summary Info dialog box when you save a new workbook.
Reset TipWizard	Clears the tips displayed in the TipWizard toolbar.
Sheets in New Workbook	The default number of sheets in a new workbook.
Standard Font	The default font for new sheets and workbooks. When you change this option, it doesn't go into affect until the next time you start *Excel.*
Size	The default font size for new sheets and workbooks. When you change this option, it doesn't go into affect until the next time you start *Excel.*
Default File Location	The directory *Excel* uses by default when you open or save a file.
Alternate Startup File Location	A directory that contains files you want opened automatically when you start *Excel.*
User Name	The name *Excel* uses in scenarios, views, file sharing, and the Summary Info dialog box.

Figure 4-5 How to set the General options

Summary

- The Options command of the Tools menu lets you access tabs that you can use to change the *Excel defaults*.
- The View tab of the Options dialog box lets you change the defaults for options that affect the display of the *Excel* window or the workbook window.
- The Calculation and Edit tabs of the Options dialog box let you change the defaults for options that affect the operation of *Excel*.
- The General tab of the Options dialog box lets you change the defaults for new workbooks.

Chapter 5

How to enter, edit, and format the data in a worksheet

When you create a worksheet, you enter labels and values into many of its cells. And you align and format these labels and values so they are displayed properly. Obviously, the entry, formatting, and editing techniques you use can have a large effect on how efficiently you use *Excel*. That's why this chapter presents these techniques in detail.

To start, you'll learn all the methods and rules for entering labels, values, dates, and times. Next, you'll learn how to align and format the labels and values that you enter. Then, you'll learn how to edit any label or value. Last, you'll learn how to enter a series of labels or values into a range by using the Fill command or the AutoFill feature.

How to enter labels and values

When you use *Excel*, you can enter labels and values into a worksheet in three different ways. In addition, you can use a variety of entry formats that aren't available in many spreadsheet programs.

The three basic entry methods Figure 5-1 summarizes the three methods that you can use for entering labels and values into the cells of a worksheet. The most basic method is called *direct cell entry*. To use it, you just move the cell pointer to the cell, type the data, and press the Enter key or an arrow key to complete the entry. As you type, the entry appears in the cell and in the entry area of the formula bar. If you want to cancel the entry before you complete it, you can press the Esc key.

When you use *range entry*, you begin by highlighting the range. Then, you type the data in the first cell in the range and press the Enter key to move the cell pointer to the next cell in the range so you can enter data there. When you enter data into the last cell in a column within the range, the cell pointer advances to the first cell in the next column. *Excel* continues advancing the cell pointer each time you press the Enter key until it reaches the end of the range. When you use range entry, you can still use the Esc key to cancel an entry. But you shouldn't use the arrow keys to complete an entry for a cell when you're using range entry. If you do, the highlighted range is deselected and the range entry process ends.

When you use *formula bar entry*, you make the cell entry in the entry area of the formula bar, not in the cell itself. To use this method, you first move the cell pointer to the cell you want. Then, you click the mouse on the entry area. This lets you type the data in the formula bar. To complete the entry, you can press the Enter key or click on the Enter box to the left of the

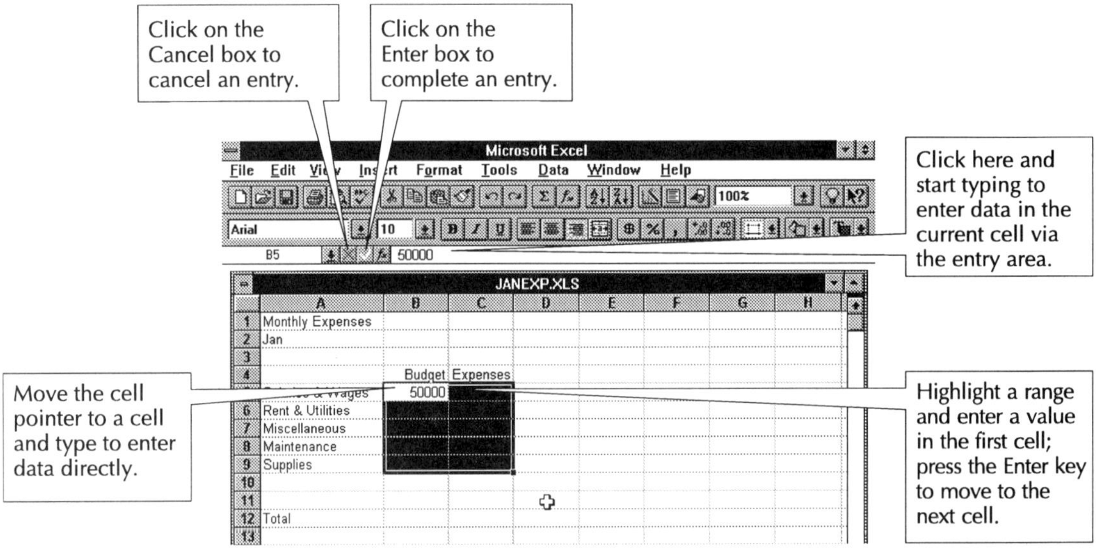

The three basic entry methods

Name	Description
Direct cell entry	Select a cell, type the entry directly in the cell, and use the Enter key or an arrow key to complete the entry.
Range entry	Highlight a range of cells. Then, type the first entry directly in the cell and use the Enter key to move to the next cell in the range. You can also move the cell pointer within the selected range by pressing Shift+Enter, Tab, and Shift+Tab. Continue in this way until you've entered all the cells in the range.
Formula bar entry	Select a cell, click in the entry area on the formula bar, and type the entry. To complete the entry, you can use the Enter key or an arrow key, or you can click the Enter box on the formula bar.

The keystrokes for completing and canceling entries

Keystroke	Function
Enter	Completes an entry and moves the cell pointer to the cell below.
Shift+Enter	Completes an entry and moves the cell pointer to the cell above.
Tab	Completes an entry and moves the cell pointer to the cell to the right.
Shift+Tab	Completes an entry and moves the cell pointer to the cell to the left.
Arrow	Completes an entry and moves the cell pointer in the direction of the arrow; if a range was highlighted, deselects the range.
Esc	Cancels the entry you're making before you complete it.

Figure 5-1 How to enter data into a cell

entry area. Similarly, to cancel an entry, you can press the Esc key or click on the Cancel box.

Because entering data always requires the use of the keyboard, you can usually enter data more efficiently if you use the keyboard instead of the mouse. That's why you should use direct cell entry or range entry as described in figure 5-1. Although you can use the Enter and Cancel boxes with these entry methods, it's more efficient to use the Enter key or an arrow key to complete an entry and the Esc key to cancel an entry.

Valid entry formats for labels, values, dates, and times Figure 5-2 summarizes the valid entry formats that you can use with *Excel*. For the most part, you don't need to worry about entry formats because *Excel* interprets entries that contain letters as labels and entries that are numbers as values. However, if you make an entry like "Nov 4," *Excel* will interpret it as a date value, not as a label. If you want to use a number, a date, or a time as a label, start the entry with an apostrophe.

How to align labels and values

By default, a label is aligned on the left of its cell and a value is aligned on the right of its cell. However, you can use toolbar buttons or the Format Cells dialog box to tell *Excel* how a label or a value should be aligned in its cell.

The easiest way to align labels and values is to use one of the buttons in the Formatting toolbar summarized in figure 5-3. To align the entries in a range, you just highlight the cells before you click on the button. If you want to right-align the labels in a range of cells, for example, you can highlight the range and click on the Align Right button. To return the labels to their default alignment, click on the Align Right button again.

The last button in figure 5-3 lets you center the data in a cell across a range of columns as illustrated in figure 5-4. In this example, the label is centered across four columns. Note that when you center a label as in this example, the value is still stored in the cell where you entered it. In this case, the label is stored in cell B3.

Another way to change the alignment of the entries in a range of cells is to use the Alignment tab in the Format Cells dialog box as summarized in figure 5-5. As you can see, you have more alignment options when you use the Format Cells dialog box than you do when you use toolbar buttons. However, most of the additional options in the Alignment tab are more than most *Excel* users need, although some of them are occasionally useful. If

Valid formats for label entries

All characters are valid.

Notes

- An entry that contains a letter is treated as a label, unless *Excel* interprets it as a date or time.
- If you want to use a entry as a label that *Excel* doesn't recognize as a label, you can first apply the Text format to the cell. Or, you can start the entry with an apostrophe (').

Valid formats for value entries

Valid characters	**Example**
The digits 0-9	189
A leading plus or minus sign	-97
One decimal point (period)	-123.45
A leading dollar sign	$123.45
Commas in appropriate places	1,234,567
A trailing percent sign	21.2%

Valid formats for date entries

3-Jul-93	July 3, 1993	7/3/93
3-Jul	July 3	7/93
Jul-93		7-3-93

Notes

- If a date is entered in a format other than those listed, *Excel* may display it using one of the default formats.
- Depending on the cell format, *Excel* may convert a date entry into a serial number that represents the number of days that have elapsed since a starting date. (The default starting date is January 1, 1900.) Then, to display this number in a useful form, you format the cell with a date format.
- You can type a date and a time in the same cell, separated by a space.

Valid formats for time entries

10:15	10:15 am	10:15 pm	13:35
10:15:30	10:15:30 am	10:15:30 pm	13:35:20

Notes

- Depending on the cell format, *Excel* may convert a time entry into a decimal number that represents the portion of the day that has elapsed since midnight. To display this number in a useful form, you format the cell with a time format.
- You can type a date and a time in the same cell, separated by a space.

Figure 5-2 The valid entry formats for labels, values, dates, and times

Procedure

1. Highlight the cell or range of cells that contains the data you want to align.
2. Click on one of the toolbar buttons for alignment.

Button	Function
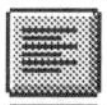	Left-align
	Center
	Right-align
	Center data across a range of columns

Note

If you click on one of these buttons after the data is already aligned with that format, the data is returned to the default alignment.

Figure 5-3 How to use buttons in the Formatting toolbar to change data alignment

you select the Fill option, for example, *Excel* repeats the entry in the display so it fills the entire cell. If you use the options in the Vertical group, you can align an entry at the top, center, or bottom of a cell. If you use the options in the Orientation group, you can change an entry so it is vertical. And if you use the Wrap Text option, text that would normally spill over to the next column is continued on a new line in the cell. When this happens, *Excel* automatically adjusts the row's height to accommodate the new line.

Although it's usually more efficient to align labels and values after you enter them, you can also apply an alignment to a range of cells before you make the entries. If, for example, you highlight a range of cells and use the toolbar button for right alignment, the labels that you enter into these cells will be right-aligned.

How to format values

Excel can display numbers, dates, times, and the results of formulas according to any of the numeric formats shown in figure 5-6. You can apply a numeric format to a cell before or after you enter data into it. If you enter the value 12345 into a cell that has the first Currency format shown in figure 5-6, for example, it's displayed as $12,345. If you experiment with the different formats, you shouldn't have any trouble figuring out what the symbols in each format mean.

1. Enter the label in the left-most column and highlight the columns you want the label centered across:

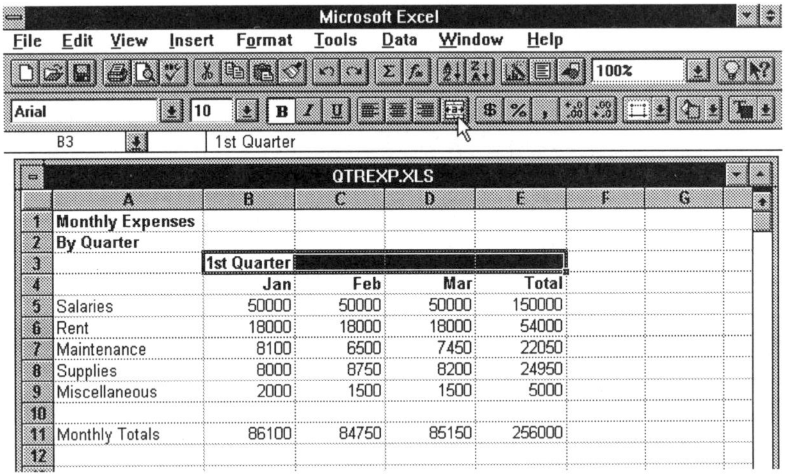

2. Click on the Center Across Columns button and the label is centered across the columns you highlighted:

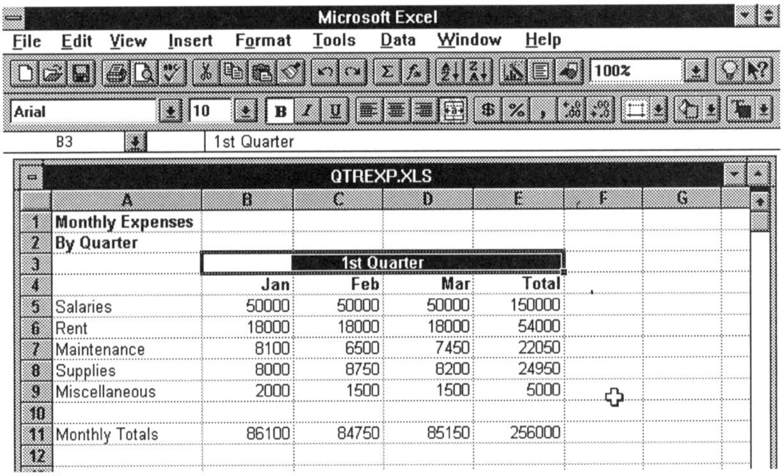

Figure 5-4 How to use the Center Across Columns button to center a label across a range of columns

Three ways to access the Alignment tab of the Format Cells dialog box

- Select the Cells command from the Format menu and click on the Alignment tab.
- Select the Format Cells command from the shortcut menu and click on the Alignment tab.
- Press Crtl+1 and click on the Alignment tab.

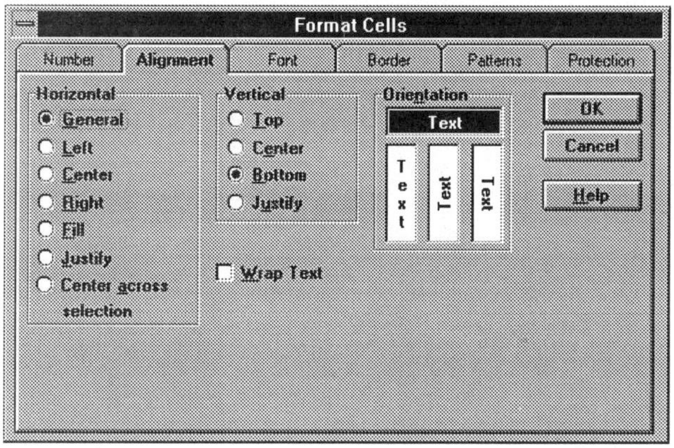

Option	Function
Horizontal	
General	Aligns labels to the left and values to the right.
Left	Aligns both labels and values to the left.
Center	Centers both labels and values.
Right	Aligns both labels and values to the right.
Fill	Repeats the entry in the display so that it fills the entire cell without changing the actual contents of the cell.
Justify	Aligns wrapped text to both the left and right. If the text is long and isn't already wrapped, *Excel* wraps it for you.
Center Across Selection	Centers an entry over a range of columns.
Vertical	
Top	Aligns the entry at the top of the cell.
Center	Aligns the entry at the center of the cell.
Bottom	Aligns the entry at the bottom of the cell.
Justify	Aligns wrapped text to both the top and bottom of the cell. If the text is long and isn't already wrapped, *Excel* wraps it for you.
Wrap Text	Causes entries that would normally spill over to the next column to wrap to the next line in the cell. The row height is adjusted automatically.
Orientation	Provides for different orientations of an entry.

Figure 5-5 How to use the Format Cells dialog box to change data alignment

Category	Displays
Number	A number with fixed decimal places with or without commas.
Accounting	A number in a variety of accounting formats.
Date	A date in a variety of formats.
Time	A time in a variety of formats.
Percentage	A number with fixed decimal places followed by a percent sign.
Fraction	A number as a fraction.
Scientific	A number in scientific notation.
Text	The text of a formula rather than the calculated result.
Currency	A number with fixed decimal places, a leading currency symbol, and commas if necessary.
All	All available formats.
Custom	Custom formats you create.

Figure 5-6 The numeric formats available with *Excel*

For business worksheets, the numeric format categories that you use most often are Number, Percentage, and Currency. For a date or time, you also need the Date or Time category. And you may occasionally want to use the Text category for auditing the data in a worksheet as described in

Sample format codes	Cell contents	Cell display
0	458	458
0.00	458	458.00
#,##0_);(#,##0)	45874	(45,874)
_(* #,##0_);_(* (#,##0);_(* "-"_);_(@_)	456789.12	456,789
_(* #,##0.00_);_(* (#,##0.00);_(* "-"??_);_(@_)	456789.12	456,789.12
_($* #,##0_);_($* (#,##0);_($* "-"_);_(@_)	456789.12	$ 456,789
m/d/yy	1/2/1991	1/2/91
d-mmm	1/2/1991	2-Jan
mmm-yy	1/2/1991	Jan-91
h:mm	10:50:00 AM	10:50
h:mm AM/PM	10:50:00 AM	10:50 AM
h:mm:ss AM/PM	10:50:00 AM	10:50:00 AM
0.00%	.0012	0.12%
0%	.12	12%
0.00%	.1245	12.45%
# ?/?	.5	1/2
# ?/?	1.5	1 1/2
# ??/??	10.5	10 1/2
0.00E+00	2.3E-23	2.30E-23
0.00E+00	12.5236	1.25E+01
##0.0E+0	-23.2114	-23.2E+0
@	12*25	12*25
@	=A14+A1	=A14+A1
@	=SUM(I9:I13)	=SUM(I9.I13)
$#,##0_);($#,##0)	123785.56	$123,787
$#,##0.00_);($#,##0.00)	123785.56	$123,785.56
$#,##0.00_);($#,##0.00)	-21455.23	($21,455.23)
All available format codes are displayed.		
Depends on the custom formats you have created.		

chapter 18. On the other hand, you probably won't ever need formats in the Accounting, Fraction, and Scientific categories. The All category includes numeric formats from all of the other categories, and the Custom category includes formats you create yourself.

Button	Function	Cell display before	Cell display after
	Applies a Currency format to the selected cells.	123.45	$123.45
	Applies a Percentage format to the selected cells.	.25	25%
	Applies a Number format with commas to the selected cells.	1234567	1,234,567
	Each time you click, adds one decimal place to the numeric format.	123	123.0
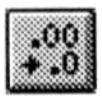	Each time you click, removes one decimal place from the numeric format.	123.0	123

Figure 5-7 The buttons in the Formatting toolbar you can use to apply numeric formats to a range of cells

How to apply formats to cells The easiest way to change the format of the values in a cell or a range of cells is to use the toolbar buttons shown in figure 5-7. The first three buttons apply the indicated format to the selected cells. The last two buttons change the number of decimal places in the numeric format.

You can apply any of the numeric formats in figure 5-6 using the Number tab from the Format Cells dialog box as illustrated in figure 5-8. From this dialog box, you select the appropriate category, then you choose the specific format you want. You can also apply some of the formats using the keyboard shortcuts shown in figure 5-8.

You can also create your own custom formats from this dialog box. To do that, type the format code in the Code text box. If you want to create a format for a social security number, for example, type ###-##-####. Figure 5-9 presents some examples of custom formats you might want to create.

To create a custom format, you need to understand the symbols used in the format codes. If you had trouble understanding any of the sample formats presented in figure 5-6, you may want to take a few minutes to find out about the different symbols. For a description of all the symbols you can use, search for "format codes, number" in online Help, then select the "Number Format Codes" topic.

How to use General format for data entry The default format for the cells in a new worksheet is General. When you enter values, dates, and times into cells with this format, *Excel* changes the format of the cells so they correspond to the data you entered. This is illustrated in figure 5-10. If you enter 1,234 into a cell with General format, for example, the value 1234

Three ways to access the Number tab of the Format Cells dialog box

- Select the Cells command from the Format menu and click on the Number tab.
- Select the Format Cells command from the shortcut menu and click on the Number tab.
- Press Crtl+1 and click on the Number tab.

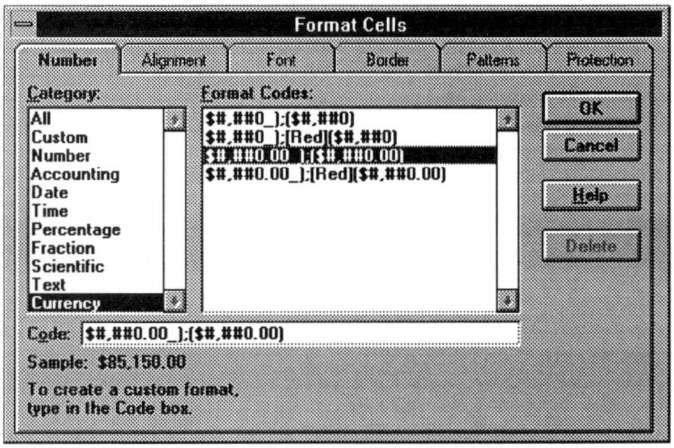

Operation

- To change the format of a selected range of cells, select a category from the Category list box, then select a specific format from the Format Codes list box.
- To create a custom format, type the format code in the Code text box. When you click on the OK button, the new format is stored in the Custom category and in the category that's currently highlighted. To delete a custom format, highlight it and click on the Delete button.

Shortcut Keys

Key combination	Format category	Format code
Ctrl+Shift+~	All	General
Ctrl+Shift+!	Number	0.00
Ctrl+Shift+@	Time	h:mm
Ctrl+Shift+#	Date	d-mmm-yy
Ctrl+Shift+$	Currency	$#,##0.00_);[Red]($#,##0.00)
Ctrl+Shift+%	Percentage	0%
Ctrl+Shift+^	Scientific	0.00E+00

Figure 5-8 How to use the Format Cells command or its keyboard shortcuts to change the format of a range of cells

Format code	Cell contents	Cell display	Description
(###)###-####	4154778569	(415)477-8569	Telephone number
###-##-####	584458966	584-45-8966	Social Security Number
#####-####	947114585	94711-4585	9-digit Zip Code
mmmm d, yyyy	7/2/94	July 2, 1994	Date with month spelled out

Figure 5-9 Examples of custom format codes

is stored in the cell and the format of the cell is changed to a Number format with a comma and zero decimal places. Similarly, if you enter 12.3% into a cell with General format, the value .123 is stored in the cell and the format of the cell is changed to a Percentage format. Although it's not shown in this figure, you can also change a General format to Scientific format by entering a value with a valid scientific format.

When you enter a date into a cell with General format using one of the patterns shown in figure 5-10, the format of the cell is changed to one of the date formats. In addition, your entry is converted into a serial number that gets stored in the cell. The serial number represents the number of days that have passed since January 1, 1900 (or January 1, 1904 if you changed the default). For instance, the date number for July 3, 1993 is 34153. By using serial numbers instead of actual dates, *Excel* makes it easy for you to perform arithmetic operations on the date. If you subtract one date from another, for example, you can tell how many days have elapsed between the two.

When you enter a time into a cell with General format using one of the formats shown in figure 5-10, the format of the cell is changed to one of the time formats. In addition, your entry is converted into a decimal number that represents the fractional portion of the day that has passed since midnight. For instance, .25 represents 6:00 AM; .5 represents 12:00 noon; and .75 represents 6:00 PM. So you can perform arithmetic operations on times just as you can on dates.

General format is probably most useful when you want to make entries with varying formats into a few cells. Then, you can enter data and format the cells at the same time. When you want to enter a range of values that all have the same format, though, you're better off applying the proper format to the cells first and then entering the data. That way, you don't have to enter the extra characters that are required for proper formatting in cells with General format.

Value entry

Your entry	Value stored	Value displayed	New format category	Format code
123.45	123.45	123.45	General	General
-123.45	-123.45	-123.45	General	General
1,234	1234	1,234	Number	#,##0
1,234.56	1234.56	1,234.56	Number	#,##0.00
-1,234	-1234	-1,234	Number	#,##0
1,234.567	1234.567	1,234.57	Number	#,##0.00
$1234	1234	$1,234	Currency	$#,##0_);[Red]($#,##0)
$1,234	1234	$1,234	Currency	$#,##0_);[Red]($#,##0)
$1234.56	1234.56	$1,234.56	Currency	$#,##0.00_);[Red]($#,##0.00)
$1,234.56	12345.56	$1,234.56	Currency	$#,##0.00_);[Red]($#,##0.00)
$-1,234	-1234	($1,234)	Currency	$#,##0_);[Red]($#,##0)
$1,234.567	1234.567	$1,234.57	Currency	$#,##0.00_);[Red]($#,##0.00)
.123%	.00123	0.12%	Percentage	0.00%
1.23%	.0123	1.23%	Percentage	0.00%
12.3%	.123	12.30%	Percentage	0.00%
1234%	12.34	1234%	Percentage	0%

Date entry

Your entry	Value stored	Value displayed	New format category	Format code
3-jul-93	34153	3-Jul-93	Date	d-mmm-yy
3-jul	34153	3-Jul	Date	d-mmm
jul-93	34153	Jul-93	Date	mmm-yy
july 3, 1993	34153	3-Jul-93	Date	d-mmm-yy
july 3	34153	3-Jul	Date	d-mmm
7/3/93	34153	7/3/93	Date	m/d/yy
7/93	34153	Jul-93	Date	mmm-yy
7-3-93	34153	7/3/93	Date	m/d/yy

Time entry

Your entry	Value stored	Value displayed	New format category	Format code
10:15	0.427083	10:15	Time	h:mm
10:15:30	0.427431	10:15:30	Time	h:mm:ss
10:15 am	0.427083	10:15 AM	Time	h:mm AM/PM
10:15:30 am	0.427431	10:15:30 AM	Time	h:mm:ss AM/PM
10:15 pm	0.927083	10:15 PM	Time	h:mm AM/PM
10:15:30 pm	0.927431	10:15:30 PM	Time	h:mm:ss AM/PM
13:35	0.565972	13:35	Time	h:mm
13:35:20	0.566204	13:35:20	Time	h:mm:ss

Figure 5-10 How to use the General format for data entry

Three ways to begin editing

- Double-click on the cell you want to edit.
- Move the cell pointer to the cell you want to edit and press F2.
- Move the cell pointer to the cell you want to edit and click in the entry area of the formula bar.

Two ways to end editing

- Press the Enter key.
- Click on the Enter box: 

Two ways to cancel editing

- Press the Esc key.
- Click on the Cancel box: 

Figure 5-11 How to begin, end, and cancel an edit operation

How to edit the contents of a cell

When you want to change the data you've entered into a cell, you can just re-enter it. Then, your new entry replaces the old entry. Often, though, it's more efficient to *edit* the contents of the cell. This means that you change only those characters in the old entry that need to be changed.

Figure 5-11 summarizes the methods you can use to begin, end, and cancel an edit operation. As you can see, you can begin the editing process in three ways. Usually, it's most efficient to either double-click on the cell you want to edit or to move the cell pointer to the cell and press the F2 key. This lets you edit the entry directly in the cell. Then, when you've made the changes you want to make, you can press the Enter key to complete the editing operation. Or, if you decide to cancel the editing operation, you can press the Esc key.

Figure 5-12 presents the keys you can use to edit the contents of a cell. All of these keys work the same way they do with most programs. For instance, to change from *insert mode* to *typeover mode* and back again, you press the Insert key. When typeover mode is active, the cursor changes from an insertion point to a block that marks the character that you're going to type over.

Key	Function
Left-arrow	Moves the cursor left one character.
Right-arrow	Moves the cursor right one character.
Backspace	Erases the character to the left of the cursor.
Delete	Erases the character to the right of the cursor.
Home	Moves the cursor before the first character.
End or Down-arrow	Moves the cursor after the last character.
Ctrl+arrow	Moves the cursor one word in the direction of the arrow.
Insert	Toggles between insert and typeover mode.
Esc	Cancels the edit operation.

Figure 5-12 The keys you can use to edit the contents of a cell

How to enter a sequence of labels or values

Excel provides two techniques you can use to enter a sequence of labels or values into a range of cells. The Fill Series command lets you enter a sequence of values. The AutoFill feature lets you enter a sequence of labels or values based on an example you provide. You can also create custom sequences for use with the AutoFill feature.

How to use the Fill Series command Figure 5-13 presents a procedure for using the Fill Series command. Then, figure 5-14 shows you how to use this command to enter a sequence of months into a range. After you enter the starting value in the first cell and set the entries in the dialog box the way you want them, you click on the OK button to complete the command. Then, *Excel* fills the cells with the sequence of values you specified.

How to use the AutoFill feature Another way to enter a data sequence into a range of cells is to use the AutoFill feature as illustrated in figure 5-15. When you use this feature, you generally need to enter the first two entries in the sequence. If, for example, you want to enter a sequence of odd numbers from 1 through 21, you need to enter 1 in the first cell in the range and 3 in the second cell. And if you want to enter a sequence of dates, you need to enter two dates. However, *Excel* can generate some sequences, like the one in figure 5-15, based on a single starting value. This example illustrates the versatility of the AutoFill feature.

Procedure

1. Enter the starting value in the worksheet.
2. Select the Fill command from the Edit menu, then select Series from the Fill submenu and this dialog box appears:

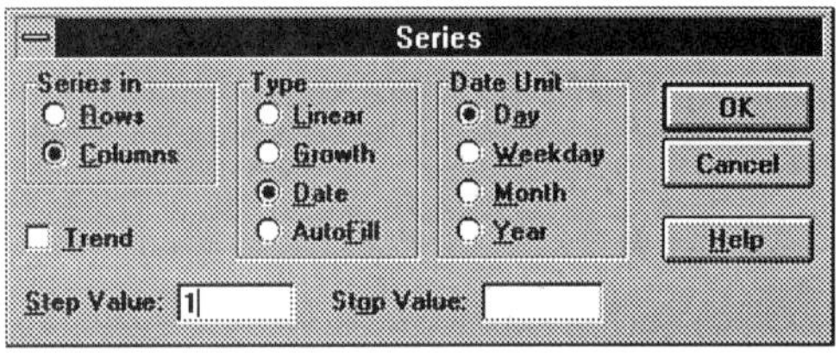

3. Select a Series In option:

Option	Function
Rows	Places the series in rows.
Columns	Places the series in columns.

4. Select a Type option:

Option	Example
Linear	1, 2, 3, 4...
Growth	2, 4, 8, 16, 32...
Date	1/7/92, 1/14/92, 1/21/92...
AutoFill	Q1, Q2, Q3, Q4, Q1...

5. If you're creating a date series, select a Date Unit option:

Option	Example
Day	2-May, 3-May, 4-May...
Weekday	10/7/93, 10/8/93, 10/11/93, 10/12/93...
Month	3-Jul-93, 3-Aug-93, 3-Sep-93....
Year	Oct-93, Oct-94, Oct-95...

6. Enter appropriate values in the Step Value and Stop Value text boxes.
7. Click on the OK button.

Notes

- If you create a sequence of dates or times, *Excel* displays them in the format you use for the starting value. You can use any of the available date and time formats.
- If you prefer not to supply the Stop Value explicitly, an alternative is to highlight a range that contains the cells you want to fill before you issue the Fill Series command. Then, *Excel* ends the Fill operation when it reaches the end of the range.

Figure 5-13 How to use the Fill Series command

1. To create a series of months from April of 93 to March of 96, enter Apr-93 in the first cell. Next, select the Fill Series command from the Edit menu. In the Series dialog box, select the Columns, Date, and Month options. Then, enter Apr-96 as the Stop Value and click on the OK button:

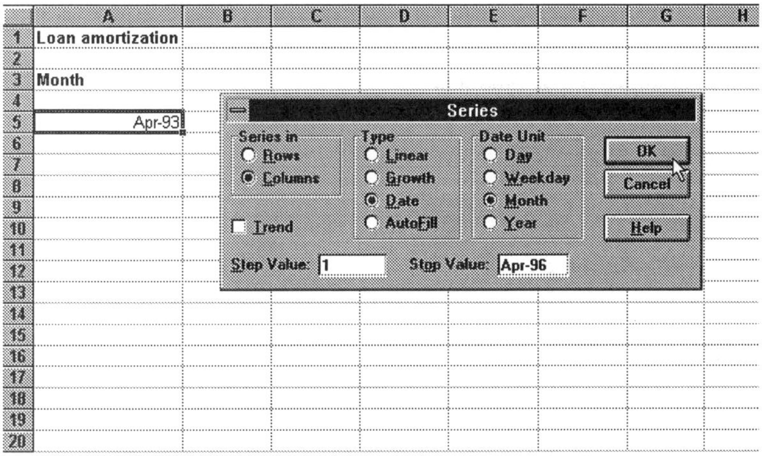

2. *Excel* creates the series of months down the column:

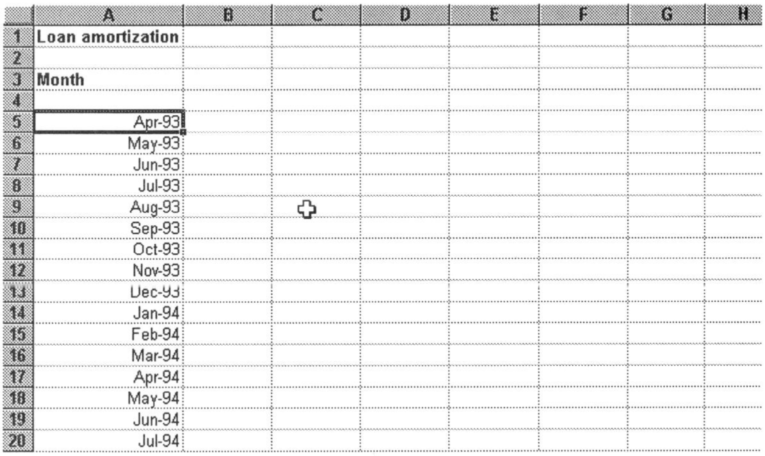

Note

If you select the Series In Rows option, *Excel* creates the series across the row.

Figure 5-14 How to enter a sequence of months using the Fill Series command

Procedure

1. Enter the first one or two values or labels, depending on the series, and highlight them. Then, place the mouse pointer over the fill handle until the pointer turns into a cross:

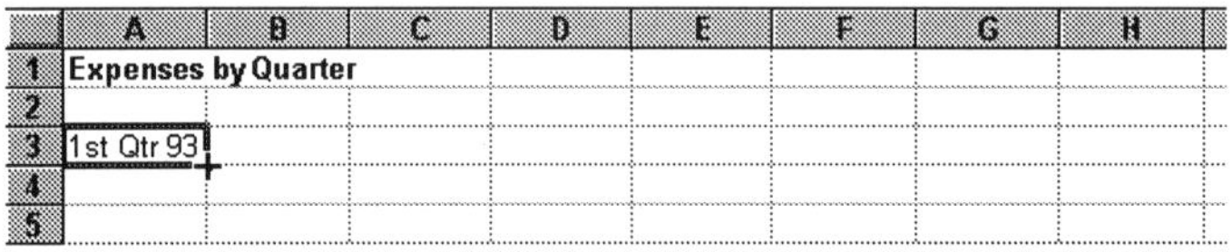

2. Drag the fill handle across the range you want to fill:

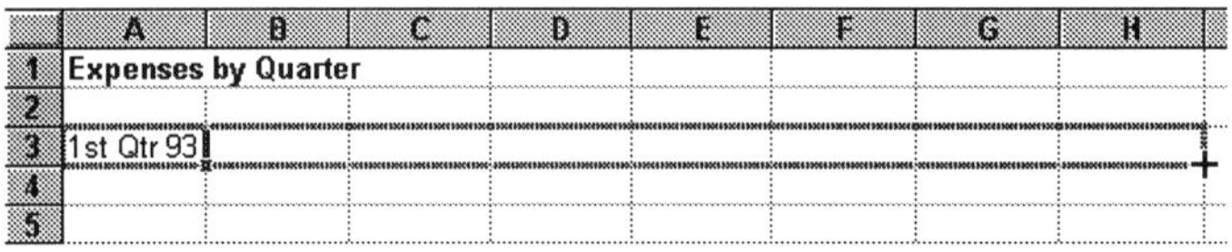

3. *Excel* interprets the series and fills in the range accordingly:

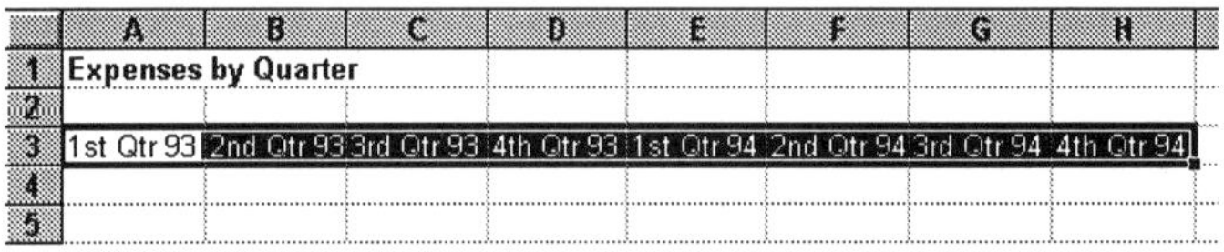

Notes

- If you enter a single label that *Excel* doesn't recognize as part of a series, it will copy the label into the range.
- If you enter a single value, *Excel* will copy the value into the range. To create a series of consecutive values from a single value, hold down the Ctrl key as you drag the fill handle.

Figure 5-15 How to use the AutoFill feature

How to create a custom AutoFill sequence If you frequently use a sequence of values that neither the Fill Series command or the AutoFill feature can handle, you can create a custom sequence. To set up a custom sequence, you use the Custom Lists tab from the Options dialog box as shown in figure 5-16. Once you set up a custom list, you can use it to create a sequence by entering an item from the list, then using the AutoFill feature to fill a range of cells.

Perspective

When you start a new worksheet, the default format is General. The General format is useful when you want to enter data that requires a special

Procedure

1. Enter the custom sequence you want to create in the worksheet and highlight it:

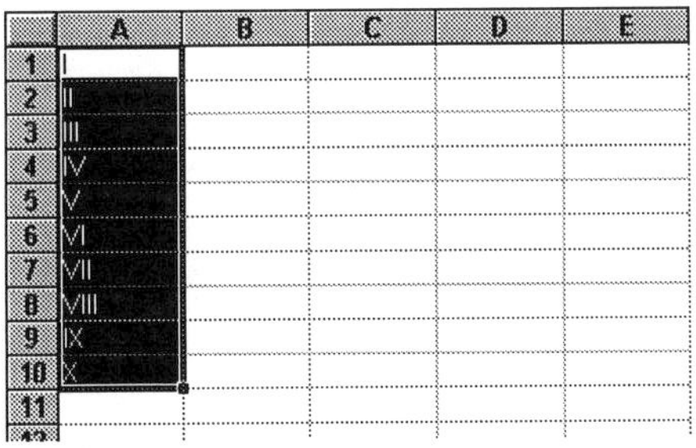

2. Select the Options command from the Tools menu, then click on the Custom Lists tab and this dialog box appears:

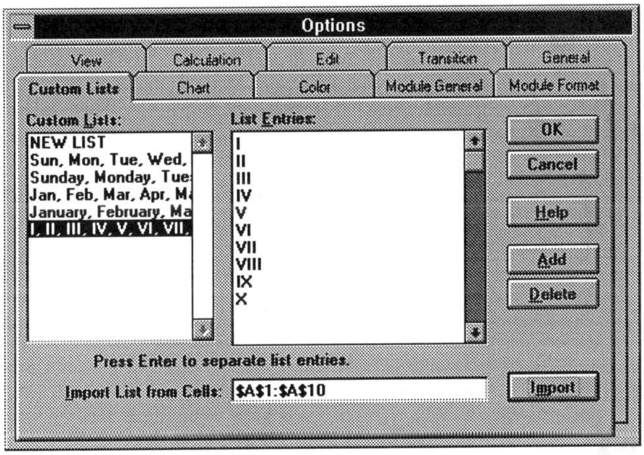

3. The range that contains the list appears in the Import List From Cells text box. Click on the Import button to create the list. The new list appears at the bottom of the Custom Lists list box and in the List Entries dialog box.
4. Click on the OK button to exit from the dialog box.

Notes

- You can also create a custom list by selecting the NEW LIST option from the Custom Lists list box and typing the list into the List Entries list box.
- To edit a custom sequence, highlight the sequence in the Custom Lists list box and enter the changes in the list that appears in the List Entries list box.
- To delete a custom sequence, highlight the sequence in the Custom Lists list box and click on the Delete button.

Figure 5-16 How to create a custom AutoFill sequence

format, like those in the Percentage, Date, and Time categories. By entering the right characters, you can enter the data and convert the format of the cell from General to the appropriate format in a single operation.

When you enter a range of values that require the same format, though, you shouldn't enter the extra characters that tell *Excel* what the General format should be changed to. Instead, you should format the range with the appropriate numeric format either before or after you enter the values. That way, you won't waste time entering the extra formatting characters (the dollar signs, commas, or percent signs), and you can be sure that the formats are the same throughout the range.

When you format the data in a worksheet, keep in mind that you can format more than one range at a time by using a *nonadjacent selection* of ranges. To make a nonadjacent selection, just hold down the Ctrl key as you highlight the ranges. Once all the ranges are highlighted, you can use the toolbar buttons or the Number tab from the Format Cells dialog box to format the values in these ranges.

Summary

- You can enter data into a worksheet by using *direct cell entry*, *range entry*, or *formula bar entry*. Usually, the first two methods are more efficient than formula bar entry because you don't have to switch your hand from the keyboard to the mouse as you move from cell to cell.
- You can align a label or a value after you enter it by selecting its cell, then clicking on one of the alignment buttons or using the Alignment tab from the Format Cells dialog box.
- You can format a cell before or after you enter data into it.
- When you use the General format, you can format a value as you enter it by including commas, a dollar sign, or a percent sign.
- When you use the General format, you can format a date or time when you enter it by using a valid date or time entry format.

Chapter 6

How to enter and edit the formulas and functions of a worksheet

An introduction to the types of functions

- Date & Time
- Statistical
- Financial
- Math & Trigonometry
- Logical
- Database & List Management
- Text
- Engineering, Information, Lookup & Reference, and DDE & External

When and how to use relative, absolute, or mixed references in a formula

- What happens when you copy formulas with relative, absolute, and mixed references
- How to create a relative, absolute, or mixed reference
- When and how to use a relative reference in a formula
- When and how to use an absolute reference in a formula
- When and how to use mixed references in a formula

How to detect and correct circular references

Perspective

Summary

When you want to perform calculations in a worksheet, you use *formulas*. To help simplify the task of creating formulas, *Excel* provides a set of built-in formulas, called *functions*. Functions perform a variety of operations, such as adding the values in a range and getting the average of the values in a range.

In this chapter, you'll learn how to enter formulas and functions and the three types of references they can contain. You'll also learn how to use some of the most common functions, and you'll be introduced to the different types of functions. Finally, you'll learn how to detect and correct common formula errors called *circular references*.

If you understand basic algebra, the material in this chapter shouldn't be difficult for you. If you don't, some of the mathematical notation may be confusing. For most business worksheets, though, the formulas are relatively simple, so the mathematical notation isn't a problem.

How to enter formulas

Figure 6-1 summarizes what you need to know to enter formulas into a worksheet. Before you can enter formulas, you need to know their basic format. You should also know the three ways to identify a cell used in a formula. And you should know how to use parentheses so that *Excel* performs the operations in a formula in the correct sequence.

The basic format of a formula A typical formula consists of the formula indicator, numbers, cell references, and arithmetic operators. For example, the formula to multiply the contents of cell B3 by 100 is =100*B3. Figure 6-1 lists all the operators you can use in a formula.

When you enter a formula, you must first type the formula indicator, an equal sign (=). The formula indicator tells *Excel* you're entering a formula and not a label. You can also begin a formula with a plus sign (+), which is the *Lotus 1-2-3* formula indicator. When you press the Enter key to complete the formula, *Excel* converts the plus sign to an equal sign.

How to enter cell references *Excel* provides two basic methods for entering cell references into a formula. The most direct way is to type the reference. If, for example, you want to include the value in cell B5 in a formula, you type *B5*.

An easier and less error-prone method for entering cell references is to use the cell pointer to identify the cells you want to include. This technique is illustrated in figure 6-2. To move the cell pointer to each cell in a formula, you can use either the mouse or the pointer-movement keys.

General procedure

1. Begin the formula by entering an equal sign (=) or a plus sign (+). If you enter a plus sign, *Excel* converts it to an equal sign when you press the Enter key.
2. Type the first value in the formula or identify the first cell.
3. Type an arithmetic operator.
4. Type the next value or identify the next cell.
5. Continue entering operators and values or cell references until the formula is complete.
6. Press the Enter key.

Three ways to identify a cell used in a formula

1. Use the mouse to select the cell.
2. Use the pointer-movement keys to move the cell pointer to the cell.
3. Type the cell reference into the formula.

The arithmetic operators you can use in a formula

Operator	Meaning	Order of precedence
+	Positive number	1
-	Negative number	1
^	Exponentiation (raising to the power of)	2
*	Multiplication	3
/	Division	3
+	Addition	4
-	Subtraction	4

Parentheses

You can use parentheses whenever you want to clarify the sequence in which operations will be performed. The operations in the innermost sets of parentheses are performed first.

Examples

Formula	Description
=C5-B5	Subtracts the contents of cell B5 from the contents of cell C5.
=C3+C4+C5	Adds the contents of cells C3, C4, and C5.
=SUM(C3:C5)	Adds the contents of cells C3 through C5.
=(C5-B5)/B5	First, subtracts the contents of cell B5 from the contents of cell C5; then, divides the result by the contents of cell B5.
=.065*D10	Multiplies the contents of cell D10 by .065.

Figure 6-1 How to enter formulas

1. To begin the formula, enter = in the cell. Then, move the cell pointer to the first cell you want to use in the formula and *Excel* includes the cell reference in the formula:

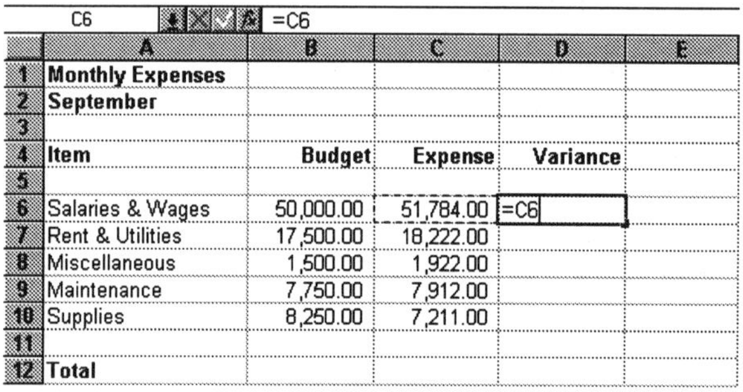
C6 =C6

	A	B	C	D	E
1	Monthly Expenses				
2	September				
3					
4	Item	Budget	Expense	Variance	
5					
6	Salaries & Wages	50,000.00	51,784.00	=C6	
7	Rent & Utilities	17,500.00	18,222.00		
8	Miscellaneous	1,500.00	1,922.00		
9	Maintenance	7,750.00	7,912.00		
10	Supplies	8,250.00	7,211.00		
11					
12	Total				

2. Enter the next operator. Then, move the cell pointer to the next cell you want to use in the formula and *Excel* includes the cell reference in the formula:

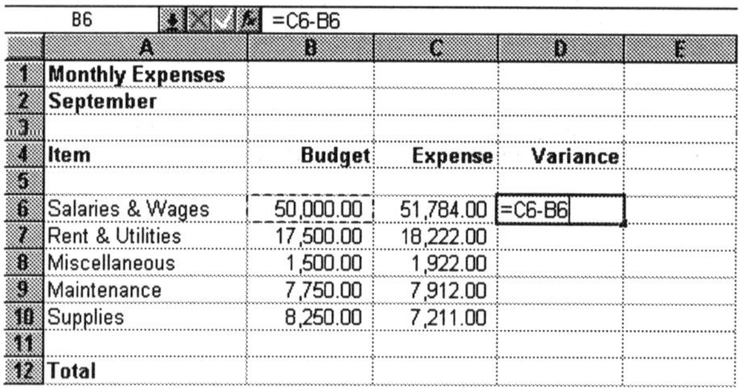
B6 =C6-B6

	A	B	C	D	E
1	Monthly Expenses				
2	September				
3					
4	Item	Budget	Expense	Variance	
5					
6	Salaries & Wages	50,000.00	51,784.00	=C6-B6	
7	Rent & Utilities	17,500.00	18,222.00		
8	Miscellaneous	1,500.00	1,922.00		
9	Maintenance	7,750.00	7,912.00		
10	Supplies	8,250.00	7,211.00		
11					
12	Total				

3. Press the Enter key and *Excel* replaces the formula in the cell with its value:

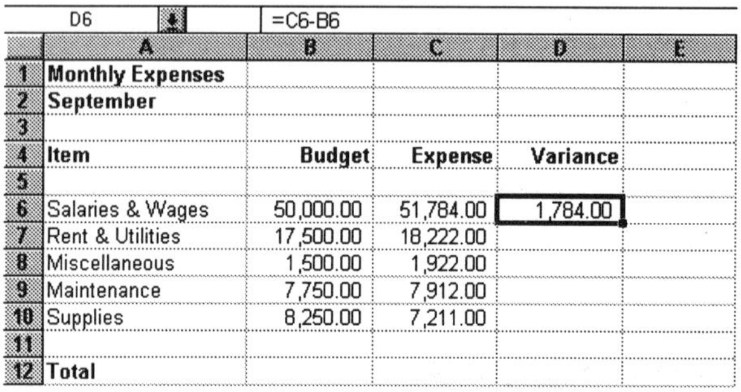
D6 =C6-B6

	A	B	C	D	E
1	Monthly Expenses				
2	September				
3					
4	Item	Budget	Expense	Variance	
5					
6	Salaries & Wages	50,000.00	51,784.00	1,784.00	
7	Rent & Utilities	17,500.00	18,222.00		
8	Miscellaneous	1,500.00	1,922.00		
9	Maintenance	7,750.00	7,912.00		
10	Supplies	8,250.00	7,211.00		
11					
12	Total				

Figure 6-2 How to use the cell pointer to enter cell references in a formula

When and how to use parentheses within a formula When *Excel* calculates the value of a formula, it does the operations within the formula in their *order of precedence*. As you can see in figure 6-1, multiplication

Formula	Value without parentheses	Value with parentheses
=(10+3)*5	25	65
=(9+9)/3	12	6
=(-9+9)/3	-6	0
=(2+3)*5^2	77	125
=((2+3)*5)^2	77	625

Figure 6-3 How parentheses affect the way *Excel* interprets a formula

and division operations are done before addition and subtraction operations. And, exponentiation ("raising to the power of") is done before multiplication and division.

Notice in figure 6-1 that numbers denoted as positive or negative are evaluated before any exponentiation, multiplication, division, addition, or subtraction is performed. So in the formula -3^2+9/3, the first operation is to treat the three as a negative three; the second operation is to raise the negative three to the power of two; the third operation is to divide nine by three; and the last operation is to add the two results together. The resulting value is 12 (9+3=12).

If two or more operators within a formula have the same order of precedence, the operations are done from left to right. In the formula 9*9+3/3, for example, the first operation is nine times nine (9*9=81); the second operation is three divided by three (3/3=1); and the last operation adds the two results together (81+1=82).

When the operations within a formula aren't going to be evaluated the way you want them to be, you can use parentheses to override the order of precedence. This is illustrated by the examples in figure 6-3. When a formula contains parentheses, *Excel* calculates the expressions in the parentheses before it uses its order of precedence and its left-to-right rule. If one set of parentheses is contained within another set, *Excel* calculates the value of the expression in the innermost set of parentheses first. Within a set of parentheses, the order of precedence still applies. And after all the expressions contained in parentheses are calculated, the order of precedence still applies.

You can also use parentheses when a formula gets so complicated that it's hard for you to figure out what the sequence of operations is going to be. By using parentheses, you can be sure a formula works the way you want it to. Whenever you use parentheses in a formula, however, you must make sure that you enter an equal number of left and right parentheses. If you don't, *Excel* won't accept the formula when you press the Enter key.

How to enter functions

Figure 6-4 summarizes what you need to know to enter functions into a worksheet. Although it's not indicated in this figure, you can enter a function as part of a formula or by itself. In most cases, however, you'll use functions by themselves. When you enter a function by itself, be sure to start it with the formula indicator to distinguish it from a label.

The syntax of a function When you enter a function, you must be sure to use its correct format, or *syntax*. I'll present the syntax for some specific functions later in this chapter. For now, you should know that every function begins with a function name, such as SUM. For most functions, the function name is followed by a set of parentheses that contains one or more *arguments*. If a function requires more than one argument, the arguments must be separated by a comma. Even if a function doesn't require arguments, you must still type a pair of parentheses after the function name.

Many of the functions require a range as an argument. I'll show you how to identify a range in a moment. A few of the functions require a cell reference. To enter a cell reference into a function, you can use one of the techniques listed in figure 6-1 for identifying a cell. If a function requires any other type of argument, you have to type it in.

How to enter a range If a function requires a range as one of its arguments, you can identify the range using any of the techniques listed in figure 6-4. The easiest way to identify a range is to highlight it with the mouse. Or, you can use one of the cell pointer techniques. You can also identify a range by typing the reference of the first cell followed by a colon and the last cell reference. For example, B5:B14 is a typical range entry. Finally, you can identify a range by using its name. I'll show you how to use range names in the next chapter.

If the range you're entering is the final argument in the function, you can press the Enter key to complete the formula and *Excel* automatically adds the right parenthesis to the function. This technique is useful when you don't have to enter additional operations in the formula after the function.

General procedure

1. Type = (the equal sign), the name of the function, and a left parenthesis.
2. Enter the first argument.
3. If the function requires another argument, type a separator (a comma).
4. Continue entering arguments and separators until the function is complete.
5. Type a right parenthesis.

The format of a function

=function-name([argument-1 [,argument-2...]])

The types of arguments you can use in a function

Type	Example
range	B6:B10
range name	BUDGET
cell reference	B12
value	12
text	"Budget"
condition	C12>B12

Five ways to identify a range used in a function

1. Highlight the range with the mouse.
2. Move the cell pointer to one corner of the range; type a colon (:); and move the pointer to the other corner of the range.
3. Move the cell pointer to one corner of the range. Then, hold down the Shift key while you move the pointer to the other corner of the range.
4. Type the cell reference for one corner of the range; type a colon (:); and type the cell reference for the other corner of the range.
5. Type the range name. See chapter 7 for details.

Figure 6-4 How to enter a function

Three shortcuts for entering functions

Excel 5.0 provides three shortcuts that can make entering functions easier. First, you can use the AutoSum button on the Standard toolbar to insert a SUM function automatically. Second, you can use a keyboard shortcut to insert placeholders for a function's arguments into the function. And third, you can select a function using the Function Wizard.

How to use the AutoSum button Like the previous version of *Excel*, *Excel 5.0* provides a toolbar button called AutoSum that makes it easy to add SUM functions to your worksheets. Figure 6-5 shows how to use the AutoSum button. Because the SUM function is one you'll use frequently in your worksheets, you'll want to take advantage of this toolbar button.

In most cases, you'll use AutoSum by placing the cell pointer below or to the right of the data you want summed and clicking on the AutoSum button in the Standard toolbar as illustrated in the procedure in figure 6-5. Then, *Excel* inserts the SUM function along with a range argument. By default, *Excel* adds the cells above the cell if there are values both above and to the left of the cell.

If the range of cells you want to add contains blank cells, you can't use this technique. That's because *Excel* assumes it's reached the end of the range when it finds a blank cell. To sum a range of cells that contains blank cells, you have to highlight the range before you click on the AutoSum button. Then, *Excel* sums the range and places the function in the next blank cell below or to the right of the range. You can also use this technique to add the values in the cells to the left of the cell where you want to place the SUM function if there are also values above that cell.

You can also use AutoSum to enter SUM functions into a range of cells. This is a useful skill if you need to sum more than one column or row of data. To sum columns, highlight a range below the columns of data where you want to place the SUM functions. To sum rows, highlight a range to the right of the rows of data. Then, click on the AutoSum button and *Excel* enters the SUM functions.

How to use a keyboard shortcut for entering arguments If you know the name of a function but you can't remember its arguments, you can use the keyboard short Ctrl+Shift+A to help you enter the arguments. Figure 6-6 shows you how to do that. Notice that to use this keyboard shortcut, you must first enter an equal sign and the name of the function. Then, when you press Ctrl+Shift+A, *Excel* inserts placeholders for the function's arguments along with separators and parentheses. Notice that the placeholders indicate the types of arguments to be entered. The SUM function in figure 6-6, for example, requires numeric arguments. In general, these placeholders aren't much help for simple functions, but they can be helpful for more complex functions.

When *Excel* inserts the placeholders for a function, it also highlights the placeholder for the first argument so you can enter it immediately. In

Procedure

1. Move the cell pointer to a cell below or to the right of the cells to be summed and click on the AutoSum button:

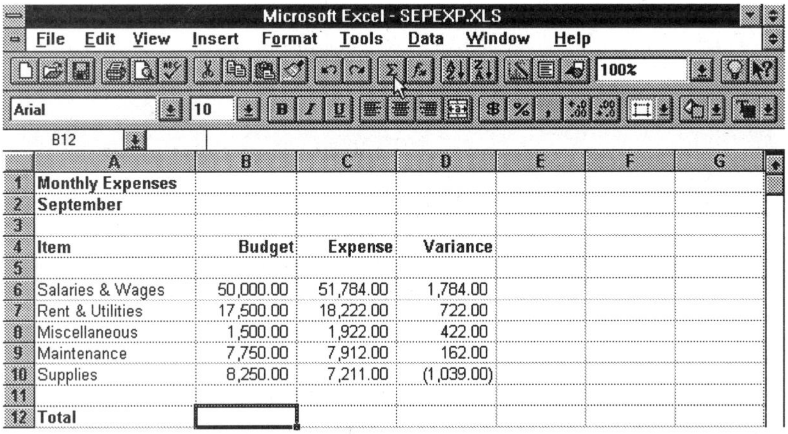

	A	B	C	D	E	F	G
1	Monthly Expenses						
2	September						
3							
4	Item	Budget	Expense	Variance			
5							
6	Salaries & Wages	50,000.00	51,784.00	1,784.00			
7	Rent & Utilities	17,500.00	18,222.00	722.00			
8	Miscellaneous	1,500.00	1,922.00	422.00			
9	Maintenance	7,750.00	7,912.00	162.00			
10	Supplies	8,250.00	7,211.00	(1,039.00)			
11							
12	Total						

2. *Excel* inserts the SUM function with a range argument:

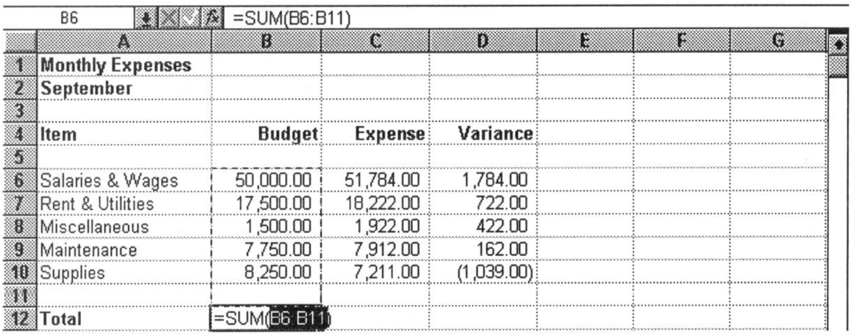

	A	B	C	D	E	F	G
1	Monthly Expenses						
2	September						
3							
4	Item	Budget	Expense	Variance			
5							
6	Salaries & Wages	50,000.00	51,784.00	1,784.00			
7	Rent & Utilities	17,500.00	18,222.00	722.00			
8	Miscellaneous	1,500.00	1,922.00	422.00			
9	Maintenance	7,750.00	7,912.00	162.00			
10	Supplies	8,250.00	7,211.00	(1,039.00)			
11							
12	Total	=SUM(B6:B11)					

3. Press the Enter key and the result is displayed:

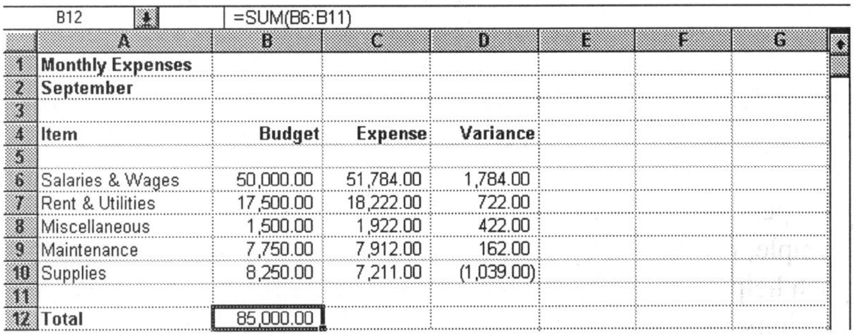

	A	B	C	D	E	F	G
1	Monthly Expenses						
2	September						
3							
4	Item	Budget	Expense	Variance			
5							
6	Salaries & Wages	50,000.00	51,784.00	1,784.00			
7	Rent & Utilities	17,500.00	18,222.00	722.00			
8	Miscellaneous	1,500.00	1,922.00	422.00			
9	Maintenance	7,750.00	7,912.00	162.00			
10	Supplies	8,250.00	7,211.00	(1,039.00)			
11							
12	Total	85,000.00					

Figure 6-5 How to use the AutoSum button (part 1 of 2)

Notes

- If the worksheet contains values in the cells both above and to the left of the current cell, AutoSum sums the cells above. To sum the cells to the left, highlight the range and click on the AutoSum button. *Excel* inserts the SUM function into the first blank cell to the right of the range.
- If you don't highlight a range, *Excel* includes the range from the first cell above or to the left of the current cell that contains a value up to the first cell that is blank or doesn't contain a value.
- If the range you want to sum contains blank cells, highlight the range and click on the AutoSum button. *Excel* inserts the SUM function into the first blank cell below or to the right of the range.
- If the range argument *Excel* inserts is incorrect, you can change it by entering or highlighting a different range.
- To enter SUM functions into a range of cells, highlight a range below the columns of data or to the right of the rows of data you want to sum before you click on the AutoSum button.

Figure 6-5 How to use the AutoSum button (part 2 of 2)

figure 6-6, for example, the placeholder *number1* is highlighted. If you want to sum a range of cells, you can replace the first placeholder with a range by using any of the techniques in figure 6-4. If the function requires additional arguments, you can edit the function in the cell or formula bar to replace the remaining placeholders. Be sure to delete any placeholders and separators you don't need.

How to use the Function Wizard If you need to use a function but you can't remember its name or the arguments it requires, you may want to use the Function Wizard as illustrated in figure 6-7. When you access the Function Wizard, it displays a dialog box that lets you select the function you want to enter. Then, when you select the function and press the Finish button, *Excel* inserts the function along with the placeholders and separators for any arguments it requires in the current cell.

Just as it does when you use the keyboard shortcut to insert placeholders in a function, *Excel* highlights the placeholder for the first argument so you can enter it immediately. Then, you can edit the function in the formula bar to replace or delete the remaining placeholders.

The Next button in the Function Wizard dialog box opens a second dialog box to help you enter arguments into the function. For most functions, it's faster and more efficient to bypass this dialog box and enter the arguments directly into the worksheet. However, this dialog box can be helpful for entering complex functions.

Procedure

1. Type = and the name of the function. Then, press Ctrl+Shift+A and *Excel* inserts the placeholders for the function's arguments along with separators and parentheses:

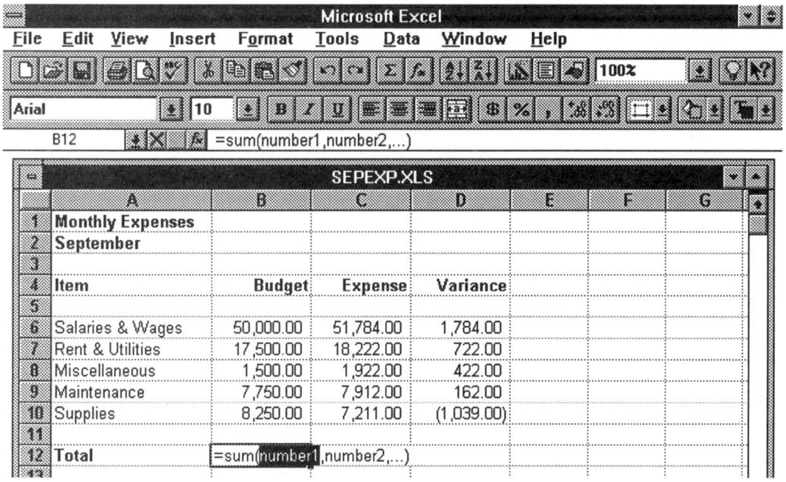

2. Enter the arguments for the function and press the Enter key to complete the function.

Note

When *Excel* inserts the placeholders, it highlights the first one so you can enter the argument immediately. If you need to enter more arguments, highlight the appropriate placeholders and enter the arguments using the mouse and the editing keys. Delete any placeholders and separators you don't need.

Figure 6-6 How to use a keyboard shortcut to enter the arguments of a function

The Function Wizard also lets you edit a function or a formula that contains a function. If you select a cell that contains a function and access the Function Wizard, the Editing Function dialog box appears. From this dialog box, you can replace or edit the arguments of the function. However, it's usually faster just to double-click on the cell that contains the function and edit the arguments directly in the worksheet.

Procedure

1. Move the cell pointer to the cell where you want to enter the function, and access the Function Wizard using one of the techniques listed in part 2. Then, this dialog box appears:

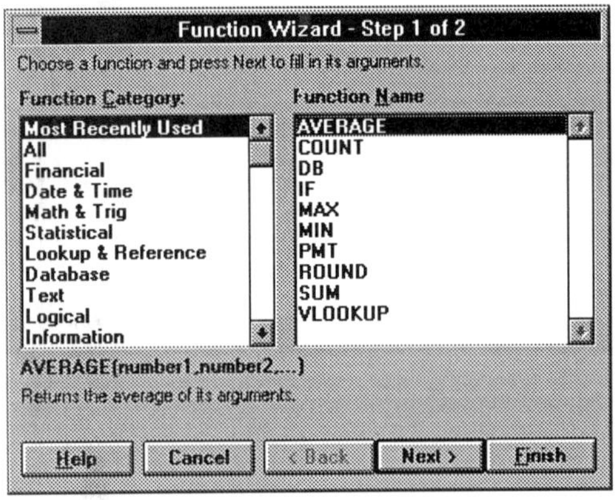

2. Select a category from the Function Category list box. The default is the category you selected a function from the last time you used the Function Wizard.
3. Select the function you want from the Function Name list box.
4. Click on the Finish button and *Excel* inserts the function name and parentheses into the worksheet. If the function requires arguments, *Excel* also inserts the placeholders for them along with separators:

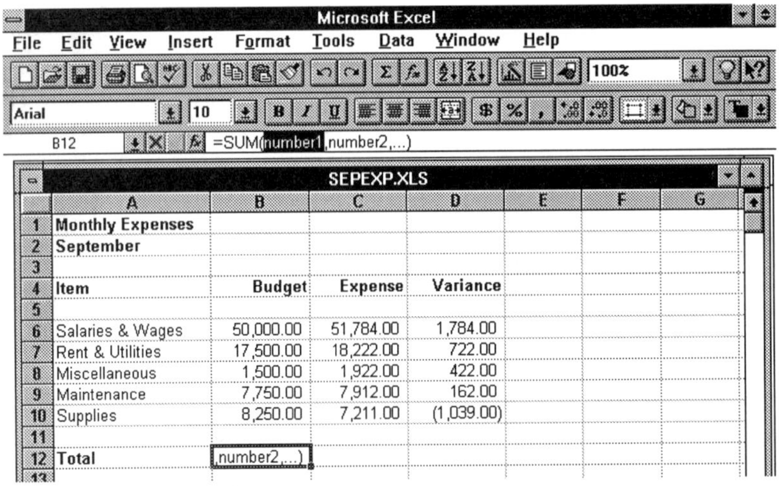

5. Enter the arguments for the function and press the Enter key to complete the function.

Figure 6-7 How to use the Function Wizard to enter a function (part 1 of 2)

Four ways to access the Function Wizard

- Click on the Function Wizard button in the Standard toolbar: 
- Select the Function command from the Insert menu.
- Press Shift+F3.
- Click on the Function Wizard button that appears in the formula bar when you type = in a cell.

Notes

- When you highlight a function in the Function Name list box, the format and description of the function is displayed below the list boxes.
- If a function doesn't require any arguments, *Excel* completes the entry when you click on the Finish button from the Function Wizard dialog box.
- When *Excel* inserts the function, it highlights the placeholder for the first argument so you can enter it immediately. If you need to enter more arguments, highlight the appropriate placeholders in the formula bar and enter the arguments using the mouse and the editing keys. Delete any placeholders and separators you don't need.
- The Next button displays a second Function Wizard dialog box that you can use to enter arguments into a function you aren't familiar with:

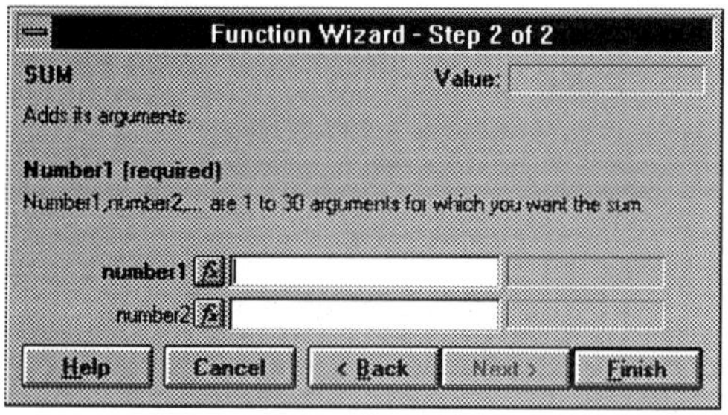

For simple functions, this dialog box can be more confusing than it is helpful. However, it can be helpful for complex functions because it provides a description of each argument.

Figure 6-7 How to use the Function Wizard to enter a function (part 2 of 2)

The functions you're most likely to use

Figure 6-8 presents six useful functions. Although *Excel* provides more than 200 functions, these are the ones you'll probably use most often.

The TODAY and NOW functions The TODAY function returns the current date according to your computer's internal clock. The date appears in this form: mm/dd/yy. You can use one of *Excel*'s date formats to change the appearance of the date.

Function name	Syntax (arguments)	Function
TODAY	TODAY()	Returns the current date value according to the computer's clock.
NOW	NOW()	Returns the current date and time value according to the computer's clock.
SUM	SUM(range)	Adds the values in the specified range.
AVERAGE	AVERAGE(range)	Calculates the average of the values in the specified range.
COUNT	COUNT(range)	Counts the number of cells in the specified range that contain numeric values.
ROUND	ROUND(value,decimal-places)	Rounds the value specified in the first argument to the number of decimal places specified in the second argument.

Figure 6-8 Six useful functions

The NOW function is similar to the TODAY function, but it returns the date and time. The date and time appear in this form: mm/dd/yy hh:ss. Although this is the only format *Excel* provides for a date and time in a single cell, you can apply any date or time format to the cell. If you apply a date format that doesn't include the time, however, only the date is displayed in the cell. And if you apply a time format that doesn't include the date, only the time is displayed. The date and time returned by the NOW and TODAY functions are updated whenever *Excel* recalculates the worksheet.

The SUM, AVERAGE, and COUNT functions Figure 6-9 presents a worksheet that uses the SUM, AVERAGE, and COUNT functions. Here, the total sales are calculated with a SUM function, the average sale is calculated with an AVERAGE function, and the number of sales is calculated with a COUNT function. As you can see, the range specified for each function is the same: C3:C14.

In figure 6-9, you may notice that the COUNT function returned a value of 9 even though there are 12 cells in the specified range. That's because three of the cells are empty, and the COUNT function doesn't count empty cells. In addition, the AVERAGE function doesn't factor in empty cells in its calculations. Besides empty cells, cells that contain labels won't be counted by the SUM, AVERAGE, and COUNT functions.

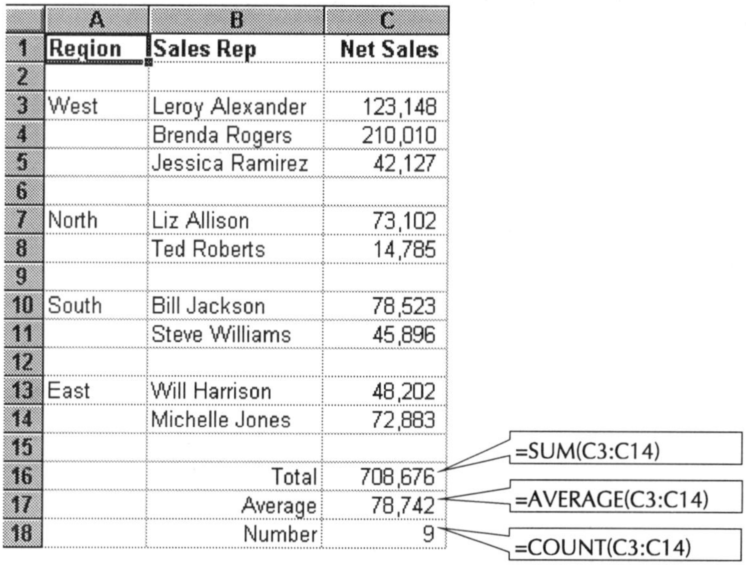

	A	B	C
1	Region	Sales Rep	Net Sales
2			
3	West	Leroy Alexander	123,148
4		Brenda Rogers	210,010
5		Jessica Ramirez	42,127
6			
7	North	Liz Allison	73,102
8		Ted Roberts	14,785
9			
10	South	Bill Jackson	78,523
11		Steve Williams	45,896
12			
13	East	Will Harrison	48,202
14		Michelle Jones	72,883
15			
16		Total	708,676
17		Average	78,742
18		Number	9

Figure 6-9 A worksheet that uses the SUM, AVERAGE, and COUNT functions

The ROUND function Unlike the other functions in figure 6-8, the ROUND function requires two arguments. The first argument is the value to be rounded. This can be the value itself, the cell reference of the value, or a formula that creates a value. The second argument is the number of decimal places you want the rounded value to contain.

Figure 6-10 illustrates the operation of the ROUND function. Notice in the fourth ROUND function that the second argument is a negative number. In that case, the number is rounded to the left of the decimal point. The last two examples in figure 6-10 show how you can use a formula or function as the first argument of a ROUND function.

You should know that if the value in a cell contains more decimal places than the cell format calls for, *Excel* automatically rounds the value that's displayed. However, only the displayed value changes. The actual value remains the same, and *Excel* continues to use that value in its calculations. When you use the ROUND function, however, *Excel* rounds the actual value, not just the value that's displayed. Then, any calculations *Excel* does using this value will have different results than if the value wasn't rounded. So be sure that's what you want to do before you use the ROUND function.

ROUND function	Resulting value
=ROUND(2437.289,2)	2437.29
=ROUND(2437.289,0)	2437
=ROUND(2437.289,4)	2437.289
=ROUND(2437.289,-1)	2440

Examples of ROUND functions that use a formula or function as an argument

=ROUND(C5/D5,1)

=ROUND(SUM(B4:B14),2)

Figure 6-10 How the ROUND function works

An introduction to the types of functions

Although I just presented the six most commonly used functions, there are many more you may want to use in your worksheets. These functions are divided into the eleven categories that follow, and figure 6-11 shows you examples of typical functions from each category. If you want specific information on any of the functions, you can use *Excel*'s online Help.

In addition to the functions in the categories in figure 6-11, you can create your own functions, called *user-defined functions*. To create a user-defined function, you use *Excel's Visual Basic* program. For more information on this program, refer to *Excel*'s online Help.

Date & Time The date and time functions perform operations that are related to the date and time. You already learned how to use two of these functions: NOW and TODAY. *Excel* also provides a variety of other date and time functions that perform date and time calculations.

Statistical The statistical functions perform statistical operations. You already learned how to use the AVERAGE and COUNT functions. However, *Excel* provides dozens of other statistical functions that perform operations such as calculating the standard deviation of the values in a range and performing forecasting, probability, ranking, and significance calculations. Many of these functions perform complicated calculations, and you'll need a strong background in statistics to use them.

Function category	Typical functions	Examples
Date & Time	Get the current date and time. Get the current date only. Convert a label that looks like a date to its date value.	NOW TODAY DATEVALUE
Statistical	Get the average of the values in a range. Count the numbers in a range. Estimate the standard deviation of the values in a range.	AVERAGE COUNT STDEV
Financial	Calculate the periodic payment required to pay off a loan. Calculate the future value of a series of equal payments.	PMT FV
Math & Trigonometry	Get the total of the values in a range. Round a value. Take the square root of a value. Return the integer portion of a value. Get the sine, cosine, or tangent of an angle.	SUM ROUND SQRT INT SIN COS TAN
Logical	Take one action if a condition is true; take another if it's false.	IF
Database & List Management	Get the average of the values in a field. Get the total of the values in a field. Count the numbers in a field.	DAVERAGE DSUM DCOUNT
Text	Count the characters in a text argument. Convert all the letters in a text argument to uppercase. Get a specified number of characters from the beginning of a text argument.	LEN UPPER LEFT
Engineering	Convert a number from one system to another. Convert a decimal number to a hexadecimal number. Convert a hexadecimal number to a decimal number.	CONVERT DEC2HEX HEX2DEC
Information	Return specified information about a cell, such as its contents or location. Return a true value if the argument or the cell it refers to contains text.	CELL ISTEXT
Lookup & Reference	Count the number of columns in a range. Count the number of rows in a range.	COLUMNS ROWS
DDE & External	Connect to an external source, perform a query, and return the results.	SQLREQUEST

Figure 6-11 The eleven types of functions

Financial The financial functions perform operations such as calculating periodic payments and future values. If your specialty is finance, you shouldn't have trouble using these functions because they use terminology and perform operations that you are already familiar with. Even if your specialty isn't finance, though, some of these functions may be useful to you.

Math & Trigonometry The mathematical and trigonometric functions perform operations such as summing a range of values, rounding a value, and getting the square root of a value. Although SUM, ROUND, and SQRT are the three functions you're most likely to use, *Excel* provides dozens of others. Because many of these functions perform complicated calculations, you'll need a strong background in mathematics to use them.

Logical The logical functions perform calculations based on logical formulas and true/false values. The most commonly used logical function is IF. Figure 6-12 presents the syntax of this function along with the operators and logical functions you can use in its first argument.

If you review the syntax of the IF function, you'll see that the first argument represents a test. If the test is true, the second argument is performed. If the test is false, the third argument is performed.

By using the conditional operators in figure 6-12, you can set up a test that compares two values. This is illustrated in the worksheet in figure 6-13. Here, the IF functions in cells E6 through E14 determine the commission rate for each sales representative. If a representative's total sales (in column D) are 200,000 or more, the commission rate is eight percent (0.08). Otherwise, the commission rate is seven percent (0.07).

You can also use the logical functions in figure 6-12 to combine conditional tests. If you wanted to base the commission rate in figure 6-13 on the sales from both product groups instead of from the total sales, for example, you could enter an IF function like this:

```
=IF(AND(B6>=100000,C6>=100000),0.08,0.07)
```

Here, the commission rate is set to eight percent if the sales for both product groups are 100,000 or more; and it's set to seven percent if the sales for either product group is less than 100,000. In other words, both conditions must be true for the test to be true. In contrast, when you use the OR logical function, the test is true if either condition is true. When a function appears within another function as in the example above, the function is said to be a *nested.*

The syntax of the IF function

=IF(test,true-action,false-action)

The conditional operators you can use in the *test* argument of an IF function

Operator	Meaning	Condition test example
=	Equals	B4=C4
<>	Does not equal	D12<>3.14
>	Greater than	B4>C4
<	Less than	1000<D12
>=	Greater than or equal to	F21>=1000
<=	Less than or equal to	F21<=20000

The logical functions you can use in the *test* argument of an IF function

Function	Syntax (arguments)	Meaning	Example
AND	AND(test-1,test-2,...)	Returns a true value if all all its arguments are true.	=IF(AND(B6>=100000,C6>=100000), 0.08,0.07)
OR	OR(test-1,test-2,...)	Returns a true value if any of its arguments are true. Returns a false value if all its arguments are false.	=IF(OR(B6>=100000,C6>=100000), 0.08,0.07)
NOT	NOT(test)	Reverses the value of its argument. So, if the argument is true, NOT will return a false value. If the argument is false, NOT will return a true value.	=IF(NOT(D6<200000),0.08,0.07)

Figure 6-12 The IF function and the conditional operators and logical functions you can use in its first argument

Database & List Management The database and list management functions perform calculations on the entries in a database or list. Many of these functions have non-database counterparts. For example, the DSUM function sums the values in a field of a database or list. You'll probably never have to use these functions because you can use *Excel*'s list processing features to perform the same calculations more easily.

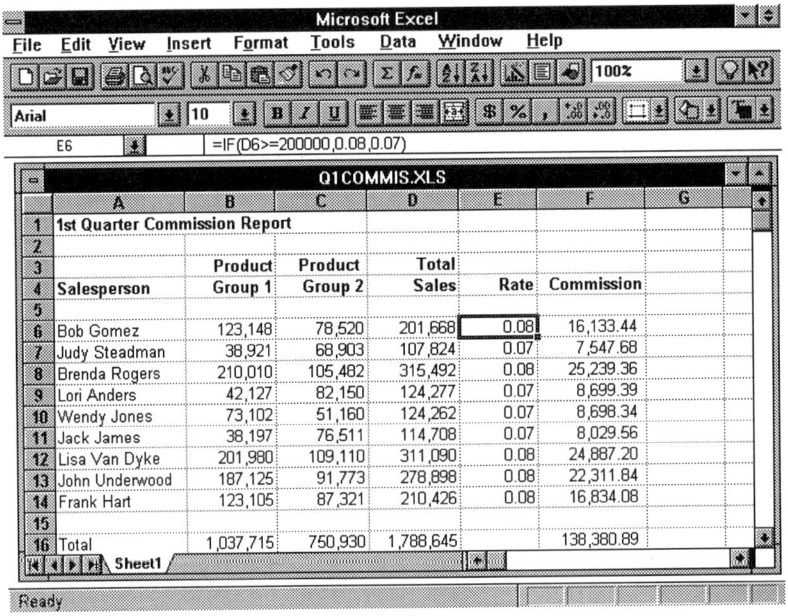

Figure 6-13 An IF function that sets the commission rate based on the total sales

Text The text functions perform operations on the text in one or more cells. For example, the LEN function returns the numbers of characters in a text argument, and the UPPER function converts all the characters in a text argument to uppercase. You may occasionally find some use for a few of these functions.

Engineering, Information, Lookup & Reference, and DDE & External It's unlikely that you'll ever need to use these types of functions in your business worksheets. As you'd guess, engineering functions perform engineering operations. The information functions return information about your worksheet. For example, the CELL function returns information about a cell, such as its contents or location. The lookup and reference functions return information about ranges and arrays. For example, the COLUMNS function can count the number of columns in a range. And the DDE and external functions provide advanced technical features for programers.

Type of reference	Example	Meaning when copied	Sample formula
Relative	A3	Adjust both the column and row.	=A3+B3
Absolute	$A$3 $C$17	Adjust neither the column nor the row.	=$A$3+B3 =$C$17*.07
Mixed	B$12	Adjust the column but not the row.	=B$12*B3
	$D2	Adjust the row but not the column.	=$D2/365

Figure 6-14 The three types of references you can use in a formula

When and how to use relative, absolute, or mixed references in a formula

Figure 6-14 summarizes the three types of cell references you can use in formulas: relative, absolute, and mixed. Although the type of reference doesn't affect the results of a formula when it's in its original cell, it does determine how a formula is copied from one cell to another. In this topic, then, you'll learn what happens when you copy formulas with the three types of references. Next, you'll learn how to create the three types of references. Finally, you'll learn when to use each of the three types in formulas.

What happens when you copy formulas with relative, absolute, and mixed references The first type of cell reference is a *relative reference.* When a relative reference is copied, the row and column in the reference are adjusted relative to the cell that it's copied to. If, for example, a formula is copied two cells to the right and three cells down, a relative reference in the formula is changed so it points to a cell two cells to the right and three cells below the original reference. This is the kind of reference you'll use most often.

The second type of cell reference is an *absolute reference.* When it's copied, the reference isn't adjusted at all. An absolute reference is identified by a dollar sign ($) to the left of the column identifier and another dollar sign to the left of the row identifier as in $B$5. You probably won't need to use this type of reference often, but it's useful in some situations.

The third type of cell reference is a *mixed reference.* In a mixed reference, either the column or row identifier is a relative reference, and the

Methods

1. Type the dollar signs as needed in the formula.
2. Press the F4 (Absolute) key to cycle through reference formats. If the cursor is on a reference to cell B4, for example, it gets changed as follows with four repetitions of the F4 key:

   $B$4

   B$4

   $B4

   B4

Note

You can use these methods as you enter or edit a formula.

Figure 6-15 Two ways to create an absolute or mixed address

other identifier is an absolute reference. Thus, $C7 is a mixed reference with an absolute column identifier and a relative row identifier. Similarly, D$10 has an absolute row identifier and a relative column identifier. As you might guess, the relative identifier is adjusted when a mixed reference is copied, but the absolute identifier isn't. Like absolute references, you probably won't use mixed references often, but they can save you time in some situations.

How to create a relative, absolute, or mixed reference When you type a cell reference into a formula without using dollar signs, you create a relative reference. You also create a relative reference when you identify a cell used in a formula by pointing at it. To create an absolute or mixed reference, you can use one of the techniques in figure 6-15. First, you can type the dollar signs where you want them. Second, you can use the F4 (Absolute) key to cycle through the four combinations for a cell reference. Note that you can use these techniques either as you enter or edit a formula.

When and how to use a relative reference in a formula Generally, you use relative references in formulas. Then, when you copy the formulas, *Excel* adjusts the references so they work correctly in their new locations. For example, figure 6-16 shows what happens when you copy a formula with relative references down a column. Here, I started by entering the formula =C6-B6 in cell D6. Then, I copied cell D6 to the range D7:D10. Since the references in the formula are relative, *Excel* interprets the formula to mean, "Get the number that's one column to the left in the same row as

Part 1: The formula =C6-B6 is entered into cell D6.

D6 | =C6-B6

	A	B	C	D
1	**Monthly Expenses**			
2	**September**			
3				
4	**Item**	**Budget**	**Expense**	**Variance**
5				
6	Salaries & Wages	50,000.00	51,784.00	1,784.00
7	Rent & Utilities	17,500.00	18,222.00	
8	Miscellaneous	1,500.00	1,922.00	
9	Maintenance	7,750.00	7,912.00	
10	Supplies	8,250.00	7,211.00	

Part 2: When the formula in cell D6 is copied to cells D7 through D10, *Excel* adjusts the column and row references.

D6 | =C6-B6

	A	B	C	D
1	**Monthly Expenses**			
2	**September**			
3				
4	**Item**	**Budget**	**Expense**	**Variance**
5				
6	Salaries & Wages	50,000.00	51,784.00	1,784.00
7	Rent & Utilities	17,500.00	18,222.00	722.00
8	Miscellaneous	1,500.00	1,922.00	422.00
9	Maintenance	7,750.00	7,912.00	162.00
10	Supplies	8,250.00	7,211.00	(1,039.00)

=C6-B6
=C7-B7
=C8-B8
=C9-B9
=C10-B10

Figure 6-16 How *Excel* adjusts relative references when a formula is copied

this cell; then, subtract from it the number that's two columns to the left in this row." When the formula is copied, *Excel* modifies the cell reference to establish the same relationship in the new location. As a result, the row identifiers are increased as the formula is copied down the column, but the column identifiers stay the same.

When and how to use an absolute reference in a formula Figure 6-17 presents a worksheet that uses a formula with an absolute reference. Here, the formula =B6*(1+$D$1) is entered in cell C6. This formula multiplies

Part 1: The formula =B6*(1+$D$1) is entered into cell C6.

C6 | =B6*(1+$D$1)

	A	B	C	D
1	**Monthly Expenses**		**% Increase**	5%
2	**Budget Planning**			
3				
4	**Item**	**Current**	**Projected**	
5				
6	Salaries & Wages	50,000.00	52,500.00	
7	Rent & Utilities	17,500.00		
8	Miscellaneous	1,500.00		
9	Maintenance	7,750.00		
10	Supplies	8,250.00		

Part 2: When the formula in cell C6 is copied to cells D7 through D10, *Excel* doesn't adjust the reference to cell D1.

C6 | =B6*(1+$D$1)

	A	B	C	D
1	**Monthly Expenses**		**% Increase**	5%
2	**Budget Planning**			
3				
4	**Item**	**Current**	**Projected**	
5				
6	Salaries & Wages	50,000.00	52,500.00	
7	Rent & Utilities	17,500.00	18,375.00	
8	Miscellaneous	1,500.00	1,575.00	
9	Maintenance	7,750.00	8,137.50	
10	Supplies	8,250.00	8,662.50	

=B6*(1+$D$1)
=B7*(1+$D$1)
=B8*(1+$D$1)
=B9*(1+$D$1)
=B10*(1+$D$1)

Figure 6-17 How to use an absolute reference in a formula so the cell reference isn't adjusted when the formula is copied

the value in the column to its left by a value of one plus the value in cell D1. Because D1 is entered as an absolute reference, it doesn't change when the formula is copied down the C column. As a result, all the values in column B are multiplied by a value of one plus the value in cell D1. Since column B contains monthly expenses and cell D1 contains the value 5%, the values in column C indicate the monthly expenses if the budget is increased by five percent. To see how the budget would look if it was increased by ten percent, all you would have to do is enter the value 10% in cell D1.

I hope it's obvious why you can't use a relative reference for cell D1 in the example in figure 6-17. If you did, the cell reference would be adjusted to cell D2 when the formula was copied to cell D7; it would be adjusted to cell D3 when the formula was copied to cell D8; and so on. Since D2 and D3 don't contain acceptable values, this wouldn't work at all.

You can see, then, how you can use an absolute reference when you want to use a value in one fixed cell in the formulas for other cells. When you change the value in the one fixed cell, all the other cells are adjusted accordingly. This is useful when you create many types of worksheets for what-if analysis.

When and how to use mixed references in a formula Occasionally, you need to use a mixed reference so that only one portion of the reference is adjusted when you copy it. Figure 6-18 presents a worksheet with a formula that requires two mixed references. This worksheet shows the effect of budget increases of four, five, and six percent. The formulas in the range of cells from C6 to E10 use mixed references, so they always refer to column B to get the current budget amount, and they always refer to row 4 to get the percentage increase.

I started this worksheet by entering the formula =$B6*(1+C$4) into cell C6. As you can see, $B6 is a mixed reference: it uses an absolute column ($B) and a relative row (4). That way, the column will always be B even if the formula is copied into other columns, but the row will vary as the formula is copied to other rows. The other mixed reference in this formula, C$4, is just the opposite. It uses a relative column (C) and a fixed row ($4). So when this cell is copied, the column will vary as the formula is copied to other columns, but the row will stay the same even if the formula is copied to other rows.

In part 2 of figure 6-18, you can see the effect of copying this formula down to cells C7 through C10, then across to cells D6 through E10. If you study this worksheet for a moment, you'll see that the formula has been adjusted correctly in each of the cells it was copied to. Although mixed references can be useful in situations like this, using them can be tricky. So you need to take extra care when you use them.

How to detect and correct circular references

A *circular reference* occurs when a formula refers to itself. In other words, the formula tries to include the result of its calculation in the calculation. This is illustrated by the worksheet in figure 6-19. Here, the formula in cell

Part 1: The formula =$B6*(1+C$4) is entered into cell C6.

C6 | =$B6*(1+C$4)

	A	B	C	D	E
1	**Monthly Expenses**				
2	**Budget Planning**				
3					
4	**Item**	**Current**	**4%**	**5%**	**6%**
5					
6	Salaries & Wages	50,000.00	52,000.00		
7	Rent & Utilities	17,500.00			
8	Miscellaneous	1,500.00			
9	Maintenance	7,750.00			
10	Supplies	8,250.00			

Part 2: When the formula is copied to cells C7 through C10 and to cells D6 through E10, the mixed references are adjusted so the formula still works correctly.

E15

	A	B	C	D	E
1	**Monthly Expenses**				
2	**Budget Planning**				
3					
4	**Item**	**Current**	**4%**	**5%**	**6%**
5					
6	Salaries & Wages	50,000.00	52,000.00	52,500.00	53,000.00
7	Rent & Utilities	17,500.00	18,200.00	18,375.00	18,550.00
8	Miscellaneous	1,500.00	1,560.00	1,575.00	1,590.00
9	Maintenance	7,750.00	8,060.00	8,137.50	8,215.00
10	Supplies	8,250.00	8,580.00	8,662.50	8,745.00

=$B6*(1+C$4)
=$B6*(1+D$4)
=$B6*(1+E$4)
=$B10*(1+C$4)
=$B10*(1+E$4)

Figure 6-18 How to use mixed references in a formula so it works correctly when it is copied

B12 is =SUM(B6:B12). This is a circular reference because the formula in cell B12 contains a reference to cell B12.

When a circular reference occurs, the displayed value is usually inaccurate. That's why *Excel* always alerts you to this condition by displaying *Circular*: followed by a cell reference in the status bar. If you examine the contents of the cell that contains the circular reference, you can usually determine the problem. Then, you edit the cell to remove the circular reference. The message in the status bar will disappear unless there's another circular reference in the worksheet. If the worksheet contains another circular reference, *Excel* displays its cell reference once you've corrected the previous one.

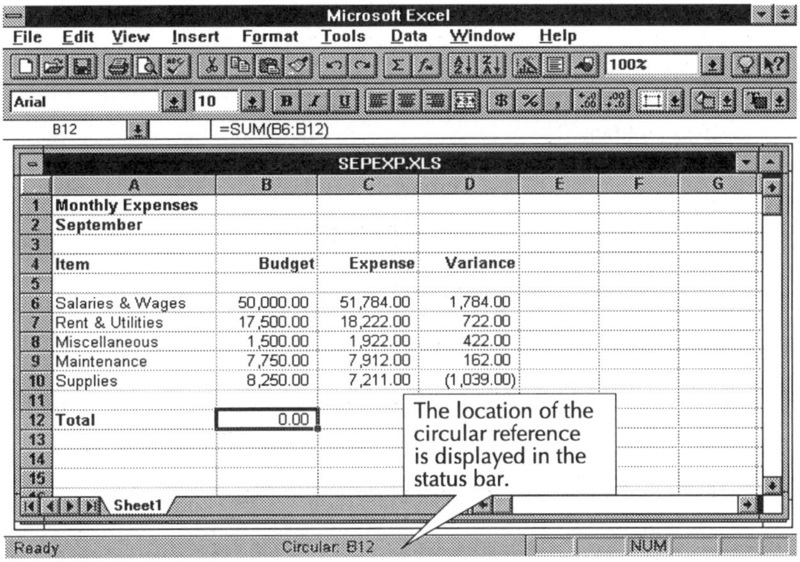

Figure 6-19 A worksheet that contains a circular reference in a SUM function

Perspective

Although most formulas and functions are relatively simple, it's still easy to make errors as you enter them into a worksheet. In fact, it's common for a finished worksheet to contain one or more errors. Worse, the more complicated a worksheet is, the more likely it is to contain errors...and the less likely they are to be detected.

To help prevent errors from going unnoticed, you should double-check the formulas in your worksheets to make sure they work correctly. To help you do that, *Excel* provides some special features for *auditing* a worksheet. In chapter 18, you can learn how to use these features.

Summary

- Most formulas consist of numbers, operators, and cell references. A formula must begin with a formula indicator, the equal sign (=). If you enter a plus sign (+) as the formula indicator, *Excel* converts it to an equal sign when you complete the formula.
- You can enter a cell reference into a formula or function by typing it or by moving the cell pointer to the cell you want to include.

- If you don't use parentheses in a formula, *Excel* uses its *order of precedence* to determine the order in which it performs operations: positive and negative evaluation first, then exponentiation, then multiplication and division, then addition and subtraction. You can use parentheses to change this order.
- A function consists of the function's name, followed by arguments that are enclosed in parentheses and separated by commas. If a function doesn't require arguments, you must still include the parentheses.
- You can identify a range used in a function by highlighting it with the mouse, by using one of the cell pointer techniques, by typing it, or by entering a range name.
- You can use the AutoSum button on the Standard toolbar to quickly add SUM functions to your worksheet.
- You can use the keyboard shortcut Ctrl+Shift+A to help you enter the arguments of a function after you enter an equal sign and the name of the function.
- You can use the Function Wizard to select the function you want and enter the function name, parentheses, argument placeholders, and separators into your worksheet.
- The TODAY, NOW, SUM, AVERAGE, COUNT, and ROUND functions are six of the over 200 functions *Excel* provides.
- The functions that come with *Excel* are divided into eleven categories: date and time, statistical, financial, math and trigonometry, logical, database and list management, text, engineering, information, lookup and reference, and DDE and external. You can also create your own functions using *Excel*'s *Visual Basic* program.
- The IF function lets you perform one of two actions depending on the result of a conditional test.
- When you copy a *relative reference*, its row and column references are adjusted relative to the cell where it's copied. When you copy an *absolute reference*, the row and column references aren't adjusted. And when you copy a *mixed reference*, either the row or column reference is adjusted, but not both.

- You can use the F4 (Absolute) key as you enter or edit a reference to change it to various combinations of fixed, relative, and mixed references.
- *Excel* displays the message *Circular:* followed by a cell reference in the status bar to tell you that the worksheet contains a circular reference in the cell.

Chapter 7

How to edit a worksheet with maximum efficiency

When you *edit* a worksheet, you make changes to it. For instance, you may decide to insert a row or column into a worksheet, to move a range of data from one area in a worksheet to another, or to hide one or more columns so they won't be printed or so you can work more easily with a large worksheet. To a large extent, how efficiently you can perform editing operations like these determines how productive you can be with *Excel.*

In this chapter, you'll learn how to perform the most useful editing functions in the most efficient ways. As you will see, *Excel* often provides more than one way for doing most of these functions. When you complete this chapter, you'll be able to decide which methods work best for you.

How to repeat or undo the last operation

If you want to repeat your last editing action, *Excel* usually lets you do so. Also, if you make a mistake while you're editing a worksheet, you can usually undo the last operation you performed. For example, you can undo a find and replace operation if you discover that it didn't work the way you wanted it to. Just be sure to undo it before you perform another operation since *Excel* keeps track of only the last operation you performed.

To repeat or undo an operation, you can use one of the techniques in figure 7-1. Note, however, that you can't repeat or undo every operation. If the operation can't be repeated or undone, the message "Can't repeat" or "Can't Undo" appears in the Edit menu in place of the Repeat or Undo commands.

How to move the cell pointer

As you enter and edit the data in a worksheet, you need to move the cell pointer to the area of the worksheet where you want to work. Usually, you do that using direct mouse or keyboard actions. In some situations, however, you may want to move the cell pointer using the Go To command or the Name box.

With the mouse The simplest way to move the cell pointer is to click on a cell with the mouse. If the cell you want to move to isn't currently displayed, you have to use the scroll bars to display it. Since I showed you how to use the scroll bars in chapter 1, I won't repeat that information here.

Three ways to issue the Repeat command

- Select the Repeat command from the Edit menu.
- Press F4.
- Click on the Repeat button in the Standard toolbar: 

Note

Not all actions can be repeated. When that's the case, the words "Can't Repeat" appear dimmed in the Edit menu in place of the Repeat command.

Three ways to issue the Undo command

- Select the Undo command from the Edit menu.
- Press Crtl+Z.
- Click on the Undo button in the Standard toolbar: 

Note

Not all actions can be undone. When that's the case, the words "Can't Undo" appear dimmed in the Edit menu in place of the Undo command. Actions you can't undo include cell pointer movement, recalculation using the F9 key, and deletion of a worksheet.

Figure 7-1 How to repeat or undo your last operation

With the keyboard You can also move the cell pointer using the keyboard as summarized in figure 7-2. Here, the only keystroke combinations that may be confusing are the End+Home combination (which can also be done by pressing the End key followed by the Home key) or the End+Arrow combination (which can also be done by pressing the End key followed by an Arrow key). If you experiment with these combinations, you'll quickly see how useful they can be. When you use End+Down-arrow, for example, *Excel* moves the cell pointer to the last cell in the column before the next blank cell. As a result, this combination can be useful when you want to highlight a range.

With the Go To command If you're working in a large worksheet, you may want to use the Go To command to move the cell pointer directly to any area of the worksheet as summarized in figure 7-3. As you can see, you can use this command to move the cell pointer to a specific cell by entering

Keystrokes	Function
Right-arrow or Tab	Moves the cell pointer right one cell.
Left-arrow or Shift+Tab	Moves the cell pointer left one cell.
Down-arrow or Enter	Moves the cell pointer down one cell.
Up-arrow or Shift+Enter	Moves the cell pointer up one cell.
Home	Moves the cell pointer to the first column of the current row.
Ctrl+Home	Moves the cell pointer to cell A1.
Ctrl+End or End+Home	Moves the cell pointer to the last row and column in the worksheet.
Page-up or Page-down	Moves the cell pointer up or down one screen.
Alt+Page-up or Alt+Page-down	Moves the cell pointer left or right one screen.
Ctrl+Arrow or End+Arrow	Moves the cell pointer in the direction of the arrow to a cell that contains data and is next to a blank cell or to the last cell in the column or row.

Figure 7-2 The keystroke combinations for moving the cell pointer

a cell reference in the Reference text box. Or, you can move to and highlight a named range by selecting it from the Go To list box. You can also select special types of cells using the Go To Special dialog box.

With the Name box Another way to move the mouse pointer is to click on the Name box (on the left side of the formula bar), type in a cell reference, and press the Enter key. The Name box also provides the most convenient way to go to a named range, as you'll see later in this chapter.

How to work with columns and rows

Some of the functions you perform in a worksheet involve entire rows or columns. For example, you often need to change the width of a column to accommodate the data it contains. Also, you frequently need to add rows and columns to a worksheet. And you may want to hide or expose one or more columns or rows to make it easier to use a large worksheet.

How to change the width of one or more columns Often, you enter data that is too wide for a column. If the data is a label, it spills over into adjoining columns unless those columns already contain data. If the data is

Two ways to access the Go To dialog box

- Select the Go To command from the Edit menu.
- Press F5.

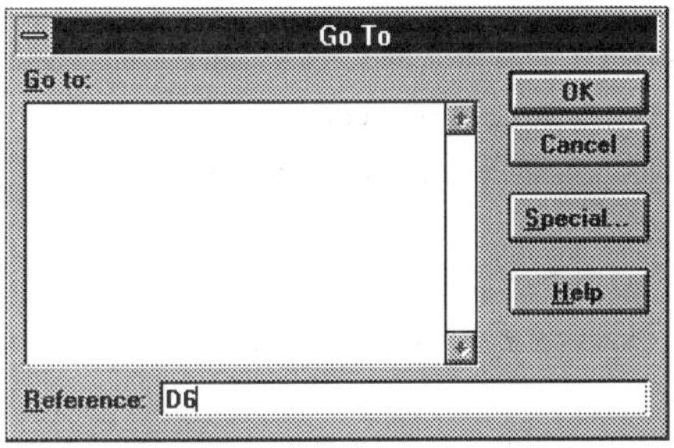

Operation

- To move the cell pointer to a specific cell, enter the cell reference in the Reference text box.
- To move the cell pointer to a named range, highlight the range name in the Go To list box. When you click on the OK button, *Excel* highlights the range.
- To select a special type of cell, click on the Special button and choose an option from the Go To Special dialog box:

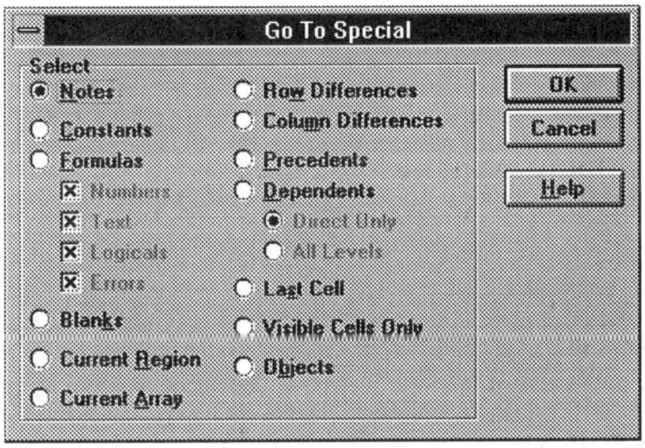

Figure 7-3 How to use the Go To command to move the cell pointer

numeric, how it's displayed depends on the cell's format. Sometimes, it's displayed in exponential notation, but that's usually not what you want. Other times, the value can't be displayed at all, and pound signs are displayed across the cell. If one of these situations occurs, you simply need to widen the column.

The easiest way to change the width of one or more columns is to use the mouse as illustrated in figure 7-4. First, select the columns or rows, then place the pointer in the worksheet frame on the separator line to the right of

Procedure

1. Select the columns you want to change by dragging the mouse pointer over the column letters in the worksheet frame.
2. Place the mouse pointer on the separator line to the right of the column letter for one of the columns you selected. When the pointer is in the correct position, it will change to a double-headed arrow:

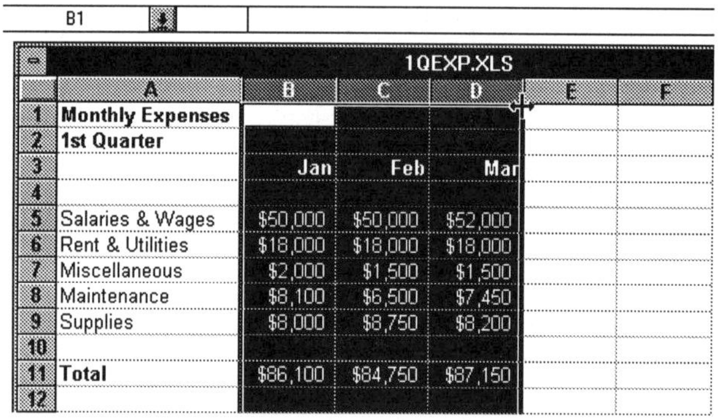

3. Drag the double-headed arrow to the column width you want:

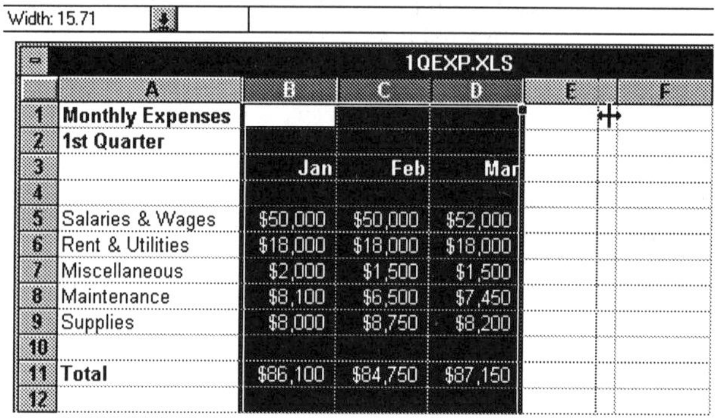

Notes

- You can change the width of a single column without selecting it first. Simply drag the appropriate separator line.
- You can change the width of one or more columns to accommodate the largest entry by double-clicking on the separator line instead of dragging it.

Figure 7-4 How to use the mouse to change the width of one or more columns

one of the columns so the pointer changes to a double-headed arrow. Then, drag the columns or rows to the desired size. As you drag, the width of the column (in characters) is displayed in the Name box.

How to use the Column Width command

1. Select the columns you want to change.
2. Select the Column Width command from the Format or shortcut menu and this dialog box appears:

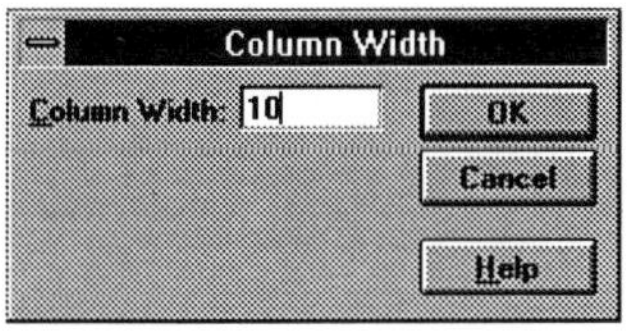

3. Enter the number of characters that you want displayed in the columns and click on the OK button.

Notes

- You don't have to select entire columns to use the Column Width command from the Format menu. Instead, you can highlight a range that includes at least one cell from each column that you want to change.
- The number in the Column Width dialog box refers to the number of characters that can be displayed using the standard font set with the Options command of the Tools menu. For fonts that are smaller, more characters will fit in a column than the number shown. For larger fonts, fewer characters will fit in a column than the number shown.

How to use the Column AutoFit Selection command

1. Highlight at least one cell in each column that you want to change.
2. Select the Column AutoFit Selection command from the Format menu, and *Excel* adjusts the column widths to accommodate the largest entry in each column.

Figure 7-5 How to use menu commands to change the width of one or more columns

You can also use the mouse to adjust the column width so it accommodates the largest entry. To do that, position the pointer as described above so it changes to a double-headed arrow. Then, double-click without moving the pointer.

Another way to change the width of one or more columns is to use the menu commands summarized in figure 7-5. To change the column width to a specific number of characters, you use the Column Width command in the Format or shortcut menu. To adjust the column width so it accommodates the largest entry, you use the Column AutoFit Selection command in the Format menu.

How to insert rows

1. Select the rows below where you want to insert new rows by dragging the mouse pointer over the row numbers in the worksheet frame. The number of rows you select will be the number of rows that are inserted:

	A	B	C	D	E
1	**Monthly Expenses**				
2	**1st Quarter**				
3					
4		**Jan**	**Feb**	**Mar**	
5	Salaries & Wages	$50,000	$50,000	$52,000	
6	Rent & Utilities	$18,000	$18,000	$18,000	
7	Miscellaneous	$2,000	$1,500	$1,500	
8	Maintenance	$8,100	$6,500	$7,450	
9	Supplies	$8,000	$8,750	$8,200	
10					
11	**Total**	$86,100	$84,750	$87,150	
12					
13					

2. Select the Rows command from the Insert menu or the Insert command from the shortcut menu or use the keyboard shortcut (Ctrl++), and *Excel* inserts the rows:

	A	B	C	D	E
1	**Monthly Expenses**				
2	**1st Quarter**				
3					
4		**Jan**	**Feb**	**Mar**	
5	Salaries & Wages	$50,000	$50,000	$52,000	
6	Rent & Utilities	$18,000	$18,000	$18,000	
7					
8					
9	Miscellaneous	$2,000	$1,500	$1,500	
10	Maintenance	$8,100	$6,500	$7,450	
11	Supplies	$8,000	$8,750	$8,200	
12					
13	**Total**	$86,100	$84,750	$87,150	

How to insert columns

Use the procedure above, but select the columns to the right of where you want to insert the new columns. Then, select the Columns command from the Insert menu or the Insert command from the shortcut menu, or use the keyboard shortcut (Ctrl++).

Note

You can also insert columns or rows by first selecting a range that contains the number of columns or rows you want to insert. Then, when you start the Insert command from the shortcut menu, a dialog box is displayed that lets you specify whether you want to insert columns or rows.

Figure 7-6 How to insert rows and columns

How to insert or delete one or more columns or rows Figure 7-6 shows you how to insert one or more rows or columns. To do that, you can select the Rows or Columns command from the Insert menu or the Insert command from the shortcut menu when complete rows or columns are highlighted. You can also use the keyboard shortcut (Ctrl++). Notice that to insert new rows, you select the rows below where you want them inserted.

How to delete rows

1. Select the rows you want to delete:

	A	B	C	D	E
1	**Monthly Expenses**				
2	**1st Quarter**				
3					
4		**Jan**	**Feb**	**Mar**	
5	Salaries & Wages	$50,000	$50,000	$52,000	
6	Rent & Utilities	$18,000	$18,000	$18,000	
7					
8					
9	Miscellaneous	$2,000	$1,500	$1,500	
10	Maintenance	$8,100	$6,500	$7,450	
11	Supplies	$8,000	$8,750	$8,200	
12					
13	**Total**	$86,100	$84,750	$87,150	

2. Select the Delete command from the Edit or shortcut menu or use the keyboard shortcut (Ctrl+-), and *Excel* deletes the rows:

	A	B	C	D	E
1	**Monthly Expenses**				
2	**1st Quarter**				
3					
4		**Jan**	**Feb**	**Mar**	
5	Salaries & Wages	$50,000	$50,000	$52,000	
6	Rent & Utilities	$18,000	$18,000	$18,000	
7	Miscellaneous	$2,000	$1,500	$1,500	
8	Maintenance	$8,100	$6,500	$7,450	
9	Supplies	$8,000	$8,750	$8,200	
10					
11	**Total**	$86,100	$84,750	$87,150	
12					
13					

How to delete columns

Use the procedure above, but select the columns you want to delete.

Note

You can also delete columns or rows by first selecting a range that contains the number of columns or rows you want to delete. Then, when you start the Delete command, a dialog box is displayed that lets you specify whether you want to delete columns or rows.

Figure 7-7 How to delete rows and columns

To insert new columns, you select the columns to the right of where you want them inserted. The number of rows or columns you select indicates the number of rows or columns *Excel* inserts. So if you select two rows, *Excel* inserts two rows above the ones you selected.

Figure 7-7 presents the procedure for deleting columns and rows. To do that, you select the columns or rows you want to delete and issue the Delete command from the Edit or shortcut menu. You can also use the keyboard shortcut (Ctrl+-).

How to hide one or more columns or rows

Method 1

1. Select the columns or rows you want to hide.
2. Place the mouse pointer on the separator line in the worksheet frame to the right of the selected columns or below the selected rows. When the mouse pointer changes to a double-headed arrow, drag it to the left for columns or up for rows until zero is displayed in the Name box. When you release the mouse button, the columns or rows are hidden.

Method 2

Place the mouse pointer on the separator line in the worksheet frame to the right of the columns or below the rows you want to hide. When the pointer changes to a double-headed arrow, drag it to the left past the columns you want to hide or up past the rows you want to hide. When you release the mouse button, the columns or rows are hidden.

How to expose one column or row at a time

Place the mouse pointer in the worksheet frame just to the right of the separator line that is to the right of the column you want to expose or just below the separator line that is below the column you want to expose. When it is in the correct position, it turns into a double-headed arrow with a white center line. Then, drag it to the right to expose one column and set the column width, or drag it down to expose one row and set the row height.

Figure 7-8 How to use the mouse to hide or expose columns and rows

You can also use the Insert command from the shortcut menu or the Delete command from the Edit or shortcut menu when a range of cells is highlighted instead of complete rows or columns. Then, a dialog box is displayed that lets you specify whether you want to insert or delete rows or columns. If you're using a mouse to select the range, though, it's easier to highlight the complete rows or columns before you issue the command and skip the dialog box.

How to hide or expose one or more columns or rows As you work on a worksheet, it often makes sense to hide one or more columns or rows instead of deleting them. Then, you can display two columns side-by-side when they're separated by other columns. And when you print the worksheet, the hidden columns aren't printed. Later, when you want to display or print the hidden columns or rows, you can expose them.

The easiest way to hide or expose columns or rows is to use the mouse techniques presented in figures 7-8. These techniques are similar to those for changing the width of one or more columns. To hide columns, for example, you first select the columns you want to hide. Then, you drag the separator line in the worksheet frame that's to the right of the columns to the left until zero is displayed as the width in the Name box. When you release the mouse button, the columns are hidden. You use a similar technique to hide rows.

Another way to hide columns or rows with the mouse is to drag a separator line without first selecting the columns or rows. For example, to hide columns, you can drag a separator line to the left over the adjacent columns, thus hiding them. And to expose one column at a time, you can drag the separator line to the right. If you experiment with these mouse methods, you'll see that they're quite easy to use, even if they're confusing at first.

You can also use the Column Hide and the Row Hide commands in the Format menu to hide columns or rows as summarized in figure 7-9. Notice that when you use these commands, you don't have to select entire columns or rows as you do when you use the mouse methods. Instead, you highlight one or more cells in each column or row that you want to hide.

To expose columns or rows using menu commands, you first have to indicate which columns or rows you want to expose. To do that, highlight a range that includes at least one cell from the column to the left and the column to the right of the hidden columns or from the row above and the row below the hidden rows. You can't do this, however, when the column you want to expose is column A or the row is row 1. In that case, you have to use the Go To command or the Name box to go to a cell in the hidden column or row. Then, issue the Column Unhide or the Row Unhide command from the Format menu to expose the columns or rows.

How to move and copy data

Excel provides four methods for moving and copying data. First, you can use the drag-and-drop method. Second, you can use the clipboard method. Third, you can use the AutoFill feature. And fourth, you can use the Fill Right, Fill Left, Fill Up, and Fill Down commands in the Edit menu.

With the drag-and-drop method Figure 7-10 presents the procedures for moving or copying data with the drag-and-drop method. The only difference between moving and copying data is that you hold down the Ctrl key as you drag the data to perform a copy operation. To move data, you just drag it. You can tell if you're copying data when you drag it because a plus sign (+) appears next to the mouse pointer.

How to hide columns

1. Select the columns you want to hide:

	A	B	C	D	E	F	G	H
1	**Monthly Expenses**							
2								
3								
4		**Jan**	**Feb**	**Mar**	**Apr**	**May**	**Jun**	**Jul**
5	Salaries & Wages	$50,000	$50,000	$52,000	$52,000	$52,000	$52,000	$52,000
6	Rent & Utilities	$18,000	$18,000	$18,000	$18,000	$18,000	$18,000	$18,000
7	Miscellaneous	$2,000	$1,500	$1,500	$1,500	$1,500	$2,250	$2,100
8	Maintenance	$8,100	$6,500	$7,450	$5,500	$7,300	$8,900	$8,500
9	Supplies	$8,000	$8,750	$8,200	$7,800	$7,500	$8,350	$8,400
10								
11	**Total**	$86,100	$84,750	$87,150	$84,800	$86,300	$89,500	$89,000
12								

2. Select the Column Hide command from the Format menu or the Hide command from the shortcut menu for one or more highlighted columns, and *Excel* hides the columns:

	A	E	F	G	H	I	J	K
1	**Monthly Expenses**							
2								
3								
4		**Apr**	**May**	**Jun**	**Jul**	**Aug**	**Sep**	**Oct**
5	Salaries & Wages	$52,000	$52,000	$52,000	$52,000	$53,500	$52,000	$52,000
6	Rent & Utilities	$18,000	$18,000	$18,000	$18,000	$18,000	$18,000	$18,000
7	Miscellaneous	$1,500	$1,500	$2,250	$2,100	$1,250	$1,750	$1,500
8	Maintenance	$5,500	$7,300	$8,900	$8,500	$4,200	$5,200	$6,450
9	Supplies	$7,800	$7,500	$8,350	$8,400	$8,400	$6,800	$7,550
10								
11	**Total**	$84,800	$86,300	$89,500	$89,000	$85,350	$83,750	$85,500
12								

How to expose columns

1. Select the columns to the left and right of the hidden columns you want to expose.
2. Select the Column Unhide command from the Format menu or the Unhide command from the shortcut menu for one or more highlighted columns, and *Excel* exposes the columns.

How to hide or expose rows

To hide rows, use the procedure above for hiding columns, but select the rows you want to hide and issue the Row Hide command from the Format menu or the Hide command from the shortcut menu. To expose rows, select both the row above and below the hidden rows you want to expose and issue the Row Unhide command from the Format menu or the Unhide command from the shortcut menu.

Notes

- To expose column A or row 1, use the Go To command or the Name box to go to a cell in that column or row before issuing the Unhide, Column Unhide, or Row Unhide command.
- You can also hide columns or rows by first selecting a range that contains at least one cell in each column or row you want to hide, then issuing the Hide, Column Hide, or Row Hide command.

Figure 7-9 How to use the menu commands to hide or expose columns and rows

How to move the data in a range

1. Highlight the cells that contain the data you want to move.
2. Place the mouse pointer on the outline of the cells so that the pointer turns into an arrow:

	A	B	C	D	E
1	**Monthly Expenses**				
2	**1st Quarter**				
3					
4		Jan	Feb	Mar	
5	Salaries & Wages	$50,000	$50,000	$52,000	
6	Rent & Utilities	$18,000	$18,000	$18,000	
7	Miscellaneous	$2,000	$1,500	$1,500	
8	Maintenance	$8,100	$6,500	$7,450	
9	Supplies	$8,000	$8,750	$8,200	
10					
11	**Total**	$86,100	$84,750	$87,150	
12					

3. Press and hold down the mouse button as you drag the outline of the cells to another location:

	A	B	C	D	E
1	**Monthly Expenses**				
2	**1st Quarter**				
3					
4		Jan	Feb	Mar	
5	Salaries & Wages	$50,000	$50,000	$52,000	
6	Rent & Utilities	$18,000	$18,000	$18,000	
7	Miscellaneous	$2,000	$1,500	$1,500	
8	Maintenance	$8,100	$6,500	$7,450	
9	Supplies	$8,000	$8,750	$8,200	
10					
11	**Total**	$86,100	$84,750	$87,150	
12					

4. Release the mouse button and the data is moved to its new location:

	A	B	C	D	E
1	**Monthly Expenses**				
2	**1st Quarter**				
3		Jan	Feb	Mar	
4					
5	Salaries & Wages	$50,000	$50,000	$52,000	
6	Rent & Utilities	$18,000	$18,000	$18,000	
7	Miscellaneous	$2,000	$1,500	$1,500	
8	Maintenance	$8,100	$6,500	$7,450	
9	Supplies	$8,000	$8,750	$8,200	
10					
11	**Total**	$86,100	$84,750	$87,150	
12					

How to copy the data in a range

Use the same procedure as above, but hold down the Ctrl key as you drag the range. Notice that a plus sign (+) appears next to the arrow to indicate a copy operation.

How to move or copy entire rows or columns

Use the same procedure you use for moving or copying a range of cells, but select the rows or columns first by dragging the mouse pointer over the row numbers or column letters in the worksheet frame.

Figure 7-10 How to use the drag-and-drop feature to move or copy data

By default, *Excel* asks you to confirm a move or copy operation if the new location already contains data. However, you can turn this feature off if you want *Excel* to automatically replace the existing data. To do that, deselect the Alert Before Overwriting Cells option in the Edit tab of the Options dialog box.

With the clipboard Figure 7-11 presents the procedures for moving or copying data using the clipboard. The only difference between moving and copying data using this technique is that you use the Cut command to move data, and you use the Copy command to copy data. When you use either of these commands, *Excel* stores a copy of the data in the clipboard. Then, to complete the move or copy operation, you move the mouse pointer to the new location and press the Enter key or use the Paste command to copy the data from the clipboard. If you used the Cut command to place the data in the clipboard, the data is then removed from its original location.

In most cases, you select the location for the paste operation by placing the cell pointer in the upper left corner of the range. But you can also highlight the range where you want to copy or move the data. When you do, however, the destination range must be exactly the same size and shape as the source range. If it's not, a dialog box appears stating that the areas are different shapes and the operation isn't performed.

With the AutoFill feature Figure 7-12 presents the procedure for using the AutoFill feature to copy data. Notice that this procedure is the same as the procedure you use to fill a range with a series using the AutoFill feature. The difference is that in this case, *Excel* doesn't recognize the data you're copying as part of a series. So it copies the data instead.

With the Fill commands Figure 7-13 presents the procedures for using the Fill Down, Fill Right, Fill Up, and Fill Left commands. To use one of them, highlight the cells that contain the data you want to copy as well as the adjacent cells that you want to copy the data to. Then, issue the command. The commands that are active on the Fill submenu depend on the range you highlighted.

How to work with ranges

Excel provides many commands for operating on a range of cells. For instance, the Cut and Copy commands in the Edit menu work on a range of cells, and the Cells command in the Format menu applies to a range of

How to move the data in a range

1. Highlight the cells that contain the data you want to move:

	A	B	C	D	E
1	**Monthly Expenses**				
2	**1st Quarter**				
3					
4		**Jan**	**Feb**	**Mar**	
5	Salaries & Wages	$50,000	$50,000	$52,000	
6	Rent & Utilities	$18,000	$18,000	$18,000	
7	Miscellaneous	$2,000	$1,500	$1,500	
8	Maintenance	$8,100	$6,500	$7,450	
9	Supplies	$8,000	$8,750	$8,200	
10					
11	**Total**	$86,100	$84,750	$87,150	
12					

2. Click on the Cut toolbar button, select the Cut command from the Edit or shortcut menu, or use the keyboard shortcut (Ctrl+X) to copy the contents of the highlighted cells to the clipboard.
3. Select the cell in the upper left corner of the range where you want to move the data:

	A	B	C	D	E
1	**Monthly Expenses**				
2	**1st Quarter**				
3					
4		**Jan**	**Feb**	**Mar**	
5	Salaries & Wages	$50,000	$50,000	$52,000	
6	Rent & Utilities	$18,000	$18,000	$18,000	
7	Miscellaneous	$2,000	$1,500	$1,500	
8	Maintenance	$8,100	$6,500	$7,450	
9	Supplies	$8,000	$8,750	$8,200	
10					
11	**Total**	$86,100	$84,750	$87,150	
12					

4. Click on the Paste toolbar button, select the Paste command from the Edit or shortcut menu, use the keyboard shortcut (Ctrl+V), or press the Enter key to paste the data in the new location and delete the data from its original location:

	A	B	C	D	E
1	**Monthly Expenses**				
2	**1st Quarter**				
3		**Jan**	**Feb**	**Mar**	
4					
5	Salaries & Wages	$50,000	$50,000	$52,000	
6	Rent & Utilities	$18,000	$18,000	$18,000	
7	Miscellaneous	$2,000	$1,500	$1,500	
8	Maintenance	$8,100	$6,500	$7,450	
9	Supplies	$8,000	$8,750	$8,200	
10					
11	**Total**	$86,100	$84,750	$87,150	
12					

How to copy the data in a range

Use the same procedure you use for moving data, except click on the Copy toolbar button, select the Copy command from the Edit or shortcut menu, or use the keyboard shortcut (Ctrl+C) to copy the data to the clipboard.

Figure 7-11 How to use the clipboard to move or copy data

Procedure

1. Select the cell or range of cells that contains the data you want to copy, and place the mouse pointer over the fill handle so the pointer turns into a cross:

B11 =SUM(B5:B9)

	A	B	C	D	E
1	**Monthly Expenses**				
2	**1st Quarter**				
3		**Jan**	**Feb**	**Mar**	
4					
5	Salaries & Wages	$50,000	$50,000	$52,000	
6	Rent & Utilities	$18,000	$18,000	$18,000	
7	Miscellaneous	$2,000	$1,500	$1,500	
8	Maintenance	$8,100	$6,500	$7,450	
9	Supplies	$8,000	$8,750	$8,200	
10					
11	**Total**	$86,100			
12					

2. Drag the fill handle across the range you want to copy the data to:

B11 =SUM(B5:B9)

	A	B	C	D	E
1	**Monthly Expenses**				
2	**1st Quarter**				
3		**Jan**	**Feb**	**Mar**	
4					
5	Salaries & Wages	$50,000	$50,000	$52,000	
6	Rent & Utilities	$18,000	$18,000	$18,000	
7	Miscellaneous	$2,000	$1,500	$1,500	
8	Maintenance	$8,100	$6,500	$7,450	
9	Supplies	$8,000	$8,750	$8,200	
10					
11	**Total**	$86,100			
12					

3. Release the mouse button and the data is copied into the range:

B11 =SUM(B5:B9)

	A	B	C	D	E
1	**Monthly Expenses**				
2	**1st Quarter**				
3		**Jan**	**Feb**	**Mar**	
4					
5	Salaries & Wages	$50,000	$50,000	$52,000	
6	Rent & Utilities	$18,000	$18,000	$18,000	
7	Miscellaneous	$2,000	$1,500	$1,500	
8	Maintenance	$8,100	$6,500	$7,450	
9	Supplies	$8,000	$8,750	$8,200	
10					
11	**Total**	$86,100	$84,750	$87,150	
12					

Note

If *Excel* recognizes the starting entry as part of a series, it continues the series in the extended range instead of copying the data. If that's not what you want, hold down the Ctrl key as you drag the fill handle.

Figure 7-12 How to use the AutoFill feature to copy data to adjacent cells

How to copy data to the right

1. Highlight a range that includes the data you want to copy and the cells to the right where you want to copy it:

B11 =SUM(B5:B9)

	A	B	C	D	E
1	**Monthly Expenses**				
2	**1st Quarter**				
3		**Jan**	**Feb**	**Mar**	
4					
5	Salaries & Wages	$50,000	$50,000	$52,000	
6	Rent & Utilities	$18,000	$18,000	$18,000	
7	Miscellaneous	$2,000	$1,500	$1,500	
8	Maintenance	$8,100	$6,500	$7,450	
9	Supplies	$8,000	$8,750	$8,200	
10					
11	**Total**	$86,100			
12					

2. Select the Fill Right command from the Edit menu or use the keyboard shortcut (Ctrl+R), and the data is copied:

B11 =SUM(B5:B9)

	A	B	C	D	E
1	**Monthly Expenses**				
2	**1st Quarter**				
3		**Jan**	**Feb**	**Mar**	
4					
5	Salaries & Wages	$50,000	$50,000	$52,000	
6	Rent & Utilities	$18,000	$18,000	$18,000	
7	Miscellaneous	$2,000	$1,500	$1,500	
8	Maintenance	$8,100	$6,500	$7,450	
9	Supplies	$8,000	$8,750	$8,200	
10					
11	**Total**	$86,100	$84,750	$87,150	
12					

How to copy data down

1. Highlight a range that includes the data you want to copy and the cells below where you want to copy it.
2. Select the Fill Down command from the Edit menu or use the keyboard shortcut (Ctrl+D), and the data is copied.

How to copy data to the left

1. Highlight a range that includes the data you want to copy and the cells to the left where you want to copy it.
2. Select the Fill Left command from the Edit menu and the data is copied.

How to copy data up

1. Highlight a range that includes the data you want to copy and the cells above where you want to copy it.
2. Select the Fill Up command from the Edit menu and the data is copied.

Figure 7-13 How to use the Fill commands to copy data to adjacent cells

How to insert a range of cells

1. Highlight the range where you want to insert the new cells:

1546	2938	2984	2783
1934	3940	584	1984
3584	1038	987	638
945	498	2931	2984
1258	3985	4873	1985
2396			987

2. Select the Cells command from the Insert menu or the Insert command from the shortcut menu or use the keyboard shortcut (Ctrl++), and this dialog box appears:

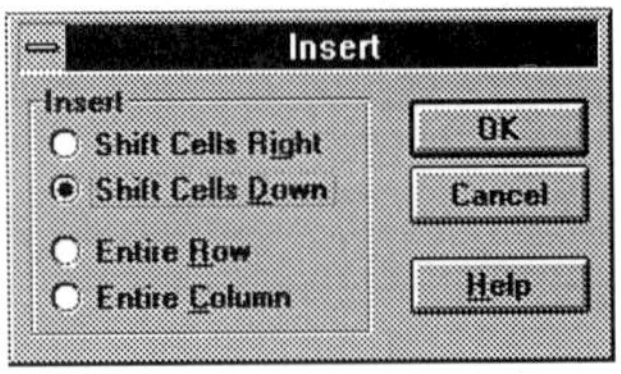

3. Select the Shift Cells Right or Shift Cells Down option to indicate where you want to shift the existing data when the cells are inserted.
4. Click on the OK button, and *Excel* inserts the range of cells and shifts the data in the direction you specified:

1546	2938	2984	2783
1934	3940	584	1984
3584	1038	987	638
945			2984
1258	498	2931	1985
2396	3985	4873	987

How to delete a range of cells

Use the same procedure you use to insert a range of cells, but select the Delete command from the Edit or shortcut menu or use the keyboard shortcut (Ctrl+-).

Figure 7-14 How to insert or delete a range of cells

cells. In this topic, you'll learn how to use some other commands that are useful for working with ranges.

How to insert or delete a range of cells When you need to insert cells in a worksheet, you usually insert entire rows and columns. Occasionally, though, you may need to insert a range of cells. If, for example, you're entering columns of data, you may omit figures from one or more columns accidentally. If so, you can insert blank cells so you can enter the missing data as illustrated in figure 7-14.

Use the Delete key

1. Highlight the range of cells that contains the data you want to delete.
2. Press the Delete key. Then, the contents of the cells are deleted, but not the formatting applied to those cells.

Use the Clear command

1. Highlight the range of cells that contains the data you want to delete.
2. Select the Clear Contents command from the Edit menu or the shortcut menu.

Note

To delete the cell formatting and notes along with the data from the selected range, select the Clear All command from the Edit menu.

Figure 7-15 Two ways to delete data from a range of cells

Note in step 3 in figure 7-14 that you have to tell *Excel* which direction to shift the data that's in the range where you want to insert the blank cells. Your choices are to shift it to the right or shift it down. The option you choose depends on the specific situation. In figure 7-14, I selected the Shift Cells Down option because I omitted the data for a row in two columns.

Figure 7-14 also presents the procedure for deleting a range of cells. Basically, you use the Delete command from the Edit or shortcut menu. Then, you have to select an option from the Delete dialog box to tell *Excel* whether data should be shifted from below or to the right of the deleted cells to fill the range.

How to delete the data from a range of cells Figure 7-15 presents two methods for deleting the data from a range of cells. First, you can highlight the range and press the Delete key. Then, *Excel* deletes the contents of the cells, but leaves any formats or notes you may have applied to the cells.

Second, you can use the Clear command from the Edit menu. When you use this command, you must specify what you want to clear by choosing the right subcommand. To remove just the cells' contents, select Contents. Or, you can select Formats to clear the formats you have applied to the cell, Notes to remove the notes for the cell, or All to remove everything. Since you can use the Delete key to delete the cell contents, you'll probably use the Clear command only if you want to delete the formats or notes from a range of cells but you want to leave the cells' contents in place.

How to change formulas to values Occasionally, you want to convert the formulas in a range to their calculated values. For instance, suppose you created a worksheet that displays total sales calculated by adding values from several columns. Then, if you decide you want to delete the columns that the total sales are calculated from, you must first convert the total sales formulas to values. Otherwise, you'll lose the total sales data.

Figure 7-16 presents two methods for converting formulas to values. First, you can press the F9 (Calc) key while you're editing a cell that contains a formula. Second, you can copy a range that contains formulas to the clipboard and paste the values of the formulas back into the worksheet using the Paste Special command. You'll want to use this technique if you need to change the formulas in several cells to values.

How to transpose data Figure 7-17 presents the procedure for transposing data (that is, switching a column of data to a row of data or vice versa). This is useful when you start a worksheet one way and decide that it would work better if the rows and columns were transposed. Notice that you can't overlap the original range with the new range, and any existing data in the new range is replaced.

How to set the view so it works best for you

In chapter 4, you learned how to use the options in the View tab of the Options dialog box to set defaults that determine whether features like the status bar and sheet tabs are displayed in the application and document windows. In this chapter, I'll assume that you already know how to use these options, so I won't present them again. Instead, I'll show you how to use the commands for changing the view that are available from the View and Window menus. Figure 7-18 presents these commands.

How to hide or display the formula bar, the status bar, or the toolbars The first two commands on the View menu, Formula Bar and Status Bar, let you hide or display the formula bar or the status bar. If either of these commands has a check mark in front of it, that means the feature is displayed. To hide the feature, select the command.

When you select the Toolbars command from the View menu, Excel displays a dialog box that lets you hide or display any of *Excel*'s toolbars. In addition, this dialog box lets you customize the toolbars. Chapter 20 covers the use of toolbars in detail, so I won't say anything more about them here.

Use the F9 (Calc) key

1. Double-click on the cell that contains the formula you want to change, or place the cell pointer on the cell and press the F2 (Edit) key:

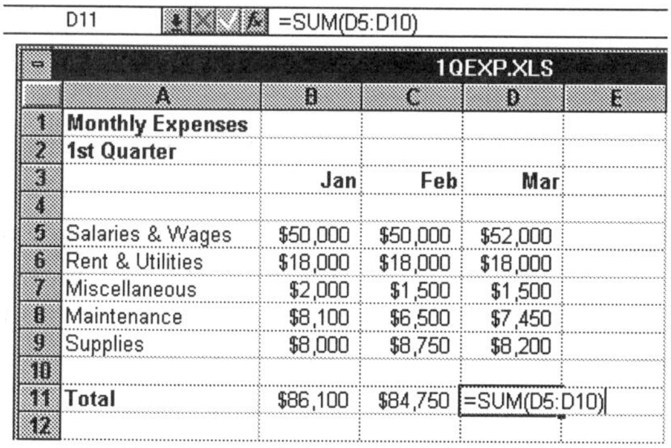

D11 =SUM(D5:D10)

1QEXP.XLS

	A	B	C	D	E
1	**Monthly Expenses**				
2	**1st Quarter**				
3		**Jan**	**Feb**	**Mar**	
4					
5	Salaries & Wages	$50,000	$50,000	$52,000	
6	Rent & Utilities	$18,000	$18,000	$18,000	
7	Miscellaneous	$2,000	$1,500	$1,500	
8	Maintenance	$8,100	$6,500	$7,450	
9	Supplies	$8,000	$8,750	$8,200	
10					
11	**Total**	$86,100	$84,750	=SUM(D5:D10)	
12					

2. Press the F9 (Calc) key and *Excel* replaces the formula with its calculated value:

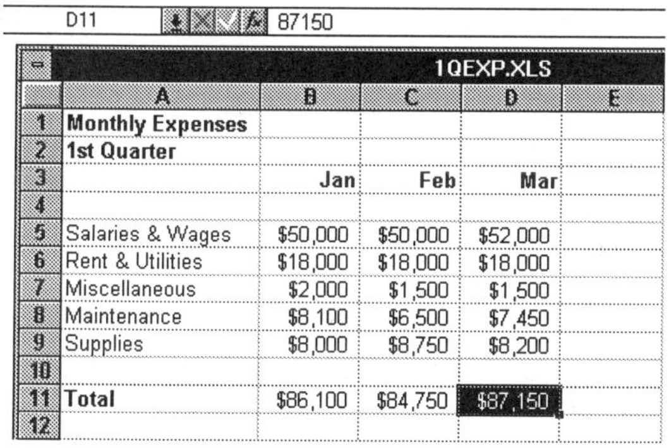

D11 87150

1QEXP.XLS

	A	B	C	D	E
1	**Monthly Expenses**				
2	**1st Quarter**				
3		**Jan**	**Feb**	**Mar**	
4					
5	Salaries & Wages	$50,000	$50,000	$52,000	
6	Rent & Utilities	$18,000	$18,000	$18,000	
7	Miscellaneous	$2,000	$1,500	$1,500	
8	Maintenance	$8,100	$6,500	$7,450	
9	Supplies	$8,000	$8,750	$8,200	
10					
11	**Total**	$86,100	$84,750	$87,150	
12					

3. Press the Enter key or click on the Enter box to accept the value.

Use the Paste Special command

1. Highlight the range that contains the formulas and copy it to the clipboard.
2. Select the Paste Special command from the Edit or shortcut menu and this dialog box appears:

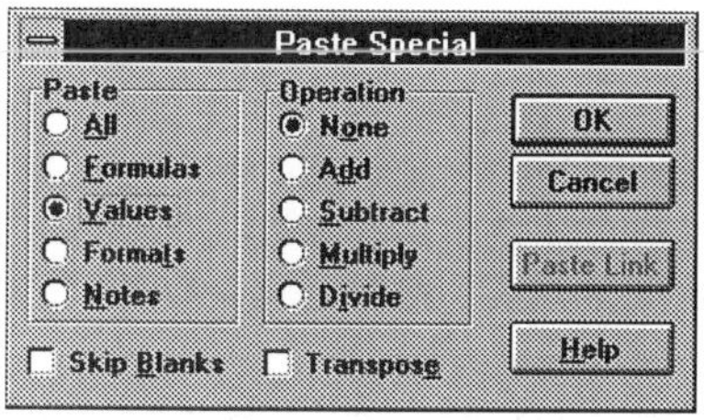

3. Select the Values option in the Paste group.
4. Click on the OK button and *Excel* replaces the formulas with their calculated values.

Figure 7-16 Two ways to change formulas to values

Procedure

1. Highlight the range of cells you want to transpose and copy it to the clipboard:

	A	B	C	D	E
1	Monthly Expenses				
2	1st Quarter				
3		Jan	Feb	Mar	
4					
5					
6					
7					

2. Select the cell in the upper left corner of the range where you want the transposed data to appear:

	A	B	C	D	E
1	Monthly Expenses				
2	1st Quarter				
3		Jan	Feb	Mar	
4					
5					
6					
7					

3. Select the Paste Special command from the Edit menu or the shortcut menu and select the Transpose option from the command's dialog box.
5. Click on the OK button and *Excel* transposes the data:

	A	B	C	D	E
1	Monthly Expenses				
2	1st Quarter				
3		Jan	Feb	Mar	
4	Jan				
5	Feb				
6	Mar				
7					

Note

You cannot overlap the original range with the new range.

Figure 7-17 How to transpose a range of cells

How to zoom in or out of the display Figure 7-19 shows you how to use the Zoom command in the View menu to increase or decrease the size of the display. As you can see, this dialog box lets you select from several magnification settings. In addition, you can choose the Fit Selection option to adjust the magnification so the current selection fills the display. Or, you can specify your own setting in the Custom text box. You can also select a magnification setting from the drop-down list box in the Standard toolbar.

The View menu

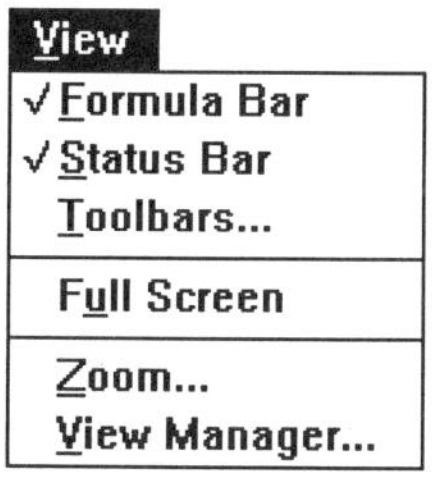

Command	Function
Formula bar	Displays or hides the formula bar.
Status bar	Displays or hides the status bar.
Toolbars	Displays or hides any or all of the toolbars that are available with *Excel*; customizes toolbars.
Full Screen	Toggles between the default display and full-screen display where *Excel*'s application window is maximized and the title bar, the Standard and Formatting toolbars, the formula bar, and the status bar are hidden.
Zoom	Changes the magnification of the current window.
View Manager	Creates, applies, and deletes views (sets of display options) for the current worksheet.

The Window menu

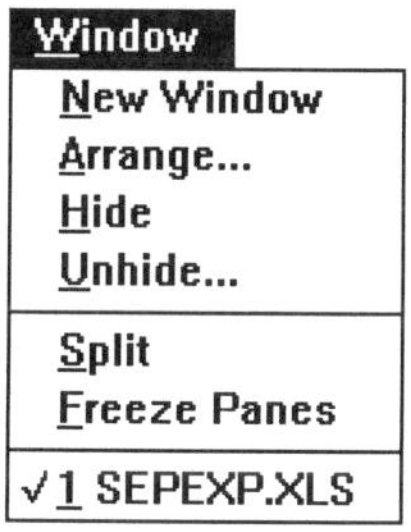

Command	Function
Split	Splits the window into two or four panes so you can work on more than one area of a worksheet at the same time.
Freeze Panes	Freezes one or more rows or columns so they're not scrolled off the screen.

Figure 7-18 The View and Window menu commands for changing the display

How to display a worksheet in full-screen view Figure 7-20 shows you how to use the Full Screen command in the View menu to display a worksheet in full-screen view. As you can see, the toolbars, the formula bar, the status bar, and the title bar are all hidden in this view so you can see as much of the worksheet as possible. In this view, *Excel* displays the floating Full Screen toolbar that contains a single button. If you click on this button, *Excel* returns the display to normal view. You can also return to normal view by selecting the Full Screen command again.

Access

Select the Zoom command from the View menu.

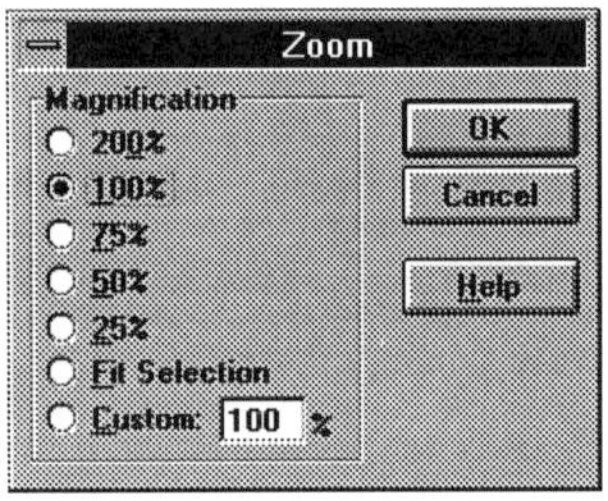

Operation

- Select a percent option to display the worksheet at the indicated magnification.
- Select the Fit Selection option to adjust the magnification so that the current selection fills the display.
- Use the Custom option to specify a custom magnification setting.

Figure 7-19 How to zoom in or out of the display

How to freeze one or more rows or columns When the column and row headings are scrolled off the screen, it can be difficult to remember what data each row or column contains. In that case, you can use the Freeze Panes command in the Window menu to "freeze" one or more columns and rows on the screen so you can always see them. The use of this command is summarized in figure 7-21. After you issue this command to freeze rows or columns, it's replaced in the Window menu by the Unfreeze Panes command. Then, you issue this command to remove the panes and return the display to normal.

How to view more than one area of a worksheet at the same time Occasionally, you may find yourself scrolling back and forth between two areas of a worksheet. For example, you may need to compare the values in two columns of a worksheet that you can't display on the screen at the same time. To eliminate this problem, you can use the horizontal or vertical split boxes or the Split command in the Window menu to divide the document window into panes. Then, you can see two areas of the worksheet at once.

Figure 7-22 shows you how to use the vertical and horizontal split boxes. By default, the *vertical split box* is located in the lower right corner

Access

Select the Full Screen command from the View menu.

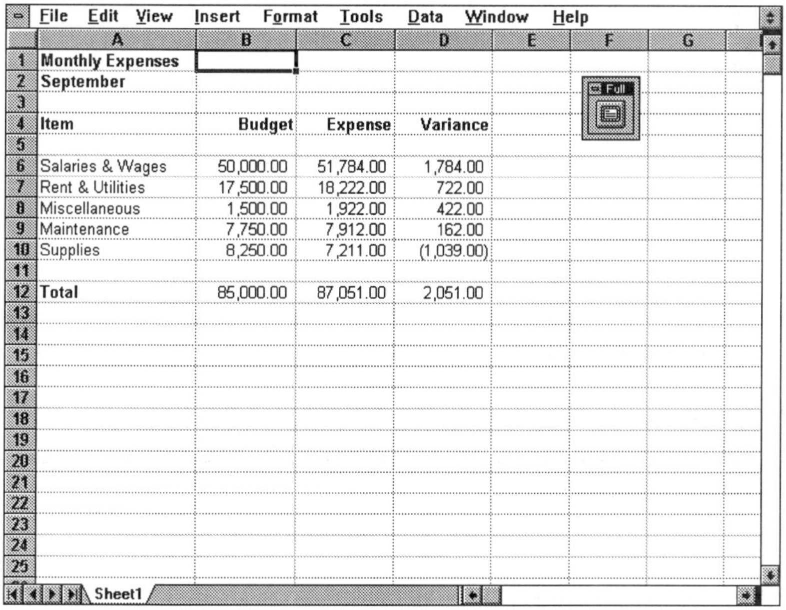

Note

To switch back to the normal view, select the Full Screen command again or click on the button in the floating Full Screen toolbar.

Figure 7-20 How to display a worksheet in full-screen view

of the document window, and the *horizontal split box* is located in the upper right corner of the document window. To use one of the split boxes, drag it to the location where you want to split the window. Or, double-click on the split box to split the window to the left or above the current cell. To split the window into four panes, use both the vertical and horizontal split boxes.

When you split the window using the vertical split box, vertical scrolling in the two panes is automatically synchronized. Similarly, when you split the window using the horizontal split box, horizontal scrolling is synchronized. And, if the screen is split both vertically and horizontally, scrolling is synchronized in two of the panes at any given time depending on which scroll bar you use.

How to freeze columns

1. Place the cell pointer in row 1 of the column to the right of the last column you want to freeze:

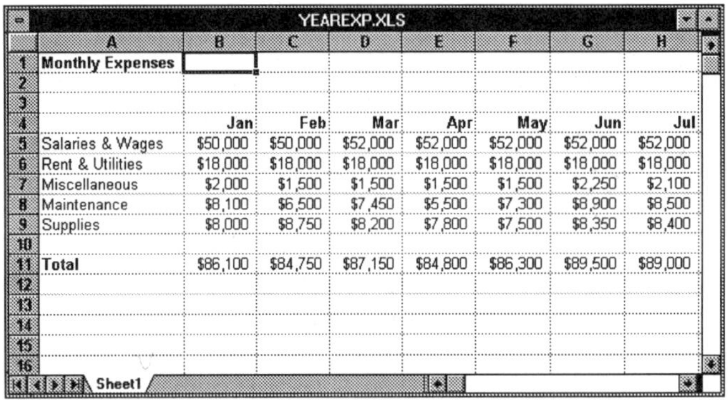

YEAREXP.XLS

	A	B	C	D	E	F	G	H
1	Monthly Expenses							
2								
3								
4		Jan	Feb	Mar	Apr	May	Jun	Jul
5	Salaries & Wages	$50,000	$50,000	$52,000	$52,000	$52,000	$52,000	$52,000
6	Rent & Utilities	$18,000	$18,000	$18,000	$18,000	$18,000	$18,000	$18,000
7	Miscellaneous	$2,000	$1,500	$1,500	$1,500	$1,500	$2,250	$2,100
8	Maintenance	$8,100	$6,500	$7,450	$5,500	$7,300	$8,900	$8,500
9	Supplies	$8,000	$8,750	$8,200	$7,800	$7,500	$8,350	$8,400
10								
11	Total	$86,100	$84,750	$87,150	$84,800	$86,300	$89,500	$89,000

Sheet1

2. Select the Freeze Panes command from the Window menu. Now, the frozen columns are always displayed when you scroll:

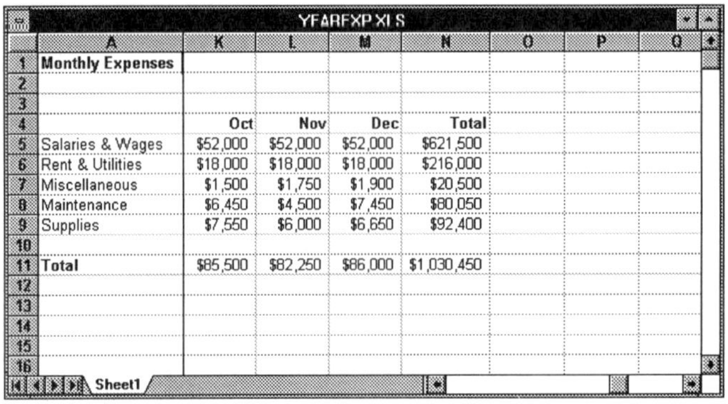

YEAREXP.XLS

	A	K	L	M	N	O	P	Q
1	Monthly Expenses							
2								
3								
4		Oct	Nov	Dec	Total			
5	Salaries & Wages	$52,000	$52,000	$52,000	$621,500			
6	Rent & Utilities	$18,000	$18,000	$18,000	$216,000			
7	Miscellaneous	$1,500	$1,750	$1,900	$20,500			
8	Maintenance	$6,450	$4,500	$7,450	$80,050			
9	Supplies	$7,550	$6,000	$6,650	$92,400			
10								
11	Total	$85,500	$82,250	$86,000	$1,030,450			

Sheet1

How to freeze rows

1. Place the cell pointer in column A of the row below the one you want to freeze.
2. Select the Freeze Panes command from the Window menu.

How to freeze both columns and rows

1. Place the cell pointer in the column to the right of the last column you want to freeze and in the row below the last one you want to freeze.
2. Select the Freeze Panes command from the Window menu.

How to unfreeze columns and rows

Select the Unfreeze Panes command from the Window menu. This command replaces the Freeze Panes command when columns or rows are frozen.

Figure 7-21 How to freeze or unfreeze columns and rows

Two ways to split a window vertically

- Click and drag the vertical split box to where you want to split the window:

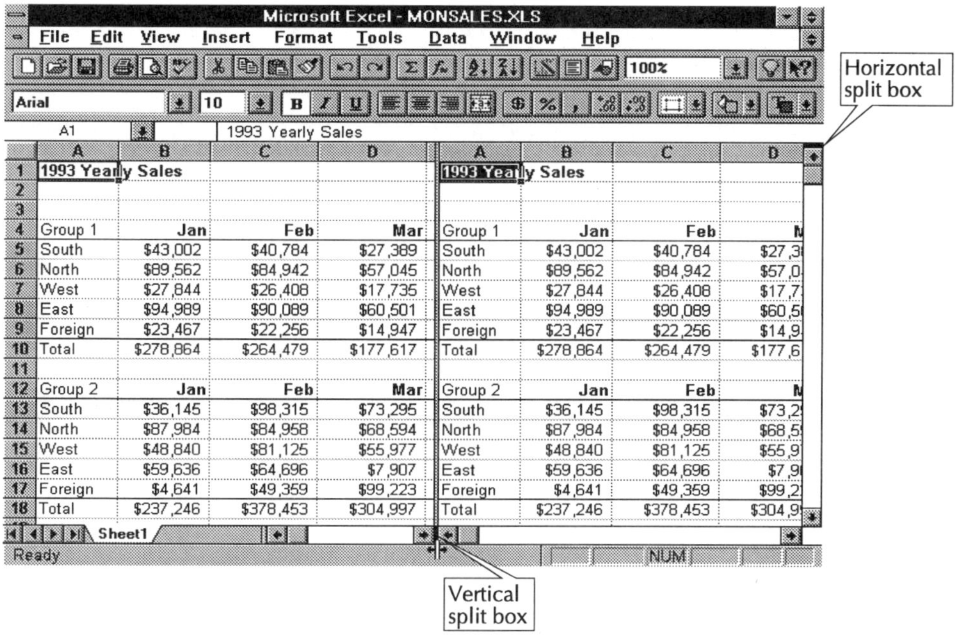

- Double-click on the vertical split box to split the window to the left of the current cell.

Two ways to split a window horizontally

- Drag the horizontal split box to where you want to split the window horizontally.
- Double-click on the horizontal split box to split the window above the current cell.

Two ways to unsplit a window

- Drag a split box back to its original position.
- Double-click on the split box.

Note

You can divide a window into four panes by splitting it both vertically and horizontally.

Figure 7-22 How to use the vertical and horizontal split boxes to split or unsplit the document window

Figure 7-23 presents the procedure for using the Split command. As you can see, where you place the cell pointer determines where *Excel* splits the window. Note that if you place the cell pointer anywhere except in column A or row 1, *Excel* splits the window into four panes.

How to split the window vertically

1. Place the cell pointer in row 1 of the column to the right of where you want to split the window.
2. Select the Split command from the Window menu, and *Excel* splits the window vertically.

How to split the window horizontally

1. Place the cell pointer in column A of the row below where you want to split the window.
2. Select the Split command from the Window menu, and *Excel* splits the window horizontally.

How to split the window into four panes

1. Place the cell pointer in the column to the right of where you want to split the window and in the row below where you want to split the window.
2. Select the Split command from the Window menu, and *Excel* splits the window into four panes.

How to unsplit a window

Select the Remove Split command from the Window menu. This command replaces the Split command when the window is split.

Figure 7-23 How to use menu commands to split or unsplit the document window

The easiest way to return a document window to a single pane is to drag the vertical or horizontal split box back to its original location. This works whether you used a split box or the Split command to split the window. You can also return the window to a single pane by selecting the Remove Split command from the Window menu. This command replaces the Split command after you split the window.

How to save and retrieve worksheet view settings Figure 7-24 describes how to use the View Manager command in the View menu to save, retrieve, and delete groups of view settings, called *views*. When you create a new view, all you have to do is give it a name. Then, *Excel* records the zoom percentage, frozen panes, the window's size and position, the print area, and the current active cell. By default, current print settings and hidden rows and columns are also recorded with the view, but you can override those defaults if you want to.

How to work with range names

Because *range names* are easier to remember than actual cell references, you can use them with the Go To command or the Name box to move easily to an area of a worksheet. Range names can also make it easier to execute *Excel* commands and to create formulas.

Access

Select the View Manager command from the View menu and this dialog box appears:

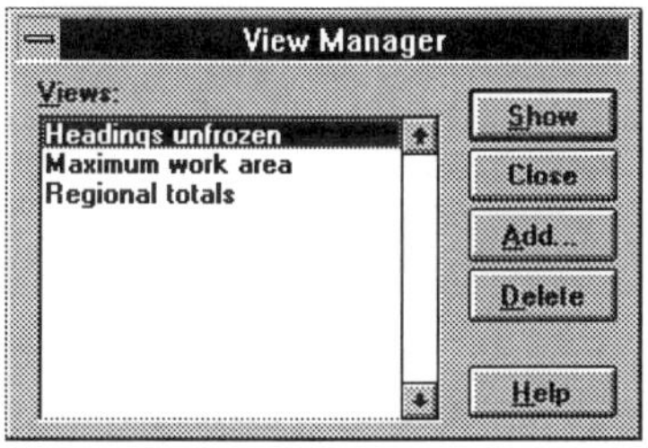

Operation

- To create a new view that uses the worksheet's current view options, click on the Add button and supply a name for the new view in the dialog box that appears.
- To retrieve a different view and apply its options to the worksheet, select the view from the Views list box and click on the Show button.
- To delete a view, select it from the Views list box and click on the Delete button.

Notes

- The first time you access the View Manager for a worksheet, the Views list is empty.
- Views you create with the View Manager are associated with the current worksheet. You can create different views for different worksheets in the same workbook.
- If you didn't perform a complete installation of *Excel*, the View Manager command may not be present in the View menu. That's because the View Manager is an add-in program that doesn't have to be installed. See chapter 24 to find out how to install add-in programs.

Figure 7-24 How to use the View Manager to create, retrieve, and delete views

How to create and delete range names Figure 7-25 presents the procedure for using the Name Define command in the Insert menu to name a range of cells. The name you assign to a range can be up to 255 characters long and can't contain any spaces. Although you can include numbers and special characters in range names, you shouldn't begin a range name with a number or a special character other than the underscore or the backslash. And you shouldn't create range names that look like cell references because *Excel* won't be able to distinguish them from actual cell references. Finally, you can't include hyphens in range names.

You can also delete range names from the Define Name dialog box shown in figure 7-25. To do that, highlight the ranges you want to delete and click on the Delete button.

Procedure

1. Highlight the range of cells you want to name:

	A	B	C	D	E	F	G	H
1	**Monthly Expenses**							
2								
3								
4		**Jan**	**Feb**	**Mar**	**Apr**	**May**	**Jun**	**Jul**
5	Salaries & Wages	$50,000	$50,000	$52,000	$52,000	$52,000	$52,000	$52,000
6	Rent & Utilities	$18,000	$18,000	$18,000	$18,000	$18,000	$18,000	$18,000
7	Miscellaneous	$2,000	$1,500	$1,500	$1,500	$1,500	$2,250	$2,100
8	Maintenance	$8,100	$6,500	$7,450	$5,500	$7,300	$8,900	$8,500
9	Supplies	$8,000	$8,750	$8,200	$7,800	$7,500	$8,350	$8,400
10								
11	**Total**	$86,100	$84,750	$87,150	$84,800	$86,300	$89,500	$89,000
12								

2. Select the Name Define command from the Insert menu and this dialog box appears:

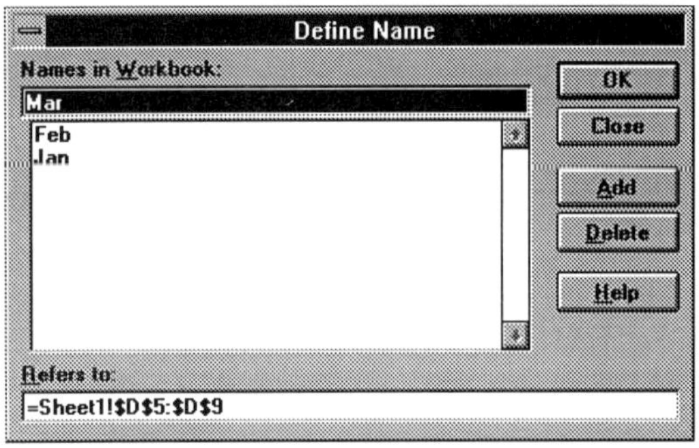

3. Enter the name of the range in the Names In Workbook text box.
4. Click on the OK button to name the range.

Rules for creating range names

- The name can consist of 255 characters or less.
- Don't use a name that's a valid cell reference.
- The first character must be a letter, an underscore character, or a backslash.
- Don't include spaces or hyphens in the name.

Notes

- If you want to add two or more range names without closing the dialog box, click on the Add button instead of the OK button after you enter the first range name. Then, the range name you just created appears in the Names In Workbook list box. To name another range, enter its name in the Names In Workbook text box and the range it occupies in the Refers To text box. Then, click on the Add button if you want to add another range name, or click on the OK button to complete the command and return to the worksheet.
- You can also name a 3-D range of cells. For more information on 3-D ranges, see chapter 9.
- To delete a named range, highlight the range name in the Names In Workbook list box and click on the Delete button.

Figure 7-25 How to name a range of cells

1. Highlight the range of cells you want to name, including the cells you want to assign as labels:

	A	B	C	D	E	F	G	H
1	**Monthly Expenses**							
2								
3								
4		Jan	Feb	Mar	Apr	May	Jun	Jul
5	Salaries & Wages	$50,000	$50,000	$52,000	$52,000	$52,000	$52,000	$52,000
6	Rent & Utilities	$18,000	$18,000	$18,000	$18,000	$18,000	$18,000	$18,000
7	Miscellaneous	$2,000	$1,500	$1,500	$1,500	$1,500	$2,250	$2,100
8	Maintenance	$8,100	$6,500	$7,450	$5,500	$7,300	$8,900	$8,500
9	Supplies	$8,000	$8,750	$8,200	$7,800	$7,500	$8,350	$8,400
10								
11	**Total**	$86,100	$84,750	$87,150	$84,800	$86,300	$89,500	$89,000
12								

2. Select the Name Create command from the Insert menu and this dialog box appears:

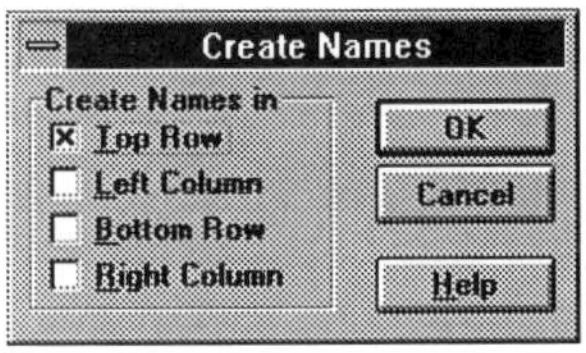

3. Select an option to tell *Excel* where the cells you want to use as labels are located.
4. Click on the OK button to name the ranges.

Figure 7-26 How to assign labels as range names for a range of cells

Figure 7-26 shows you how to use the Name Create command in the Insert menu to assign labels in the worksheet as the range names for adjacent cells. Notice that the labels you want to use to name the ranges must be in the top or bottom row or the left or right column of the highlighted range. Then, when you issue the Name Create command, the labels are assigned as range names to the cells in the adjacent rows or columns.

How to move to a named range If you use named ranges in a worksheet, you can use the Name box or the Go To command to move the cell pointer to a range as described in figure 7-27. To use the Name box, simply click on its drop-down arrow and select the named range from the list that's displayed. To use the Go To command, select it from the Edit menu or press F5. Then, select the named range from the list that's displayed. In either case, *Excel* moves to and selects the named range.

How to enter a range name into a formula or a dialog box Once you create a range name, you can use it in formulas and commands that operate on cells in that range. One way to enter a range name into a formula or

Use the Name box

1. Click the Name box's drop-down arrow to display a list of the range names in the current workbook:

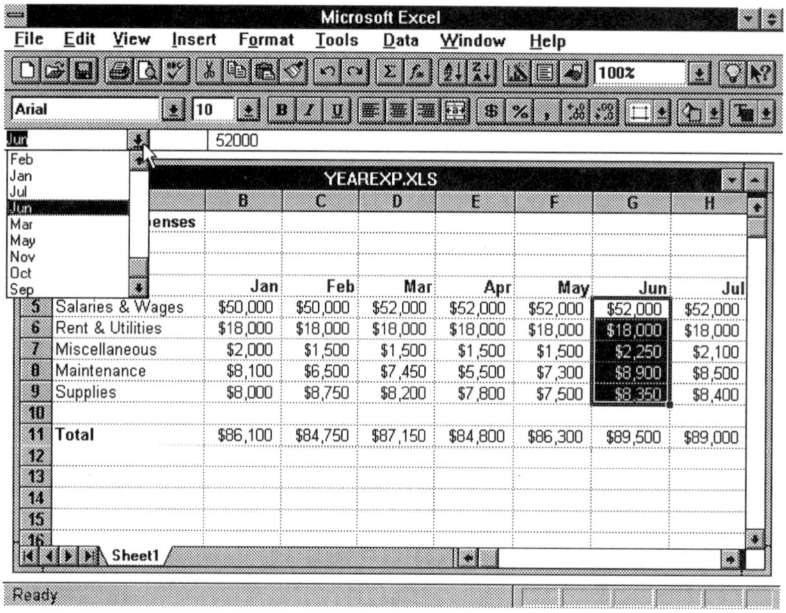

2. Select the range name you want to move the cell pointer to and *Excel* selects the entire named range.

Use the Go To command

Select the Go To command from the Edit menu, or use the keyboard shortcut (F5) to start the command. Then, select the range name from the list that's displayed.

Figure 7-27 Two ways to move the cell pointer to a named range

dialog box is to type it. However, you can also use the methods shown in figures 7-28 and 7-29. The first method uses the Name box to display a list of the available range names. The second method uses the Name Paste command in the Insert menu to display a dialog box that shows all the range names in the current workbook.

How to replace references with range names In addition to entering range names into formulas, you can replace cell references to named ranges in existing formulas. To do that, you use the Name Apply command in the

1. Enter the formula up to the point where you need to refer to the named range.
2. Click on the Name box's drop-down arrow, and select the range name from the list that's displayed:

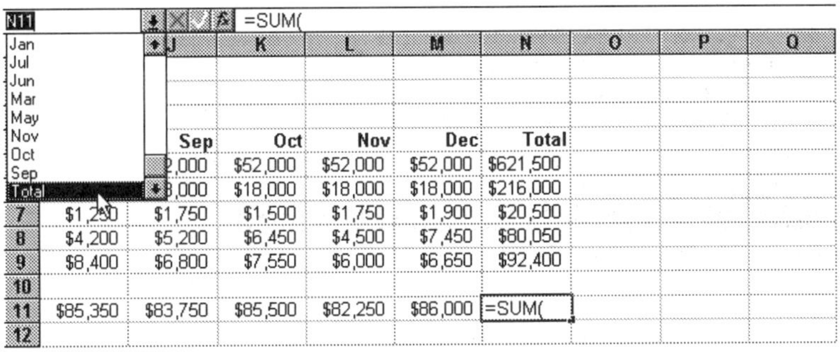

3. The range name is entered into the formula:

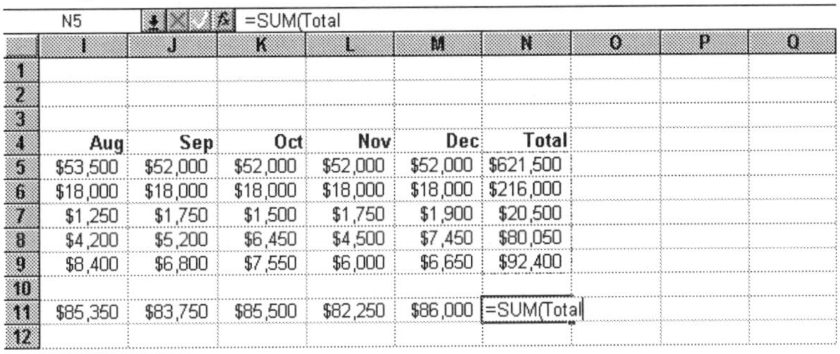

Figure 7-28 How to use the Name box to enter a range name into a formula

1. Enter the formula up to the point where you need to refer to the named range.
2. Press the F3 (Name) key or select the Name Paste command from the Insert menu, and this dialog box appears:

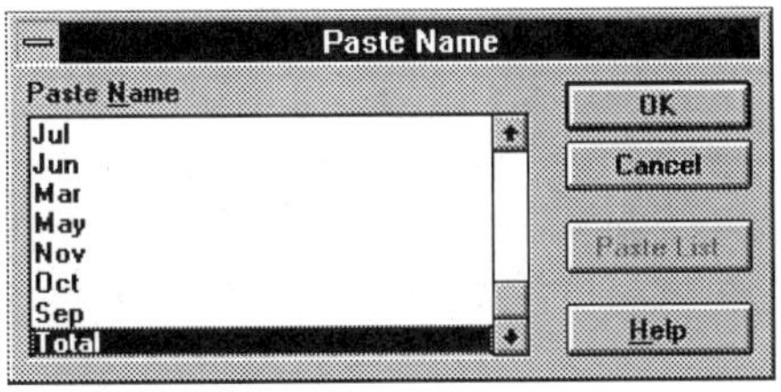

3. Select the range name from the Paste Name list box.
4. Click on the OK button and *Excel* enters the name into the formula.

Figure 7-29 How to use the Name Paste command to enter a range name into a formula

Insert menu as illustrated in figure 7-30. Note that although you can apply selected range names to a selected area of a worksheet, the default is to apply all the defined range names to the entire worksheet.

How to search for and replace data

Figure 7-31 presents the procedures for using the Find and Replace commands in the Edit menu. For either command, you begin by specifying the text you want to find. For a Replace operation, you also specify the replacement text. Then, you can select several options that determine how *Excel* performs the search.

If *Excel* finds an occurrence of the text you specified, it displays the Find or Replace dialog box again. For a find operation, you can then choose to find the next occurrence, end the operation, or begin a replace operation. For a replace operation, you can find the next occurrence, replace the text, replace all occurrences of the text, or end the operation.

Since a replace operation can drastically change a document in just a few seconds, there are two precautions you may want to take. First, you can save your workbook before you perform a replace operation. Then, if the replace doesn't work quite right, you can close the workbook without saving the changes. Second, you can replace the current occurrence the first couple of times instead of replacing all occurrences right away. That way, you can make sure the operation is working the way you want it to before you change the entire worksheet.

How to sort the data in a worksheet

Sorting the data in a worksheet can sometimes make it easier to use and interpret. Because the data you sort will often be organized in a list, chapter 15 covers sorting in detail. But you may occasionally want to sort data that isn't in list form. That's what you'll learn to do in this chapter.

Figure 7-32 summarizes the procedure for sorting the data in a range of cells. When you sort a range of cells, you begin by selecting the range to be sorted. This range is called the *data range*. Then, you start the Sort command and identify the *primary sort key*. The primary sort key specifies the column you want to sort the data by. If you want to sort on two or more columns, you identify the *secondary sort keys*. For each key you specify, you also select the Ascending or Descending option to indicate the sort order.

Procedure

1. If you want to limit the area that the range names are applied to, highlight a range. The default is to apply the selected range names to the entire worksheet.
2. Select the Name Apply command from the Insert menu, and this dialog box appears:

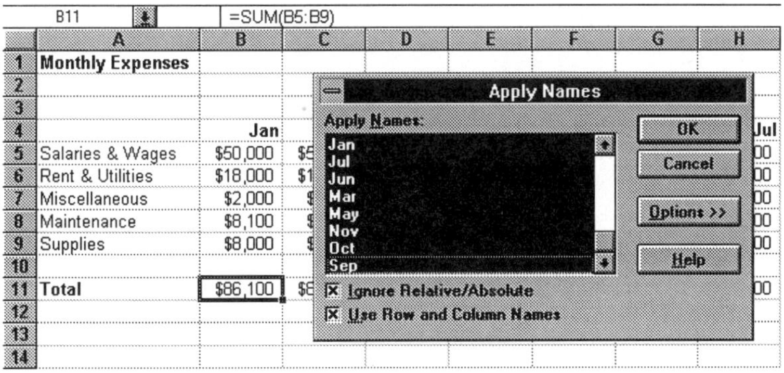

3. Deselect any range names in the Apply Names list box that you don't want to use in place of cell references. By default, all the range names are selected.
4. Click on the OK button and *Excel* replaces all cell references to the selected ranges with their range names:

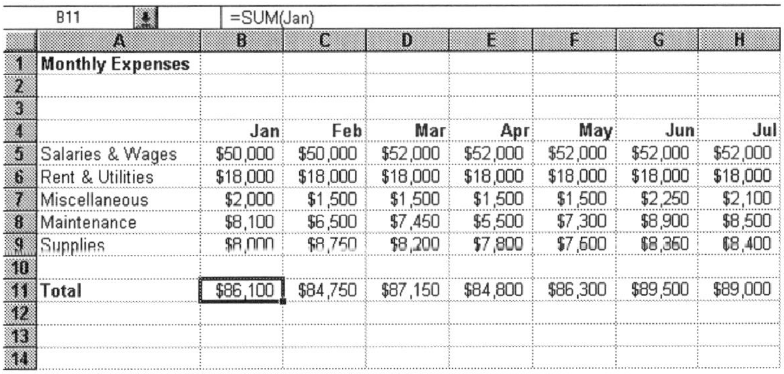
B11 =SUM(Jan)

	A	B	C	D	E	F	G	H
1	Monthly Expenses							
2								
3								
4		Jan	Feb	Mar	Apr	May	Jun	Jul
5	Salaries & Wages	$50,000	$50,000	$52,000	$52,000	$52,000	$52,000	$52,000
6	Rent & Utilities	$18,000	$18,000	$18,000	$18,000	$18,000	$18,000	$18,000
7	Miscellaneous	$2,000	$1,500	$1,500	$1,500	$1,500	$2,250	$2,100
8	Maintenance	$8,100	$6,500	$7,450	$5,500	$7,300	$8,900	$8,500
9	Supplies	$8,000	$8,750	$8,200	$7,800	$7,600	$8,360	$8,400
10								
11	Total	$86,100	$84,750	$87,150	$84,800	$86,300	$89,500	$89,000
12								
13								
14								

Notes

- If the Ignore Relative/Absolute option is selected, *Excel* replaces references with range names regardless of the reference type.
- If the Use Row And Column Names option is selected, *Excel* replaces references with the range names for the column or row that contains the cells in the range if a range name can't be found for the exact range.
- The Options button expands the Apply Names dialog box and displays additional options for applying range names.

Figure 7-30 How to replace references with range names

How to perform a find operation

1. If you want to search a selected range, highlight the range. Otherwise, *Excel* will search the current worksheet.
2. Select the Find command from the Edit menu and this dialog box appears:

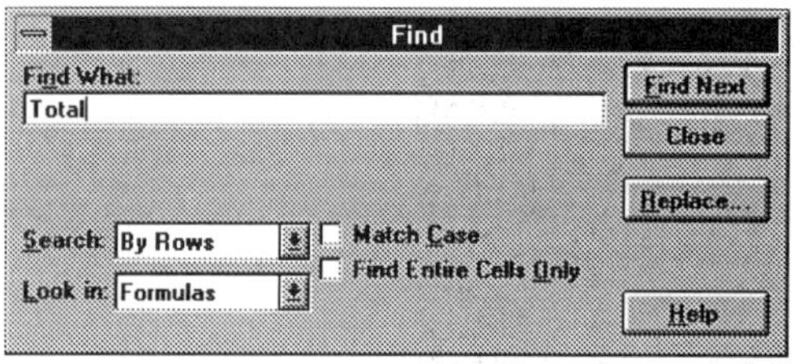

3. Enter the text you want to search for in the Find What text box.
4. Specify how you want *Excel* to search:
   - Select an option from the Search drop-down list box. The options are By Rows and By Columns.
   - Select an option from the Look In drop-down list box. The options are Formulas, Values, and Notes.
   - To search for text that matches the case of the text in the Find What text box, select the Match Case option.
   - To look for cells that contain exactly what's specified in the Find What text box with no additional characters, select the Find Entire Cells Only option.
5. Click on the OK button and *Excel* locates the first occurrence of the text.
6. To find the next occurrence, click on the Find Next button. To start a replace operation, click on the Replace button. To end the Find operation, click on the Close button.

How to perform a replace operation

1. If you want to search a selected range, highlight the range. Otherwise, *Excel* will search the current worksheet.
2. Select the Replace command from the Edit menu and this dialog box appears:

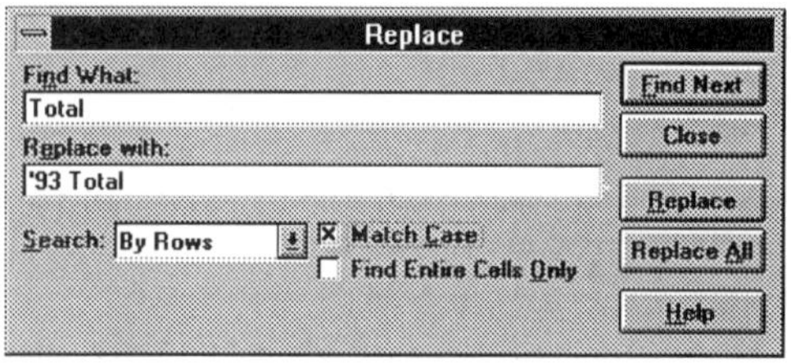

3. Enter the text you want to search for in the Find What text box, and enter the replacement text in the Replace With text box.
4. Specify the Search, Match Case, and Find Entire Cells Only options as appropriate.
5. To replace the text one occurrence at a time, click on the Find Next button. Then, when *Excel* finds the next occurrence of the text, click on the Replace button. Or, to replace all occurrences of the text, click on the Replace All button.

Figure 7-31 How to search for and replace data

Procedure

1. Select the rows you want to sort.
2. Select the Sort command from the Data menu and this dialog box appears:

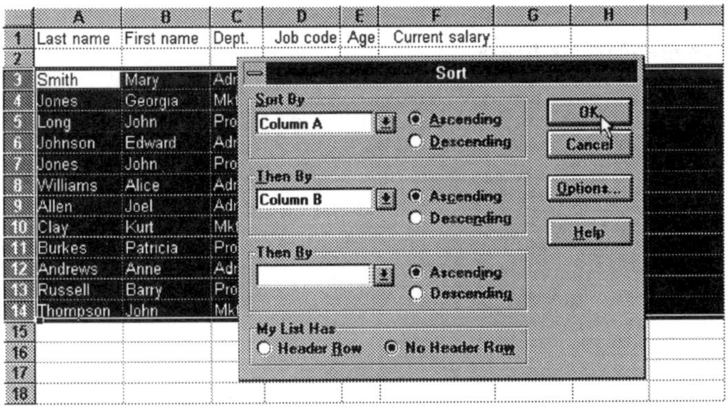

3. Select the column you want to use as the primary key from the drop-down list box in the Sort By group, and select the Ascending or Descending option from that group.
4. If you want to sort by more than one key, select the column you want to use for each secondary key from the drop-down list boxes in the Then By groups, and select the Ascending or Descending option from that group.
5. Click on the OK button and *Excel* sorts the selected rows:

	A	B	C	D	E	F	G	H	I
1	Last name	First name	Dept.	Job code	Age	Current salary			
2									
3	Allen	Joel	Admin	2	25	$30,000			
4	Andrews	Anne	Admin	3	30	$34,000			
5	Burkes	Patricia	Prod	1	52	$28,500			
6	Clay	Kurt	Mktg	2	43	$41,250			
7	Johnson	Edward	Admin	2	30	$33,250			
8	Jones	Georgia	Mktg	3	43	$47,500			
9	Jones	John	Prod	2	33	$31,400			
10	Long	John	Prod	3	52	$39,900			
11	Russell	Barry	Prod	2	33	$31,500			
12	Smith	Mary	Admin	1	23	$24,600			
13	Thompson	John	Mktg	1	50	$26,500			
14	Williams	Alice	Admin	1	50	$28,900			
15									

Notes

- The options in the My List Has group indicate whether or not the data is organized in list form. If it is, the data range should include a header row. See chapter 15 for more information on sorting lists.
- To sort data only in selected columns, select a range that includes only those columns before you issue the Sort command. Then, the order of the data in other columns in the affected rows doesn't change.
- The Options button displays another dialog box that lets you specify additional options for the sort operation. You usually don't need to use these options.

Figure 7-32 How to sort the data in a range of cells

How to group and outline the data in a worksheet

If a worksheet is so large that it's awkward to use, you may find *Excel*'s outlining feature helpful. This is especially true if the worksheet consists of detail data and summary data. After you outline a worksheet with this kind of structure, you can hide as much detail as you like so you can focus on the summary data.

How you outline a worksheet depends on how it's organized. If your worksheet contains subtotals that define groups of data, you can use the automatic outlining feature. I'll show you how to use this feature in a moment. If your worksheet doesn't contain subtotals, you have to define the groups you want to include in the outline manually. Since this isn't a common situation, I won't describe that technique in this book. Finally, if the worksheet is organized in list form, you can generate subtotals and an outline automatically. I'll show you how to do that in chapter 15.

Figure 7-33 presents the procedure for using the Auto Outline command to create an outline. When you use this command, *Excel* analyzes the cell references in the formulas in the worksheet to determine how to group and outline the data. As you can see in the figure, *Excel* can outline data both by rows and by columns.

When a worksheet is in outline form, controls appear to the left of the worksheet if there are groups of rows in the outline and above the worksheet if there are groups of columns. You can use these controls or the related menu commands to hide and show information in an outline as described in figure 7-34. This figure also describes how to remove an outline from a worksheet.

How to check the spelling in a worksheet

Figure 7-35 shows you how to use the spell checking feature to check for misspelled words and duplicate words in areas that contain text, including the current worksheet, charts, and text blocks. When you run the spell checker, the default is to check the current worksheet. But if you want to check only a specific range, you can highlight that range before you start the spell checker.

Once you start the spell checker, *Excel* begins searching for errors. Whenever it finds a word it can't identify, it displays a dialog box that lets you decide how to handle the error. There, you can replace the unknown word with the one that *Excel* suggests, or you can select a replacement from the list of alternatives. If the list doesn't include the correct word, you can type it in the Change To text box. Then, you can replace the current occur-

Procedure

1. If you want to limit the area that's outlined, highlight a range. The default is to outline the entire worksheet.
2. Select the Auto Outline command from the Group and Outline submenu of the Data menu, and *Excel* outlines the data:

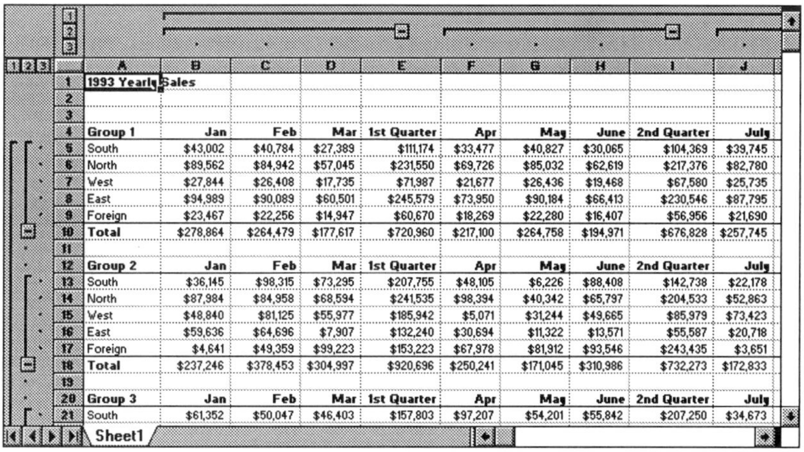

	A	B	C	D	E	F	G	H	I	J
1	1993 Yearly Sales									
2										
3										
4	Group 1	Jan	Feb	Mar	1st Quarter	Apr	May	June	2nd Quarter	July
5	South	$43,002	$40,784	$27,389	$111,174	$33,477	$40,827	$30,065	$104,369	$39,745
6	North	$89,562	$84,942	$57,045	$231,550	$69,726	$85,032	$62,619	$217,376	$82,780
7	West	$27,844	$26,408	$17,735	$71,987	$21,677	$26,436	$19,468	$67,580	$25,735
8	East	$94,989	$90,089	$60,501	$245,579	$73,950	$90,184	$66,413	$230,546	$87,795
9	Foreign	$23,467	$22,256	$14,947	$60,670	$18,269	$22,280	$16,407	$56,956	$21,690
10	Total	$278,864	$264,479	$177,617	$720,960	$217,100	$264,758	$194,971	$676,828	$257,745
11										
12	Group 2	Jan	Feb	Mar	1st Quarter	Apr	May	June	2nd Quarter	July
13	South	$36,145	$98,315	$73,295	$207,755	$48,105	$6,226	$88,408	$142,738	$22,178
14	North	$87,984	$84,958	$68,594	$241,535	$98,394	$40,342	$65,797	$204,533	$52,863
15	West	$48,840	$81,125	$55,977	$185,942	$5,071	$31,244	$49,665	$85,979	$73,423
16	East	$59,636	$64,696	$7,907	$132,240	$30,694	$11,322	$13,571	$55,587	$20,718
17	Foreign	$4,641	$49,359	$99,223	$153,223	$67,978	$81,912	$93,546	$243,435	$3,651
18	Total	$237,246	$378,453	$304,997	$920,696	$250,241	$171,045	$310,986	$732,273	$172,833
19										
20	Group 3	Jan	Feb	Mar	1st Quarter	Apr	May	June	2nd Quarter	July
21	South	$61,352	$50,047	$46,403	$157,803	$97,207	$54,201	$55,842	$207,250	$34,673

Notes

- When *Excel* creates an outline, it analyzes the cell references in formulas and constructs the outline accordingly. When the cell references point up or down, *Excel* groups rows. When the cell references point left or right, *Excel* groups columns. As a result, both columns and rows can be outlined in a worksheet as in the example above.
- If your worksheet doesn't already include the subtotals needed to use the Auto Outline command, you can use the Group command in the Group and Outline submenu of the Data menu to create groups manually. Or, if the data is in list form, you can use the Subtotals command in the Data menu to add subtotals to the list and outline the data.

Figure 7-33 How to use the Auto Outline command to create an outline

rence or you can replace all remaining occurrences; you can ignore the current occurrence or all remaining occurrences; or you can add the word to the user dictionary.

Notice that the Spelling dialog box contains three options. The Add Words To option specifies the dictionary words are added to when you click on the Add button. The Always Suggest option determines whether or not replacement words are listed in the Suggestions list box. And the Ignore UPPERCASE option determines whether or not *Excel* checks the spelling of words that are in uppercase. Normally, these options are set the way you want them, but you can change them at any time.

How to remove an outline

Select the Clear Outline command from the Group and Outline submenu of the Data menu.

Three ways to hide information in an outline

- Click on an outline symbol that shows a number to hide all of the detail information in the outline below that level.
- Click on an outline symbol that shows a minus sign to hide all of the detail information subordinate to the associated outline item.
- Select a cell in a summary row or column for the outline level you want to hide, then select the Hide Detail command from the Data menu.

Three ways to show information in an outline

- Click on an outline symbol that shows a plus sign to display all of the information at the level directly subordinate to the associated outline item.
- Click on an outline symbol that shows a number to show all of the information in the outline at that level and above.
- Select a cell in a summary row or column for the outline level you want to expand, then select the Show Detail command from the Data menu.

The worksheet outline in figure 7-33 with all detail information hidden

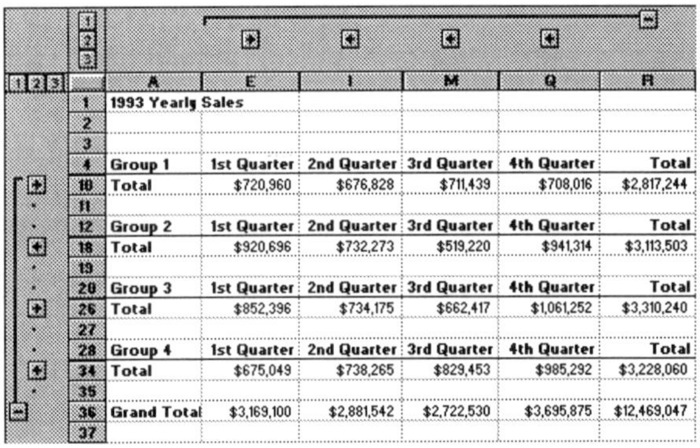

	A	E	I	M	Q	R
1	1993 Yearly Sales					
2						
3						
4	Group 1	1st Quarter	2nd Quarter	3rd Quarter	4th Quarter	Total
10	Total	$720,960	$676,828	$711,439	$708,016	$2,817,244
11						
12	Group 2	1st Quarter	2nd Quarter	3rd Quarter	4th Quarter	Total
18	Total	$920,696	$732,273	$519,220	$941,314	$3,113,503
19						
20	Group 3	1st Quarter	2nd Quarter	3rd Quarter	4th Quarter	Total
26	Total	$852,396	$734,175	$662,417	$1,061,252	$3,310,240
27						
28	Group 4	1st Quarter	2nd Quarter	3rd Quarter	4th Quarter	Total
34	Total	$675,049	$738,265	$829,453	$985,292	$3,228,060
35						
36	Grand Total	$3,169,100	$2,881,542	$2,722,530	$3,695,875	$12,469,047
37						

Figure 7-34 How to remove an outline or hide and show information in an outline

Perspective

As I said at the start of this chapter, *Excel* often offers two or more methods for accomplishing the same editing function. If you like to use a mouse, for example, you can perform all the editing functions without ever using the keyboard. But if you like to use the keyboard, you can perform all of the editing functions without using the mouse. Either way, you should be able to do your editing functions quicker and better than you've ever done them before.

1. If you want to limit the area that's checked for spelling errors, highlight a range. The default is to check the current worksheet.
2. Select the Spelling command from the Tools menu, press F7, or click on the Spelling button in the Standard toolbar: 
3. *Excel* checks the worksheet, and when it encounters an error, this dialog box appears:

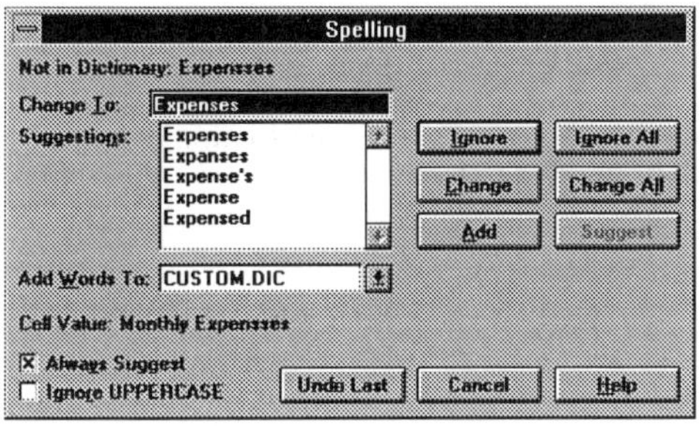

4. Perform one of the following actions:
   - To replace the word, select the new word from the Suggestions list box or type the word in the Change To text box and click on the Change button.
   - To replace all remaining occurrences of the word, select the new word from the Suggestions list box or type the word in the Change To text box and click on the Change All button.
   - To skip the word without changing it, click on the Ignore button.
   - To skip all remaining occurrences of the word, click on the Ignore All button.
   - To add the word to the dictionary in the Add Words To text box, click on the Add button.
   - To display replacement words in the Suggestions list box, click on the Suggest button. Then, click on one of the other buttons to replace or skip the word or add it to the dictionary.
5. When the spelling check is complete, this dialog box appears:

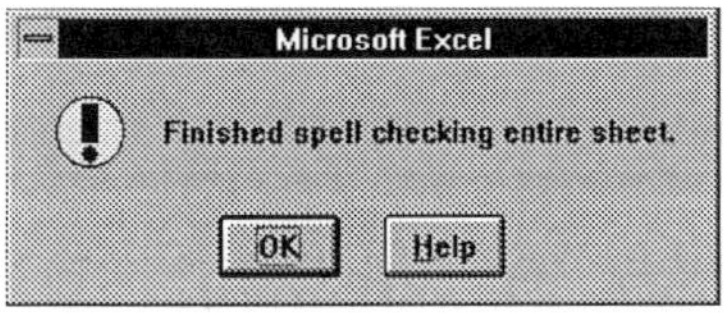

6. Click on the OK button to end the spelling check.

Notes

- The Add Words To option lets you add words to a user dictionary.
- The Always Suggest option determines whether or not replacement words are listed in the Suggestions list box when a word isn't found in the dictionary.
- The Ignore UPPERCASE option determines whether or not words that are in uppercase are checked.
- The Undo Last button reverses the last change and returns you to the word that was changed so you can make another selection.
- If *Excel* finds a duplicate word, the Change and Change All buttons change to Delete and Delete All.

Figure 7-35 How to check the spelling in a worksheet

Summary

- To repeat the last operation, use the Repeat command in the Edit menu, its keyboard shortcut (F4), or the Repeat button on the Standard toolbar.
- To undo the last operation, use the Undo command in the Edit menu, its keyboard shortcut (Ctrl+Z), or the Undo button on the Standard toolbar.
- To move the cell pointer in a worksheet, use the mouse, the keyboard, the Go To command, or the Name box.
- To change the width of one or more columns, use the mouse to drag the separator line to a new size, or use the Column Width command in the Format menu.
- To insert one or more columns or rows, use the Columns or Rows command in the Insert menu, the Insert command from the shortcut menu, or the keyboard shortcut (Ctrl++).
- To delete one or more columns or rows, use the Delete command in the Edit or shortcut menu, or use the keyboard shortcut (Ctrl+-).
- To hide or expose one or more columns or rows, use the mouse techniques, the Column Hide or Row Hide command in the Format menu, or the Hide command in the shortcut menu. To expose columns or rows, use the mouse technique, the Column Unhide or Row Unhide command in the Format menu, or the Unhide command in the shortcut menu.
- To move and copy data from one area of a worksheet to another, drag it with the mouse, use the Cut, Copy and Paste commands in the Edit menu or the shortcut menu, use the keyboard shortcuts (Ctrl+X, Ctrl+C, and Ctrl+V), or use the buttons on the Standard toolbar for these commands.
- To copy data to adjacent cells, use the AutoFill feature or the Fill Right, Fill Down, Fill Left, or Fill Up commands in the Edit menu.
- To insert a range of cells, use the Cells command in the Insert menu, the Insert command in the shortcut menu, or the keyboard shortcut (Ctrl++).
- To delete a range of cells, use the Delete command in the Edit or shortcut menu or the keyboard shortcut (Ctrl+-).
- To delete the contents of a cell, use the Delete key. To delete the contents of a cell, its format, its notes, or all of the above, select an appropriate command from the Clear submenu of the Edit menu.

- To replace the formula in a cell with its calculated value, press the F9 (Calc) key as you edit the cell. To change the formulas in a range of cells to values, copy the formulas to the clipboard, then issue the Paste Special command to copy the values back into the range.
- To copy a column of data to a row or vice versa, use the Transpose option of the Paste Special command.
- To display or hide the formula bar, the status bar, or the toolbars, use the Formula Bar, Status Bar, or Toolbars command in the View menu.
- To enlarge or reduce the size of the display, use the Zoom command in the View menu.
- To display a worksheet in full-screen view, use the Full Screen command in the View menu.
- To freeze one or more rows or columns on the screen so you can always see them, use the Freeze Panes command in the Window menu.
- To split the document window into two or four *panes,* use the *vertical* and *horizontal split boxes* or the Split command in the Window menu.
- To create or delete *range names*, use the Name Define command in the Insert menu. To assign labels as range names for a range of cells, use the Name Create command in the Insert menu.
- To move the cell pointer to a named range, use the Name box or the Go To command in the Edit menu.
- To enter a range name into a formula or a dialog box, type it, select the range name from the Name box drop-down list, or press the F3 (Name) key and select the range name from the list that's displayed.
- To replace cell references in existing formulas with range names, use the Name Apply command in the Insert menu.
- To search for or replace data in a worksheet, use the Find or Replace command in the Edit menu.
- To sort the rows in a range of cells, use the Sort command in the Data menu.

- To outline the data in a worksheet that contains subtotals, use the Auto Outline command from the Group and Outline submenu of the Data menu. To hide and reveal parts of the outline, use the Hide Detail and Show Detail commands in the Data menu or use the outline control buttons that appear with the worksheet. To remove an outline, use the Clear Outline command from the Group and Outline submenu of the Data menu.
- To check the spelling in a worksheet, use the Spelling command in the Tools menu, press F7, or click on the Spelling button in the Standard toolbar.

Chapter 8

How to format a worksheet to improve its appearance

In chapter 5, you learned some basic techniques for formatting the labels and values of a worksheet. In particular, you learned how to align labels and how to apply different number formats to values. And in chapter 7, you learned how to change the width of a column so the data it contains is displayed appropriately. In this chapter, you'll learn some additional ways to format your worksheets to make them more effective.

Most of the commands you use to format your worksheets are available from the Format menu. In this chapter, you'll learn about five of these commands: Cells, Row Height, Row AutoFit, AutoFormat, and Style. The other commands in this menu are covered in other chapters of this book. You'll also learn about the Fill Justify command in the Edit menu in this chapter. Although you can use these menu commands to perform most of the formatting functions, *Excel* provides other ways to perform many of the same functions as you'll see throughout this chapter.

How to change the font, font size, or font attributes for a range of cells

The term *font* refers to the type you use for the data in a worksheet. For example, the type that's used in the worksheets throughout this chapter is a font called Arial. Each font comes in a variety of sizes. The standard unit of measure for font size is a *point*, which is 1/72 of an inch. The data in the worksheets in this chapter use 10-point type.

All new workbooks use a default font and font size. The starting defaults are Arial for font and 10-point for font size. You can change these defaults so that new workbooks use the font and font size you want by using the Options command in the Tools menu. Chapter 4 shows you how to use this command, so I won't present it again here.

How to use the Font and Font Size boxes You can change the font and font size with toolbar boxes in the Formatting toolbar. Figures 8-1 and 8-2 show you how to do that. To change the font, highlight the cell or range of cells you want to change and click on the arrow next to the Font toolbar box. Then, *Excel* opens a drop-down list that contains all the available fonts as illustrated in figure 8-1. To change the font, click on the one you want or move the highlight to it and press the Enter key. To change the font size, you use the same procedure, but you click on the Font Size toolbar box as illustrated in figure 8-2.

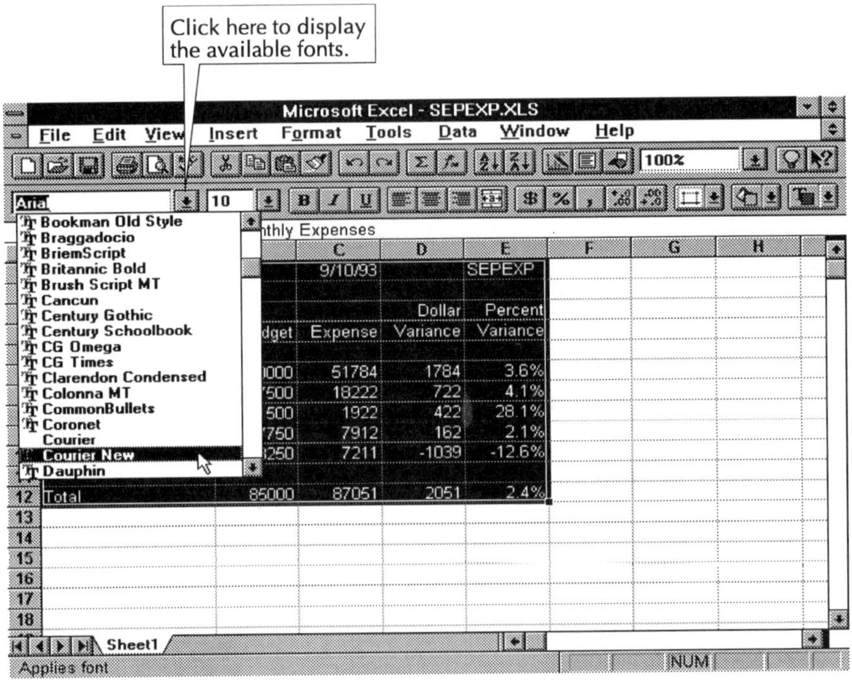

Procedure

1. Highlight the cell or range you want to format.
2. Click on the arrow next to the Font box in the Formatting toolbar to display a list of available fonts.
3. To select a font, click on it or highlight it and press the Enter key.

Notes

- You can also change the font of selected text by editing a cell and selecting the text, then selecting the font.
- The fonts available to you depend on which fonts you have installed through *Windows.*

Figure 8-1 How to use the Font box in the Formatting toolbar to change the font for a cell or range

You can also change the font or font size for selected text in a cell. To do that, highlight the text while you're editing the cell. Then, use the Font and Font Size toolbar boxes to change the font and font size of the selected text.

Not all the fonts listed in figure 8-1 come with *Excel*, so the list on your system probably won't look the same. One of the benefits of *Windows* is its integrated font management feature. With this feature, any font you install in *Windows* is available to all *Windows* applications.

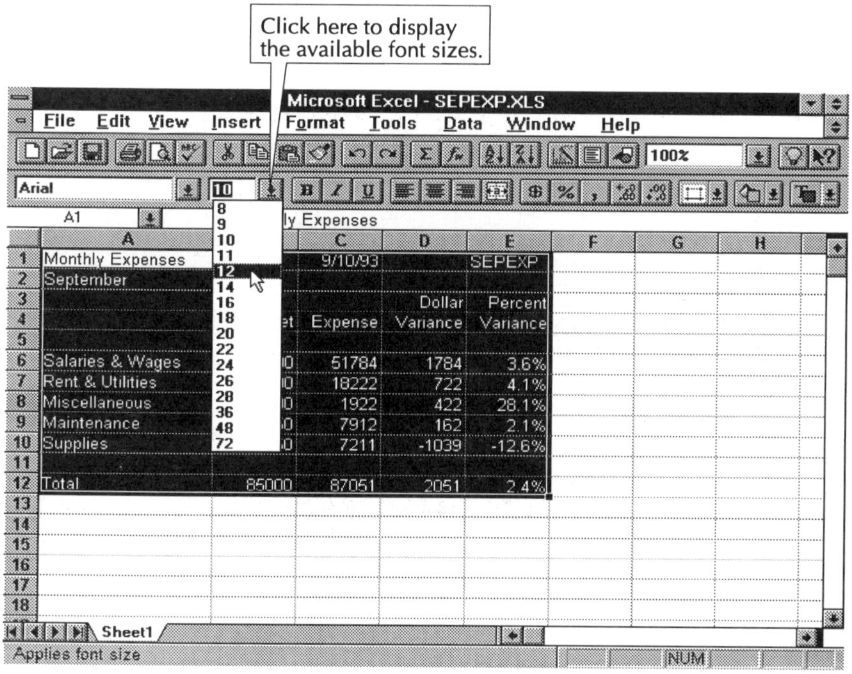

Procedure

1. Highlight the cell or range you want to format.
2. Click on the arrow next to the Font Size box in the Formatting toolbar to display a list of available font sizes.
3. To select a size, click on it or highlight it and press the Enter key.

Notes

- You can also change the font size of selected text by editing a cell and selecting the text, then selecting the font size.
- The sizes available to you depend on the individual font you want to change.

Figure 8-2 How to use the Font Size box in the Formatting toolbar to change the font size for a cell or range

How to use the toolbar buttons and keyboard shortcuts to change font attributes *Excel* provides four buttons in the Formatting toolbar you can use to change the font *attributes* of a cell: Bold, Italic, Underline, and Color. Figure 8-3 presents these toolbar buttons along with their keyboard shortcuts. To apply any of these attributes, highlight the cells you want to change and click on the appropriate toolbar button or press the appropriate keys. You can also change the font attributes for selected text using these buttons by selecting the text while you're editing the cell that contains it.

How to change a font attribute

Highlight the cell or range you want to format, and click on one of the toolbar buttons or use one of the keyboard shortcuts:

Attribute	Button	Keyboard shortcut
Bold		Ctrl+B
Italic		Ctrl+I
Underline		Ctrl+U
Color	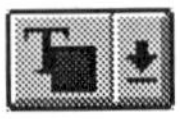	

Notes

- If you click on the Font Color button, *Excel* applies the default color or the last color you applied using this button to the current selection. (The color to be applied appears inside the square on the button.) To apply a different color, click on the arrow on the right side of the button and select a color from the palette that appears:

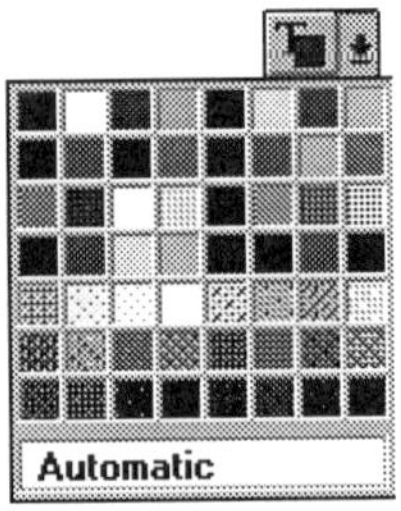

  To keep this palette open, drag it off of the toolbar.
- You can also change the attributes of selected text by editing a cell and selecting the text, then clicking on a button or using one of the keyboard shortcuts.

Figure 8-3 How to use the buttons in the Formatting toolbar or the keyboard shortcuts to change font attributes

The color that's applied when you click on the Font Color button is the color that's displayed inside the square on the button. If you want to apply a different color, click on the arrow on the right side of the button and select a color from the palette that's displayed. If you need to apply several different colors to a worksheet, you may want to keep this palette open by dragging it off of the toolbar.

How to use the Font tab of the Format Cells dialog box You can also change the font, font size, and font attributes by using the Font tab of the Format Cells dialog box as shown in figure 8-4. From this dialog box, you can access two formatting options you can't access using the default

Three ways to access the Font tab of the Format Cells dialog box

- Select the Cells command from the Format menu and click on the Font tab.
- Select the Format Cells command from the shortcut menu and click on the Font tab.
- Press Ctrl+1 and click on the Font tab.

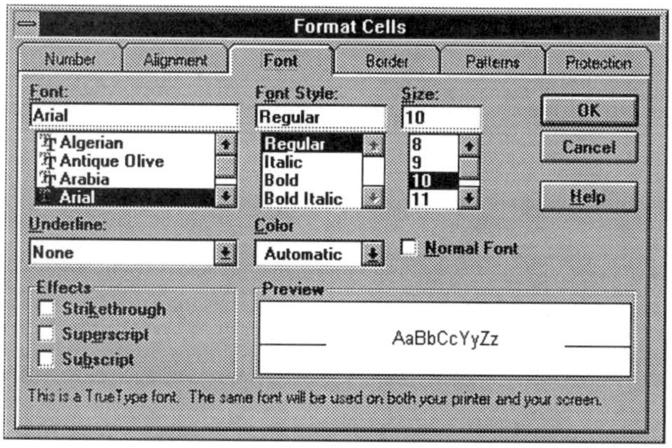

Operation

- To change the font and set its size, select an option from the Font and Size list boxes.
- To apply an attribute or combination of attributes like bold or bold and italics, select an option from the Font Style list box.
- To apply an underline, select an option from the Underline drop-down list box.
- To change the font color, select a color from the Color drop-down list box.
- To apply special formats, select an option from the Effects group.
- To restore all settings to those in the Normal style, click on the Normal Font option.

Notes

- The Font tab offers two formatting options you can't access through the default Formatting toolbar: (1) you can select from four different underlines, and (2) you can apply strikethrough, superscript, and subscript attributes to a font.
- You can see what the selections you make look like in the Preview box before you accept them and apply them to your worksheet.
- You can also change the font, font size, and font attributes of selected text by editing a cell and selecting the text, then accessing the Format Cells dialog box.
- The fonts, sizes, and colors that are available to you depend on your PC.

Figure 8-4 How to use the Font tab to change the font, font size, and font attributes

Formatting toolbar. First, you can select four different types of underlines from the Underline drop-down list box. Second, you can apply strike-through, superscript, and subscript effects using the options in the Effects group. You can also return the font settings to their defaults by selecting the Normal Font option.

Procedure

1. Select the rows you want to change by dragging the mouse pointer over the row numbers in the worksheet frame.
2. Place the mouse pointer on the separator line below the row number for one of the rows you selected. When the pointer is in the correct position, it will change to a double-headed arrow:

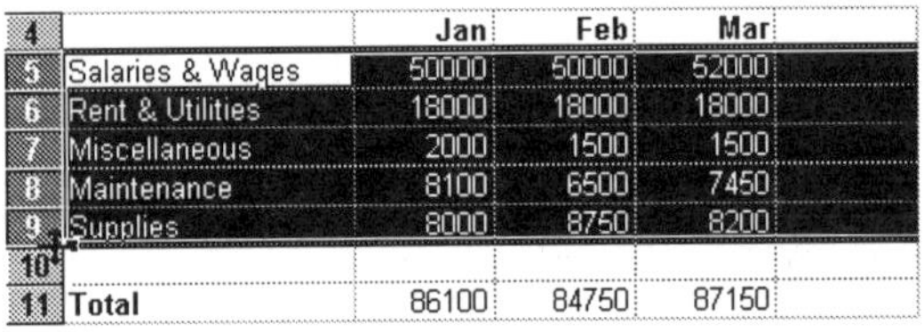

		Jan	Feb	Mar	
4					
5	Salaries & Wages	50000	50000	52000	
6	Rent & Utilities	18000	18000	18000	
7	Miscellaneous	2000	1500	1500	
8	Maintenance	8100	6500	7450	
9	Supplies	8000	8750	8200	
10					
11	Total	86100	84750	87150	

3. Drag the double-headed arrow up or down to the height you want:

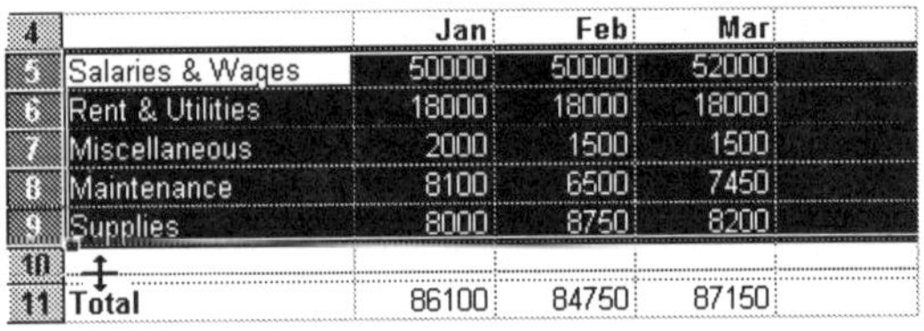

		Jan	Feb	Mar	
4					
5	Salaries & Wages	50000	50000	52000	
6	Rent & Utilities	18000	18000	18000	
7	Miscellaneous	2000	1500	1500	
8	Maintenance	8100	6500	7450	
9	Supplies	8000	8750	8200	
10					
11	Total	86100	84750	87150	

Notes

- You can change the height of a single row without selecting it first. Simply drag the appropriate separator line.
- You can change the height of one or more rows to accommodate the largest entry by double-clicking on the separator line instead of dragging it.

Figure 8-5 How to use the mouse to change the height of one or more rows

How to change the height of one or more rows

Normally, you don't have to change the row height because *Excel* adjusts it automatically depending on the font and font size you use. But if you ever need to change the height of one or more rows, you can do so using a mouse technique that's similar to the one for changing the width of a column.

Figure 8-5 presents the procedure for using this mouse technique. As you can see, you just select the rows and drag a separator line to change the height of the rows. As you do that, *Excel* displays the new height in points in the Name box of the formula bar. You can also change the height of one or more rows to accommodate the largest font by double-clicking on a separator line instead of dragging it.

How to use the Row Height command

1. Select the rows that you want to change.
2. Select the Row Height command from the Format or shortcut menu and this dialog box appears:

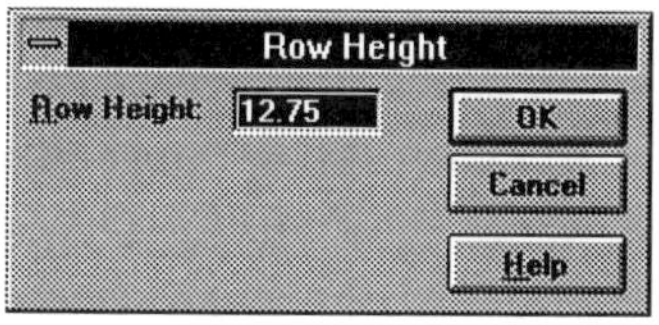

3. Enter the height of the row in points and click on the OK button.

Note

You don't have to select entire rows to use the Row Height command from the Format menu. Instead, you can highlight a range that includes at least one cell from each row you want to change.

How to use the AutoFit command

1. Highlight at least one cell in each row that you want to change.
2. Select the Row AutoFit command from the Format menu, and *Excel* adjusts the row heights to accommodate the largest font in each row.

Figure 8-6 How to use menu commands to change the height of one or more rows

You can also change the height of one or more rows using the menu commands summarized in figure 8-6. To change the height of one or more row to a specific number of points, you use the Row Height command in the Edit or shortcut menu. To change the height of one or more rows so that they accommodate the largest font in each row, you use the Row AutoFit command in the Edit menu.

How to split a long string of text into two or more rows

In chapter 5, you learned how to wrap a long string of text so that it appears on two or more lines in a single cell instead of spilling over into the next column. The Fill Justify command in the Edit menu provides a similar feature. When you use this command, however, the text is split into two or more rows instead of two or more lines in a single row. In addition, this command lets text spill over into the number of columns you specify.

Figure 8-7 shows you how to use the Fill Justify command to split a long string of text into two or more rows. In the example in this figure, I split the text so that it's confined to three columns. To do that, I highlighted the cell that contains the data along with the next two columns in the

Procedure

1. Highlight a range that includes the cell that contains the text you want to split and the columns you want the data limited to:

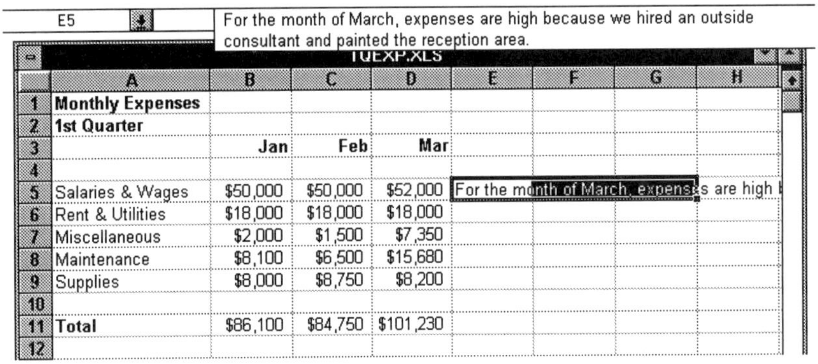

E5 | For the month of March, expenses are high because we hired an outside consultant and painted the reception area.

1QEXP.XLS

	A	B	C	D	E	F	G	H
1	**Monthly Expenses**							
2	**1st Quarter**							
3		**Jan**	**Feb**	**Mar**				
4								
5	Salaries & Wages	$50,000	$50,000	$52,000	For the month of March, expenses are high			
6	Rent & Utilities	$18,000	$18,000	$18,000				
7	Miscellaneous	$2,000	$1,500	$7,350				
8	Maintenance	$8,100	$6,500	$15,680				
9	Supplies	$8,000	$8,750	$8,200				
10								
11	**Total**	$86,100	$84,750	$101,230				
12								

2. Select the Fill Justify command from the Edit menu, and *Excel* splits the text so that it's confined to the columns you highlighted:

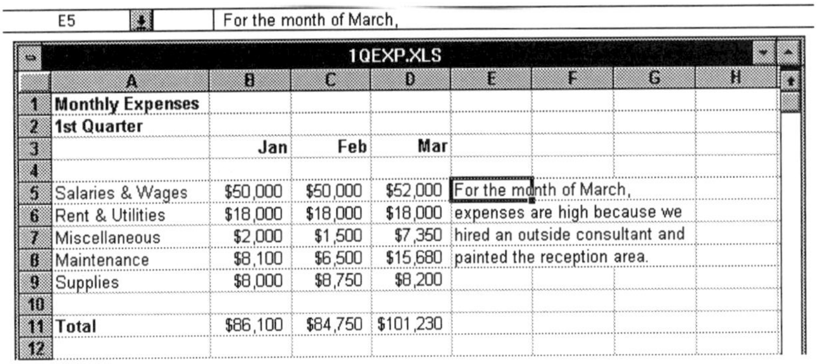

E5 | For the month of March,

1QEXP.XLS

	A	B	C	D	E	F	G	H
1	**Monthly Expenses**							
2	**1st Quarter**							
3		**Jan**	**Feb**	**Mar**				
4								
5	Salaries & Wages	$50,000	$50,000	$52,000	For the month of March,			
6	Rent & Utilities	$18,000	$18,000	$18,000	expenses are high because we			
7	Miscellaneous	$2,000	$1,500	$7,350	hired an outside consultant and			
8	Maintenance	$8,100	$6,500	$15,680	painted the reception area.			
9	Supplies	$8,000	$8,750	$8,200				
10								
11	**Total**	$86,100	$84,750	$101,230				
12								

Note

You can also use the Fill Justify command on a range that includes more than one row. However, all the cells that contain data must be the left-most cells of the highlighted range.

Figure 8-7 How to split a long string of text into two or more rows

worksheet. Then, when I issued the Fill Justify command, *Excel* split the text into four rows so that the text in each row occupies no more than three columns.

How to add borders, colors, and patterns to a worksheet

Occasionally, you need to do more than just change the font, font size, and font attributes of a worksheet to make it effective. Sometimes, you need to add a border around a range of cells to make it stand out from the rest of the

Operation

- To apply the default border or the last border you applied using the Borders button, highlight the cell or range you want to format and click on the Borders button:

The picture on the Borders button indicates the border to be applied.

- To apply a border other than the one shown on the Borders button, highlight the cell or range you want to format. Then, click on the arrow on the right side of the button and select a border from the palette that appears:

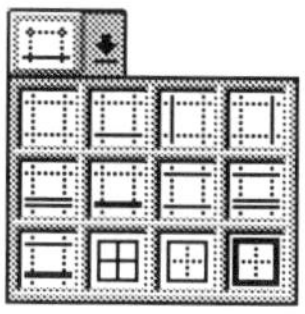

Note

You can keep the border palette open by dragging it off of the toolbar.

Figure 8-8 How to use the Borders button in the Formatting toolbar to add a border to a range

worksheet. And, if a worksheet is particularly complex or its appearance is particularly important, you may need to add colors or patterns. One note of caution, though: Don't overdo it. If you use too many of these features, your worksheets will look busy and they won't be as effective.

Borders Figure 8-8 shows you how to use the Borders button in the Formatting toolbar to add a border to a range of cells. This button is similar to the Font Color button you learned about earlier in this chapter. To use it, you can click on the button to apply the default border or the last border you applied using this button. Or, you can click on the arrow on the right side of the button and select a different border from the palette that's displayed. You can also keep the border palette open by dragging it off of the toolbar.

Although the Borders button is easy to use, it provides a limited number of border options. If you want to add a border that's not available from this button, you can use the Border tab of the Format Cells dialog box as shown in figure 8-9. From this tab, you can select which sides of each cell in the range will have a border; you can select the line style for the border; and you can select the color of the border.

If you modify a range of cells that already has a border, you might be confused to see that some of the options in the Border group are shaded. If an option is shaded, it means that only some of the cells in the range have

Three ways to access the Border tab of the Format Cells dialog box

- Select the Cells command from the Format menu and click on the Border tab.
- Select the Format Cells command from the shortcut menu and click on the Border tab.
- Press Ctrl+1 and click on the Border tab.

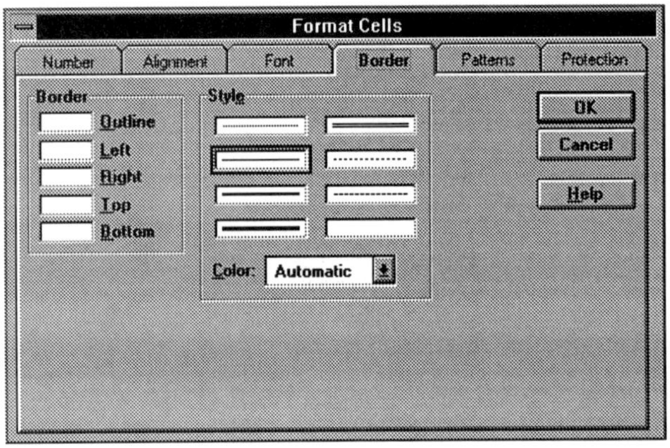

Operation

- To add a border to a range of cells, select the appropriate Border options: Outline, Left, Right, Top, or Bottom.
- To change the line style for a border, select a style from the Style group after you select the Border option. The style you select is then used as the default for any additional border options you select.
- To change the color for a border, select a color from the Color drop-down list box. The color you select is then used as the default for any additional border options you select.

Figure 8-9 How to use the Border tab to add borders to a range

that border. For example, if the range of cells is outlined, that means some of the cells have a border on the left edge, some have a border on the right edge, some have a border on the top edge, some have a border on the bottom edge, and some have a mixture of borders. In that case, the Left, Right, Top, and Bottom options are shaded.

Figure 8-10 presents four examples that use different types of borders. You can create any of these borders using either the Borders button or the Border tab. If you study these examples, I think you'll appreciate the versatility of the borders feature.

Colors and patterns *Excel* lets you add a variety of colors and patterns to any part of a worksheet. You learned how to apply a color to text earlier in this chapter. Now, you'll learn how to apply colors and patterns to one or more cells. To do that, you can use the Color button in the Formatting toolbar, or you can use the Patterns tab in the Format Cells dialog box.

Border options	Result

Left, Right, Top, and Bottom selected for cells A4 to D11.

	A	B	C	D	E
1	**Monthly Expenses**				
2	**1st Quarter**				
3					
4		**Jan**	**Feb**	**Mar**	
5	Salaries & Wages	$50,000	$50,000	$52,000	
6	Rent & Utilities	$18,000	$18,000	$18,000	
7	Miscellaneous	$2,000	$1,500	$1,500	
8	Maintenance	$8,100	$6,500	$7,450	
9	Supplies	$8,000	$8,750	$8,200	
10					
11	**Total**	$86,100	$84,750	$87,150	
12					

Outline selected for cells B5 to D11.

	A	B	C	D	E
1	**Monthly Expenses**				
2	**1st Quarter**				
3					
4		**Jan**	**Feb**	**Mar**	
5	Salaries & Wages	$50,000	$50,000	$52,000	
6	Rent & Utilities	$18,000	$18,000	$18,000	
7	Miscellaneous	$2,000	$1,500	$1,500	
8	Maintenance	$8,100	$6,500	$7,450	
9	Supplies	$8,000	$8,750	$8,200	
10					
11	**Total**	$86,100	$84,750	$87,150	
12					

Bottom selected for cells B4 to D4 and B9 to D9.

	A	B	C	D	E
1	**Monthly Expenses**				
2	**1st Quarter**				
3					
4		**Jan**	**Feb**	**Mar**	
5	Salaries & Wages	$50,000	$50,000	$52,000	
6	Rent & Utilities	$18,000	$18,000	$18,000	
7	Miscellaneous	$2,000	$1,500	$1,500	
8	Maintenance	$8,100	$6,500	$7,450	
9	Supplies	$8,000	$8,750	$8,200	
10					
11	**Total**	$86,100	$84,750	$87,150	
12					

Left, Right, Top, and Bottom selected for cells B4 to D4; Outline selected for cells B5 to B11, C5 to C11, and D5 to D11.

	A	B	C	D	E
1	**Monthly Expenses**				
2	**1st Quarter**				
3					
4		**Jan**	**Feb**	**Mar**	
5	Salaries & Wages	$50,000	$50,000	$52,000	
6	Rent & Utilities	$18,000	$18,000	$18,000	
7	Miscellaneous	$2,000	$1,500	$1,500	
8	Maintenance	$8,100	$6,500	$7,450	
9	Supplies	$8,000	$8,750	$8,200	
10					
11	**Total**	$86,100	$84,750	$87,150	
12					

Figure 8-10 Four examples of a worksheet that uses borders

Operation

- To apply the default color and pattern or the last color and pattern you applied using the Color button, highlight the cell or range you want to format and click on the Color button:

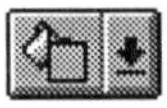

The color and pattern in the square on the button indicates the color and pattern to be applied.

- To apply a color or pattern other than the one shown on the Color button, click on the arrow on the right side of the button and select a color from the palette that appears:

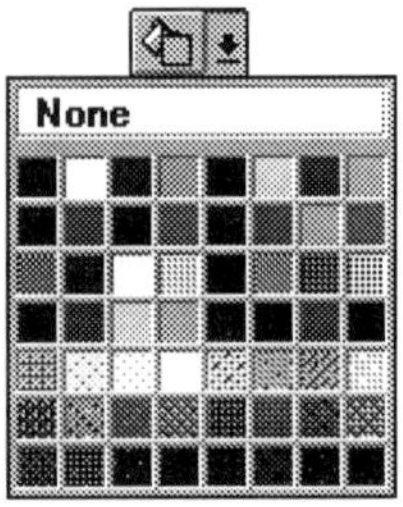

Note

You can keep the color palette open by dragging it off of the toolbar.

Figure 8-11 How to use the Color button in the Formatting toolbar to apply colors and patterns to a range

Figure 8-11 shows you how to use the Color button to apply colors and patterns to a range of cells. This button is similar to the Font Color and Borders buttons you learned about earlier in this chapter. If you click on it, *Excel* applies the default color, or the last color and pattern you applied using this button, to the selected range. And if you click on the arrow on the right side of the button, you can choose a color and pattern from the palette that's displayed. You can keep this palette open by dragging it off of the toolbar.

Figure 8-12 shows you how to apply colors and patterns to a range using the Patterns tab. From this tab, you can select the color and pattern you want to apply from those that are displayed. To apply a different pattern or pattern color, select an option from the Pattern drop-down list box.

Even if you don't have a color printer, you may want to use the color and pattern features. In particular, you can use them to highlight areas of a worksheet with different shades of gray. You can also use them to produce a special effect of white text on a black background.

Three ways to access the Patterns tab of the Format Cells dialog box

- Select the Cells command from the Format menu and click on the Patterns tab.
- Select the Format Cells command from the shortcut menu and click on the Patterns tab.
- Press Ctrl+1 and click on the Patterns tab.

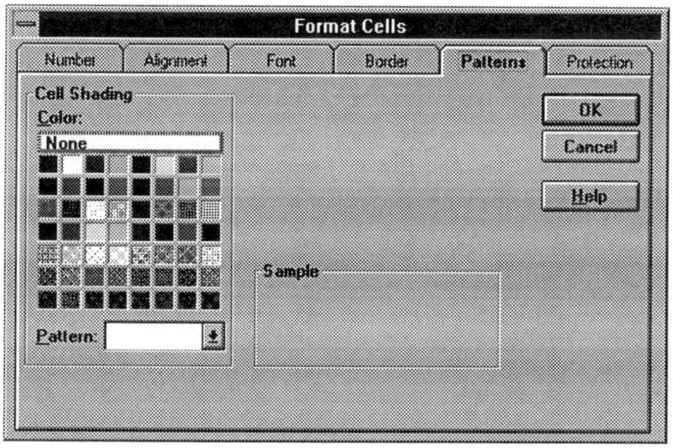

Operation

- To change the background color of the range, select an option from the Color palette.
- To apply a pattern and pattern color to the range, select an option from the Pattern drop-down list box.

Note

The selections you make appear in the Sample box so you can see what they look like before you apply them to the selected range.

Figure 8-12 How to use the Patterns tab to apply colors and patterns to a range

How to copy and delete formats

When you create a worksheet, you usually want ranges that contain similar data to have the same formats. For example, you probably want all the column and row headings to look the same. To format multiple ranges, you can highlight all the ranges at once, then apply the formats. Or you can format one range, then copy the formats to the other ranges. To copy formats, you can use the Format Painter or the Paste Special command in the Edit menu.

How to use the Format Painter to copy formats Figure 8-13 shows you how to copy formats using the Format Painter button in the Standard toolbar. Before you click on this button, be sure the cell pointer is on the cell that contains the formats you want to copy. Then, click on the button and highlight the range where you want to copy the formats. When you do, *Excel* copies alignment, font settings, borders, colors, patterns, protection status, and number formats to the range. It doesn't copy column widths or row heights.

You can also use the Format Painter to copy formats to two or more ranges. To do that, you double-click on its button after you place the cell pointer on the cell that contains the formats you want to copy. Then, you can highlight as many ranges as you want, and *Excel* pastes the formats to the ranges. When you're done copying the formats, click on the Format Painter button again to turn the feature off.

How to use menu commands to copy and delete formats You can also use the Paste Special command in the Edit menu to copy formats from one range to another as illustrated in figure 8-14. To use this command, you copy a cell that contains the formats you want to use to the clipboard. Then, you select the range you want to copy the formats to, and you use the Paste Special command to apply the formats from the clipboard to the selected range.

Figure 8-14 also presents the Clear Formats command. You use this command to remove formats from selected cells. Then, the cells return to their default formats.

How to use styles

A *style* is a combination of number format, font, alignment, borders, patterns, and protection status that's applied to a cell. (You'll learn about protection statuses in chapter 24.) If you use a certain style frequently, you can name it and save it so you can apply it to other areas of a worksheet or to other workbooks.

How to create and use styles If you find yourself using the same combination of formats often, you may save some time by naming the formats as a style. Then, instead of copying the formats from one range to another, you can apply the style. You can also change a style if you decide it's not what you want. And you can rename or delete a style. You perform all of these operations using the Style command in the Format menu as shown in figure 8-15.

Procedure

1. Place the cell pointer on the cell that contains the formats you want to copy.
2. Click on the Format Painter button in the Standard toolbar, and the cursor changes into the Format Painter cursor:

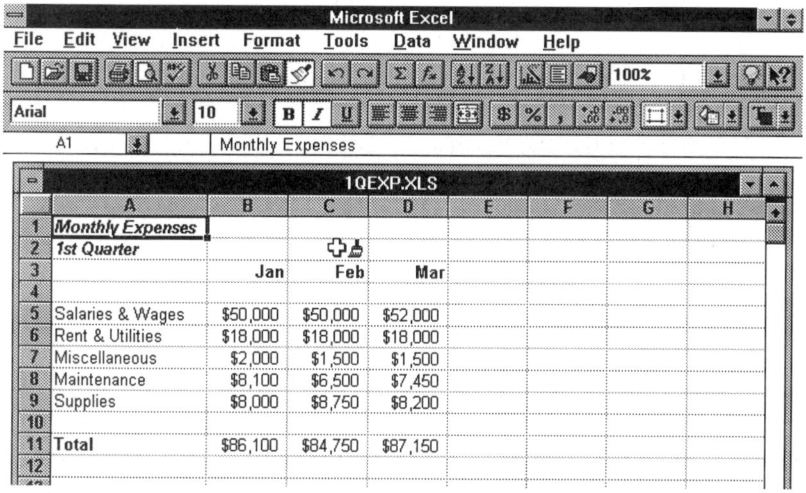

3. Use the mouse to select the range where you want to copy the formats:

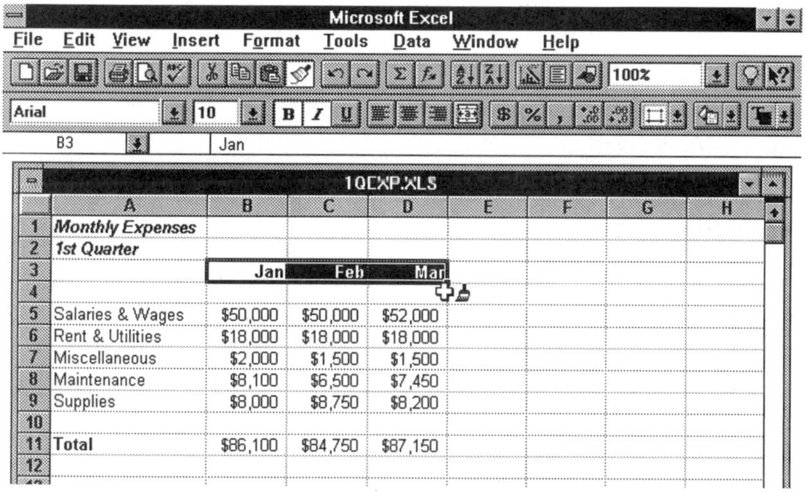

Figure 8-13 How to use the Format Painter to copy formats (part 1 of 2)

4. Release the mouse button and the formats are applied to the range:

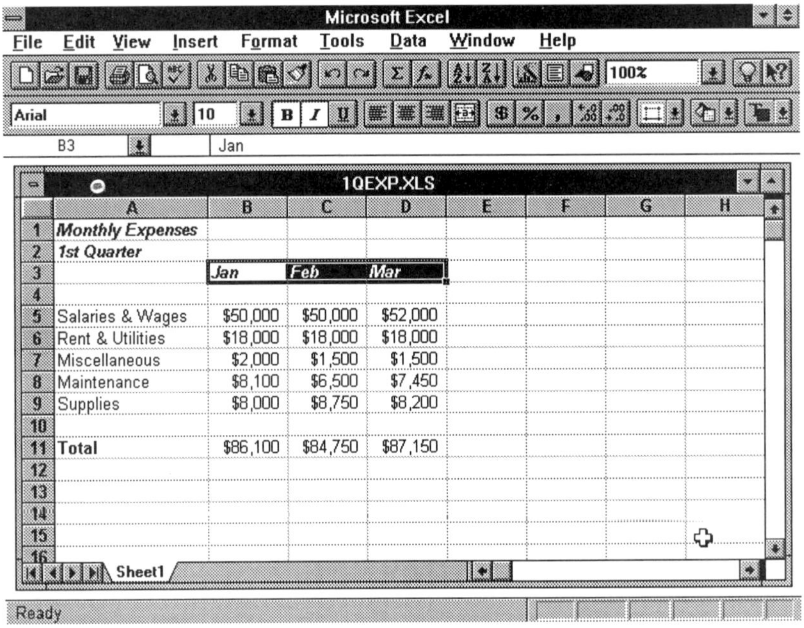

Note

To paste the selection more than once, double-click on the Format Painter button. Then, repeat steps 3 and 4 to paste the selection as many times as you like. To end the operation, click on the Format Painter button again.

Figure 8-13 How to use the Format Painter to copy formats (part 2 of 2)

The easiest way to create a style is to apply the formats you want to include in the style to a cell, then issue the Style command and enter a name for the style. Then, to apply the style to a range, select the range, issue the Style command, and select the style from the Style Name drop-down list box. When you create or apply a style, you can also use the options in the Style Includes group to exclude any of the formats. If you deselect any of these options when you create a style, the associated formats aren't included in the style. And if you deselect any of these options when you apply a style, the associated formats aren't applied.

How to copy formats

1. Place the cell pointer on the cell that contains the formats you want to copy.
2. Copy the cell to the clipboard.
3. Highlight the range where you want to copy the formats.
4. Select the Paste Special command from the Edit menu or the shortcut menu and this dialog box appears:

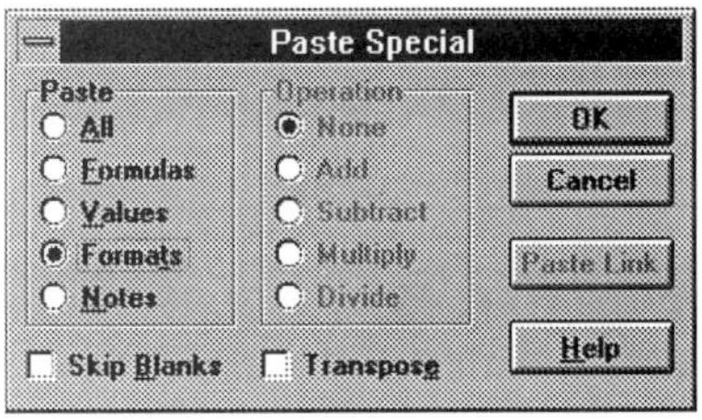

5. Select the Formats option in the Paste group, and click on the OK button to copy the formats to the selected range.

How to delete formats

1. Highlight the range of cells that contains the formats you want to delete.
2. Select the Clear Formats command from the Edit menu.

Figure 8-14 How to use menu commands to copy and delete formats

The easiest way to change a style is to apply the new formats to a cell. Then, select the Style command and enter the name of the style in the Style Name text box. Note that when you use this method, you have to type in the style name even if it's already displayed in the Style Name text box. Then, the formats in the selected cell are displayed in the Style Includes group. To change the style, click on the Add button and confirm your selection. When you do, *Excel* applies the new formats to all the cells that are formatted with the selected style. Note that you can change any of the built-in styles using this technique as well as any styles you create. For instance, you might want to change the worksheet defaults by changing the Normal style.

You can also create or change a style using the Modify button in the Style dialog box. When you use this button, you don't have to select a cell that contains the formats you want to include in the style. Instead, you select the formats from the Format Cells dialog box, which is displayed when you click on the Modify button.

How to create a style

1. Place the cell pointer on the cell that contains the formats you want the style to contain.
2. Select the Style command from the Format menu and this dialog box appears:

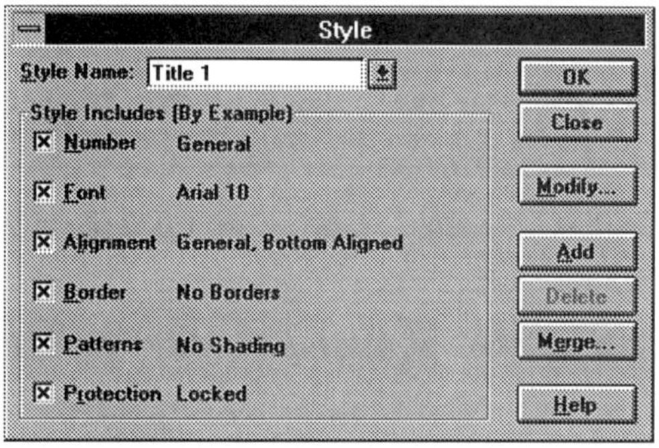

3. Enter the name you want to give to the style in the Style Name drop-down list box.
4. Click on the OK button.

How to apply a style

1. Select the cell or range you want to format with a style.
2. Select the Style command from the Format menu and the Style dialog box appears.
3. Select a style from the Style Name drop-down list box, and a description of the formats included in the style appears in the Style Includes group.
4. Click on the OK button and the style is applied.

How to change a style

1. Select a cell that contains the new formats.
2. Select the Style command from the Format menu and the Style dialog box appears.
3. Type the name of the style you want to change in the Style Name drop-down list box, and a description of the new formats appears in the Style Includes group.
4. Click on the Add button to change the style, and *Excel* displays a dialog box that asks if you want to redefine the style.
5. Click on the Yes button, then click on the OK button from the Style dialog box and all the cells with that style are updated with the new formats.

How to rename a style

1. Select a cell that's formatted with the style you want to rename.
2. Select the Style command from the Format menu and the Style dialog box appears. The style applied to the current cell appears in the Style Name text box.
3. Type in a new name and click on the OK button.

Figure 8-15 How to work with styles (part 1 of 2)

How to delete a style

1. Select the Style command from the Format menu and the Style dialog box appears.
2. Select the style you want to delete from the Style Name drop-down list box.
3. Click on the Delete button, and the style is deleted. All the cells with the selected style are changed to their default format.
4. Click on the OK button to close the Style dialog box.

Notes

- When you create or apply a style, you can deselect any of the options in the Style Includes group. Then, for a create operation, the formatting for that option isn't included in the style. For an apply operation, the formatting isn't applied to the current selection.
- You can click on the Add button to create a style without applying it to the current selection and without exiting from the Style dialog box.
- You can also create or change a style by clicking on the Modify button. Then, *Excel* displays the Format Cells dialog box so you can change any of the format options.
- The Merge button lets you copy styles from another workbook into the current workbook. See figure 8-16 for details.

Figure 8-15 How to work with styles (part 2 of 2)

How to copy styles from another workbook Figure 8-16 summarizes the procedure for copying styles from one workbook to another. When you copy styles, you *merge* the styles from a *source workbook* into a *destination workbook*. To do that, both workbooks must be open and the destination workbook must be current.

To merge styles, you select the Style command from the Format menu, then click on the Merge button in the Style dialog box. From the Merge Styles dialog box, you select the source workbook. Note that when you merge styles, you can't select the styles you want to merge; *Excel* merges all of the styles in the source document with the styles in the destination document. This can cause a problem if both worksheets have styles with the same names. In that case, *Excel* displays a dialog box that asks if you want to replace the styles in the destination document. If you don't, click on the No button and *Excel* cancels the operation. Then, you can rename the styles in the destination document and perform the merge operation again.

If you frequently use the same set of styles for your workbooks, you'll want to use the merge feature to copy the styles from one workbook to another instead of creating the styles for each new workbook. Then, you'll spend less time formatting your workbooks, and your workbooks will be more consistent.

Procedure

1. Open the workbook that contains the styles you want to copy (the source workbook).
2. Switch to the workbook where you want to copy the styles (the destination workbook).
3. Select the Style command from the Format menu and the Style dialog box appears.
4. Click on the Merge button and this dialog box appears:

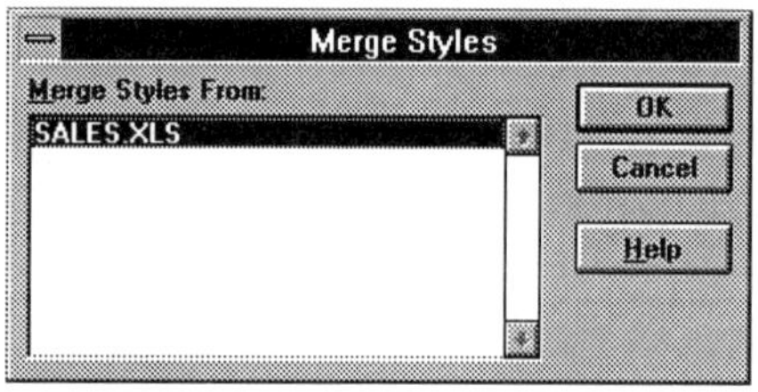

5. Select the name of the workbook that contains the styles you want to copy.
6. Click on the OK button, and *Excel* adds the styles in the source workbook to the styles in the destination workbook.

Note

If the source workbook contains a style that has the same name as a style in the destination workbook, a message box appears that asks if you want to merge styles that have the same names. If you answer *yes*, the style from the source workbook replaces the one in the destination workbook. If you answer *no*, the operation is canceled.

Figure 8-16 How to copy styles from another workbook

How to use autoformats

Excel comes with 16 *autoformats* that you can use to format ranges in your worksheets. To apply an autoformat, you use the AutoFormat command as illustrated in figure 8-17. Note that when you apply an autoformat, you can omit any of the formats it contains. To do that, you click on the Options button and deselect the formats you don't want to apply.

Figure 8-17 also shows you how to remove autoformats from a range of cells. To remove an autoformat immediately after you apply it, select the Undo AutoFormat command from the Edit menu. To remove an autoformat after you perform other operations, highlight the range that contains the autoformat, then issue the AutoFormat command and select the None option from the Table Format list box.

How to apply an autoformat

1. Highlight the range of cells you want to format.
2. Select the AutoFormat command from the Format menu and this dialog box appears:

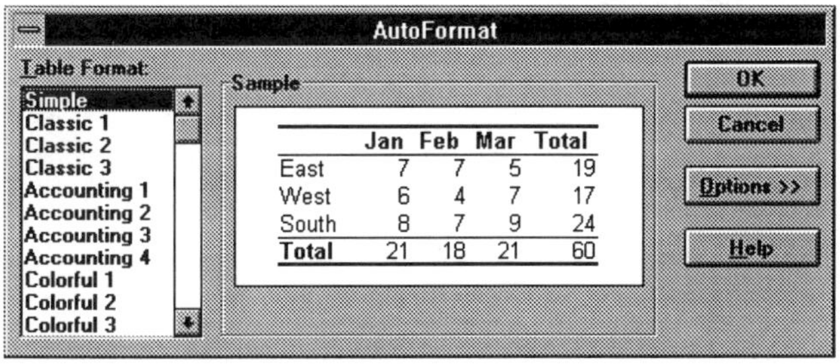

3. Select one of the table formats from the Table Format list box, and click on the OK button to apply the format to the selected range.

Notes

- When you click on the Options button, controls appear that let you remove the following formats from those that are applied: number formats, borders, font attributes, colors and patterns, alignments, and column widths and row heights.
- The selections you make appear in the Sample box so you can see what they look like before you apply them to the selected range.

Two ways to remove an autoformat

- Select the Undo AutoFormat command from the Edit menu immediately after applying the autoformat.
- Select the range that's formatted with the autoformat, then select the AutoFormat command from the Format menu and the AutoFormat dialog box appears. Select the None option from the Table Format list box and click on the OK button.

A worksheet formatted with two different table formats

Classic 1

	A	B	C	D	E
1	**Monthly Expenses**		*9/10/93*		*SEPEXP*
2		**September**			
3				***Dollar***	***Percent***
4		*Budget*	*Expense*	***Variance***	***Variance***
5					
6	Salaries & Wages	50000	51784	1784	3.6%
7	Rent & Utilities	17500	18222	722	4.1%
8	Miscellaneous	1500	1922	422	28.1%
9	Maintenance	7750	7912	162	2.1%
10	Supplies	8250	7211	-1039	-12.6%
11					
12	**Total**	85000	87051	2051	2.4%

List 1

	A	B	C	D	E
1	*Monthly Expenses*		*9/10/93*		*SEPEXP*
2	*September*				
3				*Dollar*	*Percent*
4		*Budget*	*Expense*	*Variance*	*Variance*
5					
6	Salaries & Wages	50000	51784	1784	3.6%
7	Rent & Utilities	17500	18222	722	4.1%
8	Miscellaneous	1500	1922	422	28.1%
9	Maintenance	7750	7912	162	2.1%
10	Supplies	8250	7211	-1039	-12.6%
11					
12	**Total**	85000	87051	2051	2.4%

Figure 8-17 How to apply and remove an autoformat

Perspective

If you use the techniques presented in this chapter, you'll quickly be able to format your worksheets so they're easy to read and interpret. But again, I want to caution you not to get carried away. For most worksheets, you probably won't need to use many of the formatting techniques presented in this chapter. In most cases, changing the font, font size, and font attributes of the titles and headings of a worksheet is enough to make the worksheet effective. So, you can save the other features for those special occasions when you really need to make an impression.

As a general guideline, you shouldn't spend any more time formatting your worksheets than you do entering its data. If you do, you're probably putting too much emphasis on the appearance of the worksheet, or you're not working as efficiently as you could be.

Summary

- To change the *font* or font size, click on the Font or Font Size box in the Formatting toolbar and select a font or size from the list that's displayed.
- To boldface, italicize, underline, or change the color of a cell entry, click on the appropriate toolbar button or use the appropriate keyboard shortcuts.
- You can also use the Font tab in the Format Cells dialog box to change the font, font size, or font attributes.
- To change the height of a row, use the mouse, the Row Height command in the Format or shortcut menu, or the Row AutoFit command in the Format menu.
- To split a long string of text into two or more rows, use the Fill Justify command in the Edit menu.
- To customize your worksheets with borders, colors, and patterns, you can use the appropriate toolbar buttons or the Borders and Patterns tabs in the Format Cells dialog box.
- To copy formats from one range of cells to another, use the Format Painter button or the Paste Special command in the Edit or shortcut menu. To delete the formats from a range of cells, use the Clear Formats command in the Edit menu.

- To create and use styles, use the Style command in the Format menu.
- To apply an *autoformat*, use the AutoFormat command in the Format menu.

Chapter 9

How to work with more than one worksheet at a time

So far, the material in this section has taught you how to work with single worksheets. But with *Excel 5.0 for Windows*, you can work with two or more worksheets at the same time. When you do that, it's easy to share data between worksheets.

This chapter presents two methods for working with more than one worksheet at a time. First, you'll learn how to use a workbook that contains two or more worksheets. Second, you'll learn how to work with worksheets in two or more workbooks at the same time.

How to work with more than one worksheet in a single workbook

Figure 9-1 presents a workbook that contains four worksheets. Although you can't tell from the figure, the first three worksheets contain sales figures for each month in the first quarter of the year, and the last worksheet contains the total sales figures for the first quarter. To create and use a workbook like this, you need the skills that follow.

How to use the workbook window controls for more than one worksheet Figure 9-2 identifies the workbook window controls you can use when you're working with more than one worksheet in a single workbook. The controls you'll use most often are the sheet tabs that display the names of the worksheets. You can use these tabs to move from one worksheet to another or to change a worksheet's name. By default, *Excel* names the worksheets Sheet1, Sheet2, Sheet3, and so on. I'll show you how to change the worksheet names so they're more meaningful in just a moment.

If a workbook contains so many worksheets that *Excel* can't display their tabs all at once, you can use the tab-scroll arrows to scroll the tabs left and right. The left-most tab-scroll arrow displays the first tab in the work-book. The right-most tab-scroll arrow displays the last tab in the workbook. The other two tab-scroll arrows display the next tab to the left and the right. If you want to increase or decrease the size of the tab area, you can drag the tab splitter.

How to change worksheet names Figure 9-3 shows you how to change a worksheet name. When you work with multiple worksheets, you'll probably find it helpful to change the worksheet names to indicate what's in each worksheet. If Sheet1 contains sales information for January, for example, you might change the worksheet name to January or Jan.

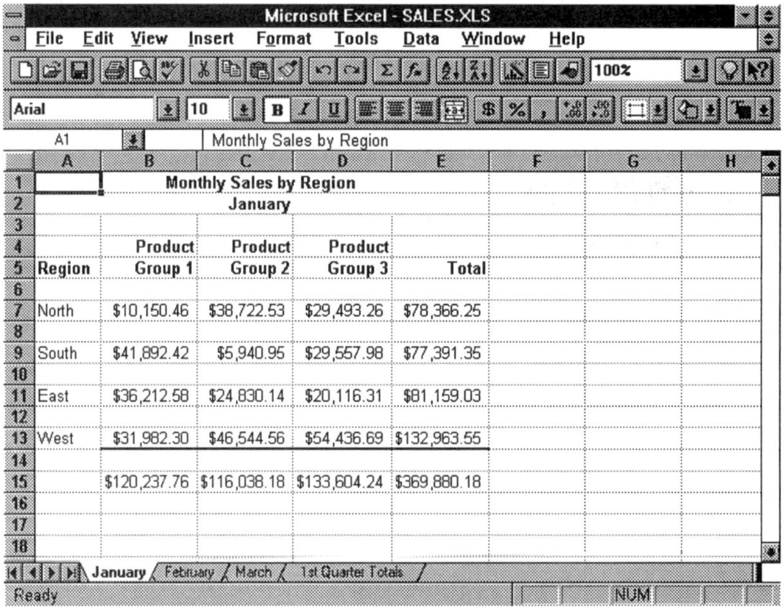

Figure 9-1 An *Excel* workbook that contains four worksheets

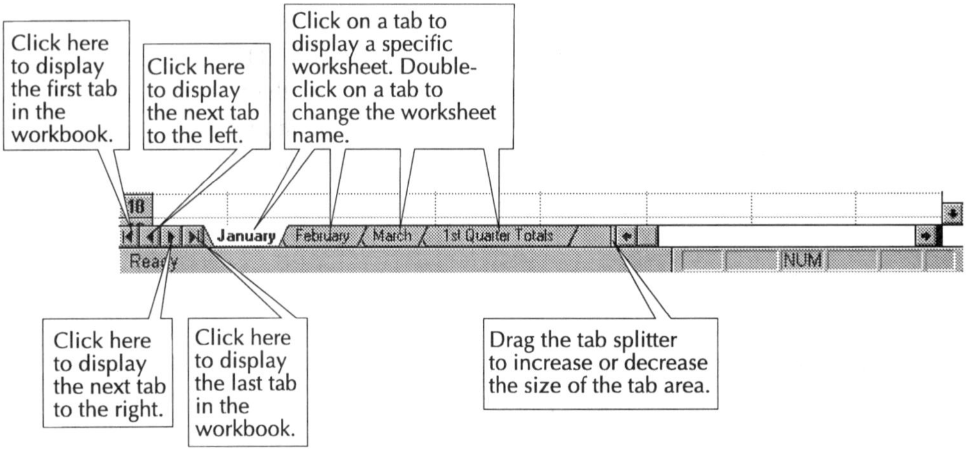

Figure 9-2 The workbook window controls for working with more than one worksheet

Three ways to access the Rename Sheet dialog box

- Double-click on a tab.
- Click the right mouse button on a tab and select the Rename command from the shortcut menu that appears.
- Select the Sheet Rename command from the Format menu.

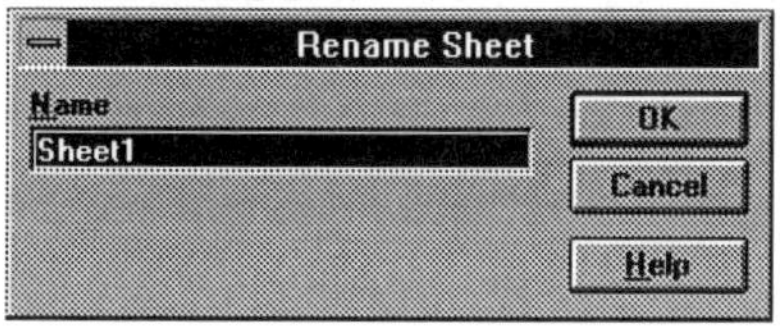

Note

A worksheet name can consist of up to 31 characters.

Figure 9-3 How to change a worksheet name

Keystrokes	**Function**
Ctrl+Page-up	Moves to the previous worksheet.
Ctrl+Page-down	Moves to the next worksheet.

Figure 9-4 The keystroke combinations for moving from one worksheet to another

How to move from one worksheet to another The easiest way to move from one worksheet to another is to click on the tab for the worksheet you want to display. However, if you have a large number of worksheets or your worksheet names are long, you may not be able to see all the worksheet tabs at one time. In that case, you can use the tab-scroll arrows I showed you in figure 9-2 to display the tab for the worksheet you want to move to. You can also move from one worksheet to another by using the keystroke combinations presented in figure 9-4.

How to display more than one worksheet at a time Sometimes, it's easier to work with multiple worksheets if you can see more than one of them at the same time. That way, you can move back and forth between them more easily, and you can see how a change in one worksheet affects the others.

Figure 9-5 shows you the procedure for displaying more than one worksheet at a time. As you can see, you use the New Window command in the Window menu to create windows to display the worksheets. And, you use the Arrange command in the Window menu to arrange the windows on the screen. Figure 9-6 shows you examples of the different Arrange options.

When you use the Arrange command to display more than one worksheet, you can switch to another window by clicking on it. When you switch to another window in a configuration where the windows are overlapped, *Excel* brings the window to the top of the stack so you can see all of it. To maximize, move, resize, or close the windows, you can use the *Windows* techniques presented in chapter 1.

The New Window command lets you create as many new windows as you need. However, if you try to display more than three or four windows using the Tile, Vertical, or Horizontal arrangement, the windows will be too small for you to use them effectively. If you need to display more than four worksheets, the Cascade arrangement is usually the most helpful.

How to select a group of worksheets Many of the functions *Excel* provides for working with more that one worksheet can operate on two or more worksheets at the same time. For example, you can add or delete several worksheets at a time, or you can format several worksheets at the same time. Before you can issue a command that operates on two or more worksheets, however, you have to group the worksheets. Figure 9-7 shows you how to do that.

As you can see in the figure, you can select both adjacent and non-adjacent groups of worksheets. When you select a group, *Excel* displays the word "Group" in the title bar of the worksheet window. You can tell which worksheets are included in the group because the tabs for all of the selected worksheets are highlighted. To ungroup the worksheets, use one of the techniques in figure 9-7.

How to add or delete worksheets By default, a workbook contains 16 worksheets. If you need to add or delete worksheets, you can use the procedures in figure 9-8.

When you add a worksheet, *Excel* inserts it before, or in front of, the current worksheet. So if the current workbook contains 4 worksheets and the current worksheet is Sheet1, *Excel* adds Sheet5 in front of Sheet1. Notice that when you delete worksheets, *Excel* asks you to confirm the operation to be sure that's what you want to do.

Procedure

1. For each additional worksheet you want to display, select the New Window command from the Window menu to open another window for the workbook.
2. Select the Arrange command from the Window menu and this dialog box appears:

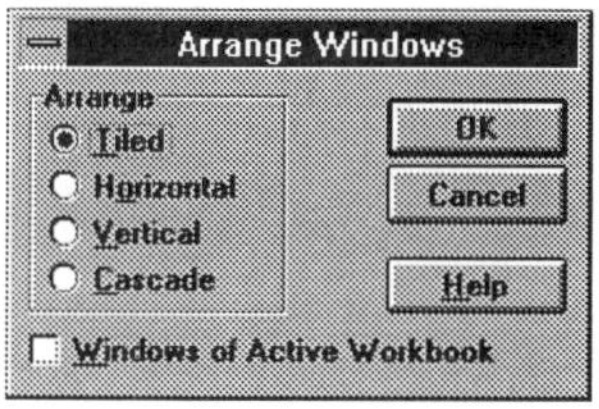

3. Choose an option from the Arrange group (see figure 9-6 for details), and select the Windows Of Active Workbook option so the windows that contain other open workbooks aren't displayed.
4. Click on the OK button, and *Excel* displays all the windows on the screen with the current worksheet in each window.
5. Select the worksheet you want to display in each window by clicking on the window to activate it, then clicking on a sheet tab:

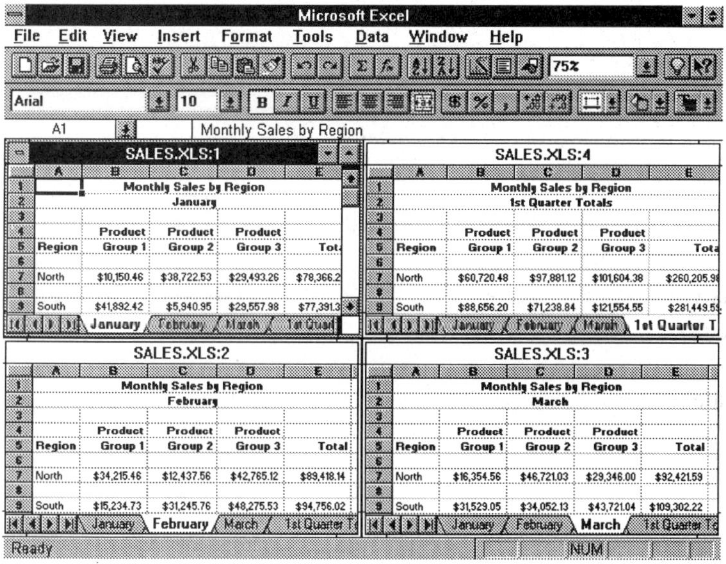

Notes

- When you open a new window for a workbook, *Excel* displays the number of the window after the file name in the title bar.
- To change the screen back so it displays only one worksheet at a time, click on the maximize button in any of the worksheet windows.
- You can also activate a window by pressing Ctrl+F6 to switch to the next window or by selecting the window name from the list at the bottom of the Window menu.

Figure 9-5 How to display more than one worksheet at a time

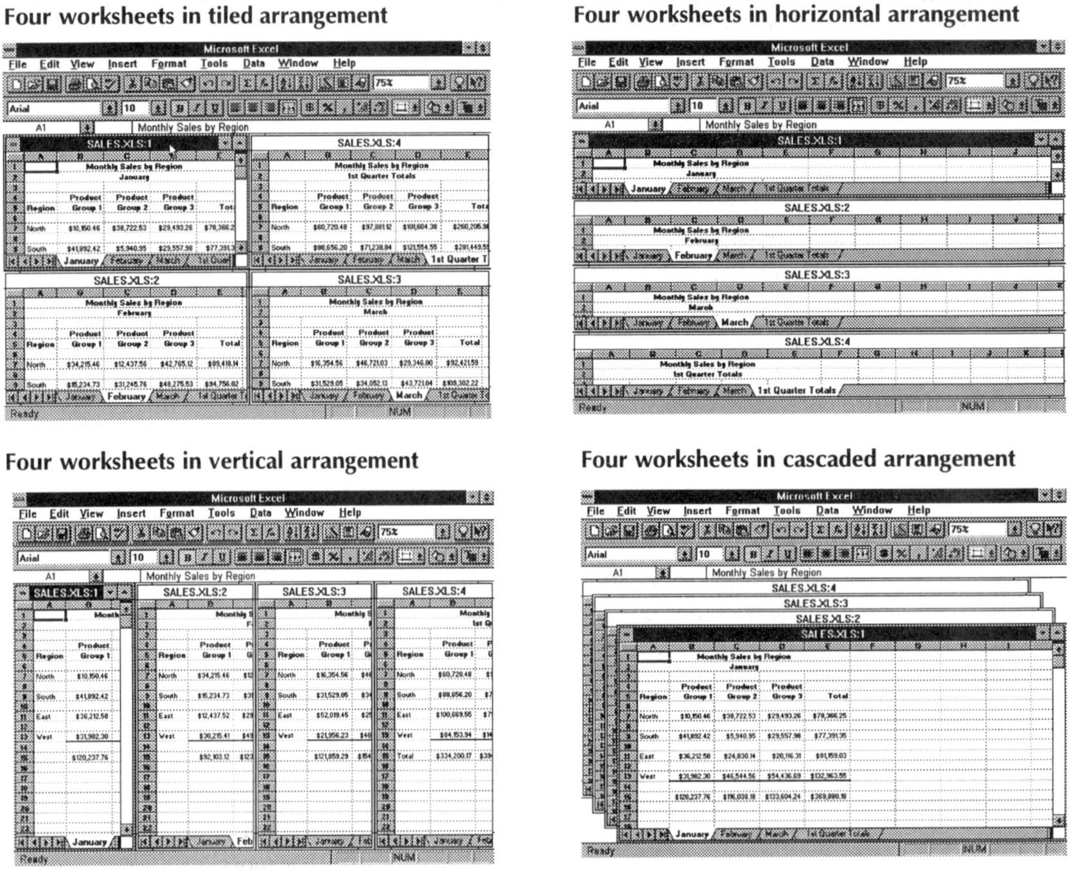

Figure 9-6 Examples of the four Arrange options

How to move or copy worksheets *Excel* provides two methods for moving and copying the worksheets in a workbook. First, you can use the drag-and-drop method presented in figure 9-9. Second, you can use the Move or Copy Sheet command presented in figure 9-10. When you use either of these methods, you can move or copy more than one worksheet at the same time by selecting a group of worksheets. You can also use either of these methods to move or copy worksheets to another workbook. You'll learn how to do that later when I show you how to work with worksheets from two or more workbooks.

How to select a group of adjacent worksheets

1. Click on the tab of the first worksheet in the group.
2. Hold down the Shift key and click on the tab of the last worksheet in the group.

How to select a group of non-adjacent worksheets

Hold down the Ctrl key and click on the tab for each worksheet you want to include in the group.

How to select all the worksheets in a workbook

Select the Select All Sheets command from the shortcut menu that's displayed when you click the right mouse button on a sheet tab.

Two ways to ungroup worksheets

- Click on the tab for a worksheet that isn't in the group.
- Select the Ungroup Sheets command from the shortcut menu that's displayed when you click the right mouse button on a sheet tab.

Note

When you select a group of worksheets, *Excel* displays the word "Group" to the right of the file name in the title bar and highlights all the tabs for the selected worksheets.

Figure 9-7 How to group or ungroup worksheets

How to enter, edit, and format data in more than one worksheet at the same time When you group two or more worksheets using the techniques in figure 9-7, any changes you make to one worksheet in the group affect the other worksheets in the group. If two or more worksheets in a workbook have the same layout, then, you can enter the labels for all of them and format all of them at the same time. You can also enter formulas and functions in the worksheets using this technique. And if you need to make any changes that affect all of the worksheets in the group, you can edit the data in one worksheet and *Excel* will apply the changes to the other worksheets.

If you use this technique to enter, edit, and format worksheets, the only data you'll have to enter in individual worksheets is the values and labels that change from one worksheet to the next. You may also want to apply special formatting to one or more worksheets that you don't want to apply to the others. Before you do that, be sure to ungroup the worksheets using one of the techniques in figure 9-7. Then, you can enter, edit, and format the data in individual worksheets without affecting the other worksheets in the workbook.

How to add a worksheet using the Worksheet command in the Insert menu

1. Click on the tab of the worksheet before which you want to add a worksheet.
2. Select the Worksheet command from the Insert menu.

How to add a worksheet using the Insert command in the shortcut menu

1. Click the right mouse button on the tab for the worksheet before which you want to add a worksheet, and a shortcut menu appears.
2. Select the Insert command and this dialog box appears:

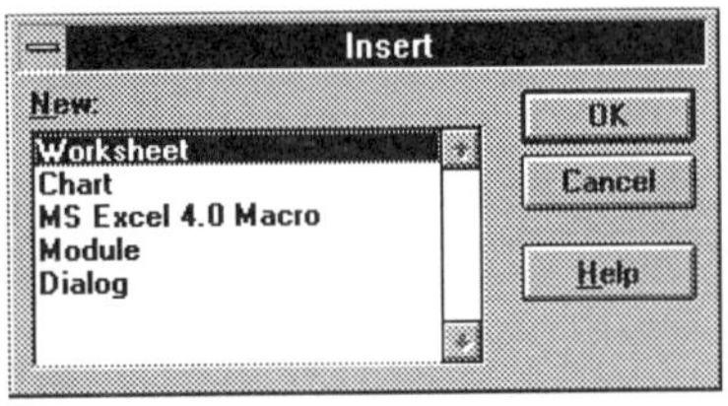

3. Select the Worksheet option from the New list box.
4. Click on the OK button.

Note

You can add more than one worksheet by selecting an adjacent group of worksheets that contains the number of worksheets that you want to insert. The new worksheets are inserted in front of the first worksheet you select.

How to delete worksheets

1. Select the worksheets that you want to delete.
2. Select the Delete Sheet command from the Edit menu, or select the Delete command from the shortcut menu that's displayed when you click the right mouse button on a sheet tab, and this dialog box appears:

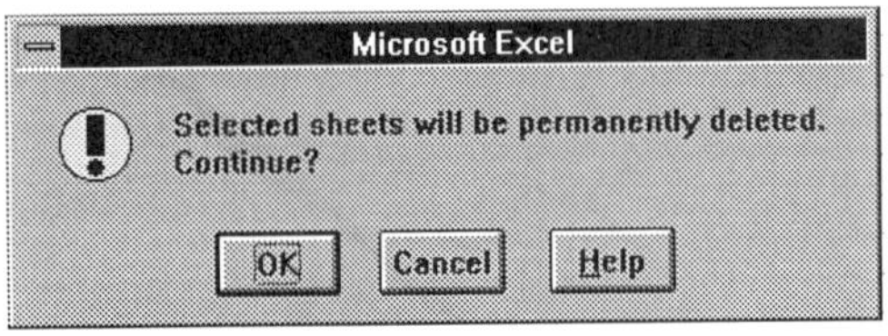

3. Click on the OK button to delete the worksheets.

Figure 9-8 How to add or delete one or more worksheets

How to enter and edit formulas and functions that refer to other worksheets In general, the procedures for entering and editing formulas and functions in a workbook that contains more than one worksheet are the same as the procedures for entering and editing them in a single

How to move a worksheet

1. Position the pointer over the tab of the worksheet you want to move, and press and hold the mouse button. A small black arrowhead appears above the row of tabs marking where the worksheet will be inserted:

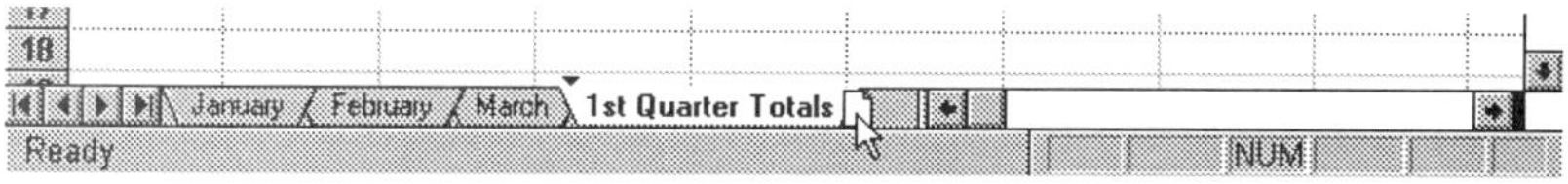

2. Drag the worksheet so the arrowhead points to the location where you want to move it:

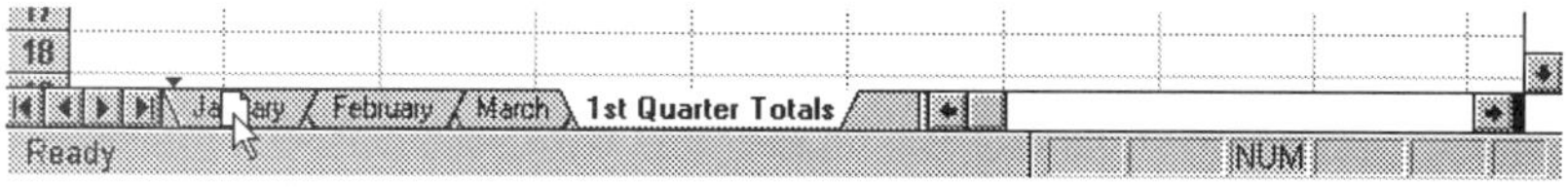

3. Release the mouse button and the worksheet is moved to the new location:

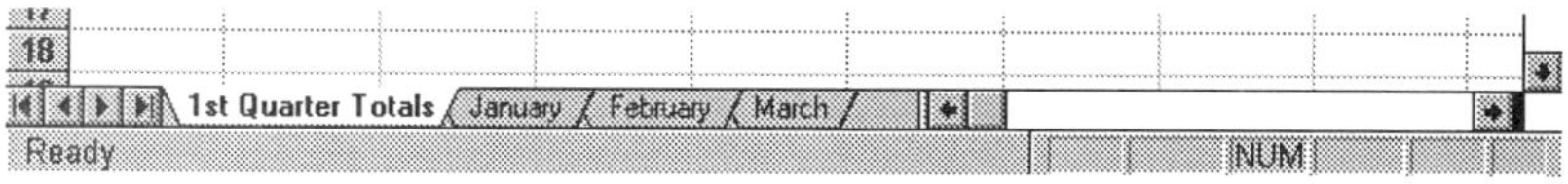

How to copy a worksheet

Use the same procedure as above, but hold down the Ctrl key as you drag the worksheet. A plus sign appears inside the worksheet pointer to indicate a copy operation.

Notes

- You can move or copy more than one worksheet at a time by selecting a group, then dragging the tab of one of the selected worksheets to the new location.
- You can also move or copy worksheets to another open workbook. To do that, the tabs for both workbooks must be visible on the screen.
- You can also move or copy worksheets to a new workbook. To do that, select the worksheets and drag them outside the workbook window.

Figure 9-9 How to use the drag-and-drop feature to move or copy one or more worksheets

worksheet. The only difference is that if a formula or function refers to a cell in another worksheet, you need to identify the worksheet that contains that cell. To do that, you precede the cell reference with the worksheet name followed by an exclamation point. For example,

Sheet1!A1

refers to cell A1 in the worksheet named Sheet1, and

Sheet1:Sheet3!B4:B7

refers to the range of cells from B4 to B7 in the range of worksheets from Sheet1 to Sheet3. A range like this that includes cells from two or more worksheets is called a *3-D range*.

How to move a worksheet

1. Select the worksheets you want to move.
2. Select the Move or Copy Sheet command from the Edit menu, or select the Move or Copy command from the shortcut menu that's displayed when you click the right mouse button on a sheet tab. Then, this dialog box appears:

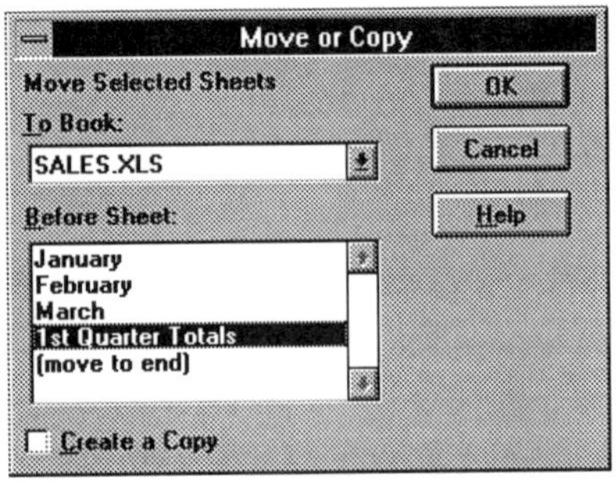

3. Select the worksheet before which you want to move the worksheet from the Before Sheet list box.
4. Click on the OK button.

How to copy a worksheet

Use the same procedure as above, but select the Create A Copy option from the Move or Copy dialog box.

Notes

- You can also move or copy worksheets to another open workbook. To do that, select the workbook where you want to move or copy the worksheets from the To Book drop-down list box.
- You can also move or copy worksheets to a new workbook. To do that, select the New Workbook option from the To Book drop-down list box.

Figure 9-10 How to use the Move or Copy Sheet command to move or copy one or more worksheets

Although you can type in a cell reference with the appropriate worksheet names, it's usually easier to use the cell pointer to identify the cell or range you want to include. To identify a cell or a range that consists of cells in a single worksheet, you just switch to the worksheet and highlight the range using the mouse or the keyboard. Then, *Excel* automatically includes the worksheet name in the reference.

To identify a 3-D range, you use the technique presented in figure 9-11. Here, I entered a SUM function to calculate the sum of the values in cell B7 in each of the first three worksheets, named January, February, and March,

Procedure

1. Enter the function up to the point where you want to insert the 3-D reference:

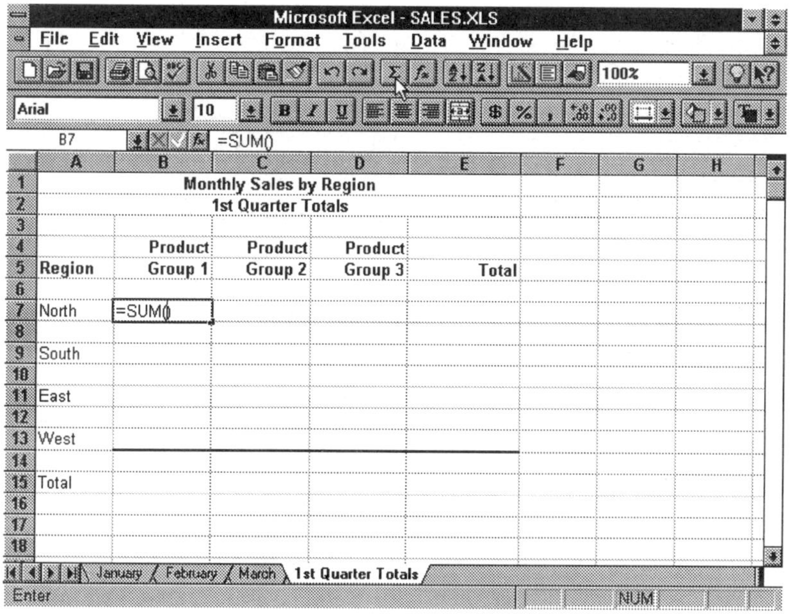

2. Click on the tab for the worksheet that contains the first cell in the 3-D range, and move the cell pointer to that cell:

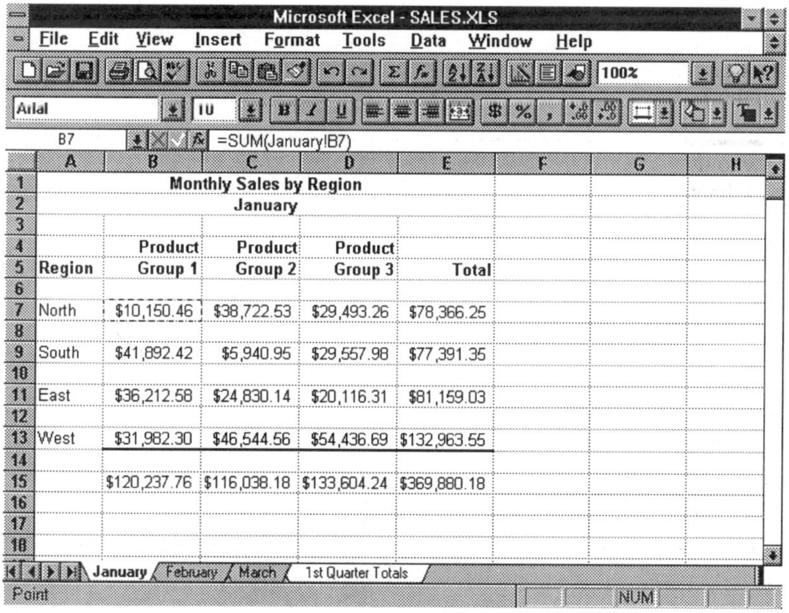

Figure 9-11 How to enter a 3-D reference into a function (part 1 of 2)

3. Press and hold the Shift key, then click on the tab for the worksheet that contains the last cell in the range:

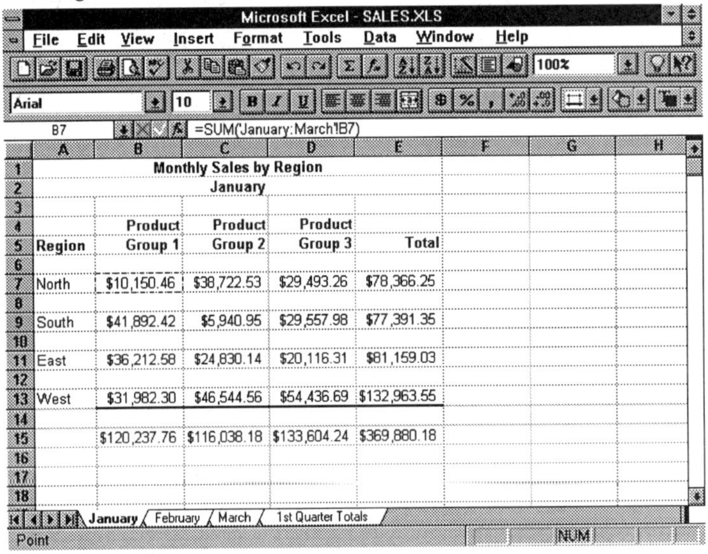

4. Press the Enter key to accept the reference and *Excel* completes the function:

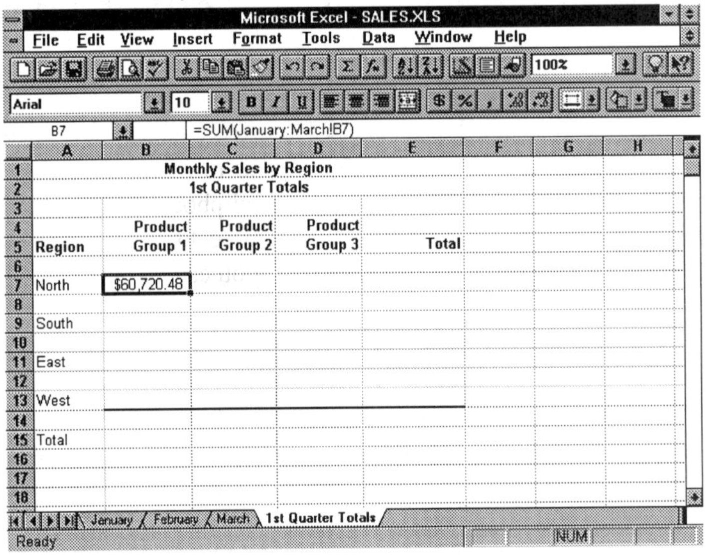

Notes

- You can also select a 3-D range that consists of a range of cells from two or more worksheets. To select the range in the first worksheet, use the mouse or any of the keyboard techniques.
- *Excel* provides no way to extend a range to other worksheets using the keyboard. You have to use the mouse.

Figure 9-11 How to enter a 3-D reference into a function (part 2 of 2)

1. Select a group of worksheets that includes the worksheet that contains the data you want to copy and the worksheets you want to copy the data to.
2. Select the cell or range that contains the data you want to copy.
3. Select the Fill Across Worksheets command from the Edit menu and this dialog box appears:

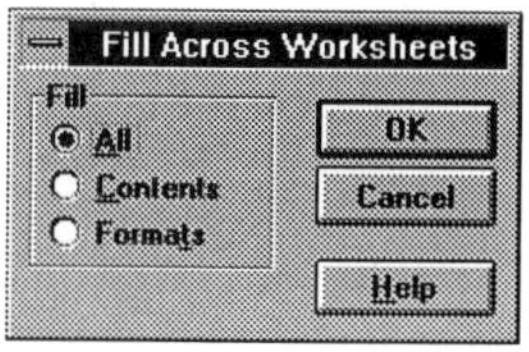

4. Select a Fill option and click on the OK button.

Figure 9-12 How to copy data from one worksheet to the same location in other worksheets

and I stored the result in cell B7 of the last worksheet. Note that you can also use this technique to select a range of cells in each of the worksheets. Although you can use either the mouse or the keyboard to select the cell or range in the first worksheet, you can use only the mouse to extend the range to the other worksheets.

How to move or copy data from one worksheet to another To move or copy data from one worksheet to another, you use the clipboard and the Cut, Copy, and Paste commands just as you do to move or copy data within a single worksheet. The only difference when you're working with two worksheets is that after you copy the data to the clipboard from the first worksheet, you have to move to the second worksheet to paste it. Since the data remains in the clipboard after you paste it, you can duplicate the data in several worksheets if you need to.

You can also copy data from a cell or range in one worksheet into the same location in other worksheets. To do that, you use the Fill Across Worksheets command illustrated in figure 9-12. Notice that before you use this command, you have to group the worksheet that contains the data you want to copy with the worksheets you want to copy the data to. Then, when you issue the command, *Excel* copies the data in the range you select to the same range in the other worksheets in the group.

How to hide one or more worksheets

1. Select the worksheets you want to hide.
2. Select the Sheet Hide command from the Format menu.

How to expose a worksheet

1. Select the Sheet Unhide command from the Format menu and this dialog box appears:

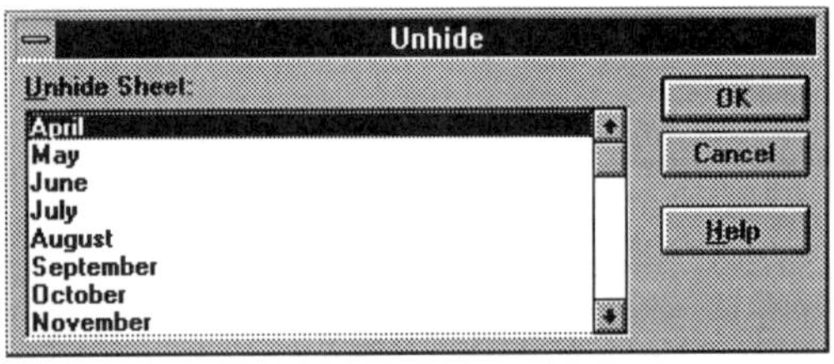

2. Highlight the worksheet you want to expose in the Unhide Sheet list box.
3. Click on the OK button.

Notes

- If a workbook contains a single worksheet, you can't hide it.
- You can expose only one worksheet at a time.

Figure 9-13 How to hide or expose worksheets

How to hide or expose worksheets Figure 9-13 presents the procedures for hiding and exposing worksheets. As you can see, you can hide more than one worksheet at the same time by selecting a group. However, you can expose only one worksheet at a time. Also note that if a workbook contains only one worksheet, you can't hide it.

How to work with named ranges Normally, a name you create for a range of cells is defined at the workbook level. In other words, you can use the name throughout the workbook to refer to the range it identifies. Because of that, you can't assign the same name to two different ranges in a workbook, even if the ranges are in different worksheets.

If you want to use the same name for two or more ranges in different worksheets of the same workbook, you can define them at the sheet level.

To do that, you precede the range name with the worksheet name. For example, the name

Sheet1!North

refers to the range associated with the name North in the worksheet named Sheet1. Once you define a name at the worksheet level, you can refer to it from any worksheet in the workbook. Note that if you refer to a named range from the worksheet where it's defined, however, you don't need to include the worksheet name in the reference.

How to work with worksheets from two or more workbooks

If two or more related worksheets have the same layout and contain related information, you'll almost certainly want to store them in the same workbook. Occasionally, though, you may want to use worksheets in two or more different workbooks at the same time. To do that, you need the skills that follow.

How to open two or more workbooks and switch between them To use worksheets from two or more workbooks at the same time, you have to open the files that contain them. To do that, you can issue the Open command for each file. Or, if the files are stored in the same directory, you can open them all at once. To do that, hold down the Ctrl key as you select the files from the Open dialog box. Or, to select a range of files, select the first file, then hold down the Shift key and select the last file. *Excel* creates a document window for each file you open.

By default, you can see only one document window at a time because they overlay one another. To display a workbook other than the current one, then, you have to switch to it. Figure 9-14 presents two ways to switch to another workbook. If you use the Window menu, you can switch to any open workbook. If you use Ctrl+F6, *Excel* displays the next workbook in sequence.

How to display two or more workbooks at the same time If you want to display all of the open workbooks at the same time, you can use one of the Arrange options you saw in figure 9-6. When you issue the Arrange

Method 1: Select the workbook you want to switch to from the Window menu:

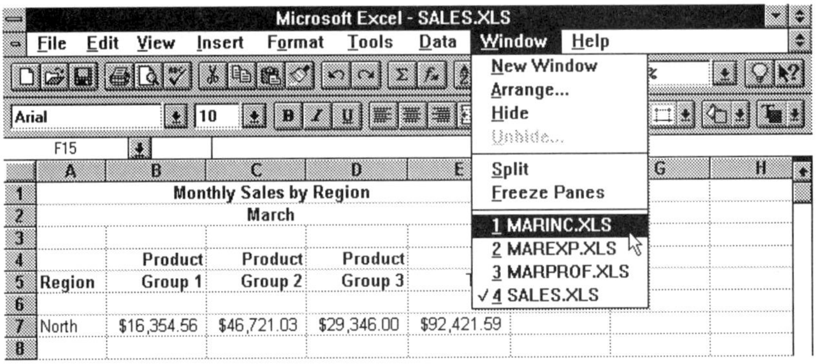

Method 2: Press Ctrl+F6 to display the next workbook.

Figure 9-14 Two ways to switch from one workbook to another

command, be sure that the Windows Of Active Workbook option isn't selected. Otherwise, *Excel* will display only the windows in the current workbook. The default is to display the windows for all open workbooks.

When you use the Arrange command to display the windows for open workbooks, you can switch to another window by clicking on it. When you switch to another window in a configuration where the windows are overlapped, *Excel* brings the window to the top of the stack so you can see all of it. To maximize, move, resize, or close the windows, you can use the *Windows* techniques presented in chapter 1.

How to move or copy worksheets from one workbook to another Earlier in this chapter, you learned how to use the drag-and-drop feature and the Move or Copy Sheet command to move and copy worksheets within a workbook. Figures 9-9 and 9-10 present these techniques. You can also use these techniques to move and copy worksheets to another workbook.

To use the drag-and-drop feature to move or copy worksheets from one workbook to another, both workbooks must be open and the sheet tabs in both workbooks must be visible. Then, you can drag the worksheet from one workbook to the other. You can also move or copy worksheets to a new workbook by dragging them outside the workbook window and releasing

1. Place the cell pointer on the cell that contains the data you want to move or copy, and cut or copy the data to the clipboard.
2. Switch to the other workbook and place the cell pointer on the cell where you want to paste the data.
3. Select the Paste Special command from the Edit menu and this dialog box appears:

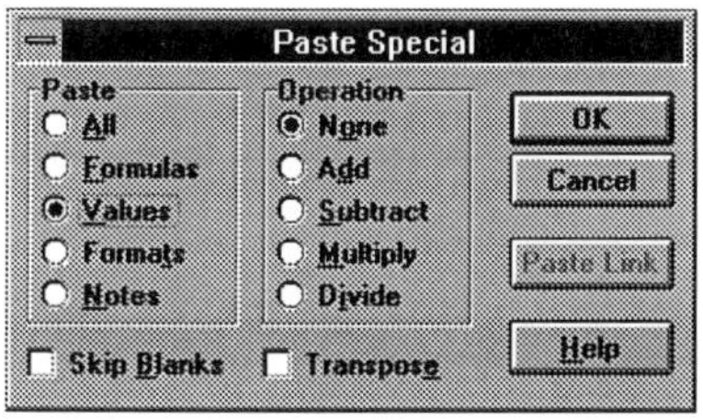

4. Select the Values option from the Paste group.
5. Click on the OK button and the value of the data in the clipboard is inserted.

Figure 9-15 How to paste a formula from one workbook as a value in another workbook

the mouse button. Then, *Excel* creates a new workbook for the selected worksheets.

To use the Move or Copy Sheet command to move or copy worksheets from one workbook to another, you select the destination workbook in the To Book drop-down list box of the Move or Copy dialog box. Then, you select the worksheet before which you want to insert the worksheets from the Before Sheet list box. You can also move or copy worksheets to a new workbook by selecting the New Book option from the To Book drop-down list box.

How to move or copy data from one workbook to another If you want to move or copy data from one workbook to another, you use the clipboard. Just issue the Cut or Copy command, switch to another workbook, and issue the Paste command. You need to be careful, however, if you're moving or copying a cell that contains a formula. If you want to paste the value instead of the formula, you need to use the Paste Special command presented in figure 9-15. When you use this command, you select the Values option from the Paste group. Then, *Excel* places the value of the formula in the current cell.

How to link cells between workbooks Although you can copy data from one workbook to another using the procedures I just presented, the copied data is independent of the original data. That means that if you update the original data, it has no affect on the copied data. If you want to, however, you can *link* the cells that contain the data in the two workbooks so that when the original data is changed, the copied data is updated.

You'll use two operations to link cells from one workbook to another. If you want simply to "copy" the data from one workbook to another, you can use the Paste Special command as presented in figure 9-16. When you use the Paste Link option of this command, *Excel* automatically includes a reference to the linked workbook in the cell reference. You can see this workbook reference in the entry area of the formula bar in the screen at the bottom of the figure.

If you want to refer to another workbook in a formula or function, you can use one of the techniques in figure 9-17. First, you can use the cell pointer to select the cell or highlight the range in the workbook that you want to refer to. This technique is illustrated in figure 9-18. To use this technique, both workbooks must be open. Second, you can type in the workbook reference using the format indicated in the second method in figure 9-17. To use this technique, the workbook that you're referring to doesn't have to be open.

Once you've established links to other workbooks, you want to be sure the links are updated when the data changes. As you can see in figure 9-19, *Excel* updates the workbook links automatically when the Calculation option is set to Automatic. If you don't want workbook links to be updated automatically, you need to change the Calculation option to Manual.

Whenever you open a workbook that contains a link to a closed workbook, a dialog box appears that asks if you want to re-establish the links between the workbooks. If you click on the Yes button and the Calculation option is set to Automatic, the linked data is updated. If the Calculation option is set to Manual, *Excel* re-establishes the link but doesn't update the data. Then, you have to press the F9 key to update the data. The data is also updated when you save the workbook if the Recalculate Before Save option is selected.

1. Open the workbook that contains the cell you want to refer to, and copy the data to the clipboard:

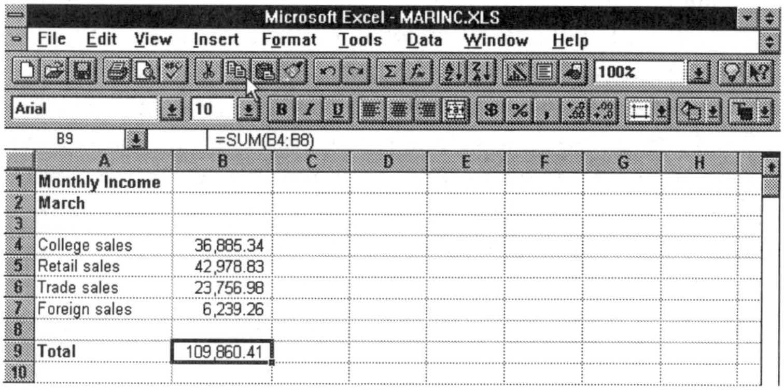

2. Switch to the workbook where you want to place the reference, and place the cell pointer on the appropriate cell.
3. Select the Paste Special command from the Edit menu and this dialog box appears:

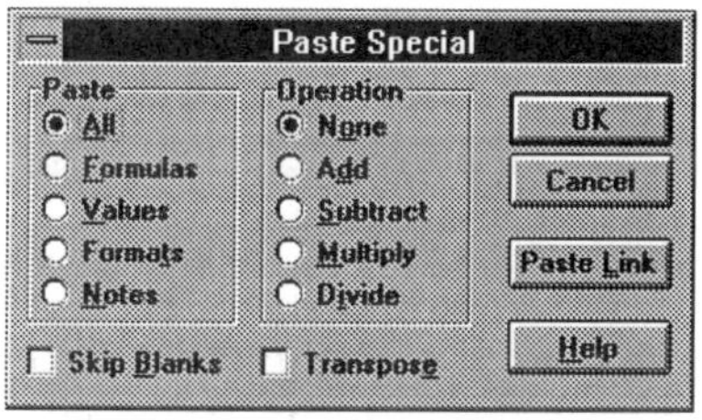

4. Click on the Paste Link button and the workbook reference is inserted into the worksheet:

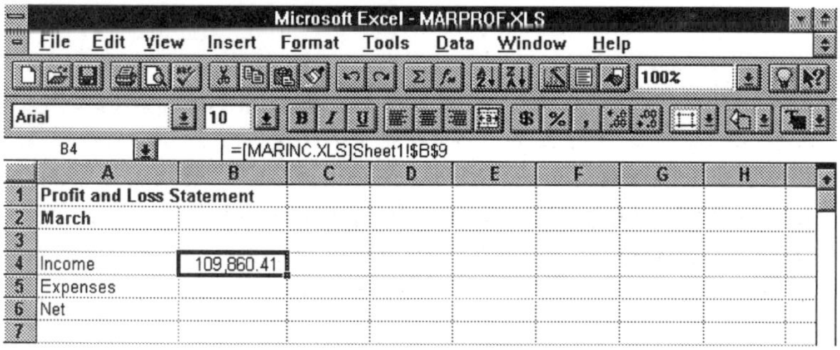

Figure 9-16 How to link a cell in one workbook to a cell in another workbook

Use the cell pointer

1. Open both workbooks.
2. Enter the formula that will contain the workbook reference up to the point where you want to refer to the other open workbook.
3. Switch to the other workbook and highlight the range you want to refer to.

Type it in

Enter the formula that will contain the workbook reference up to the point where you want to refer to the other workbook, and type in the reference using this format:

[filename.xls]sheetname!range

Notes

- To make switching between workbooks easier, arrange the workbook windows so you can see both of them.
- You can type in a reference for any workbook, whether or not it's open.

Figure 9-17 Two ways to enter a workbook reference in a formula or function

Perspective

In most cases, it's more efficient to store two or more related worksheets in a single workbook. Then, the worksheets are easier to work with, and you don't have to worry about whether or not the links have been updated. When you include more than one worksheet in a single workbook, however, all the worksheets are in internal memory at the same time. As a result, your PC will require more memory to accommodate the worksheets and may run more slowly. In that case, it may be more efficient to store each worksheet in its own workbook.

1. Open the workbook that will contain the SUM function and the workbook you want to refer to in the function, and arrange the workbook windows so you can see both of them. Then, begin the SUM function by clicking on the AutoSum button or by typing it:

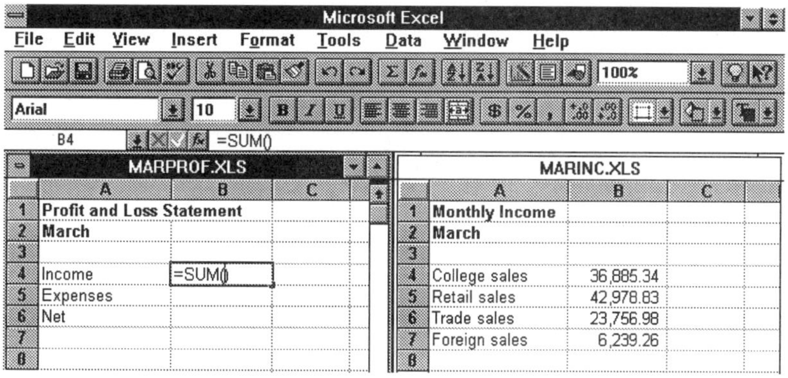

2. Highlight the range in the other workbook you want to refer to, and the workbook reference is included in the SUM function:

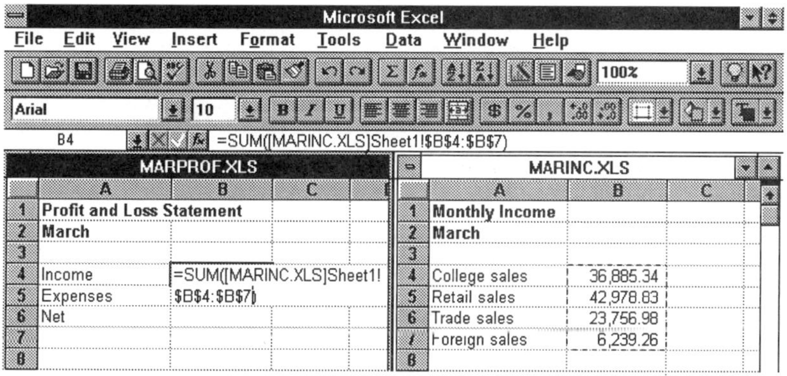

3. Press the Enter key to complete the formula:

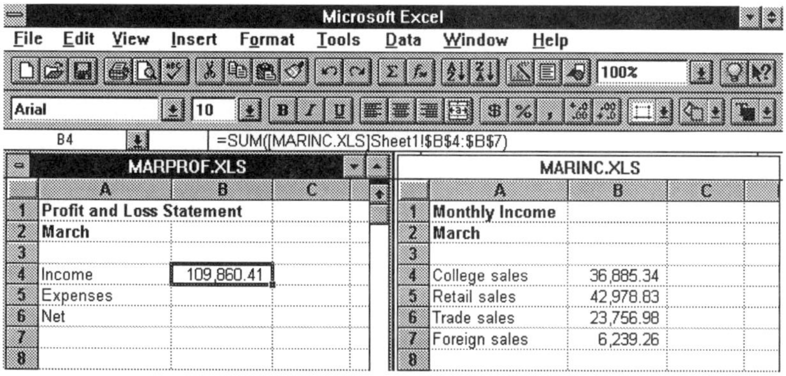

Figure 9-18 How to enter a SUM function that refers to a range in another open workbook

If the Calculation option is set to Automatic

- If the workbook that contains the link and the workbook it's linked to are both open, any changes you make to the linked data are reflected in the workbook that contains the link.
- If you open a workbook that contains a link to another workbook, a dialog box appears that asks if you want to re-establish the links. Click on the Yes button and the linked data is updated.

If the Calculation option is set to Manual

1. Open the workbook that contains the links, and a dialog box appears that asks if you want to re-establish the links.
2. Click on the Yes button and the links are re-established, but the linked data isn't updated.
3. Press the F9 key at any time to update the workbook links.

Notes

- If the Recalculate Before Save option is selected along with the Manual option, the linked data is automatically updated when you save the workbook.
- You can set the Calculation option using the Calculation tab in the Options dialog box. See chapter 4 for details.

Figure 9-19 How to update workbook links

Summary

- You can use the controls on the workbook window to switch to another worksheet, change a worksheet name, scroll the sheet tabs, and increase or decrease the size of the tab area.
- To change a worksheet name, double-click on the sheet tab or select the Rename command from the shortcut menu, and enter the name.
- To move to another worksheet, click on its tab or use the key combinations.
- To display more than one worksheet at the same time, create a new window for each worksheet using the New Window command in the Window menu and arrange the windows using the Arrange command in the Window menu.
- To select a group of worksheets, hold down the Ctrl key as you click on the sheet tabs.
- To add a worksheet to a workbook, use the Worksheet command in the Insert menu or the Insert command in the shortcut menu.
- To delete worksheets, use the Delete Sheet command in the Edit menu or the Delete command in the shortcut menu.

- To move or copy worksheets within a workbook or from one workbook to another, use the drag-and-drop feature, the Move or Copy Sheet command in the Edit menu, or the Move or Copy command in the shortcut menu.
- You can enter, edit, and format data in more than one worksheet at a time by grouping the worksheets. Then, any changes you make to one worksheet in the group are reflected in the other worksheets in the group.
- A reference to a cell in another worksheet must include the worksheet name, like this: Sheet2!D4. A reference to a range that includes cells from two or more worksheets is called a *3-D range*. A 3-D reference looks like this: Sheet1:Sheet3!A4:D4.
- You can move or copy data from one worksheet to another using the clipboard and the Cut, Copy, and Paste commands. You can also copy data to other worksheets using the Fill Across Worksheets command in the Edit menu.
- To hide worksheets, use the Sheet Hide command in the Format menu. To expose worksheets, use the Sheet Unhide command in the Format menu.
- To open two or more workbooks at the same time, issue the Open command. Then, *Excel* opens a workbook window for each workbook.
- To switch from one workbook to another, select the workbook name from the Window menu or press Ctrl+F6.
- To display all the open workbooks on the screen at the same time, use the Arrange command in the Window menu.
- To move and copy data from one workbook to another, use the clipboard and the Cut, Copy, and Paste commands. To copy a formula from one workbook and paste it as a value in another workbook, use the Paste Special command in the Edit menu.
- To link a cell in one workbook to a cell in another workbook, use the Paste Link option of the Paste Special command.
- To enter a reference to another workbook in a formula or function, highlight a range in the workbook or type in the workbook reference.
- If the Calculation option is set to Automatic, workbook links are updated automatically. If the Calculation option is set to Manual, you can update workbook links by pressing the F9 key.

Chapter 10

How to print a worksheet

In this chapter, you'll start by reviewing the basic procedure for printing worksheets. Then, you'll learn how to preview a worksheet and how to insert and remove page breaks. Finally, you'll learn how to use the tabs of the Page Setup command to set up your worksheets so they look the way you want them to when they're printed.

So you'll have some idea of what you can do with the *Excel* printing features, figure 10-1 shows a worksheet that was printed with *Excel*'s defaults. Then, figure 10-2 shows the same worksheet after I changed the page breaks, changed the margins so the worksheet is centered, added a header, added titles to each page, and removed the footer and grid lines. Since most of these features are easy to use, you should take advantage of them whenever they're appropriate.

How to print all or part of a worksheet

Figure 10-3 presents the dialog box you use to print all or part of a worksheet. As you can see, you can use the Print dialog box to print a selection, a selected worksheet, or all the worksheets in the current workbook. If you select an embedded chart before you start the Print command, you can also use it to print just the chart.

The other print options let you print selected pages and multiple copies. You can also change the page setup of the worksheet by clicking on the Page Setup button. You can preview the printed worksheet by clicking on the Print Preview button. And you can select another printer by clicking on the Printer Setup button.

How to preview a worksheet before you print it

Figure 10-4 shows you how to preview a worksheet before you print it so you can make sure the pages are going to look the way you want them to. As you can see, you can use the buttons at the top of the display to perform several functions. For example, you can use the Zoom button to switch between full-page and magnified view. You can also switch between these two views by clicking anywhere on the page.

The Margins button at the top of the preview screen lets you change the page margins, the margins for the headers and footers, and the widths of the columns in the printed worksheet. When you click on this button, dotted lines with handles at each end appear at each margin. Handles also appear at the right side of each column. You can see these lines and handles in figure 10-4. To change a margin or a column width, place the pointer over a

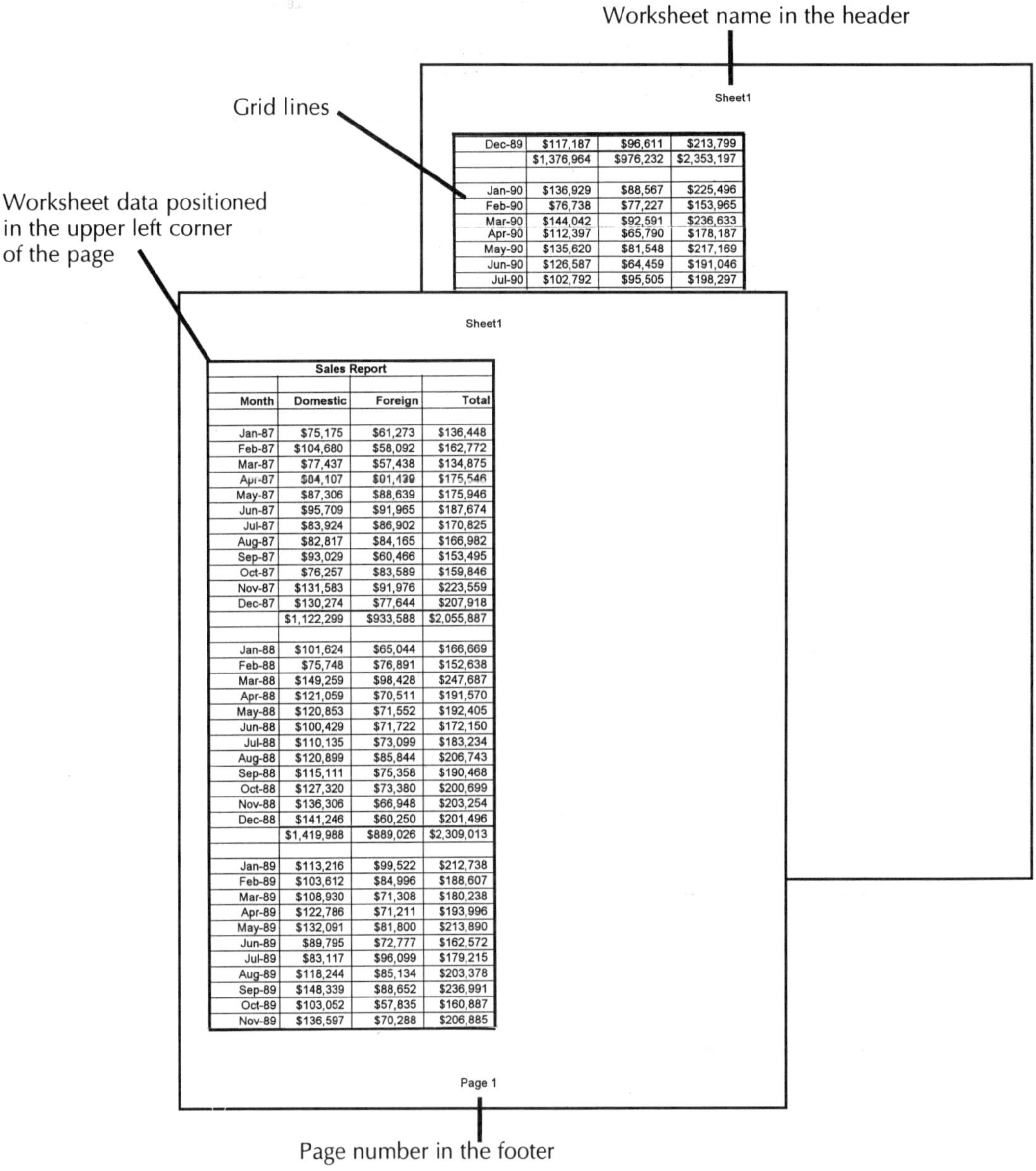

Dec-89	$117,187	$96,611	$213,799
	$1,376,964	$976,232	$2,353,197
Jan-90	$136,929	$88,567	$225,496
Feb-90	$76,738	$77,227	$153,965
Mar-90	$144,042	$92,591	$236,633
Apr-90	$112,397	$65,790	$178,187
May-90	$135,620	$81,548	$217,169
Jun-90	$126,587	$64,459	$191,046
Jul-90	$102,792	$95,505	$198,297

Sales Report			
Month	Domestic	Foreign	Total
Jan-87	$75,175	$61,273	$136,448
Feb-87	$104,680	$58,092	$162,772
Mar-87	$77,437	$57,438	$134,875
Apr-87	$84,107	$91,439	$175,546
May-87	$87,306	$88,639	$175,946
Jun-87	$95,709	$91,965	$187,674
Jul-87	$83,924	$86,902	$170,825
Aug-87	$82,817	$84,165	$166,982
Sep-87	$93,029	$60,466	$153,495
Oct-87	$76,257	$83,589	$159,846
Nov-87	$131,583	$91,976	$223,559
Dec-87	$130,274	$77,644	$207,918
	$1,122,299	$933,588	$2,055,887
Jan-88	$101,624	$65,044	$166,669
Feb-88	$75,748	$76,891	$152,638
Mar-88	$149,259	$98,428	$247,687
Apr-88	$121,059	$70,511	$191,570
May-88	$120,853	$71,552	$192,405
Jun-88	$100,429	$71,722	$172,150
Jul-88	$110,135	$73,099	$183,234
Aug-88	$120,899	$85,844	$206,743
Sep-88	$115,111	$75,358	$190,468
Oct-88	$127,320	$73,380	$200,699
Nov-88	$136,306	$66,948	$203,254
Dec-88	$141,246	$60,250	$201,496
	$1,419,988	$889,026	$2,309,013
Jan-89	$113,216	$99,522	$212,738
Feb-89	$103,612	$84,996	$188,607
Mar-89	$108,930	$71,308	$180,238
Apr-89	$122,786	$71,211	$193,996
May-89	$132,091	$81,800	$213,890
Jun-89	$89,795	$72,777	$162,572
Jul-89	$83,117	$96,099	$179,215
Aug-89	$118,244	$85,134	$203,378
Sep-89	$148,339	$88,652	$236,991
Oct-89	$103,052	$57,835	$160,887
Nov-89	$136,597	$70,288	$206,885

Figure 10-1 A worksheet printed using *Excel*'s defaults

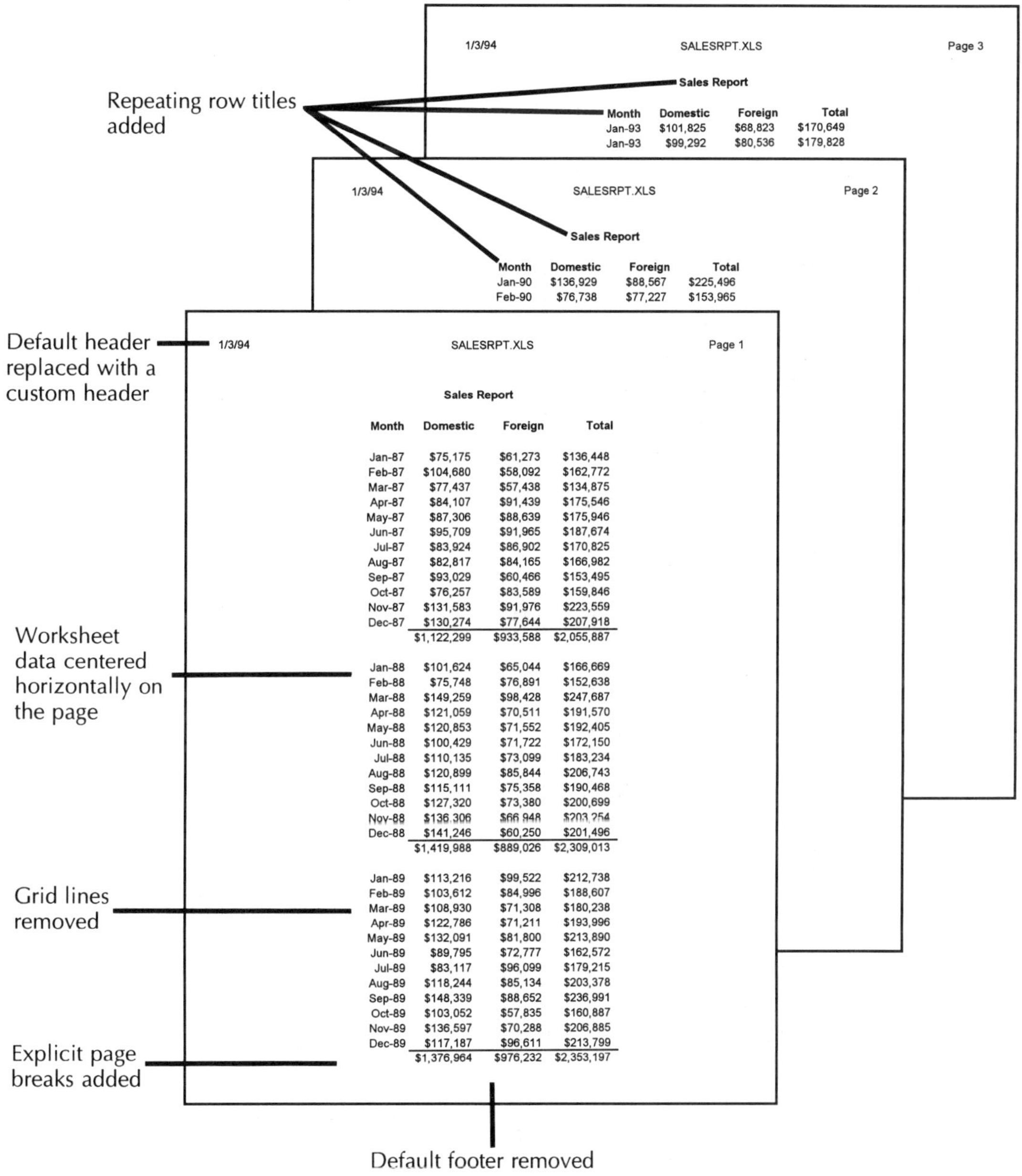

Figure 10-2 A worksheet that uses several of *Excel*'s printing features

Three ways to access the Print dialog box

- Select the Print command from the File menu.
- Press Ctrl+P.
- Click on the Print button from the Print Preview window or any of the tabs in the Page Setup dialog box.

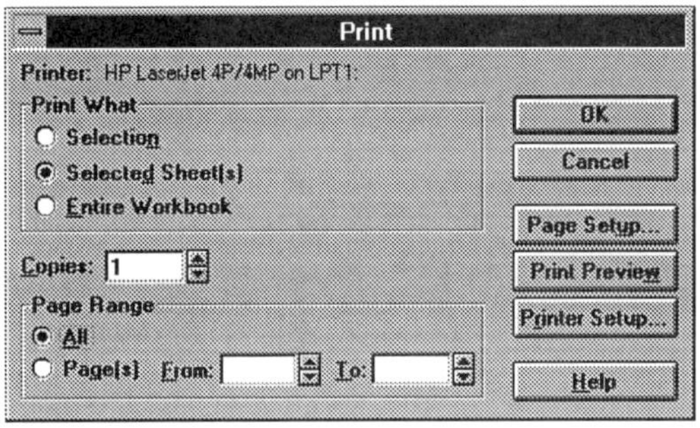

Print What group

The default is to print the current worksheet, unless you select a range or a chart before issuing the Print command. You can also print the entire workbook.

Copies option

The default is to print one copy.

Page Range group

The default is to print all the pages, but you can also select a range of pages.

Notes

- You can click on the Page Setup button to change the page setup, you can click on the Print Preview button to preview the printed worksheet, and you can click on the Printer Setup button to select another printer.
- You can print the current worksheet according to the settings you previously selected by clicking on the Print button in the Standard toolbar: 

Figure 10-3 How to print all or part of a worksheet

handle and drag it. Although you can also change the margins using the Page Setup command as you'll see later in this chapter, you can see the effect immediately if you change them from the preview screen.

Three ways to access the Print Preview window

- Click on the Print Preview button in the Standard toolbar: 
- Select the Print Preview command from the File Menu.
- Click on the Print Preview button in the Print dialog box or any of the tabs in the Page Setup dialog box.

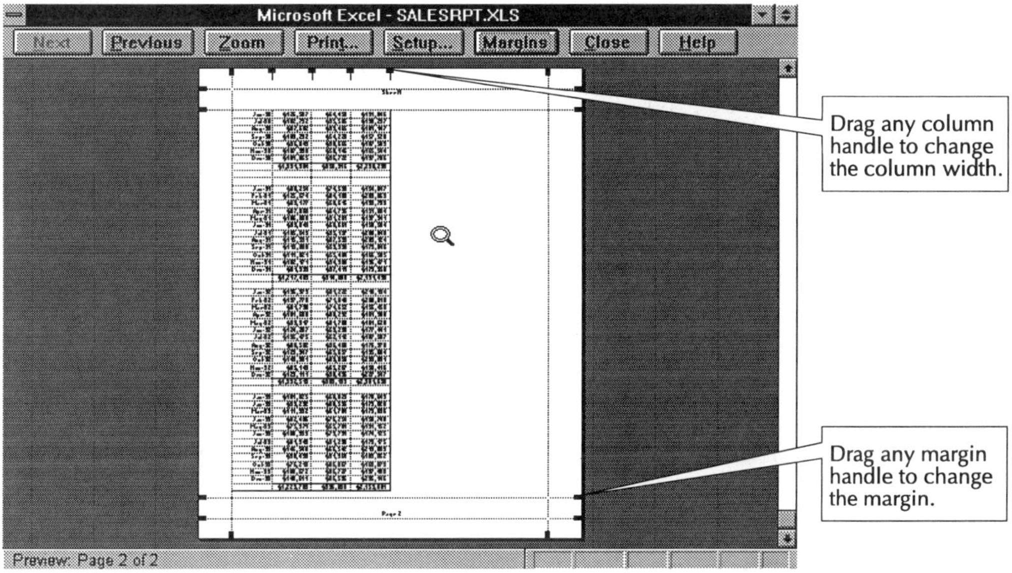

Button	Function
Next	Displays the next page.
Previous	Displays the previous page.
Zoom	Toggles between full-page and magnified view.
Print	Displays the Print dialog box.
Setup	Displays the Page Setup dialog box.
Margins	Displays handles you can use to adjust the margins and column widths.
Close	Closes the Print Preview window and returns to the current worksheet.
Help	Displays Help information for the Print Preview window.

Notes

- You can use the arrow keys or the scroll bars to move from one page to another in full-page view or to move around a page in magnified view.
- You can click on any area of a page in full-page view to magnify it. Click again to return to full-page view.
- To change a margin or column width, place the pointer over the appropriate handle and drag it.

Figure 10-4 How to preview a worksheet

How to change page breaks

By default, *Excel* automatically inserts *horizontal page breaks* based on the settings for the top and bottom margins and *vertical page breaks* based on the settings for the left and right margins. *Excel* represents page breaks with dashed lines in the worksheet, but only after you preview a worksheet or after you print it for the first time. If you can't see the page breaks in your worksheets, you need to select the Automatic Page Breaks option in the View tab of the Options dialog box.

Often, though, the automatic page breaks don't occur where you want them to. In that case, you can insert your own page breaks as summarized in figure 10-5. To insert a page break, you use the Page Break command in the Insert menu. As you can see, where you place the cell pointer prior to issuing the Page Break command determines where *Excel* places the page break.

Later, if you want to delete a page break, you move the cell pointer to the row immediately below or to the column immediately to the right of the page break, and you select the Remove Page Break command from the Insert menu. You should know that you can remove only the page breaks you insert, not the automatic page breaks *Excel* inserts.

How to set the Page options

Figure 10-6 presents the Page tab of the Page Setup dialog box. You can use this tab to change the orientation, quality, and first page number of the printed output as well as the paper size. You can also use this tab to size a worksheet so it fits on fewer pages.

How to change the print orientation, paper size, first page number, and print quality To change the orientation of a worksheet, you select the Portrait or Landscape option from the Page tab of the Page Setup dialog box. If you select Landscape, your worksheet will print sideways on the paper. This is useful when your worksheet is too wide to fit across the paper, but it will fit sideways. The default orientation is Portrait, which prints up and down on the paper.

You can also specify the size of paper you want to use and the print quality by selecting options from the Paper Size and Print Quality drop-down list boxes. The options that are available depend on the printer you're using. Finally, you can change the page number that's printed on the first page of the printed output by selecting an option from the First Page Number drop-down list box. The default is Auto, which means that *Excel* uses the page number of the first page you're printing in the document.

How to insert a vertical page break

1. Place the cell pointer in row 1 of the column to the right of where you want to insert the page break.
2. Select the Page Break command from the Insert menu.

How to insert a horizontal page break

1. Place the cell pointer in column A of the row below where you want to insert a page break.
2. Select the Page Break command from the Insert menu.

How to insert both a vertical and a horizontal page break

1. Place the cell pointer in the column to the right of where you want a vertical page break and in the row below where you want a horizontal page break.
2. Select the Page Break command from the Insert menu.

How to remove a page break

Place the cell pointer in the column to the right or in the row below the page break you want to remove, and select the Remove Page Break command from the Insert menu.

Notes

- If you can't see the automatic page breaks in your worksheet, use the Options command from the Tools menu to select the Automatic Page Breaks option in the View tab.
- You can delete only those page breaks you insert using the Insert Page Break command. You can't delete automatic page breaks.
- You can remove all the manual page breaks in a worksheet at once by highlighting the entire worksheet and issuing the Remove Page Break command.

A worksheet that shows a horizontal page break after row 46

43	Nov-89	$136,597	$70,288	$206,885
44	Dec-89	$117,187	$96,611	$213,798
45		$1,376,964	$976,232	$2,353,197
46				
47	Jan-90	$136,929	$88,567	$225,496
48	Feb-90	$76,738	$77,227	$153,965
49	Mar-90	$144,042	$92,591	$236,633

Figure 10-5 How to insert or delete page breaks

How to size a worksheet so it fits on the page If a worksheet doesn't fit on a page, you can adjust its margins or orientation to make it fit. If that doesn't work, you can try one of the options in the Scaling group of the Page tab. Using these options, you can adjust both the height and the width of the printed output.

The Adjust To option lets you reduce or enlarge the printed output by a percent of the original size. And the Fit To option lets you specify the

Two ways to access the Page tab of the Page Setup dialog box

- Select the Page Setup command from the File menu and click on the Page tab.
- Click on the Page Setup button from either the Print dialog box or the Print Preview window, and click on the Page tab.

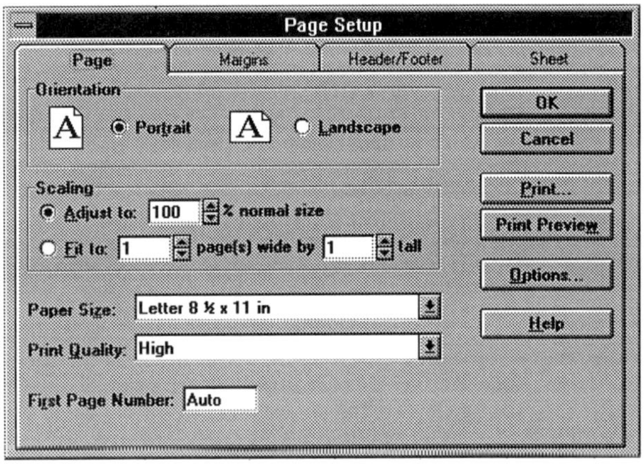

Orientation group

To print on the paper so that the longer side is vertical, select the Portrait option. To print on the paper so that the longer side is horizontal, select the Landscape option.

Scaling group

You can adjust the size of the printed document from 10 to 400 percent of its original size, or you can specify the number of pages wide and tall you want the document printed on.

Other options

You can change the paper size, the print quality, and the first page number. The default option for the first page number is Auto, which means that *Excel* will use the number of the first page you're printing in the worksheet.

Notes

- You can click on the Print button to print the worksheet, and you can click on the Print Preview button to preview the printed worksheet.
- If you click on the Options button, *Excel* displays a dialog box that lets you set options specific to the selected printer.

Figure 10-6 The Page tab of the Page setup dialog box

number of pages wide and tall you want the printed output to occupy. If you use these options, keep in mind that the more data you try to fit on a page the less readable it becomes.

Two ways to access the Margins tab of the Page Setup dialog box

- Select the Page Setup command from the File menu and click on the Margins tab.
- Click on the Page Setup button from either the Print dialog box or the Print Preview window, and click on the Margins tab.

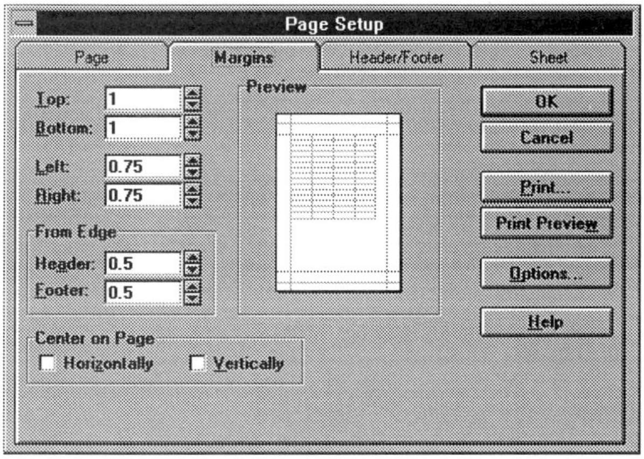

Top, Bottom, Left, and Right options

Enter the measurements for these margins in inches.

From Edge group

Enter the distance from the top of the paper to the header and from the bottom of the paper to the footer in inches.

Center On Page group

Select one or both options to center the worksheet horizontally, vertically, or both.

Notes

- The Preview box shows the current margins.
- You can click on the Print button to print the worksheet, and you can click on the Print Preview button to preview the printed worksheet.
- If you click on the Options button, *Excel* displays a dialog box that lets you set options specific to the selected printer.

Figure 10-7 The Margins tab of the Page Setup dialog box

How to set the Margins options

Figure 10-7 shows the Margins tab of the Page Setup dialog box. From this tab, you can change the margins on the page by entering values in the Top, Bottom, Left, and Right spin boxes. You can also adjust the amount of space between the edge of the paper and the header and footer by entering values in the Header and Footer spin boxes. If you want to center the worksheet horizontally, vertically, or both, select the appropriate options in the Center On Page group. You can see the results of your selections in the Preview box.

How to set the Header/Footer options

The worksheet in figure 10-1 shows *Excel*'s default *header* (the worksheet name) and *footer* (the page number). To change the header or footer, you use the options in the Header/Footer tab of the Page Setup dialog box shown in figure 10-8. As you can see, *Excel* provides a variety of options for you to choose from. However, you can also create custom headers and footers.

To create a custom header or footer, you use the procedure presented in figure 10-9. If you want to modify an existing header or footer, select it from the drop-down list box before you click on the Custom Header or Custom Footer button. If you want to create a header or footer from scratch, select the None option from the drop-down list box.

You can enter data in any the three sections of the Header or Footer dialog box. If you enter data in the first text box, it's placed at the left margin. If you enter data in the second text box, it's centered on the page. And if you enter data in the third text box, it's placed at the right margin.

To include special information like the current date and page number in a header or footer, you use the buttons in the middle of the dialog box. Just place the insertion point where you want to insert the information and click on the button. When you do, *Excel* inserts a code that's replaced with the appropriate information when the worksheet is printed.

The first button in the middle of the Header and Footer dialog boxes lets you change the font of the header or footer. To use this button, select the text you want to format and click on the button. Then, a dialog box appears that lets you change the font, font size, font attributes, and special effects of the selected text.

Because using a header makes it easy for you to print the date at the top of a worksheet, you may want to use headers for all your worksheets, even the ones that are only one page long. That way, you don't have to use the NOW function to put the date in the worksheet. You may also want to include the name of the workbook file in your worksheet headers so you'll always know what file the worksheet is stored in. To promote efficiency, you can use a standard format for your headers so all your worksheets print with a standard heading.

Two ways to access the Header/Footer tab of the Page Setup dialog box

- Select the Page Setup command from the File menu and click on the Header/Footer tab.
- Click on the Page Setup button from either the Print dialog box or the Print Preview window, and click on the Header/Footer tab.

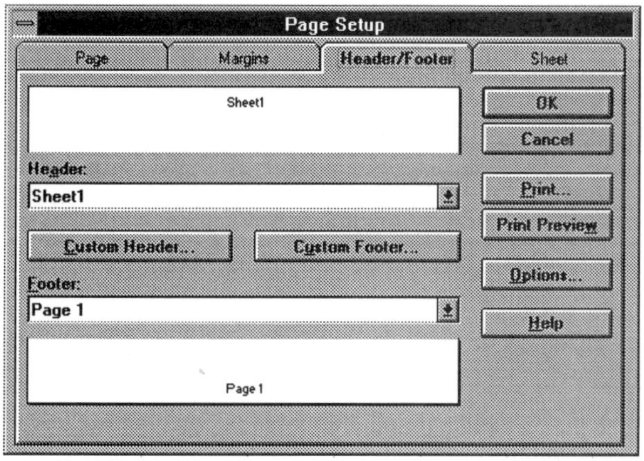

Option	Function
Header	Lets you select from a list of pre-defined headers:

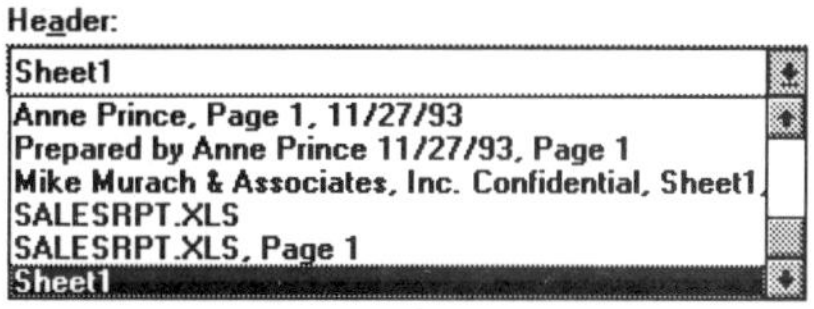

	A preview of your selection is shown in the area above this option.
Custom Header	Lets you create a custom header. See Figure 10-9 for more information.
Custom Footer	Lets you create a custom footer. See Figure 10-9 for more information.
Footer	Lets you select from a list of pre-defined footers. The choices are the same as the choices for pre-defined headers. A preview of your choice is shown in the area below this option.

Notes

- You can click on the Print button to print the worksheet, and you can click on the Print Preview button to preview the printed worksheet.
- If you click on the Options button, *Excel* displays a dialog box that lets you set options specific to the selected printer.

Figure 10-8 The Header/Footer tab of the Page Setup dialog box

How to create a custom header

1. Access the Header/Footer tab of the Page Setup dialog box.
2. Select the pre-defined header that you want to customize from the Header drop-down list box or, to create a header from scratch, select (none) from the list.
3. Click on the Custom Header button and the Header dialog box appears:

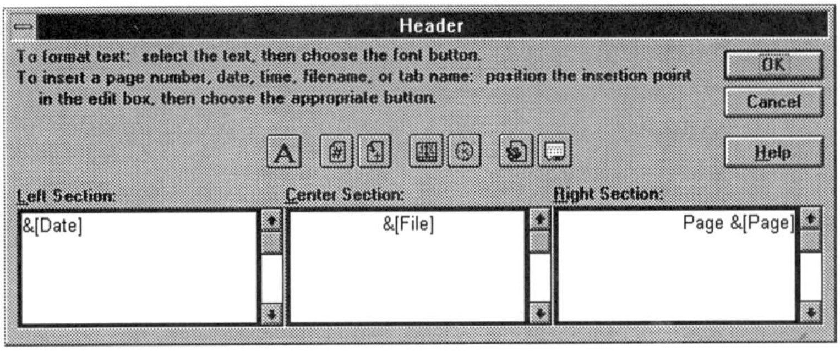

4. Enter any text you want in the Left Section, Center Section, and Right Section boxes, or click on one of the following buttons to insert special information.

Button	Code inserted	Function
	&[Page]	Inserts the page number.
	&[Pages]	Inserts the total number of pages.
	&[Date]	Inserts the date.
	&[Time]	Inserts the time.
	&[File]	Inserts the file name.
	&[Tab]	Inserts the worksheet tab name.

5. Click on the OK button, and you're returned to the Header/Footer tab of the Page Setup dialog box.

How to create a custom footer

Use the same procedure as above, but select a footer from the Footer drop-down list box and click on the Custom Footer button.

Note

You can change the font and font attributes of selected text by clicking on the text button: 

Figure 10-9 How to create a custom header or footer

How to set the Sheet options

Figure 10-10 presents the Sheet tab of the Page Setup dialog box. From this tab, you can select a specific area of the worksheet to be printed; you can select titles to be printed on each page of the printed output; you can specify that grid lines, notes, or row and column headings are to be printed; and you can specify the order in which the pages are printed.

How to print a specific area of a worksheet If you want to print a specific area of a worksheet, you'll usually select that area before you issue the Print command. However, if you always print the same area of the worksheet, you can avoid having to select that area every time by entering the range in the Print Area text box of the Sheet tab. To enter a range in this text box, you can type it in or you can click on the box and select the range in the worksheet.

How to print titles on each page of a worksheet When you print a worksheet that contains two or more pages, you may want to repeat the column headings on each page to make the worksheet easier to read. That's what I did for the worksheet in figure 10-2. In addition, I included the report title on each page. If a worksheet is too wide for all the columns to print on one page, you may also want to print the row headings on each page. The rows and columns you repeat on each page of a printout are called *print titles*.

You identify the print titles for a worksheet by entering a range in the Rows To Repeat At Top and Columns To Repeat At Left text boxes. You can enter a range in these boxes either by typing them in or by clicking on the box and selecting the rows or columns in the worksheet. If you type in a range, it must include at least one cell from each row or column that you want to repeat.

How to print the gridlines, notes, or row and column headings and set other print options The options in the Print group of the Sheet tab let you select whether or not the gridlines, notes, or row and column headings are printed. In addition, you can specify if you want to print in draft quality or if you're printing to a black and white printer. The Gridlines option is the only one that is selected by default. In most cases, you'll want to turn this option off.

How to change the print order The last two options in the Sheet tab determine the order in which *Excel* prints multiple-page worksheets. If you select the Down, Then Across option, *Excel* prints all of the pages that

Two ways to access the Sheet tab of the Page Setup dialog box

- Select the Page Setup command from the File menu and click on the Sheet tab.
- Click on the Page Setup button from either the Print dialog box or the Print Preview window, and click on the Sheet tab.

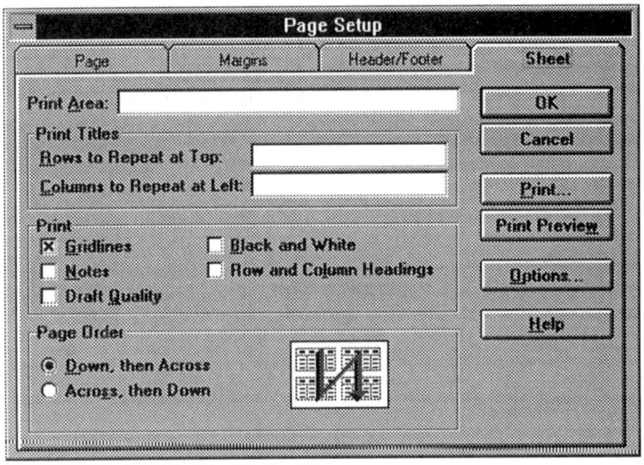

Print Area option

To print a specific area of the worksheet, click on the text box, then highlight a range in the worksheet or type in the range.

Print Titles group

To print the contents of one or more columns or rows in the worksheet on each page, click on the appropriate text box, then highlight the columns or rows in the worksheet or type in a range. If you type in a range, it must include at least one cell from each column or row you want to print.

Print group

To print grid lines, notes, or row and column headings, select the appropriate option. To print a draft-quality copy of the worksheet on a dot-matrix printer, select the Draft Quality option. If you're printing to a black and white printer, select the Black And White option.

Page Order group

Determines the order in which pages are printed if the worksheet is more than a single page wide and tall. The sample to the right of these options illustrates the selected order.

Notes

- You can click on the Print button to print the worksheet, and you can click on the Print Preview button to preview the printed worksheet.
- If you click on the Options button, *Excel* displays a dialog box that lets you set options specific to the selected printer.

Figure 10-10 The Sheet tab of the Page Setup dialog box

contain the leftmost columns of the worksheet first. Then, when it reaches the bottom of the worksheet, it prints all of the pages that contain the next group of columns to the right. It continues this process until it reaches the last column of the worksheet. If you select the Across, Then Down option, *Excel* prints all of the pages that contain the top-most rows first, followed by the pages that contain the next group of rows, and so on. This feature can help you organize your printed copies according to your worksheet's layout.

Summary

- To print all or part of a worksheet, select the Print command from the File menu or press Ctrl+P. If you've already specified the print settings, you can also click on the Print button in the Standard toolbar to print the worksheet.
- To preview a worksheet, select the Print Preview command from the File menu, click on the Preview button from the Print dialog box or any of the tabs in the Page Setup dialog box, or click on the Print Preview button in the Standard toolbar.
- To insert a horizontal or vertical page break, position the cell pointer and select the Page Break command from the Insert menu. To delete a page break that you've inserted, position the cell pointer and select the Remove Page Break command from the Insert menu.
- You can use the Page tab of the Page Setup dialog box to change the print orientation, scaling, paper size, print quality, and first page number for the printed output.
- You can use the Margins tab of the Page Setup dialog box to change the margins and to center the printed page.
- You can use the Header/Footer tab of the Page Setup dialog box to change the header and footer that are printed.
- You can use the Sheet tab of the Page Setup dialog box to specify the print area; add titles to a printed page; print the gridlines, notes, and row and column headings; and specify the print order.

Section 3

Charts and graphics

The three chapters in this section present the skills you need for enhancing a worksheet with charts and graphics. In chapter 11, you'll learn the basic skills for creating and modifying a chart. Then, in chapter 12, you'll learn some advanced charting techniques. And in chapter 13, you'll learn how to enhance a worksheet or a chart with graphics like arrows, circles, and boxes. Since both the charting and graphics features are easy to use, most *Excel* users should know enough about them so they can use them whenever they're appropriate.

Chapter 11

How to create and modify a chart

Most of this book focuses on the worksheet capability of *Excel* 5.0 because that's its most useful one. But its charting capability shouldn't be overlooked. Often, charting the data in a worksheet can make it easier to understand.

For example, figure 11-1 presents a simple worksheet and a *column chart* that has been created from it. Here, the chart shows the levels for four types of sales over the period 1989 through 1993. You can create a column chart like this in just a minute or two.

This chapter teaches you the basic procedures and techniques for creating and modifying a chart. First, you'll learn how to create a simple chart. Next, you'll learn how to work with a chart and its components and how to make simple modifications to a chart. Finally, you'll learn how to change a chart's type, subtype, and format.

How to create a chart

Figure 11-2 presents the procedures for creating an *embedded chart* and a *chart sheet.* An embedded chart is stored in the same worksheet as the data it's based on. A chart sheet is stored in a separate worksheet in front of the current worksheet. Since you can perform most charting functions on either an embedded chart or a chart sheet, the type you use depends mostly on whether you want to print the chart on the same page as the data it's based on.

To create an embedded chart or a chart sheet, you begin by highlighting the data in the worksheet you want to include in the chart. Note that the data does not need to be in a contiguous range. In other words, you can make nonadjacent selections.

In figure 11-2, you can see that I included the column and row headings in the highlighted range. However, I excluded the report title because *Excel* won't recognize it as the title. I also excluded the row that contains the totals because I didn't want that information in the chart.

The worksheet

	A	B	C	D	E	F
1			Sales by type			
2						
3		1989	1990	1991	1992	1993
4	Retail	$472,077	$833,634	$1,101,755	$1,144,799	$1,319,306
5	College	$300,506	$263,661	$299,971	$292,105	$360,759
6	Trade	$400,116	$823,512	$960,521	$890,949	$880,819
7	Foreign	$54,097	$88,331	$130,144	$179,091	$198,685
8						
9	Total	$1,226,796	$2,009,138	$2,492,391	$2,506,944	$2,759,569
10						

The column chart

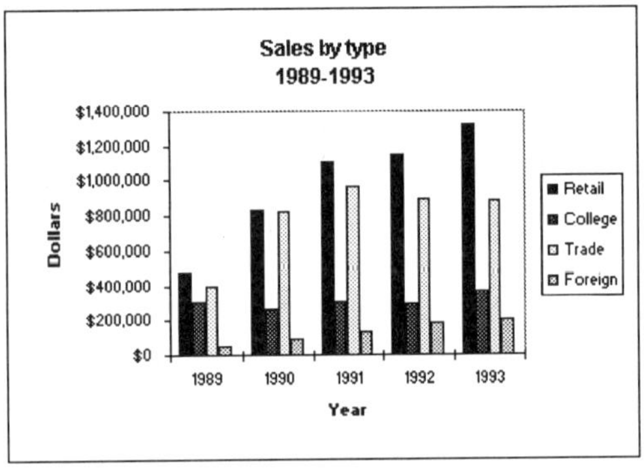

Figure 11-1 A worksheet and a column chart derived from it

After you highlight the chart range, you use the ChartWizard to create the chart. The ChartWizard lets you select from a variety of chart types and formats. It also lets you specify whether you want to chart the highlighted data by rows or by columns; it lets you specify the location of column and row headings included in the range; it lets you specify whether or not you want to include a legend with the chart; and it lets you specify chart and axis titles. Later in this chapter and in the next chapter, you'll see how you can change any of the selections you make when you create a chart.

How to work with a chart and its components

Now that you know how to create a chart, you'll want to take a minute or two to familiarize yourself with its components. Then, you'll want to experiment with the techniques for selecting, moving, sizing, and deleting a chart and its components. When you're comfortable with these techniques, you'll be ready to learn the techniques for modifying a chart.

How to create an embedded chart

1. Highlight the range of cells you want to include in the chart including row and column headings.
2. Click on the ChartWizard button  in the Standard toolbar or select the Chart On This Sheet command from the Insert menu, and place the pointer where you want the upper left corner of the chart:

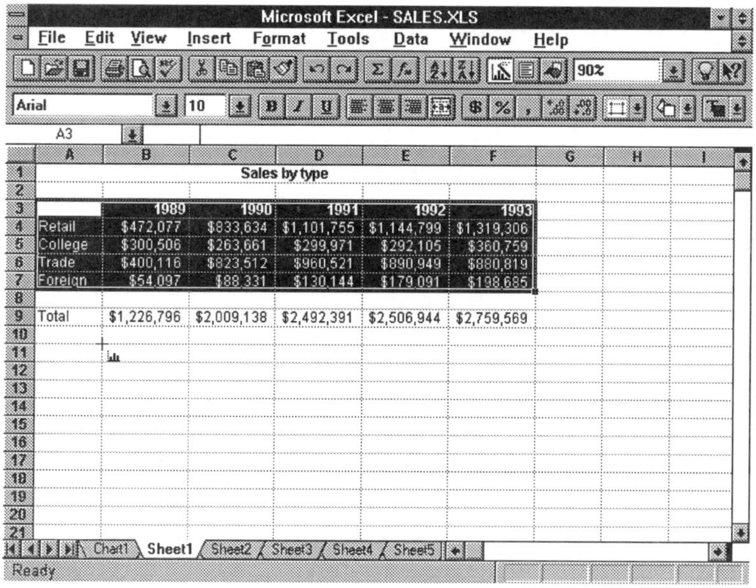

3. Release the mouse button, and this dialog box appears:

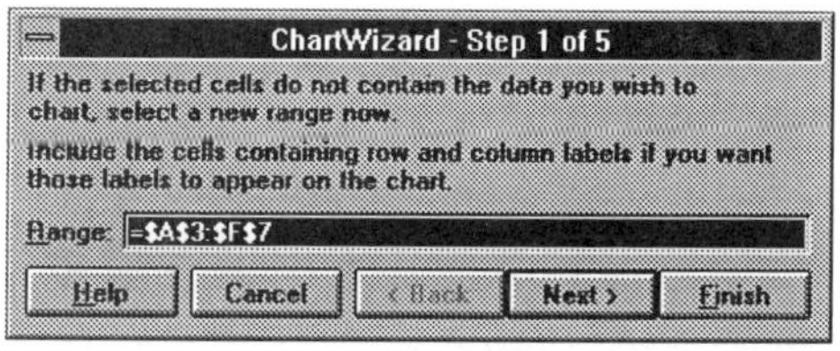

4. Verify the range, then click on the Next button and this dialog box appears:

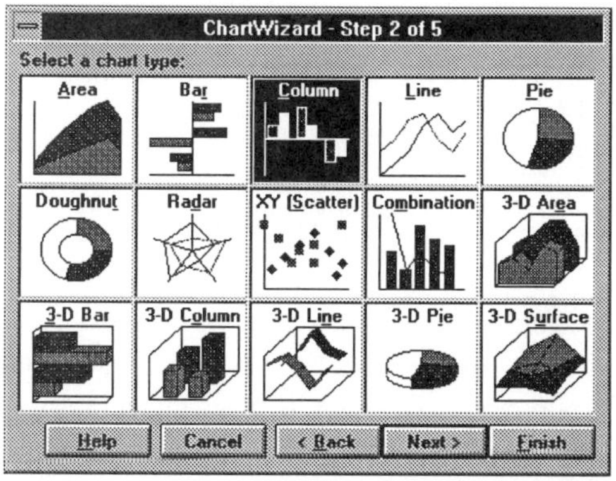

Figure 11-2 How to create a chart (part 1 of 4)

5. Select a chart type, then click on the Next button and this dialog box appears:

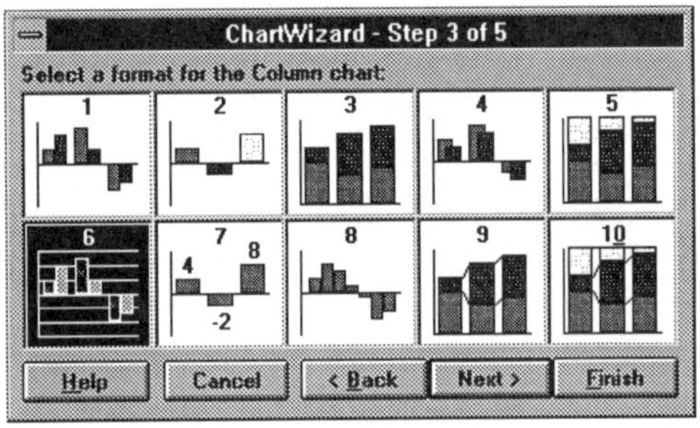

6. Select a chart format, then click on the Next button and this dialog box appears:

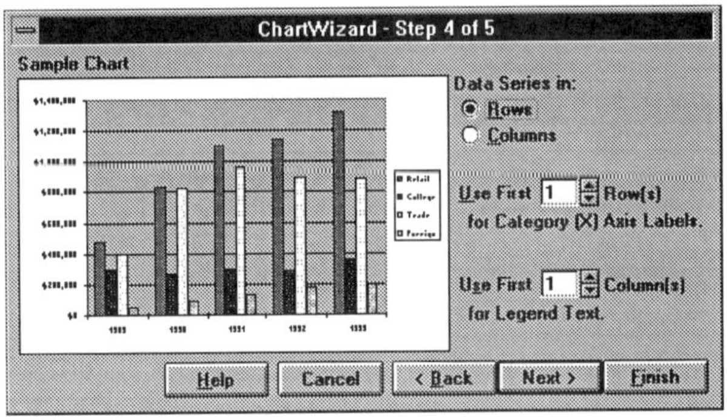

7. Change the options as necessary so the chart looks the way you want it to, then click on the Next button and this dialog box appears:

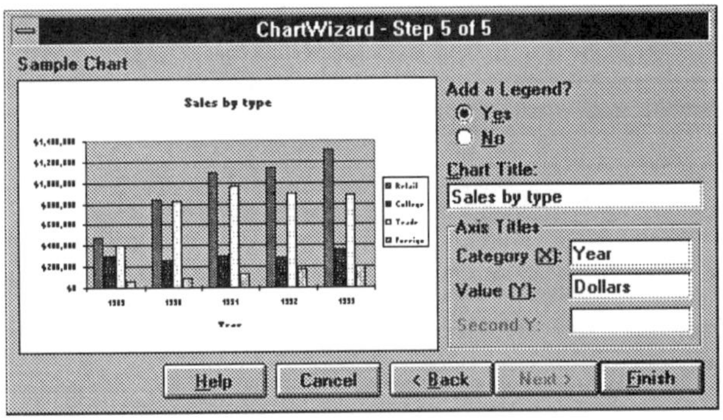

8. Select an option to indicate whether or not you want the chart to include a legend, and enter the chart and axis titles.

Figure 11-2 How to create a chart (part 2 of 4)

9. Click on the Finish button and *Excel* creates the chart:

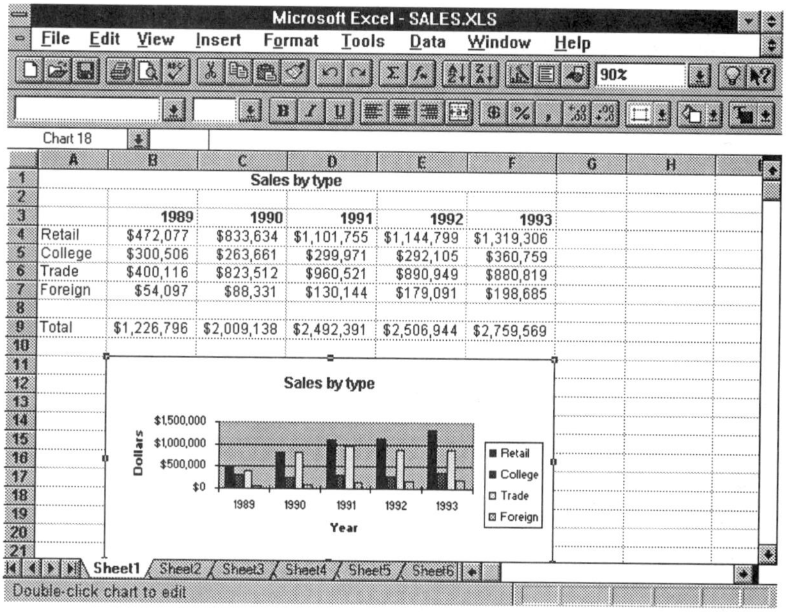

How to create a chart sheet

Use the procedure above, but, select the Chart As New Sheet command from the Insert menu in step 2. Then, when you complete the dialog boxes, *Excel* places the chart in its own worksheet:

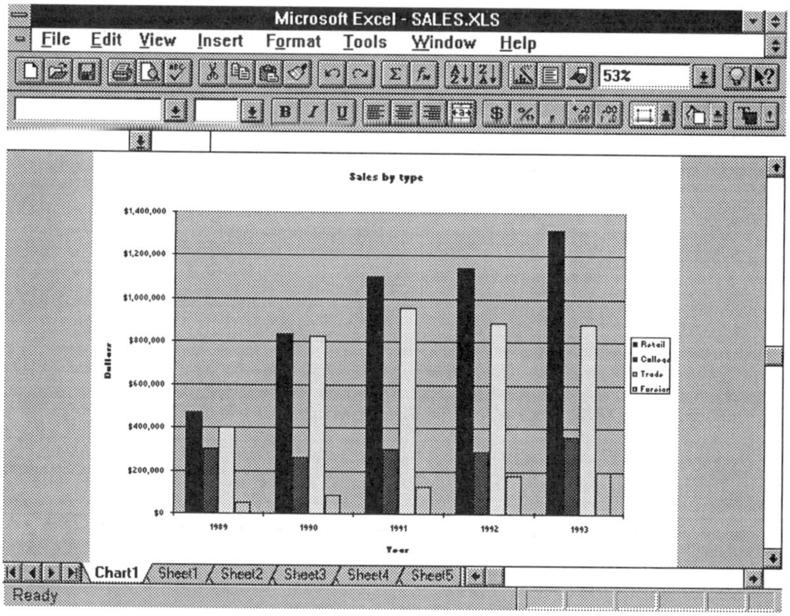

Figure 11-2 How to create a chart (part 3 of 4)

Notes

- To create a chart in a size other than the default size, click and drag the pointer until the chart outline is the size you want.
- You can also create a chart from data in nonadjacent ranges. To do that, make the nonadjacent selections before you start the ChartWizard.
- You can create a default chart in a chart sheet by highlighting the range of cells you want to include in the chart and pressing the F11 key. If *Excel* needs more information to complete the chart, it displays an appropriate dialog box. Then, you can modify the chart using the skills presented in this chapter and chapter 12.

Figure 11-2 How to create a chart (part 4 of 4)

The components of a chart Figure 11-3 presents the components of a typical chart. When *Excel* creates a chart, it plots each value in the worksheet range as a *data point*, represented by a *data marker*. These data markers are grouped into categories, with each category consisting of one data marker from each *data series*. The most important aspect of how *Excel* creates a chart is how it determines the data series and categories represented in the chart.

If the number of rows in the worksheet range is less than or equal to the number of columns in the range, *Excel* plots the values in each row as a data series and groups the values in each column into a category. That's how *Excel* plotted the data in figure 11-2, for example, since the range consists of five rows and six columns. So the data series, which are identified in the *chart legend*, are the four types of sales: Retail, College, Trade, and Foreign. And the categories, which are identified by the category names on the *x-axis*, are the five years: 1989, 1990, 1991, 1992, and 1993. If a chart contains fewer columns than rows, *Excel*'s default is to plot the values in each column as a data series and to group the values in each row into a category. If *Excel*'s default isn't what you want, you can change it from the fourth ChartWizard dialog box.

Because *Excel* groups the data markers into categories along the x-axis, this axis is also called the *category axis*. Each data marker in a chart is plotted according to the values on the *y-axis*, also called the *value axis*. In figure 11-3, for example, the height of each data marker indicates the dollar amount for a particular type of sales in a particular year.

How to select, move, size, delete, and activate a chart Figure 11-4 presents the techniques for selecting, moving, sizing, deleting, and activating a chart. As you can see, the techniques for an embedded chart and a

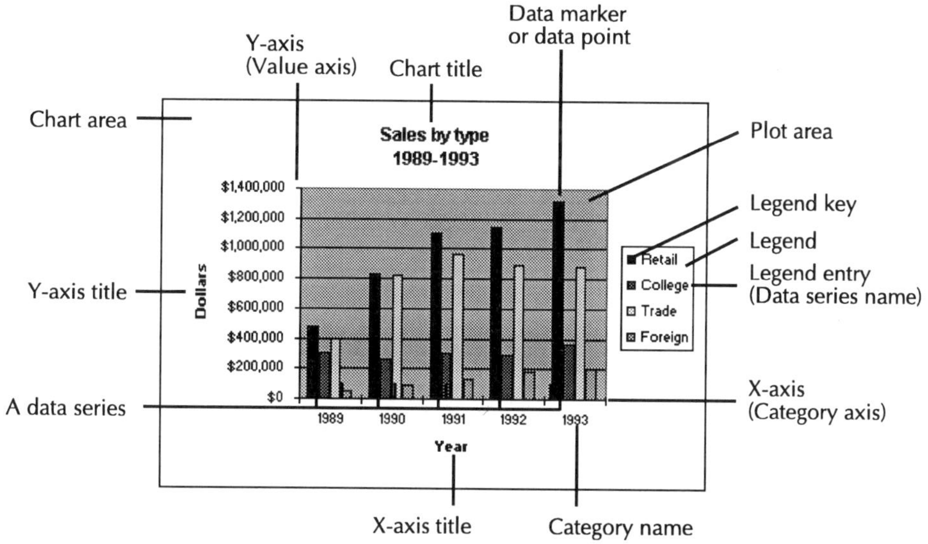

Notes

- Each value in the worksheet range is plotted as a data point, represented by a data marker. *Excel* groups the data markers into categories, with each category consisting of one data marker from each data series. If the range you select for a worksheet contains fewer columns than rows, *Excel*'s default is to chart the values in each column as a data series and to group the values in each row into a category. Otherwise, the default is to chart the values in each row as a data series and to group the values in each column into a category. You can change this default when you create a chart or after you create a chart.
- If you include the row and column headings in the range you select for a chart, *Excel* automatically adds the data series descriptions to the legend and the category descriptions to the x-axis. Otherwise, it creates defaults for the descriptions.
- *Excel* determines the measurements used along the y-axis from the values in the range you select.

Figure 11-3 The components of a chart

chart sheet are different. In most cases, you won't need to select, move, or size a chart sheet until you're ready to print it. I'll show you how to print a chart sheet in the next chapter.

When you select an embedded chart, *handles* appear at its corners and on its sides. You can size the chart by dragging any of these handles. If you want to maintain the chart's proportions when you size it, hold down the Shift key as you drag a corner handle. To move the chart, place the mouse pointer anywhere inside its border and drag it.

How to select, move, size, delete, and activate an embedded chart

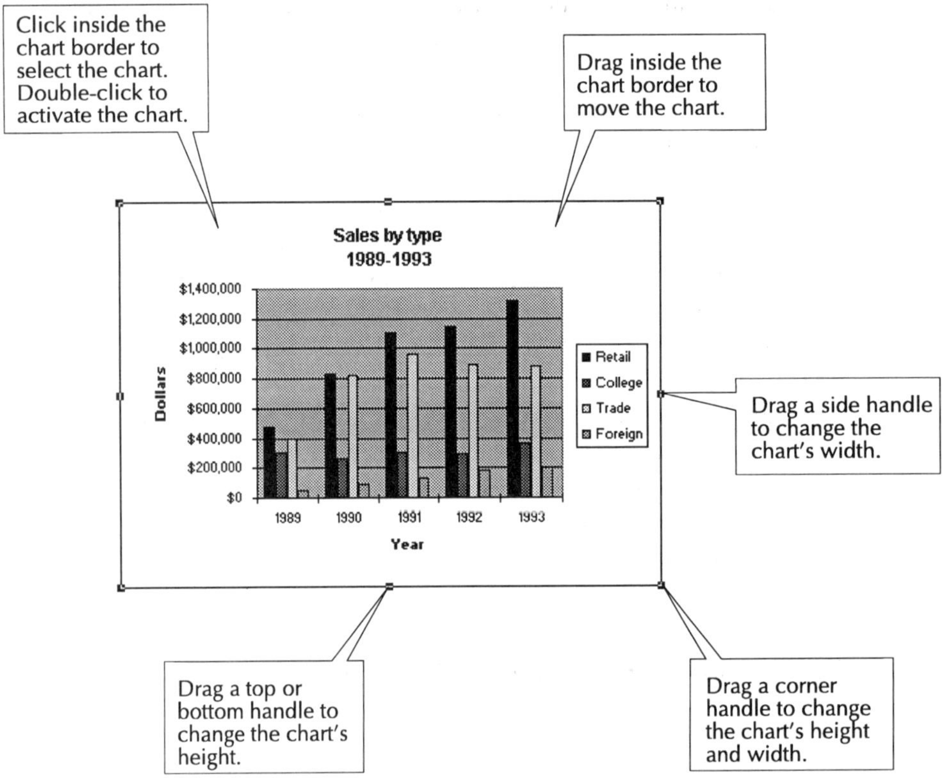

- To delete an embedded chart, select it, then press the Delete key or select the Clear command from the Edit or shortcut menu.

How to activate and delete a chart sheet

- To activate a chart sheet, click on the worksheet tab for the worksheet that contains the chart.
- To delete a chart sheet, activate the chart sheet and select the Delete Sheet command from the Edit menu.

Notes

- When you drag a corner handle to size an embedded chart, hold down the Shift key to maintain the same proportions.
- Although you can select, move, and size a chart sheet, you normally do this only to size the chart for printing. For details, see figure 12-12.

Figure 11-4 How to select, move, size, delete, and activate a chart

Before you can modify a chart, you have to activate it. To activate an embedded chart, you double-click on it. When you do, a thick border appears around it. In addition, the worksheet scroll bars disappear and *Excel*'s menus change. To activate a chart sheet, you switch to the worksheet that contains the chart. The same menus and commands that are available for an embedded chart are available for a chart sheet.

How to select, move, size, and delete chart areas and items Figure 11-5 presents the techniques for selecting, moving, sizing, and deleting the areas and items of a chart. Note that before you can perform any of these functions, you must activate the chart.

When you select a chart area, a thin border with handles appears around it. You use the border and handles to move and size the area just as you move or size a chart. When you select an item, however, a border may or may not appear around it. If a border does appear, it's thick like the border that appears around the chart, and it has handles around it that you can use to move the item. You can't size an item. If a border doesn't appear, handles appear on the item so you know it's been selected, but you can't move or size it.

How to make simple modifications to a chart

Because the ChartWizard lets you define many aspects of a chart as you create it, you may not need to modify it. However, you'll want to know how to make some simple modifications to a chart. In particular, you should know how to change the values and text included in a chart. You may also want to know how to change the placement and orientation of the legend and how to add a legend if you didn't include one when you created the chart. Likewise, you may want to know how to add chart and axis titles if you didn't include them when you created the chart.

How to change chart values and text Figure 11-6 shows you how to change the values or text in a chart. How you do that depends on whether or not the value or text is linked to the worksheet. If the value or text was included in the range you highlighted when you created the chart, it's automatically linked to the worksheet. Then, you can change it by editing the cell in the worksheet that contains the data. Otherwise, you have to edit it directly in the chart. In figure 11-6, for example, I added a second line to the chart title.

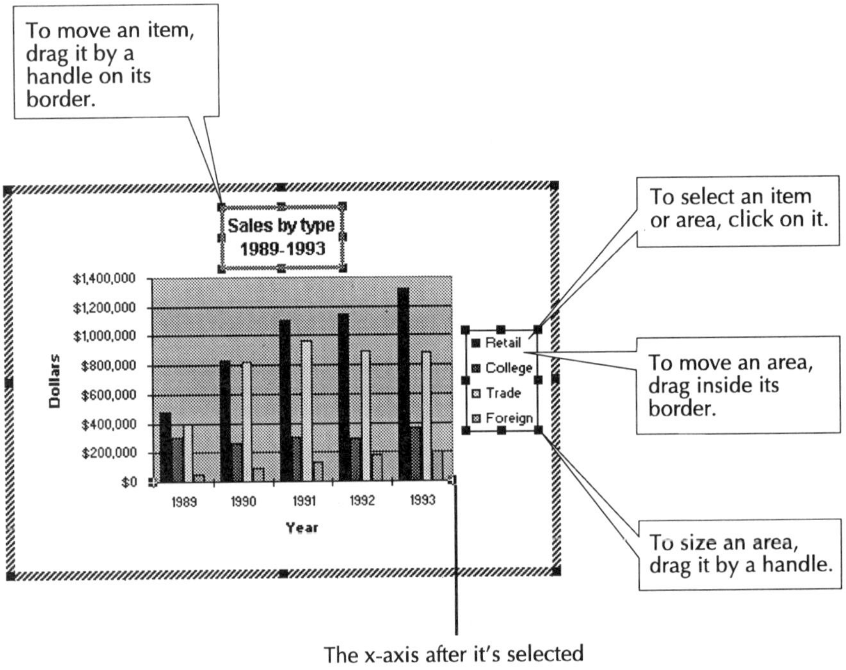

Notes

- You must activate a chart before you can select any of its items or areas.
- When you select an area, a thin border with handles appears around it, which means the area can be moved and sized. When you select an item that can be moved, a thick border with handles appears around it. When you select an item that can't be moved, handles appear on the item, but no border appears around it.
- To select a data series, click on any data marker in the series. To select an individual data point, select the data series, then click on the data marker.
- To select a legend entry or legend key, select the legend, then click on the legend entry or key.
- To cancel a selection, press the Esc key.
- To delete an area or item, press the Delete key or select the Clear command from the Edit or shortcut menu. Deleting an item or area from a chart doesn't affect the worksheet data.
- If you move or size the plot area, the axis and axis titles move with it.
- You can also use the keyboard to select items in a chart. After activating the chart, press the Up-arrow and Down-arrow keys to move between items and areas. To move between items within a group such as data points in a data series, press the Right-arrow and Left-arrow keys.

Figure 11-5 How to select, move, size, and delete chart areas and items

How to change a value or text that's linked to the worksheet

Change the data in the worksheet, and *Excel* automatically updates the chart.

How to change text that's not linked to the worksheet

1. Activate the chart.
2. Select the text item you want to change and a border appears around it:

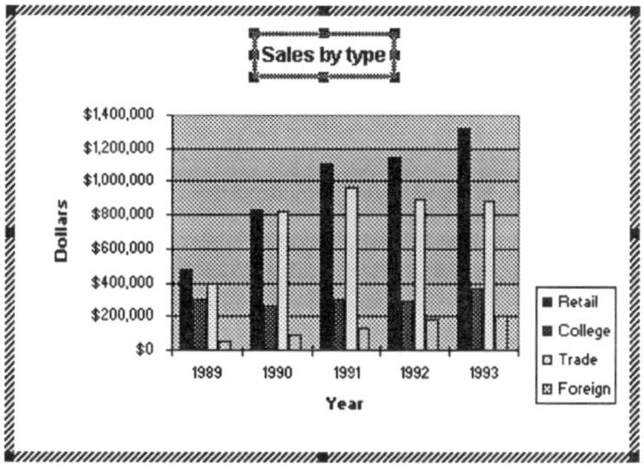

3. Click inside the border and edit the text:

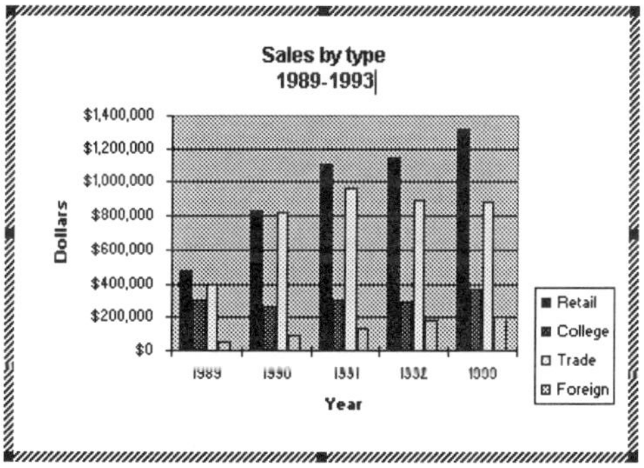

4. Click outside the item to complete the entry.

Notes

- Vertically aligned text is displayed horizontally for editing purposes.
- You can also change a value in a 2-D bar, column, line, stacked, or pie chart or a doughnut or XY chart by dragging a data marker. As you drag a data marker, its value appears in the formula bar.

Figure 11-6 How to change chart values and text

How to add a legend

Activate the chart, then select the Legend command from the Insert menu and *Excel* inserts a legend. If you highlighted the labels to be used as legend entries when you created the chart, *Excel* uses these labels in the legend. Otherwise, *Excel* uses default legend entries.

How to change the placement and orientation of the legend

1. Activate the chart.
2. Double-click on the legend, or select the legend, then select the Selected Legend command from the Format menu or the Format Legend command from the shortcut menu. Then, click on the Placement tab of the Format Legend dialog box.
3. Select one of the available options: Bottom, Corner, Top, Right, and Left.
4. Click on the OK button.

Notes

- The Top and Bottom options place the legend in one line across the top or bottom of the chart. The Corner option places the legend in the upper right corner of the chart. The Right and Left options place the legend on the right or left side of the chart.
- If the legend overlaps the plot area, *Excel* changes the size of the plot area to accomodate the legend.

Figure 11-7 How to add a legend or change its placement and orientation

How to add a legend or change its placement and orientation

Figure 11-7 shows you how to add a legend to a chart or change its placement and orientation. To add a legend, you activate the chart and select the Legend command from the Insert menu. If the range you highlighted when you created the chart included the labels that describe the data series, *Excel* automatically uses these labels as the legend entries. Otherwise, *Excel* uses default entries.

By default, *Excel* places the legend to the right of the plot area when it creates a chart. If you want to change its placement, you can drag the legend with the mouse, or you can select another option from the Placement tab of the Format Legend dialog box. If you select the Top or Bottom option, *Excel* also changes the orientation of the legend so that all of its entries appear on a single line.

How to add chart and axis titles Figure 11-8 presents the procedure for adding chart or axis titles to a chart. As you can see, the Titles dialog box lets you select which titles you want to add. When you issue this command, *Excel* inserts defaults for the titles you selected. Then, you can change the defaults using the technique described in figure 11-6.

Procedure

1. Activate the chart.
2. Select the Titles command from the Insert menu or the Insert Titles command from the shortcut menu, and this dialog box appears:

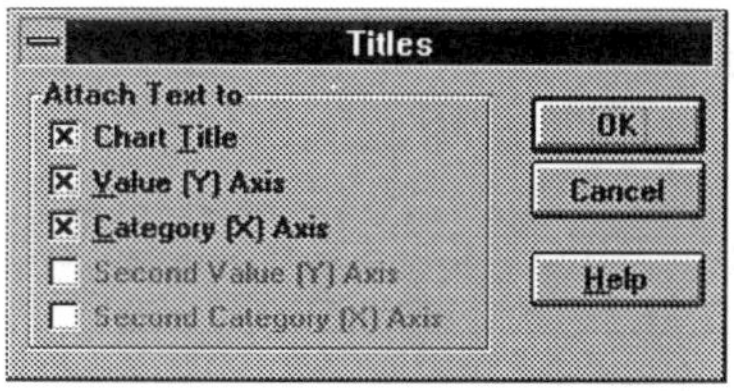

3. Select the titles you want to add.
4. Click on the OK button and *Excel* inserts default titles:

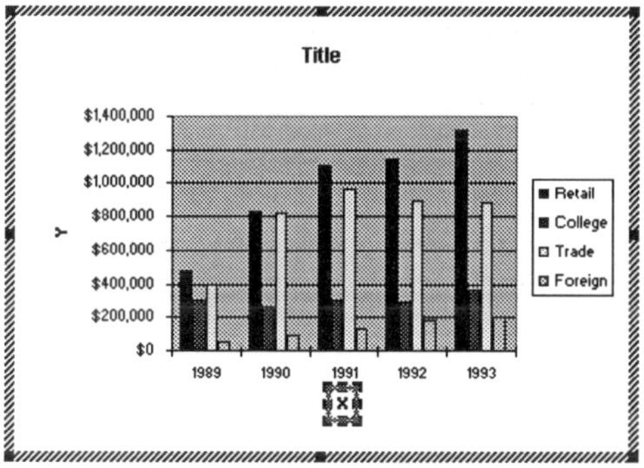

Notes

- If the text you want to include in a chart as a chart or axis title appears in the worksheet used to create the chart, you can link the title to the appropriate worksheet cells. To do that, activate the chart and select the title, then enter an equals sign (=) and a reference in the formula bar. Then, you can change the title by changing the worksheet text.
- See figure 11-6 for details on how to change a title.

Figure 11-8 How to add chart and axis titles

Instead of typing the text you want to use for chart and axis titles into the chart, you can link the titles to text that appears in the worksheet. If the text you want to use for the chart title appears in the worksheet, for example, you can link the title to the text. To do that, you select the title, then enter an equals sign (=) in the formula bar followed by the reference for the cell or range that contains the text. Then, if you change the title in the worksheet, the title is changed automatically in the chart. Most of the time, however, this isn't necessary.

How to change the chart type, subtype, and format

When you create a chart, the ChartWizard lets you specify the chart's type and format. Chart formats are like styles; they change the appearance of the chart but not the data in the chart. If you want to, you can change a chart's type or format after you create the chart. You can also change a chart's subtype, which is a variation of its type. Although each chart format is based on a chart subtype, you can change the subtype without changing the format.

Figure 11-9 shows you how to use the Chart Type command to change the chart type and subtype. Note that the subtypes that are available depend on the chart type you select. When you select a subtype, *Excel* shows you what the chart will look like in the dialog box. That way, you can be sure you select the subtype you want before you accept the selection.

Figure 11-10 shows you how to apply an *autoformat* to a chart. Notice that the formats that are available in the AutoFormat dialog box are the same as the formats that are available when you create a chart. Although *Excel* provides a variety of autoformats for each chart type, you can also create your own custom formats using the AutoFormat command. See *Excel*'s online Help for details on how to create a custom format.

Figure 11-11 presents eight types of charts that you can create with *Excel*. Although there are many others, these are the ones you'll probably find most useful. Of these eight, the column chart is the default type, and it's the type you're likely to use most often. A column chart is useful when you want to show the change in one or more data elements over time. One type of column chart is the *stacked column chart*. You can use it to show the change in individual data elements as well as the total change. A *bar chart* is similar to a column chart, but its orientation is different.

The *line* and *area charts* also show the change in one or more data elements over time. Each line in a line chart and each area in an area chart represents a data series. These types of charts are useful for showing the rate of change of one or more data elements.

You can use a *pie chart* to show how parts of data compare to the whole. Note that a pie chart can represent only one data series. In the pie chart in figure 11-11, for example, the data series is the year 1989. Because it wouldn't make sense for the legend to contain a description of a single data series, the legend for a pie chart contains a description of each slice of the pie.

Figure 11-11 also includes some *3-D charts*. Although these charts present the same information as the other charts, they can be more visually

How to change the chart type

1. Activate the chart.
2. Select the Chart Type command from the Format or shortcut menu and this dialog box appears:

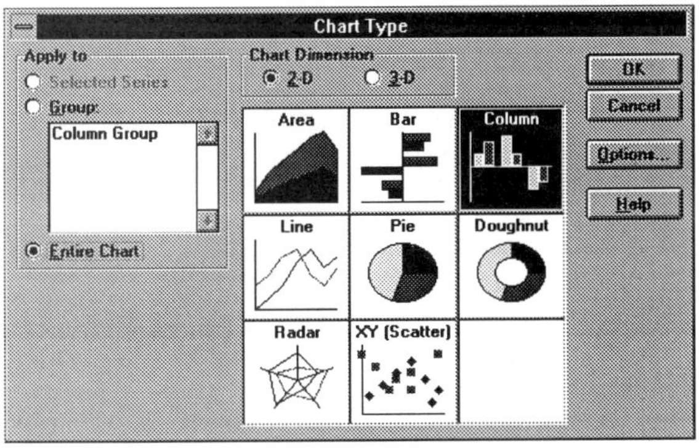

3. Select an option from the Chart Dimension group, then select a chart type from the available options.

How to change the chart subtype

1. Click on the Options button in the Chart Type dialog box, then click on the Subtype tab and this dialog box appears:

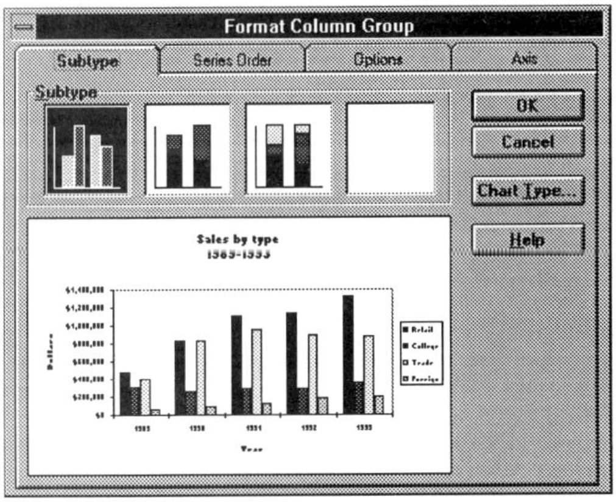

2. Select an option from the Subtype group.

Notes

- The options in the Apply To group in the Chart Type dialog box let you change the chart type for a selected data series or a chart group in addition to the entire chart. You'll learn how to use the Selected Series option in the next chapter.
- You can click on the Chart Type button in the Subtype tab to return to the Chart Type dialog box.
- You can go directly to the Format dialog box by selecting one of the Group commands from the bottom of the Format menu or one of the Format Group commands from the shortcut menu. These commands and the name of the dialog box change depending on the chart type.

Figure 11-9 How to change a chart's type and subtype

Access

Activate the chart, then select the AutoFormat command from the Format menu or the shortcut menu.

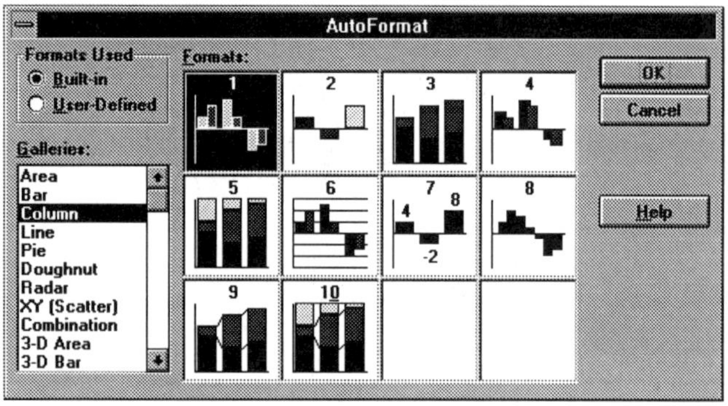

Operation

Select the Built-In option to apply a built-in format. Select the User-Defined option to apply a user-defined format. The available formats for the chart type selected in the Galleries list box are displayed in the Formats palette.

Note

You can also create your own custom formats from this dialog box. See online Help for details.

Figure 11-10 How to apply an autoformat

appealing. So you might want to use them when appearance is particularly important.

Figure 11-12 presents some charts you can use for special purposes. The *XY chart* is similar to a line chart except that both axes must be numeric. This chart is useful for showing relationships between two variables. You can also create an XY chart without the lines that connect the points. Then, it's called a *scatter chart.*

The *High-Low-Close chart* is useful for showing fluctuating data, such as stock market prices, over a period of time. The vertical lines in a High-Low-Close chart extend from the low to the high value, and the horizontal lines show the closing values. You can also create an *Open-High-Low-Close chart*, which includes the opening values.

The *radar chart* is useful for showing the similarity and uniformity of one or more data series. With this type of chart, the data is wrapped around a center point, and the y-axis stems from the center. Because radar charts can be difficult to interpret, though, you're usually better off using a column or line chart.

A column chart

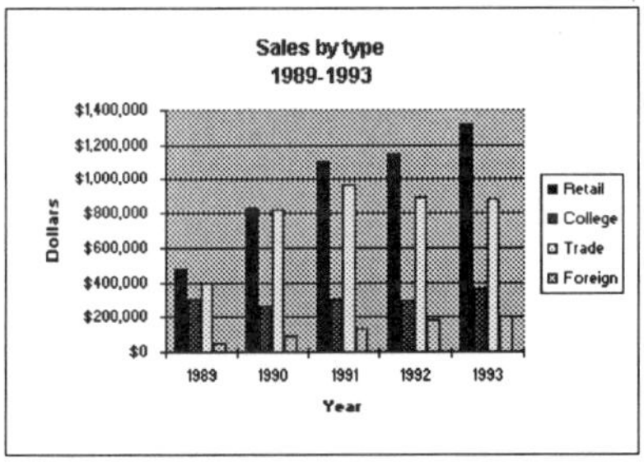

A stacked column chart

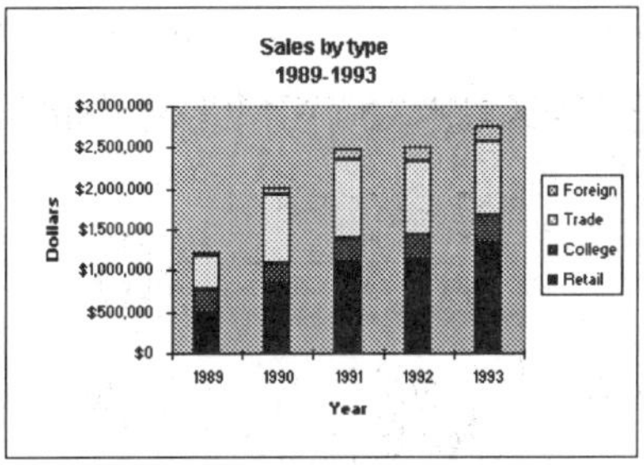

A bar chart

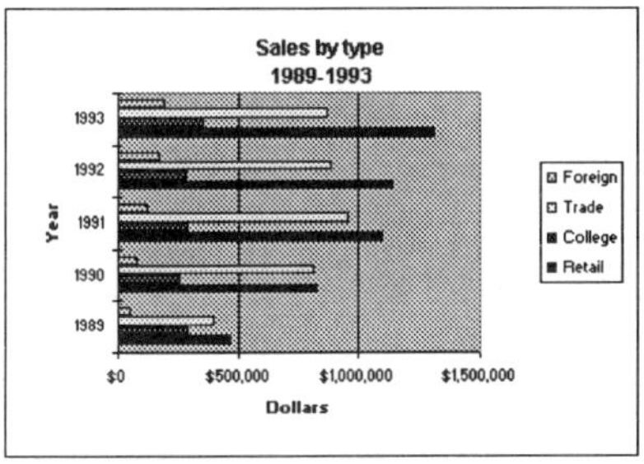

A 3-D stacked bar chart

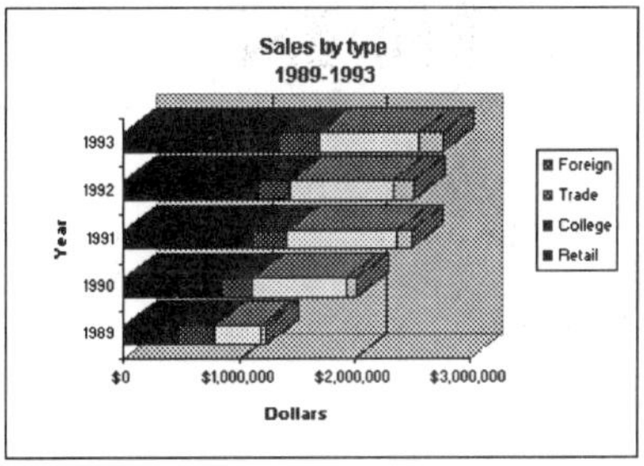

A line chart

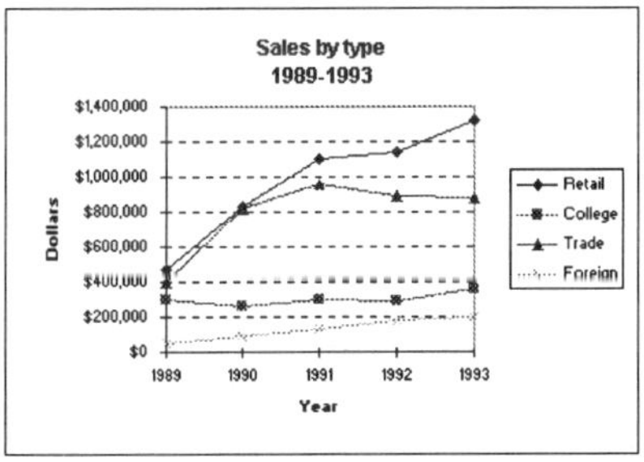

An area chart

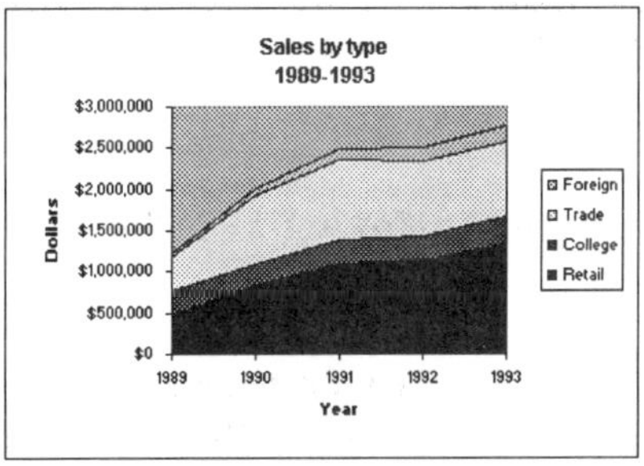

A pie chart

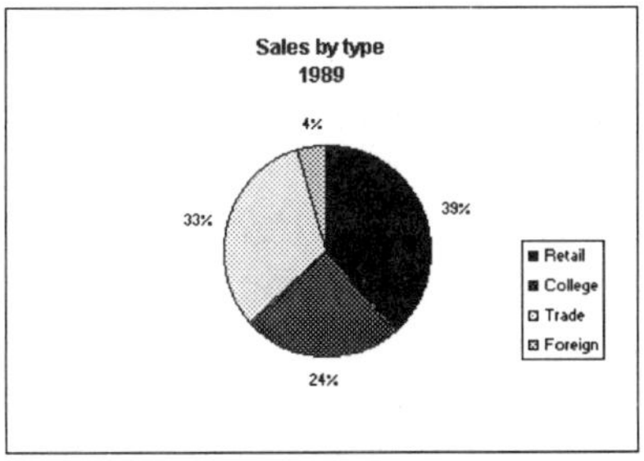

A 3-D pie chart

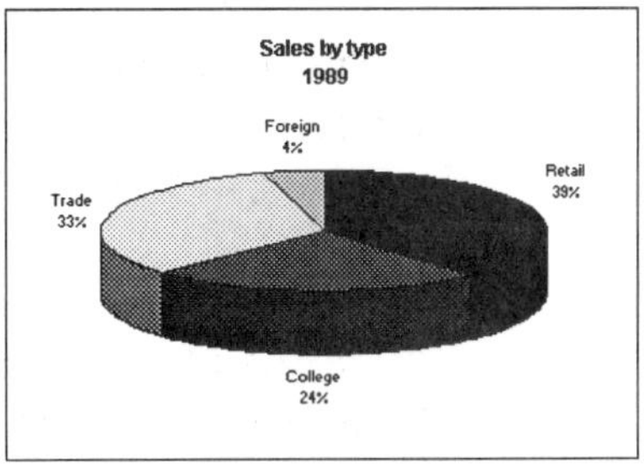

Figure 11-11 Eight charts created from the worksheet in figure 11-1

An XY chart

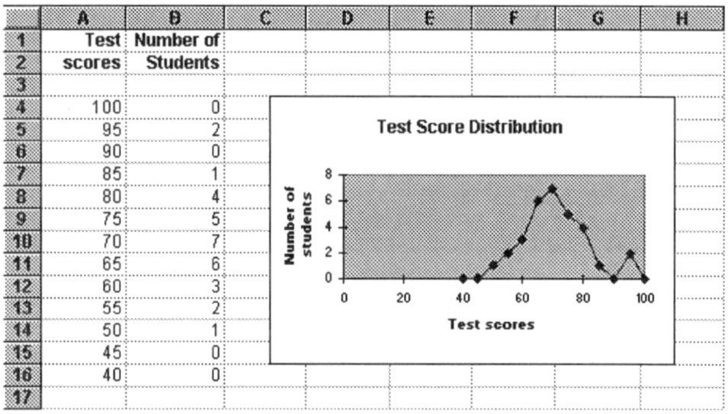

Test scores	Number of Students
100	0
95	2
90	0
85	1
80	4
75	5
70	7
65	6
60	3
55	2
50	1
45	0
40	0

A High-Low-Close chart

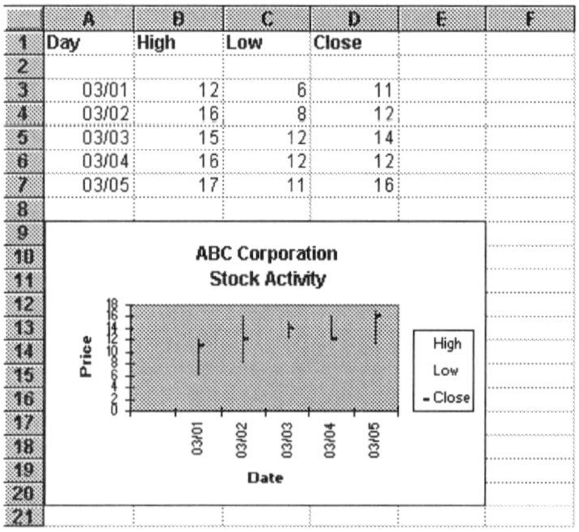

Day	High	Low	Close
03/01	12	6	11
03/02	16	8	12
03/03	15	12	14
03/04	16	12	12
03/05	17	11	16

A radar chart

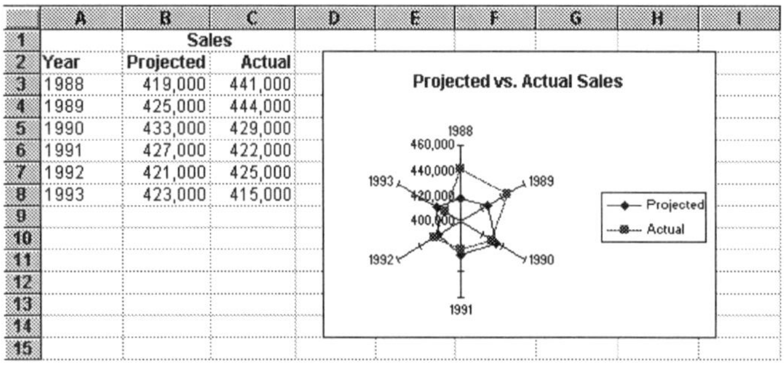

	Sales	
Year	Projected	Actual
1988	419,000	441,000
1989	425,000	444,000
1990	433,000	429,000
1991	427,000	422,000
1992	421,000	425,000
1993	423,000	415,000

Figure 11-12 Three special-purpose charts

Perspective

If you experiment with the ChartWizard, I think you'll find that you can create any simple chart in just a few seconds. If you need to create a more complicated chart, however, you'll need some additional skills. That's what you'll learn in the next chapter.

Summary

- To create an *embedded chart,* highlight a range of cells and click on the ChartWizard toolbar button or select the Chart On This Sheet command from the Insert menu. To create a chart sheet, highlight a range of cells and select the Chart As New Sheet command from the Insert menu. The range you highlight can include row and column headings, and *Excel* will use them in the chart it creates.
- A chart contains one or more categories of data, with each category containing a *data marker* or *data point* for each *data series* in the chart. *Excel* determines whether it uses the row or column data as the data series depending on the number of rows and columns in the range you highlight for the chart.
- When you select a chart by clicking on it, *handles* appear around it. You can use these handles to size the chart. You can move a chart by dragging it, and you can delete a chart or area by pressing the Delete key or by selecting the Clear command from the Edit or shortcut menu.
- To activate a chart so you can modify it, double-click on it and a heavy border appears around it. When you activate a chart, the worksheet scroll bars disappear and *Excel*'s menus change.
- To move, size, or delete an item or area of a chart, activate the chart, then select the item or area by clicking on it. The type of border that appears around the item or area determines if and how you can move or size it. To delete an item or area, press the Delete key or select the Clear command from the Edit or shortcut menu.
- To change a chart value or text that's linked to the worksheet, edit the data in the worksheet. To change chart text that's not linked to the worksheet, edit the text in the chart.

- To add a legend to a chart, select the Legend command from the Insert menu. To change the placement of the legend, use the mouse to drag it, or select an option from the Placement tab of the Format Legend dialog box.
- To add chart and axis titles to a chart, use the Titles command in the Insert menu or the Insert Titles command in the shortcut menu.
- To change a chart's type, activate the chart and use the Chart Type command in the Format or shortcut menu. To change a chart's subtype, use the Options button in the Chart Type dialog box.
- To change a chart's format, use the AutoFormat command in the Format or shortcut menu.
- The most common types of charts are the *column chart*, the *bar chart*, the *line chart*, the *area chart*, and the *pie chart*. *Excel* also provides *3-D charts* and three special-purpose charts: *XY*, *High-Low-Close,* and *radar* charts.

Chapter 12

How to use advanced charting techniques

In the last chapter, you learned how to create and make some basic modifications to a simple chart. In this chapter, you'll learn about some advanced charting techniques for creating and modifying charts. First, you'll learn how to create three special types of charts. Next, you'll learn how to add data to a chart. Then, you'll learn how to modify and enhance a chart. Finally, you'll learn how to size a chart sheet for printing. When you complete this chapter, you'll be able to create almost any chart in just a matter of minutes.

How to create three special types of charts

Although I presented a variety of charts in chapter 11, I omitted three special types you may want to use: pie charts with exploded slices, mixed charts, and charts with two y-axes.

Pie charts with one or more exploded slices Figure 12-1 presents two ways to explode the slices of a pie chart. To explode all the slices at one time, you select the pie and drag any slice away from the center of the pie. To explode one slice at a time, you select the pie, then select the slice you want to explode and drag it away from the center of the pie.

Mixed charts Figure 12-2 presents the procedure for creating a *mixed chart.* As you can see, a mixed chart is one that includes two types of charts. For example, the chart in this figure contains a column chart that shows the sales for four sales types and a line chart that shows the total sales.

To create a mixed chart, you change the chart type for one or more data series. To do that, you select the data series you want to change, then select a new chart type for the series from the Chart Type dialog box. Notice that when you select a data series before selecting the Chart Type command, the Selected Series option is selected. That means that *Excel* will change the chart type only for the selected series and not for any of the other series in the chart.

How to explode all the slices at one time

1. Activate the chart.
2. Select the pie.
3. Drag any slice of the pie away from the center and the pie is exploded:

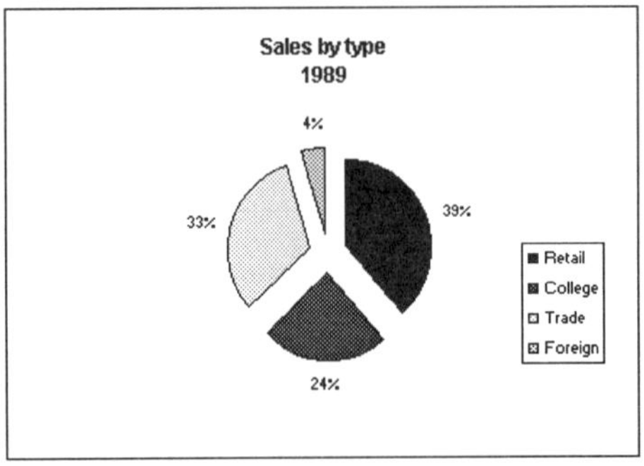

How to explode a single slice

1. Activate the chart.
2. Select the pie, then select a slice.
3. Drag the slice away from the center of the pie and it's exploded:

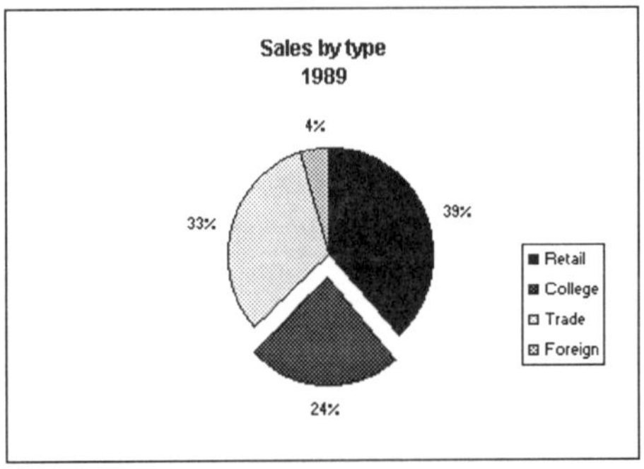

Figure 12-1 How to explode slices of a pie chart

Charts with two y-axes Figure 12-3 presents the procedure for creating a chart with two y-axes. You can use this type of chart to show the relationship between two sets of data that use different measurements. For example, the chart in figure 12-3 shows the relationship between sales and the inflation rate for a five-year period.

Procedure

1. Activate the chart.
2. Select the data series you want to chart as a different type:

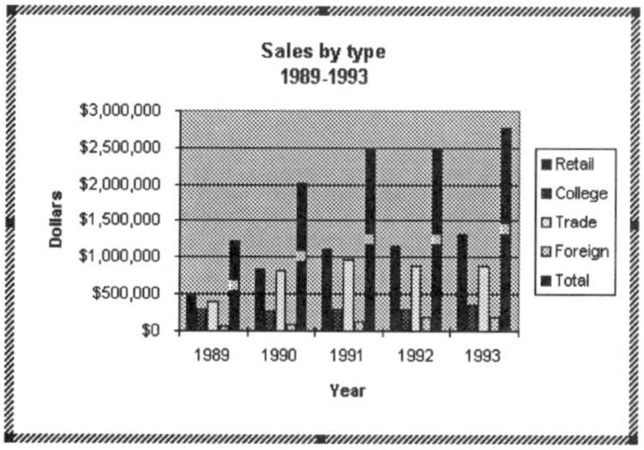

3. Select the Chart Type command from the Format or shortcut menu and this dialog box appears:

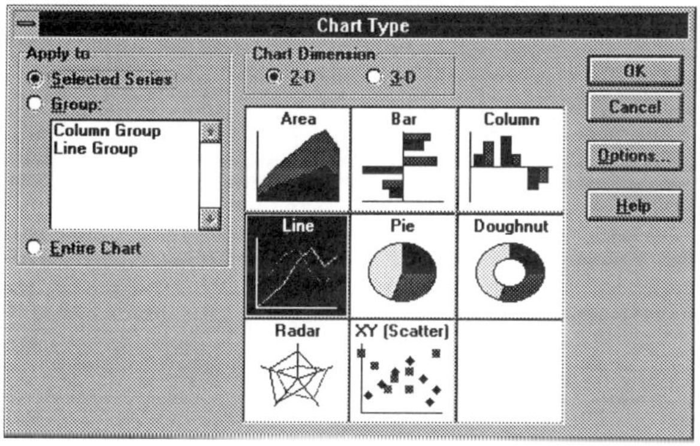

4. Select the chart type for the data series from the available options.
5. Click on the OK button and the data series is charted with the new chart type:

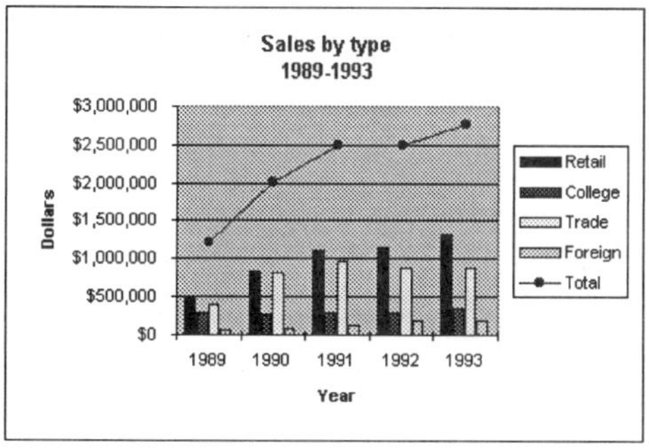

Note: You can't mix 2-D and 3-D chart types.

Figure 12-2 How to create a mixed chart

Procedure

1. Develop the chart as if all the data was going to be charted against a single axis:

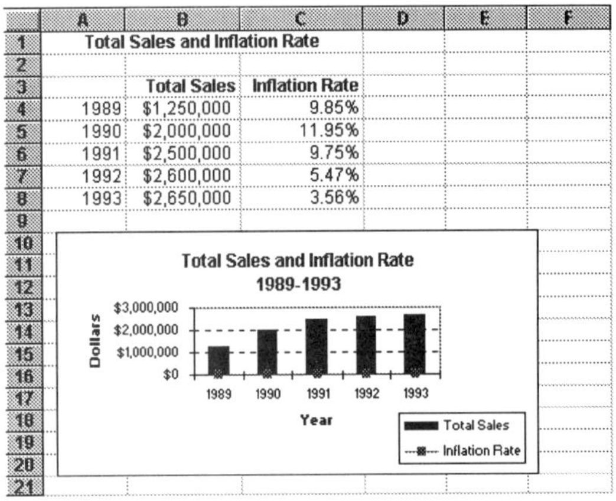

2. Activate the chart, then double click on the data series you want to plot against another axis, or select the data series and select the Selected Data Series command from the Format menu or the Format Data Series command from the shortcut menu. When the Format Data Series dialog box appears, click on the Axis tab and this dialog box appears:

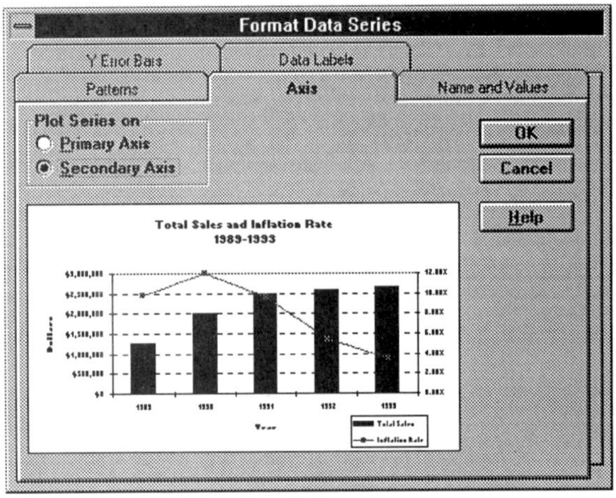

3. Select the Secondary Axis option.

Figure 12-3 How to plot a data series against a second y-axis (part 1 of 2)

4. Click on the OK button and *Excel* adds a second y-axis to the chart:

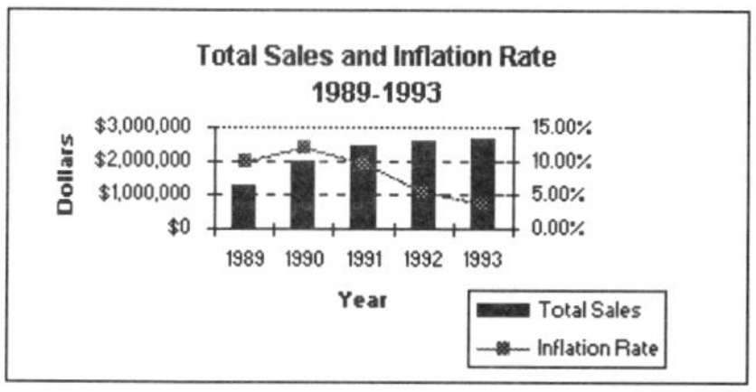

Note

When you first create the chart, the scale on the y-axis is set according to the values in the first data series. If the values in the second data series are significantly smaller, you may not be able to see the data markers unless you use a line chart. After you add the second y-axis, you can change the data series to any type of chart.

Figure 12-3 How to plot a data series against a second y-axis (part 2 of 2)

To create a second y-axis, you begin by developing the chart with a single y-axis. Then, you select the data series you want to chart against a second y-axis and access the Format Data Series dialog box. When you select the Secondary Axis option in this dialog box, *Excel* creates another y-axis using the values in the selected data series and plots the data series along that axis.

When I first tried to create the mixed chart in figure 12-3, I plotted the data as a column chart. Unfortunately, the values in the Inflation Rate data series are so small when compared to the values in the Total Sales data series that I couldn't see the data markers for that series even when I stretched the chart so that it was several screens tall. To solve this problem, I plotted the data as a line chart, then changed the Total Sales data series to a column chart. As you can see in the chart in step 1 of figure 12-3, you can see the data points for the Inflation Rate data series even though the values all appear to be zero. That way, I was able to select the data series so I could plot it against a second y-axis.

How to add data to a chart

Occasionally, you may need to add data to a chart. For example, you may want to add another data series or category. One way you can do that is by recreating the chart with the new range. If you've made any modifications to the chart or applied any special formatting, however, they are lost. In that case, you'll want to change the existing chart to include the new data.

Procedure

1. Activate the chart.
2. Click on the ChartWizard button and this dialog box appears:

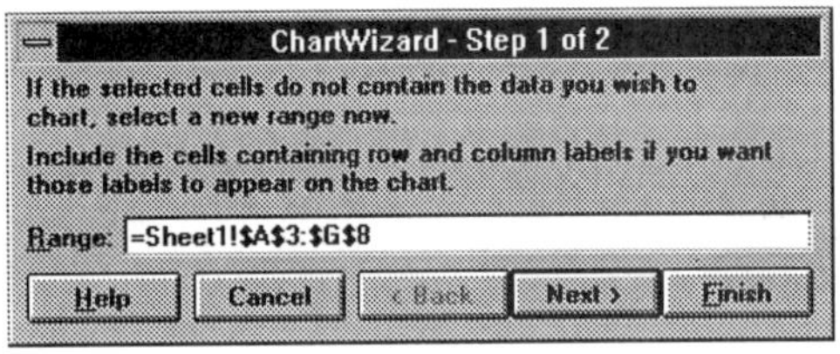

3. Highlight the new range or type the new range reference.
4. Click on the Finish button and the chart is updated to reflect the new range.

Figure 12-4 How to change a chart's range

You can add data to an existing chart in one of two ways. First, you can change the chart's range so it includes the new data. To do that, you use the ChartWizard as described in figure 12-4.

You can also add data to an existing chart using one of the techniques in figure 12-5. With the first technique, you simply highlight the data in the worksheet and drag it into the chart. Then, *Excel* automatically updates the chart range. In figure 12-5, for example, I added a new data series to the Sales-by-type chart. Note that when you use this technique, you can include row or column headings with the data just as you can when you create a chart.

If the chart is in a chart sheet, you can add data to it using the clipboard. Just copy the data from the worksheet to the clipboard and paste it into the chart sheet. Again, *Excel* updates the chart's range automatically.

Finally, you can use the New Data command to add data to an embedded chart or a chart sheet. When you use the New Data command, you specify the location of the data you want to add. Then, *Excel* adds the range you specify to the chart's range.

When you use any of the techniques in figure 12-5 to add data to a chart, *Excel* analyzes the data already in the chart to determine how to chart the new data. If *Excel* isn't able to figure out the placement or orientation of the new data, it displays the Paste Special dialog box shown in part 2 of figure 12-5. From this dialog box, you can indicate whether the new data is a data series or data points (a category), whether the data currently in the worksheet is plotted by rows or by columns, and whether the new data includes a label.

Use the mouse to add data to an embedded chart

1. Select the data you want to add and drag the outline of the selected data onto the chart:

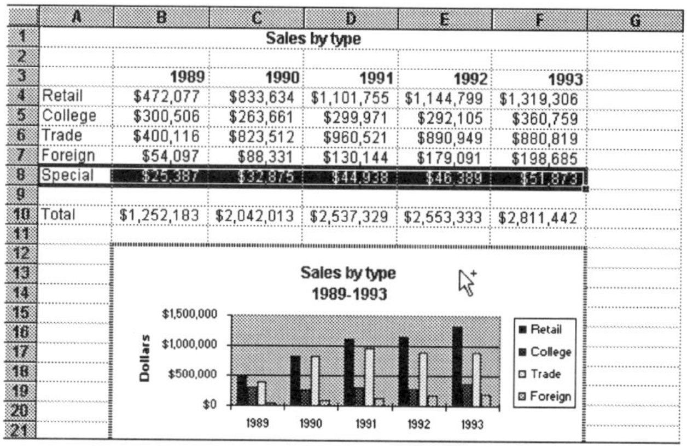

2. Release the mouse button and *Excel* adds the data to the chart:

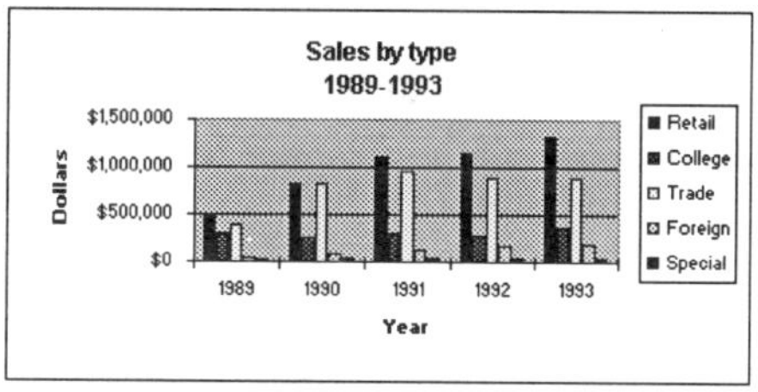

Use the clipboard to add data to a chart sheet

1. Copy the data you want to add to the chart from the worksheet to the clipboard.
2. Activate the chart sheet.
3. Select the Paste command from the Edit menu and *Excel* adds the data to the chart.

Use the New Data command to add data to an embedded chart or a chart sheet

1. Activate the chart.
2. Select the New Data command from the Insert menu and this dialog box appears:

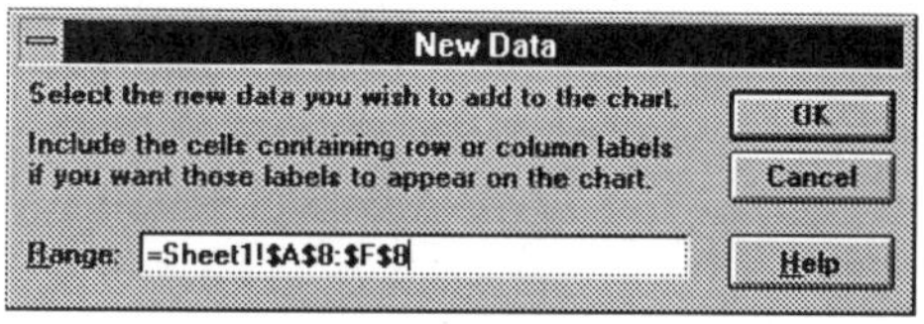

3. Select the range that contains the data you want to add or type the range reference.
4. Click on the OK button and *Excel* adds the data to the chart.

Figure 12-5 How to add a range of data to a chart (part 1 of 2)

Note

If *Excel* can't determine the placement or orientation of the new data in the chart, it displays this dialog box:

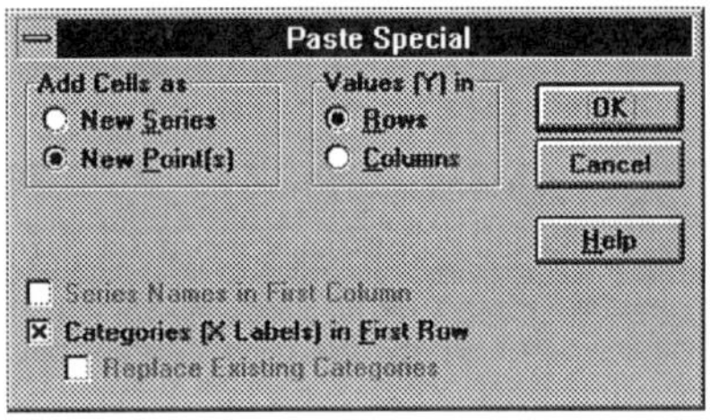

Select an option from the Adds Cells As group to tell *Excel* whether you're adding a new data series or category. Select an option from the Values (Y) In group to tell *Excel* if the data series in the chart are plotted by columns or by rows. If you included a heading in the selected range, select the Series Names In First Column or Categories In First Row option. The option that's available depends on the option you select in the Add Cells As group.

Figure 12-5 How to add a range of data to a chart (part 2 of 2)

How to modify and enhance a chart

In chapter 11, you learned how to change chart values and text, how to add a legend and change its placement and orientation, and how to add chart and axis titles. Now, you'll learn how to make additional modifications and enhancements to a chart. When you finish this part of the chapter, you'll be able to modify almost any chart so it looks just the way you want it to.

How to change the orientation of the data in a chart When you create a chart, *Excel* determines whether the rows or columns in the worksheet are used as the data series depending on the number of rows and columns in the range you select for the chart. Although the ChartWizard lets you change *Excel*'s default when you create a chart, you can also invoke the ChartWizard after you create a chart to change the orientation of the data. Figure 12-6 shows you how to do that.

When you activate a chart and click on the ChartWizard toolbar button, *Excel* displays the dialog box you saw in figure 12-4 that lets you change the chart range. If you click on the Next button from this dialog box, *Excel* displays the dialog box shown in figure 12-6. From this dialog box, you can change the orientation of the data in the chart. The chart in figure 12-6, for example, is the Sales-by-type chart after I changed the orientation from

How to change the data series from rows to columns

1. Activate the chart.
2. Click on the ChartWizard button and the first dialog box appears.
3. Click on the Next button and this dialog box appears:

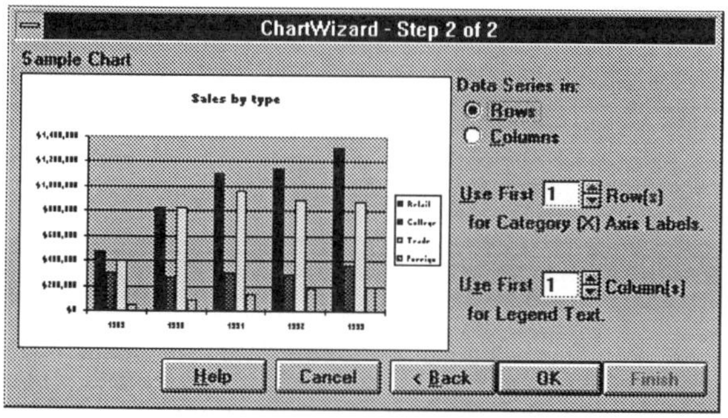

4. Select the Columns option from the Data Series In group, and change the other options if necessary.
5. Click on the OK button and *Excel* updates the chart based on your selection:

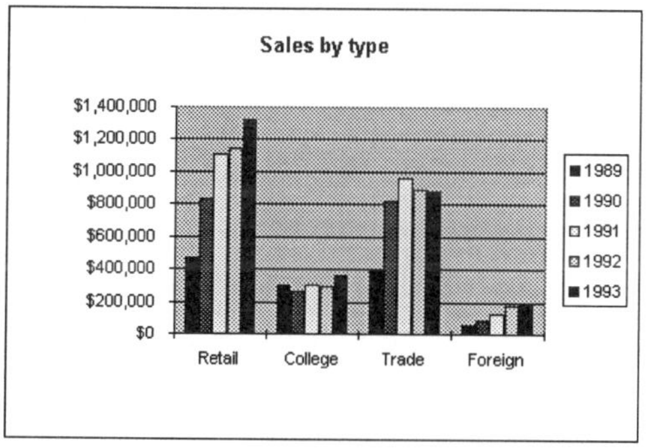

How to change the data series from columns to rows

Use the procedure above, but select the Rows option in the ChartWizard dialog box.

Figure 12-6 How to change the orientation of the data in a chart

rows to columns. As you can see, the data series and categories have been switched.

How to change the axis scales Figure 12-7 shows you how to change the scales on the both the value (Y) and the category (X) axis. In most cases, you won't need to change any of the available options because the

Three ways to access the Scale tab of the Format Axis dialog box

- Activate the chart, then double-click on an axis and click on the Scale tab.
- Activate the chart, then select an axis, select the Selected Axis command from the Format menu, and click on the Scale tab.
- Activate the chart, then select an axis, select the Format Axis command from the shortcut menu, and click on the Scale tab.

The Scale tab for the value (Y) axis

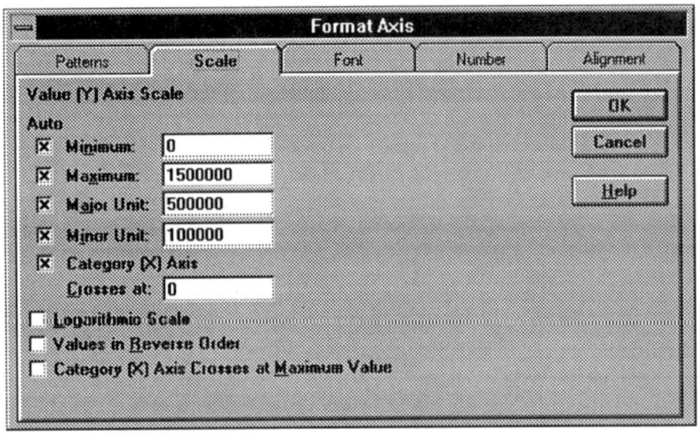

Operation

- To change the high and low values on the axis, to change the interval where values are displayed, or to change the location where the category axis crosses the value axis, enter the appropriate values in the Minimum, Maximum, Major Unit, Minor Unit, and Category (X) Axis Crosses At text boxes. If you change a value, you can return it to its default by selecting the Auto option for the value. The Major Unit and Minor Unit options also determine the placement of tick marks, tick mark labels, and gridlines. See figures 12-8 and 12-9 for details on adding these items to a chart.
- To change the scale from a standard scale to a logarithmic scale, select the Logarithmic Scale option.
- To display the values in reverse order on the axis, select the Values In Reverse Order option.
- To change the x-axis so it crosses at the maximum value on the y-axis, select the Category (X) Axis Crosses At Maximum Value option. This option overrides the Category (X) Axis Crosses At option.

Figure 12-7 How to change the axis scales (part 1 of 2)

defaults *Excel* uses are usually what you want. But you may occasionally want to change the Minimum or Maximum option for the y-axis scale, and you may want to enter different values for the Major Unit and Minor Unit

The Scale tab for the category (X) axis

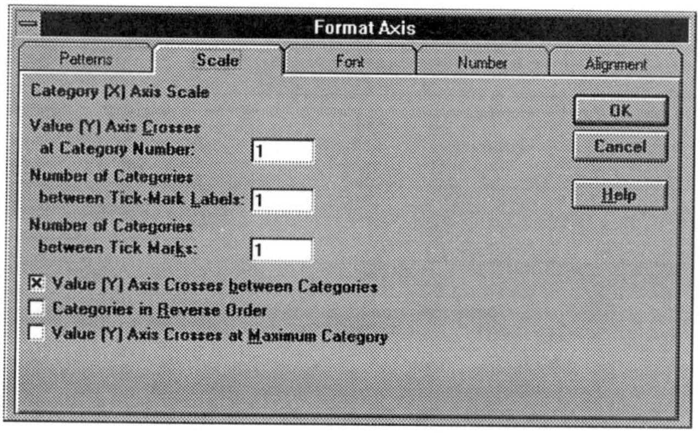

Operation

- To change the location where the y-axis crosses the x-axis, enter a category number in the Value (Y) Axis Crosses At Category Number text box.
- To change the frequency of tick marks and labels along the axis, enter a number of categories in the Number Of Categories Between Tick-Mark Labels and Number Of Categories Between Tick Marks text boxes. The Number Of Categories Between Tick Marks option also determines the major and minor intervals for the axis. *Excel* uses these intervals to determine the placement of tick marks, tick mark labels, and gridlines. See figures 12-8 and 12-9 for details on how to add these items to a chart.
- By default, the value axis crosses to the left of the selected category and the data points are plotted between tick marks. If you want to change the y-axis so that it crosses in the middle of a category and the data points are plotted on the tick marks, deselect the Value (Y) Axis Crosses Between Categories option.
- To display the categories in reverse order, select the Categories In Reverse Order option.
- To change the y-axis so that it crosses the x-axis after the last category, select the Value (Y) Axis Crosses At Maximum Category option. This option overrides the Value (Y) Axis Crosses At Category Number option.

Figure 12-7 How to change the axis scales (part 2 of 2)

options to change the major and minor intervals for the axis. You may also want to experiment with the other options to see how they affect your charts.

Two ways to access the Patterns tab of the Format Axis dialog box

- Activate the chart, then double-click on the axis and click on the Patterns tab.
- Activate the chart, then select the axis, select the Selected Axis command from the Format menu or the Format Axis command from the shortcut menu, and select the Patterns tab.

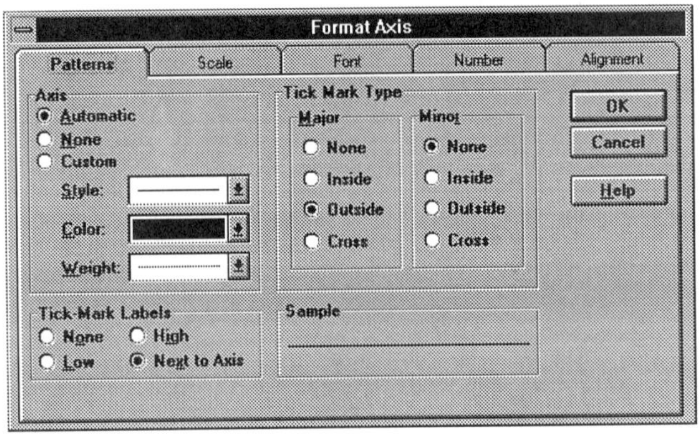

Operation

- To add tick mark labels to a chart, select the Low, High, or Next To Axis option from the Tick-Mark Labels group.
- To add tick marks at the major intervals on the axis, select the Inside, Outside, or Cross option from the Major group.
- To add tick marks at the minor intervals on the axis, select the Inside, Outside, or Cross option from the Minor group.

Figure 12-8 How to add tick marks and tick mark labels to a chart

How to add tick marks and tick mark labels to a chart By default, *Excel* includes tick marks and tick mark labels at the major intervals on each axis. If you want to include additional tick marks or labels, you use the Patterns tab of the Format Axis dialog box as shown in figure 12-8. The options you choose also determine the placement of the tick marks and labels.

How to add gridlines to a chart Figure 12-9 shows you how to add gridlines to a chart. As you can see, you can add gridlines at the major and minor intervals for each axis. The default depends on the format you selected when you created the chart.

Access

Activate the chart, then select the Gridlines command from the Insert menu or the Insert Gridlines command from the shortcut menu.

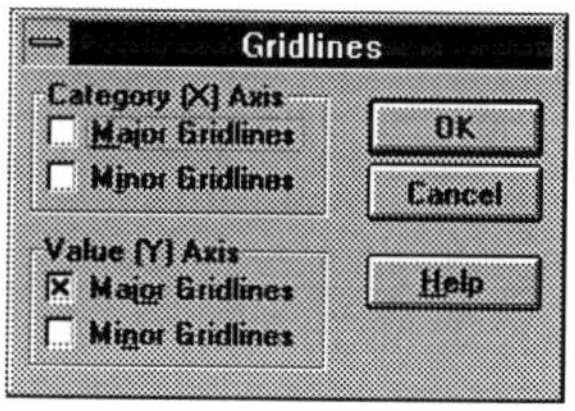

Category (X) Axis group

The options in this group determine if gridlines are included at the major and minor intervals along the x-axis.

Values (Y) Axis group

The options in this group determine if gridlines are included at the major and minor intervals along the y-axis.

Notes

- For a 3-D chart, additional options are available in this dialog box for the z-axis.
- You can control the spacing of the major and minor intervals from the Scale tab of the Format Axis dialog box as described in figure 12-7. The Scale tab is also available from the Format Gridlines dialog box. To display this dialog box, double-click on a gridline, or select a gridline, then select the Select Gridlines command from the Format menu or the Format Gridlines command from the shortcut menu.

Figure 12-9 How to add gridlines to a chart

How to add data labels to a chart You may occasionally want to add data labels to a chart to help identify one or more data points. You can add data labels to all the data points in a chart, to all the data points in a series, or to a single data point. Keep in mind, however, that data labels tend to make a chart look cluttered. So you'll want to use them sparingly.

Figure 12-10 shows you how to add data labels to a chart. The options that are available for the data labels depend on the chart type. For a chart other than a pie chart or a doughnut chart, the labels can show the actual value of the data point or the name of the category that contains the data point. The chart in figure 12-10, for example, includes data labels that show the actual dollar values for the data points in the Retail data series. For a pie

How to add data labels to all the data points in a chart

1. Activate the chart.
2. Select the Data Labels command from the Insert menu or the Insert Data Labels command from the shortcut menu, and this dialog box appears:

3. Select the appropriate options and click on the OK button.

How to add data labels to all the data points in a series

Use the procedure above, but select the data series before you select the Data Labels command.

How to add a data label to a single data point

Use the procedure above, but before you select the Data Labels command, select the data series that contains the data point you want to add a label to, then select the data point.

Notes

- You can also add data labels to a data series or data point using the Data Labels tab of the Format Data Series or Format Data Point dialog box. To access these dialog boxes, double-click on the data series or data point. The options in the Data Labels tab are the same as the options in the Data Labels dialog box.
- The Show Percent and Show Label And Percent options are available only for pie and doughnut charts.
- After you add data labels to a chart, you can edit them directly in the chart. If you do that, however, the labels will no longer be linked to the worksheet.

A column chart that contains data labels for the Retail data series

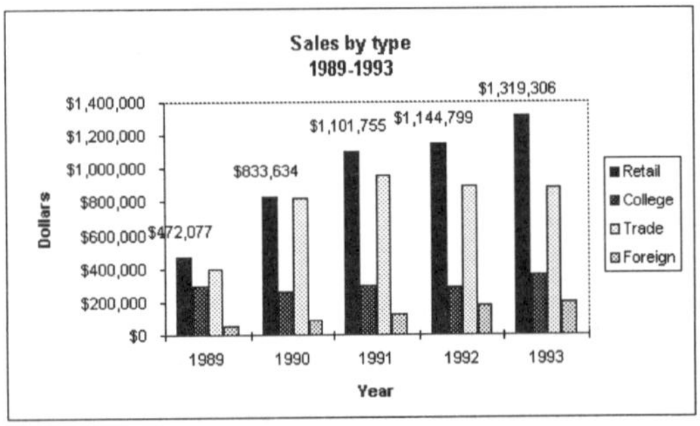

Figure 12-10 How to add data labels to a chart

Three ways to access a Format dialog box

- Double-click on the area or item you want to format.
- Select the item or area you want to format, then select the Selected... command from the Format menu for the area or item.
- Select the item or area you want to format, then select the Format command from the shortcut menu for the area or item.

The Patterns tab of the Format Chart Title dialog box

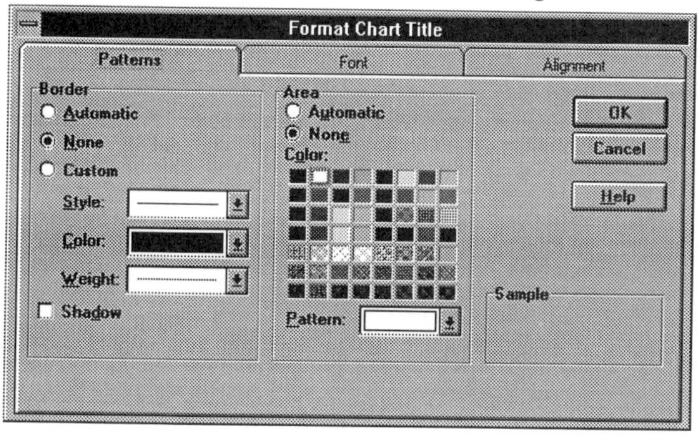

Notes

- The Selected... command in the Format menu and the Format command in the shortcut menu change depending on the item or area you select.
- You can change the default colors used in all the charts in a workbook from the Color tab of the Options dialog box. To display this dialog box, select the Options command from the Tools menu.

Figure 12-11 How to change the font, number format, alignment, and patterns used in a chart

or a doughnut chart, the data labels can also show the percent each data point is of the whole, or they can show the category name and the percent. For any chart type, you can also show the legend key next to the labels.

How to change the font, number format, alignment, and patterns used in a chart Figure 12-11 shows you how to change the font, number format, alignment, and patterns that are used in a chart. The options that are available depend on the area or item you select. As you can see in figure 12-11, for example, you can change the patterns, font, and alignment for a chart title. Although you may occasionally want to change some of these features for a chart, *Excel*'s defaults are usually satisfactory.

Three ways to access the Chart tab of the Page Setup dialog box

- Select the Page Setup command from the File menu and click on the Chart tab.
- Select the Print command from the File menu, then click on the Page Setup button from the Print dialog box and click on the Chart tab.
- Select the Print Preview command from the File menu, then click on the Page Setup button from the Print Preview dialog box and click on the Chart tab.

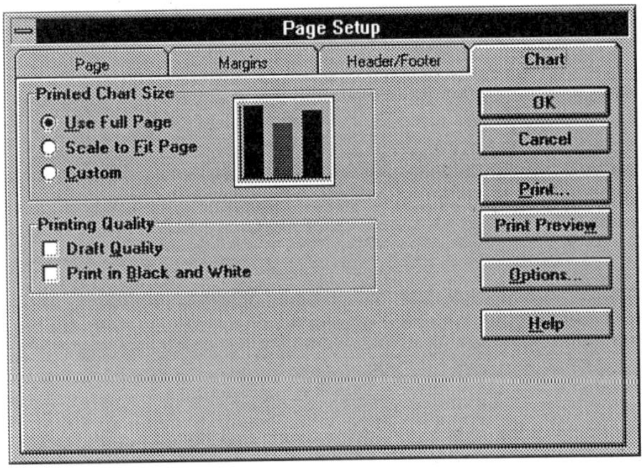

Operation

- To print the chart so that it fills the entire page, select the Use Full Page option.
- To print the chart so that it fits on the page and keeps the same proportions as on the screen, select the Scale To Fit Page option.
- To print the chart so that it is sized and positioned as it appears on the screen, select the Custom option. Then, when you select the chart, a border appears around it that lets you move and size the chart.

Note

You can also size a chart so that it fills the entire window by selecting the Sized With Window command from the View menu.

Figure 12-12 How to size a chart sheet for printing

How to size a chart sheet for printing

By default, *Excel* prints a chart sheet so that it fills the entire page. In that case, the size of the printed chart depends on the size of the paper you use. If you want to print a chart sheet in a different size, you can use the options in the Chart tab of the Page Setup dialog box as shown in figure 12-12.

The three options in the Printed Chart Size group determine the size of the printed chart. Use Full Page is the default. If you select the Scale To Fit

Page option, *Excel* prints the chart so that it fits on the page, but it keeps the same proportions that you see on the screen. If you select the Custom option, *Excel* lets you size and position the chart on the screen before you print it. To do that, you select the chart and a border with handles appears around it. Then, you can size the chart by dragging the handles, and you can move the chart by dragging it. When you print the chart, it's printed in the same size and position as it appears on the screen.

Perspective

If you experiment with the charting functions presented in this chapter, I think you'll find that you can create almost any chart in just a matter of minutes. Although some of the functions may seem complicated at first, they'll make more sense once you use them. So if you plan on using the advanced charting features of *Excel*, you should spend a few minutes experimenting with them.

Although this chapter presents the advanced charting techniques you're most likely to use, you should know that *Excel* provides other charting features. For example, it provides features that help you analyze the data in a chart, change 3-D views, and create custom data markers. If you understand the material presented in this chapter and in chapter 11, however, you won't have any trouble learning these features on your own.

Summary

- You can explode one or more slices of a pie chart by dragging them.
- To chart a selected data series with a different chart type, select the series and use the Chart Type command in the Format or shortcut menu.
- To plot a selected data series along a second y-axis, use the Axis tab of the Format Data Series dialog box.
- You can add data to a chart by changing the chart's range, by highlighting the data and dragging it onto an embedded chart, by using the clipboard to copy and paste the data onto a chart sheet, or by using the New Data command in the Insert menu.
- To change the orientation of a chart, use the ChartWizard to select another option.
- To change the scales on the x- or y-axis, use the Scale tab of the Format Axis dialog box.

- To add tick marks or tick mark labels to a chart, use the Patterns tab of the Format Axis dialog box.
- To add gridlines to a chart, use the Gridlines command in the Insert menu or the Insert Gridlines command in the shortcut menu.
- To add data labels to a chart, use the Data Labels command in the Insert menu, the Insert Data Labels command in the shortcut menu, or the Data Labels tab of the Format Data Series or Format Data Point dialog box.
- To change the font, number format, alignment, lines, colors, and patterns used in a chart, use the appropriate tabs in the Format dialog box for the selected item or area.
- To size a chart sheet for printing, use the Chart tab of the Page Setup dialog box.

Chapter 13

How to enhance a worksheet with graphics

In the last two chapters, you learned how to enhance a worksheet with a chart. Now, in this chapter, you'll learn how to further enhance a worksheet using the graphics features of *Excel.* In figure 13-1, for example, the shadowed text box is a graphics enhancement that provides some additional information. And the arrow that connects the text box to the rent value is another graphics enhancement.

In this chapter, you'll start by learning basic drawing skills. For most worksheets, these are the only skills you'll need. If you want to learn additional graphics skills, though, you can continue with the rest of the chapter. When you complete it, you'll know how to use all of the graphics features that *Excel* provides.

Basic drawing skills

In addition to charts, you can create other types of *graphic objects*. You can use the drawing features of *Excel* to draw arrows, squares, rectangles, circles, ellipses, and other shapes. You can also draw a text box like the one in figure 13-1.

To work with graphic objects in *Excel*, you use the buttons in the Drawing toolbar presented in figure 13-2. Note that most of these buttons have no menu counterparts. In particular, the twelve buttons in the first two groups that you use to draw graphic objects have no menu counterparts. So you'll need to display this toolbar before you can begin working with graphic objects. To display the Drawing toolbar, click on the Drawing button in the Standard toolbar. You can move and size this toolbar any way you like.

How to draw lines and shapes Figure 13-3 presents the different types of lines and shapes you can draw in *Excel.* As you can see, there are four types of lines: a straight line, an arc, a polyline, and a freehand drawing. The regular shapes include a square or a rectangle and a circle or an ellipse. The irregular shapes include a polygon and a freeform shape.

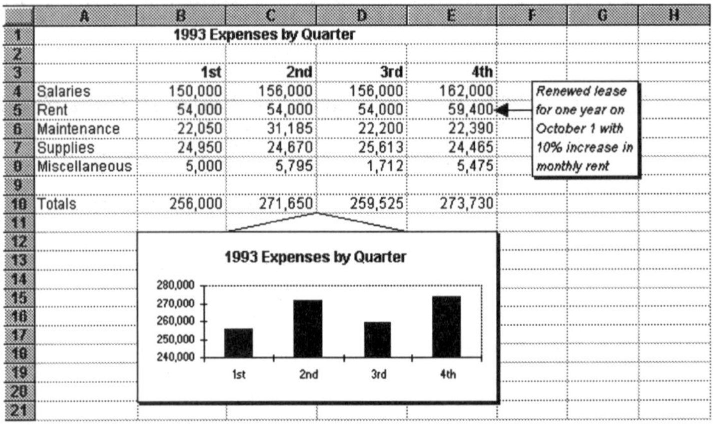

Figure 13-1 A worksheet that contains graphics

Figure 13-4 presents the procedure for drawing a straight line, an arc, or a regular shape. Once you select the button for the object you want to draw, you just place the pointer where you want to begin drawing and drag it to size the object. If you want to create a square instead of a rectangle or a circle instead of an ellipse, hold down the Shift key as you draw the object. Similarly, if you want to create a line at 45 degree angles from its starting point, hold down the Shift key as you draw. And if you want to draw a circle segment (a quarter circle), hold down the Shift key as you draw an arc. You can also snap the object to the nearest cell gridlines (the lines in the worksheet that outline the cells) by holding down the Alt key as you draw any of these objects.

Figure 13-5 presents the procedure for drawing a freehand shape. After you select the Freehand button, you hold down the mouse button and use the mouse to draw. Then, to complete the drawing, you release the mouse button.

Figure 13-6 presents the procedure for drawing and reshaping a polygon, a polyline, or a freeform shape. To create a polygon, you click the mouse button at the beginning of the first segment, then move it and click it at the end of each segment. To complete the polygon, the pointer must be positioned so that the end of the last segment is at the beginning of the first segment.

Access

Click on the Drawing button in the Standard toolbar: 

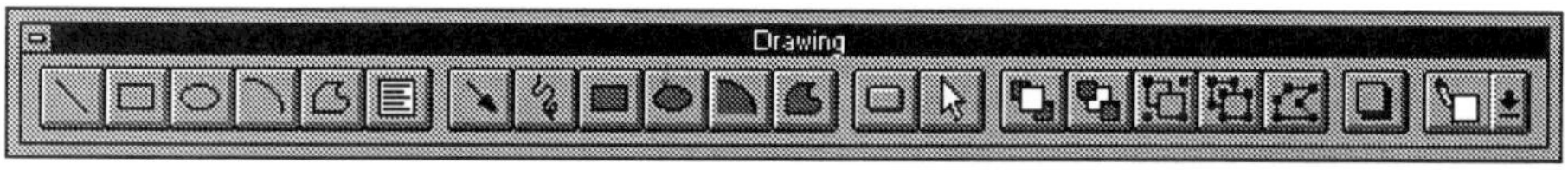

Button	Function	Button	Function
	Draws a straight line.		Creates a button. See chapter 19 for details.
	Draws a rectangle or square.		Activates selection mode.
	Draws an ellipse or circle.		Brings the selected object to the front.
	Draws an arc.		Sends the selected object to the back.
	Draws a freeform shape.		Groups selected objects.
	Creates a text block.		Ungroups a selected group.
	Draws an arrow.		Lets you reshape a polygon, polyline, or freeform object.
	Draws a freehand shape.		Adds a drop shadow to the selected object.
	Draws a filled rectangle or square.	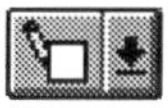	Lets you change the fill color and pattern for an object.
	Draws a filled ellipse or circle.		
	Draws a filled arc.		
	Draws a filled freeform shape.		

Notes

- You can move and size the Drawing toolbar any way you want to. To close the toolbar, click on the Drawing button again or click on the close box in the upper left corner of the toolbar.
- To draw an object, you click on the appropriate button and follow the procedures presented in this chapter. If you want to draw more than one object of the same type, double-click on the button. Then, the button remains selected until you click on it again, press the Esc key, click on another button, or click on the worksheet without dragging.
- The square shown on the Pattern button (the last button in the Drawing toolbar) indicates the default fill color and pattern.

Figure 13-2 The Drawing toolbar

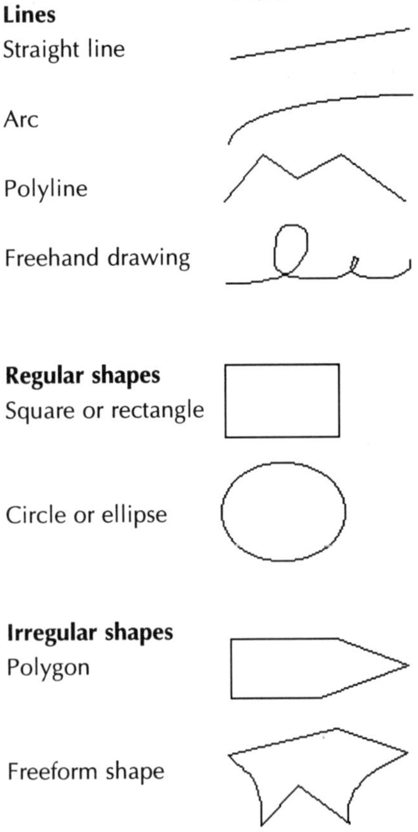

Figure 13-3 The lines and shapes you can draw in *Excel*

You create a polyline the same way you create a polygon except that the last segment doesn't have to end at the beginning of the first segment. To indicate that a polyline is complete, you double-click at the end of the last segment.

A freeform shape can contain both straight line segments and freehand segments, and it can be enclosed like a polygon or open like a polyline. To create a freehand segment, press and hold the mouse button at the beginning of the segment and continue to hold the button as you draw the segment. When you release the button, the freehand segment ends.

After you create a polygon, polyline, or freeform shape, you can reshape it if it doesn't look the way you want it to. To do that, you use the Reshape button. When you select an object with the Reshape button

Procedure

1. Click on the button in the Drawing toolbar for the object you want to draw.
2. Place the mouse pointer where you want to begin drawing the object, then drag it until the object is the desired size:

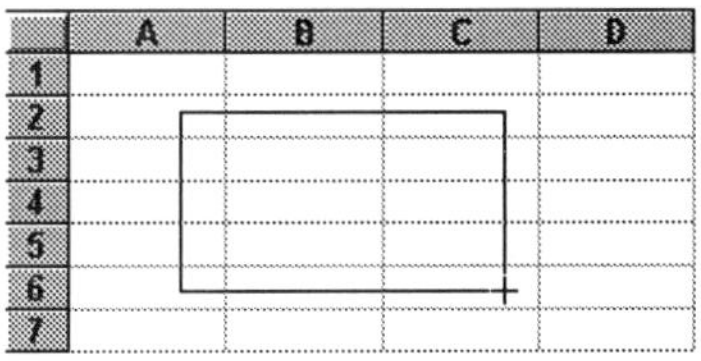

3. Release the mouse button.

Notes

- You can draw a square instead of a rectangle or a circle instead of an ellipse by holding down the Shift key as you draw.
- You can draw a line at 45 degree increments from its starting point by holding down the Shift key as you draw.
- You can draw a circle segment (a quarter circle) for an arc by holding down the Shift key as you draw.
- To snap the object to the nearest cell gridlines, hold down the Alt key as you draw.

Figure 13-4 How to draw a straight line, arc, or regular shape

1. Click on the Freehand button in the Drawing toolbar.
2. Place the pointer where you want to begin drawing the object, and press and hold the mouse button.
3. Draw the object while continuing to hold the mouse button:

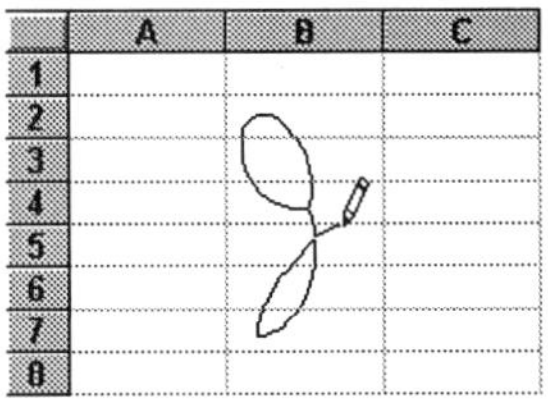

4. To complete the drawing, release the mouse button.

Figure 13-5 How to draw a freehand shape

How to draw a polygon

1. Click on one of the freeform buttons in the Drawing toolbar.
2. Place the pointer where you want to begin drawing the object, and click the mouse button.
3. Move the pointer to the end of the first segment of the drawing, and click the mouse button. Then, continue drawing segments until the starting point and ending point meet:

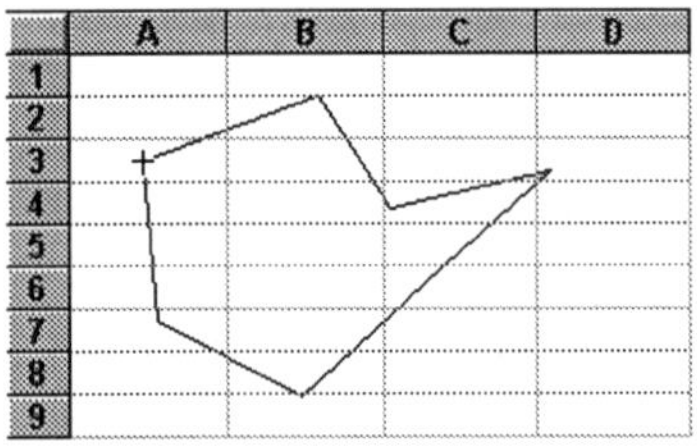

How to draw a polyline

Use the procedure above, but double-click at the end of the last segment instead of joining the starting and ending points.

How to draw a freeform shape

Use the procedures above, but hold down the mouse button to draw freehand segments.

How to reshape a polygon, polyline, or freeform shape

- To activate the reshape feature, click on the Reshape button in the Drawing toolbar. Then, select the object you want to reshape and handles appear at the ends of each line in the object:

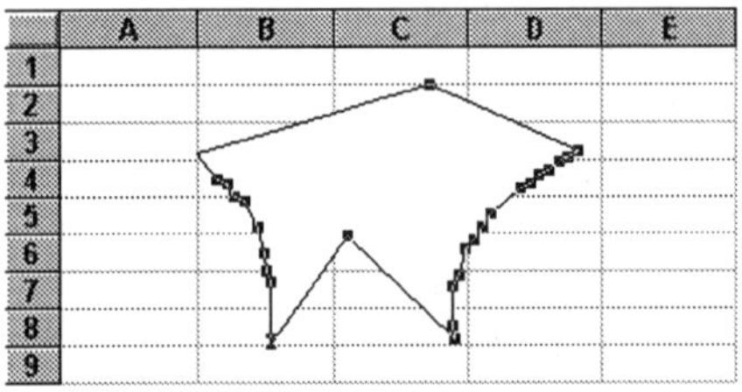

- To move a vertex (the point where two lines intersect), drag it.
- To delete a vertex, hold down the Ctrl key and click on it.
- To add a vertex, hold down the Ctrl key as you drag the line from the point where you want to add the vertex.

Note

To snap the object to the nearest cell gridlines, hold down the Alt key as you draw it.

Figure 13-6 How to draw and reshape a polygon, polyline, or freeform shape selected, handles appear at the end of each straight line segment and at various points along each freehand segment. The handles along the freehand segments indicate the ends of the straight lines that make up the segments. Each handle, then, represents the point where two lines intersect, called a *vertex*. You can move or delete a vertex or add a vertex to any line using the techniques in figure 13-6.

How to create a text box and edit and format its text Figure 13-7 presents the procedure for creating a text box and the techniques for editing and formatting the text in a text box. As you can see, creating a text box is similar to creating a rectangle. After you draw the box, though, *Excel* places a cursor inside it so you can type the text.

As you type, *Excel* automatically wraps the text to the next line when it reaches the edge of the box. If you want to move to the next line before you reach the edge of the box, press the Enter key. When you reach the bottom of the box, *Excel* scrolls the text up so you can continue typing. Then, when you're done, you need to make the box larger so you can see all the text. You'll learn how to do that in just a moment.

Once you've created a text box, you can edit and format the text any way you like. To edit the text, select the text box by clicking on it, then click in the text box and a cursor appears. Now, you can use the keyboard to change the text. To change the font, font size, and font attributes of selected text, you use the Object command in the Format menu or the Font and Font Size boxes and the font attribute buttons in the Formatting toolbar. You can also use these techniques to change the font, font size, and font attributes for all the text in a text box. To do that, select the box, but don't select specific text. You can also change the alignment of all the text in a text box using the Object command or the alignment buttons in the Formatting toolbar.

How to select, move, copy, size, and delete an object Figure 13-8 presents the techniques for selecting, moving, copying, sizing, and deleting an object. To select an object, you click on its border. You can also select a filled object by clicking anywhere inside its border. Note that if the Drawing Selection button in the Drawing toolbar is selected, *Excel* lets you select only graphic objects. If you click on a cell, it has no effect.

When you select an object, *handles* appear around it. For a straight line, a handle appears at each end. For any other object, handles appear at each corner and on each side of a box around the object. You can size an object by dragging any of its handles. If you want to maintain the object's proportions as you size it, hold down the Shift key as you drag a corner handle.

How to create a text box

1. Click on the Text Box button in the Drawing toolbar.
2. Place the pointer where you want to begin the text box, then drag it until the box is the desired size:

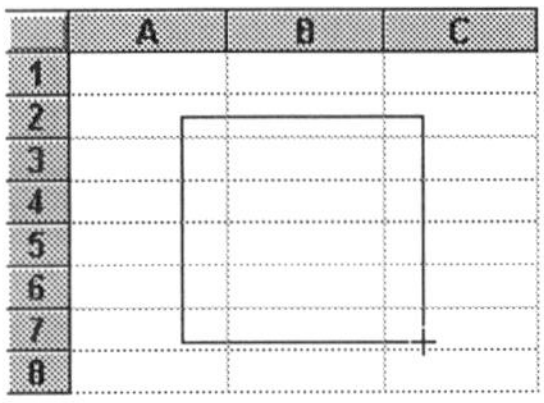

3. When you release the mouse button, a cursor is positioned inside the text box.
4. Type the text:

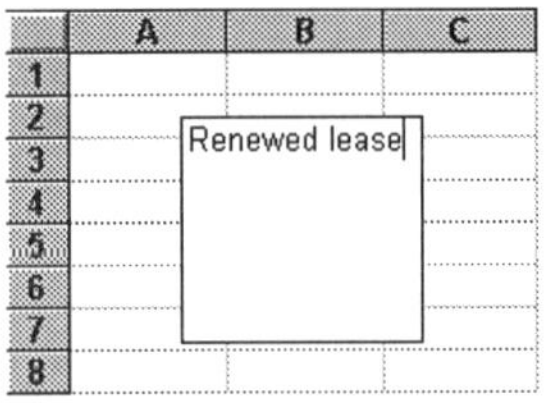

5. When you finish typing, click the pointer anywhere outside the text box to complete the operation.

How to edit and format the text in a text box

- To edit the text, select the text box, then click in the box and a cursor appears. Use the keyboard to change the text.
- To format selected text, select the Object command from the Format menu and select the appropriate options from the Font tab, or use the Font and Font Size boxes and the font attribute buttons in the Formatting toolbar.
- To format all the text in a box at once, select the box, then use the Font and Alignment tabs in the Format Object dialog box or the Font and Font Size boxes and the font attribute and alignment buttons in the Formatting toolbar.

Notes

- To snap the text box to the nearest cell gridlines, hold down the Alt key as you draw.
- To create a square text box, hold down the Shift key as you draw.
- When you enter text in a text box, it is automatically wrapped to the next line when it reaches the edge of the box. If you want to end a line before then, press the Enter key.
- When you reach the bottom of the box, the text is scrolled up so you can continue typing. To display all the text at once, you have to size the box as shown in figure 13-8.

Figure 13-7 How to create a text box and edit and format its text

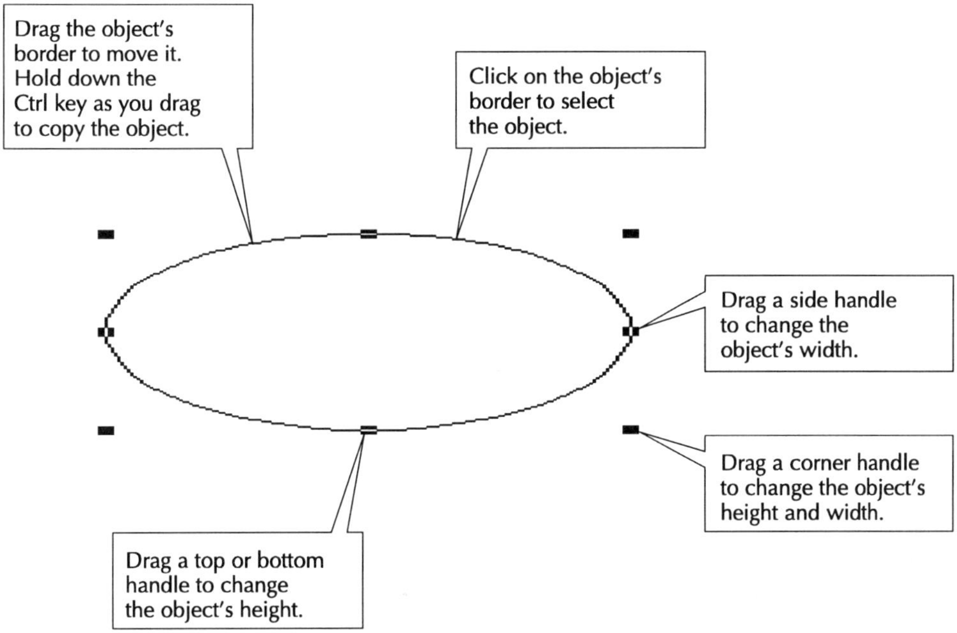

- To delete an object, select it, then press the Delete key or select the Clear command from the Edit or shortcut menu.

Notes

- If you click on the Drawing Selection button in the Drawing toolbar, you can select only graphic objects; clicking on a cell has no effect. You can also use this button to select groups of objects. See figure 13-9 for details.
- You can click anywhere inside a filled object to select it, and you can drag anywhere inside it to move or copy it.
- You can select more than one object at a time to operate on them together by holding down the Shift key as you click on each object. To remove an object from the selection, hold down the Shift key and click on the object again.
- To maintain the object's proportions when you size it, hold down the Shift key as you drag a corner handle.
- To snap an object to the nearest cell gridlines, hold down the Alt key as you move or size it.

Figure 13-8 How to select, move, copy, size, and delete an object

Procedure

1. Click on the Drawing Selection button in the Drawing toolbar.
2. Place the pointer outside all the objects you want to select, and click and drag it around all the objects:

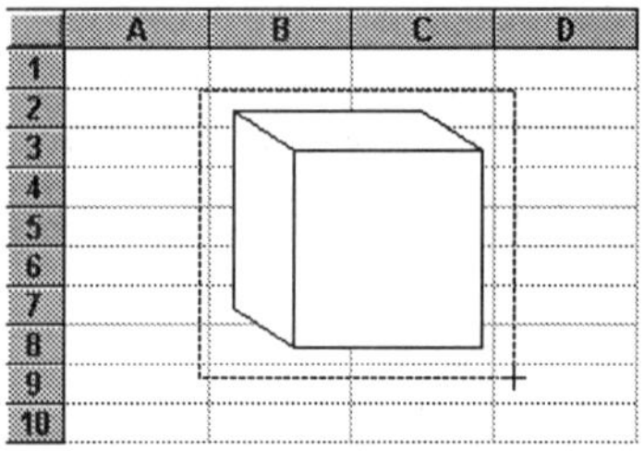

3. Release the mouse button, and all the objects are selected:

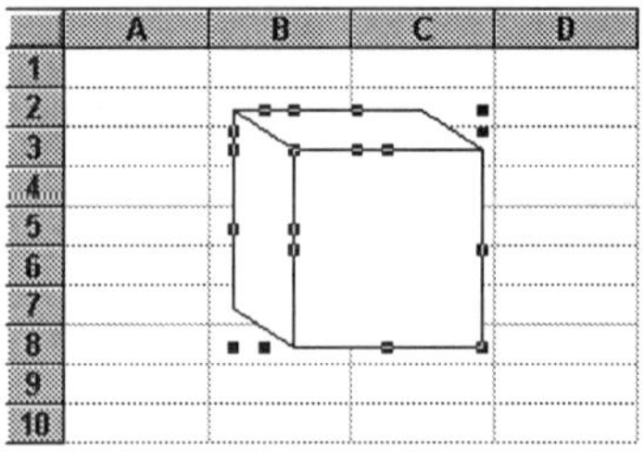

Notes

- To remove an object from the selection, hold down the Shift key and click on the object.
- The Drawing Selection button remains selected until you click on it again, press the Esc key, or double-click on a cell to select it.

Figure 13-9 How to select more than one object using the Drawing Selection button

You can move an object by placing the mouse pointer on the object's edge and dragging it. You can also move a filled object by dragging anywhere inside its border. To copy an object, hold down the Ctrl key as you drag it. If you hold down the Alt key as you move or copy an object, *Excel* snaps it to the nearest gridlines. To delete an object, select it, then press the Delete key or select the Clear command from the Edit or shortcut menu.

You can also operate on more than one object at the same time. To select each object, hold down the Shift key as you click on it. Or, you can use the Drawing Selection button as illustrated in figure 13-9. Once you select all the objects, you can move, copy, size, or delete them together. To remove an object from the selection, hold down the Shift key and click on the object again.

How to format an object Figure 13-10 shows you how to format an object. As you can see, the options in the Patterns tab that's displayed for an object depends on the object's type. For a line, you can change the line and arrowhead format. For all other objects, you can change the border format and the fill color and pattern. You can also add a drop shadow to some objects, and you can round the corners of a rectangle or text box. Note that you can hide a line or the border of another object by selecting the None option from the Line or Border group. And you can change a filled object to a transparent object by selecting the None option from the Fill group. You can also use the Drop Shadow and Pattern buttons in the Drawing toolbar and the Color button in the Formatting toolbar to format an object.

Other drawing skills

Besides the drawing features I've presented so far, *Excel* provides features for manipulating graphic objects. In particular, you can layer objects by placing one object in front of or behind another object. You can group objects so you can work on them at the same time. And you can change the way an object moves and changes size when the cells in the underlying worksheet change.

How to layer objects If you create a graphic that consists of several objects, some of the objects may overlap. By default, *Excel* places the last object you create on top of the objects already in the worksheet, but you can change that.

Figure 13-11 presents the techniques for changing the way objects are layered. When you bring an object to the front, it's placed on the top of the other objects. Similarly, when you send an object to the back, it's placed behind the other objects. How much you see of each object depends on its position in the stack.

How to group objects Figure 13-12 presents the techniques you can use to group or ungroup objects. When you create a group, you can select and manipulate all the objects in the group at the same time. Grouping also insures that none of the objects in the group are moved or sized without the other objects in the group. You can tell that the objects are grouped because handles appear around the group instead of around each object in the group.

How to change the way an object moves and changes size with the underlying cells By default, a graphic object you create in *Excel* moves and changes size with the underlying cells in the worksheet. So if

Three ways to access the Patterns tab of the Format Object dialog box

- Double-click on any object except a text box, then click on the Patterns tab.
- Select the Object command from the Format menu, then click on the Patterns tab.
- Select the Format Object command from the shortcut menu, then click on the Patterns tab.

The Patterns tab for a straight line

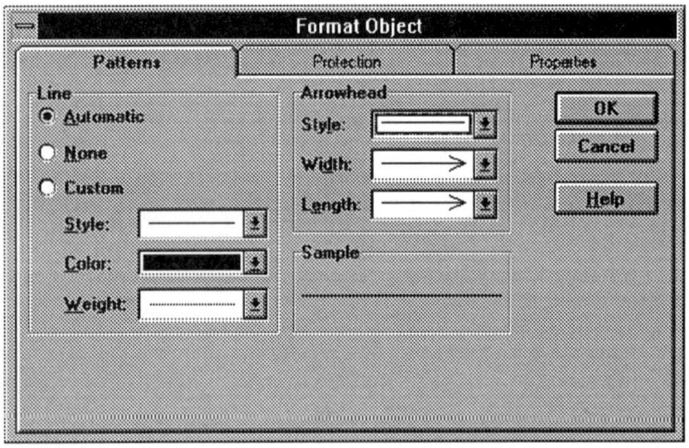

The Patterns tab for a rectangle or text box

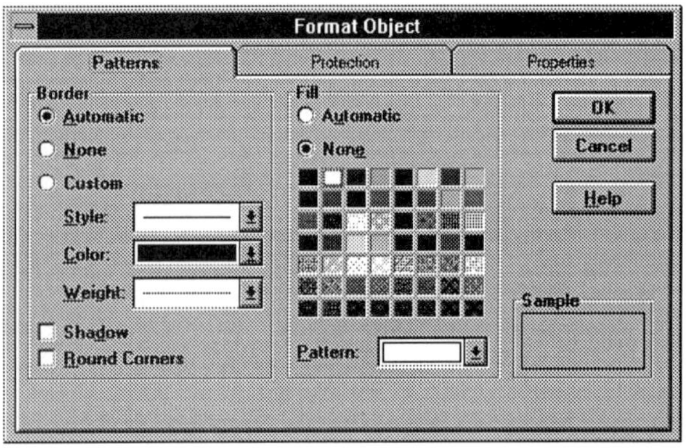

Notes

- The Patterns tab for an ellipse, a polyline, a polygon, a freehand drawing, and a freeform shape is similar to the Patterns tab for a rectangle or text box. The only difference is that the Round Corners option isn't available. The Patterns tab for an arc is also similar to the Patterns tab for a rectangle or text box. The difference is that the Shadow and Round Corners options aren't available.
- You can also use the Drop Shadow and Pattern buttons in the Drawing toolbar and the Color button in the Formatting toolbar to format an object.

Figure 13-10 How to format an object

How to bring an object to the front

1. Select the object you want to bring to the front:

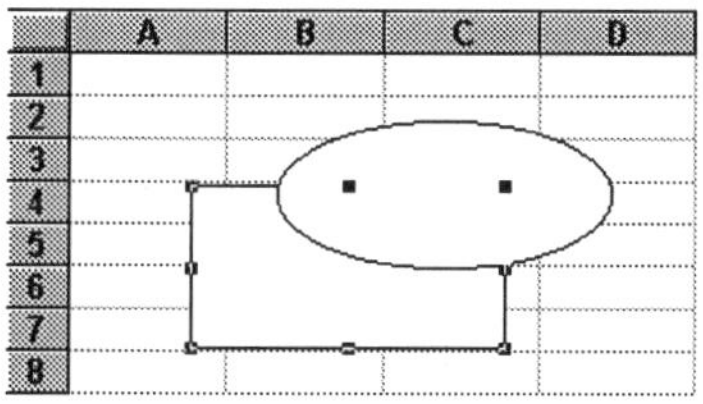

2. Click on the Bring To Front button in the Drawing toolbar or select the Bring To Front command from the shortcut menu or the Placement submenu of the Format menu, and the object is placed in front of other objects it overlaps:

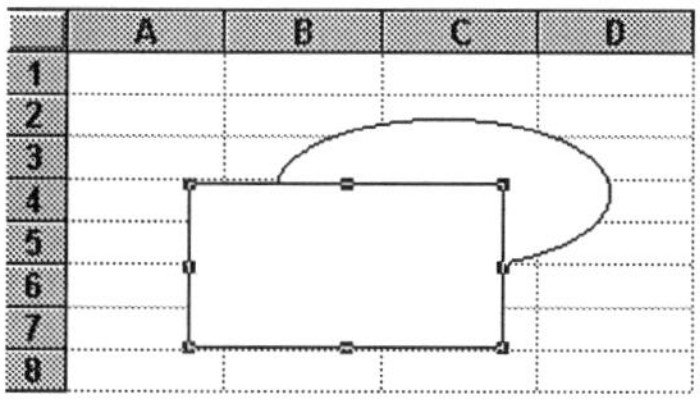

How to send an object to the back

1. Select the object you want to send to the back.
2. Click on the Send To Back button in the Drawing toolbar or select the Send To Back command from the shortcut menu or the Placement submenu of the Format menu, and the object is placed behind other objects it overlaps.

Figure 13-11 How to bring an object to the front or send it to the back

you move the underlying cells or the cells move when you insert or delete other cells, the object moves with them. And if you change the height or width of the underlying cells or insert cells in the middle of the underlying cells, the object changes size.

If you don't want an object to move or change size with the underlying cells, you can use the Properties tab of the Format Object dialog box shown in figure 13-13 to change this feature. The other options are to move but not size the object, or to neither move or size the object. Since you usually have a worksheet in final form before you add graphics to it, you may never need to use this command.

How to group objects

1. Select the objects you want to group:

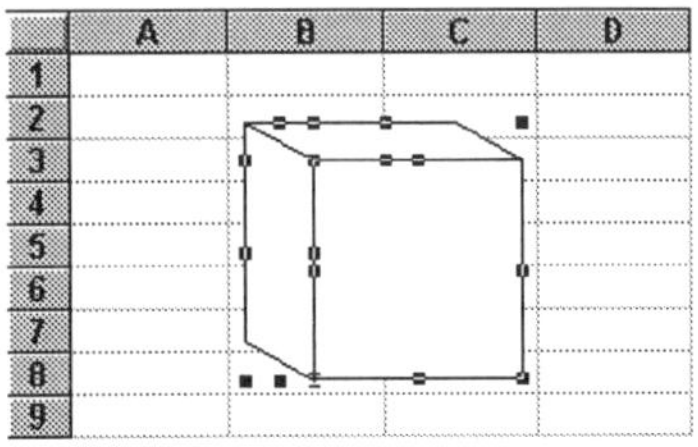

2. Click on the Group button in the Drawing toolbar or select the Group command from the shortcut menu or the Placement submenu of the Format menu, and the objects are grouped:

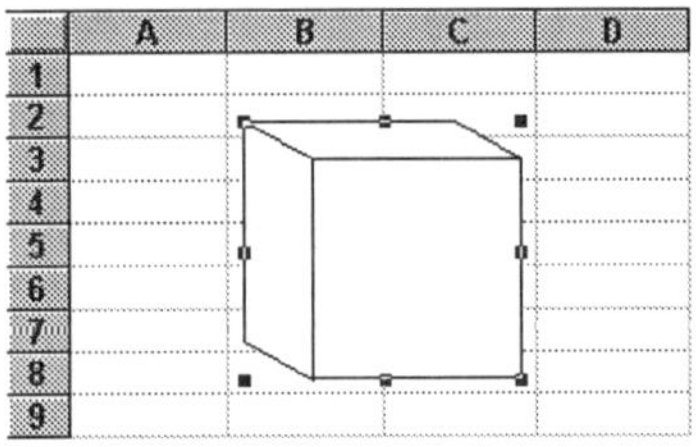

How to ungroup objects

1. Select the group of objects you want to ungroup.
2. Click on the Ungroup button in the Drawing toolbar or select the Ungroup command from the shortcut menu or the Placement submenu of the Format menu, and the objects are ungrouped.

Figure 13-12 How to group or ungroup objects

Perspective

Most worksheets don't need graphics to be effective. In fact, graphics can detract from the effectiveness of a worksheet if they're over used or not used properly. In addition, adding even minor graphics enhancements to a worksheet can take considerable amounts of time. So you should be sure there's a real need for them before you add them to a worksheet.

If you do need to add graphics enhancements to a worksheet, you should know that *Excel* can import graphics from other programs. So if you have a drawing program that comes with a clip-art library or if you've already used another program to create a drawing, you can copy it into your worksheet using the clipboard or the Picture command in the Insert menu. Once you've done that, you can select, move, copy, size, and delete it just as if you created it in *Excel*.

Access

Select the Object command from the Format menu, then click on the Properties tab.

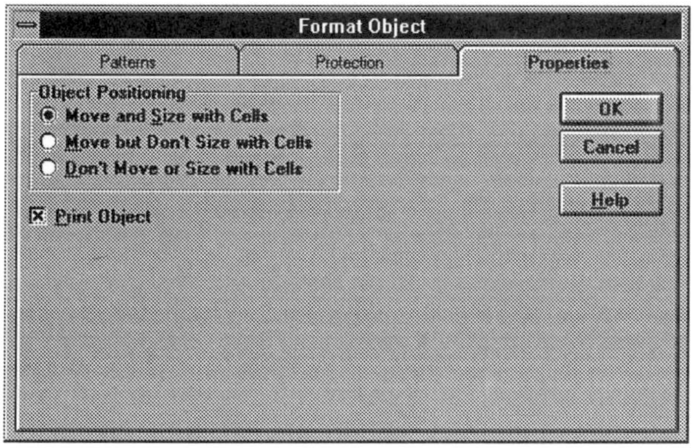

Operation

- If you select the Move And Size With Cells option, the object moves if you move the underlying cells or if the cells move when you insert or delete other cells. If you insert or delete cells in the middle of the underlying cells or you change the height or width of the underlying cells, the object changes size.
- If you select the Move But Don't Size With Cells option, the object moves but doesn't change size with the underlying cells.
- If you select the Don't Move Or Size With Cells option, the object doesn't move or change size with the underlying cells.

Figure 13-13 How to change the way an object moves or changes size with the underlying cells

Summary

- To create *graphic objects*, you use the buttons in the Drawing toolbar. To display this toolbar, click on the Drawing button in the Standard toolbar.
- When you select an object, *handles* appear around it. You can use these handles to size the object. You can also move or copy an object by dragging it, and you can delete an object by pressing the Delete key or by selecting the Clear command from the Edit or shortcut menu.
- You can select multiple objects by clicking on them while holding down the Shift key or by using the Drawing Selection button. Then, you can size, move, copy, or delete the objects at the same time.

- To change the format of a graphic object, you can use the Patterns tab of the Format Object dialog box, the Drop Shadow and Patterns buttons in the Drawing toolbar, or the Color button in the Formatting toolbar.
- After you create objects, you can layer and group them using buttons in the Drawing toolbar or commands in the Placement submenu of the Format menu.
- To change the way an object moves and changes size with the cells in the underlying worksheet, use the Properties tab of the Format Object dialog box.

Section 4

Lists and databases

Most of this book focuses on *Excel*'s spreadsheet capabilities because those are its most useful ones. However, *Excel* also includes a rich set of features for working with data organized in lists. You can think of a list as a kind of database.

This section consists of four chapters. In chapter 14, you'll learn how to set up a list and how to use filters and forms to manipulate the data in a list. In chapter 15, you'll learn how to sort a list and how to create subtotals automatically. In chapter 16, you'll learn how to create and use pivot tables. Pivot tables are a new feature of *Excel* 5.0 that let you cross-tabulate the data in a list to get different perspectives on it. And in chapter 17, you'll learn how to retrieve data from other programs into an *Excel* list. This chapter includes an introduction to *Microsoft Query*, an add-in program that comes with *Excel*.

Chapter 14

How to set up a list and use filters and forms

A *list* is a range of rows in a worksheet that contain similar data and have labeled columns. You can think of a list as a simple database where each row is a record and each column is a field. In this chapter, you'll learn how to set up a list, how to select records from a list using *Excel*'s AutoFilter and Advanced Filter features, and how to use a data form to maintain the data in a list.

How to set up a list

Figure 14-1 shows you how to set up a list. Here, you can see that the first row in a list, called the *header row*, contains a series of *column labels*, or *field names*, one for each column in the list. Each row below the header row represents one *record* in the list. And each cell in a record represents a *field*.

To create a list like this one, you start by entering the column labels. You should enter the column labels without any columns separating them, and each column label must occupy only one cell. Although the column labels in figure 14-1 start in cell A1, you can start a list anywhere in a worksheet. However, it makes sense to start a list in the upper left corner of a worksheet.

After you enter the column labels, you enter the records of the list directly under the column labels. You should enter these records with no empty rows separating them. If you need to add records later, you can do that by inserting a row or by using the data form feature presented later in this chapter.

Once the list is set up the way you want it, you can use several of the commands in the Data menu to work with it. In this chapter, I'll show you how to use the Form and Filter commands. In addition to these commands, you can use many of the commands presented in earlier chapters to maintain and format the list. For example, you can use the Rows command in the Insert menu to insert rows. You can use the Delete command in the Edit menu to delete rows. And you can use the commands in the Format menu to format the list.

How to use the AutoFilter feature to select records from a list

A major enhancement to version 5.0 of *Excel* is the AutoFilter feature. With this feature, you can display the records in a list that meet the criteria you specify by applying a *filter* to the list. Then, all the records in the list that don't meet the criteria are hidden from view, or filtered.

Procedure

1. Enter column labels (field names) in a single row to name the fields in the list.
2. Enter the data for the items in the list (records) in the rows directly below the column labels.

The Employee list

	A	B	C	D	E	F	G
1	**Last name**	**First name**	**Dept.**	**Job code**	**Age**	**Current salary**	
2	Smith	Mary	Admin	1	23	$24,600	
3	Jones	Georgia	Mktg	3	43	$47,500	
4	Long	John	Prod	3	52	$39,900	
5	Johnson	Edward	Admin	2	30	$33,250	
6	Jones	John	Prod	2	33	$31,400	
7	Williams	Alice	Admin	1	50	$28,900	
8	Allen	Joel	Admin	2	25	$30,000	
9	Clay	Kurt	Mktg	2	43	$41,250	
10	Burkes	Patricia	Prod	1	52	$28,500	
11	Andrews	Anne	Admin	3	30	$34,000	
12	Russell	Barry	Prod	2	33	$31,500	
13	Thompson	John	Mktg	1	50	$26,500	
14							

Header row (column labels)

Records

Notes

- Use labels for the column labels. Precede the column label with an apostrophe if it begins with a non-alphabetic character or if it could be mistaken for a cell reference, a formula, a value, a date, or a time.
- Use a different column label for each column in the list.
- Use the Wrap Text option in the Alignment tab of the Format dialog box if the column label is wider than the column.
- If the worksheet contains data other than the list, separate the list from the data by at least one blank row and column so *Excel* can identify it.

Figure 14-1 How to set up a list

How to find selected records Figure 14-2 shows you how to use the AutoFilter feature to display selected records from a list. When you select the AutoFilter command, *Excel* adds drop-down arrows to each cell that contains a column label. Then, you can click on these arrows to display a list of all the unique values in that column. When you select a value, *Excel* hides all the rows that don't contain that value. Then, you can apply additional filters to the list by selecting values from any of the other columns in the list.

In addition to the unique values in a column, an AutoFilter list also includes the four options listed in figure 14-2: All, Custom, Blanks, and NonBlanks. You can use these options to remove filtering from a column, specify custom selection criteria, display all the rows that don't have data in

Procedure

1. Place the cell pointer on any cell in the list.
2. Select the AutoFilter command from the Filter submenu of the Data menu, and *Excel* adds drop-down arrows to each cell in the list that contains a column label.
3. Click on the drop-down arrow for a column to access a list of the values in that column:

	A	B	C	D	E	F	G
1	Last name	First name	Dept.	Job co	A	Current sala	
2	Smith	Mary	(All)	1	23	$24,600	
3	Jones	Georgia	(Custom...) Admin	3	43	$47,500	
4	Long	John	Mktg	3	52	$39,900	
5	Johnson	Edward	Prod	2	30	$33,250	
6	Jones	John	(Blanks)	2	33	$31,400	
7	Williams	Alice	(NonBlanks)	1	50	$28,900	
8	Allen	Joel	Admin	2	25	$30,000	
9	Clay	Kurt	Mktg	2	43	$41,250	
10	Burkes	Patricia	Prod	1	52	$28,500	
11	Andrews	Anne	Admin	3	30	$34,000	
12	Russell	Barry	Prod	2	33	$31,500	
13	Thompson	John	Mktg	1	50	$26,500	
14							

4. Select one of the values in the list, and *Excel* hides all the rows that don't match that value:

	A	B	C	D	E	F	G
1	Last name	First name	Dept.	Job co	A	Current sala	
2	Smith	Mary	Admin	1	23	$24,600	
5	Johnson	Edward	Admin	2	30	$33,250	
7	Williams	Alice	Admin	1	50	$28,900	
8	Allen	Joel	Admin	2	25	$30,000	
11	Andrews	Anne	Admin	3	30	$34,000	
14							

5. Repeat steps 3 and 4 for each column you want to base the selection on.

Notes

- The drop-down list for a selected column contains all the unique values in that column in sorted order. In addition, the list contains these four options:

Option	Filtering action
All	Removes all filtering for the column.
Custom	Lets you specify custom selection criteria (see figure 14-4 for details).
Blanks	Displays rows that don't have data in the column.
NonBlanks	Displays rows that have any non-blank data in the column.

- When you use the AutoFilter feature, *Excel* highlights the row numbers of the selected rows and the drop-down arrows in the columns you based your selection on.
- When you use the AutoFilter feature on more than one column, the records displayed in the filtered list are those that match all of the values or options you selected.
- By default, *Excel* adds drop-down arrows to all the columns in a list. To add the arrows to selected columns, select the column labels before you issue the AutoFilter command.

Figure 14-2 How to use the AutoFilter feature to find selected records

Procedure

1. Move the cell pointer to the column label for the column you want to filter.
2. Type Alt+Down-arrow, and *Excel* displays the drop-down list for that column.
3. Move the highlight to the value or option you want to base the selection on using the keys listed below.
4. Press the Enter key.

Keys you can use to highlight an item

Up-arrow or Down-arrow	Moves the highlight up or down one item.
Home or End	Moves the highlight to the top or bottom of the list.
Page-Up or Page-Down	Moves the highlight up or down the height of the list box.
character	Moves the highlight to the first value in the list that starts with *character*.

Figure 14-3 How to use the keyboard to select AutoFilter criteria

the column, or display all the rows that have data in the column. I'll have more to say about the All and Custom options later in this chapter.

Although you'll usually use the mouse techniques described in figure 14-2 to apply AutoFilter criteria to a list, you can also use the keyboard techniques shown in figure 14-3. In particular, you'll want to use the last technique for highlighting a value in a drop-down list if the list contains many values. Then, you can move to the first value in the list that begins with the character you type.

How to specify custom selection criteria When you select a value from an AutoFilter drop-down list, *Excel* finds records that contain that value. In other words, Excel uses the "equals" relational operator. If you need to select records based on other relational conditions, you can select the Custom option. Then, you can specify custom selection criteria as illustrated in figure 14-4.

From the Custom AutoFilter dialog box, you can select from several relational conditions in addition to the "equals" condition. You can also specify comparison values that aren't present in the selected column. If the comparison value is a text string, it can include the asterisk (*) and question mark (?) *wildcard characters*. Finally, you can specify two comparison criteria. If you do, you must also select one of the logical operators: And or Or.

Procedure

1. Enable the AutoFilter feature for a list, and click on the drop-down arrow for the column you want to base the selection on.
2. Select the Custom option from the drop-down list and this dialog box appears:

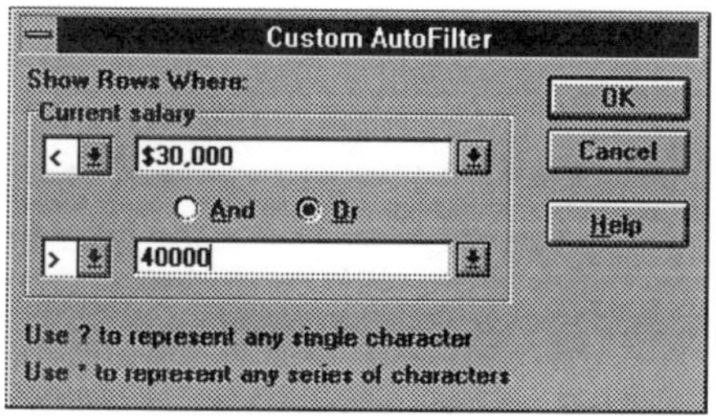

3. Specify one or two comparison criteria for the column. If you specify two criteria, choose a logical operator (And or Or).
4. Click on the OK button and *Excel* filters the list:

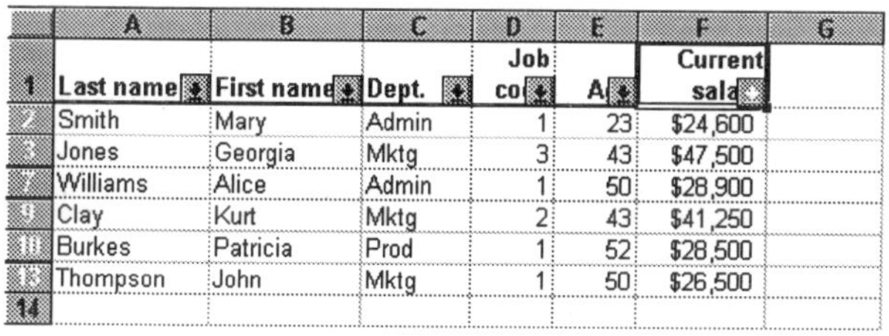

	A	B	C	D	E	F	G
1	Last name	First name	Dept.	Job co	A	Current sala	
2	Smith	Mary	Admin	1	23	$24,600	
3	Jones	Georgia	Mktg	3	43	$47,500	
7	Williams	Alice	Admin	1	50	$28,900	
9	Clay	Kurt	Mktg	2	43	$41,250	
10	Burkes	Patricia	Prod	1	52	$28,500	
13	Thompson	John	Mktg	1	50	$26,500	
14							

Notes

- Each comparison criterion consists of a relational operator and a comparison value. You can select a comparison value from the drop-down list box, which contains all the values in that column, or you can type in the comparison value.
- If the comparison value is a text string, it can include wildcard characters. The question mark wildcard (?) represents any single character, and the asterisk wildcard (*) represents any number of characters. For example, the words Jay, June, Judy, and Janice all match J*, but only June and Judy match J???.

Figure 14-4 How to use the AutoFilter feature to specify custom selection criteria

How to remove filtering from a list Figure 14-5 shows you three ways to remove filtering from a list. If you want to remove filtering that's based on a specific column, select the All option from the columns drop-down list. Then, the records that were filtered out based on the value you selected are redisplayed. If you want to remove all the filtering from a list,

How to remove the filtering based on a single column

Select the All filter option from the drop-down list for the column.

How to remove all the filtering from a list

Select the Show All command from the Filter submenu of the Data menu.

How to remove all the filtering and the AutoFilter arrows

Select the AutoFilter command from the Filter submenu of the Data menu.

Figure 14-5 How to remove filtering from a list

select the Show All command from the Filter submenu of the Data menu. Then, all the records in the list are redisplayed. And if you want to remove the filtering and the AutoFilter arrows, select the AutoFilter command from the Filter submenu of the Data menu.

How to use the Advanced Filter feature to select records from a list

When you filter a list by selecting criteria from two or more columns using the AutoFilter feature, the conditions in all the columns must be met for a record to be displayed. In other words, the implied logical operator is And. If you want to select records based on the values in one column *or* another column, you have to use the Advanced Filter feature. You can also use this feature to select records based on computed criteria and to create a results table.

How to find selected records Figure 14-6 presents the procedure for using the Advanced Filter feature to find selected records. The first step is to set up a *criteria range* that defines the records you want to select. I'll show you how to do that in a moment. Once the criteria range is set up, you issue the Advanced Filter command and identify the criteria range. Then, *Excel* hides the records that don't satisfy the criteria, just as it does when you use the AutoFilter feature. To redisplay the hidden records, issue the Show All command from the Filter submenu of the Data menu.

How to set up a criteria range Figures 14-7 and 14-8 show you how to specify two types of criteria in a criteria range: comparison criteria and computed criteria. For comparison criteria, you begin by entering the column labels for the columns you want to base the criteria on. These labels

Procedure

1. Set up the criteria range as described in figures 14-7 and 14-8.
2. Place the cell pointer on a cell in the list.
3. Select the Advanced Filter command from the Filter submenu of the Data menu and this dialog box appears:

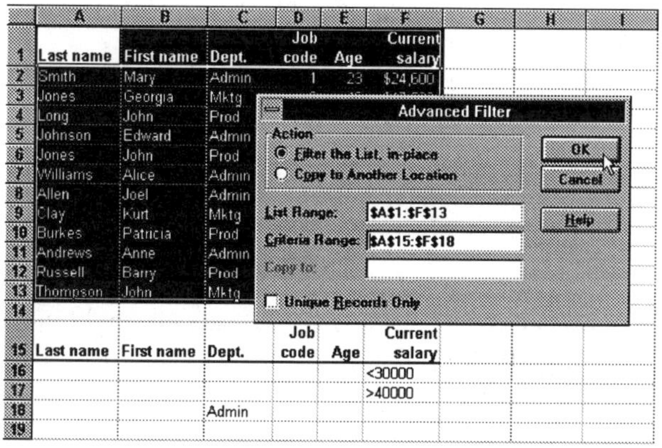

4. Enter the range that contains the criteria by typing it in or by clicking in the Criteria Range text box and selecting the range.
5. Click on the OK button and *Excel* filters the list:

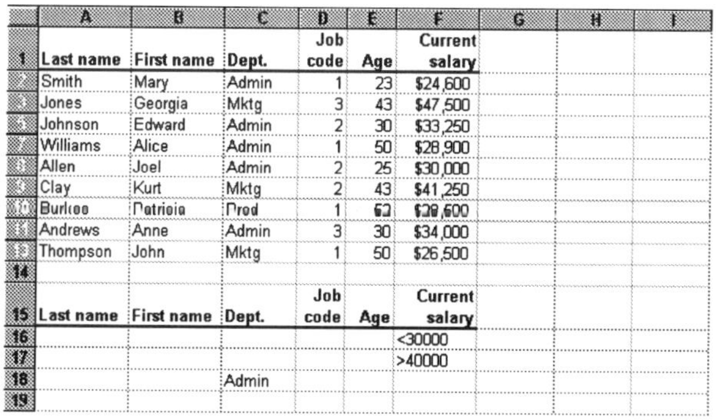

	A	B	C	D	E	F	G	H	I
1	Last name	First name	Dept.	Job code	Age	Current salary			
2	Smith	Mary	Admin	1	23	$24,600			
3	Jones	Georgia	Mktg	3	43	$47,500			
5	Johnson	Edward	Admin	2	30	$33,250			
7	Williams	Alice	Admin	1	50	$28,900			
8	Allen	Joel	Admin	2	25	$30,000			
9	Clay	Kurt	Mktg	2	43	$41,250			
10	Burkes	Patricia	Prod	1	[illegible]	[illegible]			
11	Andrews	Anne	Admin	3	30	$34,000			
13	Thompson	John	Mktg	1	50	$26,500			
14									
15	Last name	First name	Dept.	Job code	Age	Current salary			
16						<30000			
17						>40000			
18			Admin						
19									

Notes

- If the cell pointer is outside the list when you select the Advanced Filter command, you can type the range in the List Range text box, or you can click in the text box and select the range.
- If you select the Unique Records Only option, *Excel* hides duplicate records. You can select this option with or without selecting criteria.
- You can't perform successive filter operations with the Advanced Filter feature as you can with the AutoFilter feature. Each time you specify an advanced filter, *Excel* evaluates every row in the list whether or not it's hidden.
- To redisplay hidden rows, select the Show All command from the Filter submenu of the Data menu.

Figure 14-6 How to use the Advanced Filter feature to find selected records

How to specify comparison criteria

1. Enter the column label of each column you want to specify criteria for in a single row.
2. Enter a comparison condition for each column in the rows immediately below the labels. To indicate a logical And operation between two or more conditions, enter the conditions in the same row. To indicate a logical Or operation between two or more conditions, enter the conditions in different rows. The following criteria range will display all the records in the Employee list for employees who work in the Admin department and whose salary is $30,000 or more or who work in the Mktg department and whose salary is $40,000 or more:

15	Dept.	Current salary	
16	Admin	>=30000	
17	Mktg	>=40000	
18			

Notes

- An easy way to set up the column labels in a criteria range is to copy them from the list. Any labels for which you don't enter a comparison condition are ignored.
- You can omit the relational operator from an equals condition. For example, entering "Admin" is the same as entering "=Admin."
- If you want *Excel* to look for an exact match of a text value, enclose the text in quotation marks. If you don't, any values that begin with the characters will meet the condition.
- You can use the asterisk (*) and question mark wildcards (?) in a condition that tests for a text value.
- If you want two conditions for the same column to be satisfied, enter the column label twice and enter a condition in the same row in each column.
- You can combine comparison criteria and computed criteria in the same criteria range. See figure 14-8 for details on specifying computed criteria.

Figure 14-7 How to specify comparison criteria in a criteria range

must be entered in a single row. Then, you enter one or more comparison conditions for each column in the rows below these labels. If you enter the conditions for two columns in the same row, both conditions must be true for the criteria to be satisfied. If you enter the conditions in different rows, either one or the other of the conditions must be true. The comparison criteria in figure 14-7, for example, will select records from the Employee list for employees who are in the Admin department and have a salary of $30,000 or more or who work in the Mktg department and have a salary of $40,000 or more.

For computed criteria, you begin by entering a row of labels that identifies the criteria you want to base the selection on. These labels must not be the same as any of the column labels in the list. Then, you enter one or more computed conditions in each column. Each condition must refer to

How to specify computed criteria

1. Enter a label for each computed condition you want to specify in a single row. The labels must not be the same as any column label in the list.
2. Enter a computed condition for each column in the rows immediately below the labels. To indicate a logical And operation between two or more conditions, enter the conditions in the same row. To indicate a logical Or operation between two or more conditions, enter the conditions in different rows. The following criteria range will display all the records in the Employee list for employees who have an above average salary or whose salary to age ratio is more then 1000:

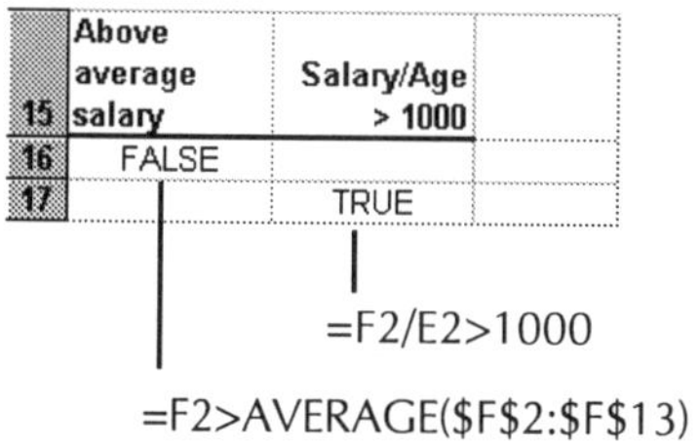

Notes

- A computed condition must evaluate to True or False and must refer to at least one column in the list. To refer to a column, enter a relative cell reference for the first row in that column (as in E2 and F2 above) or use the column label. Then, *Excel* will adjust the reference as it evaluates each row.
- If the condition refers to a cell or a range that doesn't change as *Excel* evaluates the rows, enter an absolute reference (as in $F$2:$F$13 above).
- You can combine comparison criteria and computed criteria in the same criteria range. See figure 14-7 for details on specifying comparison criteria.

Figure 14-8 How to specify computed criteria in a criteria range

at least one column in the list and must evaluate to a True or False value. The computed criteria in figure 14-8, for example, will select records from the Employee list for employees whose salary is above average or whose salary to age ratio is greater than 1000. Notice that the result of the computed condition (TRUE or FALSE) is displayed in the cell that contains the condition.

Notice that some of the cell references in the computed criteria in figure 14-8 are relative references and some of them are absolute references. If you want to refer to a column in the list, you enter a relative cell reference for the first row in the column. Then, when *Excel* evaluates the records, it adjusts the relative reference for each row. If you want *Excel* to refer to the same cell or range each time it evaluates a record, you enter an absolute reference.

Access

Select the Copy To Another Location option from the Advanced Filter dialog box.

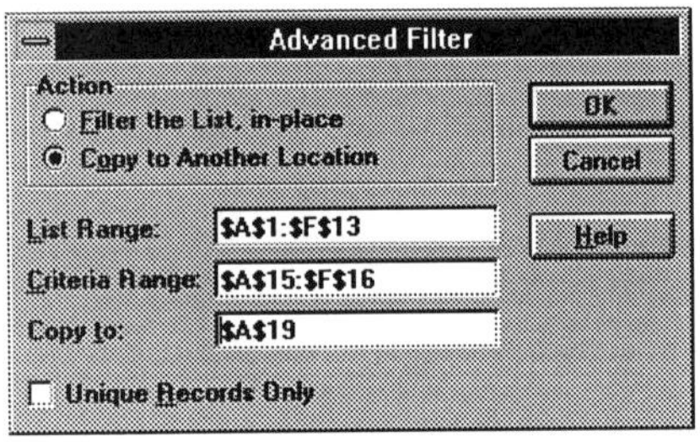

Operation

Specify the location for the results table by entering a reference for the cell in the upper left corner of the range in the Copy To text box. You can do that by typing it in or by clicking in the text box, then clicking on the cell.

Notes

- You can also enter a range in the Copy To text box. If you do, the range must include the same number of columns as the list. If all of the records that meet the criteria don't fit in the range, *Excel* asks you if you want to paste the remaining rows.
- *Excel* doesn't let you specify a Copy To location outside of the current worksheet. However, it does let you specify a List Range and a Criteria Range in another worksheet. If you want to create a results table in another worksheet, issue the Advanced Filter command from that worksheet.

Figure 14-9 How to use the Advanced Filter feature to create a results table

How to create a results table Instead of hiding the rows in a list that don't satisfy the criteria you specify, you can create a *results table.* A results table is a list that's separate from the original list and that contains only the records that satisfy the criteria. To create a results table, you select the Copy To Another Location option from the Advanced Filter dialog box, and you specify the location where you want to place the results table in the Copy To text box. This is illustrated in figure 14-9.

A results table created by the Advanced Filter command is similar to what some other spreadsheet programs (like *Lotus 1-2-3*) call a *query table.* Like a query table, a results table can be useful if you want to change the data after you select it. After you've generated a results table, for example, you can delete columns that you don't want and the columns in the original list aren't affected. You can also use other *Excel* skills to augment the results table. For instance, you can add a new field by creating a formula that's based on one or more fields in the results table.

How to use a data form to work with the data in a list

Excel's Form command lets you access a special dialog box called a *data form* to retrieve, edit, add, and delete the records in a list. When you issue this command, *Excel* builds the data form so it contains a text box for each field in the list that can be modified. In effect, the data form is a data entry and inquiry panel for the list.

How to browse, delete, change, and add records to a list Figure 14-10 shows you how to use a data form to browse, delete, change, and add records to a list. As you can see, the data form displays one record at a time. To move from one record to another, you can use the scroll bar or the Find Prev and Find Next buttons. *Excel* displays the number of the currently displayed record in the upper right corner of the data form.

To delete the current record, you click on the Delete button. When you do, the record is deleted from the list and the records beneath it are moved up to fill the empty space. To modify the current record, you simply type the changes into the appropriate text boxes and press the Enter key. Note that you can't modify fields that are protected or that contain computed values.

To add a record to the end of the list, click on the New button and *Excel* displays a blank data form. You can also display a blank data form by scrolling to the bottom of the list. Then, enter a value for each field and press the Enter key. Note that the first row below the existing list must be blank for you to add a record to the list. *Excel* won't insert a row for you.

Although it's easiest to work with a data form using the mouse, you can also use the keyboard. To move from one field to the next field, press the Tab key. To move to the previous field, press Shift+Tab. You can also move to a specific field by holding down the Alt key and pressing the underlined character in the field name.

In most cases, it's easier to add, delete, and modify the records in a list directly rather than using a data form. If you want to delete a group of records that satisfy specific criteria, for example, you can filter the list so that only those records are displayed, then delete them all at once. With a data form, you can delete only one record at a time. However, if you prefer to work with the data form, you should know that you can select the records that are displayed. Then, you can browse through selected records before you delete or modify them.

Access

Place the cell pointer on any cell in the list, and select the Form command from the Data menu.

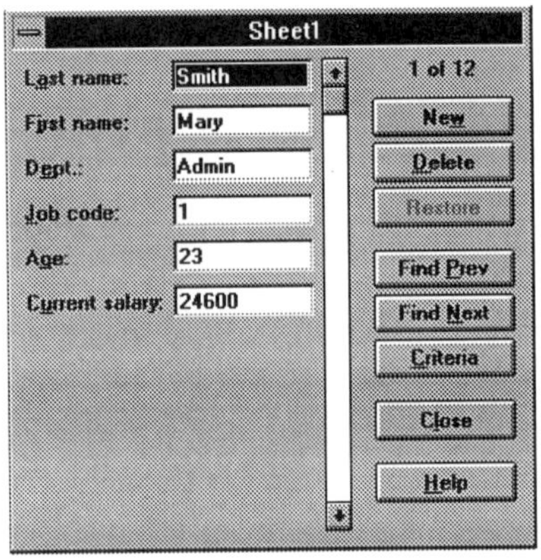

Operation

- To display the next record, click on the Find Next button. To display the previous record, click on the Find Prev button. Use the scroll bar to move to any record in the list.
- To delete the current record, click on the Delete button. *Excel* will ask you to confirm the operation.
- To modify the current record, type the changes into the text boxes in the data form and press the Enter key. To cancel the changes before you press the Enter key, click on the Restore button.
- To add a new record, click on the New button or move the scroll box down beyond the last record in the list. Then, enter the value for each field and press the Enter key. To erase the data from the data form before you press the Enter key, click on the Restore button.
- To select criteria for the records that are displayed, click on the Criteria button. See figure 14-11 for details.

Notes

- The title of the dialog box is the name of the worksheet that contains the list. The record number indicator in the upper right corner of the data form shows the number of records in the list and the position in the list of the currently displayed record.
- If a field is protected or is a computed value, it can't be modified and isn't displayed in a text box.
- You can move the focus from one field to another in the data form by pressing Tab or Shift+Tab. You can jump directly to a specific field by holding down the Alt key as you press the underlined character in the field name.
- A data form can display a maximum of 32 fields.

Figure 14-10 How to use a data form to browse, delete, change, and add records to a list

Access

Click on the Criteria button in the data form dialog box.

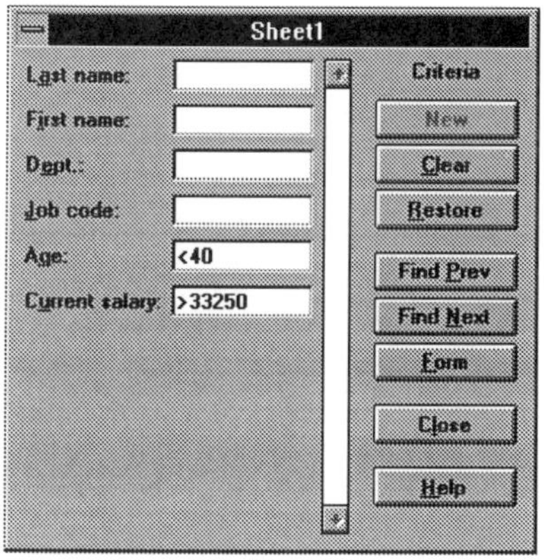

Operation

- To display selected records, type comparison or computed criteria into the appropriate text boxes. Then, press the Enter key or click on the Form button and the dialog box returns to its original form. See figures 14-7 and 14-8 for details on specifying criteria.
- To display the next selected record, click on the Find Next button. To display the previous selected record, click on the Find Prev button. If you use the scroll bar to scroll through the list, *Excel* displays all records in the list, not just those that meet the selection criteria.
- To return to the selection criteria, click on the Criteria button. Then, you can edit the criteria to change the selection, or you can remove the selection criteria from the data form by clicking on the Clear button.

Figure 14-11 How to use a data form to display selected records

How to display selected records Figure 14-11 shows how you can use a data form to retrieve records that meet specific criteria. To do that, you click on the Criteria button in the data form and enter the appropriate criteria for the fields you want to base the selection on. You can enter either comparison or computed criteria as described in figures 14-7 and 14-8. Then, press the Enter key or click on the Form button and *Excel* displays the first record that meets the criteria. To browse through the records, use the Find Prev and Find Next buttons. You can also modify and delete selected records from the data form.

Perspective

Compared to earlier releases of *Excel* and to other spreadsheet programs, the list and database features of *Excel* 5.0 presented in this chapter are versatile and easy to use. For many applications, these features provide all the functionality you need. But, as you'll see in the rest of this section, *Excel* provides additional features for working with lists and databases. On the other hand, *Excel* still isn't as powerful as most database programs. So if it's power you need, I recommend you look into buying a full-fledged database program.

Summary

- A *list* is a range of rows in a worksheet that contain similar data. The first row in a list, called the *header row*, contains *column labels* or *field names* that identify the data in each column. The remaining rows represent *records*.
- You can use basic *Excel* techniques (like inserting and deleting rows and editing the contents of cells) to work with the data in a list.
- The AutoFilter feature lets you display the records in a list that satisfy criteria you select for one or more columns in the list. Records that don't satisfy the criteria are hidden from view, or *filtered*. When you select records based on two or more columns, all of the criteria must be met for a record to be displayed.
- To use a relational operator other than "equals" to combine two conditions for the same field, you can use the Custom option that's available from the AutoFilter drop-down lists.
- To do a complex selection that AutoFilter can't handle, use the Advanced AutoFilter feature. To use this feature, you have to set up a *criteria range* that defines the records you want to select.
- The Form command displays a *data form* dialog box that you can use to add, delete, modify, and retrieve selected records from a list.

Chapter 15

How to sort and summarize the data in a list

After you set up a list in a worksheet, sorting the data can often make it easier to interpret. If you sort an employee list like the one in figure 15-1 by salary, for example, you can tell at a glance who has the highest salary and who has the lowest salary. Once you sort the data in a list, you can also summarize the data in the other columns. If you sort the list in figure 15-1 by department, for example, you can summarize the salary in each department.

In chapter 7, you learned the basic techniques for sorting the data in a range of cells. However, *Excel* makes it especially easy to sort the data in a list as you'll see in this chapter. *Excel* also makes it easy to summarize the data in a list by adding automatic subtotals. You'll learn how to do that in this chapter too.

How to sort the data in a list

You can sort the data in a list using either the Sort command in the Data menu or the toolbar buttons for sorting. I'll show you both techniques in this chapter. If you use the Sort command, you can also change the sort order.

How to use the Sort command Figure 15-1 presents the procedure for sorting the data in a list using the Sort command. If the cell pointer is positioned on any cell in the list when you issue this command, *Excel* automatically recognizes the records in the list as the *data range*. In figure 15-1, for example, you can see that *Excel* highlighted all the records in the list. Notice, however, that *Excel* didn't include the header row in the data range. Instead, it uses the column labels in that row to help you identify the sort keys for the list.

For any sort, you have to identify the column you want to use as the *primary sort key*, that is, the column you want to sort the list by. To do that, you select the column label from the Sort By drop-down list box. Then, you select the Ascending or Descending option in that group to indicate whether you want the data in that column sorted in ascending or descending order.

If you want to sort by more than one column, you can identify one or two *secondary sort keys* by choosing the appropriate column labels from the Then By drop-down list boxes. And you specify the sort order by selecting the Ascending or Descending option for each key. The list in figure 15-1, for example, is sorted by department in ascending order, and the records in each department are sorted by current salary in descending order.

Procedure

1. Place the cell pointer on any cell in the list.
2. Select the Sort command from the Data menu and this dialog box appears:

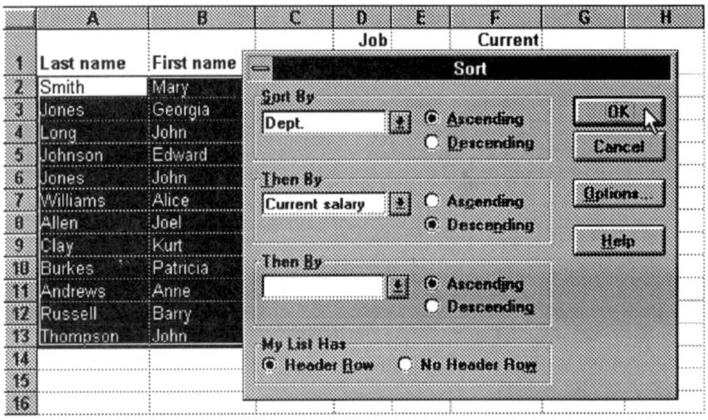

3. Select the column you want to use as the primary key from the drop-down list box in the Sort By group, and select the Ascending or Descending option from that group.
4. If you want to sort by more than one key, select the column you want to use for each secondary key from the drop-down list box in one of the Then By groups, and select the Ascending or Descending option from that group.
5. Click on the OK button and *Excel* sorts the list:

	A	B	C	D	E	F	G
1	Last name	First name	Dept.	Job code	Age	Current salary	
2	Andrews	Anne	Admin	3	30	$34,000	
3	Johnson	Edward	Admin	2	30	$33,250	
4	Allen	Joel	Admin	2	25	$30,000	
5	Williams	Alice	Admin	1	50	$28,900	
6	Smith	Mary	Admin	1	23	$24,600	
7	Jones	Georgia	Mktg	3	43	$47,500	
8	Clay	Kurt	Mktg	2	43	$41,250	
9	Thompson	John	Mktg	1	50	$26,500	
10	Long	John	Prod	3	52	$39,900	
11	Russell	Barry	Prod	2	33	$31,500	
12	Jones	John	Prod	2	33	$31,400	
13	Burkes	Patricia	Prod	1	52	$28,500	
14							

Notes

- When *Excel* recognizes the data as a list, it automatically: (1) sets the My List Has option to Header Row, (2) excludes the header row from the data to be sorted, and (3) uses column labels from the header row in the Sort By and Then By drop-down list boxes. If *Excel* doesn't recognize the data as a list, you have to select the rows you want to sort. Then, *Excel* automatically: (1) sets the My List Has option to No Header Row and (2) identifies columns with letters (like Column C and Column F) in the Sort By and Then By drop-down list boxes. See chapter 7 for details on sorting data that's not in list form.
- The Options button displays another dialog box that lets you specify additional options for the sort operation. See figure 15-3 for details.
- In the unlikely case that you want to sort by more than three key columns, do the sort in two steps. First, sort the list by the least significant keys, then sort again by the more significant keys.

Figure 15-1 How to use the Sort command to sort the data in a list

1. Numeric values in sequence (including dates, times, and results of formulas)
2. Labels in this order:
   Digits in numeric sequence
   Space
   Special characters
   Letters in alphabetic sequence
3. Empty cells

Notes

- For a descending sort, this order is reversed, except empty cells are always sorted last.
- By default, sort operations don't distinguish between uppercase and lowercase letters. To override this default, select the Case Sensitive option in the Sort Options dialog box (see figure 15-3).

Figure 15-2 The normal sort order

When you use more than one sort key, you need to be careful about the order in which you specify the keys. That's because *Excel* does the sort in the order you identify the keys. If you identify the keys in the wrong order, the sort won't work as you intended. If I had reversed the order of the two keys for the sort shown in figure 15-1, for example, the rows would have been sorted in descending order by salary before they were sorted by department. As a result, the departments wouldn't remain in separate groups like I wanted them.

How to change the normal sort order When you sort a list based on a column that contains just labels or just values, the sort works the way you would expect. When you sort a list based on a key that contains a mix of labels and values, however, the result isn't as obvious. Figure 15-2 presents the *normal sort order Excel* uses when it sorts a list in ascending sequence. As you can see, values come before labels and empty cells always come last. Within labels, numbers come before spaces, spaces come before symbols, and symbols come before letters. When you sort in descending order, the entire sort order is reversed, except empty cells still come last.

Most of the time, *Excel*'s normal sort order will sort the data the way you want it. The only problem might be if you use both uppercase and lowercase letters in a sort column. By default, *Excel* doesn't distinguish between uppercase and lowercase letters when it does a sort. If you want to override this default, you access the Sort Options dialog box as described in figure 15-3, and you select the Case Sensitive option. Then, uppercase letters will come before lowercase letters in the sort order.

Access

Select the Sort command from the Data menu and click on the Options button.

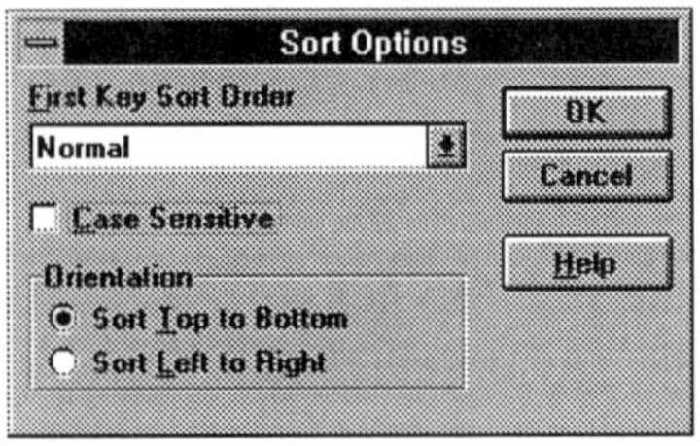

Operation

- To specify that the sort order should distinguish between uppercase and lowercase letters, select the Case Sensitive option.
- To use a different sort order for the primary key, choose one of the options in the First Key Sort Order drop-down list box.
- To sort rows based on the contents of a key column, leave the Orientation option set to Sort Top To Bottom. In the unlikely case that you want to sort columns based on the contents of a key row, change the Orientation option setting to Sort Left To Right.

Notes

- When the Case Sensitive option is selected, uppercase letters come before lowercase letters in the sort order. For example, AAA comes before aAa, which comes before aaa.
- In addition to the normal sort order, *Excel* provides sort orders that will sort the months of the year and the days of the week in both abbreviated and unabbreviated forms. You can also create your own custom sort orders using the Custom Lists tab of the Options dialog box as described in chapter 5.

Figure 15-3 How to change the sort order

The Sort Options dialog box also lets you choose a different sort order altogether or a different sort orientation. Figure 15-3 describes these options. However, it's not likely that you'll ever need to use them.

How to use the toolbar buttons for sorting Figure 15-4 presents the two buttons in the Standard toolbar you can use to sort the data in a list. The first button lets you sort a list in ascending sequence, and the second button lets you sort a list in descending sequence. When you use either of these buttons to sort a list, you position the cell pointer in the column you want to use as the sort key before you click on the appropriate button.

If you use the toolbar buttons to sort a list, you can sort by only one key at a time. If you want to sort a list by more than one key, then, you can use the Sort command, or you can do each sort in a separate step. Just be sure to

Button	Function
	Sorts the data in ascending order.
	Sorts the data in descending order.

Procedure

1. Place the cell pointer on a cell in the column you want to use as the primary key column. It can be in any row in the list.
2. Click on the appropriate toolbar button.

Notes

- *Excel* will interpret a range as a list if it has a header row and if at least one blank row and one blank column separate it from other data in the worksheet. If *Excel* can't interpret the range you want to sort as a list, select the range before you click on the toolbar button. *Excel* will use the leftmost column in the selection as the primary key.
- You can't sort data by more than one key at a time when you use the toolbar buttons. If you need to sort by more than one key, use the Sort command in the Data menu. Or, do the sort operation in multiple steps, sorting by the least significant key first and the most significant key last.

Figure 15-4 How to use the buttons for sorting in the Standard toolbar

sort by the least significant key first and by the most significant key last. If you're sorting by a primary key and one secondary key, for example, sort by the secondary key first. Otherwise, the sort won't work the way you want it to.

How to add automatic subtotals to a list

Figure 15-5 presents the procedure for adding automatic subtotals to a list. Notice that before you add subtotals, you must sort the list by the column you want *Excel* to use to determine where the subtotals are inserted. Then, when you issue the Subtotal command, *Excel* inserts a subtotal line each time the content of that column changes.

From the Subtotal dialog box, you select the column you used to sort the list, the type of summary you want to perform, and the fields you want to summarize. The same type of summary is performed for each field you select. In most cases, you'll use the Count, Sum, or Average function, but you can also select from some basic statistical functions.

When you issue the Subtotals command, *Excel* adds subtotal lines and a grand total line to your list and displays it in outline form. Then,

Procedure

1. Sort the list by the column you want *Excel* to use to determine where to insert subtotal rows.
2. Place the cell pointer on any cell in the list.
3. Select the Subtotals command from the Data menu and this dialog box appears:

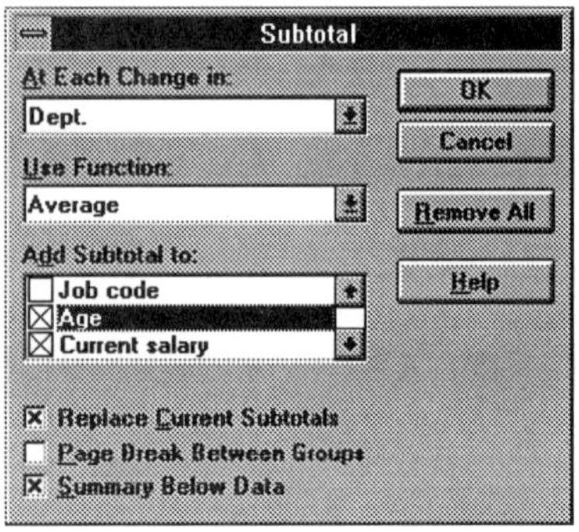

4. Select the column you want *Excel* to use to determine where to insert subtotal rows from the At Each Change In drop-down list box.
5. Select the function you want *Excel* to use in the subtotal rows from the Use Function drop-down list box.
6. Select the fields you want to summarize from the Add Subtotal To list box.
7. Click on the OK button, and *Excel* adds subtotal rows and a grand total row to the list and displays the worksheet in outline form:

	A	B	C	D	E	F	G
1	**Last name**	**First name**	**Dept.**	**Job code**	**Age**	**Current salary**	
2	Smith	Mary	Admin	1	23	$24,600	
3	Johnson	Edward	Admin	2	30	$33,250	
4	Williams	Alice	Admin	1	50	$28,900	
5	Allen	Joel	Admin	2	25	$30,000	
6	Andrews	Anne	Admin	3	30	$34,000	
7			**Admin Average**		31.6	$30,150	
8	Jones	Georgia	Mktg	3	43	$47,500	
9	Clay	Kurt	Mktg	2	43	$41,250	
10	Thompson	John	Mktg	1	50	$26,500	
11			**Mktg Average**		45.33	$38,417	
12	Long	John	Prod	3	52	$39 900	
13	Jones	John	Prod	2	33	$31 400	
14	Burkes	Patricia	Prod	1	52	$28,500	
15	Russell	Barry	Prod	2	33	$31,500	
16			**Prod Average**		42.5	$32,825	
17			**Grand Average**		38.67	$33,108	
18							

Notes

- By default, *Excel* replaces any subtotals currently in the list with the subtotals you specify. If you want to add subtotals to those that already exist, deselect the Replace Current Subtotals option.
- If you want subtotals to appear above rather than below groups of rows, deselect the Summary Below Data option.
- To remove subtotal rows from a list, click on any cell in the list, issue the Subtotals command from the Data menu, and click on the Remove All button.

Figure 15-5 How to add automatic subtotals to a sorted list you can use the outline skills you learned in chapter 7 to hide or display information in the list. To remove the subtotal lines and restore the list to its original form, access the Subtotal dialog box and click on the Remove All button.

Perspective

When you sort the data in a range, it's usually difficult to return the data to its original sequence. That's why you might want to use one of these two practices. First, if you want to save the sorted worksheet as well as the original, save it with a new file name. Before you sort the worksheet, of course, you'll want to save the original file so you don't lose the changes you've made since the last time you saved it. Then, after you save the sorted version, you can return to the original file to access the unsorted worksheet. If you want to save both the sorted and unsorted versions of the worksheet in the same workbook, copy the data to another worksheet in the same workbook before you sort it.

The second way to return a list to its original sequence is to include a column of sequence numbers in the list. To do that, you can use the AutoFill feature you learned in chapter 5 to create the sequence numbers. Then, after you sort the data, you can return the list to its original order by sorting it again using the column that contains the sequence numbers as the sort key.

Summary

- You can sort the data in a list on one or more *sort keys* using the Sort command in the Data menu. The first sort key you specify is the *primary sort key*. Any additional sort keys you specify are *secondary sort keys*.
- *Excel* uses a prescribed sequence called the *normal sort order* when it sorts columns whose cells contain a mix of letters, numbers, and special characters.
- You can use toolbar buttons to sort a list, but when you do, you can sort by only one key at a time.
- You can add automatic subtotals to a list by using the Subtotals command in the Data menu.

Chapter 16

How to use pivot tables

A *pivot table* is a table that summarizes the data in one or more fields of a list, an external database, or another pivot table. The pivot table in figure 16-1, for example, shows the average salary for three job codes in three departments.

Pivot tables are a major new feature of *Excel* 5.0. Once you get comfortable with them, you'll be able to use them to create complicated summary reports. So you can get started using pivot tables right away, the first part of this chapter teaches you basic skills for creating and using pivot tables. Then, the second part of this chapter presents some additional skills that will help you create more complicated pivot tables.

Although you can create and work with pivot tables using commands in the Data and shortcut menus and their submenus, *Excel* also provides a toolbar specifically for working with pivot tables. Figure 16-2 presents the Query and Pivot toolbar and describes its buttons. If *Excel* doesn't display this toolbar automatically when you create a pivot table, you can use the Toolbars command in the View menu to display it.

Basic skills for creating and using pivot tables

To help you understand the concepts and skills required to create and use pivot tables, you'll begin by learning how to create a simple pivot table like the one in figure 16-1. Then, you'll learn how to change the layout of a pivot table, how to change the summary function and the format of the summary data, and how to update the contents of a pivot data. Once you're comfortable with these procedures, you'll be ready to learn how to create more complicated pivot tables and use the other skills presented in this chapter.

How to create a simple pivot table When you create a pivot table, you use *Excel*'s PivotTable Wizard. Because the PivotTable Wizard walks you through the steps, creating a pivot table is as easy as selecting the fields you want it to contain. Figure 16-3 presents the procedure for using this feature.

The Employee list

	A	B	C	D	E	F	G
1	**Last name**	**First name**	**Dept.**	**Job code**	**Age**	**Current salary**	
2	Smith	Mary	Admin	1	23	$24,600	
3	Jones	Georgia	Mktg	3	43	$47,500	
4	Long	John	Prod	3	52	$39,900	
5	Johnson	Edward	Admin	2	30	$33,250	
6	Jones	John	Prod	2	33	$31,400	
7	Williams	Alice	Admin	1	50	$28,900	
8	Allen	Joel	Admin	2	25	$30,000	
9	Clay	Kurt	Mktg	2	43	$41,250	
10	Burkes	Patricia	Prod	1	52	$28,500	
11	Andrews	Anne	Admin	3	30	$34,000	
12	Russell	Barry	Prod	2	33	$31,500	
13	Thompson	John	Mktg	1	50	$26,500	
14							

A pivot table that shows the average salary for each job code in each department

	A	B	C	D	E	F
1	Average salary	Dept.				
2	Job code	Admin	Mktg	Prod	Grand Total	
3	1	$26,750	$26,500	$28,500	$27,125	
4	2	$31,625	$41,250	$31,450	$33,480	
5	3	$34,000	$47,500	$39,900	$40,467	
6	Grand Total	$30,150	$38,417	$32,825	$33,108	
7						

Figure 16-1 A pivot table created from the Employee list

The first PivotTable Wizard dialog box asks you to identify the type of source data you want to summarize. Although *Excel* lets you create a pivot table from four different sources, you'll usually use the default: an *Excel* list. Then, the next dialog box prompts you for the range that contains the list. If you place the cell pointer on a cell in the list before you start the PivotTable Wizard, *Excel* will enter the correct range for you. Otherwise, you can type in the range or select it in the worksheet.

Once you identify the list, you're ready to set up the pivot table. To do that, you drag the buttons that represent the fields in the list into the appropriate areas of the pivot table diagram in the third dialog box. If you drag a field into the Column area, it becomes a *column field*. If you drag a field into the Row area, it becomes a *row field*. The column and row fields identify the fields by which the data is summarized. In figure 16-3, the data is summarized by job code and department. If you drag a field into the Data area, it becomes a *data field*. The data field identifies the field to be summarized, in this case, the current salary. And if you drag a field into the Page area, it becomes a *page field*. I'll have more to say about page fields later in this chapter.

The Query and Pivot toolbar

Button	Function
	Accesses the PivotTable Wizard so you can create or modify a pivot table.
	Displays the PivotTable Field dialog box so you can modify the options for the selected field.
	Ungroups the values in a selected field.
	Groups selected items, or lets you group numeric items, dates, or times into ranges.
	Hides detail lines for a selected field in a pivot table.
	Shows detail lines for a selected field in a pivot table.
	Copies each page of a page field to a separate pivot table in a new worksheet in the current workbook.
	Updates the contents of the pivot table based on changes made to the source data.

Note

The Query and Pivot toolbar is displayed automatically the first time you create a pivot table. To hide it, select the Toolbars command from the View menu and deselect the Query and Pivot option.

Figure 16-2 The Query and Pivot toolbar

The last PivotTable Wizard dialog box lets you specify four pivot table options. All four of these options are selected by default, which is usually what you want. You can also indicate where you want *Excel* to place the pivot table by specifying a cell reference in the PivotTable Starting Cell text box. The default is to place the pivot table in a new worksheet in the current workbook. Finally, you can change the name *Excel* assigns to the pivot table from this dialog box.

If you study the pivot table created in figure 16-3, you'll see that the subcategories for each row and column field you selected are included as column or row labels in the pivot table. These labels are called *pivot table items*; they indicate the categories of data that are summarized in the table. For example, the Dept. column field contains three pivot table items: Admin, Mktg, and Prod.

Procedure

1. Place the cell pointer on any cell in the list you want to create the pivot table from.
2. Select the PivotTable command from the Data or shortcut menu or click on the PivotTable toolbar button, and this dialog box appears:

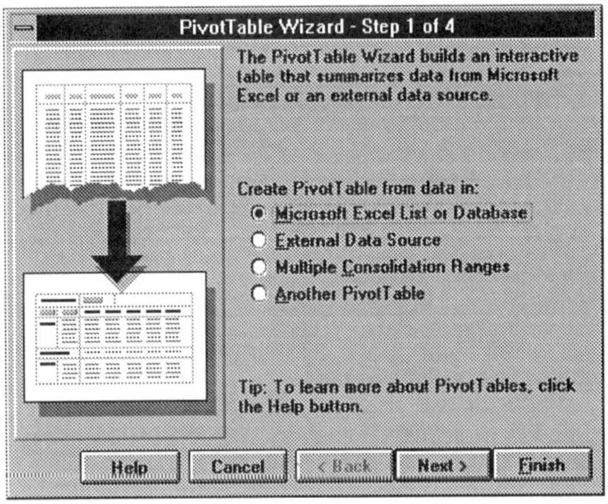

3. Click on the Next button to create the pivot table from a list, and this dialog box appears:

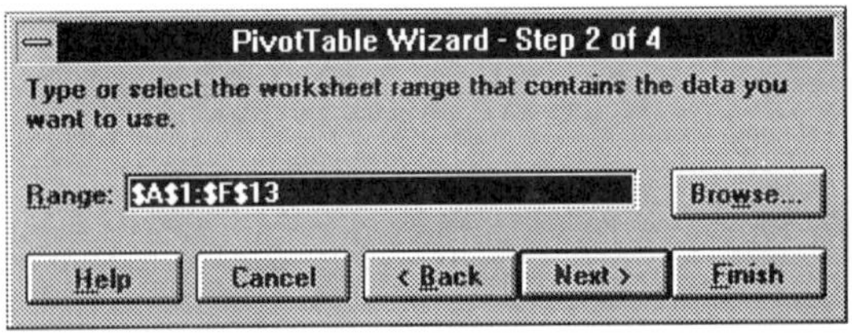

4. Make sure that the range that's displayed for the list is correct, then click on the Next button and this dialog box appears:

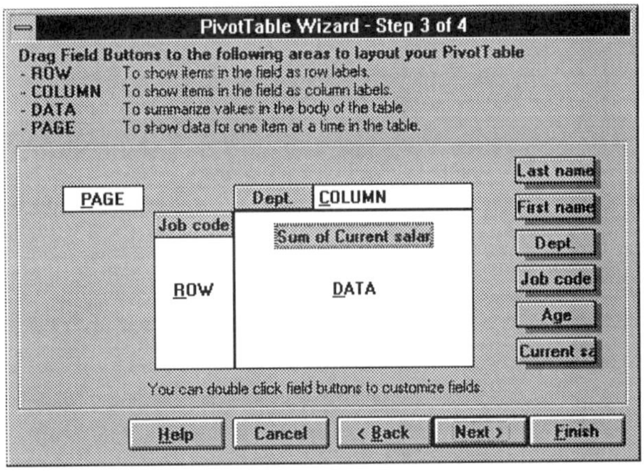

Drag the buttons for the fields you want to include in the pivot table to the proper locations as described at the top of the dialog box.

Figure 16-3 How to create a pivot table from a list (part 1 of 2)

5. Click on the Next button and this dialog box appears:

6. Deselect any options in the PivotTable Options group that aren't appropriate. Then, click on the Finish button and *Excel* builds the PivotTable according to your specifications:

	A	B	C	D	E	F
1	Sum of Current salary	Dept				
2	Job code	Admin	Mktg	Prod	Grand Total	
3	1	53500	26500	28500	108500	
4	2	63250	41250	62900	167400	
5	3	34000	47500	39900	121400	
6	Grand Total	150750	115250	131300	397300	
7						

Notes

- The Create PivotTable From Data In options in the first dialog box let you create a pivot table from sources other than a list. If you choose the External Data Source option, *Excel* invokes *Microsoft Query* so you can access an external database. (Chapter 17 introduces *Microsoft Query*.) If you choose the Multiple Consolidation Ranges option, *Excel* lets you create a pivot table that combines similarly structured data from two or more ranges. And if you choose the Another Pivot Table option, you can create a pivot table from another pivot table. If you choose one of these options, the second dialog box prompts you for the appropriate information.
- The default summary function for a numeric field is Sum. The default summary function for a non-numeric field is Count.
- *Excel* ignores any filters you may have applied to a list when it creates a pivot table from the list.
- *Excel* automatically adds subtotals and grand totals to a pivot table when you create it, so you should remove any subtotals from a list before you create a pivot table from it.
- By default, *Excel* places the pivot table in a new worksheet in the current workbook. If you want to, you can supply a specific location in the PivotTable Starting Cell text box in the last dialog box.
- By default, *Excel* saves a copy of the data on which a pivot table is based with the pivot table. If you don't want *Excel* to store this source data, deselect the Save Data With Table Layout option in the last dialog box.
- By default, *Excel* applies an autoformat to the pivot table. If you don't want to use this autoformat, deselect the AutoFormat Table option in the last dialog box.

Figure 16-3 How to create a pivot table from a list (part 2 of 2)

The *summary function* that's used in a pivot table depends on the data field you're summarizing. If the data field is numeric, the default is to use the Sum function. If the data field contains text, the default is to use the Count function. The data field I selected in figure 16-3 contains employee salaries, so the pivot table shows the sum of the current salaries for each job code in each department. I'll show you how to change the summary function in a moment.

How to change the layout of a pivot table The row and column fields you select for a pivot table and the sequence of the pivot table items within those fields determine the layout of the pivot table. If the pivot table doesn't look the way you want it to when you create it, you can change the layout. In fact, the name pivot table is based on the fact that you can "pivot" row and column fields around the data area to look at the summary data in different ways.

Figure 16-4 shows you how to change the layout of a pivot table by moving column and row fields and pivot table items. The easiest way to move a field or item is to drag it to a new location in the table. To create the pivot table in figure 16-4, for example, I dragged the Dept. label so that it's now a row field instead of a column field, and I dragged the Admin item so it's now after the Mktg item. You can also move a row or column field by accessing the third PivotTable Wizard dialog box and dragging the button for that field to a new location in the pivot table area.

How to change the summary function and the format of the summary data Figure 16-5 shows you how to use the PivotTable Field dialog box for a data field to customize a pivot table. From this dialog box, you can select from a variety of functions for summarizing the data in the pivot table. You can also change the format of the data by clicking on the Number button and selecting a format from the Format Cells dialog box that appears. And you can change the name that's used in the pivot table to describe the summary. The pivot table at the bottom of the figure shows the pivot table created in figure 16-4 after the summary function was changed to Average and a Currency format was selected.

How to update the contents of a pivot table If the source data that's summarized in a pivot table changes, the pivot table isn't automatically updated. To update a pivot table so it reflects the current state of the source data, you use the Refresh Data command. This command is available from the Data menu, the shortcut menu, and the Query and Pivot toolbar.

How to move a column or row field

With the mouse

Drag the label for a column or row field to a new position. As you drag the label, the pointer indicates whether the field will be a column or a row field, and the insert marker indicates where the field will be inserted:

	A	B	C	D	E	F
1	Sum of Current salary	Dept.				
2	Job code	Admin	Mktg	Prod	Grand Total	
3	1	53500	26500	28500	108500	
4	2	63250	41250	62900	167400	
5	3	34000	47500	39900	121400	
6	Grand Total	150750	115250	131300	397300	
7						

With the PivotTable command

1. Place the cell pointer on any cell in the pivot table.
2. Select the PivotTable command from the Data or shortcut menu or click on the PivotTable toolbar button, and the third PivotTable Wizard dialog box appears.
3. Drag the button for a column or row field to a new position.
4. Click on the Finish button, and *Excel* changes the layout of the pivot table based on the new position of the field.

How to move a pivot table item

1. Place the cell pointer on the cell that contains the label for the item you want to move.
2. Place the mouse pointer over the cell until it turns into an arrow.
3. Drag the item to a new location:

	A	B	C	D
1	Sum of Current salary			
2	Dept.	Job code	Total	
3	Admin	1	53500	
4		2	63250	
5		3	34000	
6	Admin Total		150750	
7	Mktg	1	26500	
8		2	41250	
9		3	47500	
10	Mktg Total		115250	
11	Prod	1	28500	
12		2	62900	
13		3	39900	
14	Prod Total		131300	
15	Grand Total		397300	
16				

Figure 16-4 How to change the layout of a pivot table (part 1 of 2)

When you refresh a pivot table based on an *Excel* list, you should know that only the cells in the source range you specified when you created the table are examined. If the source list has more rows or columns than it did

The pivot table in figure 16-3 after the Dept. column field was changed to a row field and the Dept. items were resequenced

	A	B	C	D
1	Sum of Current salary			
2	Dept.	Job code	Total	
3	Mktg	1	26500	
4		2	41250	
5		3	47500	
6	Mktg Total		115250	
7	Admin	1	53500	
8		2	63250	
9		3	34000	
10	Admin Total		150750	
11	Prod	1	28500	
12		2	62900	
13		3	39900	
14	Prod Total		131300	
15	Grand Total		397300	
16				

Figure 16-4 How to change the layout of a pivot table (part 2 of 2)

when the pivot table was created, you'll need to update the source range for the table before you update its contents. To update the source range, access the PivotTable Wizard to display the layout dialog box, then click on the Back button to display the dialog box that lets you specify the source range.

Other skills for working with pivot tables

The rest of this chapter presents additional skills you can use to create and work with more sophisticated pivot tables. First, you'll learn how to create pivot tables that contain more than one column, row, and data field. Then, you'll learn three skills that will make it easier for you to work with large or complicated pivot tables: how to hide and show detail data, how to group numeric data into ranges, and how to filter a pivot table using a page field.

How to create a more complicated pivot table In figure 16-4, you learned how to change the layout of an existing pivot table. However, you're not limited to simply rearranging the fields and items in a pivot table. You can also add column, row, and data fields to create a more complicated pivot table. And you can delete fields you no longer want to include in the table. Of course, you can also create a more complicated pivot table from scratch using the procedure presented in figure 16-3.

Figure 16-6 presents a pivot table that contains one row and one column field and four data fields. You can also create pivot tables that contain two

Two ways to access the PivotTable Field dialog box for a data field

- Place the cell pointer on a cell in the data area or on the cell that contains the label that describes the summary, and select the PivotTable Field command from the Data or shortcut menu or click on the PivotTable Field button in the Query and Pivot toolbar.
- Place the cell pointer on any cell in the pivot table, and access the third PivotTable Wizard dialog box by selecting the PivotTable command from the Data or shortcut menu or by clicking on the PivotTable button in the Query and Pivot toolbar. Then, double-click on the button for the data field in the data area.

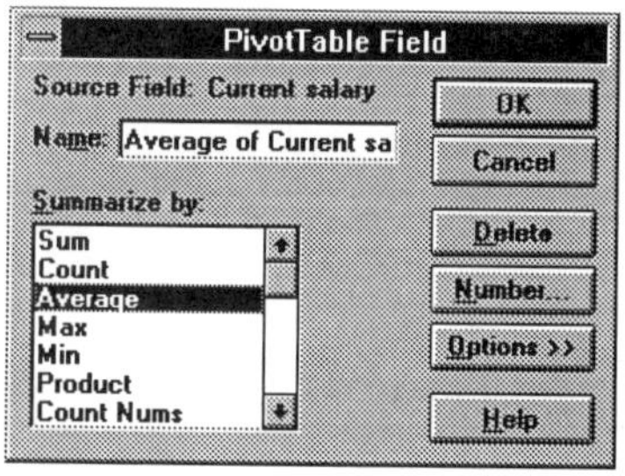

Operation

- To change the summary function, select a function from the Summarize By list box.
- To change the name of the summary field, enter a new value in the Name text box.
- To specify the number format for the summary data, click on the Number button and complete the Format Cells dialog box that appears.

The pivot table in figure 16-4 after the summary function was changed to Average and a Currency format was applied

	A	B	C	D
1	Average of Current salary			
2	Dept.	Job code	Total	
3	Mktg	1	$26,500	
4		2	$41,250	
5		3	$47,500	
6	Mktg Total		$38,417	
7	Admin	1	$26,750	
8		2	$31,625	
9		3	$34,000	
10	Admin Total		$30,150	
11	Prod	1	$28,500	
12		2	$31,450	
13		3	$39,900	
14	Prod Total		$32,825	
15	Grand Total		$33,108	
16				

Notes

- You can display the PivotTable Field dialog box to make these changes while you're creating a pivot table by double-clicking on the button for the data field in the data area of the third PivotTable Wizard dialog box.
- You can also change the name of a summary field by selecting the cell that contains the name and entering a new value.
- If you click on the Options button, *Excel* displays some additional options that let you specify advanced summarization features.

Figure 16-5 How to change a summary function and the format of the summary data

A layout for a pivot table with four data fields

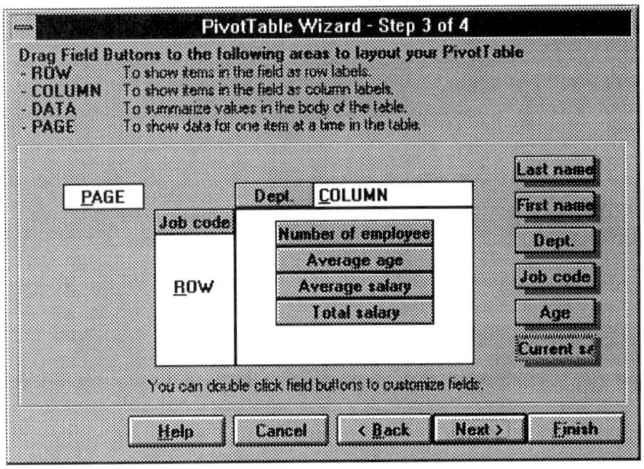

The resulting pivot table

	A	B	C	D	E	F	G
1			Dept.				
2	Job code	Data	Admin	Mktg	Prod	Grand Total	
3	1	Number of employees	2	1	1	4	
4		Average age	37	50	52	44	
5		Average salary	$26,750	$26,500	$28,500	$27,125	
6		Total salary	$53,500	$26,500	$28,500	$108,500	
7	2	Number of employees	2	1	2	5	
8		Average age	28	43	33	33	
9		Average salary	$31,625	$41,250	$31,450	$33,480	
10		Total salary	$63,250	$41,250	$62,900	$167,400	
11	3	Number of employees	1	1	1	3	
12		Average age	30	43	52	42	
13		Average salary	$34,000	$47,500	$39,900	$40,467	
14		Total salary	$34,000	$47,500	$39,900	$121,400	
15	Total Number of employees		5	3	4	12	
16	Total Average age		32	45	43	39	
17	Total Average salary		$30,150	$38,417	$32,825	$33,108	
18	Total Total salary		$150,750	$115,250	$131,300	$397,300	
19							

Notes

- To add a row, column, or data field to a pivot table from the PivotTable Wizard dialog box, drag the button for the field to the proper location in the pivot table area. To delete a row, column, or data field, drag the button for the field out of the pivot table area. You can also delete a row or column field without accessing the PivotTable Wizard by dragging the label for the field outside of the pivot table.
- You can use a different summary function for each data field in a pivot table. To change a summary function from its default, use the procedure in figure 16-5.
- You can include the same data field in a pivot table more than once. Then, you can specify a different summary function for each occurrence of the field.

Figure 16-6 How to set up a more complicated pivot table

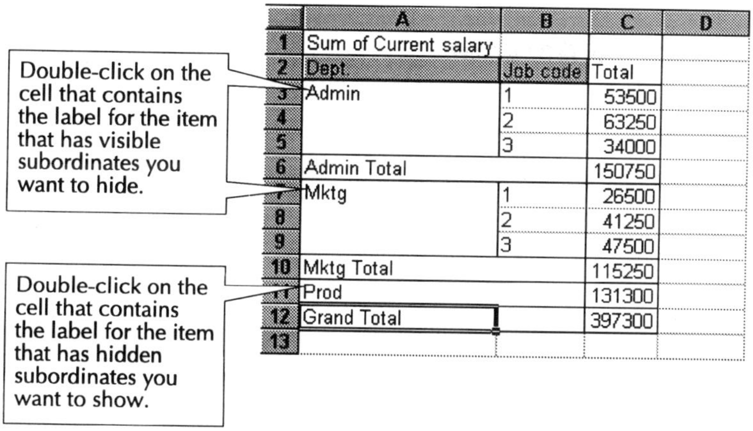

Notes

- You can also use the Hide Detail and Show Detail commands in the Group and Outline submenu of the Data or shortcut menu or the Hide Detail and Show Detail buttons in the Query and Pivot toolbar to hide and show detail data. Just move the cell pointer to the cell that contains the label for the item that has subordinate items you want to hide or show, then issue the command.
- To hide or show the details for all the items in a field, move the cell pointer to the cell that contains the label for the field, then issue the Hide Detail or Show Detail command.

Figure 16-7 How to hide and show details in a pivot table

or more row and column fields. However, keep in mind that the more fields you include in a pivot table, the more difficult it will be to interpret. As a result, it makes sense to keep pivot tables relatively simple.

How to hide and show detail data Figure 16-7 shows you how to hide and show different levels of data in a pivot table. To do that, you can simply double-click on the cell that contains the label for the item whose subordinates you want to hide or show. If you prefer, you can also use the Hide Detail and Show Detail commands to perform these functions. And you can use these commands to hide and show the detail data for all the items in a field at once.

How to group numeric items into ranges Figure 16-8 presents the procedure for grouping numeric items into ranges. In this figure, I grouped the items in the Current salary field into ranges of $10,000 dollars each. As

Procedure

1. Place the cell pointer on a cell that contains one of the numeric items you want to group:

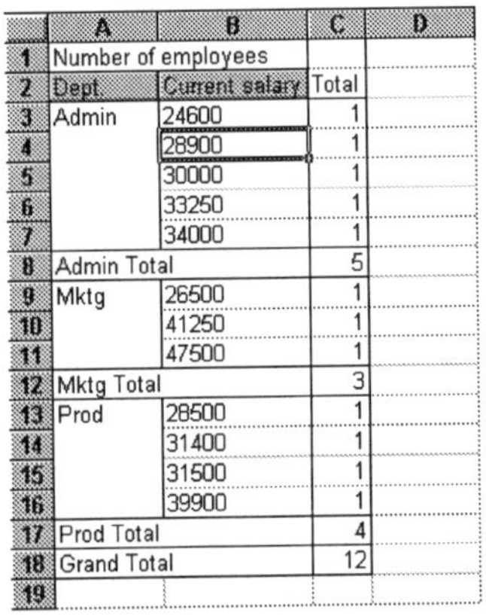

	A	B	C	D
1	Number of employees			
2	Dept	Current salary	Total	
3	Admin	24600	1	
4		28900	1	
5		30000	1	
6		33250	1	
7		34000	1	
8	Admin Total		5	
9	Mktg	26500	1	
10		41250	1	
11		47500	1	
12	Mktg Total		3	
13	Prod	28500	1	
14		31400	1	
15		31500	1	
16		39900	1	
17	Prod Total		4	
18	Grand Total		12	
19				

2. Issue the Group command from the Group and Outline submenu of the Data or shortcut menu or click on the Group button in the Query and Pivot toolbar, and this dialog box appears:

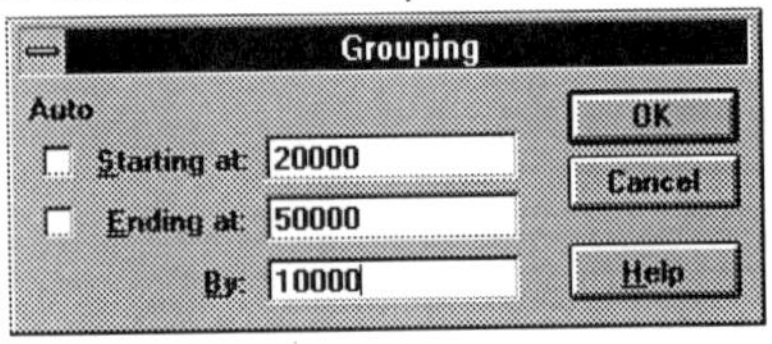

3. Enter values for the Starting At, Ending At, and By options to define the ranges for the field. Then, click on the OK button and the pivot table is changed to reflect the new ranges:

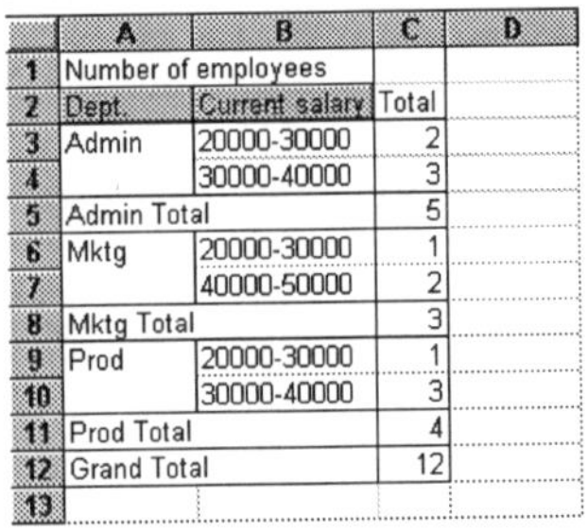

	A	B	C	D
1	Number of employees			
2	Dept	Current salary	Total	
3	Admin	20000-30000	2	
4		30000-40000	3	
5	Admin Total		5	
6	Mktg	20000-30000	1	
7		40000-50000	2	
8	Mktg Total		3	
9	Prod	20000-30000	1	
10		30000-40000	3	
11	Prod Total		4	
12	Grand Total		12	
13				

Notes

- By default, the Auto check boxes are selected, and the values for the Starting At and Ending At options are set to the lowest and highest values in the field. If you change these values, the check boxes are deselected. To return the options to their default values, click on the check boxes.
- To redisplay data in ungrouped form, select any cell that contains data for the grouped field. Then, issue the Ungroup command from the Group and Outline submenu of the Data or shortcut menu, or click on the Ungroup button in the Query and Pivot toolbar.
- You can also group dates and times into ranges, and you can create groups of selected items. For details, refer to *Excel*'s online Help.

Figure 16-8 How to group numeric items into ranges

you can see from the resulting pivot table, using ranges can help you interpret the data in a pivot table more easily. This feature is particularly useful when a pivot table field contains many separate values.

How to use a page field to filter the data in a pivot table In chapter 14, you learned how to use the AutoFilter feature to filter the data in a list. *Excel* provides a similar feature for filtering the data in a pivot table. To implement this feature, you use *page fields*.

Figure 16-9 shows you how to use a page field to filter the data in a pivot table. To create a page field, you access the layout dialog box of the PivotTable Wizard, then drag the field you want to filter into the Page area. When you click on the Finish button, *Excel* displays the field at the top of the pivot table along with a drop-down list box that contains all the items in that field. The pivot table in step 2 of figure 16-10, for example, contains a page field for the job code. To filter the table, you select an item from the drop-down list for the page field. The pivot table in step 3 of the figure, for example, shows the data for only job code 1.

Perspective

If you experiment with the pivot table functions presented in this chapter, I think you'll find that you can create almost any pivot table in just a matter of seconds. Although some of the functions may seem confusing at first, they'll make more sense once you see how they work. So if you plan on using the pivot table feature of *Excel* frequently, you should spend some time experimenting with it.

With what you've learned in this chapter, you should be able to create most of the pivot tables you'll ever need. However, there's a lot more you can do with pivot tables than what you've learned here. For example, you can sort a pivot table and you can hide or display its subtotals. But if you're comfortable with the skills you've learned here, you won't have any trouble learning how to use other pivot table features.

Procedure

1. Drag the button for the field you want to use as the page field to the Page area of the third PivotTable Wizard dialog box:

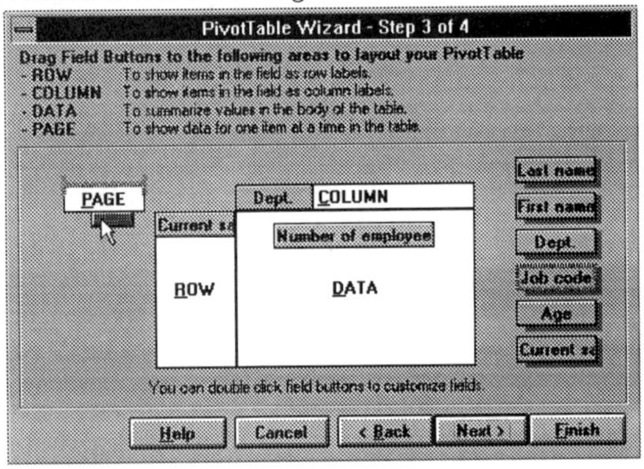

2. Click on the Finish button, and the page field appears with a drop-down list box at the top of the pivot table:

	A	B	C	D	E	F
1	Job code	(All)				
2						
3	Number of employees	Dept				
4	Current salary	Admin	Mktg	Prod	Grand Total	
5	24600	1	0	0	1	
6	26500	0	1	0	1	
7	28500	0	0	1	1	
8	28900	1	0	0	1	
9	30000	1	0	0	1	
10	31400	0	0	1	1	
11	31500	0	0	1	1	
12	33250	1	0	0	1	
13	34000	1	0	0	1	
14	39900	0	0	1	1	
15	41250	0	1	0	1	
16	47500	0	1	0	1	
17	Grand Total	5	3	4	12	
18						

3. Select a value from the drop-down list to display the data only for that value:

	A	B	C	D	E	F
1	Job code	1				
2						
3	Number of employees	Dept.				
4	Current salary	Admin	Mktg	Prod	Grand Total	
5	24600	1	0	0	1	
6	26500	0	1	0	1	
7	28500	0	0	1	1	
8	28900	1	0	0	1	
9	Grand Total	2	1	1	4	
10						

Notes

- By default, *Excel* displays the data for all values in a page field when you first create the field.
- You can also create a page field from an existing column or row field by dragging the label for that field above the pivot table to the area where the page fields are displayed. The pointer will indicate when the field is in the correct position.
- A pivot table can include more than one page field.

Figure 16-9 How to use a page field to filter a pivot table

Summary

- A *pivot table* is a table that summarizes the data in one or more fields of a list, an external database, or another pivot table based on other fields. A pivot table contains *row* and *column fields* that specify the fields by which the data is summarized and *data fields* that determine what data is summarized. You can select from several *summary functions* for each data field.
- You use the PivotTable Wizard to define a pivot table. By default, *Excel* creates the pivot table in a new worksheet in the current workbook.
- You can change the layout of a pivot table by dragging the labels for row and column fields or pivot table items from one position to another. You can also move row and column fields using the PivotTable Wizard.
- From the PivotTable Field dialog box for a data field, you can select a different summary function for the field, you can specify the format for the summarized data, and you can change the label that's used in the pivot table to identify the summary.
- To update a pivot table to reflect changes made to the source data it's based on, use the Refresh Data command in the Data or shortcut menu or the Refresh Data button in the Query and Pivot toolbar.
- To hide and show detail data in a pivot table and group numeric items into ranges, use the commands in the Group and Outline submenu of the Data or shortcut menu or the appropriate buttons in the Query and Pivot toolbar.
- You can use a *page field* to filter the data in a pivot table.

Chapter 17

How to work with data from other programs, including external databases

Occasionally, you may want to use *Excel* to access data that was created by another program. For example, the information you need may already exist as a file created by another database program. Then, you can retrieve that data into *Excel*, and you can process it as a list.

In this chapter, you'll learn three ways to access data created by another program. First, you'll learn how to use the Open command to retrieve a file that has a format *Excel* recognizes. Second, you'll learn how to open text files using the TextWizard. Finally, you'll learn how to retrieve data from an external database using the *Microsoft Query* add-in program.

How to open a file created by another application

Figure 17-1 shows you how to use the Open command to open a file created by another application. As you can see, *Excel* recognizes the formats of files created by several specific application programs. This chapter will focus on the types of files you're most likely to want to open as a list.

The procedure in figure 17-1 shows you how to open a dBase file. Because dBase is the most commonly used database file format, many programs have the ability to save files in this format. So even if you're using a program other than dBase, you may be able to save files with the dBase format and import them into *Excel* as a dBase file.

When you import a dBase file into *Excel*, each record in the file becomes one row in the worksheet and each field in a record becomes one cell in a row. In addition, *Excel* uses the field names in the database as the column labels. In other words, the file is retrieved in list format. As a result, you can immediately use the filtering, sorting, summarizing, and pivot table commands presented in the other chapters in this section to manipulate the data.

Before you open a file created by another program, you should realize that the file must be small enough to fit in an *Excel* worksheet (16,384 records or less). If the file is too big, you'll need to use the *Query* program presented later in this chapter to retrieve selected records from the file. In fact, unless you need to work with the entire file, you'll probably want to use *Query* instead of the Open command even if the file isn't too big to open. Then, you can retrieve just the records and fields you need.

Procedure

1. Select the Open command from the File menu and this dialog box appears:

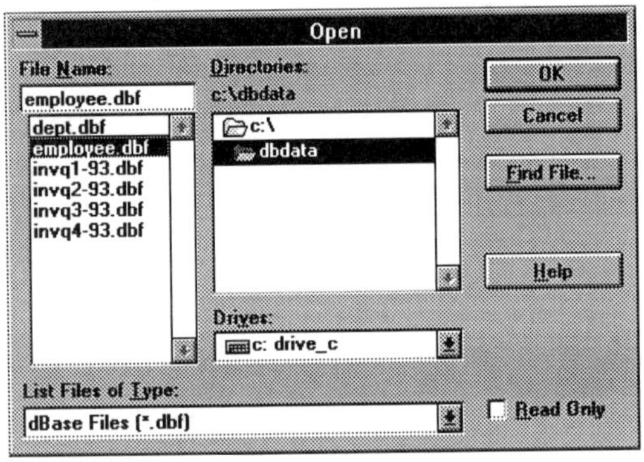

2. Select the file type of the application used to create the file you want to open from the List Files Of Type drop-down list box, then select the drive, directory, and file name. *Excel* retrieves the file and formats the data as a list:

	A	B	C	D	E	F	G
1	LAST_NAME	FIRST_NAME	DEPT	JOB_CODE	AGE	SALARY	
2	Smith	Mary	Admin	1	23	23400.00	
3	Jones	Georgia	Mktg	3	43	47500.00	
4	Long	John	Prod	3	52	39900.00	
5	Johnson	Edward	Admin	2	30	33250.00	
6	Jones	John	Prod	2	33	31400.00	
7	Williams	Alice	Admin	1	50	28900.00	
8	Allen	Joel	Admin	2	25	30000.00	
9	Clay	Kurt	Mktg	2	43	41250.00	
10	Burkes	Patricia	Prod	1	52	28500.00	
11	Andrews	Anne	Admin	3	30	34000.00	
12	Russell	Barry	Prod	2	33	31500.00	
13	Thompson	John	Mktg	1	50	26500.00	
14							

Notes

- The types of files you're most likely to open for processing as a list are:

dbf	*dBase II, III, IV*
txt	Text (text; typically tab delimited; see figure 17-2 for details)
csv	CSV (text; comma delimited)
prn	Formatted Text (text in *Lotus* PRN format; space delimited)

- You can also use the technique this figure presents to open spreadsheet documents created by programs other than *Excel* 5.0:

xls	*Excel* (5.0 and prior versions)
wks, wk1, wk3	*Lotus 1-2-3* (versions prior to 4.0)
wq1	*Quattro/Pro for DOS*
slk	SYLK (symbolic link)

When you open files of these types, *Excel* 5.0 is usually able to preserve labels, values, formulas and formats.

Figure 17-1 How to use the Open command to access a file created by another application

How to open a text file

Although many programs can store data in dBase format, some don't. However, almost all programs let you store data in text format. So you can almost always retrieve data into *Excel* as a text file. Figure 17-2 presents the procedure for doing that.

As you can see in figure 17-2, *Excel* can import two types of text files. In a *delimited text file*, the fields of the records are separated by single characters called *delimiters*. The most common delimiter is a tab character, but some programs let you use other characters. In a *fixed-width text file*, varying numbers of spaces are used in each record to align the data in columns.

When you issue the Open command for a text file, *Excel* invokes the TextWizard to help you specify how to divide and format the records into fields. In most cases, *Excel*'s assumptions about delimiters and formats are correct. So all you have to do to import a text file is accept the default values in each of the TextWizard's three dialog boxes. *Excel* even includes column labels for the fields in the records if they're contained in the first record in the text file. If the first record of the text file doesn't contain the column labels, you have to insert them into the worksheet before you can process the data as a list.

How to use *Microsoft Query* to import data from an external database

The most powerful facility *Excel* 5.0 provides for accessing the data in an external database is *Microsoft Query*. Although *Query* is a separate program, it comes with *Excel* and works as an add-in program. That means the two are tightly integrated, so they're easy to use together.

Unlike the Open command, *Query* lets you select the records that are retrieved from an external database. This means that you can access databases that contain many more records than the maximum of 16,384 *Excel* can support in a list. However, the number of records you retrieve is still restricted by the size of the worksheet.

Another advantage of *Query* is that it lets you combine data from two or more source databases (called *tables*) into one *results table*. This is called a *join* operation. Businesses that have complicated databases depend on join operations to gather and organize data in flexible ways. Although this chapter won't teach you how to perform a join operation, you shouldn't have any trouble learning how to do it on your own if you understand the information presented here.

How to import a delimited text file

1. Select the Open command from the File menu, select the txt file type option from the List Files Of Type drop-down list box, and identify the text file you want to import. Then, *Excel* displays this dialog box:

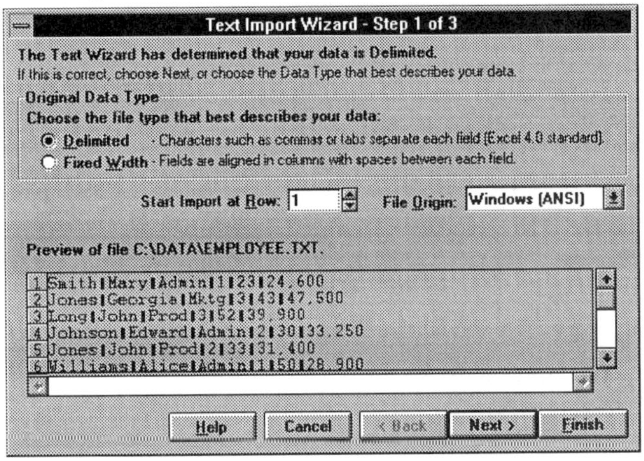

2. Change the Start Import At Row and File Origin options as necessary, then click on the Next button and this dialog box appears:

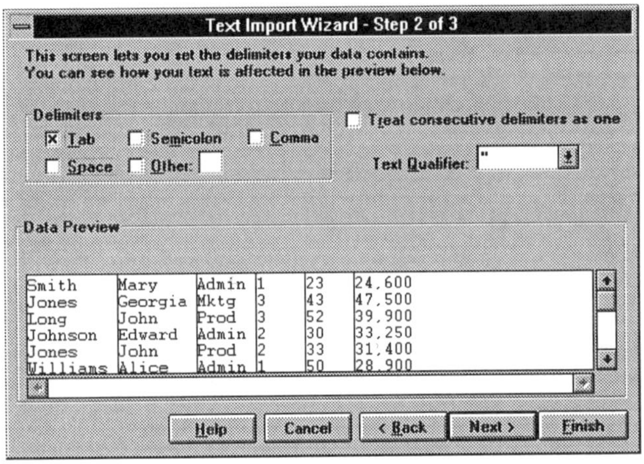

Figure 17-2 How to use the TextWizard to import a text file (part 1 of 3)

3. Select the character or characters that are used to separate the fields in each record of the text file, and *Excel* shows you how the data will be divided into columns in the Data Preview area of the dialog box. Click on the Next button and this dialog box appears:

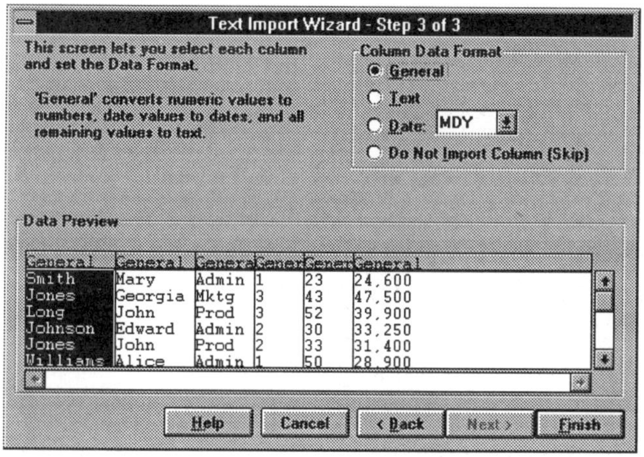

4. If you want to change the format for the data in a column, click on a column in the Data Preview area and select the format you want from the Column Data Format group. Then, click on the Finish button and *Excel* imports the file:

	A	B	C	D	E	F	G
1	Smith	Mary	Admin	1	23	24,600	
2	Jones	Georgia	Mktg	3	43	47,500	
3	Long	John	Prod	3	52	39,900	
4	Johnson	Edward	Admin	2	30	33,250	
5	Jones	John	Prod	2	33	31,400	
6	Williams	Alice	Admin	1	50	28,900	
7	Allen	Joel	Admin	2	25	30,000	
8	Clay	Kurt	Mktg	2	43	41,250	
9	Burkes	Patricia	Prod	1	62	28,600	
10	Andrews	Anne	Admin	3	30	34,000	
11	Russell	Barry	Prod	2	33	31,500	
12	Thompson	John	Mktg	1	50	26,500	
13							

Figure 17-2 How to use the TextWizard to import a text file (part 2 of 3)

To access and retrieve data from an external database, *Query* requires an *ODBC (open database connectivity) driver* for the program that created and manages the database. ODBC drivers for *dBASE*, *FoxPro*, *Access*, *Paradox*, and *SQL Server* come with *Excel*, and you can install them during set up. In addition, you can obtain ODBC drivers for *Btrieve* and *Oracle* from Microsoft. You can also expect developers of other database programs to distribute ODBC drivers for their applications.

How to import a fixed-width text file

Use the procedure for importing a delimited text file, but select the Fixed Width option from the first dialog box. Then, when you click on the Next button, this dialog box appears:

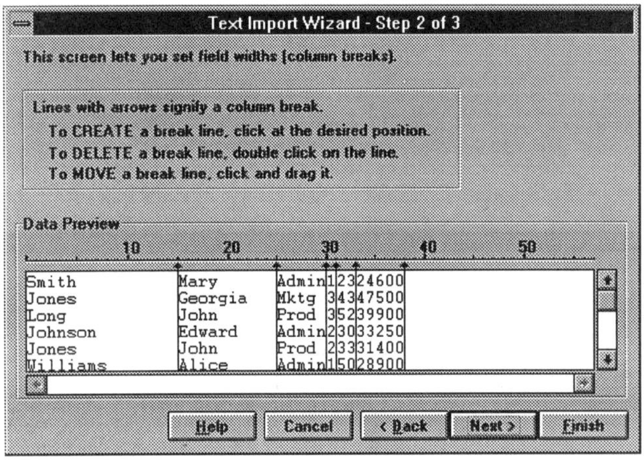

Follow the directions at the top of the dialog box to add, delete, and move the lines that indicate the column breaks.

Notes

- To omit a column from the import operation, select the column in the Data Preview area of the third dialog box and select the Do Not Import Column option from the Column Data Format group.
- If the first record in a text file contains column headings, *Excel* uses them to create column labels for the retrieved data.

Figure 17-2 How to use the TextWizard to import a text file (part 3 of 3)

How to access an external database Figure 17-3 presents the procedure for accessing an external database. First, you select the Get External Data command from the Data menu. This command starts *Query* and makes it the active program. (If the Get External Data command doesn't appear in the Data menu on your system, it means that the *Query* add-in program hasn't been installed properly. If that's the case, you can refer to chapter 24 to find out how to install the program.)

After you start the Query program, you specify the ODBC driver you want to use. Next, you specify the location and name of the external database table you want to select records from. Then, *Query* opens the file and displays a list of its fields in the *tables pane* at the top of the window.

Procedure

1. Select the Get External Data command from the Data menu to start *Query*, and this dialog box appears:

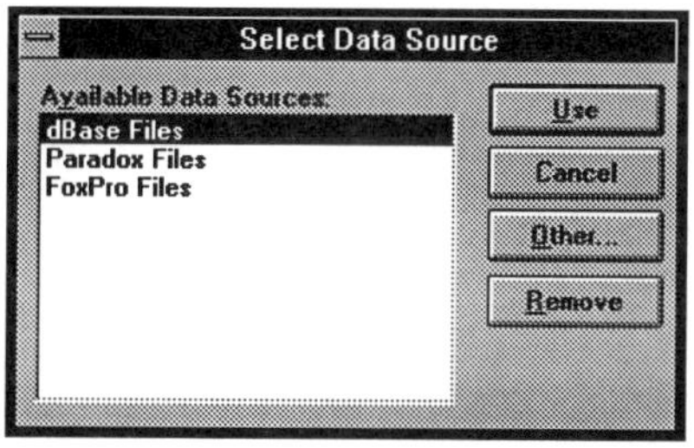

2. Select an option from the Available Data Sources list box to identify the kind of external data you want to retrieve. Click on the Use button and this dialog box appears:

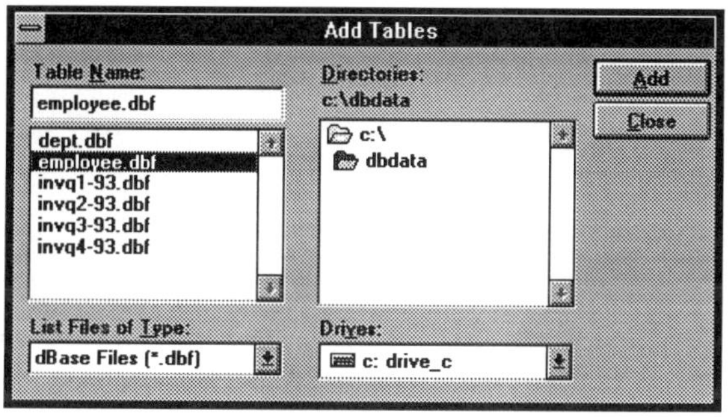

Figure 17-3 How to use *Query* to access an external database (part 1 of 2)

How to retrieve data from an external database Once you have access to an external database, you select the fields and records you want to retrieve into *Excel*. Figure 17-4 presents the procedure for doing that. Notice that as you select fields, *Query* displays the data in those fields for each record in the database in the *data pane* at the bottom of the window.

When you're done selecting the fields you want to retrieve, you specify the selection criteria for the records you want to retrieve. To do that, you can use the Add Criteria command in the Criteria menu. As you enter the criteria, they're displayed in the *criteria pane* in the middle of the window. In addition, any records that don't match the criteria are removed from the data pane.

To return the selected data to *Excel*, you use the Return Data to Microsoft Excel command in the File menu. It appears as the last command

3. Find the file you want to use in the query, then select it by double-clicking on it or highlighting it and pressing the Add button. Click on the Close button, and *Query* opens the file and displays its fields in the tables pane at the top of the window:

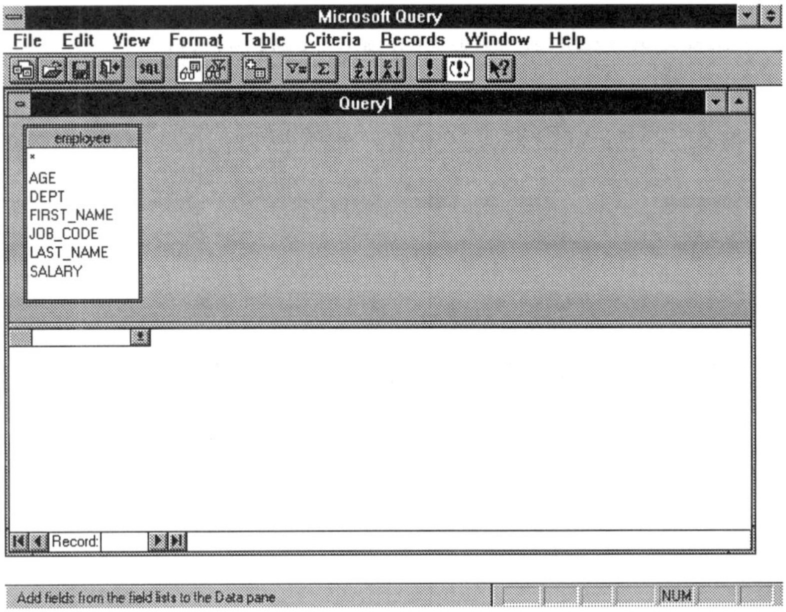

Notes

- If the source of the data you want to use isn't displayed in the Select Data Source dialog box, click on the Other button and select the source from the list that's displayed.
- You can select two or more files from the Add Tables dialog box. This is useful if you want to join data from two or more files in a single results table.

Figure 17-3 How to use *Query* to access an external database (part 2 of 2)

on the menu where you'd usually expect to find the Exit command. When you issue this command, control is returned to *Excel*. Then, *Excel* displays a dialog box that offers several options and lets you specify where you want to place the retrieved data. When you complete this dialog box, *Excel* inserts the data from the external database into the worksheet.

Procedure

1. From *Query*, select the fields you want to retrieve by double-clicking on the field names in the tables pane or by dragging the field names from the tables pane into the data pane in the lower part of the window:

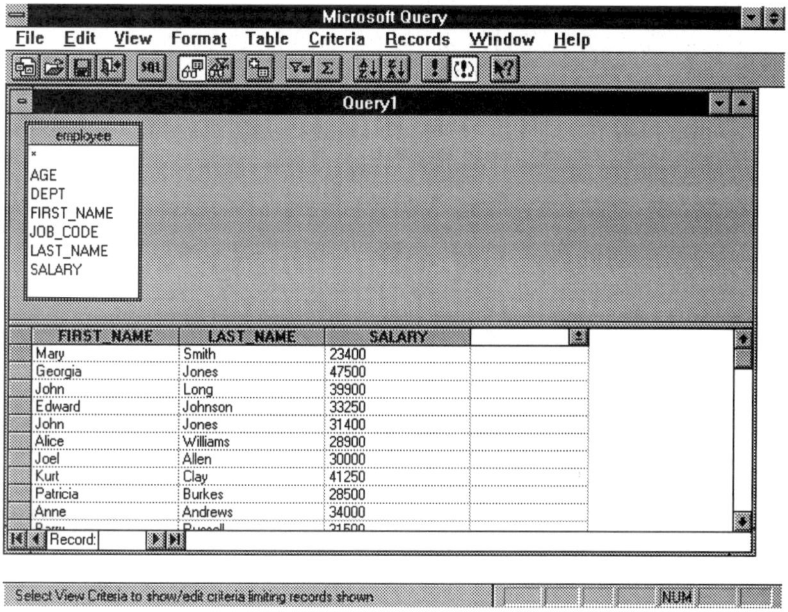

2. To specify selection criteria for the records to be retrieved, select the Add Criteria command from the Criteria menu and this dialog box appears:

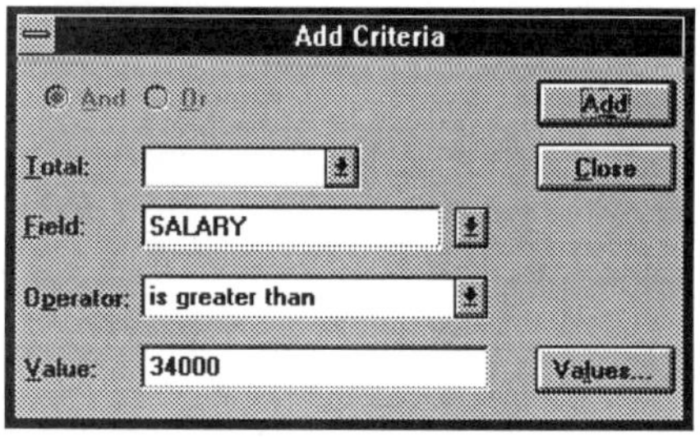

Figure 17-4 How to use *Query* to retrieve data from an external database (part 1 of 3)

3. For the first criterion, select a field and a relational operator, enter a comparison value, and click on the Add button. For each additional criterion, you must also select the And or Or option to indicate the logical relationship between the criteria. Click on the Close button, and *Query* displays the criteria in the criteria pane in the middle of the window and shows the result of the selection in the data pane:

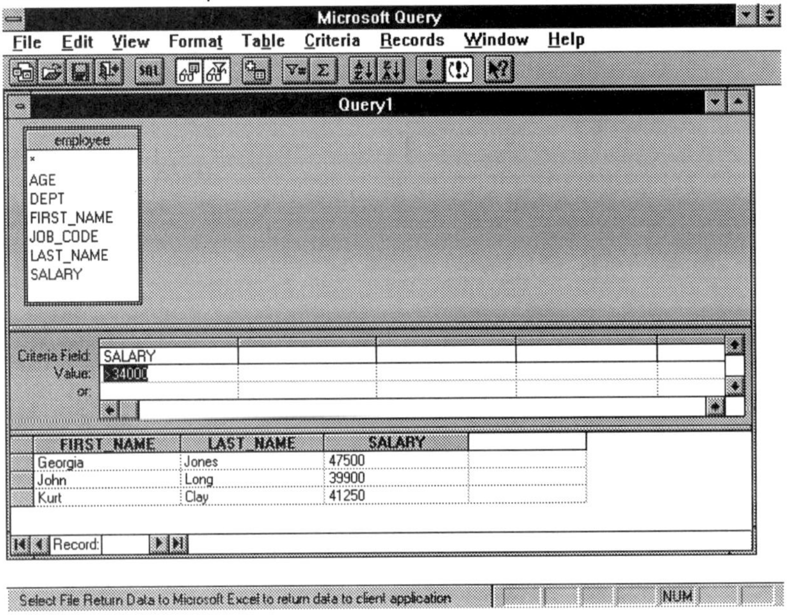

4. Select the Return Data to Microsoft Excel command from the File menu to transfer the data to *Excel*. Then, *Excel* displays this dialog box:

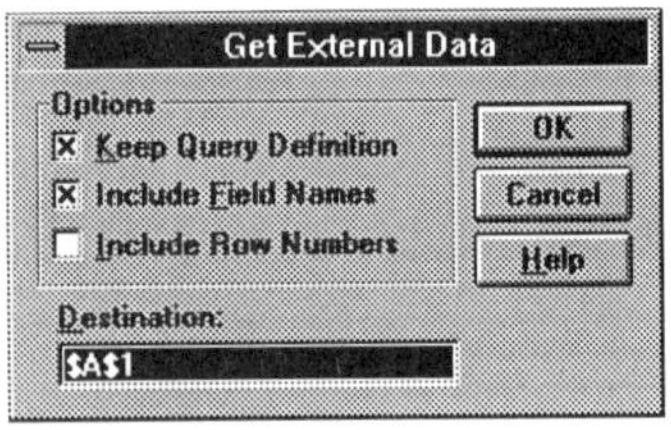

5. Choose the appropriate options, then click on the OK button and the data is inserted in the *Excel* worksheet in list form:

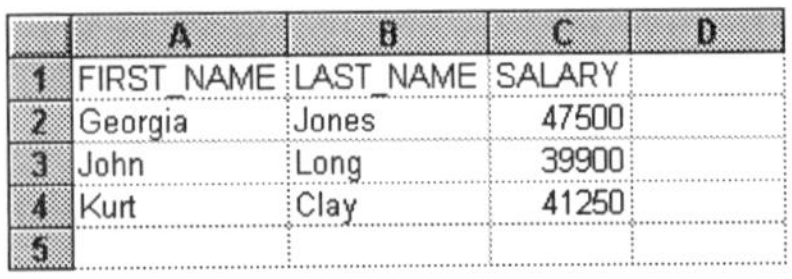

Figure 17-4 How to use *Query* to retrieve data from an external database (part 2 of 3)

Notes

- You can also use the Add Columns command in the Records menu to select fields, or you can select field names from the drop-down list box that appears in the data pane. To select all of the fields in the database, use the * option in the tables pane.
- To select a column in the data pane, click on its column heading. Then, you can delete the column by pressing the Delete key, and you can move it by dragging it to a new location.
- You can select a comparison value for a field by clicking on the Values button in the Add Criteria dialog box and selecting a value from the list that's displayed. The list includes all the values for that field that occur in the database.
- You can use the Total text box in the Add Criteria dialog box to select records based on a calculated field. See the online Help for *Query* for more information.
- You can change the criteria for a query operation by modifying it directly in the criteria pane.
- If you select the Keep Query Definition option in the Get External Data dialog box, *Excel* saves the query definition with the result data in the worksheet. This lets you update the result data later without entering the specifications for the query again.
- If you select the Include Field Names option in the Get External Data dialog box, *Excel* includes the field names from the database as column labels in the first row of the result data. In other words, the data is formatted as a list.

Figure 17-4 How to use *Query* to retrieve data from an external database (part 3 of 3)

Perspective

Although you can retrieve data from other programs into an *Excel* worksheet using the Open command, using *Microsoft Query* is usually more efficient. That's because it gives you more control over the data that's retrieved. In particular, you have control over the records and the fields that are retrieved, so you can work with just the data you need.

In addition to its retrieval functions, *Query* has many other capabilities. For example, you can use it to do calculations based on the data it retrieves. However, it's probably easier to do these calculations in *Excel* after you retrieve the selected data. You can also use *Query* to add, change, and delete records in an external database. However, I don't recommend you use it for that purpose either. Before you make changes to an external database, you need to understand its format and the commands used by the external database program. But if you know that, it's easier to create and modify the database using the database program than it is using *Query*. And if you don't understand how the external database program works, using *Query* to change a database can be dangerous. If you're not careful, you could inadvertently make changes to the database that you didn't intend to make.

Summary

- To open a database file with dBase format, use the Open command to select a file with the file type dbf. *Excel* formats the file as a list using the field names in the database as the column labels.
- To open a file with text format, use the Open command to select a file with the file type txt. *Excel* uses the TextWizard to help you specify how you want the fields in the file divided and formatted. If the first record in the file contains column headings, *Excel* formats the file as a list using the column headings as the column labels.
- To access selected data in an external database, use the *Excel* add-in program *Microsoft Query*. To access *Query*, use the Get External Data command in the Data menu. Then, from *Query*, specify the database table, fields, and criteria you want to retrieve. *Query* returns the result of the database selection to *Excel* as a list.

Section 5

Skills for special purposes

This section contains seven chapters that present the *Excel* functions and features that aren't presented in the earlier sections. Each chapter in this section presents the skills that you need for a special purpose like auditing a worksheet, creating and using recorded macros, and using the Scenario Manager. For ease of use, each chapter in this section is designed as an independent module so you can read the chapters in whatever sequence you prefer.

Chapter 18

How to audit a worksheet

It's relatively easy to make a mistake as you create or modify a worksheet. You can do that as you enter and edit formulas or as you move and copy them. That's why a high percentage of business worksheets contain one or more calculation errors. Because the worksheets look so neat and professional, though, the errors are likely to be overlooked.

When you audit a worksheet, you check it for accuracy. To do that, you check the values that you entered into the worksheet. But you also check the formulas to make sure they're working correctly. In this chapter, you'll learn how to audit a worksheet by checking its formulas.

How to display or print a worksheet that shows its formulas

Figure 18-1 presents the procedures for displaying and printing a worksheet that shows the formulas used instead of the values derived from the formulas. To display the formulas in a worksheet, you select the Formulas option from the View tab of the Options dialog box. When you do, *Excel* doubles the widths of all the columns in the worksheet and aligns all the values at the left. You may want to adjust the column widths to make the worksheet more readable. At this point, you can see which cells contain formulas, and you can check them to see whether they are correct.

When you print a worksheet that shows its formulas, you'll want to select the Row And Column Headings option from the View tab of the Page Setup dialog box. Then, when you print the worksheet, the row numbers and column letters are printed too. That way, you can tell which cells the printed formulas refer to.

How to use the Go To Special command to audit a worksheet

Figure 18-2 shows you how to use the Go To Special command to audit a worksheet. As you can see, this command can help you identify cells with specific contents. If you select the Formulas option, for example, *Excel* selects all the cells that contain formulas as illustrated in figure 18-3. Then, you can use the keystroke combinations presented in this figure to move from one highlighted cell to another.

How to display the formulas in a worksheet

1. Select the Options command from the Tools menu and click on the View tab.
2. Select the Formulas option in the Window Options group, and *Excel* displays the formulas rather than the results of the formulas in the worksheet:

	A	B	C	D	E	F
1	Monthly Expenses		34222		SEPEXP	
2	September					
3				Dollar	Percent	
4		Budget	Expense	Variance	Variance	
5						
6	Salaries & Wages	50000	51784	=C6-B6	=D6/B6	
7	Rent & Utilities	17500	18222	=C7-B7	=D7/B7	
8	Miscellaneous	1500	1922	=C8-B8	=D8/B8	
9	Maintenance	7750	7912	=C9-B9	=D9/B9	
10	Supplies	8250	7211	=C10-B10	=D10/B10	
11						
12	Total	=SUM(B6:B10)	=SUM(C6:C10)	=SUM(D6:D10)	=D12/B12	
13						

How to print a worksheet that shows its formulas

1. Select the Row And Column Headings option in the View tab of the Page Setup dialog box.
2. Print the worksheet.

Notes

- To return to normal view, deselect the Formulas option in the View tab of the Options dialog box.
- You should save the worksheet before you select the Formulas option if you expect to make any formatting changes to the worksheet when its formulas are displayed.

Figure 18-1 How to display or print a worksheet that shows its formulas

Two other options that can help you analyze the formulas in a given row or column are the Row Differences and Column Differences options. When you use these options, *Excel* compares the formulas in the row or column with a selected cell in that row or column, called the *comparison cell*. Then, *Excel* selects any cells in that row or column that don't match the pattern in the comparison cell.

Access

Select the Go To command from the Edit menu, then click on the Special button in the Go To dialog box that appears.

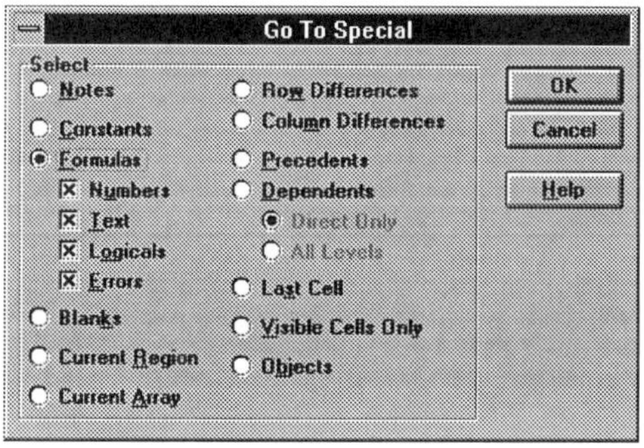

Option	Function	Keyboard shortcut
Notes	Selects cells with attached notes.	Ctrl+Shift+?
Constants	Selects cells with contents that don't start with an equals sign.	
Formulas	Selects cells with formulas that meet the criteria specified in the four check boxes that follow.	
Numbers	Selects cells with formulas that yield numbers.	
Text	Selects cells with formulas that yield text.	
Logicals	Selects cells with formulas that yield TRUE or FALSE values.	
Errors	Selects cells with formulas that yield errors.	
Blanks	Selects cells that are blank.	
Current Region	Selects all the cells in the current region, the rectangular range of cells bounded by blank rows and columns that includes the current cell.	Ctrl+* (numeric keypad)
Current Array	Selects all the cells in the current array, a rectangular range where all cells contain a formula similar to that in the current cell.	Ctrl+/
Row Differences	Selects cells in the same row as the current cell with contents that differ from the pattern in the current cell.	Ctrl+\
Column Differences	Selects cells in the same column as the current cell with contents that differ from the pattern in the current cell.	Ctrl+Shift+| (vertical bar)

Figure 18-2 How to use the Go To Special command to select cells in specific categories (part 1 of 2)

Option	Function	Keyboard shortcut
Precedents		
Direct Only	Selects cells that the formula in the current cell refer to directly.	Ctrl+[
All Levels	Selects cells that the formula in the current cell refer to directly or indirectly.	Ctrl+Shift+{
Dependents		
Direct Only	Selects cells with formulas that refer directly to the current cell.	Ctrl+]
All Levels	Selects cells with formulas that refer directly or indirectly to the current cell.	Ctrl+Shift+}
Last Cell	Selects the last cell that contains data or formatting.	
Visible Cells Only	Selects only the visible cells in the worksheet, not hidden rows or columns.	
Objects	Selects all graphic objects.	

Notes

- A selection you make using the Go To Special dialog box can include many non-adjacent cells and ranges.
- If you want to restrict the selection to cells in a specific range, select that range before you access the Go To Special dialog box. If you don't want to restrict the selection, select one cell before you access the dialog box.

Figure 18-2 How to use the Go To Special command to select cells in specific categories (part 2 of 2)

You can also use the Go To Special command to identify cell precedents and dependents. A *precedent* is a cell that's referred to by a formula. A *dependent* is a cell that contains a formula that refers to other cells. Although the Precedents and Dependents options can be useful, *Excel*'s Auditing commands and toolbar are usually more helpful for identifying and interpreting precedents and dependents.

A worksheet after the Go To Special command has been run using the Formulas option

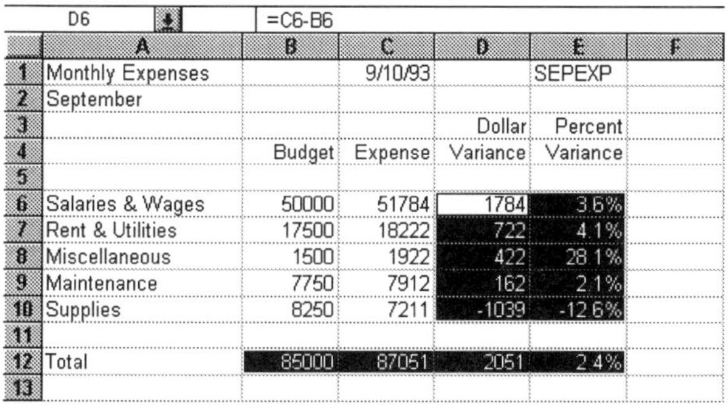

D6 =C6-B6

	A	B	C	D	E	F
1	Monthly Expenses		9/10/93		SEPEXP	
2	September					
3				Dollar	Percent	
4		Budget	Expense	Variance	Variance	
5						
6	Salaries & Wages	50000	51784	1784	3.6%	
7	Rent & Utilities	17500	18222	722	4.1%	
8	Miscellaneous	1500	1922	422	28.1%	
9	Maintenance	7750	7912	162	2.1%	
10	Supplies	8250	7211	-1039	-12.6%	
11						
12	Total	85000	87051	2051	2.4%	
13						

How to move from one highlighted cell to another

- Press Enter to go down to the next cell.
- Press Shift+Enter to go up to the previous cell.
- Press Tab to go right to the next cell.
- Press Shift+Tab to go left to the previous cell.

Notes

- Unless you want to select formulas in a specific category, leave the Numbers, Text, Logicals, and Errors options selected.
- As you move from one highlighted cell to another, you can review the formula each contains in the formula bar.

Figure 18-3 How to use the Formulas option to review the formulas in a worksheet

How to use *Excel*'s Auditing submenu and toolbar

You can also use the commands in the Auditing submenu of the Tools menu and the Auditing toolbar to audit a worksheet. This submenu and toolbar are presented in figure 18-4. Notice that you can use the last command in the Auditing submenu to display the Auditing toolbar. You'll learn how to use the rest of these commands and buttons in the remainder of this chapter.

The Auditing submenu of the Tools menu

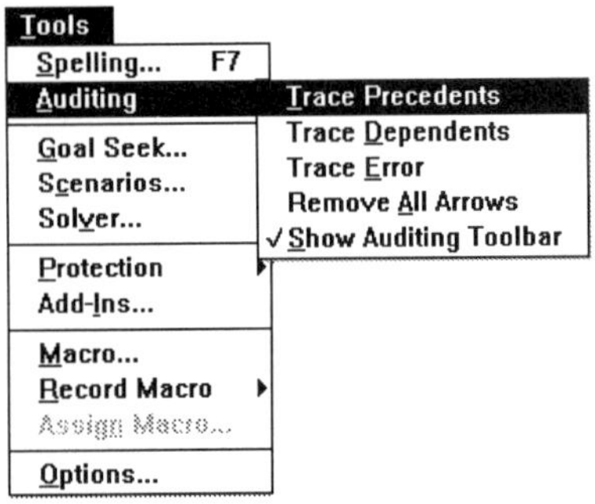

Command	Description
Trace Precedents	Draws arrows from cells that are precedents of the formula in the current cell. You can issue the command repeatedly to trace successive levels of precedents.
Trace Dependents	Draws arrows to cells that are dependents of the data in the current cell. You can issue the command repeatedly to trace successive levels of dependents.
Trace Error	Draws arrows to an error in the current cell from cells that may have caused the error.
Remove All Arrows	Removes all tracer arrows from the worksheet.
Show Auditing Toolbar	Displays or hides the Auditing toolbar.

Notes

- To use the Trace Error command, the current cell must contain an error. Red or dotted arrows point from the first precedent formula that contains an error, and blue or solid arrows point from precedents of that formula.
- *Excel* doesn't save tracer arrows when you close the workbook.
- You can double-click a tracer arrow to select the cell at the point end of the arrow. If you double-click the tracer arrow again, the cell at the opposite end of the arrow is selected.

Figure 18-4 How to use the Auditing submenu and toolbar (part 1 of 2)

How to trace precedents and dependents When you trace precedents or dependents using the Auditing commands or toolbar buttons, *Excel* adds *tracer arrows* to the worksheet. These arrows indicate the flow of data to or from the current cell. If you trace the precedents of a cell, the arrows indicate the flow of data into the formula in the current cell. If you trace the

The Auditing Toolbar

Button	Function
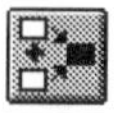	Draws arrows that trace precedents. Same as Trace Precedents command.
	Removes last set of precedent arrows drawn. Not available as a menu command.
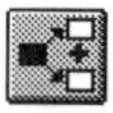	Draws arrows that trace dependents. Same as Trace Dependents command.
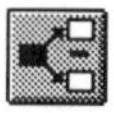	Removes last set of dependent arrows drawn. Not available as a menu command.
	Removes all tracer arrows. Same as Remove All Arrows command.
	Draws arrows that trace precedents of a formula that yielded an error. Same as Trace Error command.
	Accesses the Cell Note dialog box, which lets you add, display, or delete a note attached to the current cell.
	Displays the Info window, which contains information about the current cell.

Figure 18-4 How to use the Auditing submenu and the Auditing toolbar (part 2 of 2)

dependents of a cell, the arrows indicate the flow of data out of the current cell into other formulas in the worksheet. These arrows make it easy to see if the formulas in a worksheet are based on the correct cells.

Figure 18-5 presents the procedures for using the Trace Precedents and Trace Dependents commands and illustrates the resulting arrows. The figure also shows you how to remove one or more sets of precedent or dependent arrows. Notice that the Trace Precedents command can trace cells outside of the current worksheet. However, the Trace Dependents command can trace only cells in the current worksheet.

The first time you issue the Trace Precedents or Trace Dependents command for a selected cell, *Excel* traces the direct precedents or dependents of the cell. You can trace additional levels of precedents or dependents by using the Trace commands repeatedly. For example, figure 18-6 shows a worksheet with three levels of precedents traced. Although you may occasionally want to trace two or three levels of precedents or dependents, any additional levels are usually too complicated to interpret.

How to trace the direct precedents of the formula in a cell

1. Select the cell that contains the formula you're interested in.
2. Click on the Trace Precedents button in the Auditing toolbar or select the Trace Precedents command from the Auditing submenu of the Tools menu, and *Excel* draws tracer arrows from all cells that supply values directly to the formula:

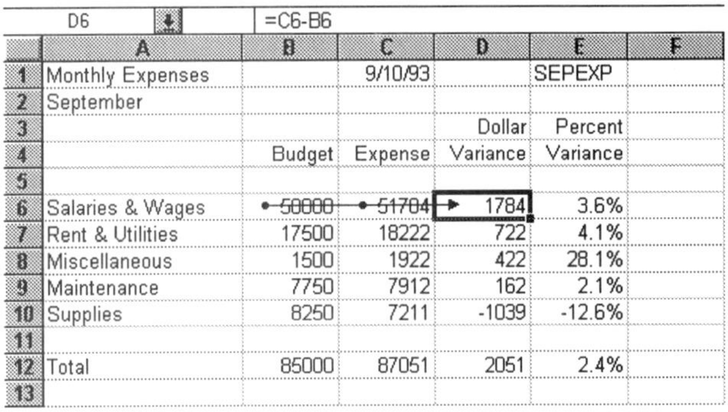

D6 | =C6-B6

	A	B	C	D	E	F
1	Monthly Expenses		9/10/93		SEPEXP	
2	September					
3				Dollar	Percent	
4		Budget	Expense	Variance	Variance	
5						
6	Salaries & Wages	50000	51784	1784	3.6%	
7	Rent & Utilities	17500	18222	722	4.1%	
8	Miscellaneous	1500	1922	422	28.1%	
9	Maintenance	7750	7912	162	2.1%	
10	Supplies	8250	7211	-1039	-12.6%	
11						
12	Total	85000	87051	2051	2.4%	
13						

How to trace the direct dependents of the data in a cell

1. Select the cell that contains the data you're interested in.
2. Click on the Trace Dependents button in the Auditing toolbar or select the Trace Dependents command from the Auditing submenu of the Tools menu, and *Excel* draws tracer arrows from the selected cell to all cells that contain formulas that refer directly to the selected cell:

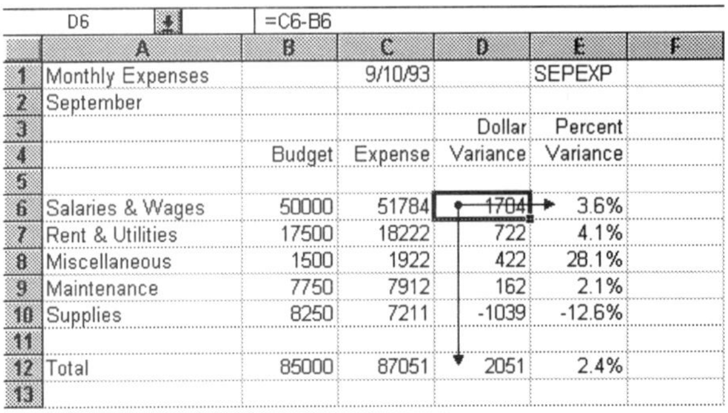

D6 | =C6-B6

	A	B	C	D	E	F
1	Monthly Expenses		9/10/93		SEPEXP	
2	September					
3				Dollar	Percent	
4		Budget	Expense	Variance	Variance	
5						
6	Salaries & Wages	50000	51784	1784	3.6%	
7	Rent & Utilities	17500	18222	722	4.1%	
8	Miscellaneous	1500	1922	422	28.1%	
9	Maintenance	7750	7912	162	2.1%	
10	Supplies	8250	7211	-1039	-12.6%	
11						
12	Total	85000	87051	2051	2.4%	
13						

Figure 18-5 How to add and remove arrows that trace precedents and dependents (part 1 of 2)

How to trace errors Figure 18-7 presents the procedure for tracing errors in a worksheet. In this example, a divide-by-zero error occurred in cell D11. Although it's easy to figure out why this error occurred without using the Trace Error command, other errors may not be so easy to find.

How to remove tracer arrows

- To remove the most recently drawn set of precedent arrows, click on the Remove Precedent Arrows button in the Auditing toolbar.
- To remove the most recently drawn set of dependent arrows, click on the Remove Dependent Arrows button in the Auditing toolbar.
- To remove all tracer arrows, click on the Remove All Arrows button in the Auditing toolbar or select the Remove All Arrows command from the Auditing submenu of the Tools menu.

Notes

- The Trace Precedents command has no effect if the active cell doesn't contain a formula.
- The Trace Dependents command has no effect if the active cell isn't referred to by any formula in the current worksheet.
- If a cell precedent resides in another worksheet, a special tracer arrow appears:

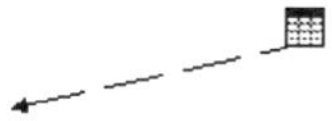

If you double-click on this arrow, the Go To dialog box appears with the workbook name, sheet name, and cell reference of the precedent. If the precedent is in the same workbook as the current worksheet or is in another open workbook, you can switch to the sheet that contains it.

Figure 18-5 How to add and remove arrows that trace precedents and dependents (part 2 of 2)

How to use cell notes Occasionally, you may want to include comments in a worksheet to describe a complex calculation or an unexpected value. One way to enter a comment is to type it directly into a cell. Another way is to enter it into a text box as described in chapter 13. If you use either of these techniques, however, the note is visible in the worksheet. If that's not what you want, you can enter the comment into a *cell note*.

Figure 18-8 presents the procedures for using cell notes. To add a note to a cell, you use the Attach Note button in the Auditing toolbar or the Note command in the Insert menu or its keyboard shortcut (Shift+F2). When a note is attached to a cell, a red rectangle called a *cell note indicator* appears in the upper right corner of the cell.

You can also use the Attach Note button or the Note command to display or delete existing notes. If you want to delete all the cell notes in a worksheet, use the Go To Special command to select all the notes, then select the Clear Notes command from the Edit menu to delete them. You can also print the cell notes in a worksheet by selecting the Notes option in the Sheet tab of the Page Setup dialog box.

The first time you trace precedents, *Excel* draws tracer arrows from the direct precedents of the current cell:

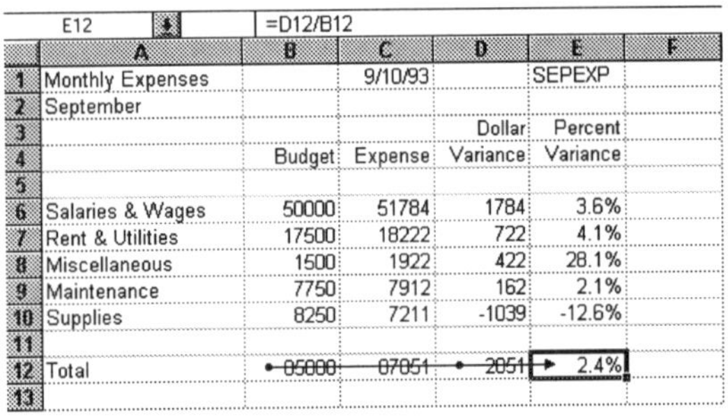

E12 =D12/B12

	A	B	C	D	E	F
1	Monthly Expenses		9/10/93		SEPEXP	
2	September					
3				Dollar	Percent	
4		Budget	Expense	Variance	Variance	
5						
6	Salaries & Wages	50000	51784	1784	3.6%	
7	Rent & Utilities	17500	18222	722	4.1%	
8	Miscellaneous	1500	1922	422	28.1%	
9	Maintenance	7750	7912	162	2.1%	
10	Supplies	8250	7211	-1039	-12.6%	
11						
12	Total	85000	87051	2051	2.4%	
13						

The second time, *Excel* draws tracer arrows to the direct precedents from their precedents:

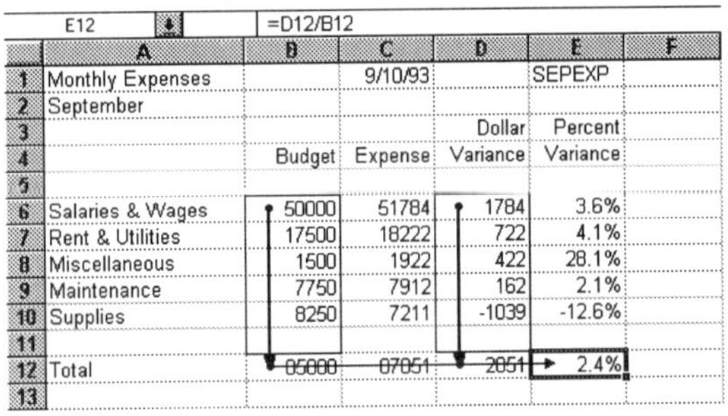

E12 =D12/B12

	A	B	C	D	E	F
1	Monthly Expenses		9/10/93		SEPEXP	
2	September					
3				Dollar	Percent	
4		Budget	Expense	Variance	Variance	
5						
6	Salaries & Wages	50000	51784	1784	3.6%	
7	Rent & Utilities	17500	18222	722	4.1%	
8	Miscellaneous	1500	1922	422	28.1%	
9	Maintenance	7750	7912	162	2.1%	
10	Supplies	8250	7211	-1039	-12.6%	
11						
12	Total	85000	87051	2051	2.4%	
13						

And the third time, *Excel* draws tracer arrows to the second-level precedents from their precedents:

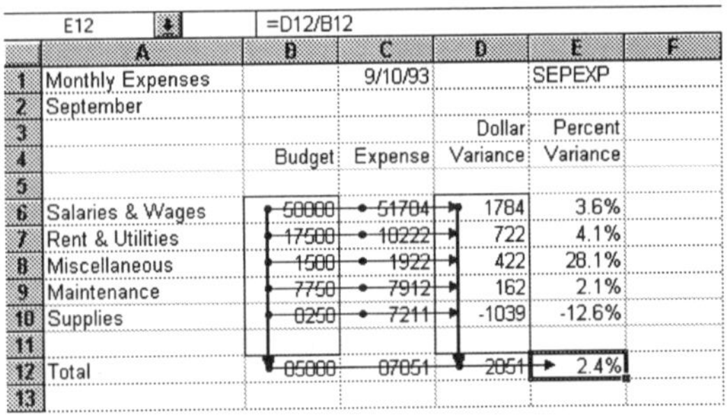

E12 =D12/B12

	A	B	C	D	E	F
1	Monthly Expenses		9/10/93		SEPEXP	
2	September					
3				Dollar	Percent	
4		Budget	Expense	Variance	Variance	
5						
6	Salaries & Wages	50000	51784	1784	3.6%	
7	Rent & Utilities	17500	18222	722	4.1%	
8	Miscellaneous	1500	1922	422	28.1%	
9	Maintenance	7750	7912	162	2.1%	
10	Supplies	8250	7211	-1039	-12.6%	
11						
12	Total	85000	87051	2051	2.4%	
13						

Note

If you add more than two or three levels of tracer arrows to a worksheet, they will probably be difficult to interpret. If you need to trace through several levels, however, you can do it by adding the arrows for the first level, then noting which cells are on the path you're interested in and removing the arrows. Then, you can trace the next level by moving the cell pointer to a cell on the first path and adding arrows again. You can repeat this procedure as many times as necessary to get to the level you want without cluttering the display with arrows.

Figure 18-6 How to trace multiple levels of precedents

Procedure

1. Select the cell that contains the error you want to trace:

D11 | =AVERAGE(D3:D9)

	A	B	C	D	E
1	Employee ID	Salary for pay period	Hours clocked during pay period	Equivalent hourly wage	
2					
3	1001	$1,750.00	83.25	$21.02	
4	1002	$1,000.00	0.00	#DIV/0!	
5	1003	$1,000.00	70.00	$14.29	
6	2001	$1,250.00	80.00	$15.63	
7	2002	$1,500.00	81.75	$18.35	
8	2003	$1,450.00	80.00	$18.13	
9	2004	$1,275.00	60.00	$21.25	
10					
11		Averages:	65.00	#DIV/0!	
12					

2. Click on the Trace Error button in the Auditing toolbar or select the Trace Error command from the Auditing submenu of the Tools menu, and *Excel* draws tracer arrows from cells that might have caused the error:

D4 | =B4/C4

	A	B	C	D	E
1	Employee ID	Salary for pay period	Hours clocked during pay period	Equivalent hourly wage	
2					
3	1001	$1,750.00	83.25	$21.02	
4	1002	$1,000.00	0.00	#DIV/0!	
5	1003	$1,000.00	70.00	$14.29	
6	2001	$1,250.00	80.00	$15.63	
7	2002	$1,500.00	81.75	$18.35	
8	2003	$1,450.00	80.00	$18.13	
9	2004	$1,275.00	60.00	$21.25	
10					
11		Averages:	65.00	#DIV/0!	
12					

Notes

- The Trace Error button or command has no effect if the active cell doesn't contain an error.
- *Excel* draws red or dotted arrows from the first precedent formula that contains an error. To that formula, *Excel* draws blue or solid arrows from its precedents.

Figure 18-7 How to trace errors

How to display or print detailed cell information If you want to display detailed information about a cell, you can open the Info window as illustrated in figure 18-9. When you open this window, *Excel* displays a variety of information about the current cell. To display information for another cell, just select the cell in the worksheet.

How to add a note to a cell

1. Select the cell you want to attach a note to.
2. Click on the Attach Note button in the Auditing toolbar, select the Note command from the Insert menu, or press Shift+F2, and this dialog box appears:

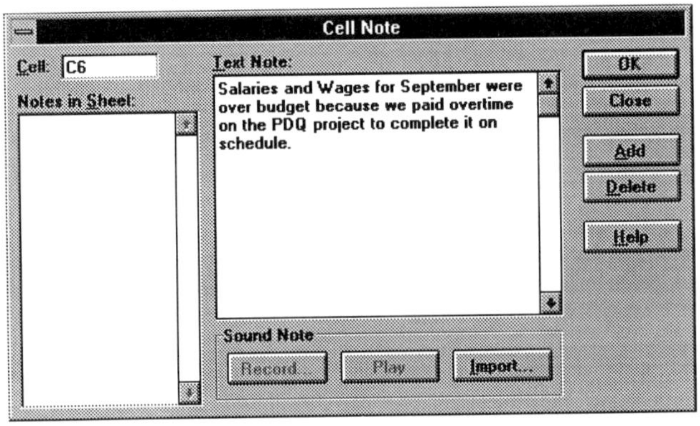

3. Enter the note in the Text Note box, or select a note from the Notes In Sheet list box to display it in the Text Note box. Edit the note if necessary.
4. Click on the OK button, and the note is added to the cell as indicated by the red rectangle in the upper right corner of the cell:

How to display a cell note

1. Select the cell that contains the note you want to display.
2. Click on the Attach Note button in the Auditing toolbar, select the Note command from the Insert menu, or press Shift+F2, and the Cell Note dialog box appears with the note for the selected cell in the Text Note box.

How to delete a cell note

Use the procedure above for displaying a cell note, then click on the Delete button.

Notes

- If you want to add more than one note, click on the Add button instead of the OK button and the Cell Note dialog box remains open. The note you just added appears in the Notes In Sheet list box. To add another note, enter the cell reference in the Cell text box, then enter the note.
- You can record, play back, or import a sound clip as a note using the buttons in the Sound Note group. These options require a sound card.
- You can delete all the notes in a worksheet by using the Go To Special command to select them, then using the Clear Notes command to delete them.
- You can print notes by selecting the Notes option in the Sheet tab of the Page Setup dialog box.
- You can remove the cell note indicator by deselecting the Note Indicator option in the View tab of the Options dialog box.

Figure 18-8 How to use cell notes

An *Excel* screen with a workbook window and the Info window

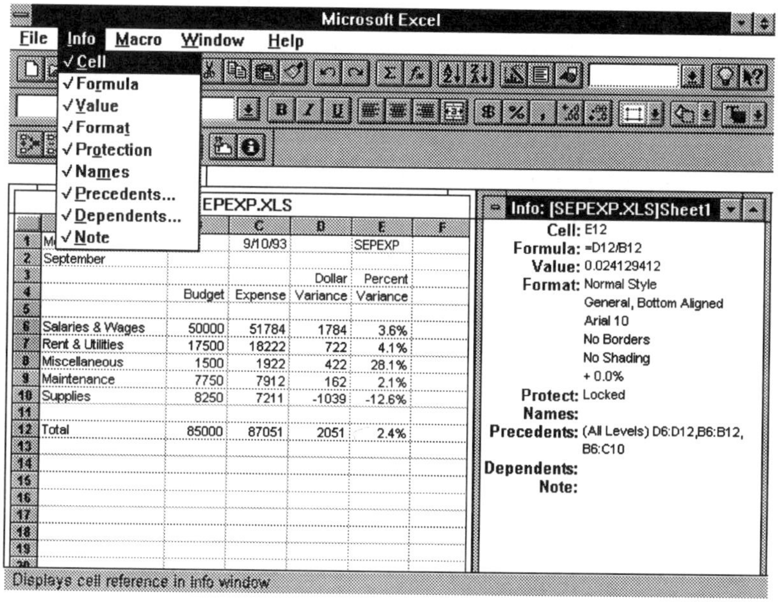

Operation

- To open the Info window, click on the Show Info Window button in the Auditing toolbar or select the Info Window option from the View tab of the Options dialog box. By default, the window displays information for the current cell.
- To display information for another cell, select the cell in the worksheet.
- To change the information that's displayed in the Info window, select or deselect the appropriate commands from the Info menu. By default, the Cell, Formula, and Note commands are selected.
- To print the information in the Info window, use the Print command in the File menu with the window active. To print information for more than one cell at the same time, select the cells in the worksheet, then switch to the Info window and issue the Print command.

Note

You can use standard techniques to switch between the Info window and the workbook window and to arrange the windows on the screen.

Figure 18-9 How to use the Info window

Notice that when the Info window is active, the *Excel* menu changes. In figure 18-9, the Info menu is pulled down. This menu contains the commands that determine what information is displayed in the Info window. In this case, all of the available information is displayed. By default, only the cell reference, formula, and note are displayed.

In general, the Info window isn't very useful. If you want to know the precedents of a cell, for example, using the Trace Precedents commands is much more effective than displaying the precedents in the Info window. However, you may want to use the Info window to create printed documentation of the cells in a worksheet. To print the contents of the Info window, activate the window, then issue the Print command from the File menu. To print information for more than one cell at the same time, select the cells in the worksheet, then switch to the Info window and issue the Print command.

Perspective

You can audit most worksheets without using the commands in this chapter. For some worksheets, though, these commands can help you audit more efficiently. That's particularly true when you're auditing someone else's worksheet or a worksheet that you haven't used in a while. But whether or not you use these commands, you should check the formulas in every worksheet you create to make sure that they are producing accurate results.

Summary

- To display a worksheet's formulas, select the Formulas option from the View tab of the Options dialog box. Then, you can use the Page Setup command to set up the printed page so it includes the column letters and row numbers.
- You can use the Go To Special command to select cells that meet specific criteria, such as all the cells that contain a formula.
- You can use the commands in the Auditing submenu of the Tools menu and the Auditing toolbar to trace cell *precedents*, *dependents*, and errors and to remove *tracer arrows*. The Auditing toolbar also contains buttons that let you add, display, or delete *cell notes* and display detailed cell information in the Info window.

Chapter 19

How to create and use recorded macros

The *macro* feature of *Excel* lets you perform a series of operations as if they were a single operation. For instance, you can create a simple macro that will put the TODAY function in a cell and format it with a date format. Later, you can perform those operations just by running the macro.

If you're like most *Excel* users, you probably won't ever develop macros for anything other than automating tasks you perform over and over, so that's what this chapter emphasizes. First, you'll learn the basic skills for recording and running macros. Then, you'll learn how to assign a macro to a button and how to move and copy macros to another workbook.

If you've developed macros for earlier releases of *Excel* or for other spreadsheet programs, you'll be interested to know that the macro capabilities of *Excel* 5.0 are based on a full-fledged programming language called *Microsoft Visual Basic Programming System, Applications Edition*, or just *Visual Basic*. You can use Visual Basic to write and test custom *Excel* applications. However, because you're not likely to need to work directly with Visual Basic, this chapter doesn't cover it. For more information, refer to the *Visual Basic User's Guide* that comes with *Excel*.

You should also know that *Excel* can open and manipulate spreadsheet files created in earlier releases of *Excel*, in *Lotus 1-2-3,* and in *Quattro Pro for DOS*, and it can successfully run macros those files contain. As a result, if you have a large investment in macros written for *Excel*, *1-2-3*, or *Quattro Pro*, you won't lose it when you move to *Excel* 5.0.

Basic skills for recording and running macros

To record and run a macro, you can use the Macro and Record Macro commands on the Tools menu, or you can use the buttons on the Visual Basic toolbar. Figure 19-1 presents this toolbar and the buttons for recording and running macros. The other buttons are for Visual Basic programming tasks that are beyond the needs of the typical *Excel* user.

How to record a macro Figure 19-2 presents the procedure for recording a macro. When you start the *Macro Recorder*, *Excel* captures every operation you perform and translates it into Visual Basic statements. As a result, you should carefully plan what you want a macro to do before you start recording it. In fact, it makes sense to practice the actions you want to automate in a macro before you record them. When you're done recording a macro, be sure to turn the Macro Recorder off so no additional operations are recorded.

Access

Select the Toolbars command from the View menu, then select the Visual Basic toolbar, or select the Visual Basic toolbar directly from the toolbar shortcut menu.

Buttons for recording and running macros

Button	Function
	Displays the Macro dialog box, which lets you select and run a macro. Same as the Macro command on the Tools menu.
	Stops the Macro Recorder. Same as the Stop Recording command on the Record Macro submenu of the Tools menu.
	Displays the Record New Macro dialog box, which lets you name, set options for, and start recording a new macro. Same as the Record New Macro command on the Record Macro submenu of the Tools menu.

Note

The other buttons on the Visual Basic toolbar are for commands related to programming in Visual Basic. If you use macros for basic tasks as described in this chapter, you'll never need to use these features.

Figure 19-1 The buttons on the Visual Basic toolbar for recording and running macros

If you use the procedure in figure 19-2 to record a macro, you can run the macro by selecting its name from a list of macros as you'll see in a moment. However, you can also assign a macro to a shortcut key or to a command on the Tools menu. To do that, you click on the Options button in the Record New Macro dialog box and the dialog box expands to include additional options. To assign a macro to a menu command, you select the Menu Item On Tools Menu option and enter a command name. To assign a macro to a shortcut key, you select the Shortcut Key option and enter the key you want to use.

By default, a recorded macro is stored in a *macro sheet* in the current workbook. The macro sheets are named Module1, Module2, and so on. If you want to change where the macro is stored, you can do that by selecting one of the options in the Store In group in the expanded Record New Macro dialog box. If you select the Personal Macro Workbook option, the macro is

Procedure

1. Position the cursor where you want to start recording.
2. Click on the Record button in the Visual Basic toolbar or select the Record New Macro command from the Record Macro submenu of the Tools menu, and this dialog box appears:

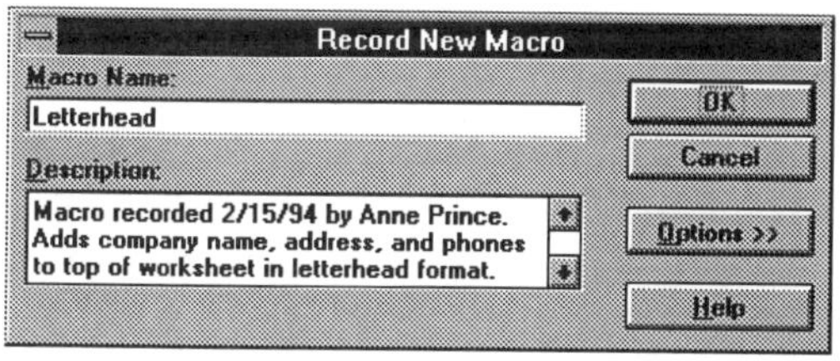

3. Enter a name and description for the macro, then click on the OK button to start the Macro Recorder and the Stop Recording button appears.
4. Perform all of the actions you want to record in the macro:

5. Click on the Stop Recording button, or select the Stop Recording command from the Record Macro submenu of the Tools menu to turn the Macro Recorder off.

Figure 19-2 How to record a macro (part 1 of 2)

stored in your *personal macro workbook*. This workbook is a file named PERSONAL.XLS that's usually in the XLSTART subdirectory of the EXCEL directory. *Excel* opens this file automatically every time it starts, so the macros it contains are always available to you. You won't notice this file is open, however, because it's hidden. That way, its window won't get in your way as you work.

Because your personal macro workbook is always open, that's where you'll want to store macros you record for your own use. If you record macros that you want others to be able to use, however, you'll want to store them in another workbook. The other two options in the Store In group

Notes

- The operations you can record in a macro include keystrokes, mouse actions, menu commands, and toolbar button selections.
- The name you assign to a macro must begin with a letter and can contain letters, numbers and underscores, but no spaces or other punctuation marks. If you don't supply a name for a new macro, *Excel* assigns one in the format Macro*x*, such as Macro4.
- The Stop Recording toolbar appears automatically when you start to record a macro, unless it's been explicitly closed after a previous recording session. If it has been closed, you can redisplay it by issuing the Toolbars command from the View menu, then selecting the Stop Recording option.
- If you click on the Options button in the Record New Macro dialog box, the dialog box is expanded to include some additional options:

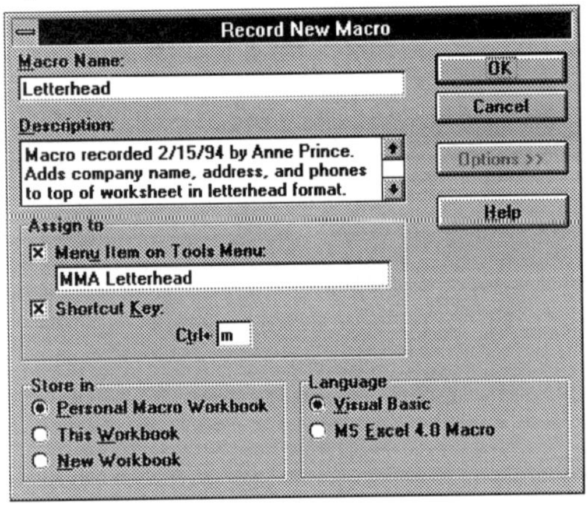

  You can add the Macro to the Tools menu by selecting the Menu Item On Tools Menu option and entering a name for the menu item, and you can assign the macro to a shortcut key by selecting the Shortcut Key option and entering the key. You can also select where the macro is stored by selecting one of the options in the Store In group. By default, the macro is stored in the current worksheet.
- By default, all cell references recorded in a macro are recorded as absolute references. If you want to record cell references as relative references, select the Use Relative References command from the Record Macro submenu of the Tools menu. You can change this option any time you want while you're recording a macro.

Figure 19-2 How to record a macro (part 2 of 2)

store a macro in the current workbook or in a new workbook. If you want to store a macro in an existing workbook other than the current workbook or your personal macro workbook, you have to copy or move it to that workbook after you record it. You'll learn how to copy or move a macro to another workbook later in this chapter.

One more setting you should be aware of when you record a macro is whether cell references are recorded as absolute or relative references. By default, all the cell references in a recorded macro are absolute. In that case, the macro is always executed on the same cells in a worksheet. If you want to record cell references as relative references, select the Use Relative References command from the Record Macro submenu of the Tools menu. Then, the current position of the cell pointer determines the cells on which the macro is executed. You can change the relative/absolute setting any time you want as you're recording a macro, so a macro can contain both relative and absolute references.

How to run a macro Figure 19-3 lists four ways to run a macro. If you assigned the macro to a keyboard shortcut or to a menu command, you can run it by typing the shortcut keys or by selecting the command from the Tools menu. You can run any macro by clicking on the Run Macro button in the Visual Basic toolbar or by selecting the Macro command from the Tools menu and selecting the macro from the Macro dialog box. The macros you can run using these techniques must be stored in your personal macro workbook or another open workbook.

You can also assign a macro to a toolbar or graphics button. I'll show you how to do that in a moment. If you assign a macro to a toolbar button, you can run the macro from any worksheet by displaying the toolbar that contains the button and clicking on it. If you assign a macro to a graphics button, you can run it only from the worksheet that contains the button.

When you run a macro, you should know that you can interrupt its execution by pressing the Esc key or the Ctrl+Break key combination at any time. You might want to do this if you accidentally run the wrong macro or if for some reason you don't want the macro to finish executing. When you interrupt a macro, *Excel* displays the Macro Error dialog box. From this dialog box, you can terminate the macro, you can continue executing the macro, you can debug the macro, or you can display the Visual Basic code for the macro.

Four ways to run a macro

- If you assigned the macro to a keyboard shortcut, type the shortcut keys.
- If you assigned a menu command to the macro, select the command from the Tools menu.
- To run any macro, click on the Run Macro button in the Visual Basic toolbar or select the Macro command from the Tools menu, and this dialog box appears:

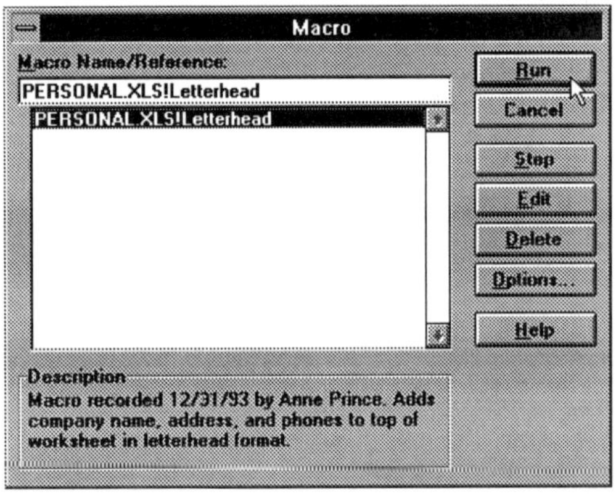

  Select the macro you want to run from the Macro Name/Reference list box, and click on the Run button.

- Assign the macro to a toolbar or graphics button, then click on the button. (See figure 19-4 for details on how to assign a macro to a button.)

Notes

- You can run a macro that's stored in any open workbook using the first three techniques. You can run a macro that's assigned to a toolbar button from any worksheet where the toolbar is displayed. And you can run a macro that's assigned to a graphics button only from the worksheet that contains the button.
- If the macro you want to run uses only absolute cell references, it doesn't matter where the cell pointer is positioned when you start it. Otherwise, you should position the cell pointer in the appropriate location before you run the macro.
- You can interrupt a macro while it's running by pressing the Esc key or Ctrl+Break. When you do, the Macro Error dialog box appears, which lets you terminate the macro, resume execution of the macro, debug the macro, or display the Visual Basic code for the macro.
- The Step button lets you monitor a macro as it runs, the Edit button lets you access and change the Visual Basic code for the macro, and the Delete button lets you delete the macro.
- The Options button displays the Macro Options dialog box where you can change the macro description, menu item, and shortcut key. Additionally, the Macro Options dialog box lets you specify a text string that describes what the macro does. *Excel* displays this description in the status bar when a menu command associated with a macro is highlighted or when the mouse pointer is over a toolbar button assigned to a macro.

Figure 19-3 How to run a macro

Other skills for using macros

After you've recorded a macro, you may want to assign it to a button to make it easier to run. And, you may want to copy or move the macro from one workbook to another to make it accessible to other users. You'll learn both of these skills in the second part of this chapter.

How to assign a macro to a button Figure 19-4 presents the procedures for assigning a macro to a toolbar button and a graphics button. In both cases, you use the Assign Macro dialog box, which lists the macros that you can assign to the button. If you like using toolbar buttons, you'll probably want to assign macros you use often to custom toolbar buttons. In contrast, you're unlikely to want to assign a macro to a graphics button. Since graphics buttons are available only from the worksheet that contains them, they're of limited use unless you're developing applications in Visual Basic.

How to copy or move a macro to another workbook When you record a macro, you can store it in the current workbook, in a new workbook, or in your personal macro workbook. If you want to store the macro in another existing workbook, you have to move or copy the macro sheet to that workbook after you record the macro. For example, you may want to copy a macro to a shared workbook so that other users can access it.

Figure 19-5 presents the procedures for moving and copying a macro to another workbook. To do that, you use the Move or Copy Sheet command in the Edit menu. When you use this command, both the source and destination workbooks must be open. In addition, if one of the workbooks is your personal macro workbook, you must reveal it before you can perform the move or copy operation. To reveal a hidden workbook, you use the Unhide command in the Window menu.

From the Move or Copy dialog box, you select the workbook you want to move or copy the selected macro sheet to, you indicate where in the workbook you want to place the macro sheet, and you indicate whether you want to move or copy the macro sheet. Note that if the workbook where you're inserting the macro sheet contains a sheet with the same name as the sheet you're inserting, *Excel* renames the sheet. For example, if the sheet you're inserting is named Module1 and the sheet already contains a sheet with that name, the new sheet is named Module1(2). If you insert another sheet named Module1, it's inserted with the name Module1(3), and so on.

How to assign a macro to a custom toolbar button

1. Select the Toolbars command from the View menu or the toolbar shortcut menu, and the Toolbars dialog box appears.
2. Click on the Customize button and the Customize dialog box appears.
3. Select the Custom option from the Categories list box, then add any button in the Custom category to any visible toolbar by dragging it into the toolbar and this dialog box appears:

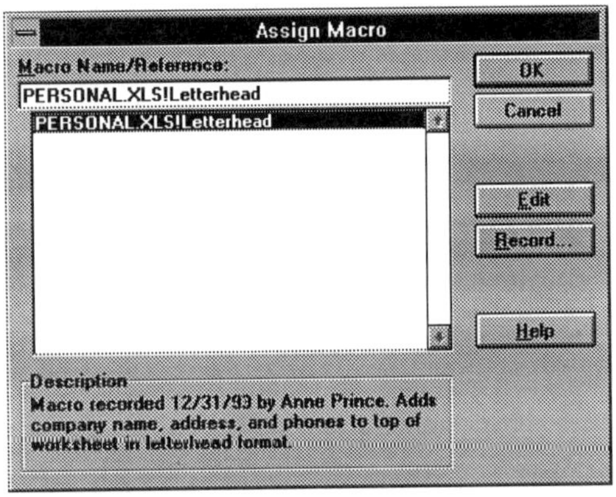

4. Select the macro you want to assign to the toolbar button.
5. Click on the OK button, and *Excel* returns you to the Customize dialog box. Click on the Close button.

How to assign a macro to a graphics button

1. Click on the Drawing button in the Standard toolbar to display the Drawing toolbar.
2. Click on the Create Button button, then drag the outline for the new button across the worksheet where you want it to appear. When you release the mouse button, *Excel* displays the Assign Macro dialog box.
3. Select the macro you want to assign to the graphics button.
4. Click on the OK button.

Notes

- You can use the techniques presented in chapter 13 to change the text on the face of a graphics button and its font, size, style, and color.
- To assign a different macro to an existing graphics button, select the button with the graphics selection tool, then select the Assign Macro command from the Tools menu and select a new macro.
- To assign a different macro to an existing toolbar button, select the button with the Customize dialog box open, then select the Assign Macro command from the Tools menu and select a new macro.
- The Edit button lets you edit a macro before you assign it to a button, and the Record button lets you record a new macro to be assigned to the button.

Figure 19-4 How to assign a macro to a button

How to move a macro sheet to another workbook

1. Open the source workbook and the destination workbook.
2. In the source workbook, select the tab for the macro sheet you want to move or copy.
3. Select the Move or Copy Sheet command from the Edit menu, and this dialog box appears:

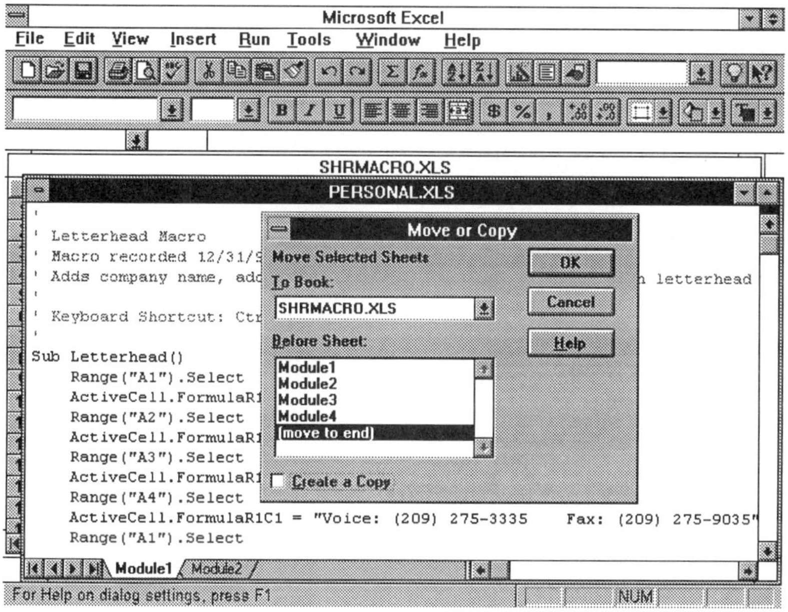

4. Select the name of the destination workbook from the To Book drop-down list box.
5. Specify where you want to insert the macro sheet in the destination workbook by selecting an option from the Before Sheet list box.
6. Click on the OK button.

How to copy a macro sheet to another workbook

Use the procedure above, but select the Create A Copy option.

Notes

- You can move or copy more than one macro sheet at a time.
- If either the source or destination workbook is your personal macro workbook (PERSONAL.XLS), you must reveal it using the Unhide command in the Window menu before you can use this procedure.
- If the destination workbook already contains a macro sheet with the same name as the sheet you're moving or copying, a number in parentheses is added to the end of the name. For example, a sheet named Module1 is inserted with the name Module1(2) to indicate that it's the second module named Module 1.

Figure 19-5 How to copy or move a macro sheet to another workbook

Perspective

Although it's easy to record simple macros, don't get carried away with this. It can easily take more time to create a macro than you'll ever save by using it. So be sure it makes sense to create a macro before you actually create it. In general, the more a macro is used, the more sense it makes to create it. What you don't want to do is to take several hours to create macros that save you several seconds each time you use them.

Before you start creating macros, you may want to check the software catalogs and documentation for *Excel* to see if a set of macros or an add-in is already available for the functions you're interested in. If, for example, you're thinking about developing macros for accounting or statistical functions, you can probably find an add-in that does what you want. For instance, *Excel*'s Data Analysis add-in lets you perform common, yet sophisticated, statistical operations. This add-in and others come with *Excel*, and many others are available for purchase. Often, buying a set of macros or an add-in can pay for itself many times over by saving you dozens of hours of development time.

Summary

- You can use a *macro* to perform a series of operations as if they were a single operation.
- To start the *Macro Recorder*, you can click on the Record New Macro button in the Visual Basic toolbar, or you can select the Record New Macro command from the Record Macro submenu of the Tools menu.
- The Macro Recorder captures the operations you perform and translates them into *Visual Basic* statements. These statements are stored as a *procedure* in a worksheet called a *macro sheet.*
- You can run a macro by clicking on the Run Macro button in the Visual Basic toolbar or by selecting the Run Macro command from the Tools menu, then selecting the macro from the Macro dialog box. You can also assign a macro to a keyboard shortcut, a command on the Tools menu, a toolbar button, or a graphics button.
- You can direct *Excel* to store a newly recorded macro in the current workbook, a new workbook, or your *personal macro workbook*. Your personal macro workbook is a file named PERSONAL.XLS that *Excel* opens automatically as a hidden file when it starts. Every macro it contains is automatically available to you.

- You can copy or move a macro sheet from one workbook to another using the Move or Copy Sheet command in the Edit menu.

Chapter 20

How to get the most from toolbars

Many of the *Excel* commands are associated with *toolbar buttons*. Because you can issue a command simply by clicking on its button, using the toolbar buttons can improve your productivity. But to get the most out of the toolbar buttons, you should display them in a way that makes them easiest for you to use. More importantly, you should customize the toolbars so the buttons you use most are available in the toolbars you use regularly. In this chapter, you'll learn how to display and customize toolbars for maximum efficiency.

How to change the toolbar display

To execute the command associated with a toolbar button, you have to display the toolbar that contains the button. You can do that using the toolbar shortcut menu or the Toolbars command in the View menu. You'll learn how to use these two techniques now. In addition, you'll learn how to change the position and configuration of the toolbar display.

How to use the toolbar shortcut menu Figure 20-1 presents the shortcut menu that's displayed when you click the right mouse button on a toolbar. Most of the commands listed in this menu are the names of toolbars. If a toolbar name has a check mark in front of it, that means that toolbar is currently displayed. To display or hide a toolbar, you click on its name.

The last two commands in the shortcut menu display dialog boxes that let you perform additional toolbar functions. You'll learn how to use the Toolbars command now, and you'll learn how to use the Customize command later in this chapter.

How to use the Toolbars command Figure 20-2 presents the dialog box that's displayed when you select the Toolbars command from the View menu or the toolbar shortcut menu. The check boxes with an "X" in them indicate the toolbars that are currently displayed. You can hide or display a toolbar by clicking on its name. From this dialog box, you can also reset a built-in toolbar to its original configuration or delete a user-defined toolbar. You can also customize a toolbar or create a new toolbar. I'll show you how to perform these two functions later in this chapter.

Access

Click on a toolbar with the right mouse button.

Command	**Function**
toolbar name	Displays or hides the named toolbar.
Toolbars	Displays the Toolbars dialog box so you can change the toolbar display.
Customize	Displays the Customize dialog box so you can customize a toolbar.

Note

Not all of the available toolbars are included in the shortcut menu.

Figure 20-1 The toolbar shortcut menu

How to change the position and configuration of a toolbar Figure 20-3 shows you how to change the position and configuration of a toolbar. As you can see, you can drag a toolbar to move it. If you drag a *docked toolbar* out of its *toolbar dock*, it becomes a *floating toolbar*. The toolbar docks are located at the top of the window between the menu bar and the formula bar, at the bottom of the window, and on the left and right sides of the window. Notice that as you drag a toolbar into the different toolbar docks, the toolbar changes size to conform to the dock. You can also change a docked toolbar to a floating toolbar or vice versa by double-clicking on the toolbar background.

A floating toolbar is a separate window that's displayed in the middle of the application window. You can move and size a floating toolbar window just as you can any other window. To hide a floating toolbar, you can use one of the techniques presented earlier in this chapter, or you can click on the close box in the upper left corner of the toolbar window.

Access

Select the Toolbars command from the View menu or the toolbar shortcut menu.

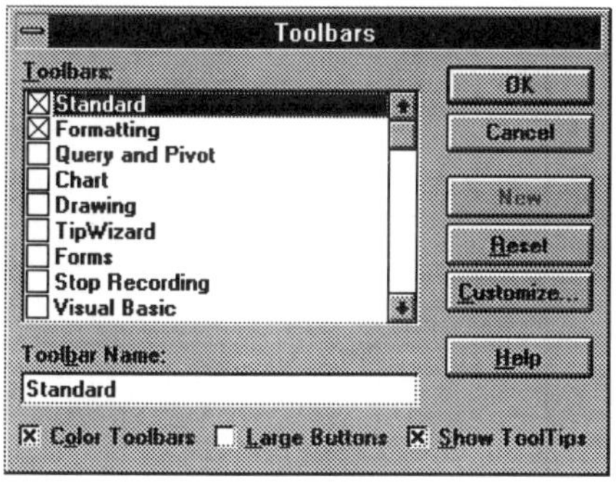

Operation

- To hide or display a toolbar, click on its name in the Toolbars list box.
- To reset a built-in toolbar to its original configuration, highlight the toolbar name in the Toolbars list box and click on the Reset button.
- To delete a user-defined toolbar, highlight the toolbar name in the Toolbars list box and click on the Delete button. The Reset button changes to Delete when you highlight a user-defined toolbar. You can't delete a built-in toolbar.
- To modify a toolbar, highlight the toolbar name in the Toolbars list box and click on the Customize button. See figure 20-4 for details.
- To create a new toolbar, enter its name in the Toolbar Name text box and click on the New button. See figure 20-5 for details.

Note

The three options at the bottom of the Toolbars dialog box let you select whether the buttons are displayed in black and white or color, the size of the buttons, and whether the name of the button is displayed when you place the pointer on it. The Large Buttons option is particularly useful if your monitor is set at a high resolution and the default button size is too small.

Figure 20-2 How to use the Toolbars command

How to customize the toolbars

Although *Excel* provides several built-in toolbars, it's likely that none of them contains all the buttons you use most frequently. Fortunately, you can change the built-in toolbars and create new toolbars that suit your needs. You can also assign a macro you create to a button, and you can edit a button's image.

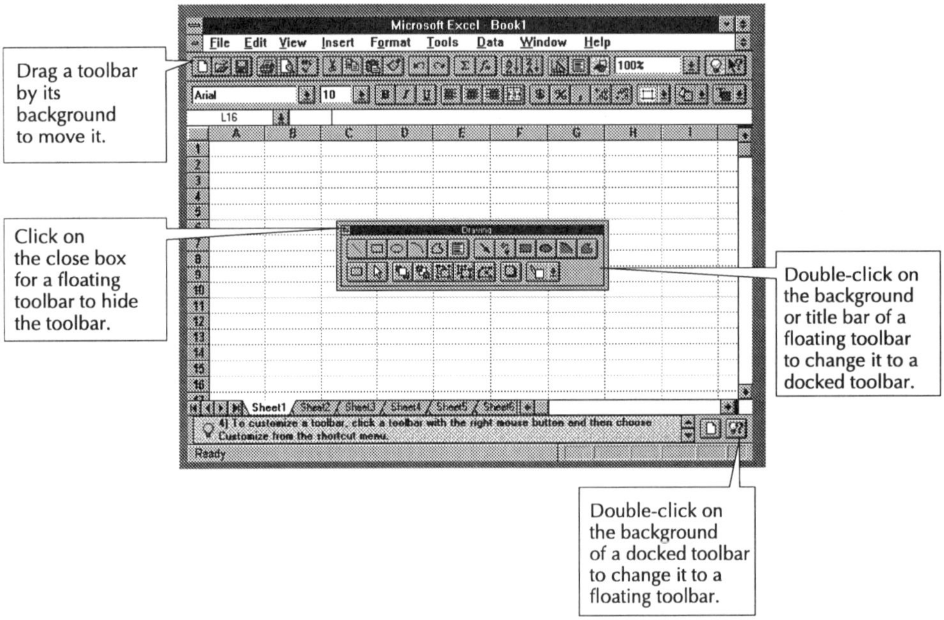

Notes

- You can dock a toolbar between the menu bar and the formula bar, at the bottom of the application window, or on the left or right side of the application window.
- A toolbar that contains a drop-down list or palette can't be docked on the left or right side of the window.
- You can move and size a floating toolbar just as you can any other window.

Figure 20-3 How to change the position and configuration of a toolbar

How to modify a toolbar To modify a toolbar, you use the Customize dialog box presented in figure 20-4. From this dialog box, you can add a button to a toolbar, you can delete a button from a toolbar, and you can move a button to a new location in the same toolbar. Note that to perform any of these operations, the toolbar you're modifying must be displayed.

How to create a new toolbar To create a new toolbar, you use the procedure presented in figure 20-5. From the Toolbars dialog box, you enter the name of the toolbar. Then, when you click on the New button, *Excel* displays the Customize dialog box along with a blank toolbar. Now, you can

Two ways to access the Customize dialog box

- Select the Customize command from the toolbar shortcut menu.
- Click on the Customize button in the Toolbars dialog box.

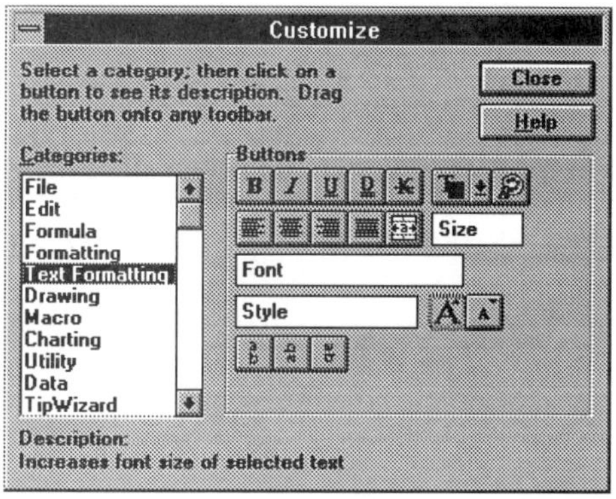

Operation

- To add a button to a toolbar, select the category that contains the button from the Categories list box and drag the button from the Buttons box to the toolbar.
- To move a button to a new location, drag it in the toolbar.
- To delete a button from a toolbar, drag it off of the toolbar.

Notes

- The toolbar you want to modify must be displayed to perform any of these operations.
- You can click on any button in the Buttons box to display a description of the button at the bottom of the dialog box. The button whose description is displayed is indicated by a dashed border.

Figure 20-4 How to modify a toolbar

use the technique presented in figure 20-4 to add buttons to the toolbar. If you need to, you can also delete and move buttons from the toolbar using the techniques in figure 20-4.

How to assign a macro to a custom button If you frequently perform a function that's not assigned to a built-in toolbar button, you may want to create a macro for that function as described in chapter 19. As you learned in that chapter, one way to run a macro is to assign it to a toolbar button. To do that, you use the procedure in figure 20-6.

1. Select the Toolbars command from the View menu or the toolbar shortcut menu, and this dialog box appears:

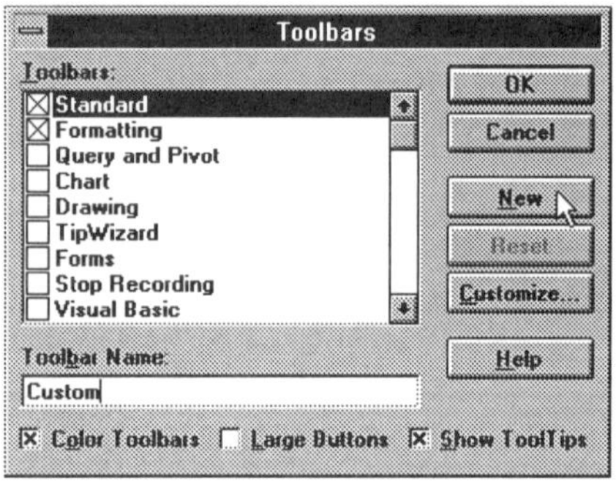

2. Enter the name of the toolbar in the Toolbar Name text box and click on the New button. *Excel* displays the Customize dialog box along with a blank toolbar:

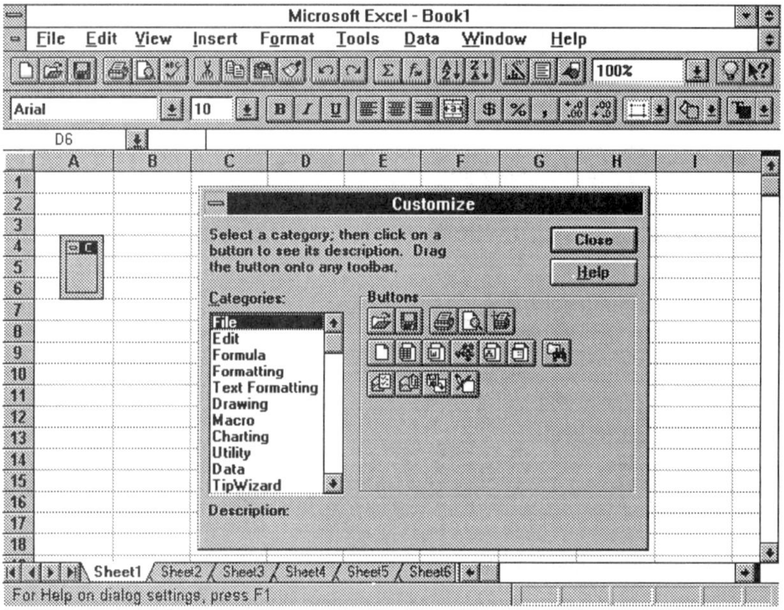

3. Use the techniques in figure 20-4 to add buttons to the new toolbar or to delete or rearrange the buttons in the toolbar:

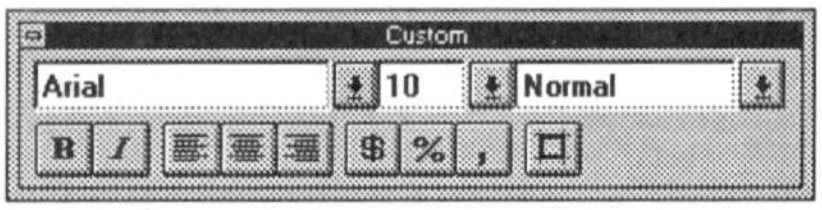

4. Click on the Close button.

Figure 20-5 How to create a new toolbar

Procedure

1. Click on the Customize button in the Toolbars dialog box or select the Customize command from the toolbar shortcut menu, and the Customize dialog box appears.
2. Select the Custom option from the Categories list box, and the buttons in the Custom category are displayed in the Buttons box:

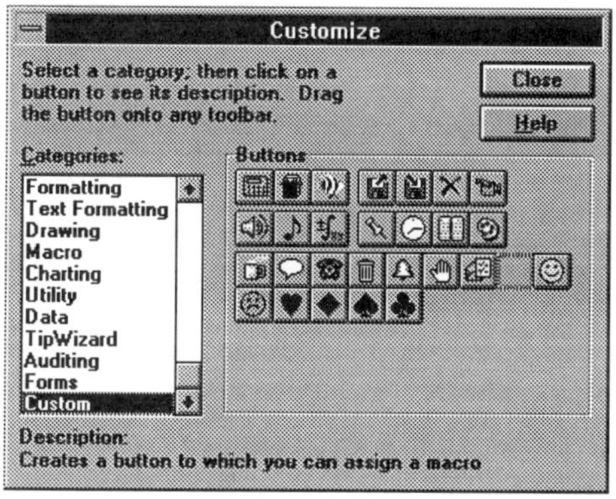

3. Add any button in the Custom category to any visible toolbar by dragging it into the toolbar, and this dialog box appears.

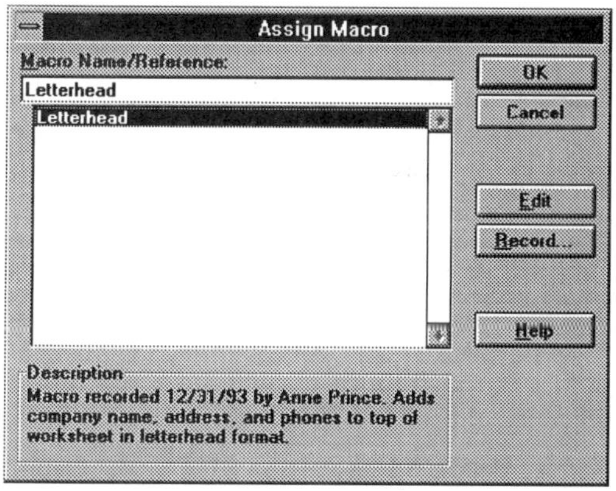

4. Select the macro you want to assign to the button.
5. Click on the OK button and *Excel* returns you to the Customize dialog box. Click on the Close button.

Notes

- You can edit a macro before you assign it to a button by clicking on the Edit button. You can also record a new macro to be assigned to the button by clicking on the Record button. See chapter 19 for details on how to record a macro.
- You can also assign a macro to a built-in button to change the button's function. However, it's best to use one of the custom buttons, which aren't assigned pre-defined functions.
- You can use the procedure in figure 20-7 to change the image of any button.

Figure 20-6 How to assign a macro to a custom button

As you can see in figure 20-6, *Excel* provides a variety of toolbar buttons that aren't assigned pre-defined functions. These buttons are available from the Custom category. When you add any of these buttons to a toolbar, *Excel* displays the Assign Macro dialog box. From this dialog box, you select the macro you want to assign to the button.

The custom button you choose to assign a macro to should be the one whose image most closely reflects the function of the macro. If none of the images are even close, you may want to select the blank toolbar button as I did in figure 20-6. In either case, once you assign a macro to the button, you can edit the button to change its image.

How to edit a button's image Figure 20-7 presents the procedure for editing a button's image. As you can see, you use the Edit Button Image command that's available from the button shortcut menu when the Customize dialog box is displayed. When you select this command, *Excel* displays the Button Editor dialog box. From this dialog box, you can edit the current button imagc or you can create a new image.

Perspective

If you like using the toolbar buttons, you should take the time to set up the toolbars you use regularly so they contain the buttons you use most often. That way, you usually don't have to switch from one toolbar to another to find the button you want to use. You may also want to experiment with the toolbar display so it's easy for you to use. On the other hand, you'll probably never need to assign a macro to a custom button. Although a custom button like the one in figure 20-6 can be useful, it's usually easier to create and use a macro without taking the time to assign it to a button.

Summary

- To display or hide a *toolbar*, select it from the toolbar shortcut menu or the Toolbars dialog box. You can also reset a built-in toolbar to its original configuration, delete a user-defined toolbar, or change the size of the toolbar buttons from the Toolbars dialog box.
- To change the position and configuration of a toolbar, drag it in the application window. You can also change a *docked toolbar* to a *floating toolbar* and vice versa by double-clicking on the toolbar background.
- To add buttons to a toolbar, delete buttons from a toolbar, move buttons in a toolbar, or create a new toolbar, use the Customize dialog box.

Procedure

1. Click on the Customize button in the Toolbars dialog box or select the Customize command from the toolbar shortcut menu, and the Customize dialog box appears.
2. Click the right mouse button on the toolbar button in the application window you want to edit, and the button shortcut menu appears:

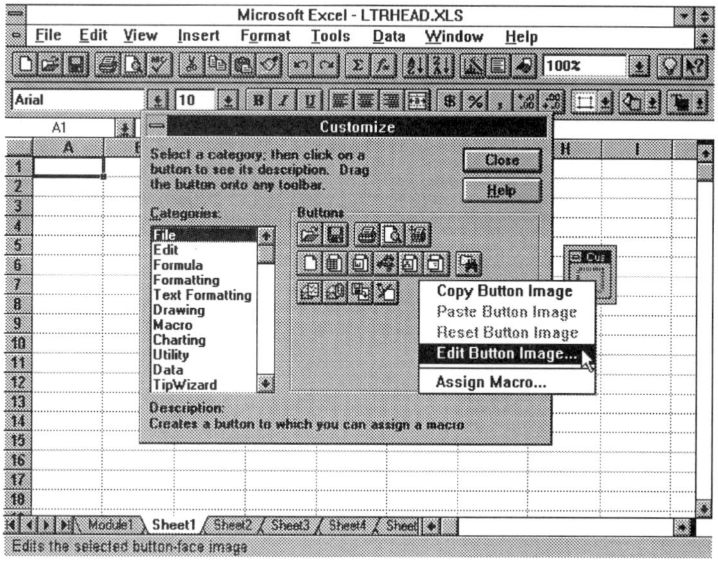

3. Select the Edit Button Image command and this dialog box appears:

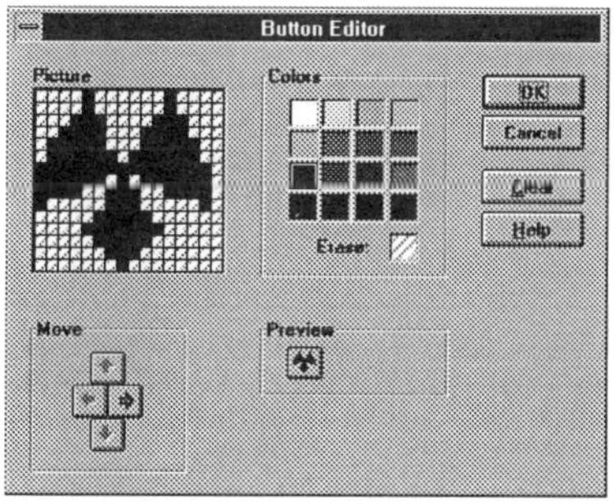

4. Edit the button image by selecting a color from the Colors box, then clicking or dragging in the Picture box where you want that color to appear.
5. Click on the OK button to change the image, and *Excel* returns you to the Customize dialog box. Click on the Close button.

Notes

- You can move an image right, left, up, or down one column or row using the arrows in the Move box.
- You can paint with the background color by clicking on the Erase box.
- You can delete the entire picture, leaving only the background color, by clicking on the Clear button.

Figure 20-7 How to edit a button's image

- To assign a macro to a custom button, use the Customize dialog box to add a custom button to a toolbar, then select the macro from the Assign Macro dialog box that's displayed.
- To edit a button's image, use the Edit Button Image command that's available from the button shortcut menu when the Customize dialog box is displayed.

Chapter 21

How to use the Scenario Manager

The *Scenario Manager* is a tool that lets you create two or more *scenarios* in a single worksheet. A scenario consists of a set of values for selected cells in a worksheet, called *changing cells*. When you display a scenario, *Excel* replaces the current values in the changing cells with the values in the scenario and recalculates the worksheet. Typically, key formulas in the worksheet depend on the values in the changing cells, so you can easily do what-if analysis by switching from one scenario to another.

In this chapter, you'll start by learning the basic skills for creating, displaying, and editing scenarios. Then, you'll learn two other skills for working with scenarios: how to merge the scenarios from two different worksheets and how to print a scenario summary report.

Basic skills for creating and using scenarios

Figure 21-1 illustrates how you can use the Scenario Manager to implement two profit and loss projections. Here, two scenarios have been created that contain different values for the cell D1, which contains the cost-of-goods-sold percentage. The first scenario is named COGS=20%, and the second is named COGS=25%. When you switch from one scenario to another, the value in the cost-of-goods-sold cell is changed, and the entire worksheet is recalculated. Because the values in row 5 in this example are derived from formulas that refer to cell D1, the change in the scenario changes the cost-of-goods-sold value at each sales level. And because the values in row 16 are derived from formulas that refer to the cells in row 5, the operating profit for each sales level changes as well.

The example in figure 21-1 is simple because it illustrates just two scenarios, and each of them replaces the value of just one cell. However, you can create scenarios that supply replacement values for up to 32 cells, and you can create a virtually unlimited number of different scenarios for a worksheet.

You can work with scenarios in two ways: using the Scenario box in the WorkGroup toolbar and using the Scenarios command in the Tools menu. When you use the WorkGroup toolbar, you can easily create and display scenarios and modify the values in the changing cells. The Scenarios command lets you perform those functions and others, such as deleting scenarios and redefining the changing cells in scenarios.

Two worksheets in the same workbook that contain profit and loss projections based on cost-of-goods-sold values of 20 and 25 percent of sales

Worksheet 1:

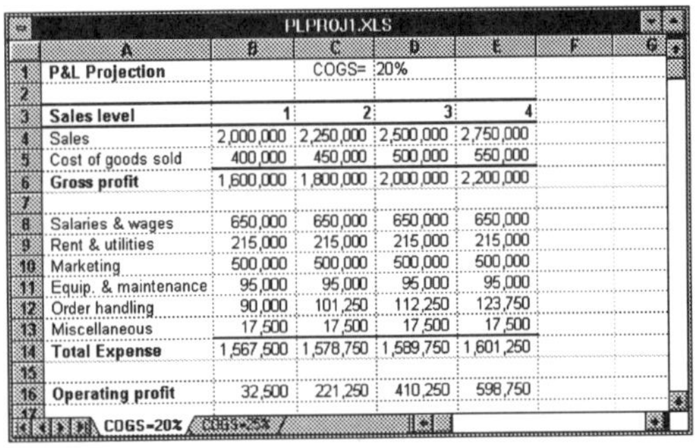

Worksheet 2:

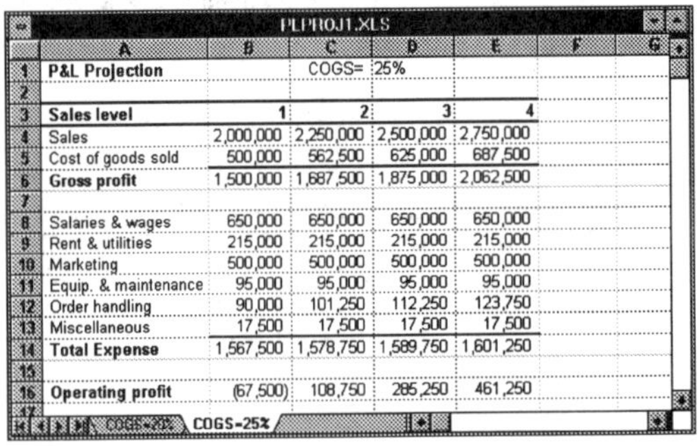

The worksheets above implemented as two scenarios in a single worksheet

Scenario 1:

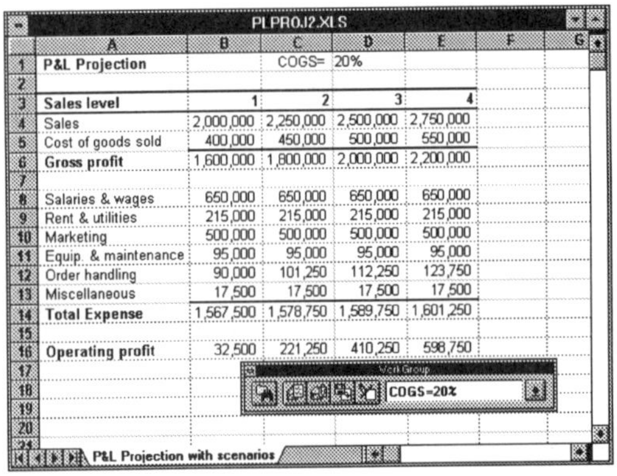

Scenario 2:

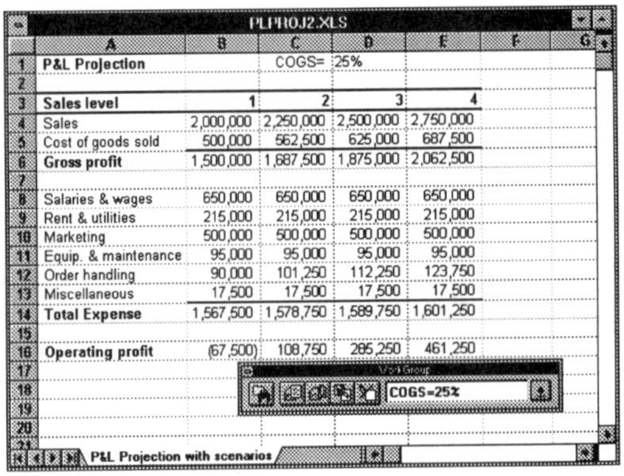

Notes

- You can create scenarios for any cells that contain values. In the example above, the changing data is a single cell (D1).
- A worksheet can have a virtually unlimited number of scenarios.
- Each worksheet in a workbook can have a different set of scenarios.

Figure 21-1 How to use scenarios

How to use the WorkGroup toolbar Figure 21-2 shows you how to use the WorkGroup toolbar to create and display scenarios and to modify the values for the changing cells in a scenario. When you use the

Access

Select the Toolbars command from the View menu and select the WorkGroup toolbar, or select the WorkGroup toolbar directly from the toolbar shortcut menu.

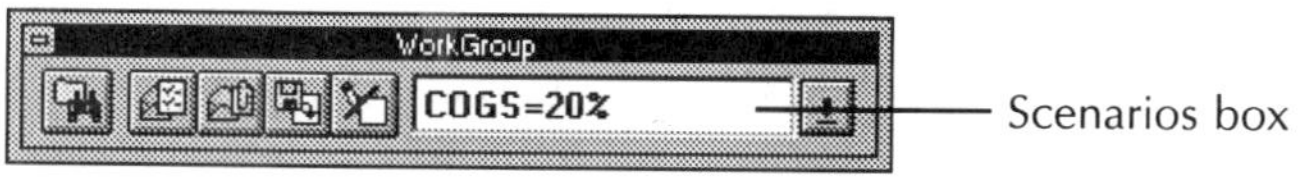

How to display a scenario

Select the scenario you want from the Scenarios drop-down list box:

How to create a new scenario

1. Enter the values for the changing cells for the scenario in the worksheet, then select the changing cells.
2. Type a name for the new scenario into the Scenarios box.
3. Press the Enter key.

How to modify the values in changing cells

1. Select the scenario you want to edit from the Scenarios drop-down list box.
2. Enter the new values for the changing cells in the worksheet.
3. Click in the Scenarios box and press the Enter key.
4. Reply to the confirmation dialog box that appears.

Notes

- You can include up to 32 changing cells in a scenario. The changing cells can be non-adjacent.
- The changing cells in a scenario should contain values, not formulas. If you use cells that contain formulas as changing cells, *Excel* replaces the formulas with their calculated values.
- You can't delete a scenario or specify different changing cells for a scenario from the WorkGroup toolbar. To perform either of these functions, you have to use the Scenarios command.
- The buttons in the WorkGroup toolbar are for features related to communications in some networked environments (like E-mail).

Figure 21-2 How to use the WorkGroup toolbar to work with scenarios

WorkGroup toolbar, you can easily move between the toolbar and the worksheet as you work with different scenarios. Notice, however, that you can't delete a scenario or redefine the changing cells for a scenario using the WorkGroup toolbar. To do that, you have to use the Scenarios command.

Access

Select the Scenarios command from the Tools menu.

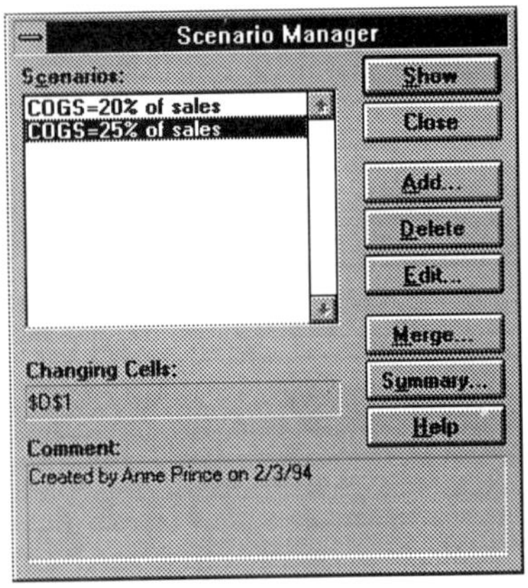

Operation

- To display a scenario in the worksheet, double-click on the scenario name in the Scenarios list box, or select the scenario name in the Scenarios list box and click on the Show button.
- To create a scenario, click on the Add button. See figure 21-4 for details.
- To delete a scenario, select the scenario in the Scenarios list box, then click on the Delete button and reply to the Delete Scenario dialog box.
- To edit a scenario, select the scenario in the Scenarios list box, then click on the Edit button. See figure 21-5 for details.
- To combine scenarios in one or more worksheets, click on the Merge button. See figure 21-6 for details.
- To create a scenario summary report, click on the Summary button. See figure 21-7 for details.

Note

The Scenario Manager dialog box remains open as you work with scenarios. To close it, click on the Close button.

Figure 21-3 How to use the Scenario Manager dialog box

How to use the Scenarios command Figure 21-3 presents the Scenario Manager dialog box that's displayed when you select the Scenarios command from the Tools menu and summarizes how you use it to work with scenarios. As you can see, you can display or delete a scenario simply by selecting the scenario and clicking on the appropriate button. The procedures for creating or editing a scenario, however, are a bit more complicated.

Figure 21-4 presents the procedure for creating a scenario using the Scenarios command, and figure 21-5 presents the procedure for editing a scenario using this command. As you can see, the Add Scenario and Edit

Procedure

1. Click on the Add button in the Scenario Manager dialog box, and this dialog box appears:

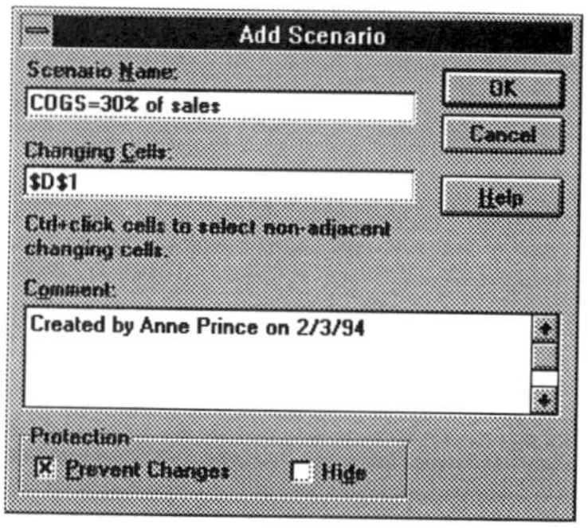

2. Type a description for the scenario in the Scenario Name text box.
3. Enter cell references for the changing cells in the Changing Cells box.
4. If you want, replace or extend the text in the Comment text box and change the settings of the Protection options.
5. Click on the OK button and the Scenario Values dialog box appears:

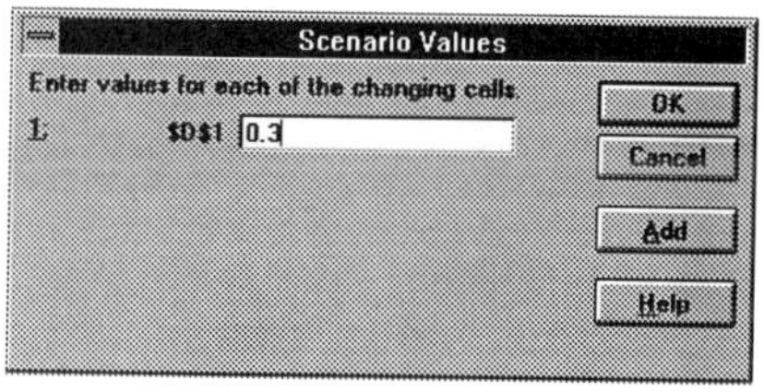

6. If necessary, enter the values for the changing cells.
7. Click on the OK button, and *Excel* returns you to the Scenario Manager dialog box.

Notes

- When the focus is on the Changing Cells text box, you can select a cell or range in the worksheet and *Excel* will enter the reference for you. If you type in the references, separate them with commas. You can include up to 32 changing cells in a scenario.
- *Excel* automatically enters the current date and user (as specified in the General tab of the Options dialog box) in the Comment box when you create a scenario.
- The comment can contain up to 255 characters and appears in scenario summary reports.
- The Prevent Changes option keeps other users from changing the scenario, and the Hide option excludes the scenario's name from the list of scenarios so it can't be displayed. These options are in effect only if the sheet is protected. (See chapter 24 for details on how to protect a worksheet.)
- Because the values in the Scenario Values dialog box default to the current values of the changing cells, you can enter the values for these cells into the worksheet before you begin this procedure.
- If you assign range names to the changing cells, the names appear in the Scenario Values dialog box instead of the cell references.
- If you click on the Add button in the Scenario Values dialog box instead of the OK button, *Excel* returns you to the Add Scenario dialog box so you can add another scenario.

Figure 21-4 How to use the Scenarios command to create a scenario

Procedure

1. Select the scenario you want to edit from the Scenarios list box in the Scenario Manager dialog box.
2. Click on the Edit button, and this dialog box appears:

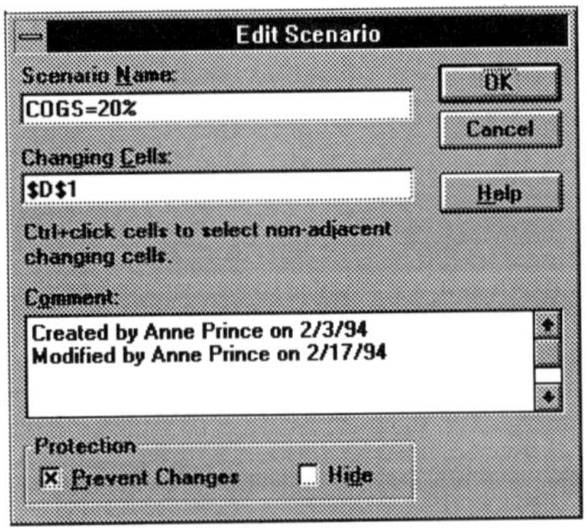

3. Modify the scenario name, changing cells, comment, and protection options as necessary.
4. Click on the OK button, and the Scenario Values dialog box appears.
5. If necessary, modify the values for the changing cells.
6. Click on the OK button, and *Excel* returns you to the Scenario Manager dialog box.

Notes

- *Excel* automatically adds the current date and user to the comments for a scenario each time you edit it.
- Because the values in the Scenario Values dialog box default to the current values of the changing cells, you can enter the values for these cells into the worksheet before you begin the edit procedure.

Figure 21-5 How to use the Scenarios command to edit a scenario

Scenario dialog boxes are identical, so once you learn how to use one, you'll have no trouble using the other. Notice that for both functions, you specify the values for the changing cells in the Scenario Values dialog box. Because the values default to the current values in the worksheet, you can enter the values into the worksheet before you create or edit the scenario.

Other Scenario Manager features

The Scenario Manager includes two other features you may want to use. First, you can merge the scenarios in two worksheets into one. Second, you can create a scenario summary report that documents the scenarios in a worksheet. You use the Scenarios command to perform both of these functions.

How to merge scenarios Figure 21-6 presents the procedure for merging the scenarios in two worksheets. You may want to use this procedure if two or more people create different scenarios in copies of the same worksheet. Then, you can merge those scenarios into a single copy of the worksheet. Note that for this procedure to yield acceptable results, the parts of the worksheets that the scenarios refer to should have the same structures.

The merge function operates on two worksheets. The *source worksheet* is the worksheet you're copying the scenarios from, and the *destination worksheet* is the worksheet you're copying the scenarios to. The workbooks that contain both of these worksheets must be open when you perform the merge operation, and the destination worksheet must be the current worksheet. Note that you can use this procedure for worksheets in two different workbooks or in the same workbook.

How to create a scenario summary report Figure 21-7 presents the procedure for creating a *scenario summary report.* A scenario summary report documents the scenarios in a worksheet and the values in the *result cells* you select. A result cell typically contains a formula that refers directly or indirectly to a changing cell.

As you can see in the figure, *Excel* creates and formats the report on a new sheet in the current workbook. Also, notice that *Excel* uses the outline feature to make it easier for you to review the report. Although this feature isn't helpful for a short report like the one in this figure, it can be helpful when the report is more complicated.

Perspective

The primary benefit of the Scenario Manager is that it helps you keep track of the different scenarios for a single worksheet. Another benefit is that it saves space. For example, to save the scenarios in figure 21-1 using the Scenario Manager, only a single cell has to be duplicated. (Of course, there's some additional overhead involved when you use the Scenario Manager.) Without the Scenario Manager, the entire worksheet must be duplicated for each combination of ranges. So if space is a critical issue on your system, the Scenario Manager can help.

Procedure

1. Open the workbooks that contain the source and destination worksheets, and make the destination worksheet the current worksheet.
2. Click on the Merge button in the Scenario Manager dialog box, and this dialog box appears:

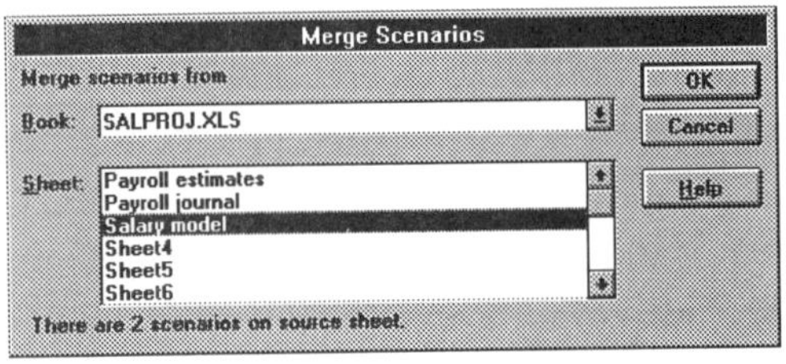

3. Select the name of the workbook that contains the scenarios you want to merge with those in the destination workbook from the Book drop-down list box.
4. Select the sheet in the source workbook that contains the scenarios you want to merge from the Sheet list box.
5. Click on the OK button.

A worksheet after payroll scenarios were merged with cost-of-goods-sold scenarios, and the Incremental Salaries scenario was displayed

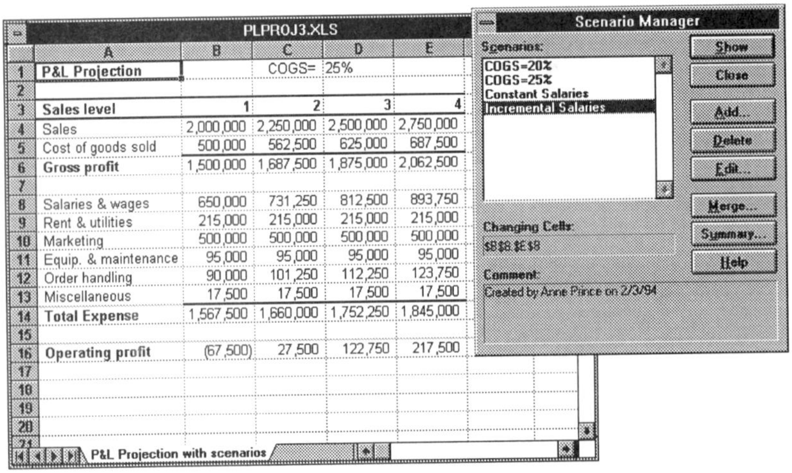

Notes

- *Excel* copies all of the scenarios from the source sheet to the destination sheet in a merge operation. If a name conflict occurs, *Excel* qualifies the name of a merged scenario with a number, its creation date, or its creator's name.
- You can merge scenarios from another sheet in the same workbook. To do that, select the current workbook from the Book drop-down list box in the Merge Scenarios dialog box.
- The source and destination sheets should have the same or similar structures. If they don't, the merged scenarios won't make sense in the context of the destination sheet, and displaying them may corrupt the destination sheet.

Figure 21-6 How to merge scenarios

Procedure

1. Display the scenarios you want reflected as current values in the summary report.
2. Click on the Summary button in the Scenario Manager dialog box, and this dialog box appears:

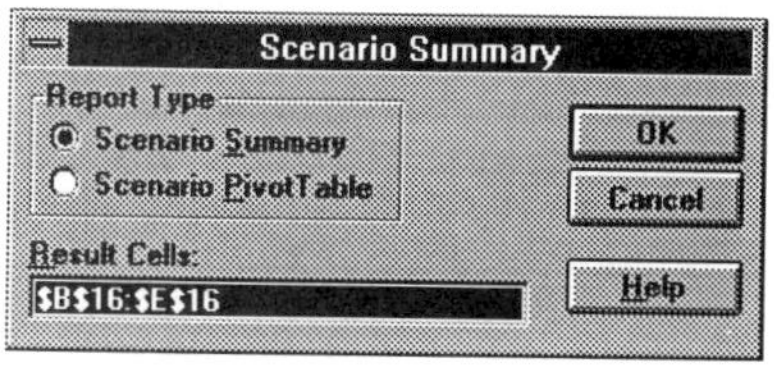

3. Select the Scenario Summary option from the Report Type group.
4. Identify the range of result cells you want represented in the report in the Result Cells text box.
5. Click on the OK button, and *Excel* creates the report in a new sheet in the current workbook:

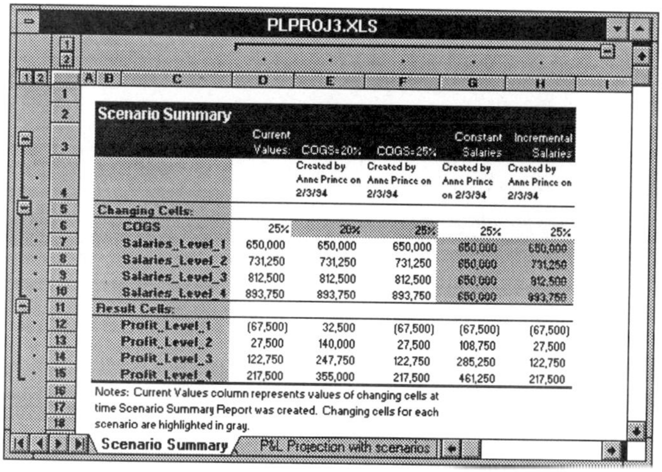

Notes

- You can use the mouse to select the result cells in the worksheet. If you type in the references, separate multiple references with commas.
- *Excel* automatically formats the scenario summary report and displays it in outline form so you can hide and reveal levels of detail.
- Values that were derived from a scenario are shaded in the summary report.
- The scenario summary report is more meaningful if you assign range names to the changing cells and result cells, as in the above example. If the cells aren't named, cell references appear in the report.
- The Scenario PivotTable option lets you create a pivot table based on the changing cells and result cells.

Figure 21-7 How to create a scenario summary report

On the other hand, one weakness of the Scenario Manager is that it doesn't provide any documentation in the worksheet itself for the scenarios that are in use. So when you print a worksheet, you have no quick way of finding out which scenarios of which ranges it represents. This forces you to provide your own documentation for printed worksheets.

Summary

- A *scenario* is a set of values for up to 32 *changing cells* that you can easily apply to a worksheet to do what-if analysis.
- To work with scenarios, you use the *Scenario Manager.* The Scenario Manager is available through the WorkGroup toolbar or the Scenarios command in the Tools menu.
- From the WorkGroup toolbar, you can create and display scenarios and modify the values for the changing cells in a scenario. With the Scenarios command, you can perform these functions, and you can delete scenarios, specify different changing cells for a scenario, merge the scenarios in two worksheets, and create *scenario summary reports.*

Chapter 22

How to use the Goal Seek and Solver commands

This chapter presents two commands that you can use for some types of business analysis: Goal Seek and Solver. Both of these commands are available from the Tools menu, and you use both of them to solve formulas. Although these commands aren't for everybody, they can be useful in some situations. The examples in this chapter will give you a good idea of how to use them.

How to use the Goal Seek command to find a value for a single variable that solves a formula

The Goal Seek command lets you find the value for a variable that's required to make the result of a formula equal to a value you specify. For example, you can use it with a proforma model to find the exact number of unit sales that are required to reach the break-even point for a product. As a result, this command can be useful for what-if analysis.

Figure 22-1 presents the procedure for using the Goal Seek command. After you set up the worksheet and start the command, you specify the cell that contains the formula you want to solve, called the *target cell*; the target value for the target cell; and the cell you want *Excel* to adjust to reach the target value, called the *changing cell*, the *adjustable cell*, or the *decision variable*. When *Excel* finds the appropriate value, it inserts that value in the changing cell and recalculates the worksheet.

How to use the Solver command

Like the Goal Seek command, the Solver command is designed to help you target the result of a formula. With the Solver command, however, you can find the answers to more complicated problems. After you learn how to use the Solver command to solve a problem, I'll show you how to create Solver reports.

A worksheet before and after the Goal Seek command is used to calculate the units that must be sold at two different price levels for profits to break even

Before

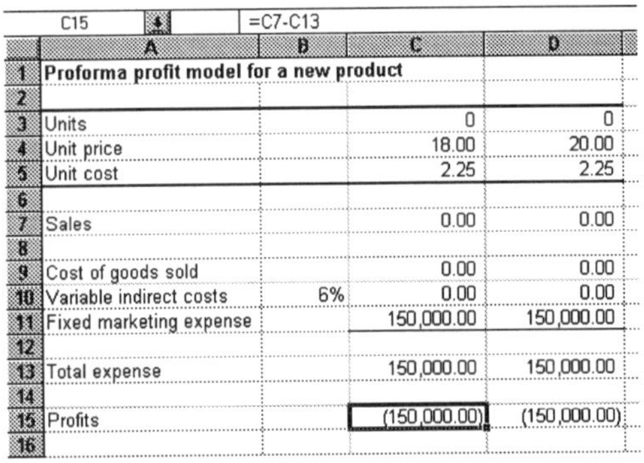

C15 =C7-C13

	A	B	C	D
1	Proforma profit model for a new product			
2				
3	Units		0	0
4	Unit price		18.00	20.00
5	Unit cost		2.25	2.25
6				
7	Sales		0.00	0.00
8				
9	Cost of goods sold		0.00	0.00
10	Variable indirect costs	6%	0.00	0.00
11	Fixed marketing expense		150,000.00	150,000.00
12				
13	Total expense		150,000.00	150,000.00
14				
15	Profits		(150,000.00)	(150,000.00)
16				

After

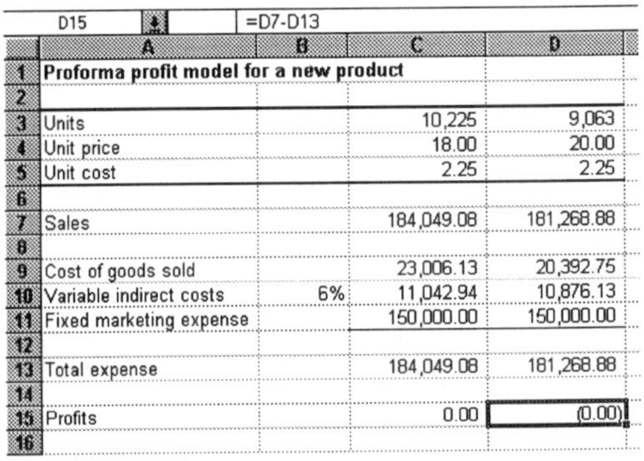

D15 =D7-D13

	A	B	C	D
1	Proforma profit model for a new product			
2				
3	Units		10,225	9,063
4	Unit price		18.00	20.00
5	Unit cost		2.25	2.25
6				
7	Sales		184,049.08	181,268.88
8				
9	Cost of goods sold		23,006.13	20,392.75
10	Variable indirect costs	6%	11,042.94	10,876.13
11	Fixed marketing expense		150,000.00	150,000.00
12				
13	Total expense		184,049.08	181,268.88
14				
15	Profits		0.00	(0.00)
16				

Procedure

1. Select the Goal Seek command from the Tools menu and this dialog box appears:

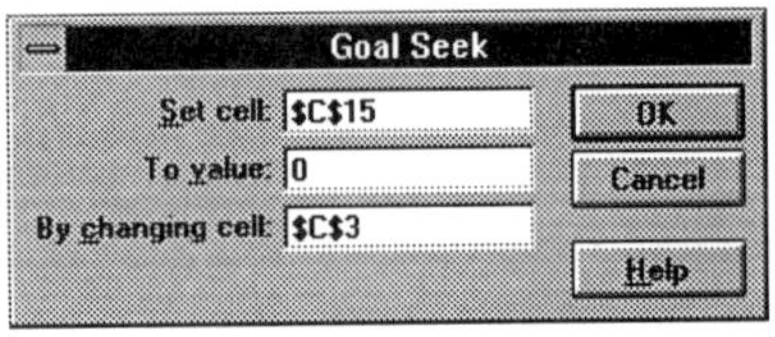

2. Specify the cell that contains the formula whose value you want to target (the target cell) in the Set Cell text box.
3. Enter the target value for the target cell in the To Value text box.
4. Specify the cell that contains the value you want *Excel* to adjust (the changing cell) in the By Changing Cell text box.
5. Click on the OK button, and *Excel* adjusts the changing cell's value so that the target cell reaches the target value and displays this dialog box:

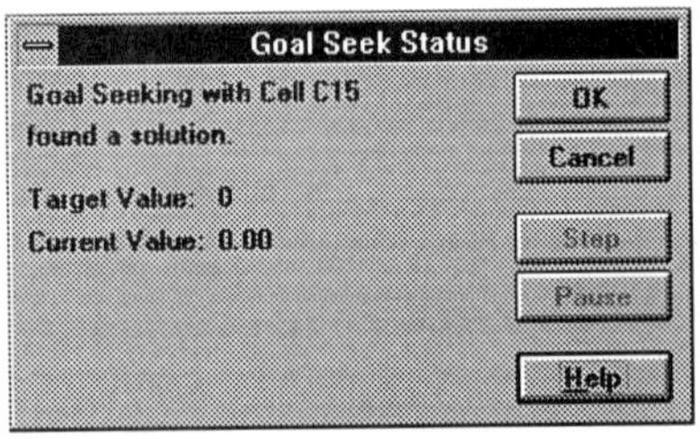

6. Click on the OK button to accept the solution, or click on the Cancel button to restore the worksheet's original values.

Figure 22-1 How to use the Goal Seek command to find a value for a single variable that solves a formula (part 1 of 2)

Notes

- The formula in the target cell must refer to the changing cell directly or indirectly.
- The Goal Seek Status dialog box displays the status of the Goal Seek operation as *Excel* performs its calculations. You can interrupt the operation by clicking on the Pause button in this dialog box. Then, you can step through the operation by clicking on the Step button, or you can continue the operation by clicking on the Continue button. (The Continue button replaces the Pause button when you click on it.)
- If *Excel* can't find a solution to the problem, it displays a message.

Figure 22-1 How to use the Goal Seek command to find a value for a single variable that solves a formula

How to find values for one or more variables that solve a formula

Figure 22-2 presents the procedure for using the Solver command to solve a problem. You'll notice that the worksheet I used in this example is the same model I used for the Goal Seek example in figure 22-1. As in that figure, I want *Excel* to determine the break-even point for a product. In this case, however, I want *Excel* to vary two cells: Units sold and Unit price. As with the Goal Seek command, the cell that contains the formula you want to solve for is called the *target cell*, and the cells you want *Excel* to adjust to solve the formula are called the *changing cells*, *adjustable cells*, or *decision variables*.

To define a Solver problem, you begin by specifying the target cell and a target value for the cell. Notice that in addition to specifying an exact value for the target cell, you can also have *Excel* search for the maximum or minimum value for the cell. This value will depend on the changing cells and *constraints* you specify.

The constraints are the logical conditions you want *Excel* to satisfy as it looks for values for the changing cells. A constraint usually involves one or more of the changing cells, but it can also involve the target cell. The example in figure 22-2, for example, specifies two constraints on the cell that contains the number of units sold: (1) it must not be greater than 30,000; and (2) it must not be less than 25,000.

When *Excel* is done searching for answers to a problem, it inserts the calculated values in the worksheet and displays the Solver Results dialog box. This dialog box lets you accept the calculated values or restore the worksheet's original values. It also lets you save the answer as a scenario and create Solver reports. If you want to learn more about scenarios, see chapter 21.

A worksheet before and after the Solver command is used to calculate the units sold and the unit price needed for profits to break even with the units sold between 25,000 and 30,000

Before

C15 =C7-C13

	A	B	C	D
1	**Proforma profit model for a new product**			
2				
3	Units		0	
4	Unit price		0.00	
5	Unit cost		2.25	
6				
7	Sales		0.00	
8				
9	Cost of goods sold		0.00	
10	Variable indirect costs	6%	0.00	
11	Fixed marketing expense		150,000.00	
12				
13	Total expense		150,000.00	
14				
15	Profits		(150,000.00)	
16				

After

C15 =C7-C13

	A	B	C	D
1	**Proforma profit model for a new product**			
2				
3	Units		25,000	
4	Unit price		8.78	
5	Unit cost		2.25	
6				
7	Sales		219,414.89	
8				
9	Cost of goods sold		56,250.00	
10	Variable indirect costs	6%	13,164.89	
11	Fixed marketing expense		150,000.00	
12				
13	Total expense		219,414.89	
14				
15	Profits		(0.00)	
16				

Procedure

1. Select the Solver command from the Tools menu and this dialog box appears:

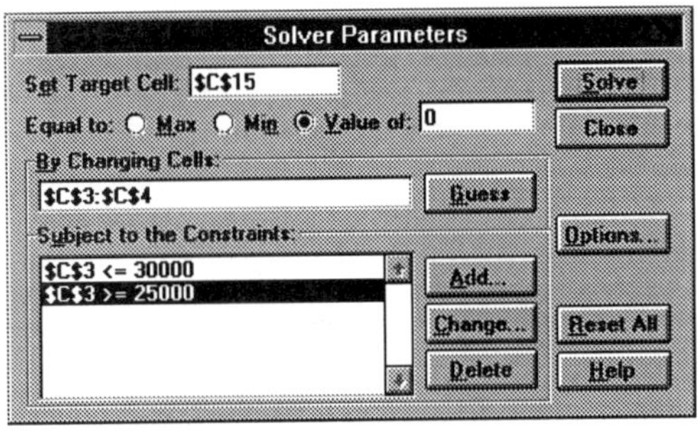

2. Specify the cell that contains the formula whose value you want to target (the target cell) in the Set Target Cell text box, and specify the target value by selecting the Max, Min, or Value Of option. If you select the Value Of option, enter a value in the text box.
3. Specify the cells that contain the values you want *Excel* to adjust (the changing cells) in the By Changing Cells text box.
4. Specify the constraints for the operation in the Subject To The Constraints box. To add a constraint, click on the Add button and this dialog box appears:

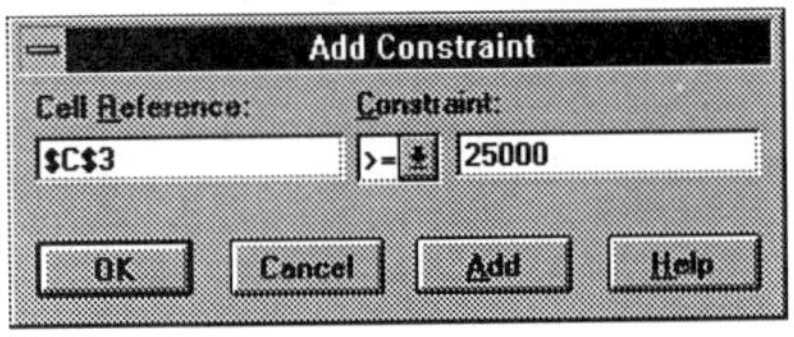

Specify a cell, an operator, and a comparison value for the constraint. Then, click on the Add button to add another constraint, or click on the OK button to return to the Solver Parameters dialog box.

Figure 22-2 How to use the Solver command to find values for one or more variables that solve a formula (part 1 of 2)

5. Click on the Solve button, and *Excel* adjusts the changing cells' values to reach the specified target value and displays this dialog box:

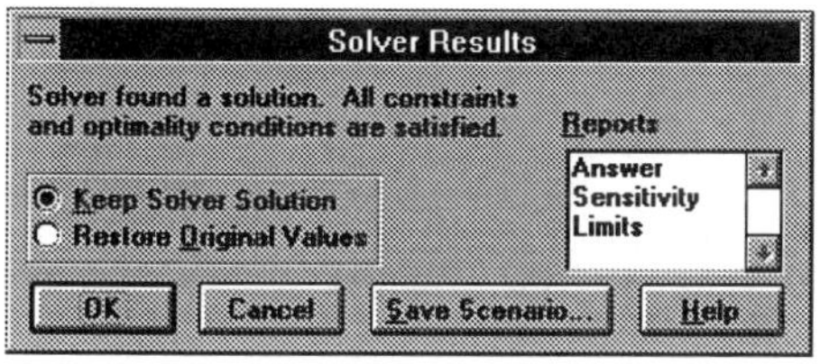

6. Click on the OK button to accept the solution, or select the Restore Original Values option and click on the OK button to restore the worksheet's original values.

Notes

- The Max and Min options in the Solver parameters dialog box let you maximize or minimize the value of the target cell. The Value Of option lets you specify a specific value for the cell.
- The target cell typically contains a formula that depends directly or indirectly on the changing cells. If the target cell doesn't contain a formula, it must be included as a changing cell. If the target cell is omitted, *Excel* finds a solution that satisfies all the constraints.
- If you click on the Guess button in the Solver Parameters dialog box, *Excel* inserts references in the By Changing Cells text box for all cells that are referred to directly or indirectly by the formula in the target cell and that don't contain formulas.
- If you click on the Options button in the Solver Parameters dialog box, the Solver Options dialog box appears. This dialog box lets you specify advanced technical features that you're unlikely to need.
- If you click on the Reset All button in the Solver Parameters dialog box, *Excel* resets all the options and values in the dialog box to their defaults.
- You can change a constraint by selecting it in the Subject To The Constraints list box in the Solver Parameters dialog box and clicking on the Change button. To delete a selected constraint, click on the Delete button.
- If *Excel* can't find an answer that satisfies all the constraints, it displays a descriptive message in the Solver Results dialog box. If this happens, you can specify different constraints or a different target value and attempt another solution.
- You can save the Solver answer as a scenario by clicking on the Save Scenario button in the Solver Results dialog box.
- If you want *Excel* to create a Solver report, select the report type from the Reports list box in the Solver Results dialog box before you click on the OK button. See figure 22-3 for more information about creating Solver reports.

Figure 22-2 How to use the Solver command to find values for one or more variables that solve a formula (part 2 of 2)

If *Excel* can't find an answer that satisfies all the constraints, it displays an error message in the Solver Results dialog box. Then, you can adjust the constraints or the target value and try to solve the problem again.

How to create Solver reports Figure 22-3 shows you how to create Solver reports from the Solver Results dialog box. When you create a report, *Excel* stores it in a new sheet in the current workbook. Then, you can print the report or save it for reference.

Perspective

As you read this chapter, you probably thought of ways you could use the Goal Seek and Solver commands with your own worksheets. If so, you'll want to take a few minutes now to try them out. In general, I think you'll find Goal Seek the more useful of the two. Most *Excel* users don't have problems so complicated that they require analysis with Solver.

In addition to Goal Seek and Solver, *Excel* offers other analytical features. For example, you can use the Table command in the Data menu to create a data table based on one or two values. And you can use the Data Analysis add-in to perform sophisticated statistical analysis. In chapter 24, you can learn more about the Table command and add-ins.

Summary

- You can use the Goal Seek command in the Tools menu to find the value that's required for a *changing cell* to make the result of the formula in a *target cell* equal to a target value.
- You can use the Solver command in the Tools menu to find the values required for one or more *changing cells* to make the result of the formula in a *target cell* equal to a target value, subject to the *constraints* you specify.

Procedure

1. Select one of the Reports options from the Solver Results dialog box:

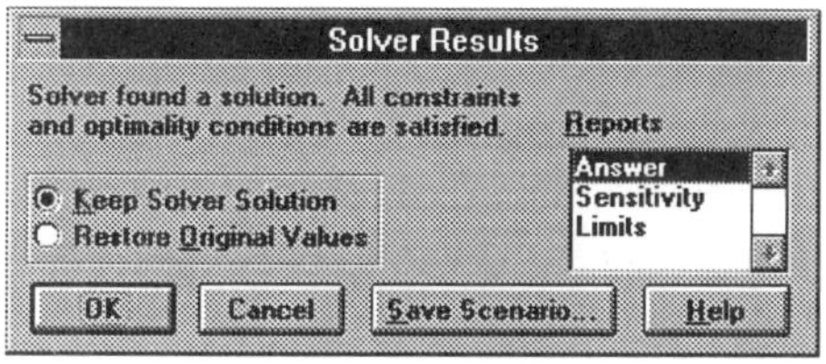

2. Click on the OK button, and *Excel* creates a report in a new worksheet in the current workbook.

Report type	**Description**
Answer	Displays information about the solution to the problem. This information includes the original and final values for target and adjustable cells and the constraints applied to reach the solution.
Sensitivity	Displays technical information on how sensitive the result of the Solver operation is to changes in the formula in the target cell or in the constraints.
Limits	Displays the high and low values for the changing cells.

An answer report for the problem in figure 22-2

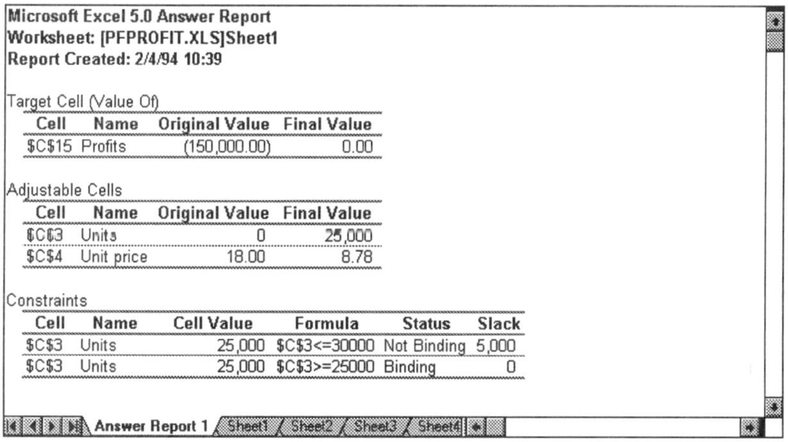

Microsoft Excel 5.0 Answer Report
Worksheet: [PFPROFIT.XLS]Sheet1
Report Created: 2/4/94 10:39

Target Cell (Value Of)

Cell	Name	Original Value	Final Value
$C$15	Profits	(150,000.00)	0.00

Adjustable Cells

Cell	Name	Original Value	Final Value
$C$3	Units	0	25,000
$C$4	Unit price	18.00	8.78

Constraints

Cell	Name	Cell Value	Formula	Status	Slack
$C$3	Units	25,000	$C$3<=30000	Not Binding	5,000
$C$3	Units	25,000	$C$3>=25000	Binding	0

Figure 22-3 How to create a Solver report

Chapter 23

How to use Object Linking and Embedding with *Excel* 5.0

The easiest way to transfer data from one program to another is to use the clipboard. If you want to copy a chart that you created in *Excel* to a document that you're working on in *Word for Windows*, for example, you switch to *Excel* and use the Copy command to copy the chart to the clipboard. Then, you switch back to *Word* and use the Paste command to insert the chart from the clipboard into the document. For most of the jobs you do, that's all you need when you want to combine the work of two or more programs.

However, *Windows* 3.1 also supports a more sophisticated mechanism for combining the work of two or more programs. It's called *Object Linking and Embedding*, or just *OLE* (pronounced *oh-lay*). When you use its linking feature to copy a chart from *Excel* to *Word for Windows*, for example, it maintains a relationship between the two programs. Then, when you update the chart in *Excel*, the chart in *Word for Windows* is updated too. When you finish this chapter, you'll know how to use OLE whenever it's appropriate for the job you're trying to do.

How OLE works

The purpose of OLE is to enable programs to work together in a way that's tightly integrated. It does that by letting you embed or link an *object* created in one program, the *server application*, into another document, the *destination document,* that's created in a *client application.* An object might be a block of text from a word processing program, a chart from a spreadsheet program, a graphic from a drawing program, or something else. You can access the object with the server application directly through the client application.

The difference between an *embedded object* and a *linked object* is subtle. When you embed an object in a destination document, the object becomes a part of the destination document although it still maintains a relationship with the program that created it. In contrast, when you link an object to a destination document, the object doesn't become a part of the destination document. Instead, it exists as a separate file that you can access independently of the client application.

If you embed a graphic that requires 100KB of storage in a workbook file that requires 20KB, for example, the size of the workbook file will jump to 120KB because the graphic becomes part of the workbook file. In contrast, if you link the two files, the size of the workbook file increases only a small amount because the graphic remains in a separate file. In this case, you see some representation of the linked document in the workbook, but the relationship between the two documents is in the form of a pointer that connects them.

Not all *Windows* programs support OLE, and those that do vary in their capabilities. Some applications can participate in an OLE relationship only as a server, others can participate only as a client, and still others can participate as both. *Excel* can participate as both a client and a server.

To complicate things, OLE is currently available in two versions. Most major Windows application now support OLE 1.0, the version introduced with *Windows* 3.1. However, since *Windows* 3.1 was released, Microsoft has distributed OLE 2.0 to software developers. OLE 2.0 is more dependable than OLE 1.0, and it offers more features. *Excel* 5.0 uses OLE 2.0, and you'll see one of its new features at the end of this chapter. However, because OLE 2.0 is so new, not many other programs use it, and almost all of those that do are Microsoft products.

How to work with linked objects

Although *Excel* can participate as a client in an OLE relationship, it's much more likely that you'll want to use *Excel* as a server. So I'll begin by showing you how to link data from an *Excel* worksheet to another application. Then, I'll show you how to link data from another application to an *Excel* worksheet.

How to link data from an *Excel* worksheet to another application

Figure 23-1 presents the procedure for linking data from an *Excel* worksheet to another application. In this case, the other application is *Word for Windows*, and the data that's being linked is an *Excel* chart.

As you can see in the figure, the procedure is simple. You copy the data you want to link to the clipboard, you switch to the other application, and you paste the link. Although the command you use to insert a link into an application differs from one application to another, the general procedure is the same.

Procedure

1. Copy the data you want to link to another application (in this case, a chart) from the *Excel* worksheet to the clipboard:

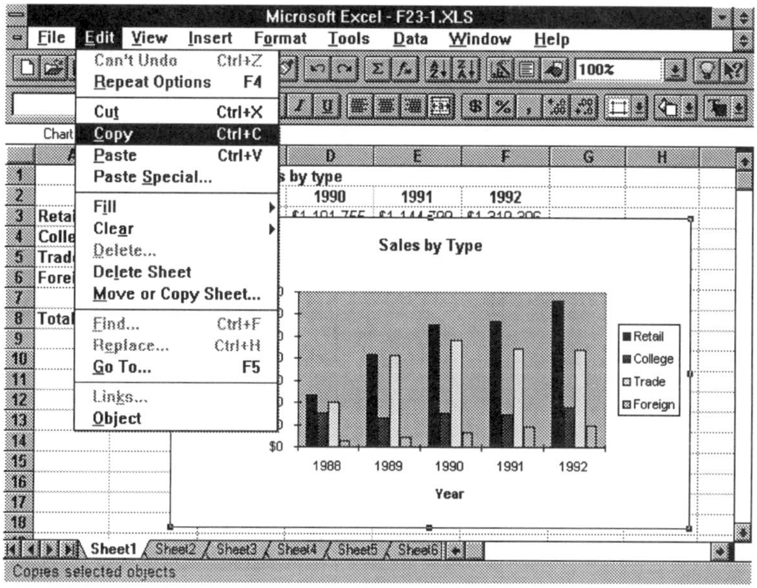

2. Switch to the client application (in this case, *Word for Windows*) and indicate the position where you want to insert the link.
3. Paste the link into the document using the appropriate command. In *Word for Windows*, you use the Paste Special command. When you select this command from the Edit menu, this dialog box appears:

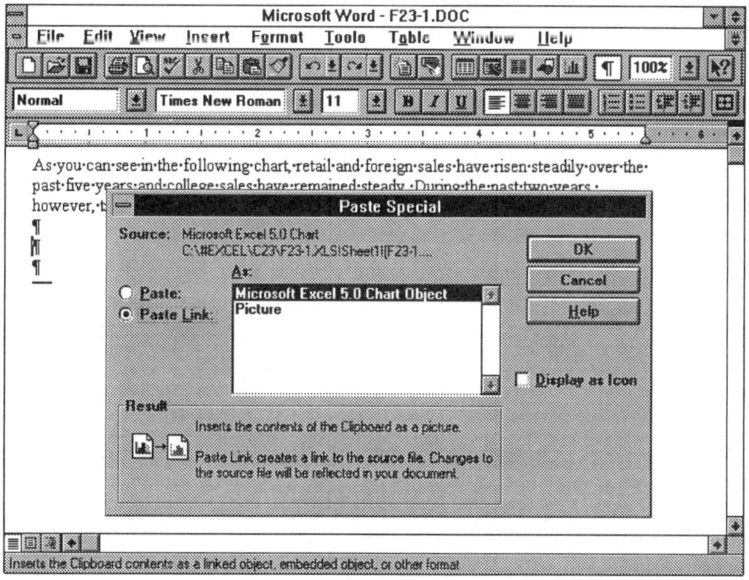

Figure 23-1 How to link data from an *Excel* worksheet to another application (part 1 of 2)

4. Select the appropriate options to link the data in the format you want. After the link has been established, the linked data appears in the client the application:

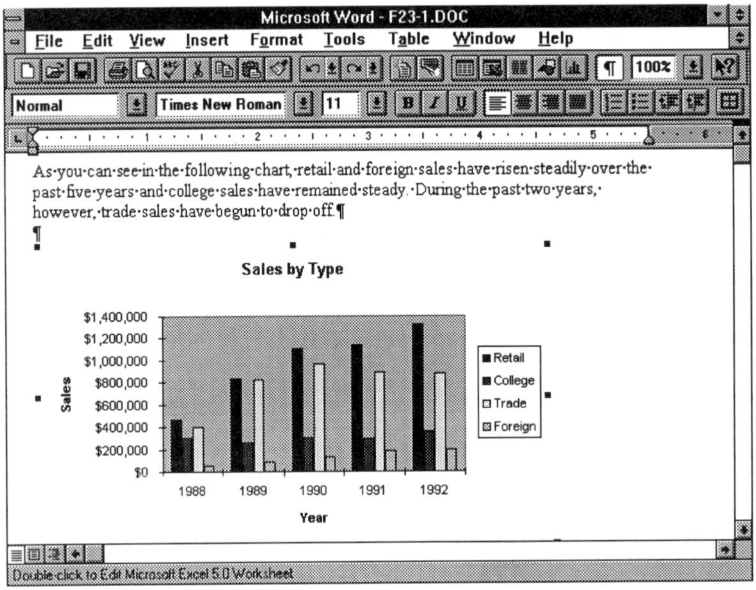

Notes

- Before you link data from an *Excel* worksheet to another application, be sure that the workbook that contains the worksheet has been saved with a permanent file name. Otherwise, the link in the destination document will point to the temporary file name, which will change when you save the workbook. As a result, the link will be lost.
- The command you use to insert a link into a client application depends on the application.
- As you use the Paste Special command in *Word for Windows* or a similar command in another application, you'll notice that the available formats vary depending on the data on the clipboard.
- Once the link is established, any change you make to the data in *Excel* is reflected in the linked data in the client application.
- To edit the *Excel* object from the client application, double-click on it. Then, *Windows* opens the *Excel* program or switches to it if it's already open, and it loads the data so you can edit it.
- When you open a document that contains a link to a changed object, the application may prompt you with a dialog box that asks if you want to update the links. Some applications update the links automatically without prompting you.

Figure 23-1 How to link data from an *Excel* worksheet to another application (part 2 of 2)

Once you establish a link to an *Excel* worksheet, any changes you make to the worksheet are reflected in the document that contains the link. If the document is open when you change the worksheet, the change is reflected immediately, and you can see it as soon as you switch back to the document. If the document isn't open when you make the change, the update is made when you open the document. Some applications, however, will ask you before they update the links to be sure that's what you want to do.

How to link data from another application to an *Excel* worksheet Figure 23-2 presents the procedures for linking data from another application to an *Excel* worksheet. As you can see, the first procedure is basically the same as the procedure in figure 23-1. It shows you how to link to selected data created in another application. The second procedure shows you how to link to an entire document created in another application. You're much more likely to use the first procedure than you are the second.

How to work with embedded objects

If you've worked with embedded objects in any *Windows* application, you won't have any trouble working with embedded objects in *Excel*. That's because the techniques you use are virtually the same, regardless of the application. The only difference may be the command you use to perform the embed operation and whether the server program can be activated in place.

How to embed an object in an *Excel* worksheet Figure 23-3 presents the procedures for embedding an existing graphic object, existing text, an existing document, and a new object in an *Excel* worksheet. As you can see, a graphic object is automatically embedded in the worksheet when you paste it using the Paste command or toolbar button. To embed text, however, you usually have to use the Paste Special command. Note that when you use this command, you want to select the format option that ends in the word *Object*. If you select another option, the object is inserted into the worksheet when you click on the Paste button instead of being embedded. Unlike an embedded object, an inserted object doesn't maintain a relationship with the application program that was used to create it.

How to establish a link to selected data created in another application

1. In the server application, copy the data you want to link to the *Excel* worksheet to the clipboard.
2. Switch to *Excel*, and place the cell pointer in the worksheet where you want to insert the link.
3. Select the Paste Special command from the Edit menu and this dialog box appears:

4. Select the Paste Link option, and select the format you want to use from the As list box.
5. Click on the OK button and the link is inserted.

How to establish a link to an entire document created in another application

1. Select the Object command from the Insert menu, then click on the Create From File tab and this dialog box appears:

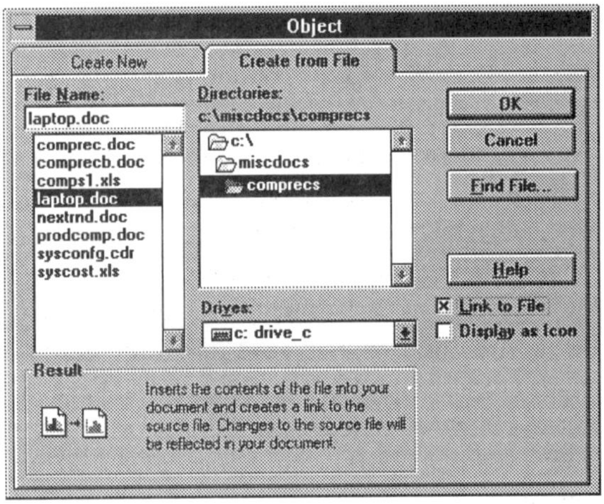

2. Identify the file you want to link to, and select the Link To File option.
3. Click on the OK button and the link is inserted.

Figure 23-2 How to link data from another application to an *Excel* worksheet (part 1 of 2)

Notes

- Before you link data from a document in another application to an *Excel* worksheet, be sure that the document has been saved with a permanent file name. Otherwise, the link in the *Excel* worksheet will point to the temporary file name, which will change when you save the document file. As a result, the link will be lost.
- The server application must be open for you to insert a link to data you've copied to the clipboard.
- The appearance of the linked data depends on the application that was used to create it. In some cases, the object appears as an icon that identifies the server application. In other cases, the object appears just as it does in the server application. If you want to display the data as an icon even though *Excel* can display it as it appears in the server application, select the Display As Icon option from the Paste Special dialog box or from the Create From File tab of the Object dialog box.
- You can edit a linked object in an *Excel* worksheet by double-clicking on it or by selecting the object, then selecting the object's name from the Edit menu. When you do, *Windows* opens the application you used to create the object or switches to the application if it's already open. Then, *Excel* loads the object so you can edit it. The way the server application appears depends on how it uses OLE features.
- You can use the Links command in the Edit menu to specify whether links are updated automatically (the default) or manually and to update manual links.

Figure 23-2 How to link data from another application to an *Excel* worksheet (part 2 of 2)

The procedure for embedding an existing document in an *Excel* worksheet is almost identical to the procedure for linking to a document presented in figure 23-2. The only difference is that you don't select the Link To File option when you want to embed the document.

To embed a new object in an *Excel* worksheet, you use the Object command in the Insert menu. When you use this command, *Windows* opens the application needed to create the type of object you select. Notice that when you create the object, you don't have to save it in a separate file. That's because the object is stored as part of the *Excel* worksheet. If you want to embed the object in other worksheets or other applications, however, you'll want to save it in a separate file so you don't have to recreate it each time you want to embed it.

How to embed an existing graphic object

1. From the server application, cut or copy the graphic object you want to embed in the *Excel* worksheet to the clipboard.
2. Switch to *Excel*, and place the cell pointer in the worksheet where you want to embed the object.
3. Click on the Paste button in the Standard toolbar, select the Paste command from the Edit menu, or use the keyboard shortcut (Ctrl+V), and the object is embedded in the worksheet.

How to embed existing text

1. From the server application, cut or copy the text you want to embed in the *Excel* worksheet to the clipboard.
2. Switch to *Excel*, and place the cell pointer in the worksheet where you want to embed the text. Then, select the Paste Special command from the Edit menu and this dialog box appears:

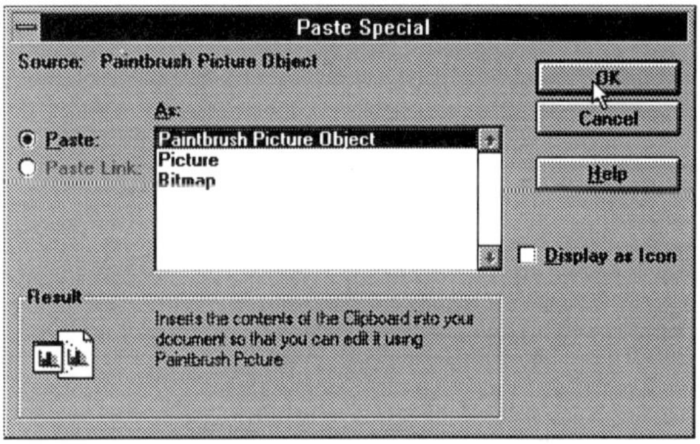

3. Select the "Object" format from the As list box, and make sure the Paste option, not the Paste Link option, is selected.
4. Click on the OK button and *Excel* embeds the text in the worksheet:

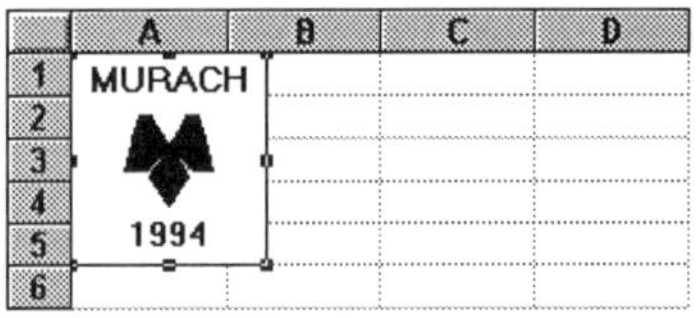

How to embed an existing document

Use the procedure in figure 23-2 for establishing a link to a document, but don't select the Link To File option.

Figure 23-3 How to embed an object in an *Excel* worksheet (part 1 of 3)

How to embed a new object

1. Place the cell pointer in the worksheet where you want to embed the new object. Then, select the Object command from the Insert menu and click on the Create New tab, and this dialog box appears:

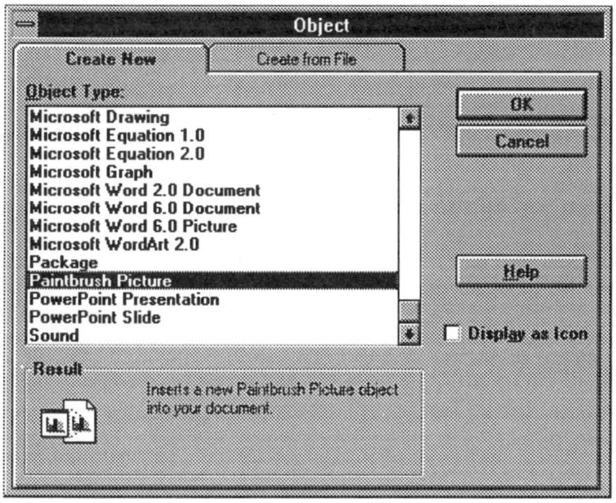

2. Select the type of object you want to create from the Object Type list box and click on the OK button. The application for the type of object you selected is opened:

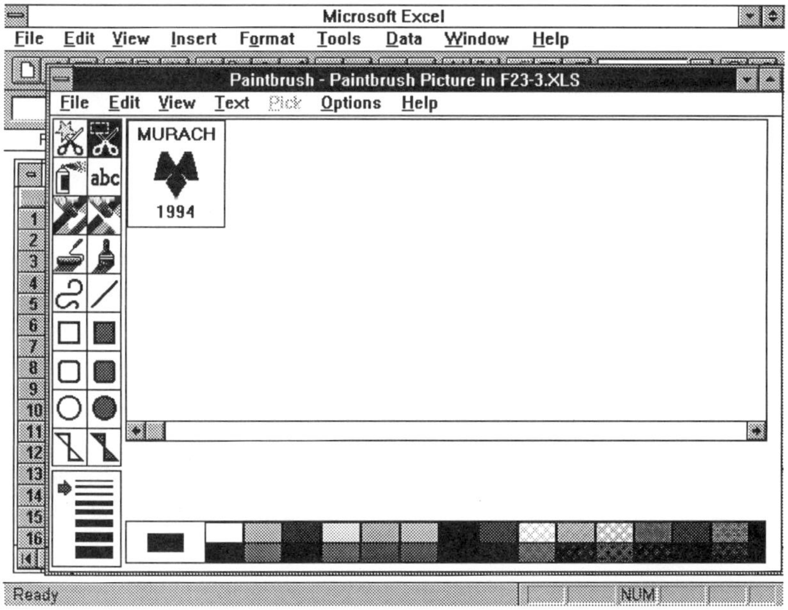

Figure 23-3 How to embed an object in an *Excel* worksheet (part 2 of 3)

3. Create the object.
4. Leave the server program and return to *Excel*. If the server program opened in a window, issue the appropriate command from its File menu (such as Update, Exit, or Exit and Return). If the server program was activated in place, click outside the object on any part of the *Excel* window.

Notes

- The format options listed in the Paste Special dialog box vary depending on the application you used to create the object you're embedding. To embed an object, select the format that ends in the word *Object*. If you select any other format, the object is inserted into the worksheet, not embedded.
- When you create an embedded object from *Excel*, the object doesn't need to be saved as a separate file since it's stored as part of the *Excel* worksheet.
- The appearance of the embedded data depends on the application that was used to create it. In some cases, the object appears as an icon that identifies the server application. In other cases, the object appears just as it does in the server application. If you want to display the data as an icon even though *Excel* can display it as it appears in the server application, select the Display As Icon option from the Paste Special dialog box or from the Create New tab of the Object dialog box.
- You can select, move, size, and delete an embedded object just as you can any drawn object.
- When the application for the embedded object is opened, it may appear in a separate window (as with Paintbrush in this example) or, if it uses OLE 2.0's in-place activation feature, it may take over the *Excel* window and change *Excel*'s menus and toolbar buttons to its own. Figure 23-4 illustrates in-place activation.

Figure 23-3 How to embed an object in an *Excel* worksheet (part 3 of 3)

How to modify an object embedded in an *Excel* worksheet The biggest advantage of embedding an object in an *Excel* worksheet versus inserting it is that you can edit it without leaving *Excel*. To do that, you use the procedure presented in figure 23-4. When you double-click on the object, *Excel* uses the embedded information to determine what server program was used to create the object.

If the server program uses OLE 1.0, a separate window is opened for the program as shown in the first part of figure 23-4. In contrast, if the server program uses OLE 2.0, the program "takes over" *Excel*'s application window and replaces *Excel*'s toolbars and menus (except File and Window) with its own, as shown in the second part of figure 23-4. This is OLE's *in-place activation* feature. To restore *Excel*'s menus and toolbars, all you have to do is click outside the activated object.

How to modify an object when the server application uses OLE 1.0

1. Double-click on the embedded object, and the application used to create the object is opened:

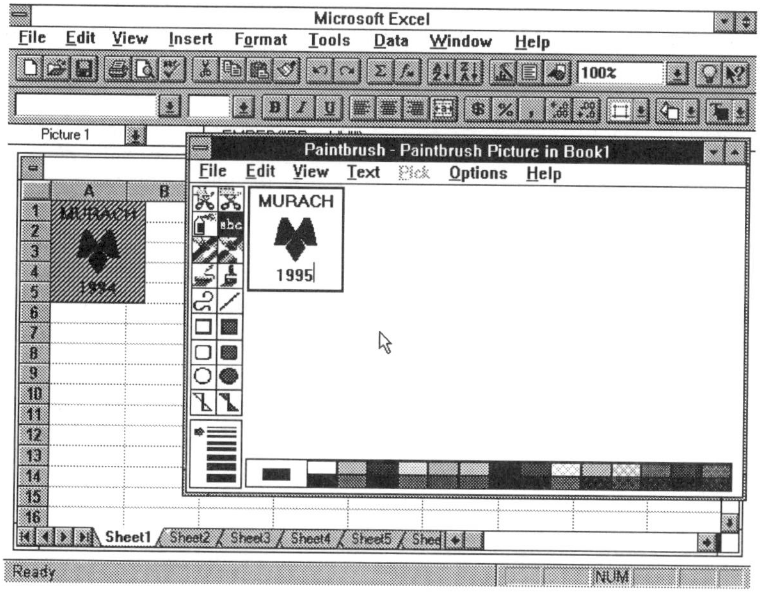

2. Modify the object, then save it and return to *Excel*. The commands or techniques you use depend on the application. When you return to *Excel*, the changes are reflected in the worksheet:

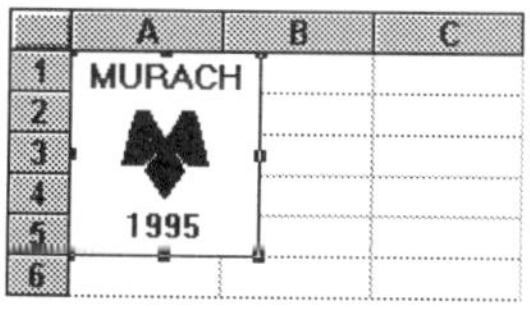

Figure 23-4 How to modify an object embedded in an *Excel* worksheet (part 1 of 3)

Perspective

Because OLE is still in its early stages of development, it isn't as useful as you might hope. First, not all applications support OLE, and many of those that do support it only partially. Second, because the programs that do support OLE use interfaces that aren't completely consistent, it's harder to work with them than it should be. In some cases, in fact, it may not work at all. And third, programs may respond so slowly when they use OLE that they'll frustrate you.

How to modify an object when the server application uses OLE 2.0's in-place activation feature

1. Double-click on the embedded object (here a *Word for Windows* 6.0 object), and the OLE 2.0-compliant server application is activated in place in the *Excel* application window:

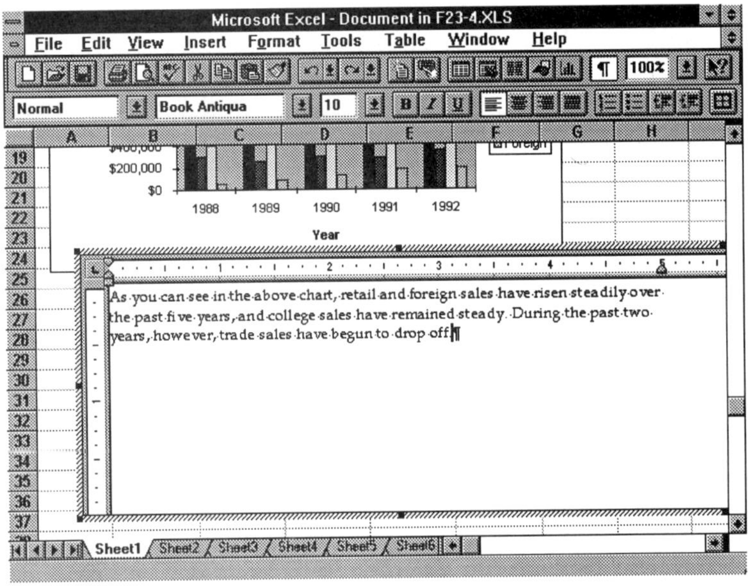

2. Modify the object from the application, then click on any part of the *Excel* document outside the object to reactivate *Excel*:

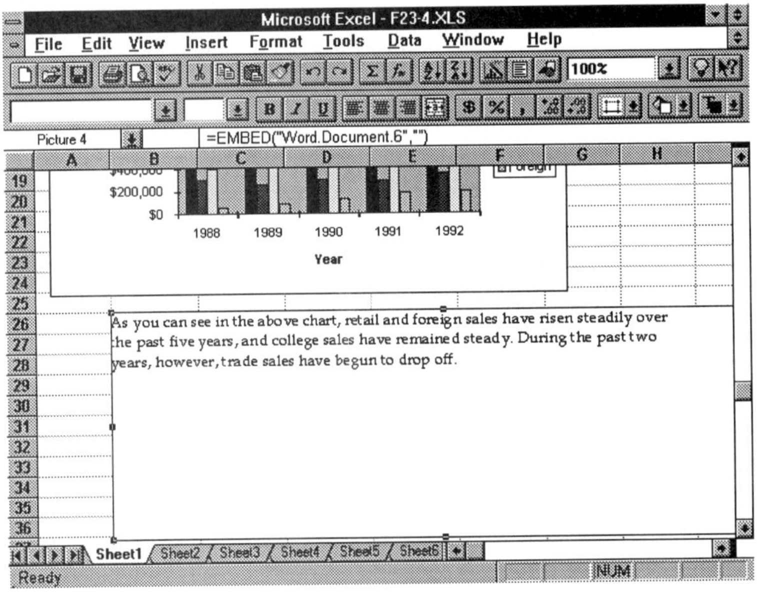

Figure 23-4 How to modify an object embedded in an *Excel* worksheet (part 2 of 3)

Notes

- You can also edit an object by selecting it, then selecting the Object command from the Edit menu.
- With in-place activation, the application window's title bar always shows *Excel* as the active program, but it reflects where the editing focus is at any given time.
- When an embedded object is activated, its application's menus, toolbars, and other features (like the word processing frame in this example) become available.

Figure 23-4 How to modify an object embedded in an *Excel* worksheet (part 3 of 3)

If you do want to use OLE in an application, you need to decide whether to use its linking or embedding feature. In general, you should link data when you want to share it between applications, and you expect that data to change. By linking the data, it's updated in the client application when it's changed in the server application. If you link data from one application to another, you'll want to experiment first to see if the links work properly. On the other hand, you should embed data when you don't need to share it with other applications, and you can't create the data in the application that you want to use it in.

Summary

- *Object Linking and Embedding* lets you *embed* or *link* an object created in a *server application* into a *destination document* created in a *client application*.
- An *embedded object* becomes a part of its destination document, while a *linked object* does not. You can access an embedded or linked object with the server application that created it directly through the destination document. To do that, you double-click on the object.
- To link data or embed existing text from another application to an *Excel* worksheet, you use the Paste Special command in the Edit menu. To embed an existing graphic object, you use the Paste command or toolbar button.
- To embed a new object in an *Excel* worksheet, you use the Object command in the Insert menu.
- OLE 2.0's *in-place activation* feature lets you edit a linked or embedded object without leaving *Excel*'s application window.

Chapter 24

Other features you ought to be aware of

If you've read the other 23 chapters in this book, you're already familiar with all but a few of *Excel*'s commands and features. You should also be quite proficient when it comes to learning new features. By now, you should see that there's an *Excel* logic behind each feature. So the more features you know, the easier it is to learn new features.

With that in mind, this chapter introduces you to the commands and features that haven't been presented in the earlier chapters. Unlike those chapters, though, this chapter doesn't present detailed information for all of the features. In some cases, it just introduces you to the capabilities that a feature provides. Then, if you need that feature, you should be able to learn how to use it on your own in just a few minutes. If you're like most *Excel* users, though, you're only going to be interested in a few of the features in this chapter. If you use the chapter plan on the facing page as a guide to this chapter, you can go directly to the features that you're interested in.

Other File menu commands

The File menu includes four commands that this book hasn't presented in detail: Save Workspace, Find File, Summary Info, and Print Report. If you work with complex sets of related *Excel* workbooks, Save Workspace and Print Report may be useful to you. And if you use *Excel* as part of a networked workgroup, Find File and Summary Info may come in handy.

Save Workspace If you use the same group of workbook files regularly, you may be able to work more efficiently if you create a workspace. A *workspace* is a file that records what workbooks are open and how their windows are arranged on the screen. When you open a workspace, all of the workbooks it contains are opened and their windows are positioned where they were when the workspace was created.

To create a workspace, you open all of the workbook files you want it to contain and arrange their windows the way you want them. Then, you issue the Save Workspace command from the File menu, and *Excel* displays the Save Workspace dialog box shown in figure 24-1. As you can see in this figure, the default name for a workspace is RESUME.XLW. Although you can change the file name, you should keep the XLW extension.

If you create a workspace file, you should know that it contains only the locations and screen positions of the workbooks and not the workbooks themselves. So you don't need to worry about workspace files taking up a lot of disk space. Because it contains only the locations and screen positions of the workbooks, however, *Excel* won't be able to find a workbook if

Access

Select the Save Workspace command from the File menu.

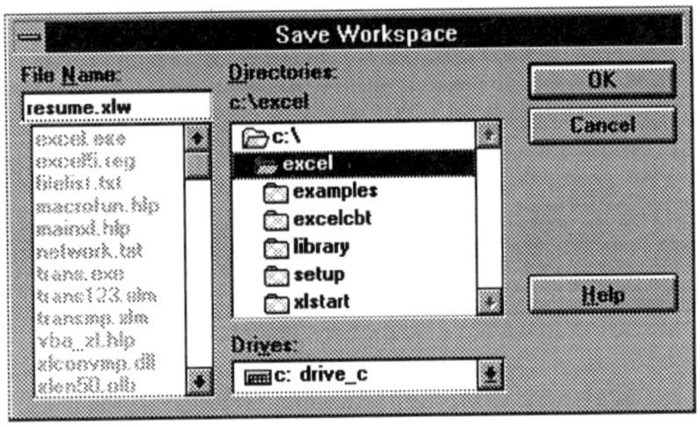

Operation

To create a workspace, open all of the workbook files you want it to contain and arrange their windows the way you want them. Then, access the Save Workspace dialog box, identify the drive and directory where you want to save the workspace, and enter a file name.

Notes

- The extension for a workspace file is XLW. *Excel* recommends RESUME.XLW as the default name for a workspace.
- To open a workspace file, use the Open command in the File menu. Then, all of the workbooks the workspace contains are opened and their windows are positioned as they were when the workspace was created.

Figure 24-1 How to create a workspace

you move or rename it. In that case, you have to recreate the workspace to update it.

To open a workspace file, you use the Open command. Because workspace files have the extension XLW, they appear by default along with workbook files in the Open dialog box.

Find File Figure 24-2 presents the Find File command. This command lets you search directory paths on your system to locate files that meet criteria you specify. Then, you can preview or open those files, and you can perform a limited set of file management operations on them. In a sense, the Find File command is like a shell program that's built into *Excel*. However, if you're comfortable working with the *Windows* File Manager, you probably won't want to use the Find File command.

Access

Select the Find File command from the File menu.

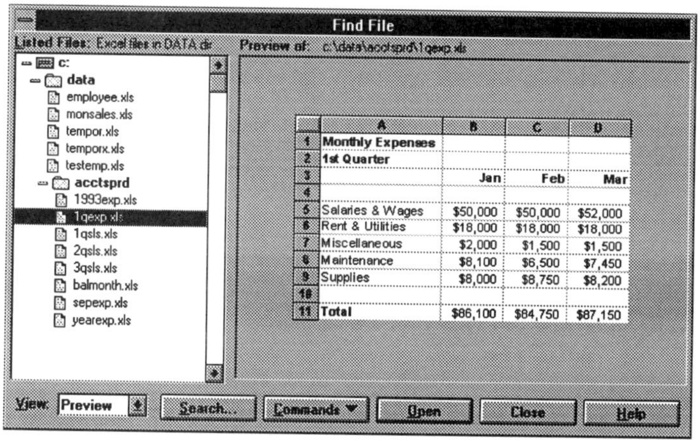

Operation

- To change the search criteria for the files listed in the Listed Files list box, click on the Search button and enter the new criteria in the Search dialog box:

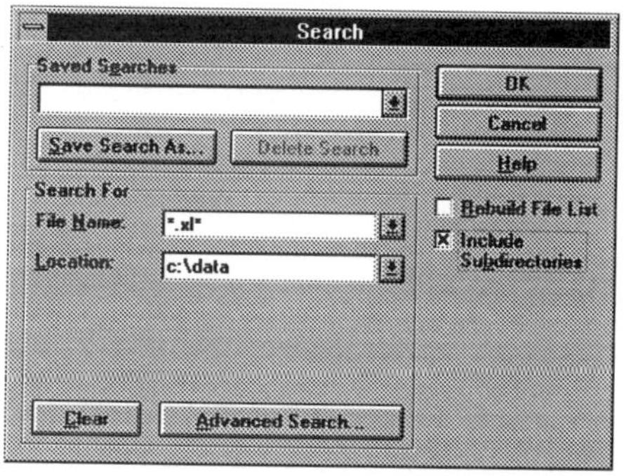

- To change the format of and the information displayed in the Find File dialog box, select an option from the View drop-down list box. The preview option displays a part of the selected file on the right side of the dialog box. The Summary option displays data entered for the selected file using the Summary Info command. And the File Info option expands the tree so it uses the entire width of the dialog box and shows the user, size, and date last saved for each file.
- To manage the files in the directory tree, click on the Commands button and *Excel* displays a menu of file management commands, including Delete and Copy.
- To retrieve and open a selected file, click on the Open button.

Notes

- The first time you select the Find File command, the Search dialog box appears so you can enter the search criteria. From then on, the Find File dialog box appears when you select this command.
- You can name and save search criteria from the Search dialog box.
- The Advanced Search button in the Search dialog box lets you specify specialized search criteria.

Figure 24-2 How to use the Find File command

Access

Select the Summary Info command from the File menu.

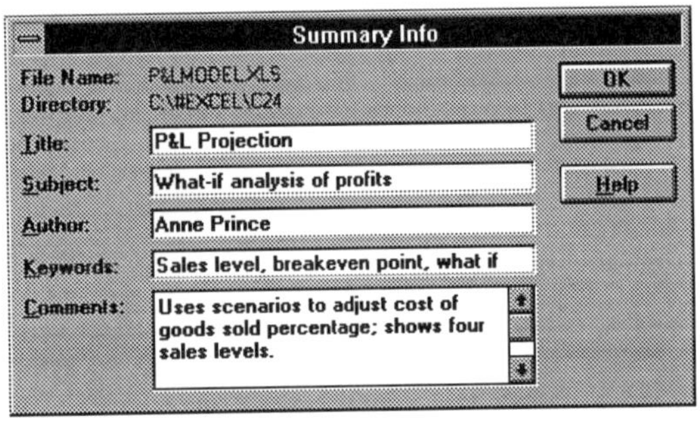

Notes

- You can enter up to 255 characters in each of the five boxes in the Summary Info dialog box.
- If the Prompt For Summary Info option in the General tab of the Options dialog box is selected, *Excel* will display the Summary Info dialog box each time you save a new file. To access the Options dialog box to turn this option on or off, select the Options command from the Tools menu.
- *Excel* automatically inserts the name of the current user in the Author box. You can set the user name in the User Name text box in the General tab of the Options dialog box. To access the Options dialog box to change this name, select the Options command from the Tools menu.
- You can search for files that contain specific summary information using the Find File command.

Figure 24-3 How to use the Summary Info command

Summary Info Figure 24-3 presents the Summary Info command. This command lets you view and enter descriptive information for the current workbook. If you use *Excel* as part of a workgroup, you can enter information in the Summary Info dialog box that can help your co-workers use the workbook. Even if you don't share workbooks with other users, you can enter notes and documentation information in the Summary Info dialog box that can help you keep track of your *Excel* files.

Print Report Figure 24-4 presents the Print Report command. This command lets you set up *reports* that contain customized printing specifications. A report can contain multiple *sections*. Each section specifies one worksheet in the current workbook, and optionally, a view and/or a scenario you want applied to that worksheet when the report is printed. The report in figure 24-4, for example, consists of two sections. Each section contains a different scenario of the same worksheet.

Access

Select the Print Report command from the File menu.

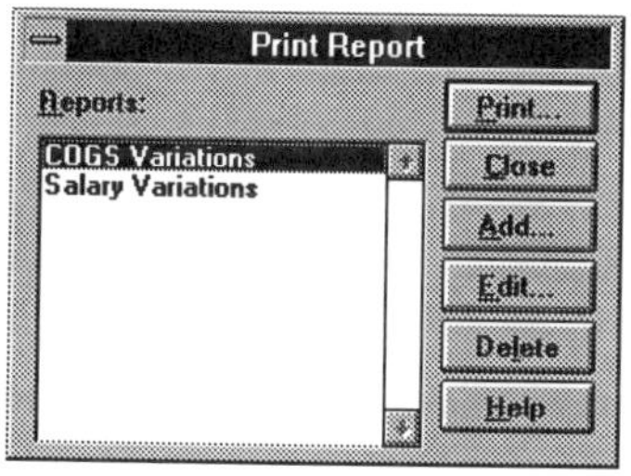

Operation

- To print a report, select it from the Reports list box and click on the Print button.
- To enter specifications for a new report, click on the Add button and complete the Add report dialog box:

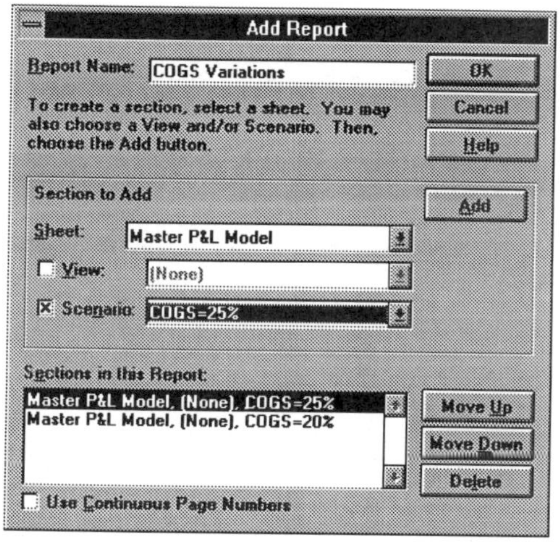

- To change the specifications for an existing report, select it and click on the Edit button. Then, complete the Edit Report dialog box. (This dialog box is identical to the Add Report dialog box.)
- To delete a report, select it and click on the Delete button.

Notes

- When you print a report, all of its sections are printed.
- You can create multiple reports in a single workbook.
- A report is saved as part of the workbook file.
- If the Print Report command doesn't appear on the File menu, you have to enable or install the Report Manager add-in.

Figure 24-4 How to use the Print Report command

Access

Select the Protect Workbook command from Protection submenu of the Tools menu.

Operation

- To prevent unauthorized users from removing workbook protection, enter a password in the Password text box.
- To prevent users from adding, deleting, renaming, moving, hiding, or displaying sheets in the workbook, select the Structure option.
- To prevent users from moving or resizing the workbook's windows, select the Windows option.

Notes

- If the current workbook is already protected, the Unprotect Workbook command appears in the Protection submenu instead of Protect Workbook. If you select the Unprotect Workbook command and the workbook is password protected, a dialog box appears that asks you to enter the password.
- Protecting a workbook does not keep unauthorized users from opening it. To do that, save the workbook with a protection password. See figure 24-8 for more information.

Figure 24-5 How to use the Protect Workbook command to protect a workbook from changes

Other Tools menu commands

The Tools menu includes two commands that this book hasn't presented in detail: Protection and Add-Ins. You'll learn about both of these commands here. In addition, you'll learn about some commands on other menus that are related to the Protection command.

Protection and related commands on other menus When you've spent many hours developing a worksheet, you don't want it to be destroyed or changed by accident. And if the data is private, you don't want unauthorized people to open the workbook file. In this topic, you'll learn how to protect the data in an entire workbook, an entire worksheet, or selected ranges within a worksheet from unauthorized use.

Figure 24-5 shows you how to protect a workbook from being changed, and figure 24-6 shows you how to protect a worksheet from being changed.

Access

Select the Protect Sheet command from the Protection submenu of the Tools menu.

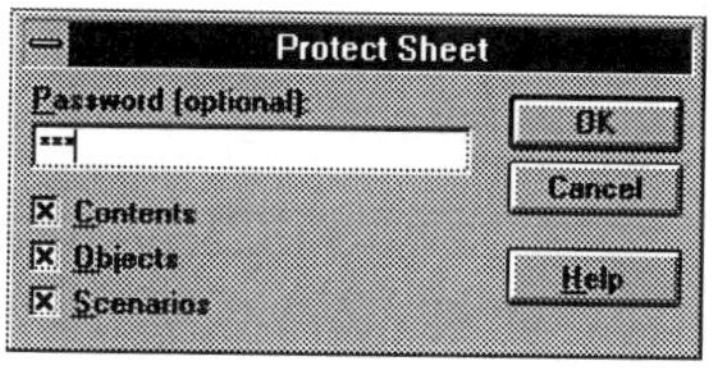

Operation

- To prevent unauthorized users from removing sheet protection, enter a password in the Password text box.
- To prevent users from changing cells or chart items, select the Contents option.
- To prevent users from changing graphic objects, select the Objects option.
- To prevent users from changing scenarios, select the Scenarios option.

Notes

- Before you use the Protect Sheet command to lock a worksheet, you can specify unlocked status for individual cell ranges and graphic objects. See figure 24-7 for more information.
- If the current worksheet is already protected, the Unprotect Sheet command appears in the Protection submenu instead of Protect Sheet. If you select the Unprotect Sheet command and the worksheet is password protected, a dialog box appears that asks you to enter the password.

Figure 24-6 How to use the Protect Sheet command to protect a worksheet from changes

As you can see, you can select different levels of protection in the Protect Workbook and Protect Worksheet dialog boxes. Workbook protection options keep users from changing the structure and layout of a workbook, and worksheet protection options keep users from changing the information in a worksheet.

You can also assign a password to a workbook or a worksheet when you protect it. Then, no one can remove the protection without entering the password, including you. So be sure to use a password that you'll remember.

By default, all of the cells and graphic objects in a worksheet are protected when you protect the worksheet. Sometimes, however, you may want to leave some of the data unprotected. Then, you can delegate the job of keeping the file up-to-date to someone else without worrying that the person will delete or change the formulas, fixed data, or objects in the worksheet.

How to unlock cells

1. Select the range of cells or the object you want to leave unlocked.
2. Select the Cells command from the Format menu, then click on the Protection tab and this dialog box appears:

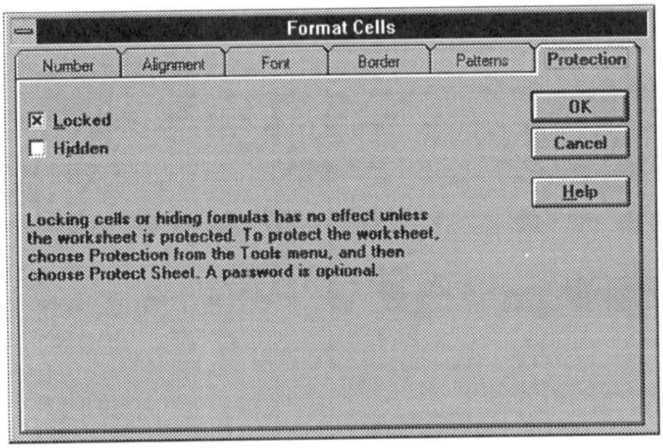

3. Deselect the Locked option and click on the OK button.
4. Repeat steps 1 through 3 for each range of cells you want to leave unlocked.
5. Protect the worksheet using the Protect Sheet command presented in figure 24-6.

How to unlock a graphic object

Use the procedure above, but select the object you want to protect and select the Object command from the Format menu.

Notes

- Although the Locked options are selected by default, *Excel* enforces locking only when you protect the worksheet using the Protect Sheet command.
- If you don't unlock cells or objects before you protect it with the Protect Sheet command, the entire worksheet is protected.
- The Hidden option in the Format Cells dialog box prevents a cell's formula from appearing in the formula bar when the contents of a worksheet are protected.
- If you select a text box, the Format Object dialog box includes the Lock Text option. This option determines whether the text inside the box is locked or unlocked. The Locked option affects only the box.

Figure 24-7 How to unlock cells or graphic objects

Figure 24-7 shows you how to use the Protection tab of the Format Cells and Format Object dialog boxes to unprotect, or unlock, cells and graphic objects. Note that you can't unlock cells or objects after a worksheet has been protected. So if you've already protected a worksheet, you have to unprotect it before you can unlock any of its cells or graphic objects.

Although protecting a workbook or worksheet using the Protection command can keep others from changing it, it doesn't keep them from accessing it and viewing its contents. And it doesn't keep them from copying the data to another workbook or worksheet where they can change it.

If you want to keep other users from opening a workbook and viewing its contents, you can assign a *protection password* to the file. And if you want to let other users make changes to a workbook but you don't want to let them save the changes in the same file, you can assign a *write reservation password*. Figure 24-8 shows you how to assign both of these types of passwords to a workbook.

After you apply a protection password to a workbook, no one can open the file without entering the password. After you apply a write reservation password to a workbook, no one can save changes to the file without entering the password. If you can't remember the password, there's no way to find out what it is. So again, be sure to use a password that you'll remember.

Add-Ins An *add-in program* is a module that expands the capabilities of *Excel*. Several add-ins come with *Excel*, and some of *Excel*'s commands (like View Manager, Print Report, Solver, and Get External Data) are implemented by add-ins. You can select which add-ins are active using the Add-Ins command as shown in figure 24-9.

When *Excel* starts, it loads the add-ins that are selected in the Add-Ins dialog box into memory. Then, their functions are available from *Excel*'s menus. If you want to use one of the add-ins that comes with *Excel* that isn't enabled by default, you can select it in the Add-Ins dialog box. If you want to use an add-in that wasn't installed when *Excel* was set up, you may be able to use the dialog box that's displayed when you click on the Browse button to identify the file. Otherwise, you can use the *Excel* Setup program to install it.

You can also disable an add-in by deselecting it in the Add-Ins dialog box. You may want to do that if you never use an add-in that's enabled by default (like Solver or Get External Data). Then, the next time you start *Excel*, that add-in isn't loaded into memory, and *Excel* may operate slightly more efficiently.

Other Data menu commands

The Data menu includes three commands that this book hasn't presented in detail: Table, Text to Columns, and Consolidate. The following topics introduce all three.

How to protect a workbook file from being opened

1. Access the Save As dialog box.
2. Click on the Options button and this dialog box appears:

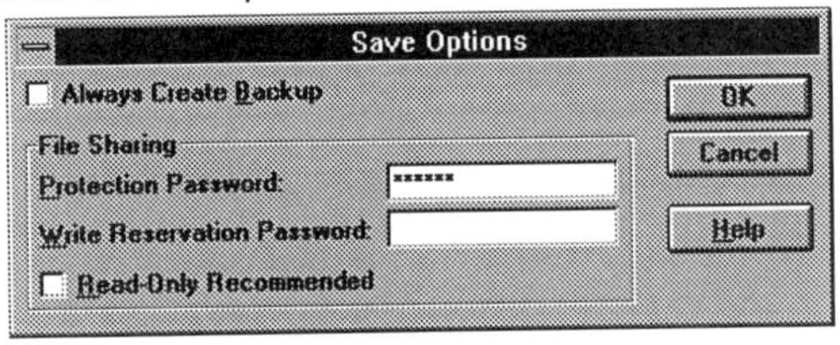

3. Enter a password in the Protection Password text box and click on the OK button.
4. Enter the password again in the Confirm Password dialog box and click on the OK button:

5. Complete the save operation from the Save As dialog box.

How to protect a workbook file from being saved

Use the procedure above, but enter a password in the Write Reservation Password text box.

Notes

- When you open a workbook file that has a protection password or save a file that has a write reservation password, you have to supply the correct password. If you can't remember the password, there's no way to find out what the password is from your PC. And there's no way to open or save the file without supplying the password.
- Although you can't save the changes you make to a file with a write reservation password to that file, you can save the changes to another file.
- If you select the Read-Only Recommended option, *Excel* displays a dialog box when you try to open the file that recommends it be opened as a read-only file. Changes made to a read-only file can't be saved in that file, so opening a file as read-only is effectively the same as opening a file with a write reservation password. However, you have the option of not following the read-only recommendation.

Figure 24-8 How to protect a workbook file from being opened or saved

Access

Select the Add-Ins command from the Tools menu.

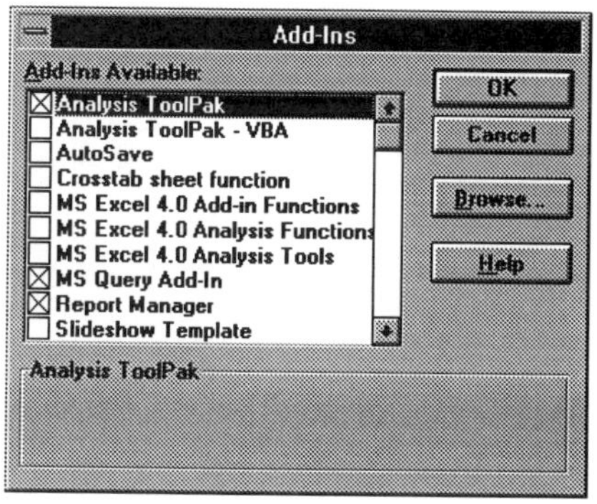

Operation

To enable an add-in so it's loaded when you start *Excel*, select the add-in from the Add-Ins Available list box.

Notes

- As you enable more and more add-ins, you expand the capabilities of *Excel*, but you also increase its memory and resource requirements. As a result, you should disable add-ins that you don't use.
- The add-ins that appear in the Add-Ins Available list box are those that were set up when *Excel* was installed on your PC. As a result, the Add-Ins dialog box on your PC may look different from the one in this figure.
- You can install additional add-ins using the Browse button or the *Excel* Setup program. The Setup program also lets you remove add-ins.
- The add-ins that come with *Excel* 5.0 are:

Analysis ToolPak	Adds statistical and engineering analysis features.
AutoSave	Saves workbooks automatically.
Microsoft ODBC Function	Adds macro features for retrieving data managed by data base programs that support Open Database Connectivity (ODBC).
Microsoft Query	Accesses *MS Query* to retrieve data from external data bases.
Report Manager	Prints reports that can contain multiple worksheets, with or without views and scenarios.
Slide Show	Works with the Slide Show template to create a slide show.
Solver	Calculates solutions to what-if problems.
View Manager	Saves and applies views.

Figure 24-9 How to enable an add-in program

Table When you use the Table command, you can create a *data table*, or *what-if* table, that depends on one or two variables. The table shows the results of substituting different values for the variables. With a one-variable data table, you can see the results of changing values on one or more formulas; with a two-variable table, you're restricted to one formula.

Figure 24-10 shows you how to set up a one- and two-variable table. As you can see, each table requires an input cell for each variable it uses. When *Excel* calculates the table, it uses these cells to temporarily store the values of the associated variables.

Each table also contains a formula that defines the calculation you want to perform for each variable or set of variables. The formula is part of the table and must be in a prescribed location. When you create a formula for a data table, the cell reference you enter for a variable in the table must refer to the input cell for the variable. In the one-variable table in the figure, for example, the formula refers to cell B15.

Figure 24-11 shows you how to calculate a data table. As you can see, once you highlight the range for the table and select the Table command, you simply identify the input cells. Then, *Excel* calculates the formula for each variable or set of variables and places the results in the table.

Although data tables may seem right for some of the analysis you do, I question their usefulness. Although they're easy to calculate, they take extra time to set up. In many cases, I think you'll find it easier to just copy the formula you want to use to all the cells in the table.

Text to Columns Figure 24-12 shows you what you can do with the Text to Columns command. As you can see, you use it to divide (or *parse*) text in one column into two or more columns. When you issue this command, it invokes *Excel*'s TextWizard. You saw how to use the TextWizard in chapter 17 when I showed you how to open a text file. The TextWizard dialog boxes for parsing text in a column are almost identical to the ones presented in that chapter. So you can refer back to figure 17-1 if you want to find out how to use these dialog boxes.

The Text to Columns command may be useful when you paste data from another application into a worksheet or when you open a text file, but you don't complete the parsing process. However, these are special cases. For the most part, the Text to Columns command is of little use.

How to set up a one-variable table

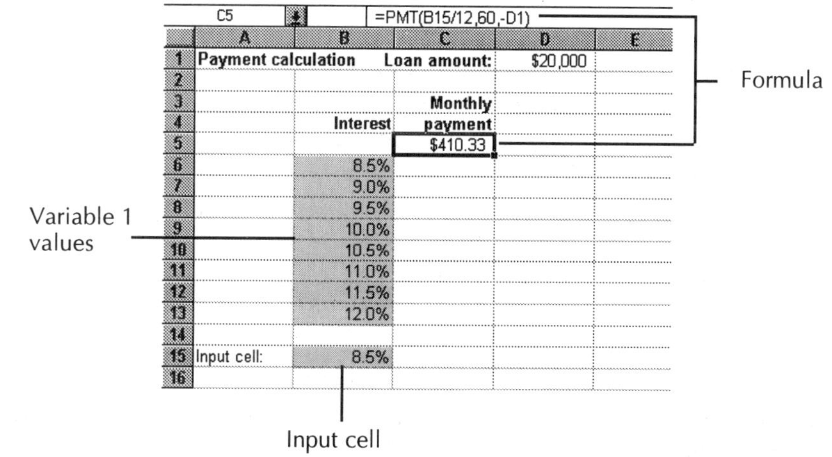

How to set up a two-variable table

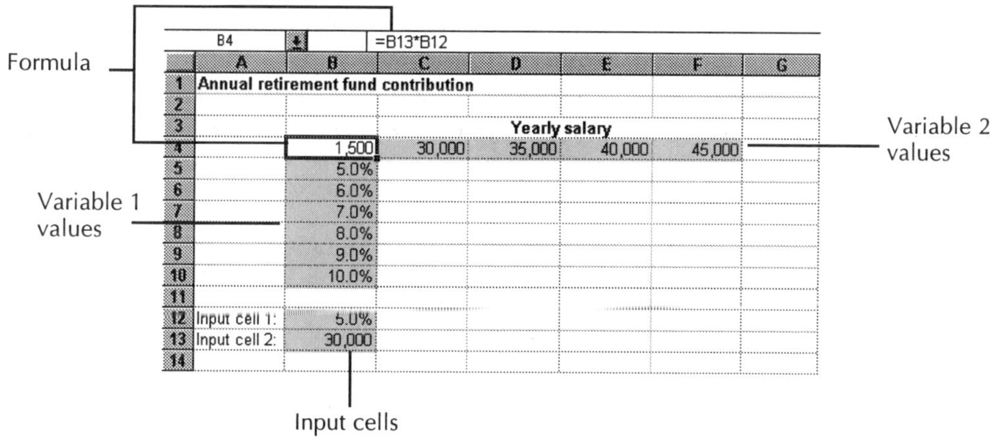

Notes

- You can also set up a one-variable table with the input values in a row instead of in a column.
- *Excel* uses the input cells to temporarily store the values of the variables they're associated with as it calculates the table.
- The formula in a data table indicates the calculation you want to perform for each variable or set of variables. The formula must refer to the input cells associated with the variables for the table.
- A one-variable table can include more than one formula. Each formula must be entered in the cell immediately to the right or below the previous formula depending on the orientation of the table.

Figure 24-10 How to set up a data table

How to calculate a two-variable data table

1. Select the range for the table, then select the Table command from the Data menu and this dialog box appears:

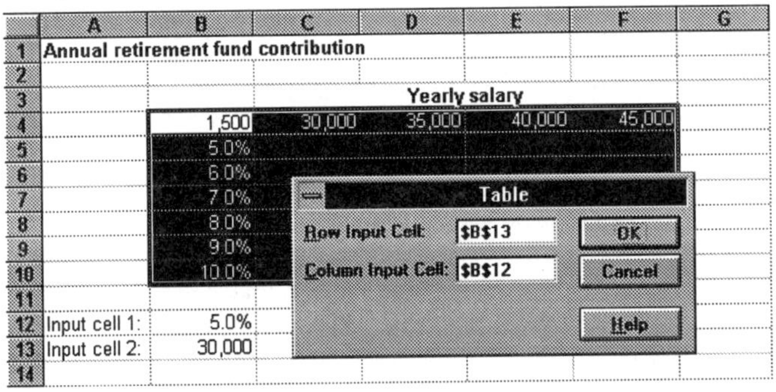

2. Enter the cell references for the input cells in the Row Input Cell and Column Input Cell text boxes.
3. Click on the OK button and *Excel* calculates the table:

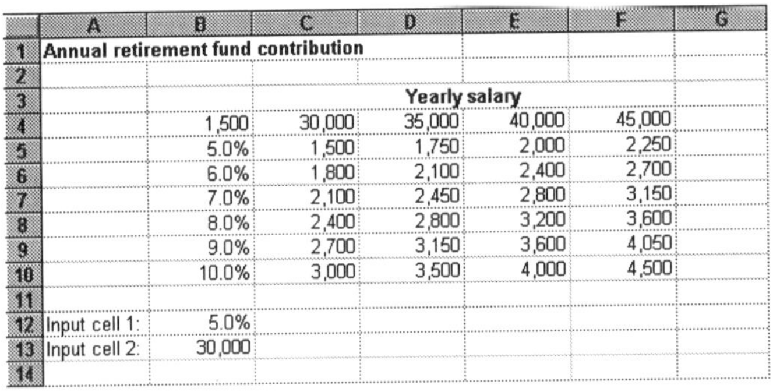

	A	B	C	D	E	F	G
1	Annual retirement fund contribution						
2							
3				Yearly salary			
4		1,500	30,000	35,000	40,000	45,000	
5		5.0%	1,500	1,750	2,000	2,250	
6		6.0%	1,800	2,100	2,400	2,700	
7		7.0%	2,100	2,450	2,800	3,150	
8		8.0%	2,400	2,800	3,200	3,600	
9		9.0%	2,700	3,150	3,600	4,050	
10		10.0%	3,000	3,500	4,000	4,500	
11							
12	Input cell 1:	5.0%					
13	Input cell 2:	30,000					
14							

How to calculate a one-variable data table

Use the procedure above, but enter a value in either the Row Input Cell or the Column Input Cell text box, not both. Which text box you enter a value in depends on the orientation of the table.

Note

Be sure to include the formula in the range you select for a one-variable table.

Figure 24-11 How to calculate a data table

A worksheet before and after one column of text is distributed across multiple columns with the Text to Columns command

Before

	A	B	C	D	E	F
1	Smith Mary Admin 1 23 24600					
2	Jones Georgia Mktg 3 43 47500					
3	Long John Prod 3 52 39900					
4	Johnson Edward Admin 2 30 33250					
5	Jones John Prod 2 33 31400					
6	Williams Alice Admin 1 50 28900					
7	Allen Joel Admin 2 25 30000					
8	Clay Kurt Mktg 2 43 41250					
9	Burkes Patricia Prod 1 52 28500					
10	Andrews Anne Admin 3 30 34000					
11	Russell Barry Prod 2 33 31500					
12	Thompson John Mktg 1 50 26500					
13						

After

	A	B	C	D	E	F
1	Smith	Mary	Admin	1	23	24600
2	Jones	Georgia	Mktg	3	43	47500
3	Long	John	Prod	3	52	39900
4	Johnson	Edward	Admin	2	30	33250
5	Jones	John	Prod	2	33	31400
6	Williams	Alice	Admin	1	50	28900
7	Allen	Joel	Admin	2	25	30000
8	Clay	Kurt	Mktg	2	43	41250
9	Burkes	Patricia	Prod	1	52	28500
10	Andrews	Anne	Admin	3	30	34000
11	Russell	Barry	Prod	2	33	31500
12	Thompson	John	Mktg	1	50	26500
13						

Notes

- The Text to Columns command uses the TextWizard, which prompts you to specify how the text in the selected column should be divided (parsed) into a number of columns. The TextWizard dialog boxes are presented in figure 17-1.
- The Text to Columns command can parse just one column of data at a time.

Figure 24-12 The operation of the Text to Columns command

Consolidate Figure 24-13 presents the procedure for consolidating the data in two or more *source areas* into a *destination area*. The source areas can all be in the same worksheet, they can be in different worksheets, or they can be in different workbooks. *Excel* consolidates the data by matching the categories in the source areas and summarizing them using the function you select from the Consolidate dialog box. Although the Consolidate command may be useful to you in some situations, it's usually worth avoiding because it's cumbersome and can lead to errors.

How to consolidate data by position

1. Place the cell pointer on the cell in the upper left corner of the range where you want to place the consolidated data.
2. Select the Consolidate command from the Data menu and this dialog box appears:

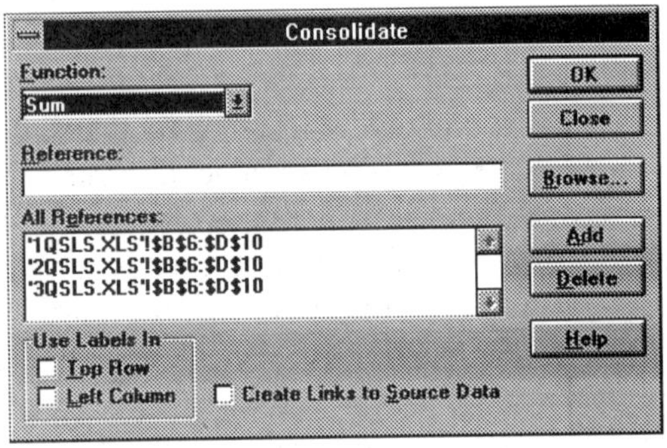

3. Select the function you want to use to summarize the consolidated data from the Function drop-down list box.
4. Specify the first source area in the Reference text box. Click on the Add button and the reference to the source area appears in the All References list box.
5. Repeat steps 3 and 4 for each source area you want to consolidate.
6. Click on the OK button and the data in all the specified source areas is consolidated.

How to consolidate data by category

Use the procedure above, but select one or both of the Use Labels In options.

Notes

- You can consolidate up to 255 source areas into a destination area. The source areas can be in the same worksheet, different worksheets, or different workbooks.
- You can specify a source area by typing in a range reference or a range name or by selecting the range from an open workbook. If the workbook that contains a source area isn't open, you can use the Browse button to select the file and enter the file reference.
- You can consolidate data by position if the categories of data in each source area are in the same relative position. If you specify the source areas by cell references, don't include labels in the source areas.
- You can consolidate data by category if the categories of data in the source areas are in different relative positions or if the source areas contain different numbers of rows or columns. The source areas you specify must include the labels for the data. You identify the position of the data labels by selecting the Top Row or Left Column option or both.

Figure 24-13 How to consolidate data

Visual Basic

When I showed you how to create and use recorded macros in chapter 19, I mentioned that macros are recorded and stored as Visual Basic procedures. Frankly, most users probably don't need or even want to know that. If you're a programmer, however, you may want to know more about Visual Basic.

Visual Basic is a powerful programming language that comes with *Excel*. It's documented in the *Visual Basic User's Guide*, a manual that comes with *Excel*, and in *Excel*'s online Help facility. Figure 24-14 presents two screens that illustrate the online Help for Visual Basic. When you use it, you can easily find how-to information for many programming tasks and reference information for all Visual Basic functions, methods, objects, properties, and statements.

If you're a programmer who's not used to working with a "visual" programming language, Visual Basic will surprise and delight you. It lets you easily create objects like dialog boxes with complicated controls that have Visual Basic procedures attached to them. So if you're an experienced programmer, you'll have no problem learning how to use Visual Basic to create *Excel* applications.

Perspective

As I said at the start of this chapter, the features presented here aren't for everyone. In fact, typical users probably won't have much use for any of them. But in case you do, the information presented in this chapter should be enough to get you started using them. Then, you can refer to the *Excel* manuals or online Help if you need more information.

Summary

- You can use the Save Workspace command in the File menu to create a *workspace* file that records all open workbooks and the arrangement of their windows on the screen. Then, you can re-open all of these workbooks in one operation by opening the workspace file.
- You can use the Find File command in the File menu to search directory paths on your system to locate files that meet criteria you specify, to preview or open those files, and to perform a limited set of file management operations on them.

The main menu for Visual Basic Help information

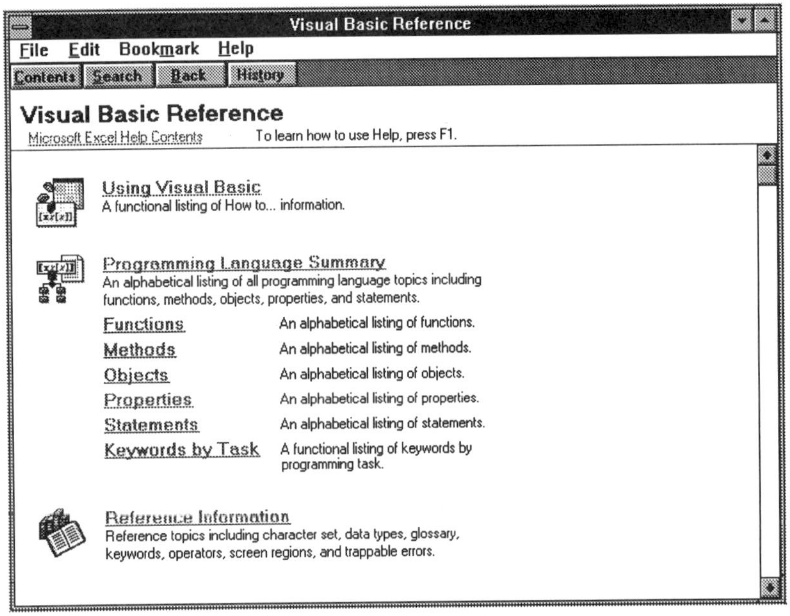

Information on how to perform a common Visual Basic programming task

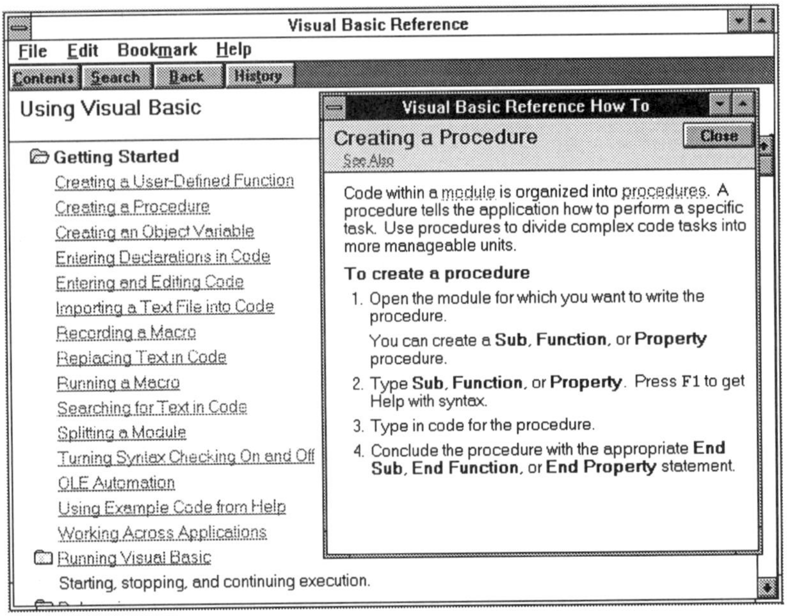

Figure 24-14 Two screens that show Visual Basic Help information

- You can use the Summary Info command in the File menu to enter and access descriptive information for the current workbook.
- You can use the Print Report command in the File menu to set up and print *reports* that contain customized printing specifications.
- You can use the Protect Workbook command in the Protection submenu of the Tools menu to prevent unauthorized changes to a workbook's structure or window arrangement.
- You can use the Protect Worksheet command in the Protection submenu of the Tools menu to prevent unauthorized changes to a worksheet's contents.
- You can leave some of the data in a worksheet unprotected by removing the locked status for selected cells or objects using the Format Cells or Format Object dialog box before you apply worksheet protection.
- You can specify a *protection password* for a workbook in the Save Options dialog box that a user must specify to open it. You can specify a *write reservation password* for a workbook in the Save Options dialog box that a user must specify to save changes to it.
- You can use the Add-Ins command in the Tools menu to enable or disable installed *add-in* programs.
- You can use the Table command in the Data menu to create a one-variable or a two-variable *data table*.
- You can use the Text to Columns command in the Data menu to *parse* data in a single column into two or more columns.
- You can use the Consolidate command in the Data menu to combine data from two or more *source areas* into a single *destination area*.
- You can use *Visual Basic*, a powerful programming language that comes with *Excel*, to create applications. You can access the Help information for Visual Basic to get complete technical documentation for the language.

Index

A

D

G

O

P

Q

R

T

Comment Form

Your opinions count

If you have any comments, criticisms, or suggestions for us, I'm eager to get them. Your opinions today will affect our products of tomorrow. And if you find any errors in this book, typographical or otherwise, please point them out so we can correct them in the next printing.

Thanks for your help.

Mike Murach

Book title: The Essential Guide: *Excel 5.0 for Windows*

Dear Mike: ____

Name ____

Company (if company address) ____

Address ____

City, State, Zip ____

Fold where indicated and tape closed.

No postage necessary if mailed in the U.S.

fold

fold

NO POSTAGE
NECESSARY
IF MAILED
IN THE
UNITED STATES

BUSINESS REPLY MAIL

FIRST-CLASS MAIL PERMIT NO. 3063 FRESNO, CA

POSTAGE WILL BE PAID BY ADDRESSEE

Mike Murach & Associates, Inc.

4697 W JACQUELYN AVE
FRESNO CA 93722-9888

fold

fold

Order Form

Our Ironclad Guarantee

To our customers who order directly from us: You must be satisfied. Our books must work for you, or you can send them back for a full refund...no questions asked.

Name (& Title, if any) ______________________

Company (if company address) ______________________

Street address ______________________

City, State, Zip ______________________

Phone number (including area code) ______________________

Fax number (if you fax your order to us) ______________________

Qty	Product code and title		*Price
Windows			
____	LWIN	The Least You Need to Know about Windows 3.1	$20.00
____	EEX5	Essential Guide: Excel 5.0 for Windows	25.00
____	MWW6	Essential Guide: Word 6.0 for Windows (available July 1994)	25.00
____	ELW4	Essential Guide: 1-2-3 Release 4 for Windows	20.00
____	WPW6	Essential Guide: WordPerfect 6.0 for Windows	25.00
Business Writing			
____	WBPC	Write Better with a PC	$19.95

Qty	Product code and title		*Price
DOS			
____	LDSR	The Least You Need to Know about DOS (2nd Ed.)	$20.00
____	DOSR	The Only DOS Book You'll Ever Need (2nd Ed.)	27.50
____	LLOT	The Least You Need to Know about Lotus 1-2-3 for DOS (covers 2.0-2.4 & 3.1)	20.00
____	GLOT	The Practical Guide to Lotus 1-2-3 for DOS (covers 2.0-2.4 and 3.0-3.4)	25.00
____	LWP	The Least You Need to Know about WordPerfect for DOS (covers 5.0 and 5.1)	20.00
____	WPTU	The WordPerfect Tutorial (covers 5.0 and 5.1)	10.00
____	EWP6**	Essential Guide: WordPerfect 6.0 for DOS	25.00
____	DWPL	DOS, WordPerfect, and Lotus Essentials	25.00

☐ Bill me for the books plus UPS shipping and handling (and sales tax within California).

☐ Bill my company. P.O.# ______________________

☐ I want to **SAVE 10%** by paying in advance. Charge to my ____Visa ____MasterCard ____American Express:
Card number ______________________
Valid thru (mo/yr) ______________________
Cardowner's signature ______________________

☐ I want to **SAVE 10% plus shipping and handling**. Here's my check for the books minus 10% ($____________). California residents, please add sales tax to your total. (Offer valid in U.S.)

To order more quickly,

Call **toll-free** 1-800-221-5528

(Weekdays, 8 to 5 Pacific Standard Time)

Fax: 1-209-275-9035

Mike Murach & Associates, Inc.

4697 West Jacquelyn Avenue
Fresno, California 93722-6427
(209) 275-3335

fold

fold

NO POSTAGE
NECESSARY
IF MAILED
IN THE
UNITED STATES

BUSINESS REPLY MAIL

FIRST-CLASS MAIL PERMIT NO. 3063 FRESNO, CA

POSTAGE WILL BE PAID BY ADDRESSEE

Mike Murach & Associates, Inc.

4697 W JACQUELYN AVE
FRESNO CA 93722-9888

fold

fold